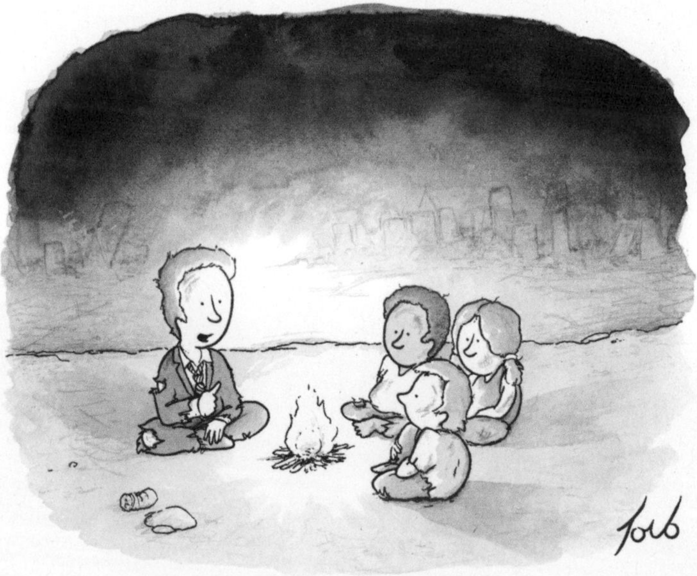

"*Yes, the planet got destroyed, but for a beautiful moment in time we created a lot of value for shareholders.*"

←   Cartoon by Tom Toro, *The New Yorker*, 2012.
→   Paper factory in Sweden, 2007. Photo by Michael Caven.

Images on cover

←↑   The first coin that depicted a woman, the Egyptian Arsinoe II Philadelphus (227–270 BC).
      It was issued posthumously by Ptolemy II, 253–246 BC, Egypt.
←   Five figures found on rock shelters in the Colombian Amazon, 11,800–12,600 years ago.
      Figures are thought to be pregnant women.
→   Icon designed by Iconoclasistas, 2015.
↓→   Image from face recognition patent 2019/0045094 A1 filed by Apple.

CAPS LOCK

HOW CAPITALISM TOOK HOLD OF GRAPHIC DESIGN, AND HOW TO ESCAPE FROM IT

Ruben Pater

They say it is love. We say it is unwaged work.
SILVIA FEDERICI

There is no document of civilisation which is not at the same time a document of barbarism.
WALTER BENJAMIN

Valiz, Amsterdam

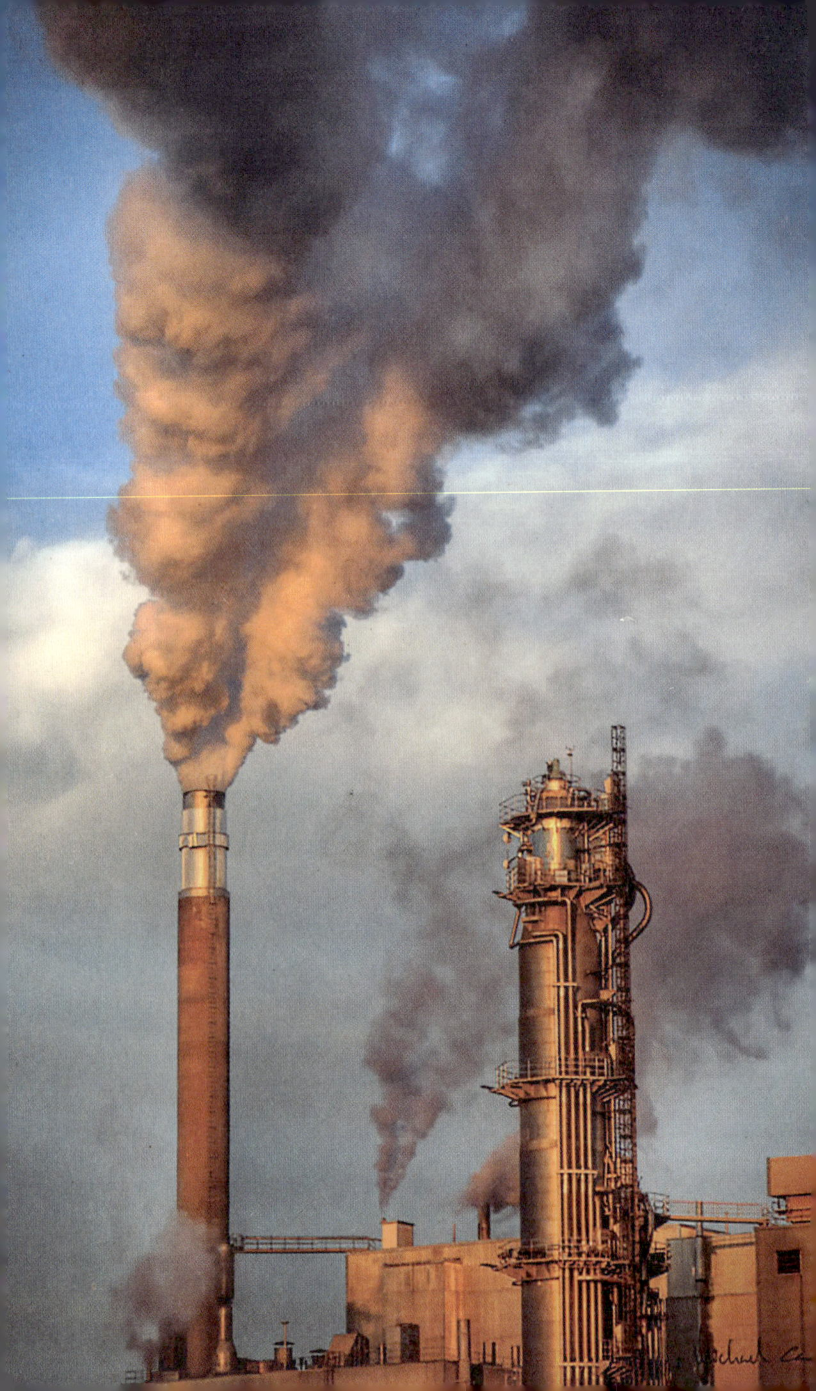

INTRO

There is no such thing as ethical graphic design under capitalism.
DESMOND WONG, DESIGNER

Apathy befalls many graphic designers when trying to imagine a design practice outside of capitalism. Desmond Wong fits in a long line of designers who have critiqued capitalism, from the *First Things First manifesto* in 1964 all the way back to William Morris (1834–1896). Through its anti-capitalist critique, graphic design has become more, not less entangled with capitalism. It seems that three centuries of this dominant economic system has paralyzed our ability to imagine alternatives. The feeling that no individual or collective can change anything until either dystopian or utopian fantasies of total collapse or full transformation, respectively, are realized.

I spent the last three years trying to answer the question if ethical graphic design can exist under capitalism. The focus is on graphic designers, but this perspective could also extend to other disciplines. The search starts by finding the origins of the current economic system, and how design has come to be so intertwined with it. Thinkers from sociology, economics, social geography, critical theory, and anthropology are consulted for the theoretical foundations. Many of them base themselves on, or are inspired by, the writings of philosopher Karl Marx (1818–1883). His critique of capitalism is widely accepted as the most detailed and thorough analysis of capitalism across the political spectrum.

Another reference point is my own twenty years of work experience as a graphic designer. I have worked in advertising, branding, infographic design, social design, speculative design, and critical design. I have made activist campaigns, annual reports for banks, and interfaces for consumer websites. I have worked under a boss, as a freelancer, I have run my own business, and have taught in design schools on several levels. From that experience I have been involved in many of the capitalist design practices mentioned in this book.

What is Capitalism Anyway?

Capitalism is an economic system that is founded on three basic principles: everything should be privately owned, all production is for the market, and people work for a wage. Based on these principles a business makes a profit and grows. Capitalism is based on ideas from the Enlightenment, in the pursuit of freeing the individual from the control of church, nobility, and family. The idea being that if all individuals would pursue their self-interest, this would best serve both them and society.

In theory, capitalism offers everyone unlimited potential but in practice only a small group of people can own the factories, crop fields, and machines needed for production. Since everything is privately owned, those with no access to the means of production have no other choice than to work for a wage. This creates a society where a minority (capitalists) has control over production, while the rest have to find a job to survive.

How does the capitalist economy work? Those who control the production—the capitalists—have to invest their profits from these 'means of production' to stay competitive, for the ultimate goal to grow. In reality they keep a lot of it for themselves, as we can see by the concentration of the world's wealth around a tiny group of 2,000 billionaires, who have more wealth than the poorest 60 percent of the world population combined.[1]

Capitalism is also called a market economy. The market is where goods and services compete with one another. By promoting products and services, graphic design plays an essential role. In theory, the free market arrives at a natural equilibrium in supply and demand, which leads to fair prices and a higher standard of living for all. Unfortunately, that hasn't been the case. The 'free' market is in reality a complex constellation of trade blocs, tariffs, and subsidies. Corporations make use of the lack of regulation by using tax havens and 'free economic zones' in low-wage countries to produce their products without the threat of unions.

Another myth of capitalism is that international markets will find a natural balance, yet economic crises are the norm rather than the exception. We have witnessed financial crashes like the one in 2008, leading to global destruction and devastation, for which the least fortunate end up paying the bill. Nor do supply

CAPS LOCK

and demand seem to create an equal marketplace. As businesses expand, sectors tend to monopolize markets. Adobe has an 80 percent market share in graphic software and Google has a 92.62 percent market share in search engines. It's not really a free market if competitors are either bought up or pushed out.

Capitalism has failed to deliver on its promise that it would create an economic system of freedom and prosperity for all. After more than three centuries, extractive industries have depleted the earth and are threatening the world's ecosystems with imminent collapse. Income inequality has increased in most developed countries since 1990.[2] Since 2014 extreme poverty has been rising with 688 million people going hungry on a regular basis.[3] Even the more privileged workers in the wealthier countries suffer from higher burnout rates and depression to meet the high productivity benchmarks. Endless consumption by the wealthy has led to an interlocking system of design, production, consumption, and waste that is nearing a point of no return.

CAPS LOCK
This book tries to understand how graphic design and capitalism have become caught in an infinite loop of creation and destruction. The central question of *CAPS LOCK* is twofold; first to historically retrace how graphic design and capitalism came to be intertwined, and secondly what strategies present themselves to unlink graphic design from capitalism, with the intended outcome of developing some kind of vision of a graphic design practice that can exist without capitalism.

Given the complexity of the relation between graphic design and capitalism, the topic cannot possibly be covered in one book. Instead of attempting a complete overview, each chapter takes a different perspective on the subject by focusing on the various roles of designers. Each role contains an historical outline, followed by practical examples. Together, the twelve roles present a cross-section of the political economy of graphic design that provides insights from different perspectives.

Design writer Guy Julier wrote that politicians often talk about the economy as one uniform entity, which is so complex it requires experts to run it.[4] In fact, design serves capitalism by devising abstract forms—infographics, money, corporate identities, branding—that hide the fact that 'the economy' is a collection of social cooperative relations between people. That's why, as a critique of design itself, this book doesn't follow the method of design theory, which usually centres designed objects. Precisely because capitalism manifests itself not only in the appearance of posters, books, or websites, but more in how they are produced, where they are they published, and how they are sold.

The first part explains how the work of graphic designers bolsters capitalism and economic relations. 'The Designer as Scribe' is about the predecessor of the typographer. The scribe or clerk was crucial in organizing complex economic societies by keeping financial records, designing coins, banknotes, stocks, and other graphic notations that instil trust in the financial system. A role that is now partly replaced by software, but is no less impactful. 'The Designer as Engineer' is about the systematic ordering of markets using graphic documents such as forms, contracts, passports, infographics, and maps. A process of standardization that allowed international markets in capitalism to function. Brands, logos, advertising, corporate identities, and interfaces are discussed in 'The Designer as Brander' and 'The Designer as Salesperson'. Further examples of contemporary work of graphic designers that each in its own way serves the commodification of all parts of society.

The second part explores how designers themselves are economic actors too. 'The Designer as Worker' and 'The Designer as Entrepreneur' take a closer look at wages, working hours, burnouts, unpaid internships, freelancing, exploitation, bosses, and the possible alternatives to these toxic work conditions. 'The Designer as Amateur' continues to question professionalism in design itself. Who can call themselves graphic designers? Who gets paid for design and who doesn't? 'The Design as Educator' explores how education prepares designers for working in capitalist conditions, and some of the alternatives that challenge the view of design education as a factory that produces graphic design workers.

The third part dives into some of the strategies that have emerged from within design in response to capitalism. 'The Designer as Hacker' looks at how the hacker ethic can change the designer's dependence on the tools and platforms made by large corporations. We also see how digital tools can intensify consumer manipulation. 'The Designer as Futurist' presents strategies by designers who want to improve society by thinking beyond what is feasible. Future design methods, such as speculative design, were intended to criticize consumerism, but have also had the reverse effect. 'The Designer as Philanthropist' is a response by designers who wish to use their skill to help others, for example social design. We find that even design with good intentions can also be neocolonial and turn out to amplify the powers of capitalism and keeping inequality in place.

Finally, 'The Designer as Activist' questions the rhetoric of activism in design, and suggests how a shift towards thinking of design as a commons may resolve some of the paradoxes that designers face. Then we leave theory behind and introduce six design collectives from around the world whose anti-capitalist practices challenge ideas of competition and exploitation. They have practiced anti-capitalist forms of graphic design for many years, and parallel to the theory this can help us understand what practical obstacles are up ahead. Brave New Alps from Italy, Common Knowledge from the UK, Cooperativa de Diseño from Argentina, Mídia NINJA from Brazil, Open Source Publishing from Belgium, and The Public from Canada. Their years of experience can provide insights and practical ideas for those who want to change their practice towards working outside of capitalism.

This Book is Neither Objective, Nor Global
Because of my personal background and experience, this book is written from a Northern European perspective, a region where capitalism and colonialism were born, and where graphic design emerged as a separate discipline. I am from the Netherlands, the country with the first stock exchange, and the first multinational corporation. As a centre of colonialism and capitalism this can give some insight about its historic foundations. Because of my background, I am relying on written sources that are either English or Dutch. This affirms the dominant Eurocentric point of view that has disproportionally influenced the design discipline. I invite the reader to be aware of this bias, and seek different sources and voices, insofar they are not yet suggested in this book.

That brings me to my second point, about neutrality. In my first book *The Politics of Design*, I proposed that there is no such thing as a neutral or objective position within design.[5] The same goes for *CAPS LOCK*, which was written from the idea that capitalism is a harmful economic system, because it destroys the planet and exploits its people. If you look at the established canon of graphic design history books, many titles celebrate design work by Western (male) designers for multinational corporations, often without mentioning the social conditions under which their work was produced. Designers that serve capitalist objectives have become so much the norm in design writing and education, that they are considered to be neutral. This book attempts to counterbalance that narrative by questioning some of the assumptions that form the basis of Western graphic design theory. The purpose of *CAPS LOCK* is to understand how graphic design and capitalism are historically related, what the effects of that relationship have amounted to, and what alternatives exist. Regardless of political persuasion or background, I believe anyone will find this book useful as an historical overview of how economy and design are related. *CAPS LOCK* is constructive but not always pleasant. It links violent events such as slavery, colonialism, exploitation, gentrification, and environmental destruction to design practices. As uncomfortable as that may be, these stories are also necessary to understand how well-intended actions can have damaging consequences.

In the final chapter more hopeful tactics appear, from six design collectives that have created, in their own way, more ethical ways of working outside of capitalism. Collectives that are setting up small-scale economies that look after the well-being of humans and their natural environment instead of pursuing profit. Designers that have found practical ways to run a design studio without bosses, working for social causes, based on solidarity and mutual trust. That provides more than a glimmer of hope that graphic design can be both meaningful and useful for humankind. Rather than waiting for politicians to realize grand ideas of utopia, these designers understand that true utopian politics already exist in the small and everyday acts of working and living together.

Ruben Pater, June 2021

CONTENTS

CAPS LOCK — Part 1

CAPS LOCK — Part 2

CAPS LOCK — Part 3

CAPS LOCK — Part 4

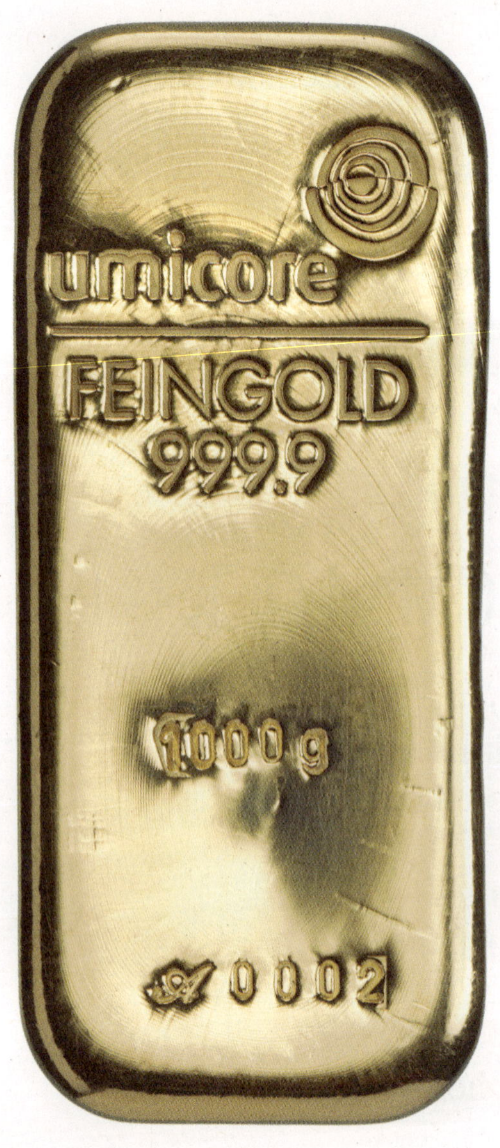

Umicore gold bar 1 kg, price $61,704.

iPhone 8 Plus, price $290.

↑ Money changer in Indonesia.
→ Carl Bloch, *Jesus Casting Out the Money Changers at the Temple*, 1874.

PART 1

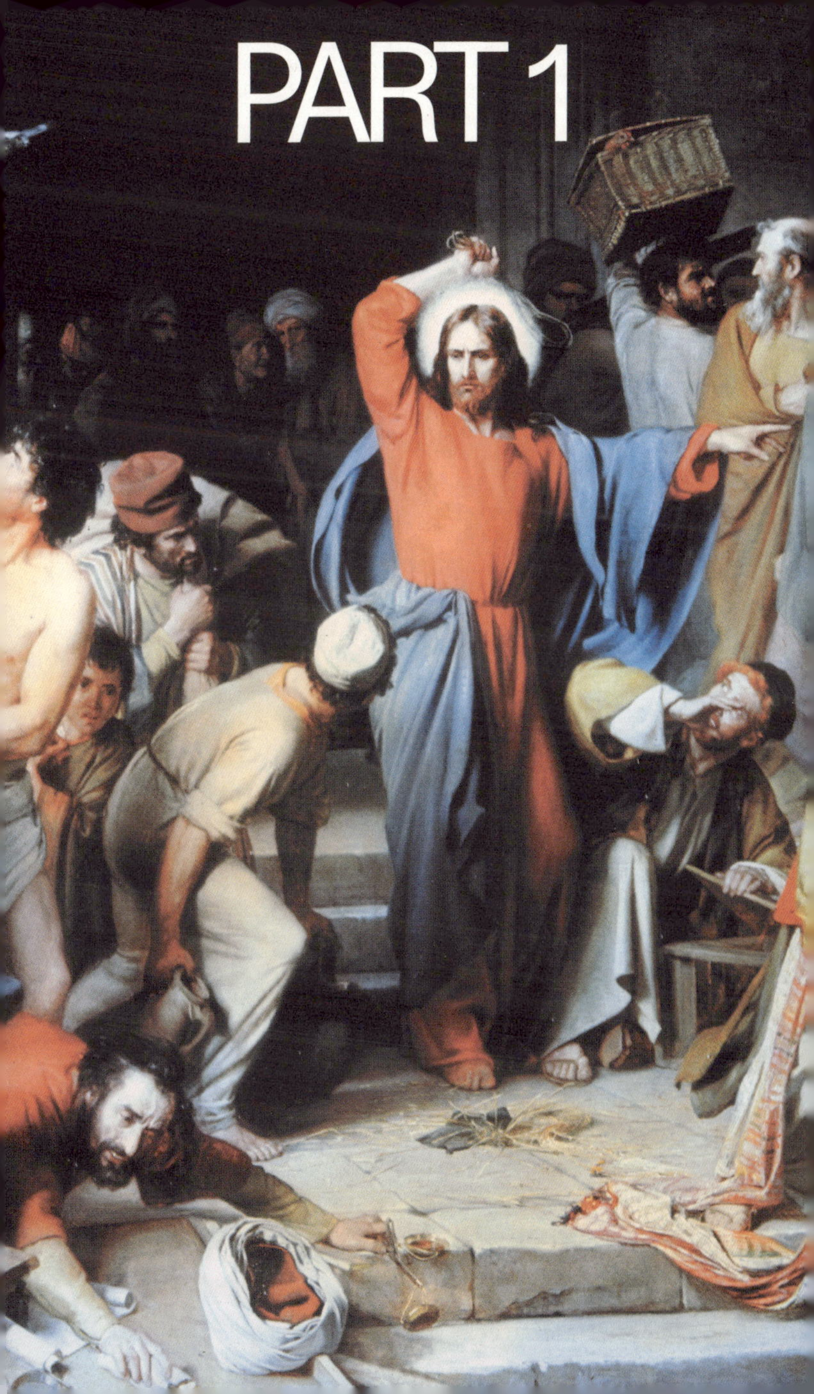

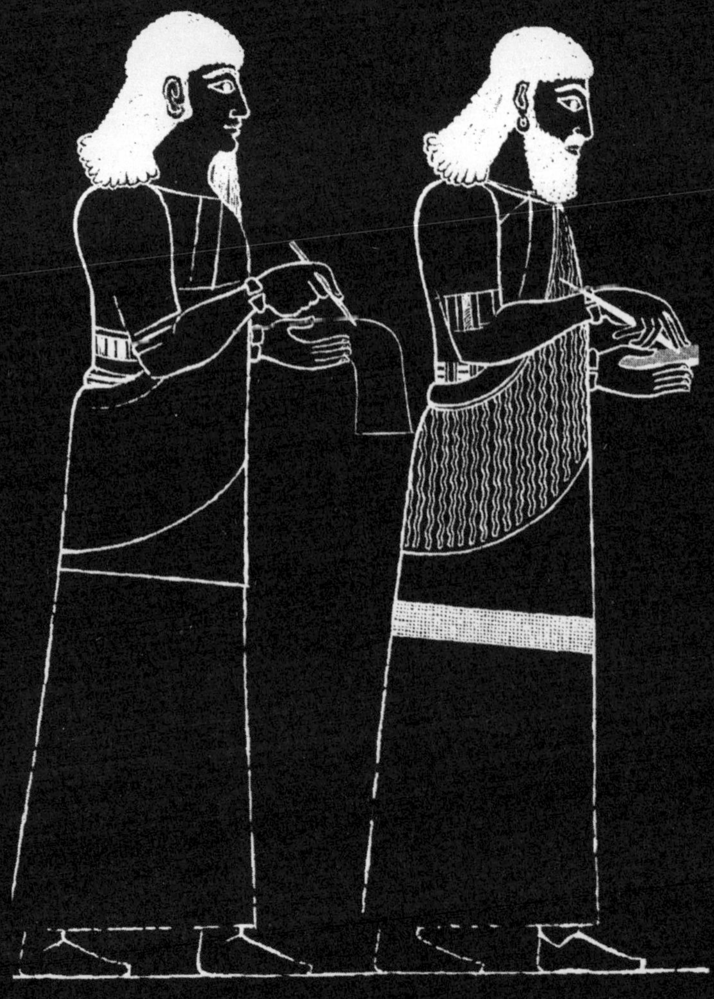

Assyrian scribes.

THE DESIGNER AS SCRIBE

Oh my hand.

*Writing is excessive drudgery. It crooks your
back, it dims your sight, it twists your
stomach and your sides.*

*Now I've written the whole thing:
for Christ's sake give me a drink.*

MEDIEVAL MONKS

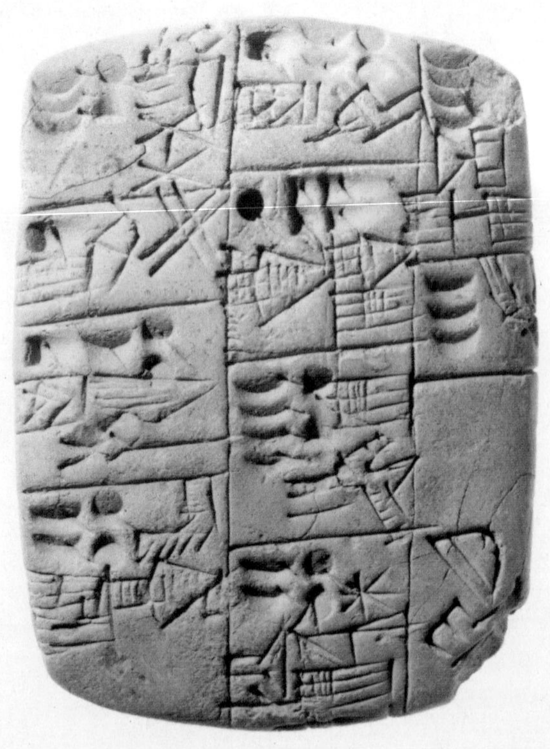

Clay tablet; record of beer; 3100-3000 BC, Uruk, shown at true size.

ON THE RECORD

A bill for the rental of a boat, the sale of an oxen, a receipt for beer. The oldest messages ever found are not diaries or love poems, but financial records. They were written on clay tablets by scribes in Mesopotamia, thousands of years before the first alphabet was invented. Mesopotamian cities like Babylon had 200,000 inhabitants, at their peak. To feed such populations, large amounts of grains were stored and traded, which required a class of trained scribes to ensure an effective financial administration.[1] The fact that these designed objects were so detailed and have survived for so long, reveals the importance of bookkeeping in managing the first large agricultural societies.

Financial records are clear examples of early graphic design. Scribes had to master skills such as consistent mark making and the ordering of information on small surfaces. The fact that these tablets predate other forms of written communication might not be coincidental. When a debt is created, stored, and traded, at some point a written record is needed to keep track of it. Economy is a system where value is exchanged based on trust, and for thousands of years scribes were responsible for creating trustworthy documents that guaranteed authenticity and authority in large societies.

This book, which is about the relation of graphic design with capitalism, begins with the designer as a scribe. Until the invention of the printing press, scribes and clerks were the only source of written communication, being typographers, lay-out specialists, and printers combined. In societies where few people were literate, this meant they had a position of power. They received an official education and their job was to systematically track and document value exchange; an indispensable task in the first large agricultural economies. In this chapter we will retrace the origins of economic notation and professional typography skills as a means to instil trust and authority in economic systems.

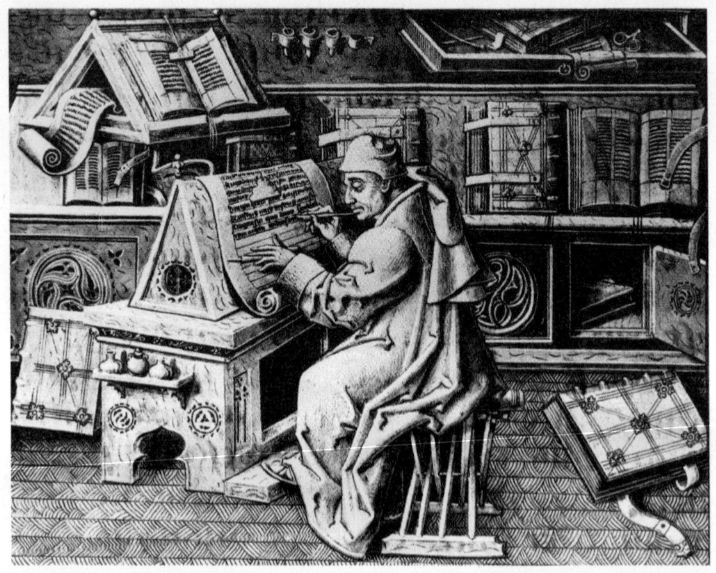

The copyist Jean Mielot in his scriptorium, fifteenth century.

The Hand of the King

In ancient Mesopotamia, scribes received their education from a very early age, and they practiced by endlessly copying tablets using a stylus with a sharp triangular tip. Tablets were small, often no more than ten centimetres wide. These documents were issued, traded, and therefore owned. Communication as a form of property was contrary to the oral culture of early primitive societies, which was a shared form of communication, as researcher and author Seth Siegelaub notes. The fact that these notation systems were owned rather than shared, indicates a changing concept about property and ownership in large early agricultural societies.[2]

Emperors and kings used scribes as an extension of their power. Scribes provided the consistency and style to convey the words of the sovereign, making their words indisputable. Different handwriting styles—called 'hands'—were developed to distinguish kingdoms or functions. In the Middle Ages, Charlemagne promoted one unified handwriting style, which thus became known as the Carolingian minuscule, the handwriting of Charlemagne. A visual identity in handwriting allowed communication to be read across long distances, and promoted the identity of the kingdom. Using well-trained scribes was therefore an act of government branding. Since very few people could write (including kings themselves) a hand also provided the necessary security for government documents. Some styles were designed to be purposefully difficult to copy, minimizing the chances of forgery, like the French Merovingian charter script and the English chancery hand.[3]

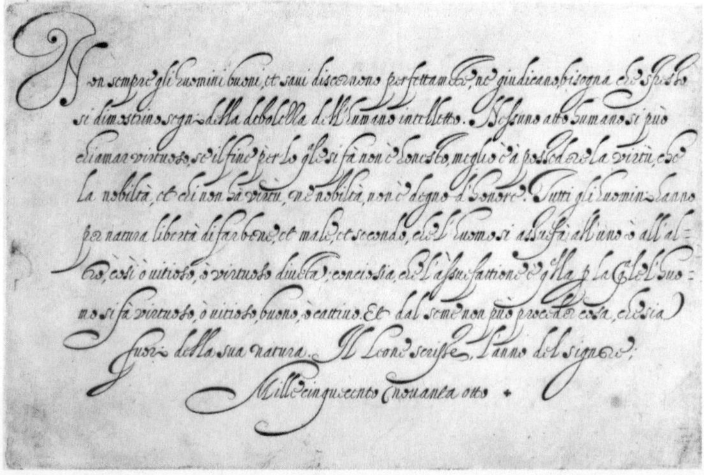

Italian chancery hand, 1598.

The Spreadsheet Never Lies

It's not just our alphabet that is rooted in financial record-keeping. The layout and ordering of information also started with financial records. In *Graphesis* (2014), Johanna Drucker explains how tabular formatting on early clay tablets reveals the first use of the design grid.[4] Just like spreadsheets today, the grids on clay tablets show a mathematical thought process. The graphical ordering of financial information commands authority, even though financial scandals have shown that mathematically correct tables in annual reports can hide a world of fraud and financial malpractice. Complex economic societies rely on consistent numerical ordering and especially in today's financialized economy where ninety percent of all money exists only in digital form, a trustworthy notation and encoding is essential.[5] Not unlike the clay tablets, financial

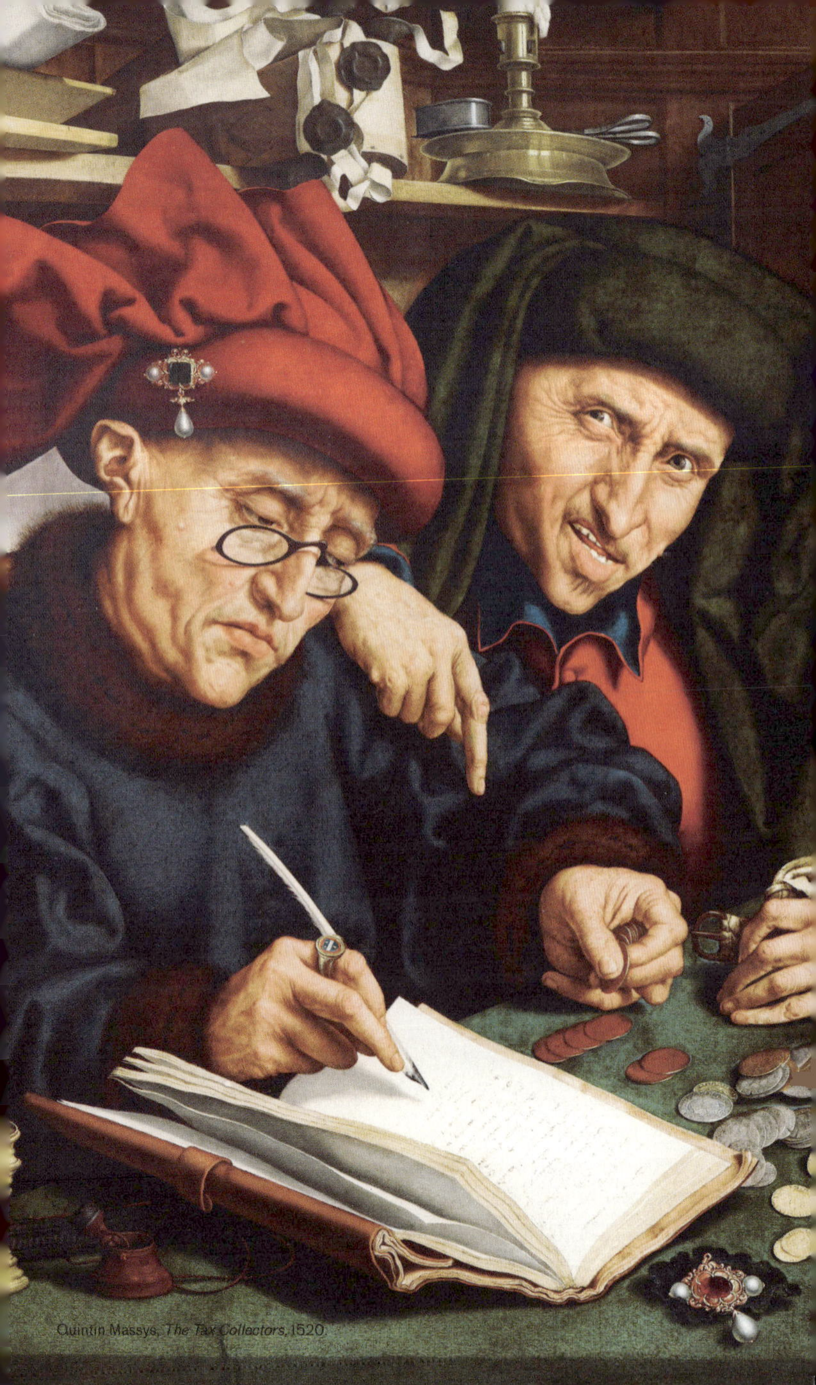

Quintin Massys, *The Tax Collectors*, 1520.

Money is the universal self-established value of all things. It has, therefore, robbed the whole world–both the world of men and nature–of its specific value. Money is the estranged essence of man's work and man's existence, and this alien essence dominates him, and he worships it.

KARL MARX, PHILOSOPHER

information today is time-stamped, encrypted, and stored in standardized formats. Whether these documents are kept in warehouses or on servers, Lisa Gitelman reminds us that even if these documents are never seen, their primary function is to serve as silent witnesses that can be summoned when needed.[6]

Financial documents are designed to look trustworthy by using style of writing or typography that is consistent, legible, and official. Documents are provided with a seal protecting the message contents, but also carry the symbol—and thus the authority—of the sovereign. State seals, national coats of arms, or bank logos still have a similar function. Finally, the date and the signature make these documents legally binding. Today, additional marks are included for machine reading—such as RFID chips, bank codes or bar codes—but similar graphic technologies can be found on tax forms, passports, and banknotes.

Computer Says No

The importance of bureaucratic documents is often overlooked, explains Lisa Gitelman in *Paper Knowledge* (2014).[7] Official documents are central to economic power whether they come in the form of financial spreadsheets or clay tablets. Trading and borrowing have always been part of society, but the moment financial information is documented and stored, it changes everything. A social relation based on trust—between neighbours, friends, or family members—suddenly becomes an abstract relation between debtor and indebted. This shift that is created through contracts and financial records makes trade between strangers easier, but also weakens social relations. For instance, you can be evicted if your payment is one day too late, or you can lose a job because you lost the hardcopy of a diploma, or you can be arrested if you lose your passport. Measures that seem utterly nonsensical and inhumane on a social level, but are perfectly in line with administrative thinking. In that sense graphic documents discipline our social behaviour to great effect.

The Breaking of Tablets

If financial records are the only existing proof of debt and wealth, then destroying such records is a revolutionary act. In the film *Batman: The Dark Knight Rises* (2012), the villain attacks the Gotham stock exchange with the intention of wiping all financial data, thereby eliminating all forms of money and debt. Such a drastic event hasn't happened yet, but records do go missing. The Australian Commonwealth Bank 'lost' 20 million bank records in 2016. Magnetic tapes on which the records were kept had disappeared or, as it turned out, had accidentally been thrown out.[8] In early Mesopotamia the destroying of financial records was actually a celebratory event. The New Year festivities in Babylon included the 'breaking of tablets'. An annual ritual to wipe debts clean and literally start with a clean slate.[9]

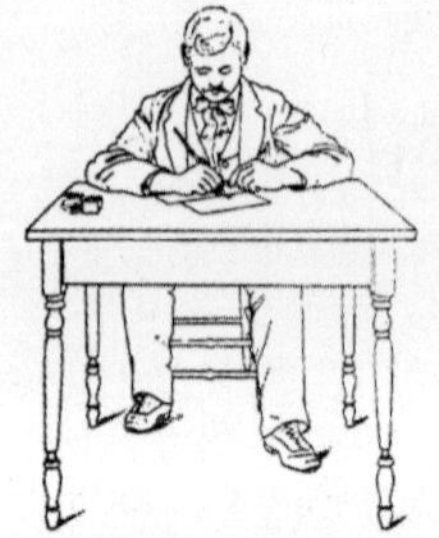
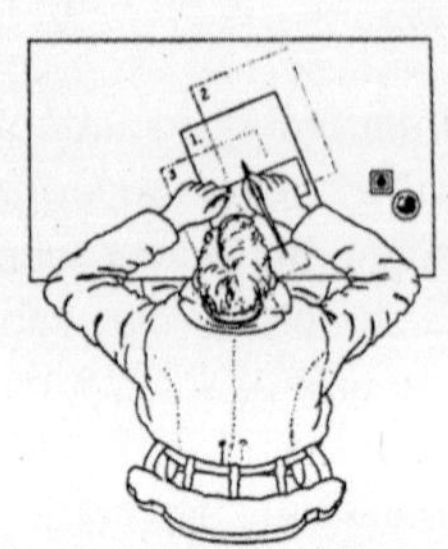
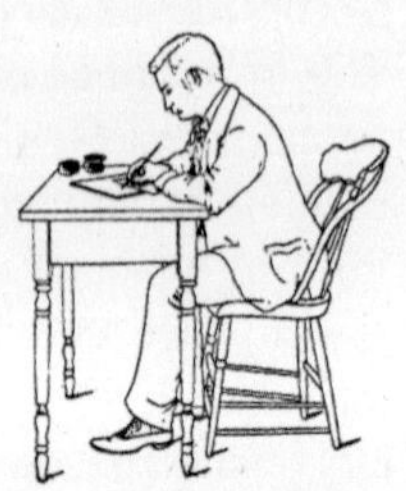

↑   Mr. Zaner's article on business penmanship, 1894.
→   Sales records from Laban Morey Wheaton's day book, 1828–1859.

Tuesday September 1st 1835 —

	$ cts $ cts
Abagail Webber Dr	
To 1 cord chips some time since 9/	1 50
„ three loads at 5/	1 2 50
Elijah H. King Dr	
To one load off chips 5/	1 00
3	
Samuel Morey Dr	
To cash pd Daniel fifteen Dollars	15 00
Henry M. Paine Dr	
To 71½ ℔ Coal delivered by Rithward at 24¢	17 20
Betsey A. Chase Dr	
To cash to pay for Bible 18/	3 00
Abagail Webber Dr	
To ½ Bush. Potatoes, new 2/6	21
To 5 lbs Lard 10d —	50 1 71
10	
Betsey A. Chase Dr	
To cash pd for Irn. L. Cambric	62
16	
To cash pd by Wife for calico	
at Boston 19/	3 17
17	
Abigail Webber Dr	
to 1 Doz. Eggs 9 —	13
to 1 Doz Eggs deliv. by Ann 9	13
Samuel Morey Dr	
To cash paid E. Babbit p order	20 00
22	
Samuel Morey Dr	
To cash paid Sophia p order	20 00
„ do. paid L. Perry Esq p order	64 41 85 41
„ pd Wild for getting Pension 6/	1 00
23	
Samuel Wrigley Dr	
To order upon Store 60/	10 00
25	
Thomas Carpenter Dr	
To paying Lieut Perry Esq 18/	3 00
29	
Samuel Morey Dr	
To cash pd Sophia forty Dollars	40 00
October 5	
Abigail Webber Dr	
to 1 lb 10 oz Lard 10d	17
to one peck potatoes, half deliv	
to day and half delivered some	
days ago — 9	11 28
Thomas Carpenter Dr	
To cash to pay L. Perry 5	8 00
Samuel Morey Dr	

Wednesday

394	Daniel Smith
	To 4 Sqares 10 by 15
152	Dauphin King
	To cash pd for your tax on
389	Oliver Clapp
	To cash towards work
506	Samuel Morey
	To cash dld Sophia
507	Abagail Webber
	To ½ Bush Potatoes d
506	Samuel Morey
	To paying L. Perry
506	Samuel Morey
	By my running Pension
	20
365	Samuel Wrigley
	to 11 notts Yarn dld
	25
344	Thomas Carpenter
	To cash five Dollar
	31
505	Samuel Morey
	To cash twenty five
365	Samuel Wrigley
	By cash paid four
402	Elijah H. King
	To ballance due Jinnot
	Nov. 3rd
365	Samuel Wrigley
	to cash
589	Oliver Clapp —
	To cash lent
	„ chips 7/6
77	David C. Bates
	To cash pd for appraisment
394	Daniel Smith
	To 1 light 10 by 15 9
	12
70	James B. Messinger
	To two lights 10 by 1
settled	George White
	To cash lent ap
507	Abagail Webber
	To 1 Bush Potatoes

TRADING INFORMATION

Beating the others to the punch has always been a deciding factor in trade. In the nineteenth century, stock broker Jim Fisk made a fortune by sending very fast ships from the US to London to go short on Confederate bonds. Since stock market news travelled by courier, his ships only had to be faster than those of the couriers, which gave Fisk an advantage before the news would reach the market.

The speed of trading changed with the invention of the ticker tape in 1867, the first electronic financial communications medium. An early kind of printer, it used electronic input from telegraph lines to print stock quotes on a continuous strip of paper. The limitations of the mechanics gave the ticker tape its unique graphic identity. For example, a stock quote would read: IBM 4S 651/4, meaning 400 shares of IBM are sold for $65.25 per share. Company names were abbreviated and capitalized and dots and numbers were added. The stock information that scrolls across screens today, is based on those early mechanical printers.

A stock exchange is where companies raise money by issuing company stock, which are essentially parts of the company itself. 'Taking the company public' is allowing others to put their money into your business, sharing both risk and reward. Retracing the shifts in the communication of financial information shows us that the search for fast information processing led to technological innovations and formal changes in notation. For instance, the way companies are listed on stock exchanges by their abbreviations.

```
SF.I.I.PR.........SE......RT.IN....ST.......USSPR.............
.............200.76....64¼.........7¾....161⅝.........200.94¼.⅜
```

```
RG.I..PR...........A.AJ..........SS.I..........ST......RG.SF.I.I..PR.....
..........200.8I½.......66.92¾.......20.99.....161⅝.............76
```

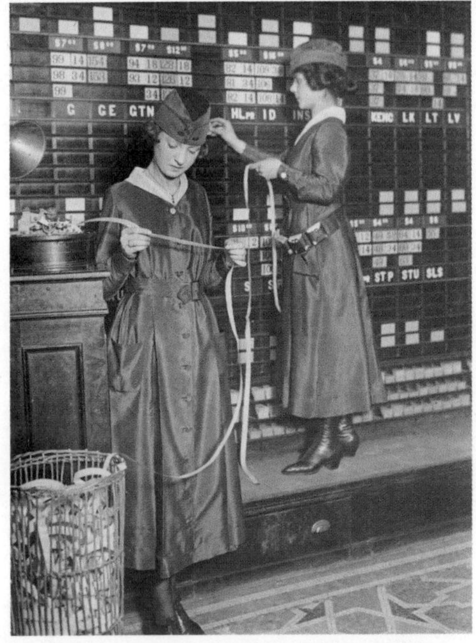

Operating the stock exchange board via ticker-tape, 1918.

Before the ticker tape, company names were shouted over the trading floor. As the number of listed companies increased, long names slowed down the speed of trading. Introduction of the ticker tape led traders to use shortened names for the faster relaying of price, thus even the communication of economic information was optimized.

Price Currents

Capitalism originated in Europe around the same time that trans-oceanic sea voyages began. Colonial journeys were expensive and extremely risky. Many ships did never return, but if they did, the profits could be considerable. The financial risks were so high that governments could not cover them and a growing class of wealthy merchants stepped in as investors. With an economy so focused on seafaring, any news on wars, shipwrecks, and pirates was crucial. The first newspapers were in fact the correspondence between investors sharing shipping and trade information. Diplomats and

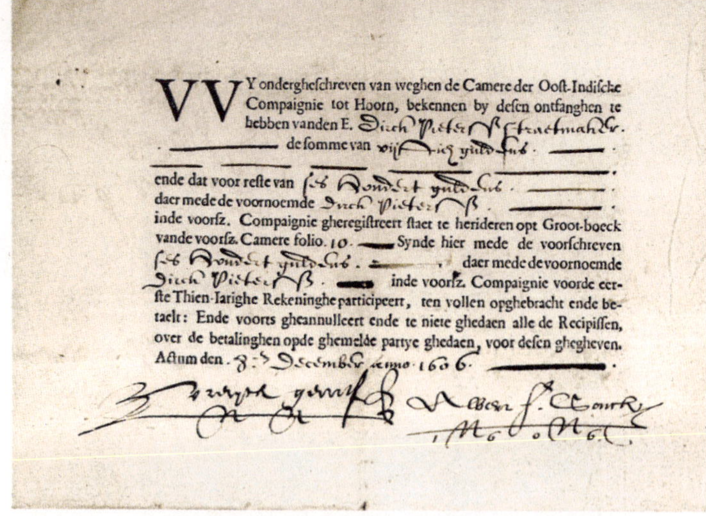

VVY onderghefchreven van weghen de Camere der Ooft-Indifche Compaignie tot Hoorn, bekennen by defen ontfanghen te hebben vanden E. _[handwritten]_ de fomme van _[handwritten]_

ende dat voor refte van _[handwritten]_ daer mede de voornoemde _[handwritten]_ inde voorfz. Compaignie gheregiftreert ftaet te heriºderen opt Groot-boeck vande voorfz. Camere folio. 10. ——— Synde hier mede de voorfchreven _[handwritten]_ daer mede de voornoemde _[handwritten]_ inde voorfz. Compaignie voorde eerfte Thien-Iarighe Rekeninghe participeert, ten vollen opghebracht ende betaelt: Ende voorts gheannulleert ende te niete ghedaen alle de Recipiſſen, over de betalinghen opde ghemelde partye ghedaen, voor defen ghegheven. Actum den. 8: 5 Decembre anno 1606. ———

↑   One of the oldest stocks ever issued from the Dutch East India Company, 1606.
→   Pricelist of the Amsterdam stock exchange, 1796. A pre-cursor of today's financial newspapers.

bankers would exchange information in private letters, thus having an advantage in trade.[10]

Stock markets began in Europe in the seventeenth century to facilitate the expansion of colonialism. The first stock exchange started in 1602 in the heart of European colonial power at the time, the city of Amsterdam. With it came financial newspapers such as the *Prijs-courant* (Price Current), which was published by stock brokers in Amsterdam in 1614, and similar journals such as *Lloyd's List* (1734) from London, and the *New-York Price Current* (1795). These featured commodity prices, insurance and exchange rates, collected and put together by clerks. The influx of wealth from the colonies led to a flourishing arts and printing industry in Europe, and the availability of cheap raw materials and wealth in combination with new technologies would kickstart the industrial revolution. We should keep in mind that this wealth came from the violent process of exploitation of people through slavery, forced labour, and the pillaging of natural resources. As Martin Luther King Jr. said in a speech in 1967: 'The fact is that capitalism was built on the exploitation and suffering of black slaves and continues to thrive on the exploitation of the poor—both black and white, here and abroad.'[11]

PRYS-COURANT der EFFECTEN,

BERICHTEN van NEGOTIATIËN, UITLOTINGE, AFLOSSINGEN en BETAALINGEN van INTERESSEN.

AMSTERDAM 2 Augustus 1796.

REPUBLIEK der VEREENIGDE PROVINTIEN.

GENERALITEIT.

	pCt.		
Oblig. op naam, met papieren	à 3 pCt.	60	à 62
——— ten lasten Frankryk onder guarantie	à 4 —	55	à 58
——— ten lasten de Provintie Groningen, idem	à 4 —	55	à 56
——— spruitende uit de Aktiën op de West-Ind. Comp.	à 3 —	54	à 58
——— Idem idem, met regt van Lyfrenten	à 5 —	60	à 65

GELDERLAND.

———	à 3	—	à —

ZEELAND.

———	à 2½	—	à —

MIDDELBURG.

———	à 3½	—	à —
———	à 3	—	à —

FRIESLAND.

———	à 3	— 50	à 52
———	à 2	— 46	à 48

UTRECHT.

———	à 3	— 54	à 56
———	à 2½	— 42	à 44

HOLLAND en WEST-FRIESLAND.

——— in blanco, Compt. 's Hage	à 2½	— 56	à 58
——— op naam en met papieren, idem	à 2½	— 56	à 54
——— in blanco, Compt. Amsterdam	à 2½	— 58	à 60
——— op naam en met papieren, idem	à 2½	— 56	à 58
———	à 3	— 60	à 62
———	à 4	— 66	à 70
———	à 5	— 76	à 84
——— Kleine Pryſen uit de Lotery van 1746	à 2½	— 56	à 58
——— Groote Pryſen uit de Lotery van 1746 en 1735	à 2	— 38	à 42
——— uit de Lotery van 1792	à 2½	— 56	à 58
——— Dertig Jaarige Renten	à 5	— 70	à 72
Wissel-Brieven, ten lasten de Staaten van Holland	à 4	— 70	à 72
Recepiſſen uit de geforceerde Geldlichting	à 2½	— 44	à 45
Recepiſſen uit de Lotery van 10 February 1796	à 2½	— 42	à 43

DIVERSE COLLEGIEN. ADMIRALITEITEN.

Oblig. Amsterdam	à 3	— 50	à 52
——— de Maas	à 3	— 50	à 51
——— Noorder-Quartier, onder guarantie van Holland	à 3	— 50	à 51
——— Friesland		— 50	à 51
——— Zeeland	à 2½	— 50	à 51
——— Last- en Veilgeld	à 4	— 70	à 71
———	à 3	— 65	à 66
———	à 2½	— 50	à 51

OOST-INDISCHE COMP.

Oblig. ten lasten diverse Kamers	à 2	— 24	à 26
———	à 2½	— 32	à 34
Recepiſſen van Anticipatie Penningen	à 3	— 20	à 24
Oblig. ſpruitende uit gemelde Recepiſſen	à 3	— 37	à 38
——— uit de Lotery van 1785		— 32	à 34

DEENEMARKEN.

		pCt.	
Oblig. op de Tollen	à 4 pCt.	96	à 98
——— op de Kroon	à 4 —	96	à 98
——— op Holstein	à 4 —	98	à 99
——— op de Deensche Leen- en Wissel-Bank	à 4 —	98	à 100

PRUISSEN.

———	à 5	— 100	à 101
——— op de Stad Dantzig	à 5	— 98	à 100

SPANJE.

———	à 4½	— 87	à 88
———	à 3½	— 73	à 74

STAATEN van AMERICA.

——— op de Vereenigde Staaten	à 5	— 99	à 100
———	à 4	— 90	à 91
——— met Premie	à 4	— 116	à 118
——— Liquidated Debts, met Premie, by Stadnitski en Stapherst	à 6	— 140	à 170
——— Idem, zonder Premie, by Diverſen	à 6	— 100	à 110
——— Differred of Uitgestelde Schulden	à 5½	— 97	à 99
——— op idem en 6 pCt. Fondſen, by Crommelin	à 5½	— 102	à 104
——— op 6 en 3 pCt. Fondſen, by Diverſen	à 5½	— 96	à 100
——— Beleening op gemelde Fondſen met Premie, by Crommelin	à 5	— 100	à 102
——— Idem idem, zonder Premie, by dito	à 4½	— 93	à 94
——— op Gronden, gelegen in de Stad Washington	à 6	— 94	à 96
——— op Akkers Land, 1 Jan. 1793, by Stadnitski	à 5	— 100	à 102
——— Idem idem, 1 Juny 1793, by dito	à 5	— 91	à 93

POOLEN.

——— op de Republiek, by de Sueth en Hogguer	à 5	— 56	à 60
——— by de Haan	à 5	— 30	à 32
——— op de Kroon	à 5	— 56	à 60
——— op Diverse Prinsen, by Hogguer, Galcher en Mulder en de Haan	à 5	— 45	à 85

SAXEN.

		St.	
——— ten lasten de Steur Ordinair	à 3	— 37	à 38
——— ten lasten de Kamer-Steur	à 2	— 36	à 37
———	à 2	— 35	à 36
——— ten lasten de Leipziger Waag	à 1	— 94	à 96 (pCt.)

Mandaaten	—	2	à 2½

WISSEL-COURS van AMSTERDAM,
1 Augustus, op de volgende STEDEN.

Stad		Koers
Madrid	uſo van 2 Maanden	81
Bilbao	Idem	80½
Cadix	Idem	81 à 80½
Sevilien	Idem	81
Lisbon	Idem	54½ à 54
Porto	1½ uſo van 3 Maanden	54 à 54
Venetien	uſo van 2 Maanden	100½
Livorno	Idem	101¼
Genua	uſo van 2 Maanden	91¾
Parys	kort	59¾
———	2 uſo	59½
Bordeaux	uſo	59¾
———	2 uſo	59½
Londen	kort	—
———	2 uſo	

Over-the-Counter

National Market System

The companies listed below reflect the volume in 100's of shares on a daily basis and the closing price and net change are reflected from the previous day based on trades as provided under the NASD National Market System.

Column 1

Stock	Div	Sales	Close	Chg.
		— A —		
A&W Bd		51	28¾—	¼
ABSs	.32	2	6½	....
ACCCp	.16	228	8¾	....
ADC		594	21¼+	⅛
ADT		993	31¾+	½
AEL		13	5¼—	½
AEPs		14	15¼—	¼
ALCh		256	⅞+	⅛
ASK		66	8⅞+	⅛
AST		2141	15¼+	⅝
AbingB	.16	3	5¾	....
AbeLinc		10	7	....
Acadin		75	3¹¹/₃₂—	¹/₃₂
Aclaims		911	6⅜—	⅛
AclwlB		952	1⁹/₃₂	+³/₃₂
Acuelo	.14	2	14¾+	¾
ACMT		14	12½+	½
AcmeSt		177	15½+	½
ActART		156	6½—	¼
ActnSv	.32	232	5¾+	¼
ActAuSt		30	2½+	⅛
Acxiom		21	21½	....
AdacLb	.16	1994	2⁹/₁₆	+¹/₁₆
Adage		408	15/16	....
Adapt		870	19—	⅛
Adingls		2	16+	½
AdiaSv	.14	7	23¼—	¼
AdobeS	.20	4616	29⅜+	⅞
Adtec		779	2¹/₁₆	—¹/₁₆
AdvCirs		578	7⅛—	¼
AdvRos		2	9½+	⅛
AdvMag		5	13+	¼
AdMkSv		22	6⅛—	¼
AdvPoly		415	5¾—	¼
AdvTel		192	13½+	¼
Advanta	.13	571	9+	⅜
AdvoSy		127	9	....
Aequtrn		104	2⅛	....
Aegon	1.39	53	54¾—	¼
AerSysl		41	⅞	—¹/₁₆
Aerovx		1019	4⅜+	⅞
AflBcCp	.32	15	4⅜+	⅛
AflBsh		602	10⅞—	¼
AgncyR		589	12⅛	....
Agnicog	.20	122	9⅜—	⅛
AirMd		306	4	....
AirWisc		174	8⅞—	⅛
Airtran	.16	338	7⅛	....
Akorn	.07	129	1⁹/₁₆—	⅛
Akzo	1.46	450	31+	⅜
AlamBc	.60	24	25¼+	¼
Alaten	1.10	3	11⅛—	⅛
Aldus		916	20½+	¼
AlexBr	.22	5	10⅜+	¼
AlexBld	.80	3174	30+	½
AlfaCp	.36	26	9¾—	½
Alico	.20	12	29½+	½
AllAms		40	1⁷/₁₆+	⅛
AlegW		634	10⅛+	⅞
AlianPh		216	9¼+	⅛
Alliant		1136	6¾	....
AlldCap	1.15	14	18	....
AldCall	.16	235	15—	⅛
AlldGp	.44	1	13+	¾
AlldRsh		9	2⅛	....
AllstFn		2	7⅜—	½
Allwsts		3166	9¼	....
Aloette	.32	755	15½	....
Alpharl		31	3/16—	⅛
AlpMic		25	3⅞	....
AltaGld	.06	1104	5⁵/₁₆	—³/₁₆
Altera		4295	9¼+	½
Altus		5	1⅛—	¼
Altos		406	8⅛—	¼
Altron		10	5	
AmcorF	.50	20	15½+	¼
Amrian		40		

Column 2

Stock	Div	Sales	Close	Chg.
AutoInf		229	4¾	....
AutoSy		30	2¼	....
Avntek		4759	2¼	....
Avatar		7	22¼+	½
Avndle	.92	432	8⅝—	¼
Aztar		3208	5¾+	⅛
AztcM	.10	45	5⅝+	⅛
		— B —		
BB&Ts	.80	53	18⅛—	⅜
BH Bulk	2.16	58	5	+ ⅛
BEIEl	.06	x566	6⅜	....
BEI		5	2½—	⅛
BF Ent		2	6¾	....
BFSNY		17	9½—	½
BHAs		168	16¼+	¼
BHABs		1629	15⅞—	⅛
BMA	1.20	x594	40½+	2¼
BMCSft		189	30¼—	¼
BMJ	.60	10	14	....
BNH	.24	18	6¼	....
BSB Bcp	.60	3	18¼	....
BT Shp		567	13¾—	¼
BTU Int		339	3¾—	⅛
Babage		1304	4¾—	⅛
Badger	.48	2	20¾+	1¼
BakerJ	.06	5062	14⅛+	½
BldLyB	.30	450	20¼	....
BaldPia		178	6⅜—	¼
Balard	.10	71	20½+	¼
Baltek	.15	122	7¼—	¼
BncPnc	1.60	241	47 +	¾
BnPops	.80	20	19¾+	½
BcpHws	1.56	126	51 —	¾
BcMiss	.84	5	20¼—	¾
Banctec		1636	18⅜+	½
BandoM	.88	30	8½—	¼
BangH	1.24	31	16	....
BankAtl		3	6¼+	¼
BkGrns	.40	6	22	....
BnkNH	.92	28	13¾—	½
BkSou	.48	156	10¾+	⅛
Bnkest		144	1⅞	....
BnkFst	.28	16	6 —	¼
BkrNte		42	2½	....
Bknth	1.08	2	16⅜+	⅛
BkIowa	1.00	7	72½	....
BkMAm		89	11¼+	⅛
BkWorc	.25	1089	16½—	¾
Banta	.56	33	22½	....
BaretRs		114	6½	....
BsTnA		4	2⅜	—³/₁₆
BasAm		5	3⅜—	⅛
BasPtrs		57	10½+	½
BselF	1.00	29	35 +	¼
BayVw	.30	12	18⅜+	⅜
BayBks	1.80	502	23½+	½
BeauCs	.15	77	14¾—	½
BeautL		47	1¾	....
Beebas	.20	10	10⅞—	⅛
BelFuse		80	3¾	....
BellW		5	4¼	....
BellSv		160	4	....
BenJer		52	13½+	¼
Benhan		110	2⅛	....
Berkley	.40	219	36 +	⅛
BerkGs	1.28	1	16½+	1
BethlBc	.57	30	11½+	¼
BetzLb	1.88	199	58 +	1
Big B	.16	159	13⅛+	¼
BigOTr		34	1⁷/₁₆+	⅛
Bindly		3	9⅞—	⅛
BingKg		5	2¼—	½
Biogn wt		2	7 +	¼
BiMedc		346	12⅞+	⅜
Biogen		1388	14⅜—	¼
Biogn pf	2.12	731	28½—	¼
Biomets		1011	21 +	½
BiotcR		65	2⅞+	⅛

Column 3

Stock	Div	Sales	Close	Chg.
CapSw	1.44	2	22 +	½
CapBcp		26	3½—	¼
CapTrs	.27	10	21 +	1
CapCrb		70	3/16	....
CrdnIDs	.08	322	21¼+	¼
CarePts		189	11 +	¼
CrePwtA		27	1¹⁷/₃₂	+⁵/₃₂
CariCm	.30	398	24⅞—	⅜
Carmik		32	12¼	....
Caringtn		652	24½+	1
Carver		86	4⅞	....
Cascdes	.60	55	17½+	⅜
CascInt		262	2⁹/₁₆+	⅛
Caseys		8	9⅜	....
CastlEn	.06	73	9¾+	¼
CasiMle		148	2⅜	....
CatoCp	.08	80	2½—	¼
Celgene		191	7¼+	¼
CellTch		70	1¹⁵/₁₆	+¹/₁₆
Celcms		249	4¾+	¼
CellCm		4530	30 +	¾
Celrln		307	22¾+	1½
Cellrlnf		53	7	....
Cencor		6	1⅞	....
CnttSB	.40	52	8⅞—	⅜
Centrbk		255	7¼	....
CentxTl		1024	19½+	⅜
Centcor		633	29 —	¼
CnBsh	.80	73	14	....
CtrCOp		27	4⅜	....
CFidBk	1.24	36	29¼+	¾
CtrlHld		13	2⅞—	¼
CJerBc	.90	11	18 +	½
CPaFin	.40	2	13½+	¼
CRsLfe	.26	37	4⅞—	¼
CnSprn		27	23¾+	½
Centuri		20	1½—	⅛
CntGld		10	13/16+	⅛
CntyBc	.30	40	3⅜	....
Cenvst	.48	18	7⅛	....
Cerdyn		54	3¼	....
Cerbco	.06	32	3⅛—	⅛
Cerner		14	13¼+	¾
Cetus		1156	15⅛	
Chalone		17	10¼+	⅜
ChncCp		5	1¾	
Chanins		10	9⅞+	⅛
ChrmSh	.12	1077	8¾—	⅛
ChrtFdl		70	2³/₁₆—	¹/₁₆
ChtFSB	.50	6	11¼+	¼
ChtOne	.52	134	15¾	....
Chrtwl		543	5/16	—¹/₃₂
ChkPt		597	10⅞—	¼
ChkTch		5	2¼	....
ChmDsg		263	12½—	½
Chemfx		161	4¾	....
ChmFin	1.00	2	33½+	1¼
Chmpwr		152	14¾	....
ChryCp	.12	86	7⅜+	⅛
ChesUts	.84	21	12 +	½
Cheshre	1.00	371	12 +	½
ChevSfl		542	3⅛—	½
ChDock	.27	23	18½—	¼
ChldDis		17	3½	
ChldWld		130	11¼—	¼
ChipsTc		3603	20½+	½
Chiron		569	26¼—	¼
Chilnd	.68	13	11 —	½
Chronr		11	1⁷/₁₆—	¹/₁₆
ChrDwt	.28	76	15⅜—	⅛
Cimflex		40	1⅝	
CinnFn	2.44	222	76 +	1⅜
CinMic		4	4½	
Cintas	.17	66	44⅜+	1
Cipher		1415	7¼+	⅛
Ciprico		21	3⅜—	⅛
Circadn		3	1⅜—	⅛
CirclFA		73	5⅜—	⅛

Column 4

Stock	Div	Sales	Close	Chg.
CtlMtg	.48	286	3⅛	....
CtrlRs		25	4	....
CnvSol		9	2⅜+	⅛
Cooker		73	2¾—	⅛
CooprD		3	2⅝	....
CooprL		54	7½	....
Coors B	.50	465	18⅜—	⅜
Copytle		250	12½+	½
Cordis		64	14 —	¼
CoreSt	1.92	2437	38⅝—	¼
CrnrFn	1.00	21	6	—¼
Cornucp		73	1⅜+	⅛
CpCapit		1319	¼	—¹/₃₂
CorpDt		20	4⅛	....
CorpSft		214	10¼—	¾
CorctCp		363	14⅝	....
CosmFr		143	6¾+	⅜
Cosmo		4	1¼+	⅛
Costar		7	15 —	¾
Costco		3390	30¾—	⅜
CtnSLf	.24	12	7¼	....
CtryLk		2	9¼—	⅛
CntyBk		24	2⅛	....
CourDis		1	4⅛+	⅛
CousPr	.60	28	15	....
Covngt		242	¾	—¹/₃₂
CrckBrl	.07	2203	29¼+	⅛
CrayCm		9053	4⅞+	¼
Crestar	1.32	246	28⅜	....
CrstFdl		192	6½	....
Criticre		26	2⅝	....
Cronus		57	12¼—	¼
CropG		31	6½+	⅜
CrosTr		448	6½+	⅛
CrwnAn		10	7⅜+	⅝
CwnBk		53	18½	....
CrwnRs		590	7⅝—	½
CulInFr		11	9⅝—	⅛
Culp	.08	4	8 —	¾
CumbFd	.48	56	13¾+	¼
Cybertk		161	6⅛	+³/₁₆
Cytogn		263	6⅛	....
Cytgn pf		115	25¼	....
		— D —		
D&N Fn	.60	161	10⅝+	1⅛
DBA		35	4⅜	....
DDI		180	3¾	....
DEP		31	7⅛	....
DF Sou		13	12¾	....
DH Tch		51	12⅛	....
DNA PI		1592	7⅛+	⅜
DS Bnc	1.60	31	17½	....
DSC		6173	12 —	⅜
DST	.16	40	10½+	½
Dahlbrg		13	11¼+	½
DlyJour		2	14¼+	½
DairyB		2	7¾	....
DaisySy		335	1⁷/₃₂	+¹/₃₂
Daka		737	½	+¹/₁₆
DalSem		2782	7⅛+	¼
DmnBio		290	15/16	—¹/₃₂
DtalO	4.15	72	3⅛—	⅛
Datflx		240	9⅞+	¼
Datkey		6	8¼+	¼
DtaMea		1	5⅞	....
DtSwtch		246	2⅛—	¼
Datphz		38	1⅛	....
Datscp		174	22¼—	⅛
Datron		48	10¼	....
Dauphn	1.42	29	29¾—	¼
Davox		32	4½	....
Dawson		14	4⅞	....
DebShp	.20	122	13⅜+	½
DeerSv	.80	1	26¼	....
Definc		86	1½—	¼
DeklbE	.20	517	31¾+	1¼
DkibGn	.45	11	40¾+	1½
DelTaco		3	3 —	¼
DelaOls		10	13	....
DellCpt		37	6⅛—	⅛
Delpinf		97	6	....
DepGty	1.56	3	26¾+	½
Dsglnc		241	2⅞—	¼
DetSys		24	6¼+	⅛
Devon		155	12 —	¼
Diagnst		1540	11⅜+	⅞
Dial Re	1.68	1	15¼+	¼

Column 5

Stock
ErleLec
Erlylnd
EsxCty
EvnSut
Evans
Everex
Exabyte
Exar
ExcelBc
EXTON
Exide
Expin
F&M
FM Nat
FDP
FHPs
FMSFn
FRPPr
FSI Int
Fabric
FairCty
FairFst
FalcOil
FamBc
FamStk
FamRst
FaradE
FrmHm
FrmHpf
Farr
Fastnls
FdScrw
Ferofls
Fibronc
FidBnc
FFdVAs
FifthTs
50-Off
FigieAs
FileNet
FnClr
FinNws
Fingmx
Finigan
FAlaBk
FstAm
FlAmBp
FtABcp
FtAFd
FtATn
FACant
FBOh
FtCapt
FtChat
FstCity
FColBn
FComB
FCmBn
FtConst
FtEstn
FtEsex
FtExec
FExpfE
FExpfF
FExpfG
FExpfH
FExwt
FtFaml
FFdGa
FtFdMic
FtFdEH
FFFtM
FtFdLaG
FtFdSB
FtFdSC
FFdAla
FFdPry
FFdPR
FtFncl
FtFnCp
FtFnHd
FtFlBk
FtGaHd
FtGoldn
FtHaws
FHomF
FtlllCp
Fstlndi
FtlntBs
FInsWi
FInlowa
FtLbty
FtMich

Abstraction of Information

The shift from the agricultural economy to a trade economy that occurred in Europe in the sixteenth and seventeenth century changed the way the economy was represented. Capital, currencies, and stock prices became more important, with their abstract graphic representation of numbers and lists, made possible by the printing industry and moveable type. The printing industry was influenced by fields such as statistics and a search for precise scientific notation in the Enlightenment period.[12]

The design of financial information today is regarded as neutral, even scientific. Financial sections of newspapers list stock prices using tabular lining figures; numerals that have equal height and width designed for the optimal reading of tables and lists. Lining figures came into existence late, and are thought to have originated from shopkeepers handwriting. In an interview with type designer Kris Sowersby—who designed the typeface for the *Financial Times*—he explains that numerals are read differently than words. 'We process words by their aggregate letters and graphemes', he says, 'but numerals are processed number by number. So, each numeric glyph should be distinct and assured in its form.'[13]

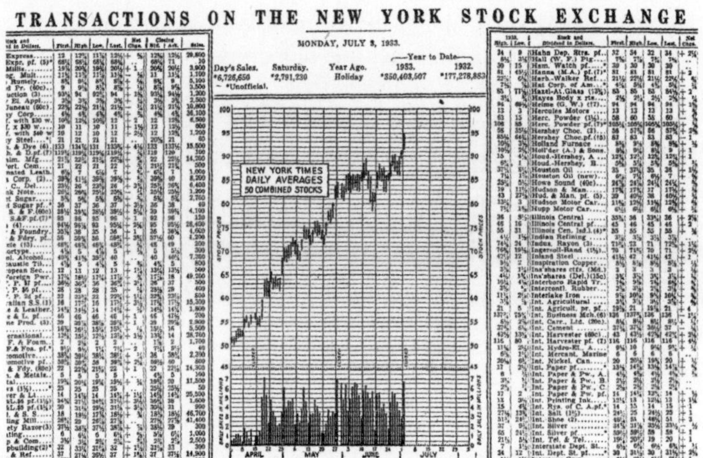

↑ Stock market information in *The New York Times*, 1933.
← Stock quotes in *The Herald Scotland's* financial section, 2000s.

The scribe is someone who documents, and therefore 'translates' daily economic transactions. We can find the language of financial data everywhere; in newspapers, on televisions screens, scrolling across outdoor billboards, on our smartphones. If stock markets were once meant for professional investors, today we are all encouraged to buy stock and become investors, either through our savings, pension plans, or mortgages.

The compact numerical graphic language of the stock market has become a representation of economy itself. Designers apply mathematical and professional rigour to financial transactions, but the form also functions to hide more about these transactions than it reveals. By representing all human economic interaction in numbers, knowledge about the underlying cultural and social value is lost. Its scientific truth makes one almost forget that behind every stock quote, every number, and every interest rate is a person working, a family being fed, someone dying, or a rainforest being cut down. We simply don't know because this is hidden behind meticulously designed and formatted tabulated numerals.

That economics can also be represented differently is shown by Gapminder, a Swedish non-profit. Dollar Street was invented by Anna Rosling Rönnlund, who wanted to compare the income of families in the world, without reducing them to statistics. Photographers went to 264 homes in 50 countries to document the objects and their owners, the faces and objects behind the statistics.[14]

We want to show how people really live. It seemed natural to use photos as data so people can see for themselves what life looks like on different income levels.

ANNA ROSLING RÖNNLUND, DESIGNER, GAPMINDER

→ Dollar Street, Gapminder. gapminder.org/dollar-street

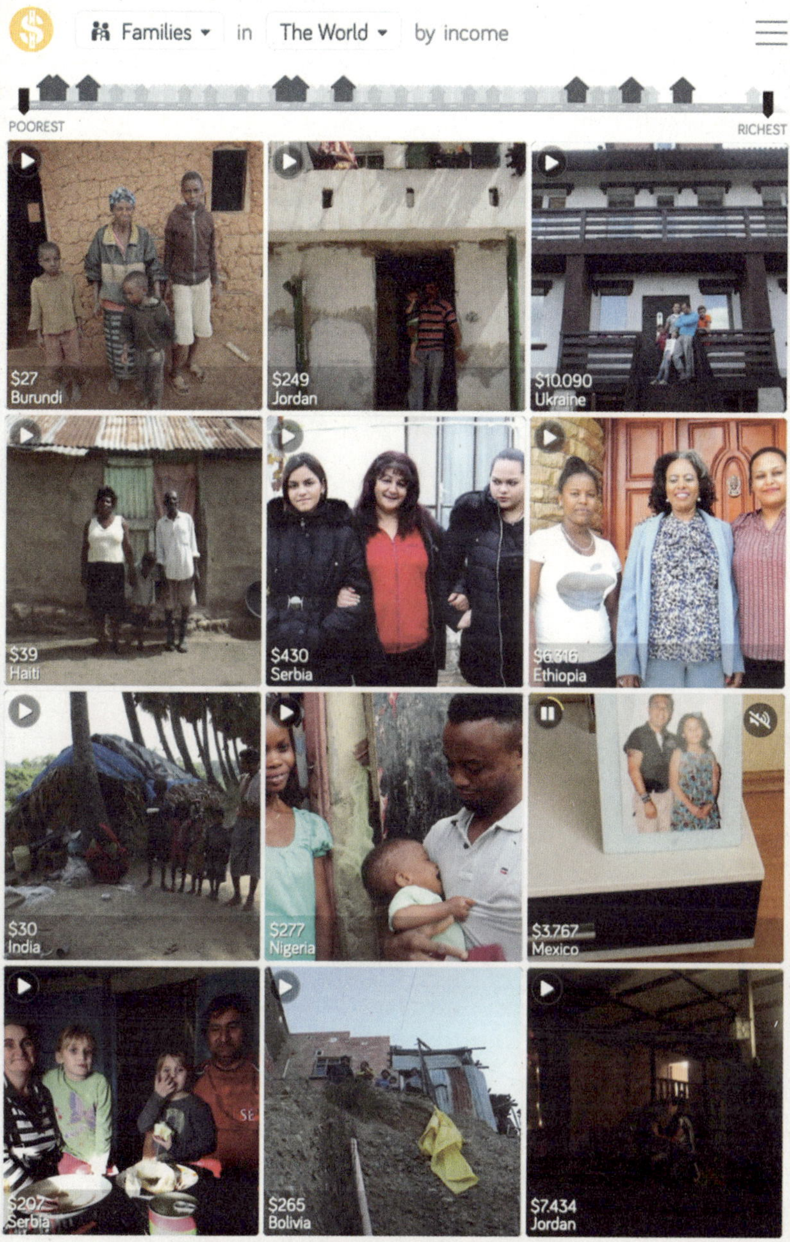

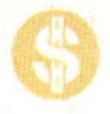

Families in The World by income
POOREST
RICHEST
$27 Burundi
$249 Jordan
$10.090 Ukraine
$39 Haiti
$430 Serbia
$6.316 Ethiopia
$30 India
$277 Nigeria
$3.767 Mexico
$207 Serbia
$265 Bolivia
$7.434 Jordan

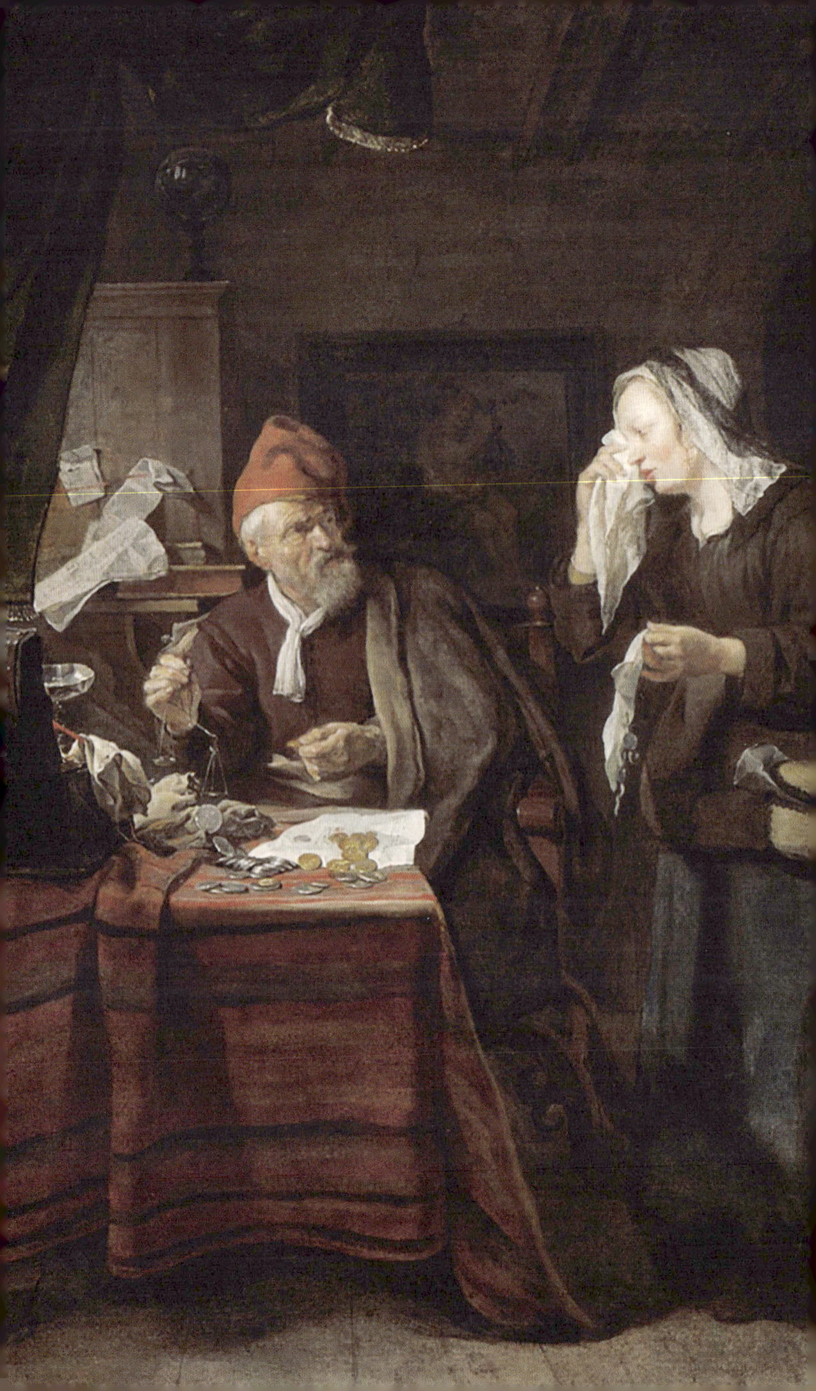

IN GOLD WE TRUST

One of capitalism's founding fathers, Adam Smith, wrote that money is a natural phenomenon that emerged from barter societies. In his theory, exchanging objects or services for one another simply became impractical when societies grew larger.[15] It is unlikely that barter societies ever existed, argues anthropologist David Graeber in *Debt: The First 5000 Years* (2011). Most archaeological evidence suggests credit was used before money existed, which could just be memorized or be stored using objects, like the clay tablets in Mesopotamia, or the knotted strings and notched strips of wood in China. Contrary to what Adam Smith asserted, money did not just naturally appear from larger societies, but was intentionally introduced by ancient kingdoms to control trade and to finance wars.[16]

Money itself is sometimes seen as the root of greed and consumerism. As money forms are designed, what role does the graphic designer have to play? For a lot of graphic designers, designing a coin or a banknote is considered a dream job. Their seductive appeal makes them popular collector's items. But limiting our focus to the aesthetics of coins and banknotes would be ignoring the more pressing question of how the work of graphic designers is needed for the functioning of our economic system. It is important to remember, as writer Jon Astbury notes: 'Money isn't real. The coins, notes and digital transfers we use to buy things are merely proxies for an abstract idea of value.'[17] The role of the designer as a scribe is to devise graphic techniques to represent economic transactions so that they are trustworthy. It is no coincidence that the word 'credit' comes from the Latin verb *credere* which means to trust, or to believe.

Earlier in this chapter the scribe was someone who documented and legitimized economic transactions in the name of the

← Gabriël Metsu, *Usurer with a Tearful Woman*, 1654.

sovereign. With the introduction of money, we find that the manual skills of the scribe are replaced with mechanical reproduction techniques to assign value and ownership. Over time, technological innovations not only help to prevent counterfeiting, but also enable more abstract forms of trust to emerge. This isn't limited to capitalism. Any large centralized economic system cannot function without designers as scribes providing the graphic language that builds trust and authority.

> ## Oh, most excellent gold! Who has gold has a treasure even helps souls to paradise.
>
> CHRISTOPHER COLUMBUS

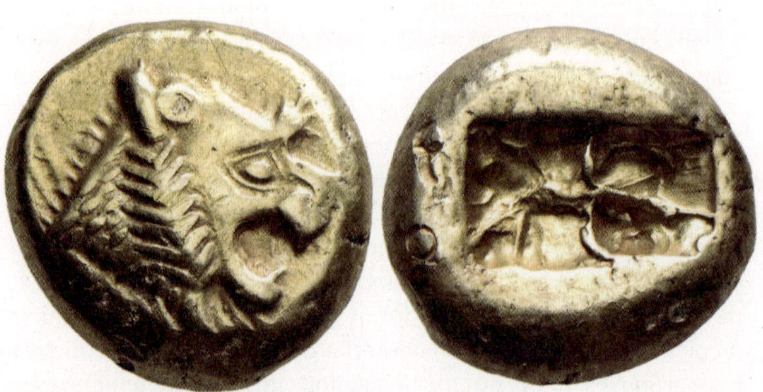

A Short History of Coinage
The first coins appeared in the kingdom of Lydia, in present-day Turkey, around 600 BC. Electrum was a naturally occurring alloy of gold and silver, which was found on the banks of a nearby river. Lumps of electrum were used to mint the first coins by stamping them with animal heads: the lion as a representation of the king. The Lydians succeeded in splitting electrum into gold and silver, which made the coins all the more popular. These silver and gold coins featured a lion attacking a bull. Notably, it is a sculpture of a bull that stands outside the Wall Street stock exchange, a symbol for aggressive financial optimism known as a bull market.

Coins were rare when they first appeared two thousand years

ago and were mostly used by merchants. The Lydia coins spread through trading with neighbouring countries and their popularity inspired the minting of coins in Greece. Each Greek city-state issued its own coins and by the fifth century BC more than one hundred mints were in operation. The gold, silver, and bronze Roman coins were widely used, and accepted far beyond its borders. The circulation of the Roman *denarii* by itself was evidence of imperial power.

One theory of why Lydian coins appeared is that they were used to pay Greek mercenary armies, according to Graeber.[18] Armies needed food and rations. Rather than sending large provisions with them or having armies plundering and pillaging the lands, it was easier to issue coins to the soldiers. Coins would give local farmers an incentive to sell their food to the soldiers, and this in turn allowed the state to demand the same coins as tax payment in return. Voilà, a market was created.

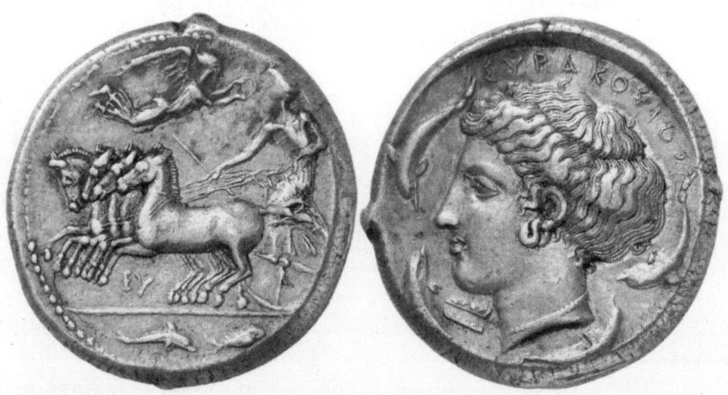

↑   Greek coins from Syracuse, 415–405 BC. Silver tetradrachme with a chariot with Nike, and on the right the head of Arethusa. Both sides are signed by the artists.

←   Lydian coins, 610–546 BC, electrum. The lion represents the king, the tails shows the denomination.

Heads or Tails

'The coin is the earliest forms of mass-produced graphic media', write Johanna Drucker and Emily McVarish in *Graphic Design History: A Critical Guide* (2009).[19] Every small kingdom or territory started issuing their own coin to raise money or to finance wars. One side (heads) was stamped with the sovereign, and the other

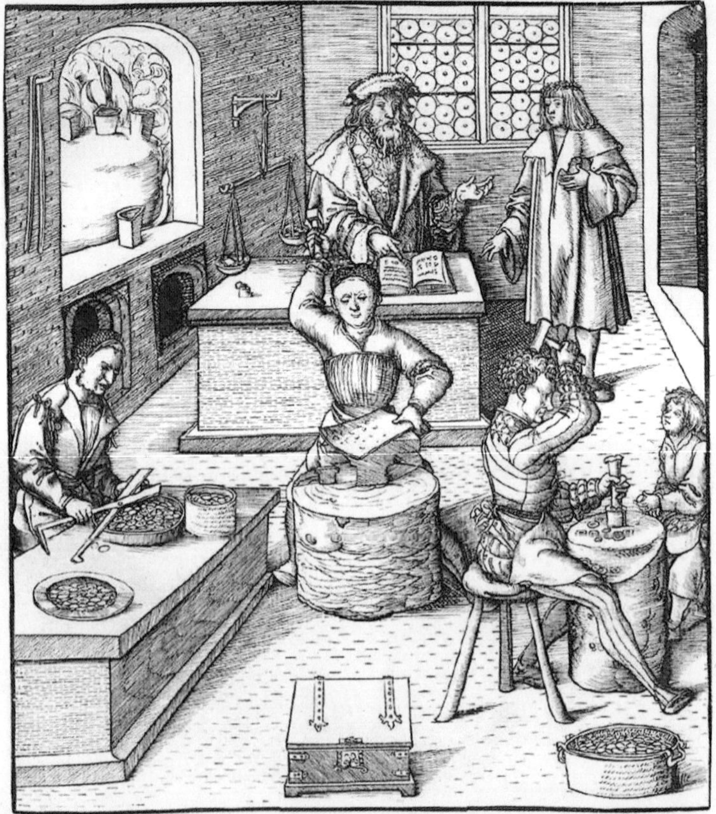

↑ The young White King learns the principles of minting. Woodcut by Leonhard Beck (c. 1480–1542).

→ A sixteenth- or seventeenth-century hoard of coin clippings discovered in Derbyshire, UK. When coins were made out of precious metals, shaving off silver or gold from coins was a punishable offense.

side (tails) featured the currency's nomination and value. The image of the sovereign would give the coin authority, guarantee its value, and warn against counterfeiting. Wherever it surfaced it promoted state power. The basic design functions of coins have not changed since.

The first person who had himself depicted on a coin was Alexander the Great. The Roman elite flaunted their wealth by having coins minted with their likeness to impress competitors. Roman Emperors were honoured by being depicted on coins after their death, also because the emperor's image in itself was respected and made coins more valuable than just their weight in gold or silver.[20] When coins or banknotes are designed today, any individual who is depicted is still subject to political debate.[21]

By the sixteenth century the number of coins that circulated was impressive. On markets in the city of Amsterdam, 388 coins from all over the world were allowed as currency. Books and posters were produced with images of coins and their nomination to help recognize them. Moneychangers weighed coins and calculated exchange rates, a much-needed profession with such diversity in currency. Counterfeiting was punishable by death, but 'clipping' was a common practice: shaving off the edges of gold and silver coins. By the seventeenth century the first silver and gold coins were designed with a milled edge to prevent clipping. Milled edges are still used and serve as extra identity marker for the visually impaired and to distinguish same-size coins.

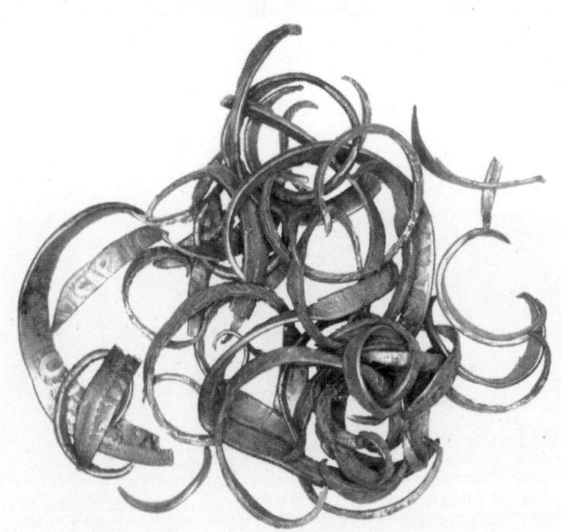

Digital Security Coin

After more than two millennia, coins are still around. The fetish that surrounds these small slices of shiny metals has reached a new level with the design of the one-pound coin in the UK in 2014. This 12-sided shaped coin features a secret digital, secure identification system with a code embedded in the top layer that becomes visible under ultraviolet light. Her Majesty's Treasury claims to it be 'the most secure circulating coin in the world'.[22] The technical document reveals the function of trust in the object and the powers that back it:

> Coins should command respect; Subject to the foregoing, coins should be small and light; A coinage system should be easily understood, in particular to help tourists, the elderly and all disability categories; Coins should be designed in such a way that counterfeits cannot easily imitate them.[23]

The introduction of coins transformed human relations, since it allowed complete strangers to engage in trade, if only they accepted coins. This meant tremendous possibilities for trade, but also diminished local forms of exchange based on trust. Historian Yuval Harari writes in *Sapiens* (2015) 'We do not trust the stranger … we trust the money she/he holds. If they run out of coins, they run out of trust.'[24] A form of trust designed by using precious metals, the face of the sovereign, and anti-counterfeiting measures.

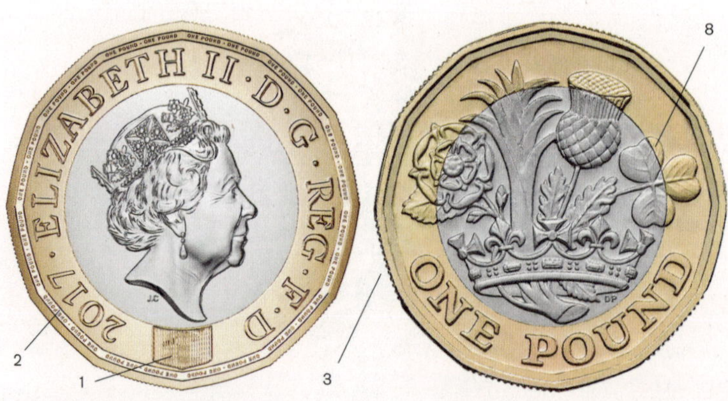

£1 coin security measures 2014

1. '£' and '1' symbols appear in different angles.
2. Micro-lettering on inside rims.
3. Milled edges.
4. Integrated Secure Identification System (ISIS). visible under ultraviolet light
5. Use of two metals.
6. Distinct 12-sided shape.
7. Electro-magnetic signature on mono-ply nickel plate.
8. Design on tails side blends from inner to outer edge.

↑   High secure £1 coin, Royal Mint, 2014.
→   Coin book from the Dutch republic with woodcut illustrations, 1622.

De halve ſtuyvers / tot viij. penningen.   De Deuyten / tot een Deuyt.

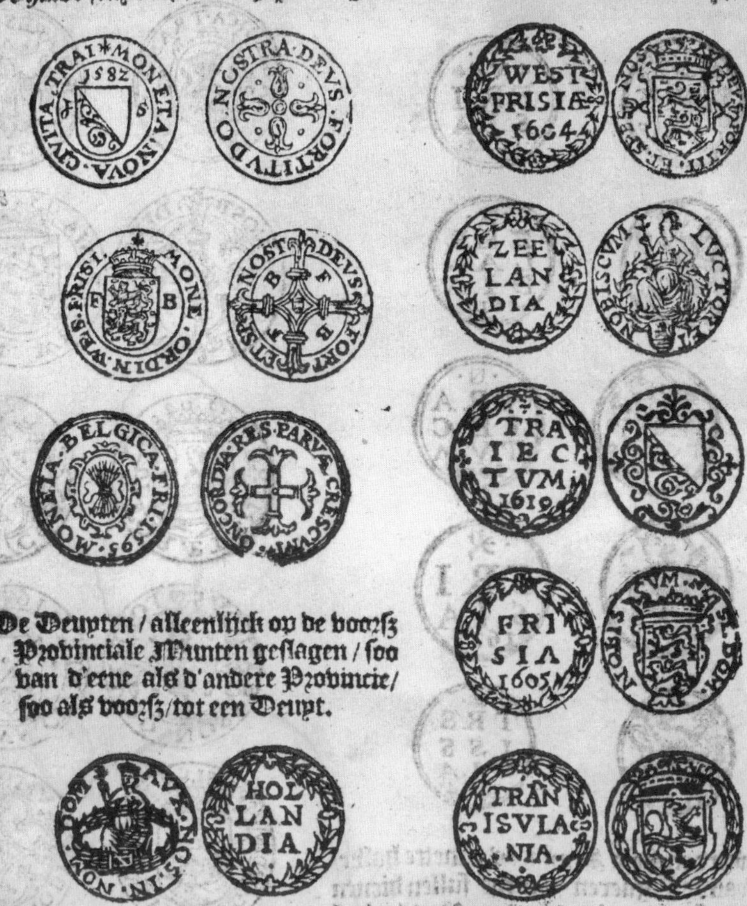

De Deuyten / alleenlijck op de voorſz Provinciale Munten geſlagen / ſoo van d'eene als d'andere Provincie / ſoo als voorſz / tot een Deuyt.

De koopere Oortgens / op eenige vande voorſz Provinciael Munten geſlagen / ende de welcke jegenwoordich voor Oortgens cours en ganck hebben / ſullen inde Provincie daer die gheſlagen zijn / alleenlijck / ende nergens anders / voor Oortgens cours ende ganck blijven behouden. Alle ander kooper-gelt / is by proviſie op eenen Penningh Hollandts gheſtelt.

FINIS.

NOTES FROM THE BANK

With their elaborate patterns, relief printing, secure embossing and foil printing techniques, banknotes are popular design objects. Noteworthy about the design of banknotes is that their basic elements have changed little, since they were introduced more than a thousand years ago. It is still a piece of paper printed with signatures and stamps using the latest printing techniques, with a government guaranteeing its value. Banknotes have the advantage over coins in that they are easier to transport and store. On the banknote we find all of the skills of the scribe for authenticating and standardizing financial records: detailed and consistent graphic forms to create a legible and portable object that can be

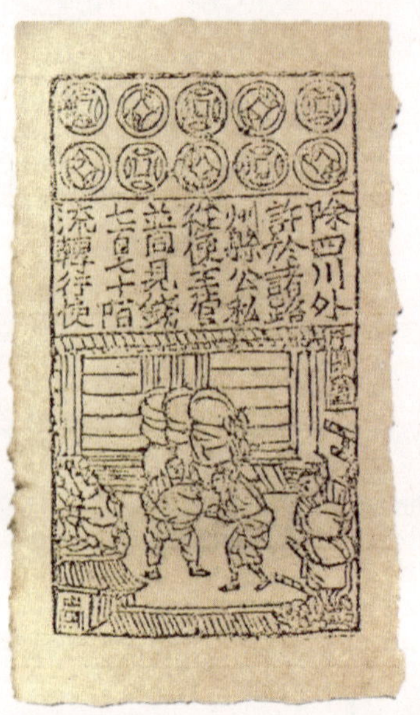

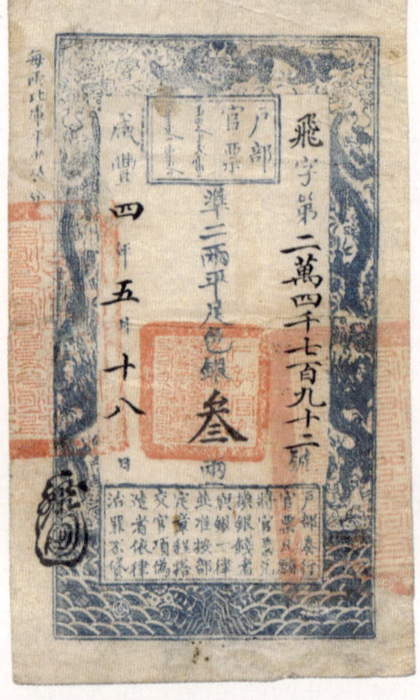

↑   Woodcut printed banknote of 770 mò of the Song Dynasty (920–1279), the first paper money.
→   Woodcut printed banknotes from the Qing Dynasty (1644–1912), Hu Pu Kuan Piao: 3-Tael, Year 4.

reproduced but not easily copied. The 50-euro banknote includes watermarks, colour-changing inks, perforations, raised printing, security threads, microprinting, a bar code, a serial number, ultraviolet ink, a hologram, and light sensitive printing. Banknote designs often include the portraits of heads of state or other important national historical figures, as studies have shown that faces on banknotes convey confidence.[25] Although they are called bank*notes*, there is little writing on them today. The most important information is basic or numerical, the serial numbers, the signature, and the country of origin—making banknotes effective in their use across cultures and languages.

The Rise of Paper Money

The first banknotes appeared in seventh-century China. Instead of having to carry around large quantities of coins, merchants were given printed notes so the coins could be safely kept in vaults. These banknotes were woodblock-printed in as many as six colours, on special paper and with state seals to avoid counterfeiting.[26]

Outside of China trade was dominated by coins for over a thousand years longer. By the thirteenth century, merchants in Europe ran into the same problems as the Chinese: the inconvenience of carrying large amounts of coins. Italian moneychangers saw an opportunity and promised to keep their money safe in exchange for cash notes. These letters of exchange (*lettera di cambio*) needed the signature of both parties. Merchants often ended up not reclaiming the coins, and kept using the notes instead. The moneychangers that loaned money became the first banks.[27]

A more organized introduction of paper money didn't occur in Europe until halfway the seventeenth century. Copper had devaluated so much that some of the Swedish daler coins weighed almost 20 kilogrammes. This unwieldy 'plate money' led Sweden to issuing banknotes. The first daler banknote was large, almost A5, resembling handwritten notes. Bills had dotted lines where the name, date and signatures had to be written by the user. Banknotes were rare, and were used by rich merchants and nobility. Since each note carried the signatures of all previous users, it was like receiving an invitation from a club of wealthy gentlemen.[28]

Banknote Design

The issuing of the first banknotes was unregulated. Problems arose when many banks started printing their own notes in the nineteenth century, and, in largely illiterate societies, people often had difficulty distinguishing between fraudulent and valid banknotes. At one point 8,000 banks were issuing over 5,000 different banknotes in the US alone. Banknote designs were influenced by Romanticism in the arts and nationalist symbolism. The banknote was a canvas on which the new states could project the idealized image of the nation and its morals, with manuscript typography, ornaments, and patterns. Many banknote designs still refer to this visual language of the late eighteenth century, as this was the time when paper money started to become used frequently in everyday life. The use of portraits on banknotes took flight after the economic crises of the 1920s, when trust in the banking system and the economy had eroded. The Weimar Republic in present-day Germany saw the price of bread go up from 160 marks to 200,000,000,000 marks in just a year. This hyperinflation led to the design of emergency banknotes *(Notgeld)* to reflect the quickly changing rates. Banknotes began to portray national figures and statesmen in the hope of instilling a sense of trust.

Counterfeiting has been one of the greatest motivators for a country's need to redesign its currency.

RICHARD ZEID, DESIGNER

The Green Back

In 2003, in the midst of war-torn Baghdad, the US government flew in 363 tonnes of dollar bills from the New York Federal reserve to Baghdad's central bank. In this covert operation, a total of $12 billion was flown in on different flights, 281 million bills of $20, $50 and $100 as plastic-wrapped bricks, heavily guarded by military personnel. The money came from Saddam Hussein's financial assets and was intended to pay government employees. How much of the $12 billion actually reached the employees is unclear, but it is known that a large part of it disappeared during transport.[29]

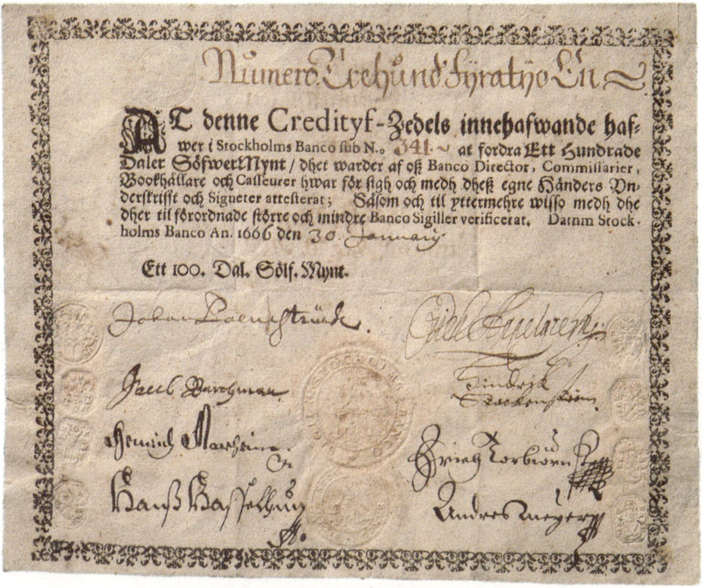

The first European banknote, the Swedish 100 daler banknote, 1666, 155 × 195 mm.

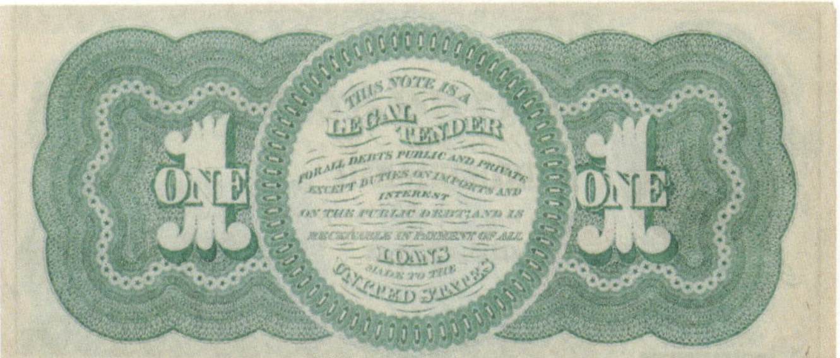

The first 'greenback' design of the US one dollar bill, 1862, 79 × 187 mm.

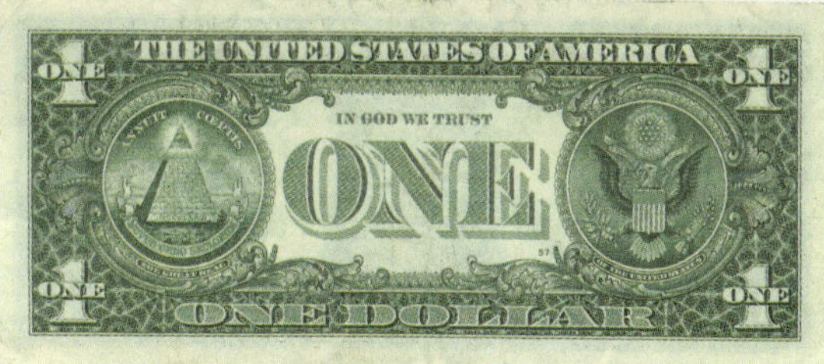

US one dollar bill, 2003, 66 × 156 mm.

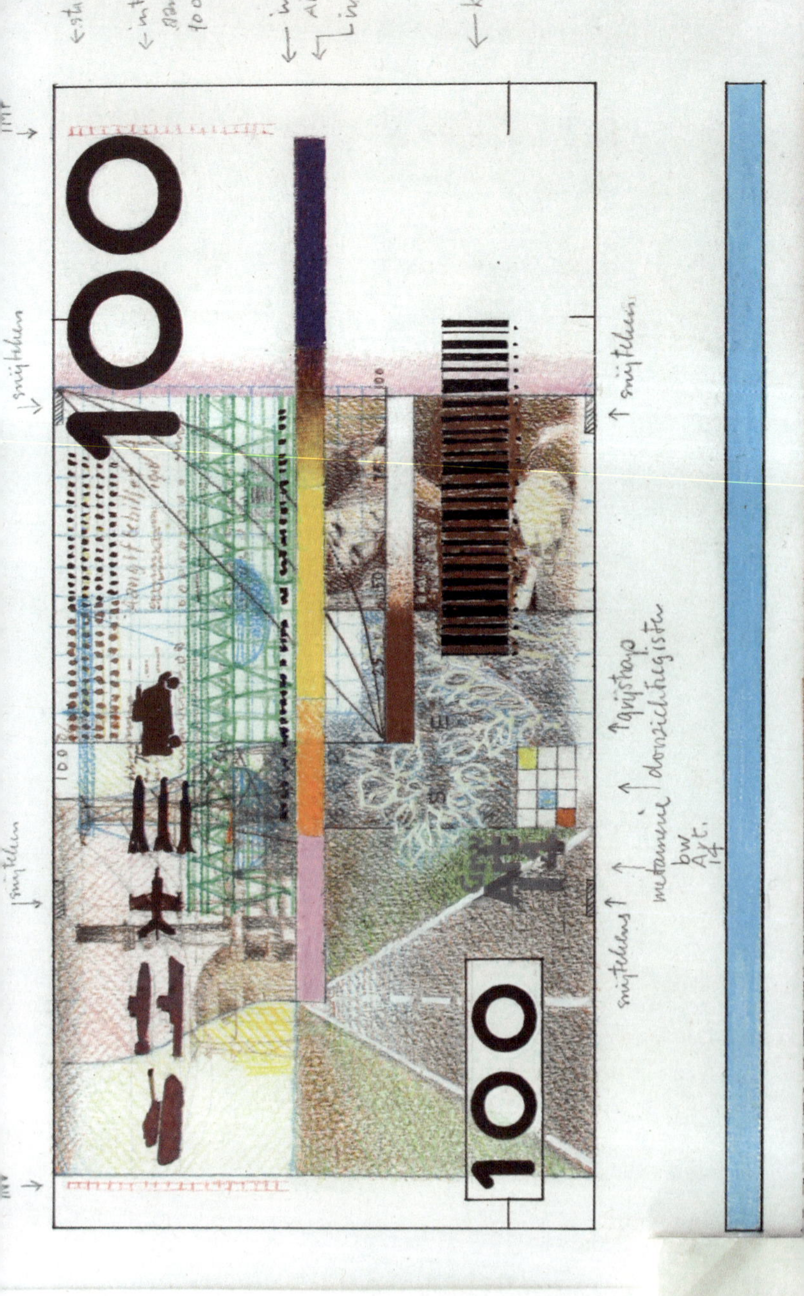

War and money have always been related. A trusted currency requires a strong government backed by military power, as a currency from an instable government is just not very trustworthy. The most widely used currency today is the US dollar, and it is considered the global currency. This dates back to World War II, when the allied countries made a plan for a financial order in the post-war world. It was then decided that exchange rates would be linked to the US dollar. This dominance of the dollar has less to do with the trustworthiness of the colour green than with the military and economic dominance of the US. Two-thirds of US currency is used abroad, and the country that supplies this currency is not coincidentally also the country with 800 military bases outside its own borders. Historically the US has not shunned away from using its military might to force a hand in economic trade. The power of a currency depends on the ability to drop bombs in any place in the world at any moment.[30]

The relation between war and money becomes evident in the designs that Jan van Toorn (1932–2020) proposed for the competition for the Dutch banknotes in 1986. He wanted to show money as a crucial element of society. The design for the

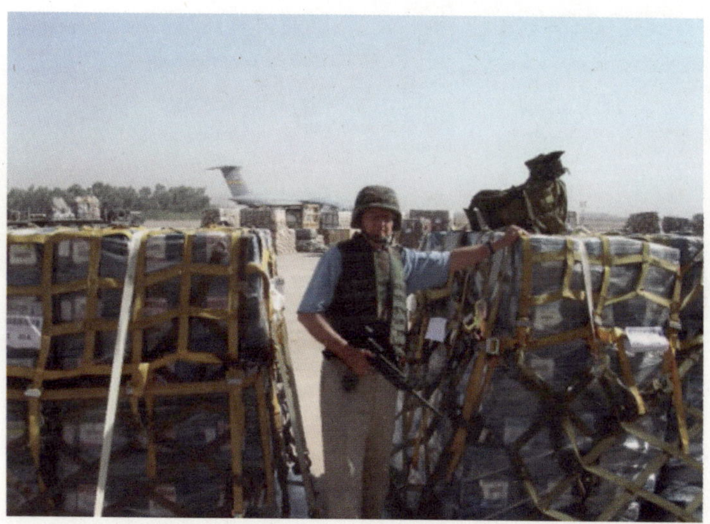

↑   Pallets of $2.4 billion in US currency arriving in Iraq, 2004.
←   Jan van Toorn, 100 guilder bank note design proposal for De Nederlandsche Bank, 1986.

100-guilder note shows a nuclear power plant and weapons; fighters, missiles, tanks, armed vehicles. This was at a time when there were mass-scale protests in the Netherlands against nuclear weapons and many Dutch were outraged with the arms race of the cold war. Van Toorn explains that he knew the banknotes would not be chosen as the competitions' winner, but that he took part in the competition for the sake of the experience.[31] His banknotes are perhaps the only ones ever designed that connect money to the state's military power.

Endnotes

At face value the banknote is an administrative document for daily economic exchange. But money ends up being much more. In popular culture we see people going crazy over stacks of bills in films, music videos, and game shows. Money isn't worth anything as an object, but it represents purchasing power, which is why it has come to symbolize power, luxury, generosity, luck, fortune, happiness, even beauty. This symbolic value is perhaps why artists and activists have often used banknotes as a medium to criticize

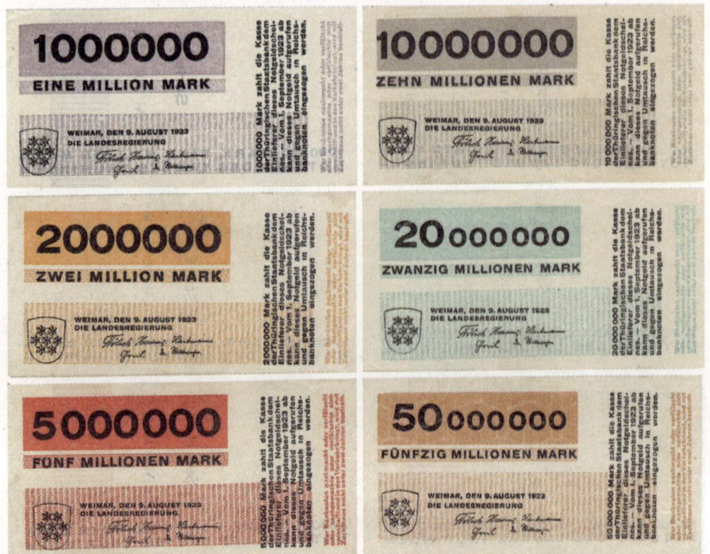

Emergency banknotes *(Notgeld)* designed by Herbert Bayer for the State Bank of Thuringia, 1923.

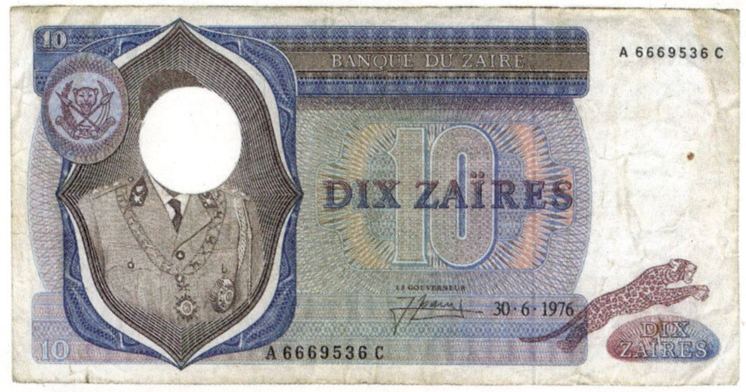

Banknote from Zaïre (present-day Democratic Republic of the Congo) with the head of Mobutu punched out after 1997, when he was ousted.

capitalism or consumerism. But singling out money as the culprit of capitalism would be missing the point of how capitalism works. Every society has used forms of money to track economic transactions, and by itself money doesn't have to be a symbol of capitalism or exploitation.

In his life-long work to understand capitalism, Karl Marx notes that the problem is not money itself, but that in capitalism money disguises social relations.[32] A dollar earned by a fourteen-year-old selling candy on the street for eight hours in the afternoon heat, is worth the same as a dollar earned in a millisecond by a stockbroker in an air-conditioned office, even though the time and efforts it took them to earn that dollar are not anywhere near comparable. What money does, is that it reduces any social or cultural association to a simple digit, which is precisely what also allows us to consume guilt-free. When we earn ten dollars, we simply have no way of finding out how the value was created that these ten dollars represent. This is why ultimately everything in capitalism can have a price tag: water, a river, CO_2 emissions, even a human life. Therefore, imagining a currency that reflects economic transactions as well as the social relations it represents, would have to coincide with an economic system that prioritizes social and human values over economic growth.

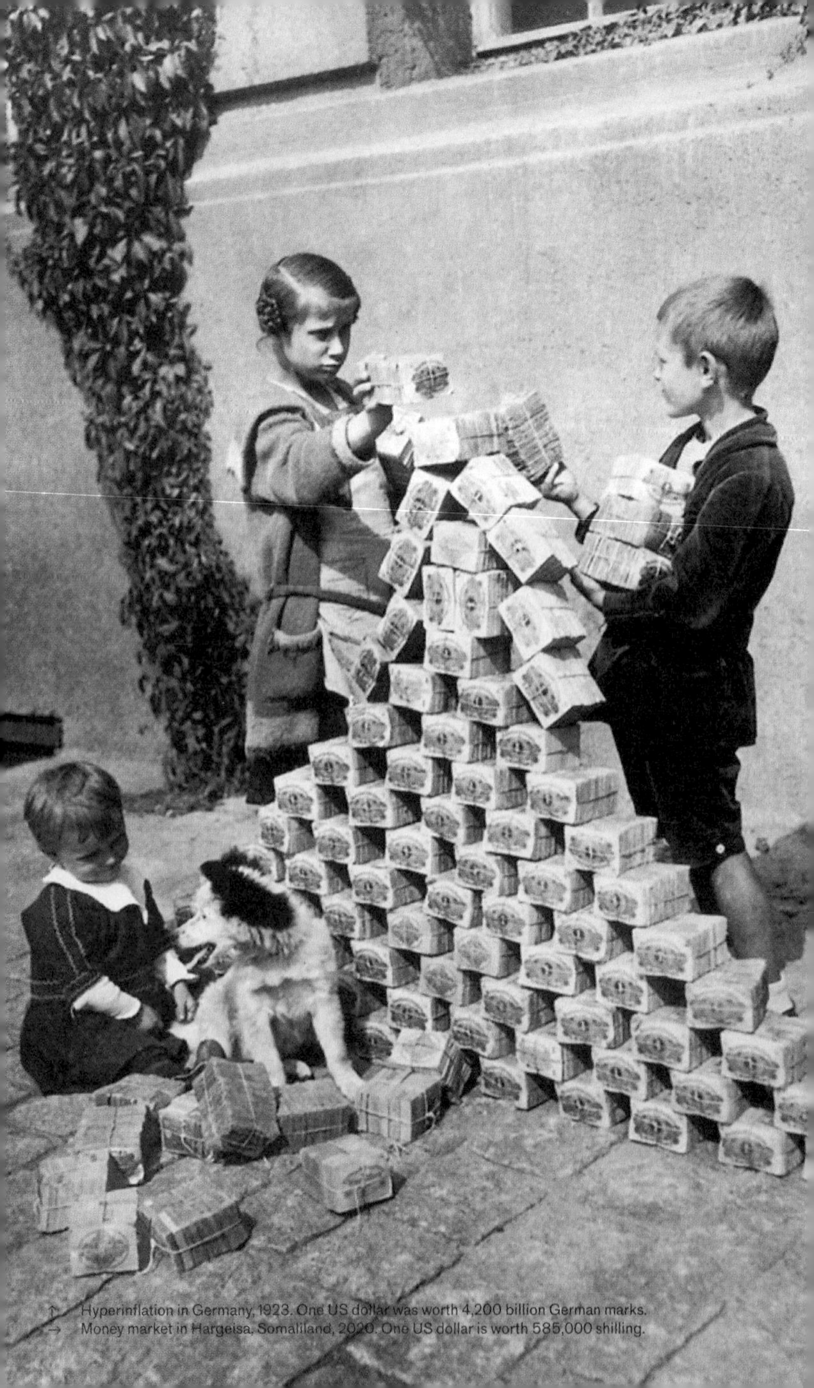

↑ Hyperinflation in Germany, 1923. One US dollar was worth 4,200 billion German marks.
→ Money market in Hargeisa, Somaliland, 2020. One US dollar is worth 585,000 shilling.

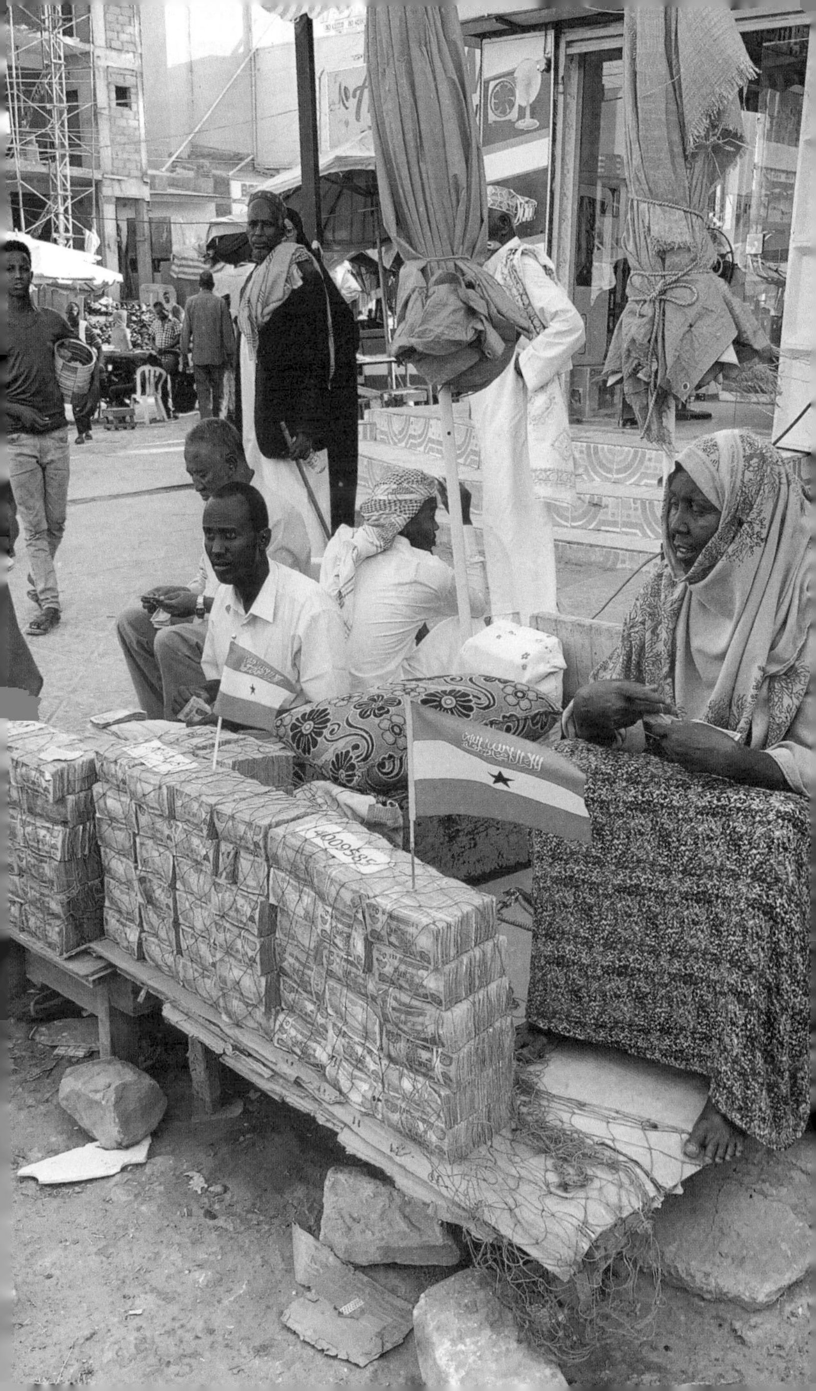
4009585

THE PLASTIC ECONOMY

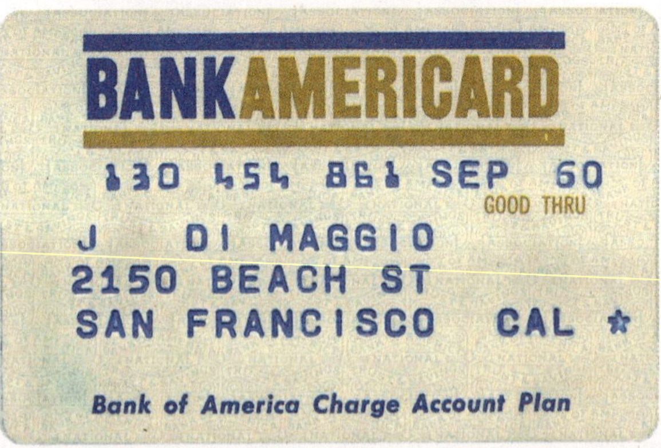

The first BankAmericard, a pre-cursor of the VISA card, 1958.

Coins and banknotes are fetishized objects, so what happens if cash disappears? The end of cash started in 1971, when the US abandoned the gold standard. As the world's global currency was no longer backed by gold, its value became solely based on trust in national governments and the global financial system. Together with the low cost of plastics and the new possibilities of information technology, this gave rise to a new form of money: the credit card. Digital technology made it possible to replace the authority and security provided by the designer as a scribe with binary information. The graphic designer no longer assigns trust or prevent counterfeiting in virtual currency forms, but has to manufacture positive associations in order to encourage spending.

Credit cards were invented in 1921 but did not reach high circulation until the 1960s. The first successful credit card was the BankAmericard (the precursor of the VISA card) issued by the Bank of America in 1958. In the same year American Express became the first credit card that could be used outside of the US.

Credit card companies used aggressive marketing to gain a market share. The BankAmericard was mailed to more than a million people in California, among whom the entire population of Fresno. It was a success. Two years later, cardholders in Fresno had spent $60 million with their new cards.[33]

Before the credit card, small loans existed in the form of store credit or family and community loans. Credits cards introduced easy and portable forms of credit, making debt an easy way to enjoy luxuries people could not yet afford. Credit cards turned out to be an extremely profitable business, since credit card companies found a loophole which allowed them to charge sky-high interest rates. Today a third of cardholders pay interest rates of 20% or higher.[34] Credit card debts have grown exponentially since 1950 from nothing to over $1 trillion today, with an average of $8,402 per US household.

As Light as a Free-Floating Dollar

The form of the credit card perfectly illustrates virtual money. Its size, its printed surface and thickness does not reveal anything about its value, which is inscribed in the digital information on the magnetic strip, or the card's chip. Value that has to be extracted by machines and has to be communicated via screens or printouts. The OCR-A typeface (1968) is especially designed to be read by machines, and the credit card's 16-digit number is not easily memorized. The invisibility of the credit card's value, hidden by its lightness and shiny surface, makes it an easy object to promote.

Its mundane appearance is an ingenious way to make money from people who have none. This is why the credit card industry flooded US households with 8 billion credit card solicitations in 2006 alone.[35] It is no longer allowed to send people free credit cards, but aggressive marketing techniques in the US persist, targeting those most vulnerable and in need of fast credit. Credit cards are also effective surveillance tools. Each time a credit or debit card is used we forfeit part of our privacy. Credit cards leave a detailed trail of our location, spending behaviour, desires, and needs, which can be marketed and sold for security or marketing purposes.

Everyday Speculation

The shift from paper to plastic card is not just a formal transformation, but an ideological one. A cash payment is done with money that you have, whereas most credit card payments take an advance on money that is expected in the future. A credit card's appearance remains the same, independent of one's bank balance, making it seem one can spend infinitely. That puts financial risk at the heart of everyday spending. Together with mortgages debts and student loans, citizens are expected to actively participate in financial risks that provide the raw material for financial speculation.[36]

With the advent of virtual money taking over physical money, the role of the scribe is outsourced to automated technology. Transactions are digitally stored and inscribed, only indirectly visible through online or offline balance sheets. Credit card users are expected to keep track of their own financial situation, betting on that job they are hoping to land, or a raise that was promised. Society expects citizens to take out loans and mortgages and invest in their

MICR (Magnetic Ink Character Recognition) E-13B, Stanford Research Institute and GE, 1958.

New Alphabet, Wim Crouwel, 1967.

OCR-A, American Type Founders, 1968.

OCR-B, Adrian Frutiger, 1968.

Typefaces designed for machine reading, or optical character recognition (OCR). Many of these were designed for automatic processing of accounting and routing information on bank checks. The OCR-A is still used on bar codes, credit cards, and bank checks.

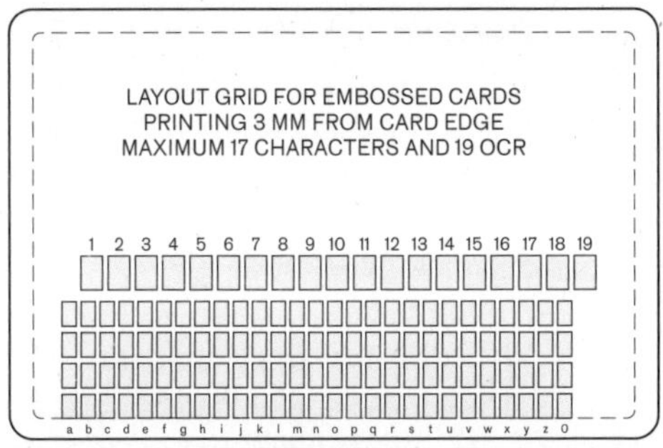

Face side

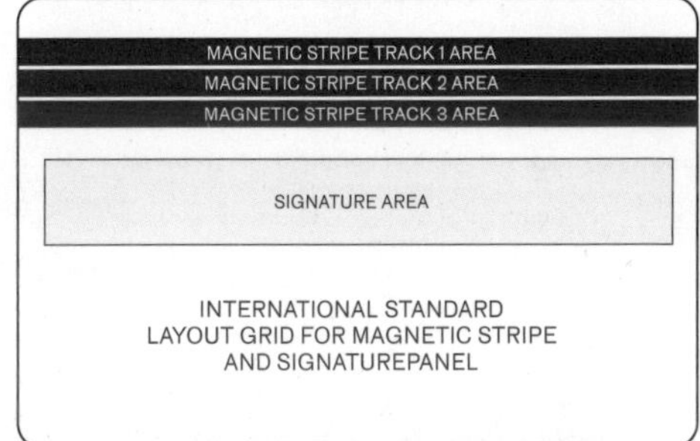

Reverse side

Design guidelines for credit cards with magnetic stripe, 86 × 54 mm, thickness 760 micron.

future. But when risk-taking leads to a crash of the financial system like in 2008, it is not citizens but banks and financial institutions who receive most of the compensation.

Titanium Plastic

The success of the credit card form has led to an almost ubiquitous use. From government identity cards, healthcare cards, to discount cards, many of us carry dozens of plastic cards around. Banks and credit card companies therefore require designers to make cards look more valuable. In the form of different spending categories, where a certain amount of money upgrades your card to a more luxurious level. Even within the world of plastic, design details like finishes, coloured plastic cores, and subtle typography can specify certain classes or bank privileges. Each category of credit is carefully designed to fit its net worth.

Take the JP Morgan Reserve card, which is made of the rare material palladium. You can get one of you have $10 million in assets. It has no printing, just inscribed information in the metal. Another prized card is the American Express Centurion card. To be eligible, you need to spend at least €250,000 with the card each year. Nicknamed the 'black card', it is made of anodized titanium with information etched in the material. There is an entire category of this credit extravagance. Cards made of pure gold, like the Kazakh Sberbank card or cards with an actual diamond inlay; the Eurasian Diamond Card Visa Infinite. A fetishized version that defies its origin as a consumer object carrying digital information that extends quick credit.

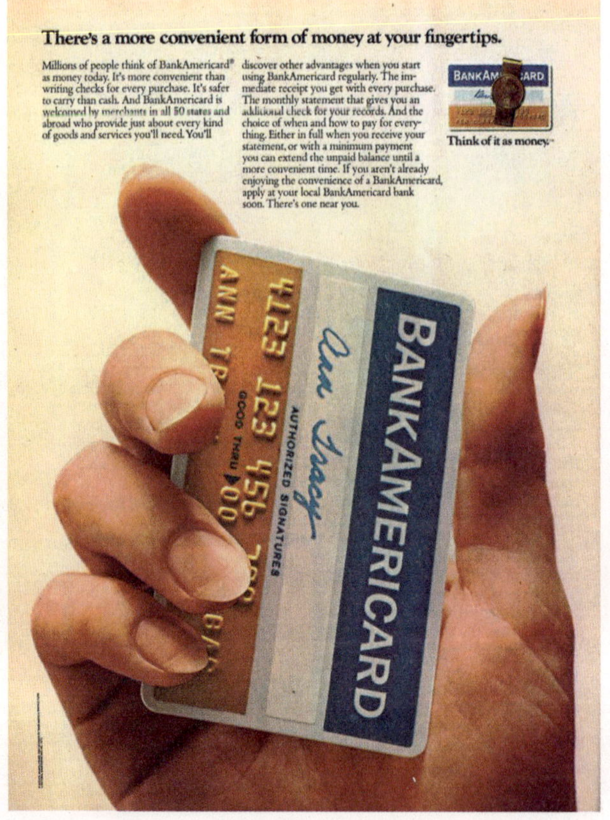

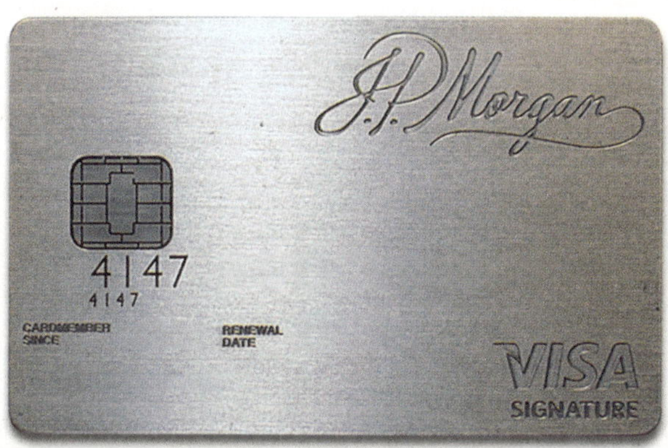

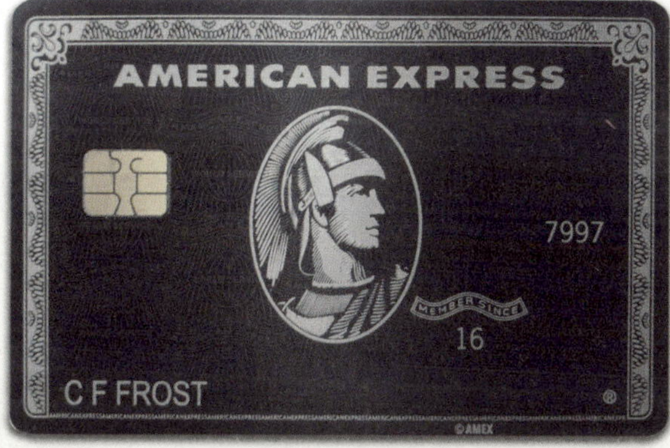

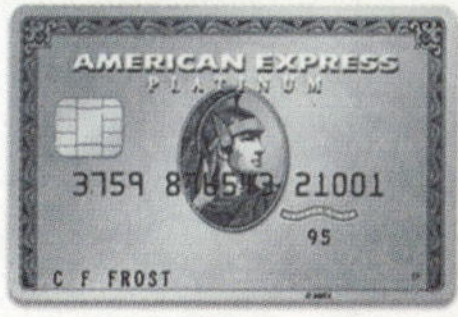

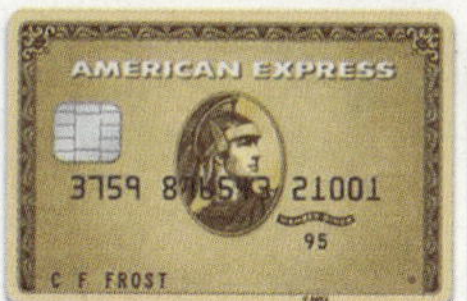

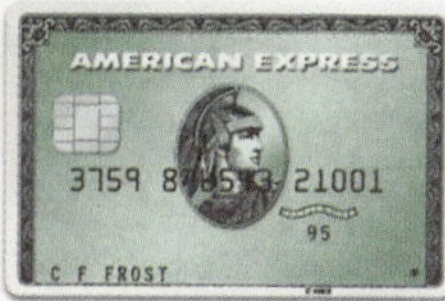

↑ JP Morgan Reserve card, made from Palladium.
↑ American Express Centurion Card, made from titanium, the most expensive credit card in the world.
↑ Three hierarchies of American Express cards, Platinum Card, Gold card, and regular card.
← Advertisement for the BankAmericard as part of the 'Fresno drop', 1958.

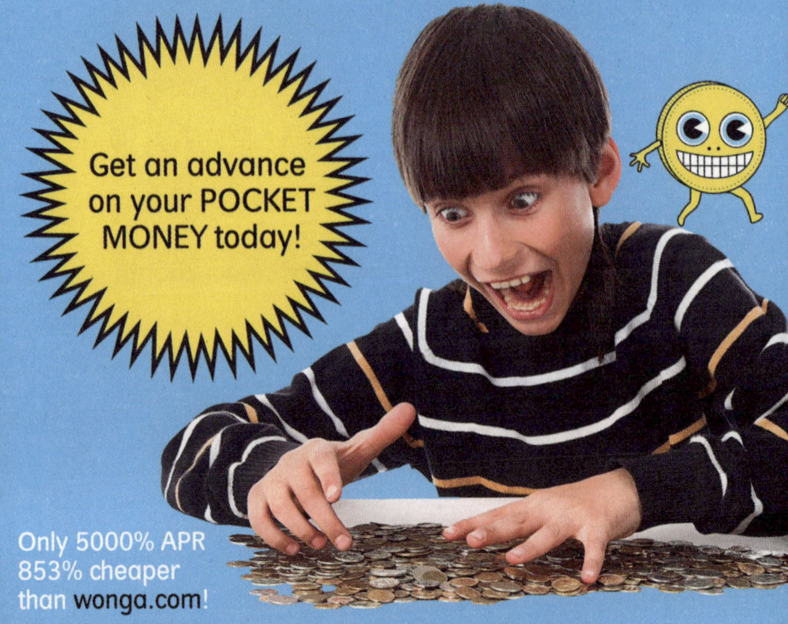

Payday Loans 4 Kids
Get an advance on your POCKET MONEY today!
Only 5000% APR 853% cheaper than wonga.com!
POCKETMONEYLOANS.COM
Representative example Amount of credit: £10 for 18 days. Interest: £24.65. Interest rate: 245%pa (fixed) Transmission fee: £6.50. Total repayment of: £40.15 plus late payment charge of £20 rolled over for next 18 days plus interest. Second missed repayment of £148
late payment charge of £20 rolled over for next 18 days plus interest. Third missed repayment of £415.01 rolled over with interest and so on and so on until we take you for everything you have and you lay awake at night with the stress boiling in your veins, going over and
what you owe and who you owe it to and what you can sell or pawn just to keep your neck above the water for another week. Representative 5000% APR, fees charged on missed payments, early repayments or non-payments with compound interest added to every last b

PLAYING WITH MONEY

Governments and banks don't like cash. It is costly to design, print, circulate, and distribute. It can be counterfeited, it is anonymous, and can be kept out of sight and control, which is why it is favoured in informal economies. Even more importantly, banks cannot gather spending data. This is why governments and banks have tried hard to abolish cash in favour of digital payment systems such as credit cards, debit cards, and payment apps. In the Netherlands more than sixty percent of all payments in 2012 were digital.[37]

Many shops and restaurants no longer accept cash, and even debit and credit cards are quickly losing terrain to banking and payment applications. Long bank account numbers, credit card numbers, verification codes and passwords have turned people to apps that use fingerprint or face recognition verification. Paying with smartphone applications provides the unique possibility for companies to link financial information to social media, location data, and contacts. Digital payment systems have tarnished the monopoly of banks, and many tech companies are now getting into finance, for example Facebook with its currency Libra, and Apple Pay. Some of these tech companies are finding new ways to turn money and finances into a game.

Money and games are never far removed, whether people are gambling, playing monopoly, betting on the stock market, or simply toss a coin. Ironically, among the first printed objects in China were banknotes and playing cards.[38] Finance itself has been compared to a game, as in the term 'casino capitalism', coined by Susan Strange in 1987.[39] Decades of innovation in the financial industry have been used to extract more profit from the financial activities of everyday citizens. Financial technology, (FinTech) is merely the latest step. Venmo is a popular payment application with more than 40 million users, that functions as a social network. Designed

←   Darren Cullen, *Pocket Money Loans*, 2013.

for friends to split bills or give group gifts, it comes with a feed where people can discuss their shared expenses. Such social paying apps are convenient, but they can also bring out unequal relationships. The Chinese payment app WePay further gamifies the paying experience by offering options such as randomized payments, and gift payments for holidays or graduation.

Media and communications researcher Rachel O'Dwyer finds this gamification of money worrying.[40] When spending money, splitting bills, or managing finances becomes a competitive activity among friends and relatives in plain sight, this may further promote and celebrate money as a person's most important quality. By doing so it can exclude or punish those who are poor or choose to live on small incomes. More importantly, alternative or non-monetary exchanges such as sharing, barter, or non-financial gifting, do not exist in these apps. Here, the role of the designer as a scribe is no longer to assign trust, but to create interfaces for websites and apps to keep users addicted to the application for as long as possible. Notifications, infinite scrolling, and limiting navigation are interface techniques borrowed from gambling, manipulating users into spending more time on the app than intended. Visual interface elements on paying apps still reference forms of trust and authority, but the design mostly serves to create positive and playful associations to nudge people into experiencing finance as entertainment, ultimately with the goal of spending more and spending often.

Your Credit Score is Excellent
In countries such as China and the US, personal privileges are increasingly influenced by credit scores, conjured up by algorithms that combine credit history and other personal details. Such scores can determine if you can buy a house, the height of your insurance rates, but are also used in dating apps, and by employers. More than half of US companies check credit scores before hiring new employees.[41]

Cathy O'Neil is a mathematician who warns against the dangers of credit scores in *Weapons of Math Destruction* (2016). Credit score systems often contain errors, like two people with the same name and birth date can be easily mixed up. Credit scores also

Today we're added up in every conceivable way as statisticians and mathematicians patch together a mishmash of data, from our zip codes and Internet surfing patterns to our recent purchases. Many of their pseudoscientific models attempt to predict our creditworthiness.

CATHY O'NEIL, MATHEMATICIAN

perpetuate class division and racial discrimination, because credit may be influenced by the neighbourhood you live in or who you are related to. In China credit scores are set up as part of a social scoring system for all citizens, where your credit and even your purchase history can influence your chances to obtain a travel visa or a government job. Although this is still in an early phase, eventually a social score could put someone on a nationwide blacklist, which currently includes no less than 13 million people. Blacklisting would prohibit you from sending your kids to certain schools, or buying train or airplane tickets.[42]

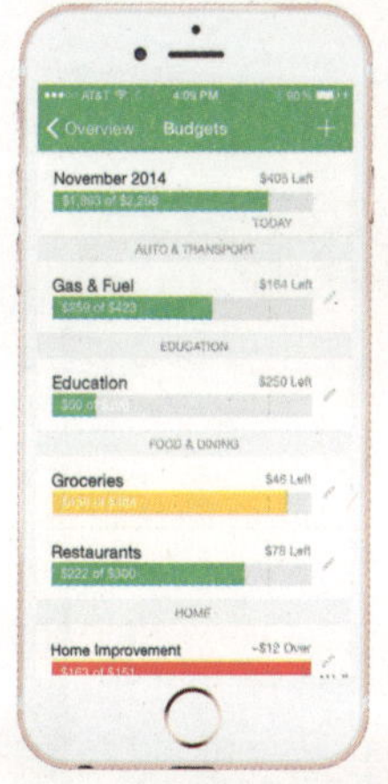
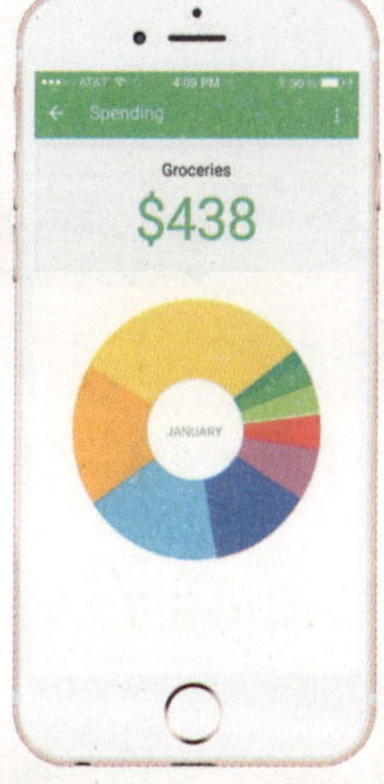
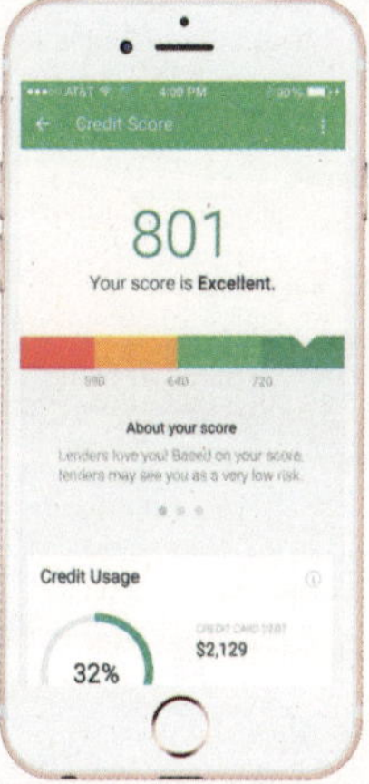

Mint personal finance app, Intuit 2007–2021.

As credit scores are becoming more important in society, companies are anticipating this by selling applications that help to manage finances. Mobile applications such as Mint keep track of all your spending, and calculate your credit score. Mint promotes this to say they are helping customers to get financially 'fit'. These apps obtain valuable insight in anyone's spending behaviour. The design of financial applications is inspired by the gambling industry.[43]

Apps such as Mint, Apple Pay, Venmo and WePay perfect this strategy, using the reliability of a spreadsheet with the fun colours and typography of gambling and computer games. The playful design obscures the function that these apps have to discipline our financial behaviour as good citizens, gather data to categorize and nudge us towards products, and posit money as the core social value.

In spite of anti-establishment rhetoric, blockchains are increasingly being developed by major corporations, banks, states and international financial institutions to secure and expedite their infrastructures.

MAX HAIVEN, RESEARCHER

→   Group chat within the Venmo payment app, 2021.
→   *Yes, gelukt* (Yes, it worked). Memes when completing transactions in the payment app Tikkie, 2021.
↓   Apple Pay website, 2020.

Those same colors show up in your spend summaries. See lots of orange? That's Food and Drinks. Pink? That's Entertainment. Looks like a fun weekend.

Learn more

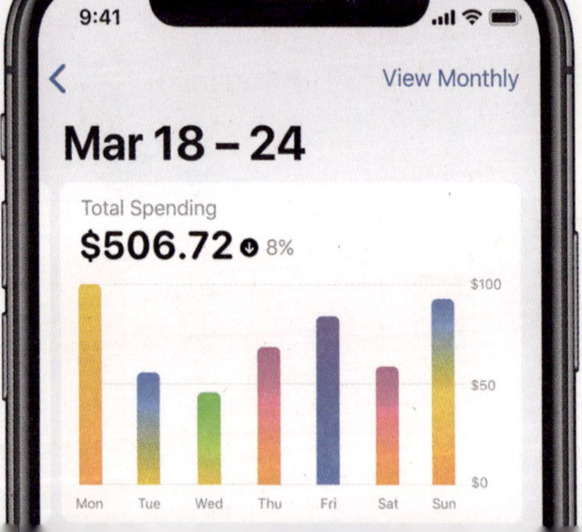

Cryptocurrencies

A much-discussed topic is cryptocurrencies, a form of money that only exists digitally. They are created and circulated outside of government control, and therefore popular for conducting informal or illicit transactions. Bitcoin (2009) was the first cryptocurrency, and by now there are about 1,800 others. Cryptocurrencies are associated with informal transactions, because some of them can be used anonymously. How cryptocurrencies exactly work is notoriously complex, and is better explained elsewhere. In the context of this book there are a few aspects worth noting: the way they create trust, and whether they are anti-capitalist or not.

Cryptocurrencies are not backed by governments (yet), and for a currency to function it needs to be trusted. What makes cryptocurrencies interesting is that trust is not forged by state power, signatures, or printing techniques, but by using computer encryption and computer networks. The blockchain is the Bitcoin database that assigns trust to each transaction. It does that by leaving a copy of each timestamped transaction on every computer in the network. Since there is not one central place where the information is stored, no single person can interfere or control the currency. Trust is outsourced to strong cryptography (mathematics) on the one hand, and the power of a multitude of computers (the collective) on the other. Blockchain, in theory, can be useful to organize large decentralized digital infrastructures without government interference.

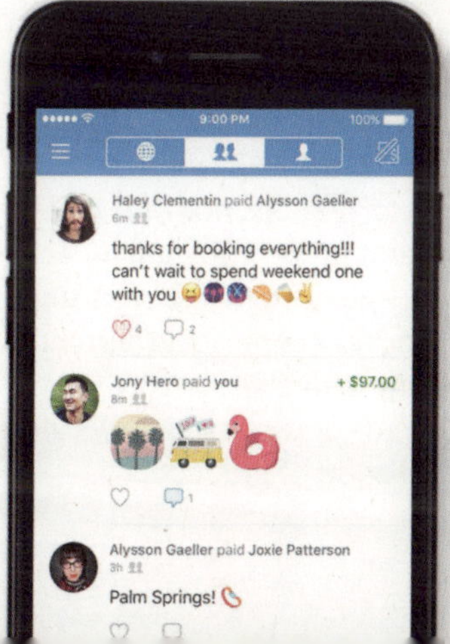

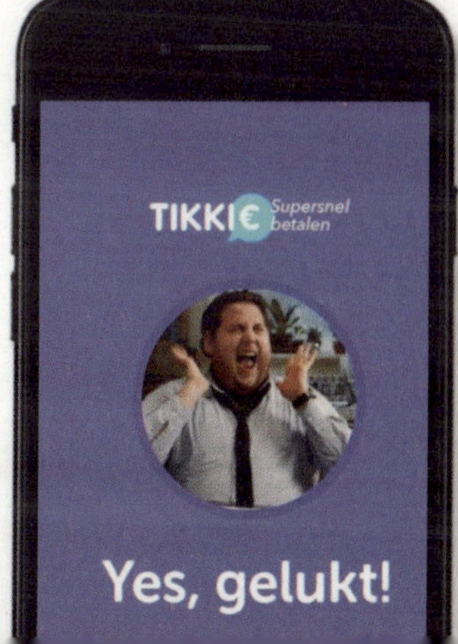

The ingenuity of cryptocurrencies to create a global currency without government interference doesn't mean they are anti-capitalist. On the contrary, the popularity of Bitcoin has driven up its value from \$0 to \$46,966 in twelve years, making early investors incredibly rich. The energy needed to 'mine' Bitcoin is proportional to how many people are mining, and today one Bitcoin transaction requires the energy nine homes consume in one year.[44] Its incredible increase in value has attracted so many interested parties, that power-consuming computer systems are custom-built to mine them.

The popularity of cryptocurrencies ignores the fact that wealth cannot be created out of nothing. As long as cryptocurrencies can be used to buy actual goods and services, the millions that Bitcoin investors have made will have to be paid for by someone, somewhere. Whether through the slow price increase of food or real estate, a higher pensioning age, or the deflation of national currencies, or the price of lithium which is needed to create the computer batteries to mine the cryptocurrencies.

Alternative Currencies

Any serious effort to create an economic system that prioritizes human and social values over profit would require a currency that is more socially embedded. Some initiatives have a go at this by using alternative or complimentary currencies. Many of these currencies, such as the Bijlmer Euro, or the Brixton Pound, are local currencies that keep value circulating in the region. These local currencies often have the same value as the national currency, the difference is that they are only issued locally and accepted locally.

For example, if you do a design job for a local beer brewery, and you spend the money at a big supermarket chain, the value created in the community by you and the brewer leaves the community. Now if instead the brewer pays you the equivalent in a local currency, you would have to spend it at local shops (the only places that accept them), and the value is kept in the community. As a benefit, local shopkeepers may be more inclined to hire you rather than a designer from far away, since you accept the local currency. The advantage of such a local economy is that any profits stay in the region, there is more contact and trade between people locally, and less costs and pollution due to transport of products.

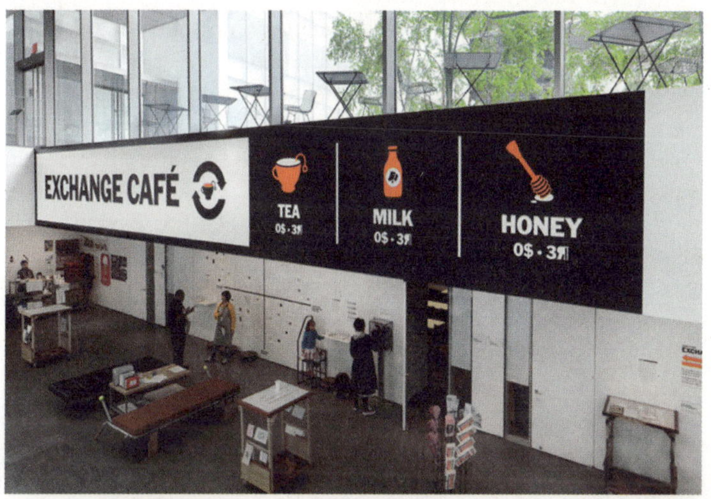

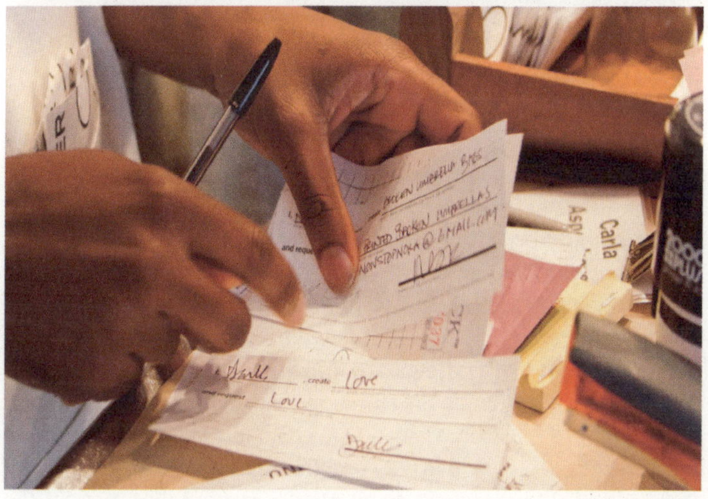

Caroline Woolard, *Exchange Café*, 2013. At Exchange Café, you will be greeted by waitstaff with direct experience working in, with, and for solidarity economies. You will be offered products with political biographies: tea carried across borders, milk distributed by prison abolitionists, and honey gifted by bees. On the wall, an emergent publication about one-on-one engagement invites contributions, and TheExchangeArchive.com shows that artworks emerge in dialog between people, not in solitary isolation. Exchange Cafe is a social space dedicated the power of one-to-one agreement. (text from artist website)

There are many alternative and local currencies in use. In 2006 there were sixteen regions in Germany where regional currencies were used instead of the Euro.[45] The last chapter of this book features the cultural network *Fora do Eixo* (off-axis) from Brazil, who have used their own $FdE currency since 2006. Some alternative currencies have their own bill designs and nominations, some are merely an upgraded version of existing bills. For example, the Bijlmer Euro was a project by artist Christian Nold to strengthen the community economy in this eastern district of Amsterdam. People could transform their €5 or €10 bill into Bijlmer Euros by pasting a sticker with an RFID chip on it. Shop owners would scan the chip and the circulation of the currency could be followed by everyone via a website.[46]

A much older alternative currency, which wields a very different form of value, is TimeBanking. This form of currency began in the US in 1827 as an experiment by Josiah Warren, whose shop would sell goods in exchange for the time it took to produce them. It is based on a very simple concept: one hour of work is equivalent to one hour of someone else's work, independent of what that work is. One hour of work by a creative director is worth the same as an hour spent by a cleaner vacuuming that same office. The currency derives its value from the resource that is scarce for all human beings, time. According to Wikipedia there are Timebanks in 34 countries, with 500 in the US alone.[47] One credit equals one hour of work, which is known as a time credit or a time dollar. When someone earns a time credit, it may be kept indefinitely with the advantage that there is never any inflation or deflation.[48]

Alternative currencies aren't legal, but national banks usually allow them to exist on a small scale. Since these currencies are not theoretical but used in very practical ways, we can learn something about different ways to create economies that respect the value of social life within communities. These kinds of small-scale experiments are also known as solidarity economy, or social and solidarity economy. The terms that are used for economic activities that are concerned with the needs and desires of people, rather than maximizing profit. This is a catch-all term for TimeBanks, barter networks, gift exchanges, community gardens, free give-away shops, sharing economies, and so on.

This chapter began with the designer as a scribe, as the one who is hired to provide graphic forms that authenticate and secure economic transactions, whether it is in the form of coins, banknotes, financial records, or stock market information. Digital forms such as credit cards or payment apps need designers to make these products desirable and encourage spending. The designer finds herself locked in a role to authenticate state economic power, only to win the public's trust. The examples given here of small-scale economic experiments may seem far removed from what a graphic designer can do. But alternative currencies and the solidarity economy show that the agency of the designer goes far beyond those roles. Designers are economic actors, we earn money and spend money, we too are subjected to a system that tries hard to ignore the social relations behind money. By spending and earning money locally, by encouraging the use of alternative currencies or setting up barter networks, you can yourself begin by creating small alternative economies that strengthen social bonds instead of designing abstract forms to represent them.

Capitalism and other systems of power are ultimately vested in how we cooperate; they can only be overcome or changed if we cooperate; not only on the level of small experimental collectives or individual subcultures, but as a society.

MAX HAIVEN, RESEARCHER

→ Lawrence Weiner, *Hour Note prototype*, 2009. Paul Glover, *Ithaca Hours*, 1991. This Ain't Rock and Roll, *Brixton Pound ten pound note*, 2011. Christian Nold, *Bijlmer Euro*, 2009. Joseph Beuys, *Kunst = KAPITAL*, 1979. Zachary Gough, *Bourdieu: A Social Currency*, 2014.

TIME BANK
60 MINUTES

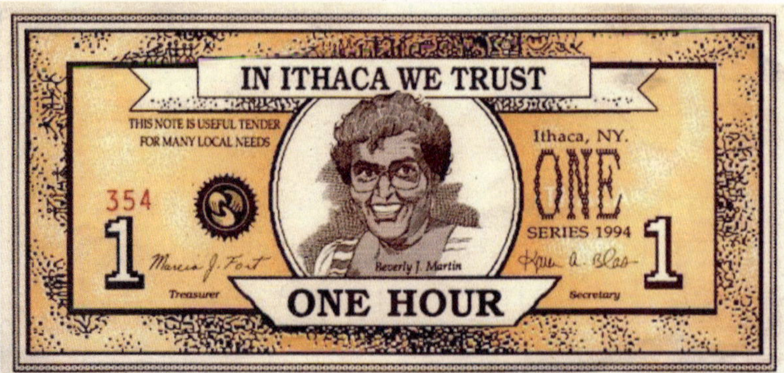

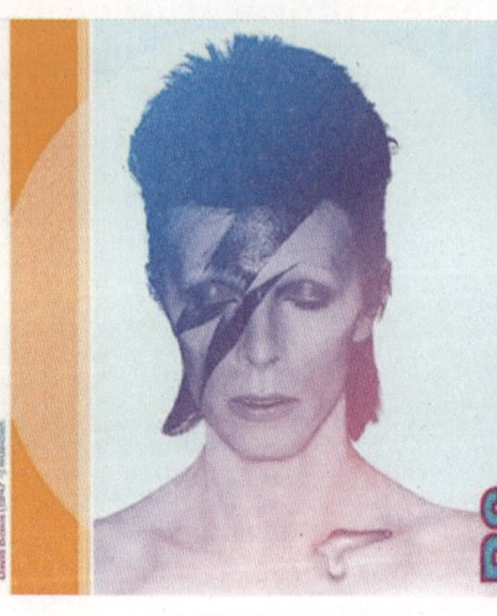

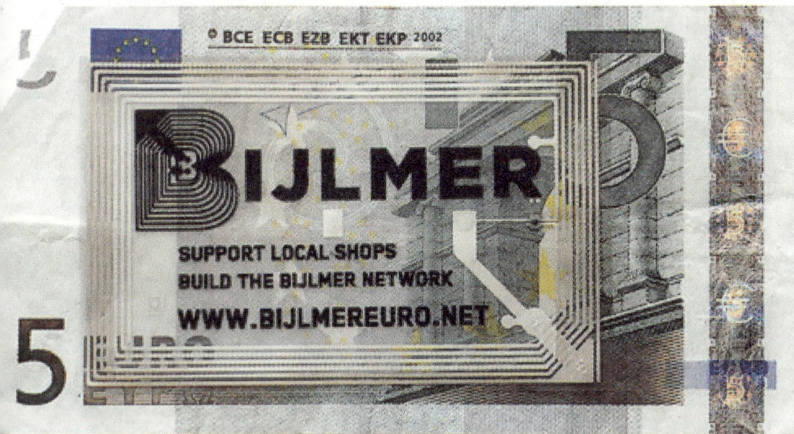
BCE ECB EZB EKT EKP 2002
BIJLMER
SUPPORT LOCAL SHOPS
BUILD THE BIJLMER NETWORK
WWW.BIJLMEREURO.NET
5
EURO

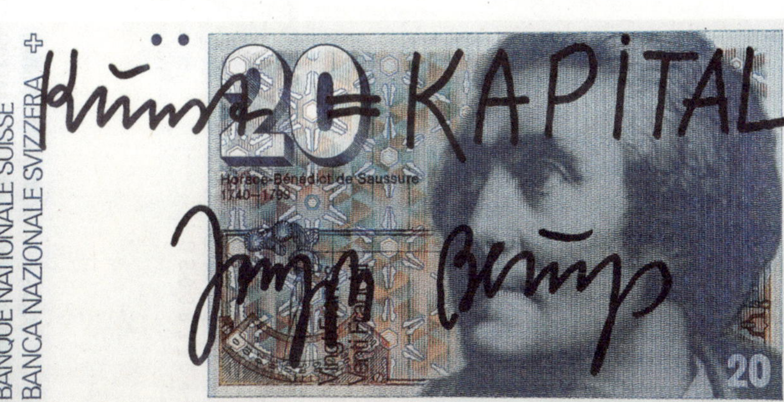
BANQUE NATIONALE SUISSE
BANCA NAZIONALE SVIZZERA
20 = KAPITAL
Horace-Bénédict de Saussure
1740—1799
20

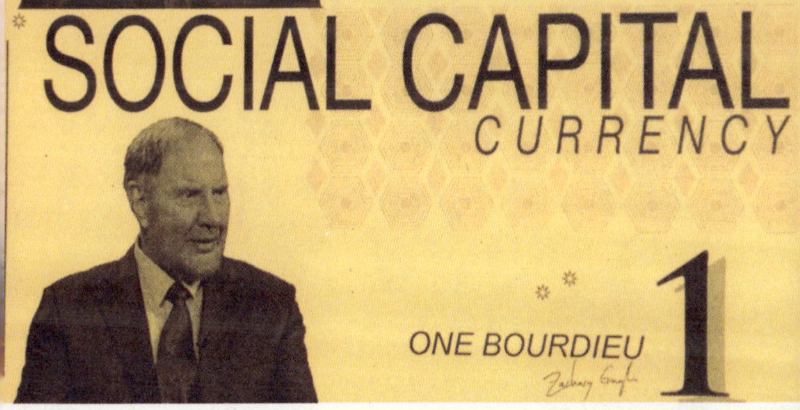
SOCIAL CAPITAL
CURRENCY
ONE BOURDIEU
1

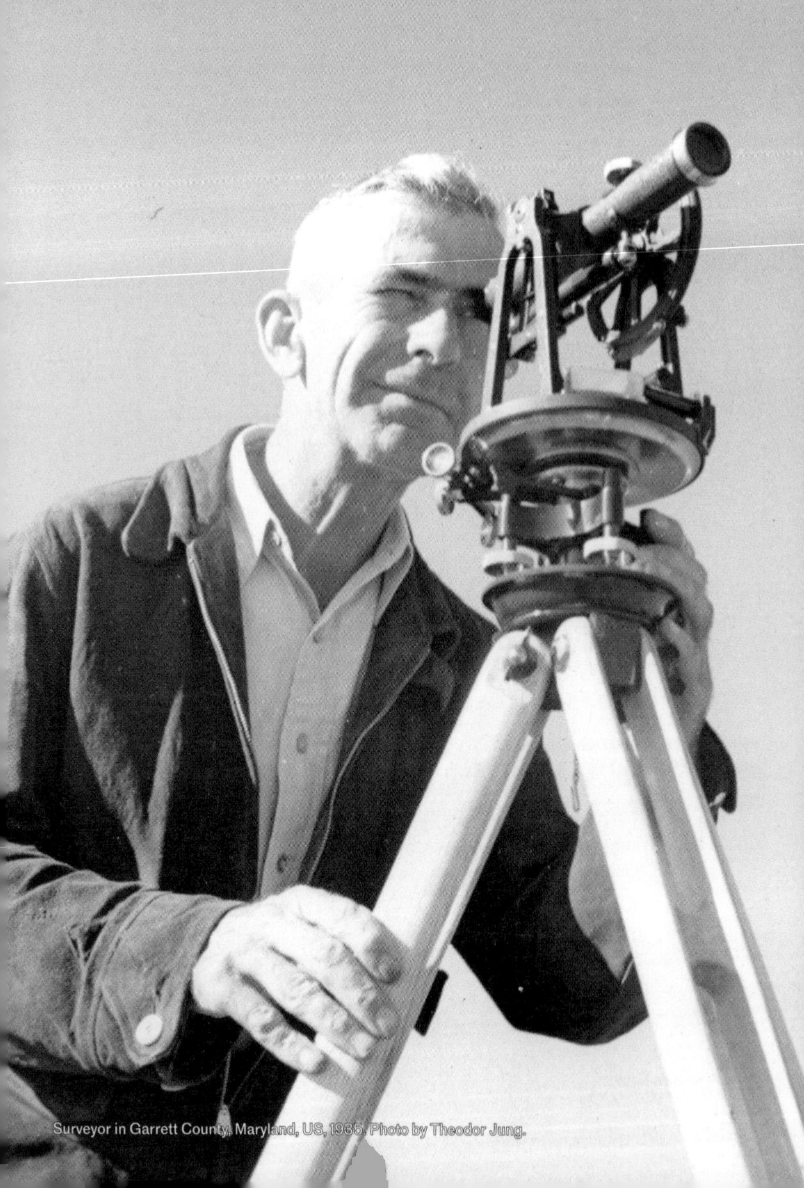

Surveyor in Garrett County, Maryland, US, 1935. Photo by Theodor Jung.

THE DESIGNER AS ENGINEER

Government has no other end,
but the preservation of property.
JOHN LOCKE

Formal languages and associational systems
are inevitable and good, becoming tyrannies only
when we are unconscious of them.
ROBERT VENTURI

Usage des Nouvelles Mesures.

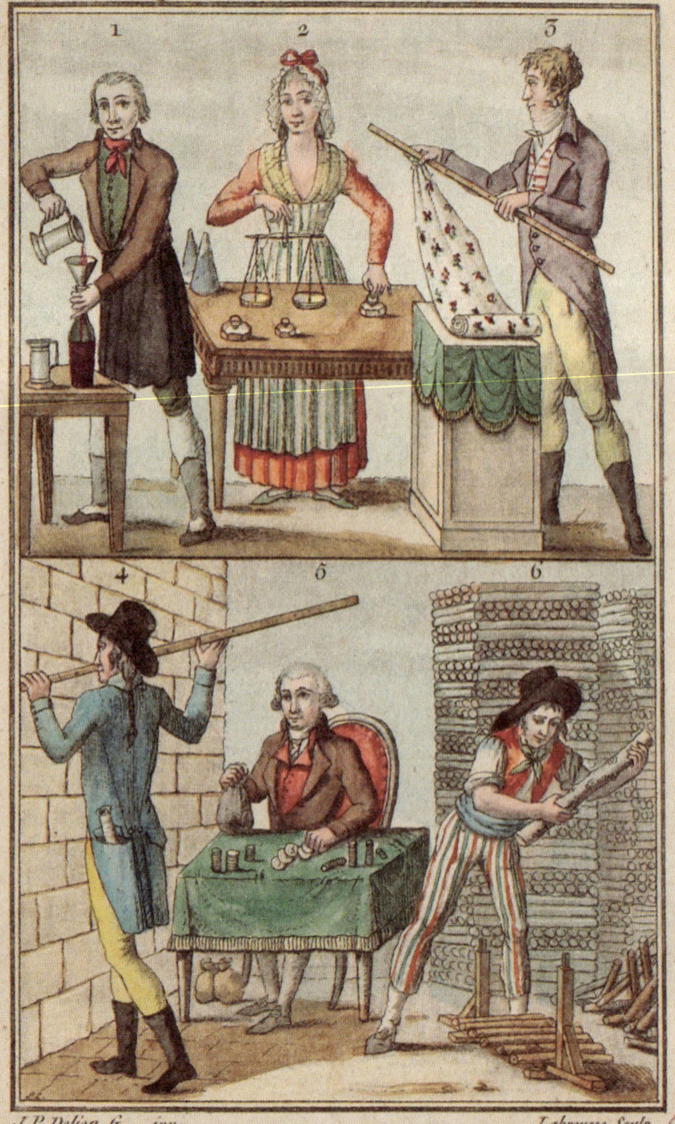

J.P. Delion G..... inv.   Labrousse Sculp.

1. le Litre (*Pour la* Pinte)   4. l'Are (*Pour la* Toise)

2. le Gramme (*Pour la* Livre)   5. le Franc (*Pour une* Livre Tournois)

3. le Mètre (*Pour l'*Aune)   6. le Stere (*Pour la* Demie Voie de Bois)

Déposé à la Bib.^{que} N^{le} le 24 Ventose An 8. | A Paris chez Delion Rue Montmartre N.º 242 près le Boulevard.

ONE SIZE FITS ALL

Every designer has to assume the role of engineer at some point. When design concepts have to be planned, organized, and executed on an industrial scale, creativity submits momentarily to strategies that solve technical problems. The objects produced by the designer as engineer are graphs, diagrams, maps, forms, manuals, and guidelines. Tools that are indispensable for governing economies and organizing industrial production. Tools that are often considered neutral, universal, and ubiquitous. Their aesthetics may be questioned, but rarely their reason for existence.

This particular role of the designer came out of the modern era that started with the Renaissance in Europe, which built on knowledge from Asia and the Middle East. Before, religion and spirituality had created a world view based on divine knowledge, until Western scientists too realized that the world could be measured, quantified, and understood through logic. This led to the age of Enlightenment, which gave birth to a culture of reason and debate that reinvigorated political and scientific life. The measuring by science created visual languages to document the resulting knowledge, but localized knowledge was also lost in the process. As James C. Scott writes 'the past three centuries as the triumph of standardized, official landscapes of control and appropriation over vernacular order'.[1]

Colonial expansion spread these ideas of knowledge across the world, which unfortunately replaced, or marginalized, indigenous and local forms of knowing. This Western idea of how knowledge is documented is so embedded in the global capitalist system today, that its legitimacy is rarely challenged. We find this in the measurements, grids, paper formats, and colour systems that are used by graphic designers.

← Coloured engraving showing the uses of the new measures of the metric system in France, 1800.

This chapter tries to understand to what extent the engineering side of graphic design serves capitalist production. What are the cultural and social values that were lost to benefit the fast growth of industrial capitalism? These questions do not seek to challenge the process of modernity, but are ways to imagine different ways of more socially embedded graphic design production.

One Size Fits All

Standardized systems are used by graphic designers to work across distances, sizes, and formats. The history of standards runs parallel to the history of economy. Before the metric system, each region in Europe used a variety of measurements specific to local trade. These were often human in more than one way. The body was often used as a measuring instrument (the elbow, the foot, the thumb) but these systems also carried cultural and social meanings.

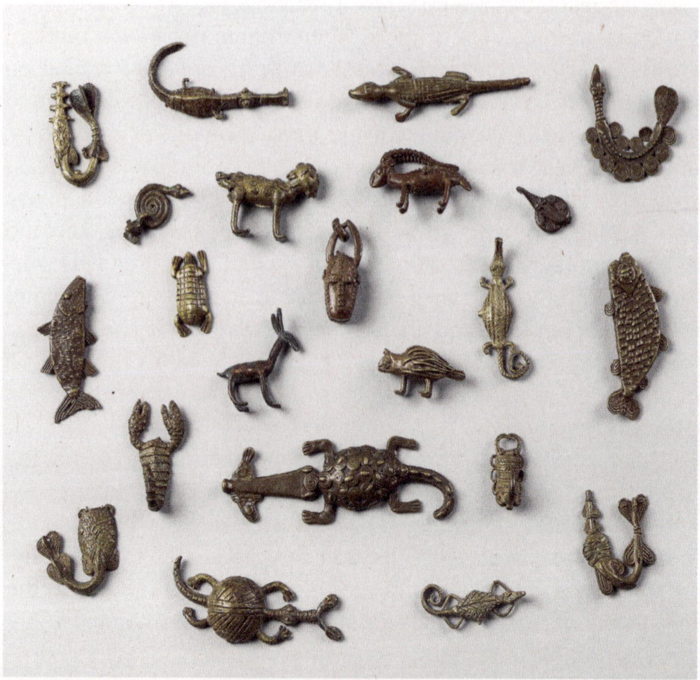

Akan gold weights from Ghana, West Africa (1400–1900). These brass figurines were used to measure gold dust.

 CAPS LOCK — Part 1

Vernacular measurement is only as precise as it needs to be for the purposes at hand. It is symbolised in such expressions as a 'pinch of salt', a 'stone's throw', 'a book of hay'.

JAMES C. SCOTT, POLITICAL SCIENTIST

Measurements evolved from the local context and not the other way around. Farmers would use different land measurements depending on the soil, the crop, and the location (sun, slope). If a farmer wanted to sell a piece of land, it made no sense to equate a hectare of sandy unfertile soil with the most productive patch. That's why measurements were used like the French *journal* (a day), which was the amount of land that could be ploughed in a single day.[2] The Ashanti in Ghana developed sophisticated measuring tools for weighing gold dust, on which their economy depended. Outstretched areas such as the Sahara knew detailed measurements for long distances, as a miscalculation would have dire consequences. These examples of pre-capitalist measurements reveal that economy is a social activity in which value is exchanged between people, creating cultural traditions and narratives in the process. Today's design systems on the other hand, are mostly the product of industrialization and economic efficiency.

One 40-millionth of the Earth's Diameter

In 1790 a commission in France was asked to come up with a new system of standards for measures and weights. In the eighteenth century over 700 measurements were used in France, and much time and effort was spent calculating the exchange of goods. Variations made measurements susceptible to those in power. For example, feudal lords demanded using small baskets for lending grain and bigger baskets when it was repaid.[3] Secondly, differences in land measurements stood in the way of a new national tax code. States depended on food supply, which required data on how much farm land there was. Anthropologist James C. Scott emphasizes in *Seeing Like a State* (1997) that local measurement practices were culturally rich and social, but not 'legible' for the state, and therefore needed to be standardized.[4]

If there is one victory of statecraft it is the metric system. The meter was calculated as 1/40,000,000th of the earth's diameter. This radical new concept of measurement shifted the scale of trade from a local to a planetary one. The new French nation state was first in the shift towards the standardization of bureaucracy and society, as the revolutionaries cried out 'one king, one law, one weight, and one measure'.[5] Although the metric system was emancipatory in its ideals—it lessened the power of aristocracy—most farmers saw it as something that was conjured up by bureaucrats, who knew nothing of local contexts. The French republic fared well with the standardization of measurements. Since the state decided how land was measured, and how crops were weighed, it could exert precise control over trade and taxes. Standardization was a way to prioritize economic efficiency over regional cultural and social relations.

Looking around any office of the western and westernized world—with the great exception of North America—one sees that the DIN and now ISO sizes have been victorious.

ROBIN KINROSS, DESIGN THEORIST

From Rags to Ratio
Paper sizes determine the work of graphic designers to a high degree. Before the invention of the current international standard of the A-formats, a great number of paper formats flourished in Western Europe. Sizes were derived from the available technology and material limitations. Parchment, which was made from animal hides, was limited to the size of the skin of the sheep and goats. When the first paper mills appeared in Europe, the size of the sheets depended on the reach of the arms of a worker holding the mould loaded with pulp.[6] Handmade paper sizes were approximate and were not referred to by their exact measurements. They would simply be known by names such as *Royale* or *Imperiale*, and the sizes of two sheets of Royale would differ by today's standards.

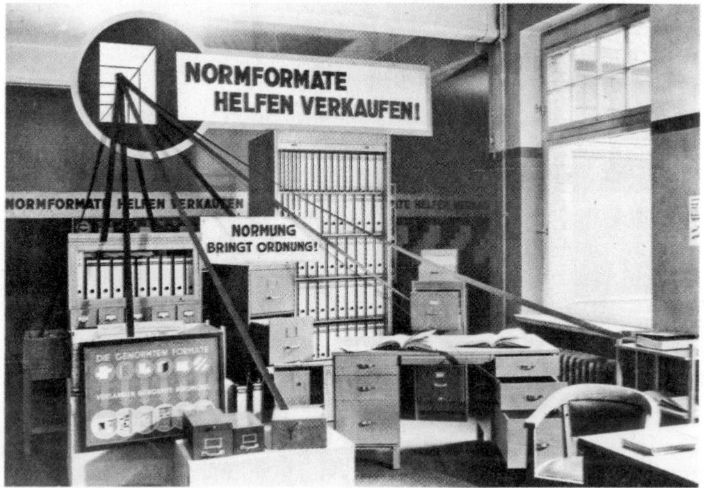

DIN paper stand at a fair in Leipzig, Germany 1932. The signs read *Normformate helfen verkaufen* (Norm formats help selling) and *Normung bringt Ordnung* (norms bring order).

It was again in France that a scientific system for paper formats was devised in line with the metric system: the A-format. It was a rational, mathematical invention based on a ratio of 1:√2, as the width of two sheets would form the length of the bigger size sheet. This invention was perfected and standardized in Germany as part of the *Deutsches Institut für Normung* (German industry norms) in 1922. The DIN system was initiated in 1917 by the manufacturers for artillery to streamline the war industry during World War I. Out of the many DIN industry standards still in use today, the best-known are the paper formats which were adopted as a world standard in 1975. Today the A-formats are the most used paper size system in the world.

In recent decades, outsourcing and digital communication have given rise to online printing services. Online bulk printers have decimated local, specialized print businesses by limiting choices in using the A formats; A6 for a postcard, A5 for a flyer, and A4 for folders. Standardization by online printers has led to lower prices for print work, which makes it more difficult for graphic designers to argue for custom sizes at local print shops. Print work is more often outsourced to low-wage countries, leading to lower costs and higher CO_2 emissions due to transport.

There is No Such Thing as Free Shipping
Another change in standardization that served capitalism was the shipping container. Because of its ubiquity the shipping container has become a symbol of the global transportation of goods. Even the volume of shipping trade itself is measured in TEU (twenty-foot equivalent), the cargo capacity of a 20-foot-long container. 90 percent of the world trade is now handled through shipping, and the low price of sea transport can be attributed to the container system.

Ports looked very different before the advent of the shipping container. Large crews of longshoremen were needed to pack cargoes into ships and these workers often lived in neighbourhoods close to the harbour. The worldwide implementation of the container in the 1960s made the large shipyard crews obsolete, and turned harbours into parking lots for cranes and trucks. In the fifteen years after the shipping container was invented, 90 percent of dockworkers in New York were laid off.[7]

Wooden containers had been in use since the 1900s for the transport of coal. It was the Vietnam War (1955–1975) that sped up their global distribution.[8] At the height of the war, more than half a million US troops were deployed in Vietnam, which required a massive logistics operation. South Vietnam did not have the infrastructure for such logistics, and the US military had difficulty supplying its troops. They hired Sealand—the first container shipping line—to take care of the transport using cubic containers called CONEX boxes.

Shipping containers for the US military accounted for half of Sealand's turnover in 1970. Pacific shipping routes carrying weapons and military material for the Vietnam war laid the groundwork for the trade of goods between Asia and the US. Sealand itself was sold to Maersk in 1999 and is now the world's largest container shipping company. Sea freight has strict guidelines for packaging, wrapping, weights, and sizes. That means containers dictate the shape of boxes and packages, and what materials are suitable for sea transport. The container has enabled the massive outsourcing of manufacturing from Europe and the US to low-wage countries, and its low cost makes it more attractive to produce far away than to produce locally, even though it would be better for the environment.

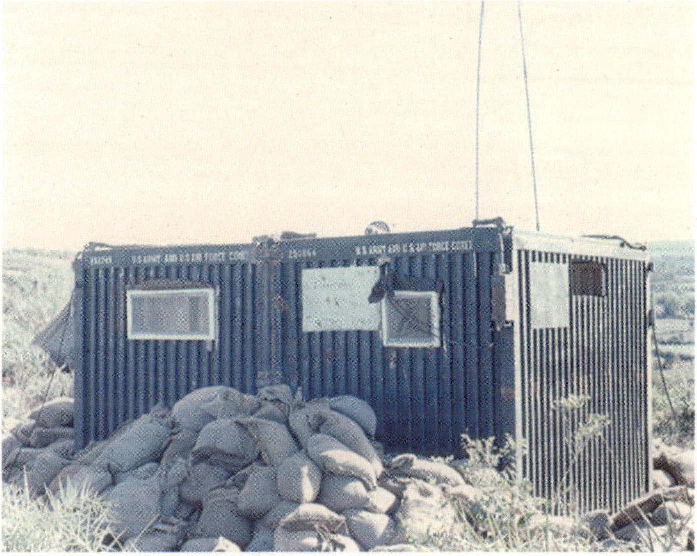

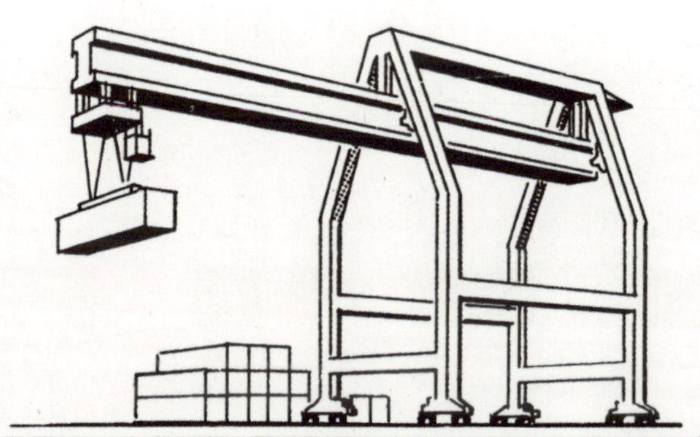

↑   Two CONEX boxes welded together, Vietnam.
↑   Container crane for CONEX boxes, image from US military document.

The Black and White Stripes

In packaging design, the bar code has been very influential. Now found on every imaginable product, the bar code was invented by engineer Joe Woodland when he was a graduate student in the US in 1952. Woodland was inspired by Morse code, and as he was sitting on Miami Beach, he drew his fingers in the sand and came up with the idea that the stripes could be thick or thin.[9] The bar code system uses optical scanning, measuring the different white spaces which correspond to a unique product.

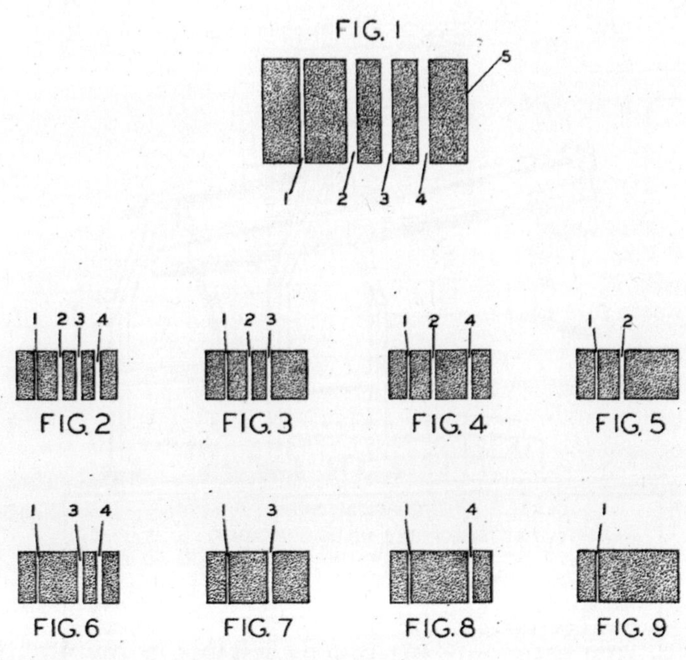

↑ Patent for the first bar code, by Joe Woodland from 1949.
→ Different bar codes.

It wasn't until the mid-1970s in the midst of the oil crisis, labour unrest, and a recession, that the bar code was implemented on a mass scale.[10] The biggest US supermarket chains held a meeting to standardize product codes. The bar code was selected out of several proposals to reverse the plummeting sales. Despite initial costs of installing bar code scanners, the profits soon outweighed the costs. The return on investment turned out to be a staggering 41,5 percent.

While economic efficiency is undoubtedly the main achievement of the bar code, the collection of consumer data is its most important legacy. Real-time sales information meant faster logistics and better insights in customer behaviour. Advertising and product development could respond to consumer demand almost immediately, with a minimum of under- or overstocking. In terms of engineering, the bar code has successfully devised a visual system that can be applied everywhere in the world independent of social contexts.

Through its ability to track consumer data, the bar code has entered all areas of life: even new-born babies are scanned in hospitals using bar codes. You can put a bar code on anything and it can be tracked, traced, and valued using computation and algorithmic efficiency. This is how the bar code has succeeded in becoming the unofficial logo of international trade.

Against Standard Living

Standards have enormous advantages, and our society could not function without them. However, the measurement systems that were used before the metric system, reveal that pre-capitalist economies contained valuable knowledge about local contexts. Vernacular knowledge that is still produced today, but often marginalized and unrecognized.

Global trade and the expansion and outsourcing of labour under capitalism could only happen thanks to standardization. The quest for lower production costs and higher profits has driven innovations such as the container and the bar code. Just two examples in a range of technologies that are devised to streamline production for optimal economic efficiency. An efficiency that is based on cheap fossil fuels, because what is efficient about a book being designed in Europe, printed in China, and sold in North America?

If we seriously want to address graphic design's involvement in the climate crisis, then perhaps efficiency and cheap mass production should not be its primary goals. Being open to local and social conditions can be a start to invite other forms of knowledge production into the graphic design profession. Allowing more informal ways of knowledge, and strengthening local production networks, can shift the focus of graphic design to a more social function of visual communication and production, instead of merely being a driver for economic growth.

The pressure for economic efficiency leads us to devising ingenious systems that organise and simplify our work because it takes less time to fit content into pre-ordained arrangements than it does to redefine a system under new conditions.

NICK BELL, DESIGNER

→ Before desktop publishing, graphic designers used typometers to measure type sizes.

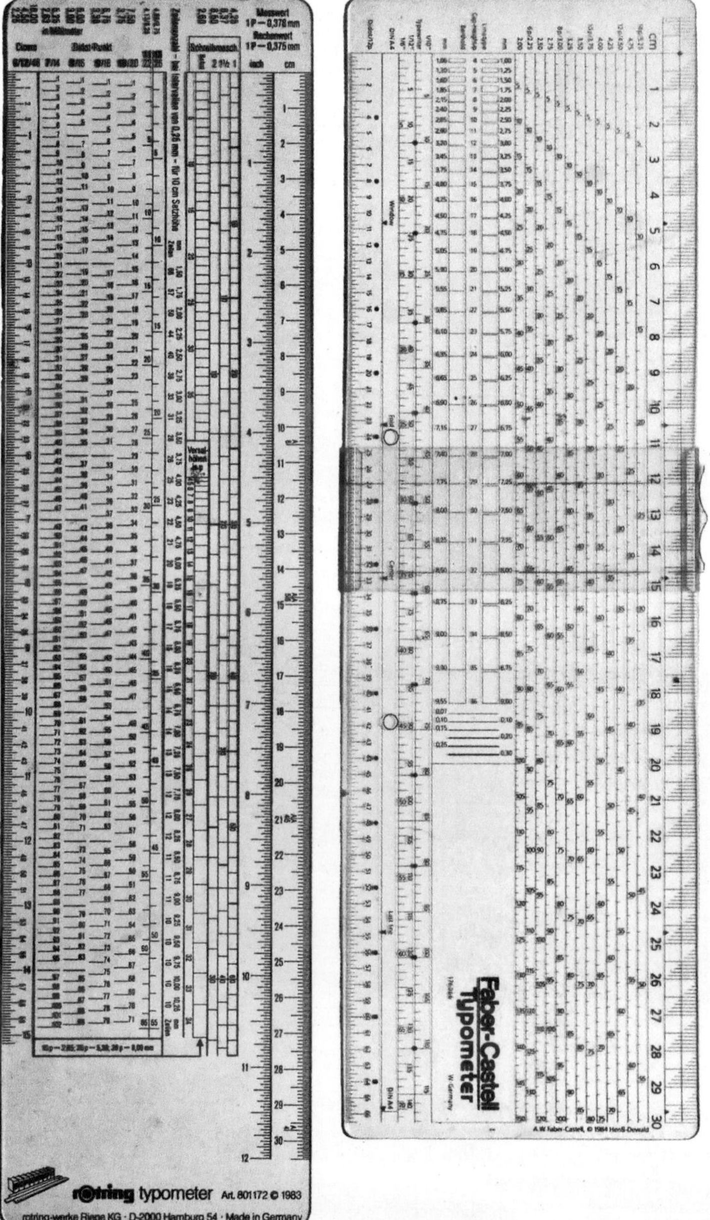

SCHEDULE 1.—Free Inhabitants in Washington Tp. **in the County of** Blackford **of** Indiana **enumerated by me, on the** 28 **day of** June 1860. Geo. S. Howell

Post Office Dundee

1	2	3	4	5	6	7	8	9	10	11	12	13
363	358	David McCleesky	43	M		Farmer	3000	760	Ohio			
		Eliz. "	43	F					N. C.			
		John "	16	M					Ind.			
		Newton "	13	"					"		1	
		Andrew J. "	11	M					"		1	
		Mary H. "	8	F					"		1	
364	654	Henry Overkiser	25	M		"	1500	201	N. Y.			
		Sarah "	24	F					Ohio			
		Simon "	5	M					"			
		Wm. A. "	3	M					"			
		Olive J. "	1	F					"			
365	355	John Sci	43	M		Black-smith	150	215	Penn.			
		Keziah "	44	F					N.			
		Benj. "	13	M					Ohio		1	
		Mary "	11	F					Ind.		1	
		Franklin "	9	M					"		1	
		George "	6	"					"		1	
366	356	William A. Boxham	26	"		Trader		450	Ohio			
		Mary A. "	19	F					"			
367		Unoccupied										
368	357	Nathan Henderson	33	M		Farmer	400	250	Ohio			
		Elizabeth "	31	F					"			
		Sarah M. "	9	"					"		1	
		Elijah P. "	7	M					"		1	
		William M. "	5	"					Ind.			
		Rebecca "	2	F					"			
369	358	Wm. F. Frazier	32	M		"	750	300	Ohio			
		Cate "	30	F					"			
		James T. "	8	M					"		1	
		Francis M. "	3	"					Ind.			
370		Unoccupied										
371	359	Mathias Roll	55	M		"			Ohio			
		Lucy "	39	F					Ind.			
		James N. "	14	M					"		1	
		Sarah E. "	11	F					"		1	
		Oscar "	9	M					"		1	
		Ward "	7	"					"		1	
		Edmund "	4	"					"			
372	360	Reuben Storms	47	"		"	2000	300	N. Y.			
		Ruth "	44	F					"			

| No. white males, 24 | No. colored males, | No. foreign born, | No. blind, | | | No. idiotic, | |
| No. white females, 14 | No. colored females, | No. deaf and dumb, | No. insane, | 7,800 | 2,475 | No. paupers, | |

THE GOOD CITIZEN

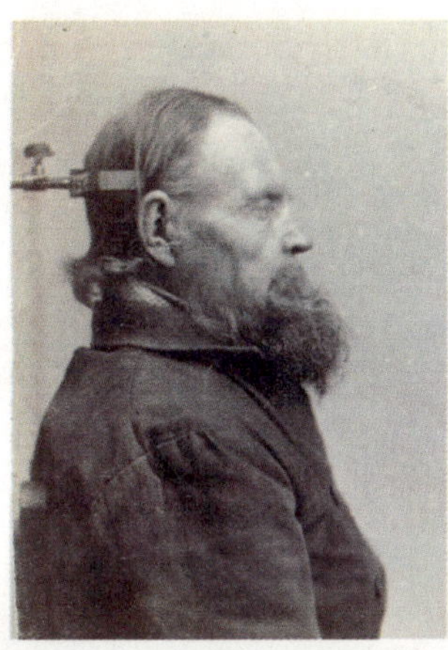

Who is a citizen and who is not? Our ideas of citizenship depends to a large extent on graphic objects such as identity cards, passports, birth and death certificates. These are designed documents with symbols, typography, and official identity points such as portrait photos, citizenship, and surnames. These developed in response the rise of the first nation states and capitalism in the eighteenth century.

Citizens were no longer divine subjects but—as John Stuart Mill and Adam Smith argued—were seen as *homo economicus* (economic beings), only pursuing their self-interest. It was during this period that the graphic forms were perfected that are considered universal and truthful, such as the first infographics, the first encyclopaedias, and official dictionaries. Nation states created bureaucracies that made use of new methods in statistics, mathematics, and a booming printing industry.

↑   Photo for identification card of prisoner 3488, Veenhuizen, the Netherlands, 1897.
←   Census document of the Washington Township in Blackford, Indiana, US, 1860.

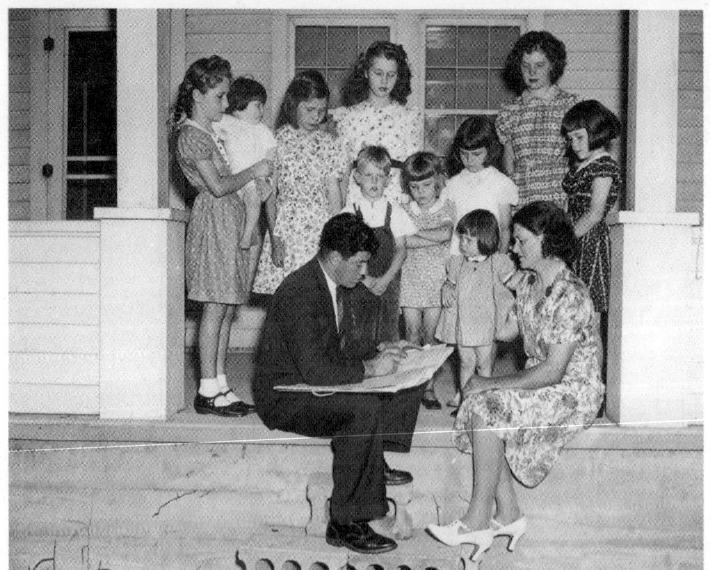

French is from Paris

At the time that Gutenberg printed his first bibles, an abundance of languages and dialects were spoken by people in Europe. Thanks to Gutenberg's invention, books could now be published in local languages, but not all languages were regarded equally. Those picked for publications depended on where printers were based, and where the centres of power were located. This is why French books were set in Parisian French, English books in London English, and the dialect of North Holland became official Dutch.

The printing industry played no small part in creating national languages, as historian and political scientist Benedict Anderson argues.[11] In 1694 the first *Dictionnaire de l'Académie française* was published in Paris, presented by Louis XIV, making Parisian French the official language of France. Since bureaucratic documents were made out in the national language, people outside the centres of power had to learn the new language when they needed to communicate with officials. Dictionaries dictated the grammar and syntax of languages, which were previously subject to permanent

↑   Information is taken down for the 1940 census, US Census Bureau, 1940s.
→   Section about race from the American Community Survey, US Census bureau, 2018.

change, while other dialects and languages were lost or marginalized.

Like standardized weights and measurements, a standardized language also enabled national markets, allowing people to communicate more effectively over long distances. It is no coincidence that the famous encyclopaedia by Diderot and d'Alembert (1751–1777) consists of entries that document industrial process, allowing work to be replicated, independent of local circumstances.[12]

⑧ Is this person a citizen of the United States?

☐ Yes, born in the United States → *SKIP to question 10a*

☐ Yes, born in Puerto Rico, Guam, the U.S. Virgin Islands, or Northern Marianas

☐ Yes, born abroad of U.S. citizen parent or parents

☐ Yes, U.S. citizen by naturalization – *Print year of naturalization*

☐ No, not a U.S. citizen

Standard Citizens

Besides standardizing measurements and language, the French republic was also known for the introduction of surnames. Official surnames were an administrative invention. Apart from a few wealthy lords with family lineages, surnames did not exist prior to the seventeenth century. People would use their first name (Mary), and in case others with the same name appeared, a simple description was added like profession (Mary Baker), physical appearance (Mary Short) or where one lived (Mary Hill). Names that could change over the course of one's life. Patronymic naming (naming family members after the oldest male) is common today, but wasn't practiced anywhere in the world before states introduced it, writes James C. Scott.[13] This wasn't a mere modernizing of the state. Surnames were used to collect taxes, to keep track of property ownership, keep police records, court orders, and organize conscription.[14]

Surnames were part of census taking, a process of systematically counting citizens for the purposes of statistical data. As a designed document, the census form does not look particularly exciting. Formatted as a precursor of a spreadsheet, we see carefully hand-written lists, organized in columns and rows. We almost forget that the census is a powerful tool in the hands of politicians. Registering citizens at an address can grant access to civil rights such as voting or receiving welfare, but it can also be used to persecute people. Census data about Japanese Americans was used in 1942 to im-prison more than a hundred thousand in special camps, of which two-thirds were US nationals.[15] During World War II in the Nether-lands, resistance fighters—among whom graphic designer Willem Sandberg—burned down the municipal administration of Amster-dam where detailed records were kept of the inhabitants and their religions. Many Jewish inhabitants were saved from deportation by the destruction of designed administration documents.

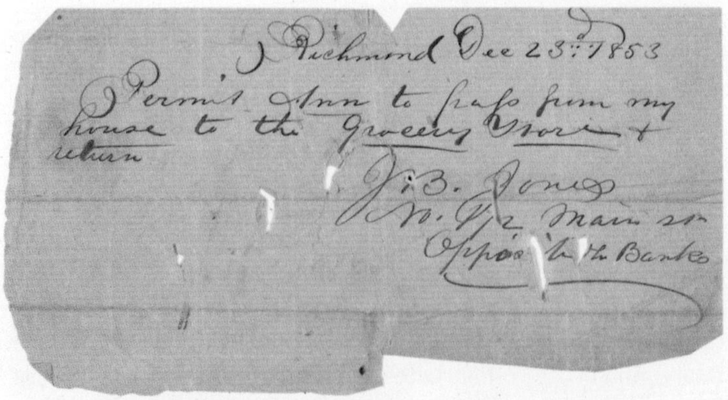

Thou Shalt Not Pass

Having no documents is synonymous for having an illegal status *(sans-papiers)*. The precursor of the passport was literally a piece of paper with a signature. They were letters signed by the sover-eign to provide diplomats or merchants with free passage. Early passports looked remarkably similar to other official papers, the

↑   Written pass for the enslaved Ann Singleton to go to the grocery store, Richmond, Virginia, 1853.
→   Printed pass issued from the Confederate government to the enslaved Bob, Richmond, Virginia, 1865.

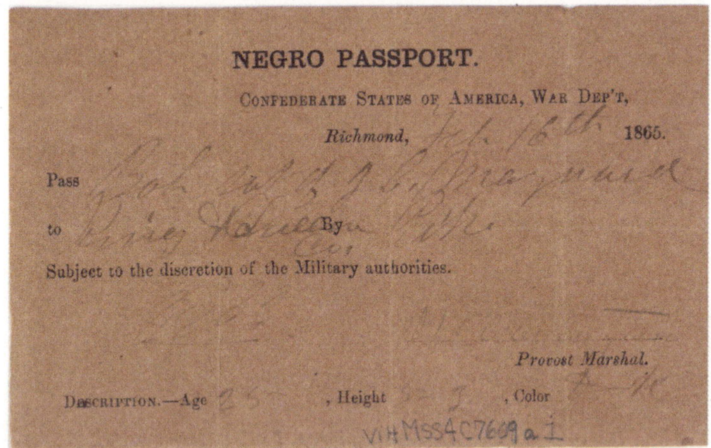

The surname was a first and crucial step toward making individual citizens officially legible, and along with the photograph, it is still the first fact on documents of identity.

JAMES C. SCOTT, POLITICAL SCIENTIST

first banknotes, and the first stock.[16] Together with the census and the national language, passports played their part in creating nation states and constructing citizenship.

Some of the first identification documents were designed to restrict movement. In the nineteenth century, Africans who were enslaved and forcefully taken to North America were not allowed to leave plantations unless they had handwritten passes. Handwriting was used as a secure technology as slaves were forbidden to learn to read or write. Literacy among slaves became a form of resistance, and runaway slaves forged slave passes to help others escape. Print technology was subsequently used to make passes more secure, as a response to increased literacy among enslaved African peoples.[17]

Passports still function as a technology to control movement. Technologies like RFID chips and face recognition are part of a control system for digital state surveillance. Designing a passport is akin to designing a surveillance tool. Graphic designers revere passports as objects, as popular design competitions for the Norwegian passport in 2017, and the Dezeen online design competition for a post-Brexit passport for Britons show. The analysis of passport designs rarely looks at the social consequences of identification, control, and restriction of movement, which can have violent consequences.

Citizenship is also a form of property under capitalism. If one brings enough money, citizenship can be purchased through a Citizenship by Investment (CIP) programme or a so-called Golden Visa. Investing $500,000 to $1 million can get you an EB-5 Visa for the US, or for investing £2 million you will be awarded a three-year stay in the UK.[18] Artist Femke Herregraven created the work Liquid Citizenship (2015), a website that lists at what prices citizenship from which countries can be bought. It criticizes the hypocrisy of immigration, by referring to illegal immigration. If you can't find a citizenship to your liking, the website suggests 'Browse smuggling routes or other possibilities in the top menu'.[19]

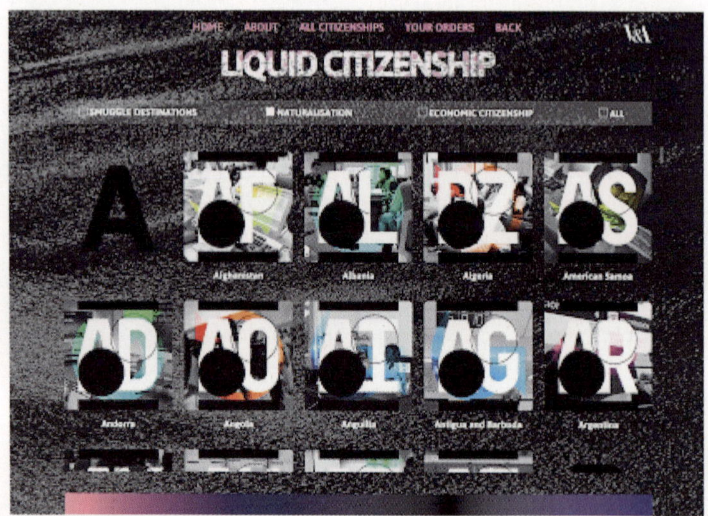

Femke Herregraven, Liquid citizenship, 2015. femkeherregraven.net/liquidcitizenship.

Dutch identity card security features

Second image of the photograph with the year of birth and a three-dimensional effect

The holder's month of birth and year of birth is shown in the form of perforations.

Fluorescent patterns, also fibres in the paper pages visible under ultraviolet light.

Tactile relief

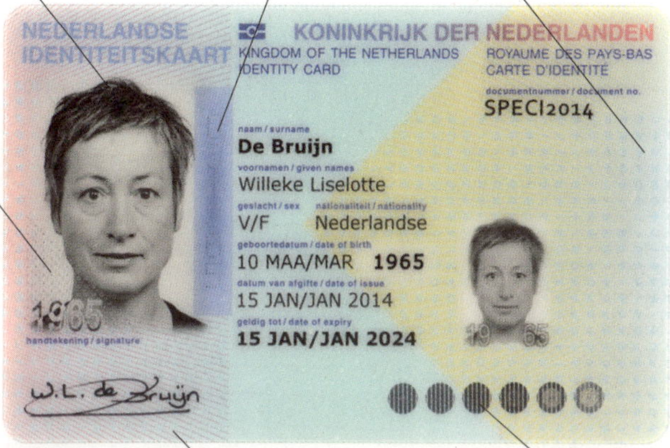

Microprinted text only visible with magnifying glass

Metallized image that can change shape and colour.

RFID chip (inside the card)
Security level: high

The chip contains a colour photograph, name, document number, nationality, a tax ID number, sex, date of birth, and date of expiry. The chip also contains a login function which allows the holder to log in to the Dutch government services like healthcare, education, or pension. Sensitive data such as medical records can be accessed using the chip.

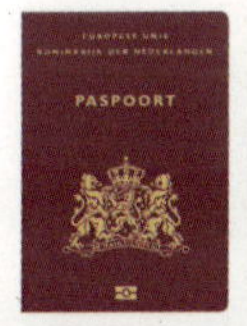

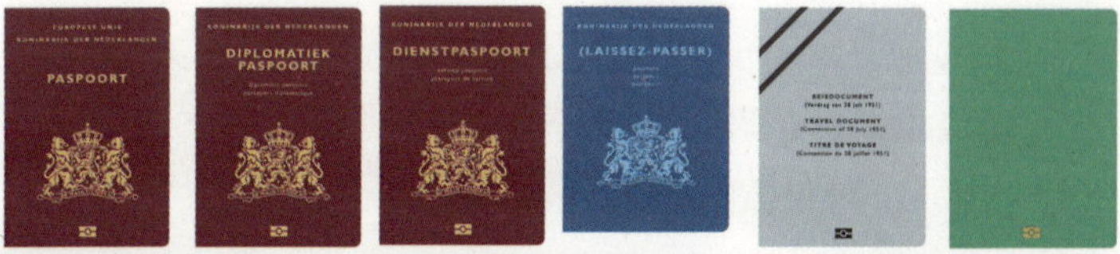

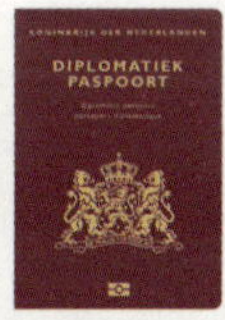

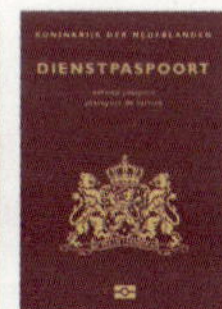

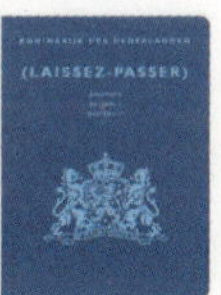

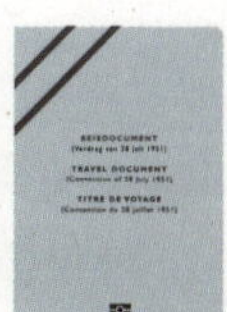

These are the six different Dutch passports, each of them having different privileges and hierarchies, such as the diplomatic passport (2), the immigrant passport (5), and the military passport (3).

DESKTOP POWER

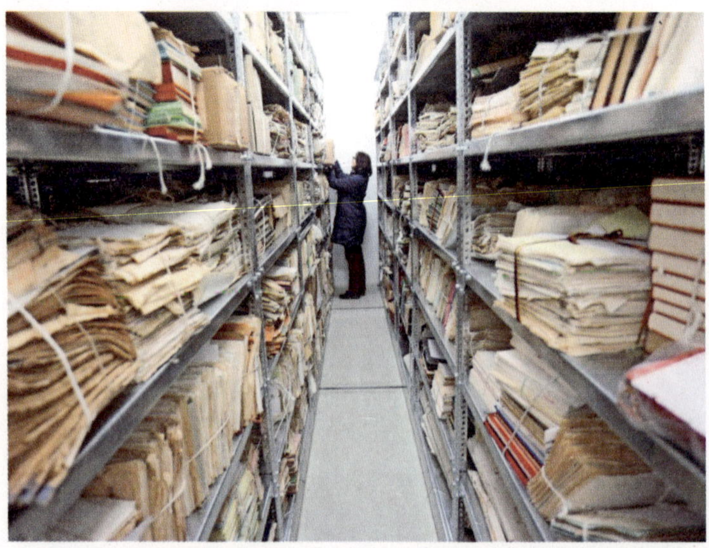

In the film *I, Daniel Blake* (2016) by Ken Loach, the main character is a 59-year-old man, caught in the horrible maze of UK bureaucracy. After having had a heart attack, his doctor forbids him to work. The unemployment agency discards this warning, with disastrous results. The film shows the stupidity and dehumanizing character of administrative thinking.[20]

Bureaucracy does not produce the most exciting designs, as David Graeber comments; paperwork is supposed to be boring.[21] Graeber, who is not a graphic designer but an anthropologist, notes how early bureaucratic documents were at least beautifully designed, written with penmanship, and specially designed stamps. Today's world of digital forms and PDF files are bare and lifeless in comparison.

As we have noted in the chapter 'The Designer as Scribe',

official documents used to require graphic forms such as calligraphy, special paper, and embossing for security and authentication. Today's documents rely on electronic security, signatures, and bar codes, which are only read by machines. If authenticity once relied on the designer's skill, it is now outsourced to optical recognition (OCR) software. The part of the design that is legible for humans has solidified in the pre-digital form design of 1980s business modernism.

Administrative documents may not be regarded as artistic, they are still designed. You could even argue that the design of an immigration form deserves greater scrutiny than a poster for an art exhibition, if we take its social impact into account. A carelessly placed text or a confusing navigation could lead to deportation or imprisonment of the applicant. In *Graphesis* (2014) Johanna Drucker looks closely at how administrative objects are designed. She notices that the graphic design of the lines, the structure, disappears from our attention. It is so generic we simply stop seeing it. Perhaps the boringness of administrative design is the entire point, the consequence of a visual strategy. An invisibility that hides the violence behind every bureaucracy.

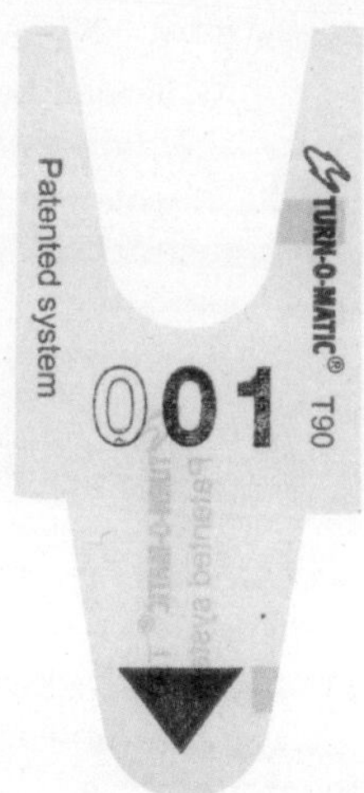

↑   Ticket from a 'Turn-o-matic' ticket, designed by Swedish designer Hans Ehrich in 1974.
←   Files from the Stasi (Staatssicherheitsdienst), the secret police in former East Germany, 2018.

The Burden of Bureaucracy

How administration becomes a tool of violence and power was studied by the French philosopher Michel Foucault. His research into prisons and mental institutes shows that we use bureaucracy to divide citizens into categories like 'the good citizen', 'the criminal', or 'the mentally ill', which then gives the state the right to take control over someone's body—surveillance, incarceration, medication, sterilization, or even murder.[22]

Graeber writes how bureaucracy is always linked to violence, even if it is invisible. Bureaucracy provides no room for discussion or negotiation, a form simply has to be filled in correctly and in time, or else. He argues that the lack of intelligence we associate with bureaucracy serves its underlying violence. This is why missing your court date, not paying a bill on time—for whatever reasonable excuse—will end up with the police on your doorstep. The force behind administration is perfectly illustrated when the inability to pay a fine in the Netherlands will produce an injunction with the headline 'You are forced to pay "In the name of the King"'.[23]

Secrecy is another by-product of administrative power. 'Every bureaucracy seeks to increase the superiority of the professionally informed by keeping their knowledge and intentions secret', wrote sociologist Max Weber.[24] Visual representations of 'official secrets'—as Max Weber calls them—can be found in the form of redacted documents, both for legal, financial, or security purposes. A request for government documents can produce pages full of blacked-out lines, as if it was abstract art. The stupidity and irrationality of bureaucratic reasoning as someone within the administration painstakingly has to go over the text line by line, rendering information useless.

It should be emphasized that administrative documents are not necessarily only a form of coercion. Documents such as contracts, citizenship, and birth certificates can provide protection and agency for people and their families. A document can extend powers and privileges without prior knowledge of age, class, gender, or race, and can therefore also be a form of emancipation. Many social struggles were fought to achieve bureaucratic rights. In many countries today, women do not have the same administrative rights as men: they cannot open a bank account, own property, or

Redacted version of Apple-HTC settlement, as part of the Apple vs. Samsung trial over patents, 2012. The redaction is intended to protect the intellectual property of both companies.

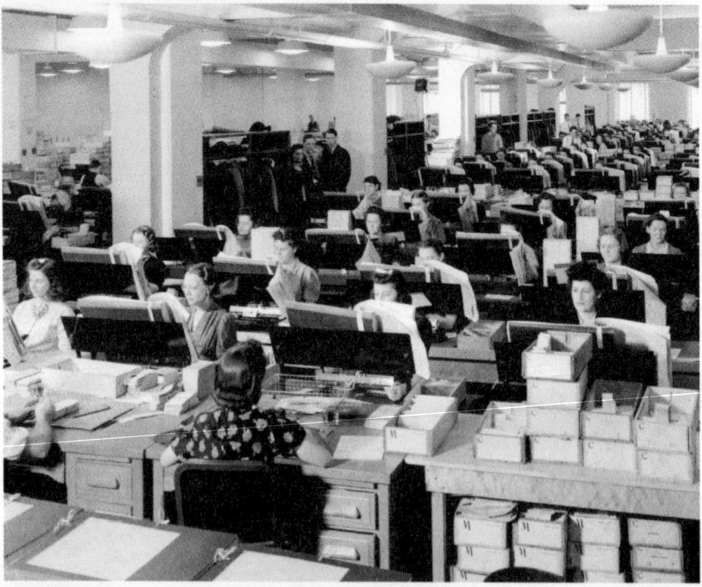

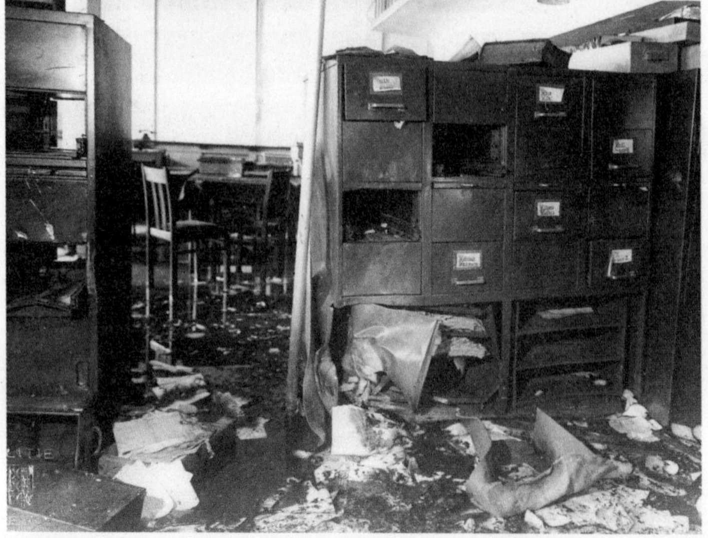

↑ US census workers transferring data to punch cards, 1940. Image by US Census Bureau.
↑ Civil registry of the municipality of Amsterdam after the firebombing by the resistance in 1943.
The intention of the attack was to prevent Dutch Jews from being tracked down. Graphic designer
Willem Sandberg was part of the resistance group that carried out the attack.

          CAPS LOCK — Part 1

even travel without male consent.[25] But achieving equality through administrative rights can also occur using more socially aware graphic documents.

> # Every bureaucracy seeks to increase the superiority of the professionally informed by keeping their knowledge and intentions secret.
>
> MAX WEBER, SOCIOLOGIST

The Critical Engineer

So far, this chapter has traced how the designer as engineer was closely involved in designing documents, standards, and supplying documents to bureaucratic systems. Disciplining citizens through civil administration happens in all large societies, but global capitalism would not have been possible without the standardization of measurements, languages, citizenship, and administrative order.

Bureaucracy is the result of a scaling of societies. When communities become too large for verbal communication and social bonds such as trust and kinship to work, graphic symbols, typography, and official documents replace the vernacular order by a bureaucratic order. The first nation states sought to unite different people by subjecting them to one superior dominant culture. Such an artificially constructed culture had to be promoted and enforced, which relied heavily on the printing press and official graphic documents. Although bureaucracy liberated people from the clutches of patriarchy and feudal control, it is still a system of hierarchy, and became a tool for oppression and control itself.

Designers as engineers hold power over printed and digitally published information by using the visual and written language of authority. Identity systems and bureaucratic documents are designed and implemented using manuals and guidelines. Social relations over long distances between citizens are replaced with contracts, birth certificates, and passports. In the same way that the assembly line alienated workers from the things they produced, bureaucracy has successfully alienated people from each other. The question is how large-scale relations of trust can be socially sensitive, without reverting to bureaucratic systems of oppression.

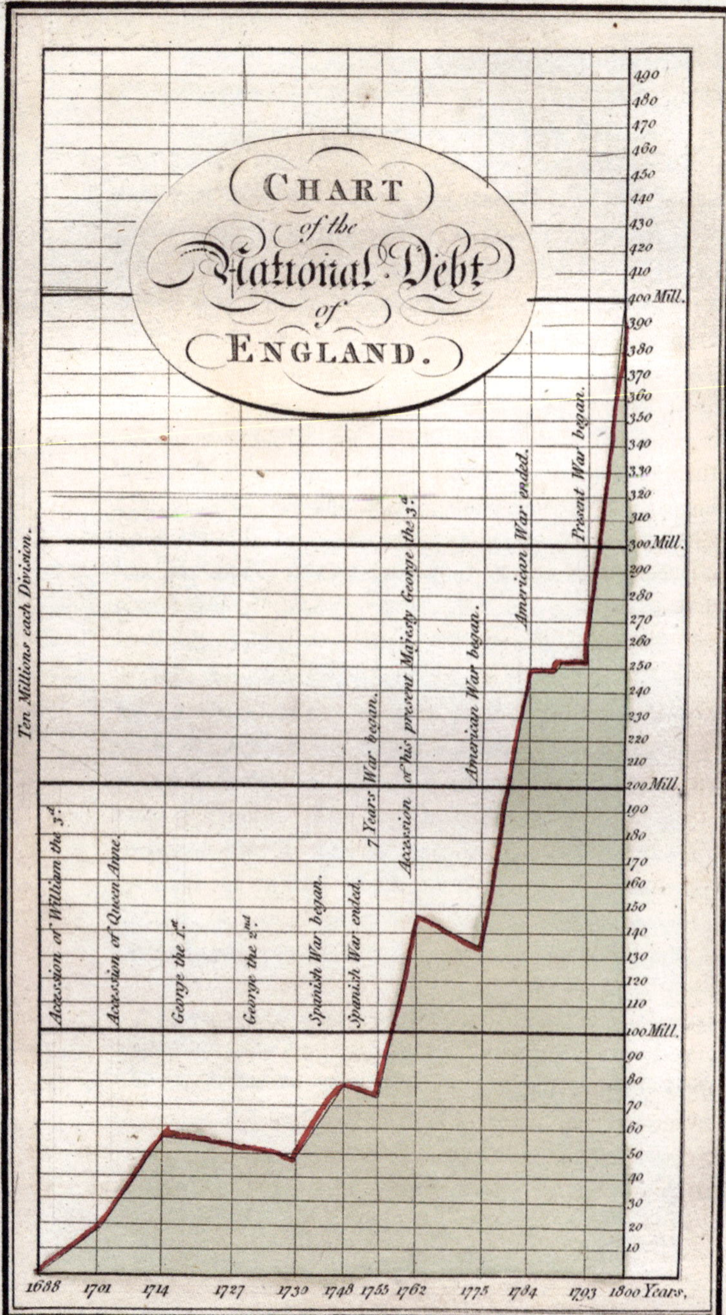

Plate 20
CHART
of the
National Debt
of
ENGLAND.
Ten Millions each Division.
Accession of William the 3.d
Accession of Queen Anne.
George the 1.st
George the 2.nd
Spanish War began.
Spanish War ended.
7 Years War began.
Accession of his present Majesty George the 3.d
American War began.
American War ended.
Present War began.
490
480
470
460
450
440
430
420
410
400 Mill.
390
380
370
360
350
340
330
320
310
300 Mill.
290
280
270
260
250
240
230
220
210
200 Mill.
190
180
170
160
150
140
130
120
110
100 Mill.
90
80
70
60
50
40
30
20
10
1688 1701 1714 1727 1739 1748 1755 1762 1775 1784 1793 1800 Years.
Neele sc. Strand.

SCIENTIFIC RHETORIC

Statistical data may be used to represent people, but that hardly satisfies individual cases. The fact that the Dutch economy grew with three percent in 2018 doesn't resonate with someone who just lost their job. Numbers have to be compared to other contexts in order to become meaningful, which is why information graphics such as pie charts, bar charts, and line graphs are so popular in economic communication.

Early forms of information graphics—or data graphics—were drawn by scientists and engineers. The first information graphics can be traced as far back as ancient Mesopotamia where mathematicians used drawings on clay tablets to explain geometry. For centuries scientific knowledge was mostly documented and shared through written text. Johanna Drucker suggests that the invention of optical instruments such as the microscope by the end of the sixteenth century helped to further the conception that science could be visual, from the scientific method of observation.[26]

Form as Data

Graphics to visualize information already existed in the Middle East, but their use accelerated in Europe with the scientific advances during the Enlightenment. Innovations in printing technology provided the accuracy and consistency needed for scientific knowledge. The new field of statistics aided the new nation states in their bureaucratic administration of taxation and population growth. Drucker and McVarish explain that administrations relied on statistics and information design to show that scientific methods were successful in managing social and cultural relations, although 'not always compatible with values of compassion'.[27]

Industrial production pioneered the standardization of formats and the idea of a universal visual language, which formed the foun-

←   Chart of the National Debt of England by William Playfair, in *The Commercial and Political Atlas*, 1786.

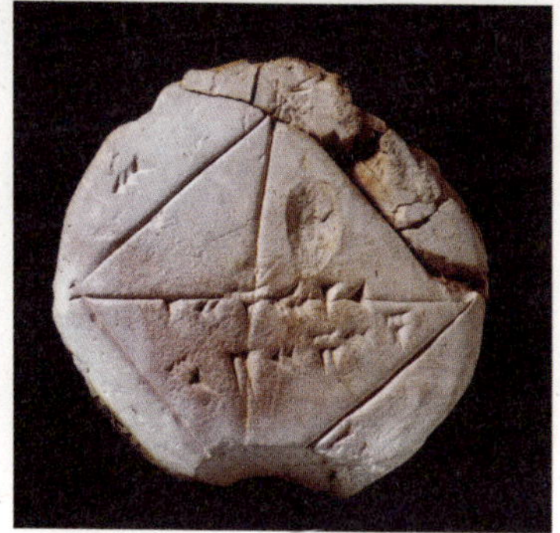

Babylonian clay tablet to learn geometry, 1800–1600 BC

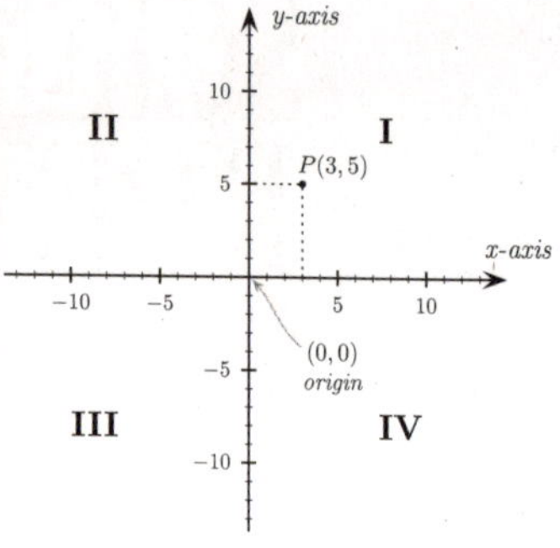

Cartesian grid, invented by René Descartes, seventeenth century.

dation of modern-day infographics. The French philosopher and mathematician René Descartes invented the x,y,z coordinate system and the rational grid in the seventeenth century. Economist and engineer William Playfair (1759–1823) developed the three most elementary information graphics; the bar graph, the pie chart and the line graph. His contemporaries were the French engineer Charles Joseph Minard and the Swiss-German mathematician J.H. Lambert, who laid the further foundations for the field of information graphics.[28] The forms that they devised have come to dominate the visual language by which science and economy are communicated.

It is noteworthy that William Playfair, the inventor of the three most important infographic formats, was both an engineer and an economist. At the end of the eighteenth century, he developed his graphics from a necessity to communicate the growth of the English economy. Following his contemporary Adam Smith, he concerned himself with the question of how to show that economic changes can be seen as long-term patterns. Playfair was able to do that successfully in his work, although he himself saw that visualizing statistical information was also prone to manipulation: 'A few seem to apprehend that there may possibly be some deception in it, of which they are not aware', he wrote.[29]

Scientific methods appeared on the factory floor at the end of the nineteenth century. Engineer Frederick Taylor came up with a method to calculate the time of each task using a stop watch, to

CAPS LOCK – Part 1

No definite and permanent advance is made in any kind of work, whether with materials or men, until use is made of measurement.

FRANK AND LILLIAN GILBRETH, ENGINEERS

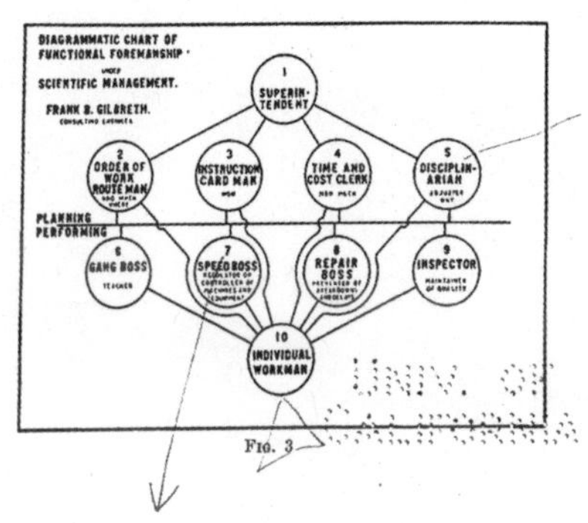

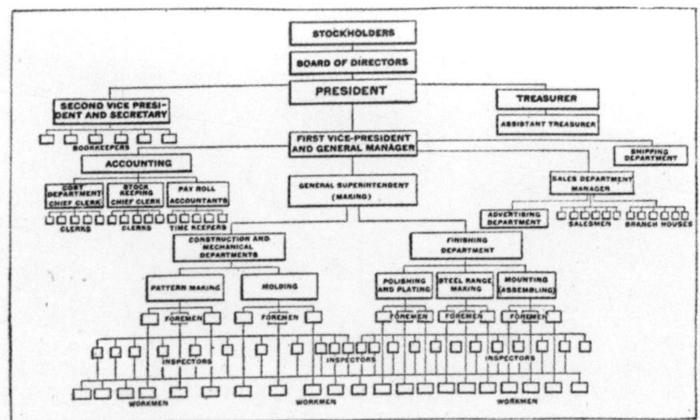

Frank B. Gilbreth and Lillian M. Gilbreth, Process charts, 1921.

apply scientific efficiency to the work process. Engineers Frank and Lillian Gilbreth were inspired by military efficiency and used drawings and photography to document the exact work movements. The use of graphic methods made the work process legible to the business bureaucracy, in efforts to speed up the work process and increase productivity. The success of his work unfortunately came at the expense of workers' well-being, who had to follow the Gilbreths meticulously planned actions within strict timeframes.[30]

The Designer as Engineer

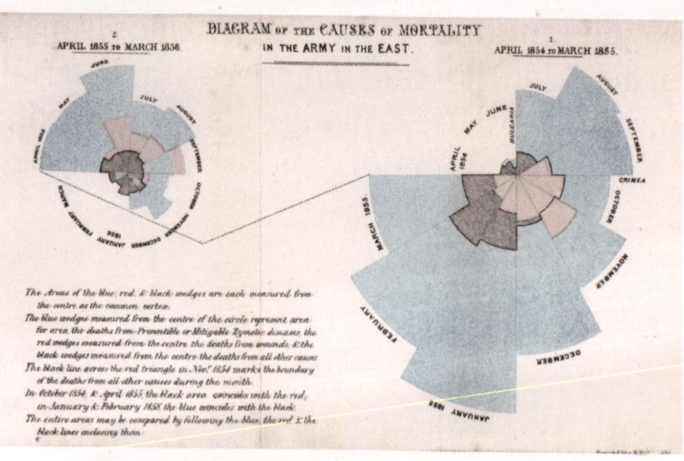

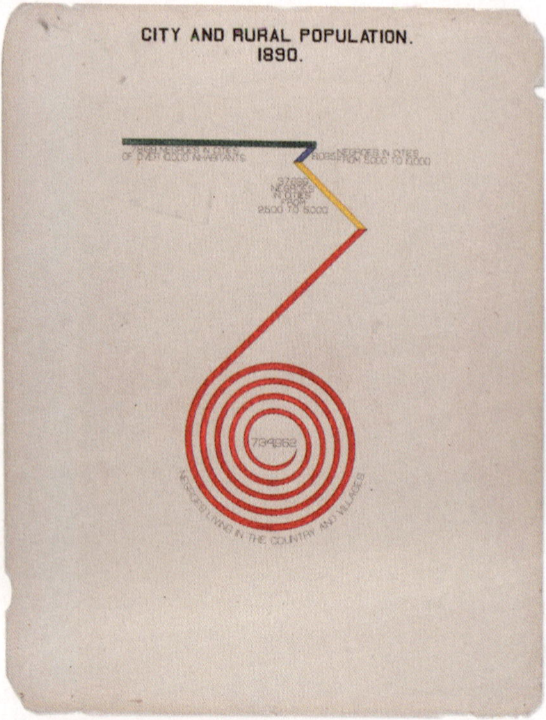

CITY AND RURAL POPULATION.
1890.

↑ Florence Nightingale, Coloured pie chart to illustrate causes of death in the British army, 1858.
↑ W.E.B. Du Bois, *City and Rural Population, 1890*. Paris, 1900.

Against the Graph

The desk of a stock trader today is like a shrine for statistics. Arrays of computer screens with lists of numbers, graphs, and bar charts. The same forms are found in the economy section of any newspaper. The field of economics often speaks through the language of mathematics, and we have gotten so used to it that it is hard to imagine alternative forms of visualizing economics. The annual report of any company is made up of spreadsheets, pie charts, and bar charts. Abstract graphic forms that say little or nothing about the well-being of workers, the social relations or the atmosphere on the work floor. A group of economy students called 'Rethinking Economics' has spoken out against the perspective that economy can only be studied using mathematics, and students do not actually learn to engage with the problems of the real world where economy happens.[31]

Many designers and artists see aesthetic value in the simplicity of infographics, while at the same understanding the limitations of graphic mathematical notation. Sociologist and civil rights activist W.E.B. Du Bois used charts to show the economic conditions of blacks in the United States, as they were underrepresented, or not represented in economic statistics. Florence Nightingale, known as the founder of modern nursing, also produced information graphics of the casualties of the Crimean War (1853–1856). She was the first to use infographics to serve a social cause, hoping her graphics would help to prevent future conflicts. If we return to the foundation of what economy is, we end up at the exchange of goods or services between people, which is a social activity. Using a mathematical visual language to represent the economy neglects the human impact, and even serves to hide violent processes such as resource extraction and exploitation.

Formal languages and associational systems are inevitable and good, becoming tyrannies only when we are unconscious of them.

ROBERT VENTURI, ARCHITECT

PROPRIÉTÉ
PRIVÉE

NO
TRESPASSING
PRIVATE
PROPERTY
KEEP
OUT

PROPRIÉTÉ
PRIVÉE
DÉFENSE
D'ENTRER

NO
TRESPASSING
THIS PROPERTY
IS PROTECTED BY
VIDEO SURVEILLANCE
PRIVATE PROPERTY
NO UNAUTHORIZED PARKING
OR WAITING. NO SOLICITING
OR LOITERING

Privatgrundstück
Betreten verboten!
PRIVAT AREA
DO NOT ENTER!
قطعة أرض خاصة
ممنوع الدخول!

VERBODEN TOEGANG
ART. 461. WETB. v. STRAFR.

GET OFF MY PROPERTY!

Owning land is for many families an important step to ensure future wealth. In feudal times, only a handful of wealthy families owned all the land, while the rest had to pay tribute or rent. Being born into nobility meant that you could live off the taxes for the rest of your life—free money for generations to come. That sounds like ancient history, but research found that in the UK, less than 1 percent of the population today still owns 66 percent of the land. Most of whom are the same dukes, barons, and earls who have owned it for centuries.[32] Maps of land ownership still reveal a history of inequality. For example in Colombia, 0.4 percent of the population owns 61 percent of the land.

The End of the Commons

One of capitalism's chief architects, Adam Smith, believed that property, together with markets and money, was the foundation on which human society was built.[33] Land ownership is perhaps not as self-evident as he made it seem. Throughout history and across cultures, we find many different forms of land use, such as land stewardship and common land. Many cultures do not believe land should be owned since it belongs to all living beings, human and non-human alike. The notion of land ownership suggests that the owners can do with it as they please, without taking the ecological value, or the cultural value, into account. Cutting up land and selling it as 'property' piece by piece has not only led to inequality but also to the unrestrained extraction of natural resources, leading to the climate crisis we are faced with today. Regarding land as property was central to the beginning of capitalism.

Lands in medieval Europe were owned by feudal lords. Part of a lord's estate (manor) was land for shared use, called the common land, or 'commons'. Peasants could have cattle graze there or grow

← Various signs protecting private property.

crops for sustenance, and hold meetings or festivals.[34] Here a public and communal life could evolve outside of the control of the market and feudal lords. Laws in seventeenth-century England, known as 'enclosure acts' ended the use of common lands, so they could be made profitable for commercial agriculture. Lands were sold to the highest bidder and by doing so, poor farmers were kicked off the land with the help of the Church and the military. Enlightenment thinkers saw this right to property as one of the main pillars of society, or, as philosopher John Locke argued; that a government's primary function is to protect private property.[35]

By the nineteenth century most of the commons in England was privatized, and many farmers left with no means to survive were forced to move to the cities to work in factories. The eviction of farmers from common land in rural Europe is regarded by many as the beginning of capitalism. The term commons would be later extended to include all cultural and natural resources that are accessible to all members of society and aren't privately owned.

Engineers and Maps

The graphic language of land ownership can be found in cadastral maps. The Romans drew detailed maps of property for taxation and to solve disputes. Roman land surveyors even created a special grid called centuration which 'turned all Europe into one vast sheet of graph paper', as Samuel Edgerton wrote.[36] These maps were intended as evidence of property in case of legal or official matters. Today's cadastral maps follow the same logic.

The French Republic played an important role in cadastral mapping. Napoleon was something of a mapping connoisseur himself, and was known to study them before battle. In 1807 he ordered the Minister of Finance to begin a detailed mapping of all property in France. Known as *cadastre napoléonien*, his ambitious plan had both financial and military intentions. Cadastral maps were needed for more precise taxation of land, but knowing the terrain in detail was also helpful in case enemies would invade. Cadastral maps reveal much about the capitalist perspective on land. Engineers who measured and mapped the plots had the tendency of drawing them more geometrically regular than they were.[37]

→   Map of a generic medieval manor with common pasture lands, 1923.

                    CAPS LOCK — Part 1

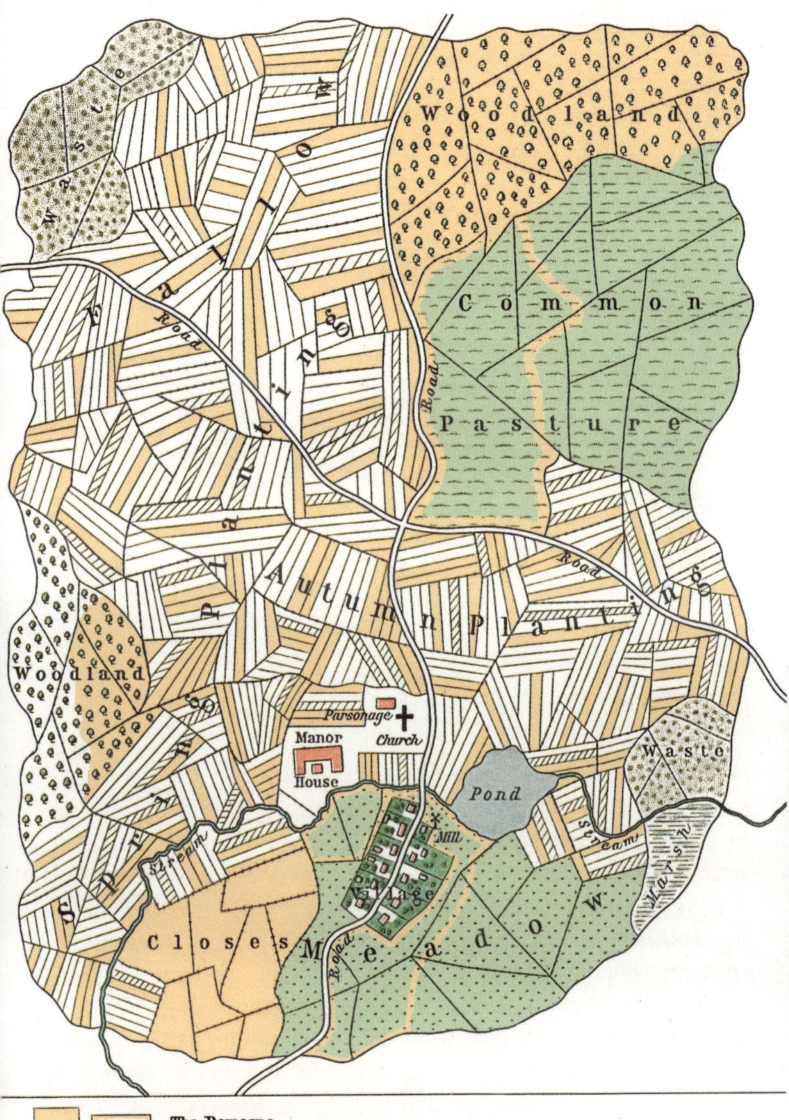

The Demesne
The glebe (i.e. strips in the open fields held by the parish church)
Later enclosures for farming and sheep-raising

This plan of a manor is wholly conventional. It is intended to show: (1) the various features that might be found in English manors (or vills) of the mediaeval period; (2) the more important changes in the agricultural system which occurred in England from the fourteenth century onward. Many of these manorial features, of course, appeared in similar domains on the continent.

The very absence of more specific adaptation to landscape or to human purpose only increased, by its very indefiniteness, its general usefulness for exchange.

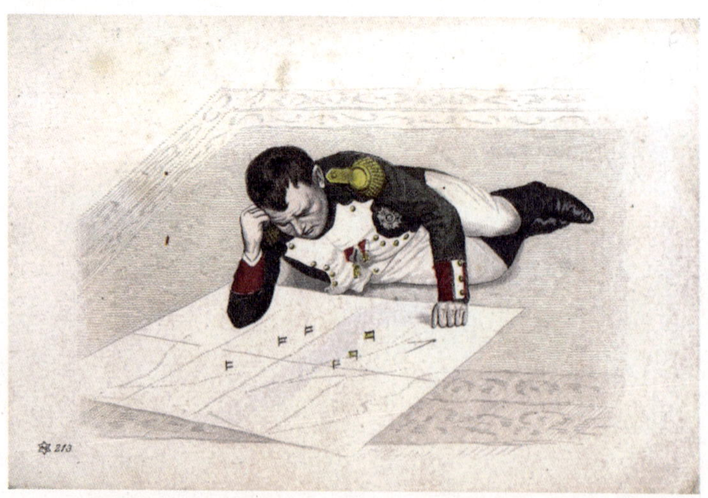

↑   Napoleon studying maps before battle.
→   Cadastral map of Auvergne-Rhône-Alpes, France, 1808.

To fit the straitjacket of property measurement, land was flattened, redrawn, and standardized through the act of mapping. James C. Scott notes that drawing an outline of a piece of land and measuring it, says nothing about the soil, the flora, the fauna, the cultural meaning, and the many kinds of other forms of value it represents.[38]

Today's cadastral system is stored in the form of geographic coordinates in digital databases. They are still an indispensable tool for legal and financial administration, and thus they represent a singular interpretation of land ownership, which doesn't allow space for alternative and non-capitalist forms of land use.

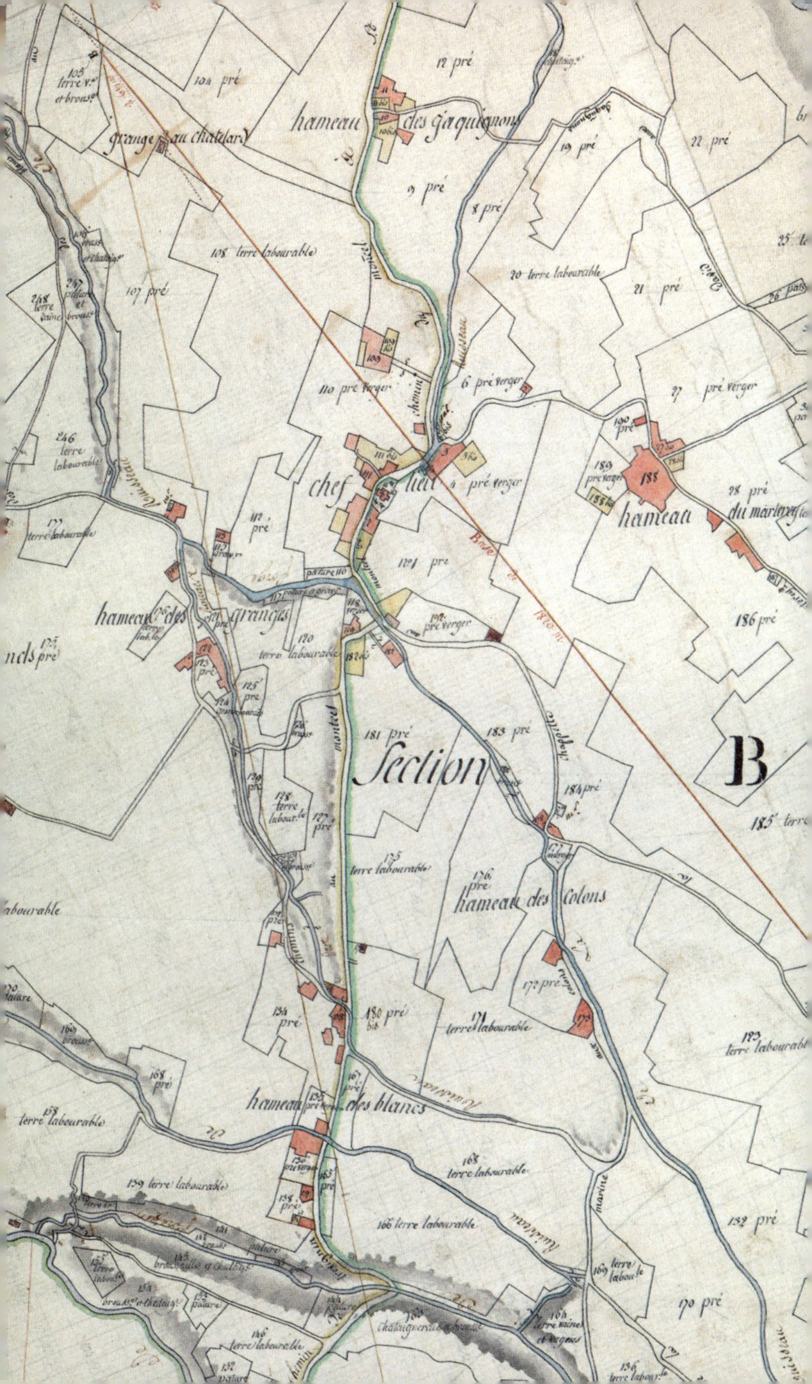

B
Section
chef lieu
hameau des Gaquignons
hameau du marlou
hameau des Colons
hameau des Granges
hameau des Blancs
grange au chatelard
105 terre v.e et breus.
247 terre v.ine et breus.
248 terre v.ine et breus.
246 terre labourable
104 pré
108 terre labourable
107 pré
172 terre labourable
12 pré
9 pré
8 pré
20 terre labourable
21 pré
25
26 pat.
19 pré
22 pré
6 pré verger
27 pré verger
28 pré verger
98 pré
190 pré
189 pré verger
188
186 pré
110 pré verger
109
103
112 pré
113 breuil
3
5 pré
4 pré verger
N.o 1 pré
114 pat.e a 110
116 pat.e a 110
118 verger
192 pré verger
120 terre labourable
121 pré
123 pré
125 pré
124 pré
126 breus
128 terre laboural.e
127 pré
175 terre labourable
176 pré
181 pré
183 pré
184 pré
185 terre
129 pré
130 breus
131 pat.re
134 pré
180 pré bis
171 terre labourable
172 pré
173
178 terre labourable
170 pré
168 terre labourable
167 pré
135 pré
168 pré
159 terre labourable
158 pré
166 terre labourable
132 pré
136 terre labour.

KANTOOR
VAN DE
HYPOTHEKEN en het KADASTER
te **AMSTERDAM**

UITTREKSEL van den Perceelsgewijzen Kadastralen
Legger der gemeente AMSTERDAM

Art. *1230.*		NAAM.	VOORNAMEN.	BEROEP.	WOONPLAATS.
Eigenaar		*Levie* *en zons.*	*Alfred* *Roemer brachestraat 5*	*spiegelfabrikant.*	*Amsterdam*
Mede-eigenaren		*de Roos* *wed. Daniel Salomon Schoyer*	*Anna Maria Catharina.*		*Amsterdam.*
Vruchtgebruiker Erfpachter Recht van opstalhouder of bezitter van het recht van gebruik en bewoning.					

POLDER, GEHUCHT of plaatselijke benaming. (Straat, gracht, enz.)	VERWIJZING NAAR HET KADASTRALE PLAN.		SOORT VAN EIGENDOM.	GROOTTE.			Bedrag der belastbare opbrengst per hectare, verminderd met den per hectare bepaalden aftrek wegens polder- en dijklasten.	Bedrag per hectare van den aftrek wegens polder- en dijklasten.	BELASTBARE OPBRENGST.		VERWIJZING naar vroegere of latere toestanden.
	Sectie.	Nommer van het perceel.		h.	a.	c.			Onge-bouwd. f.	Ge-bouwd. c.	
1.	2.	3.	4.	5.			6.	7.	8.	9.	10.
1e Oosterp. ek	S	507	huis erf			82			369	496	
id		508	id			82			369	496	
id		509	id			76			342	896	
Vrolikstraat		510	id			58			261	372	
id		511	id			53			238	372	
id		512	id			97			436	695	
id		513	id			1 19			535	694	
id		514	id			1 30			585	694	
id		515	id			1 24			558	694	
id		516	id			1 30			585	694	
1e Oosterp. ek		504	loods erf			4 72			2124	8	
id		5225	huis erf			1 83			823	61	
		1606				1606			7225	6172	
		35									
		8030									
		4818									

Property for Sale

The aftermath of the 2008 financial crisis was not unlike the enclosure of common lands. In the US risky mortgages had been sold using aggressive advertising, to people who could barely afford them. When the financial crisis hit, 10 million people were evicted from their homes.[39] Entire housing blocks stood empty as investments, while former residents were forced to sleep in cars or in tent camps.

In the capitalist system, housing and land are commodities that follow the laws of supply and demand. Since housing is almost always scarce, it becomes an object for investment. This logic creates a situation where millions are evicted from their homes, while millions of houses stand empty for investment purposes. Under capitalism a return on an investment is more important than the right to have a roof over one's head.

As rights to property are mediated through graphic objects such as maps, contracts, and signs, we accept these rights without question. Personal property is so sacred we will defend it with the help of lawyers, or dogs, or weapons, if we are to believe some of the signs on people's lawns. Property rights have turned people against each other, making them assume the roles of investors that are in constant competition for maximizing profit. If we want to think about alternatives how we can use land in a way that serves all living beings, this also means to also question the graphic representations of land itself.

> If this power is sourced in property, then the fences that divide England are not just symbols of the partition of people, but the very cause of it.

NICK HAYES, WRITER

← Cadastral extract from Amsterdam, the Netherlands, 1926.

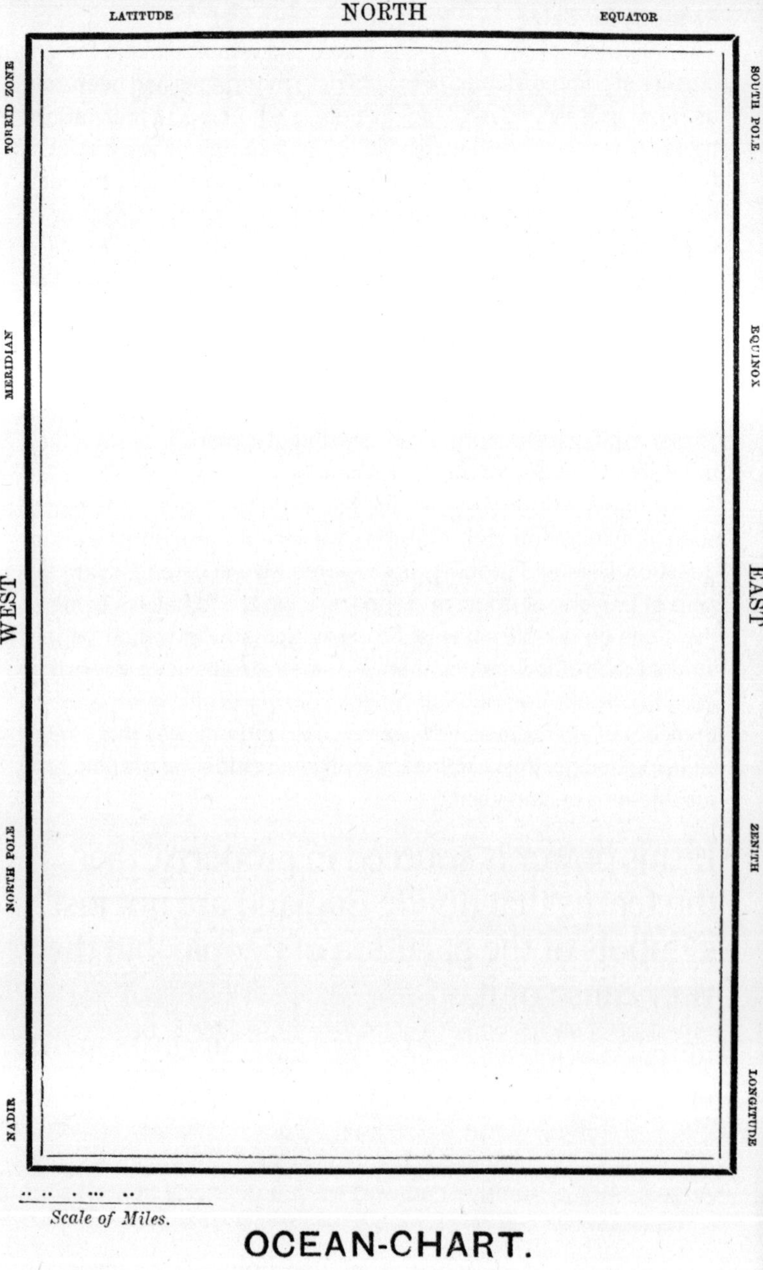

LATITUDE
NORTH
EQUATOR
TORRID ZONE
SOUTH POLE
MERIDIAN
EQUINOX
WEST
EAST
NORTH POLE
ZENITH
NADIR
LONGITUDE
Scale of Miles.
OCEAN-CHART.

TO MAP IS TO CONQUER

We find maps everywhere in our media-rich environment, but their forms are not very diverse. If you look at most maps used today, we see the offspring of colonial mapping practices. If the North is 'up', this is a remnant of maps invented in Northern Europe. If the Atlantic Ocean is left-centre, this stems from European interest in the shipping routes between the Americas and Europe. This historic perspective is relevant because of the strategic role that colonial maps have played in the forceful annexation of indigenous lands, and establishing the notion of land as property around the world. Colonial mapping practices not only established a Eurocentric worldview, but also a capitalist view of land as a form of private property that can be owned, traded, and sold.

Maps are always made from a certain viewpoint and are therefore subjective by nature. While European mapping practices rely on geographical precision for navigation, many indigenous maps create relations with the forefathers, the cosmos, the future and the past, navigating through space and time. For instance, seeing a forest as a group of living beings that are hundreds of years old, creates a very different notion of land, than if you classify it as a hectare of timber for industrial use. The maps we currently use are therefore extremely useful for navigating the seas or finding the nearest restaurant, because they were made for this purpose, but they are not very well equipped to tell us about the surrounding flora and wildlife, or what our ancestors did here. Every map is a reflection of social relations of the territory it aims to represent.

Are You on Stolen Land?
The first European who set foot on the continent later known as 'America' was trained as a mapmaker himself. Before he set off in August 1492, Columbus had worked in a cartography workshop

← Henry Holiday, Ocean-Chart. From: *The Hunting of the Snark* by Lewis Carroll, 1876.

in Lisbon. The transoceanic routes he took on his voyage would have great consequences. Before 1750, Europe was economically small, and Asia played a far bigger role in the world economy. Philosopher Walter Mignolo writes that before colonialism, the world order was 'polycentric and non-capitalist'.[40] The colonial transatlantic trade became the driver of the world economy, shifting the centre of power and knowledge to Europe.

Colonial voyages were risky and only possible through the investment from bankers and merchants. The stock that was traded on the first stock markets in Amsterdam and London were almost exclusively of the Dutch East India Company and the British East India Company. To safeguard their investments, investors received detailed reports with maps showing their new possessions. Documents convincing them colonial ventures were profitable.[41]

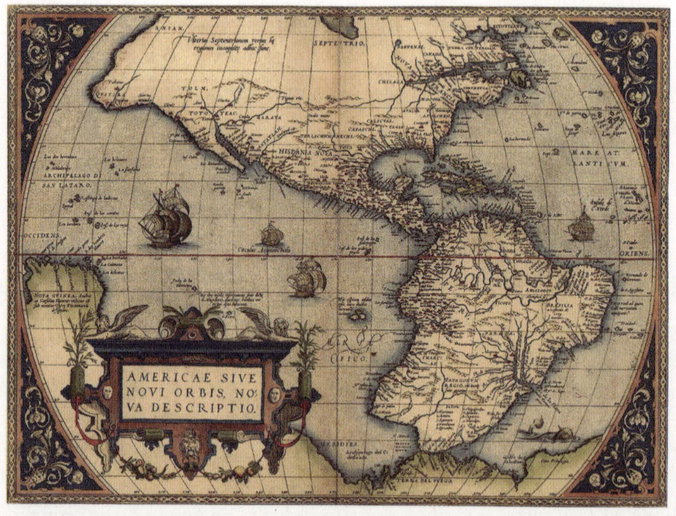

The printing press was essential for reproducing maps of these newly acquired lands. More than navigational aids, they represented the fruits of colonialism, convincing investors and the public that the enormous costs were justified, while demonstrating European superiority.

↑   Abraham Ortelius, Theatrum Orbis Terrarum, 1571–1584.
→   Ryan Vizzions, Last Child Camp Police Raid, Standing Rock Indian Reservation, 2 February 2017.

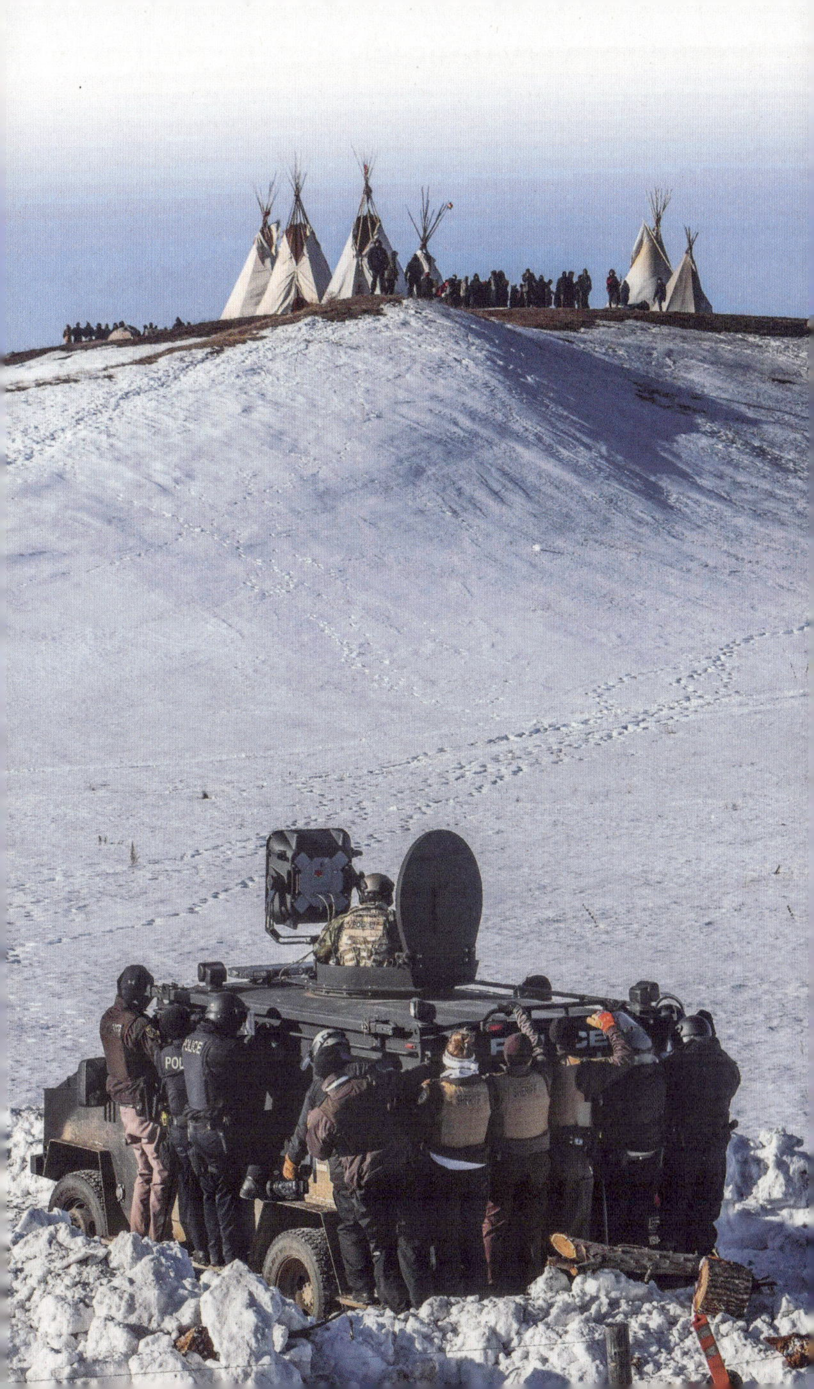

It would be very desirable that the Indians be extinguished, by miscegenation with the whites, declaring them free of tribute and other charges, and giving them private property in land.

PEDRO FERMÍN DE VARGAS, ECONOMIST

Mapping was also a tool for land grabbing. Islands and coastlines were mapped and annexed although no European had ever set foot on them. Mapping became synonymous to owning. When it turned out those lands were not uninhabited at all, the stealing of indigenous lands had to be justified. Philosopher John Locke proposed a theory that if land wasn't used efficiently enough by the owner, they could be kicked off. This theory proved its worth in the new continents were large areas of land lay idle being unproductive in the eyes of capitalism, and could therefore rightfully be occupied by settler colonists.[42]

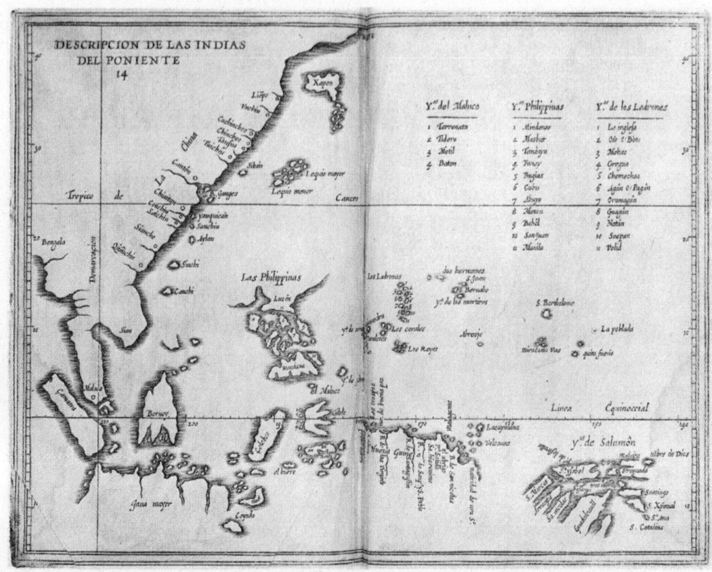

Antonio de Herrera, Map of Southeast Asia, 1622.

Here Be Savages

In precolonial times, European mapmakers had the habit of drawing dragons and octopuses at the edges to warn against falling off the earth's flat surface. When the first rumours of the existence of a new world spread, these monsters were replaced by natives that were thought to inhabit it.[43] The printing press spread stories and images of cannibals, six-armed men, centaurs, and hermaphrodites, which popularized the belief that the people inhabiting the 'new world' were of another order.[44] These wild imaginations were a precursor of how Europeans would morally defend the genocide that they unleashed on the native inhabitants.

While Adam Smith was busy writing one of the founding texts of capitalism, philosopher Immanuel Kant categorized different races according to assumed moral and physical standards, which scientifically anchored slavery as a morally just act. Colonized lands could be seized and plundered, which is exactly what Europeans did. Spanish conquerors extracted massive amounts of gold and silver from the Americas for which they used enslaved peoples and exploited the indigenous population. Mignolo writes

> ...the combination of capital, massive appropriation of land and resources, and massive exploitation of labour made it possible, for the first time in the history of the human species, to produce commodities for a global market.[45]

Besides the influx of gold and silver, plantations in the colonies flooded Europe with cheap cotton, which would in turn spark off the first industrial textile mills in the UK, the first factories of the industrial revolution.

Turtle Island

Throughout history, mapping practices have existed that were very different to the colonial and capitalist views of mapmaking. It was the influence of European mapmaking through state administration and education that marginalized other world views. The Haudenosaunee nation refer to the North American continent as 'turtle island'. Their mapping practices were radically different from European maps. For example, the Haudenosaunee do not

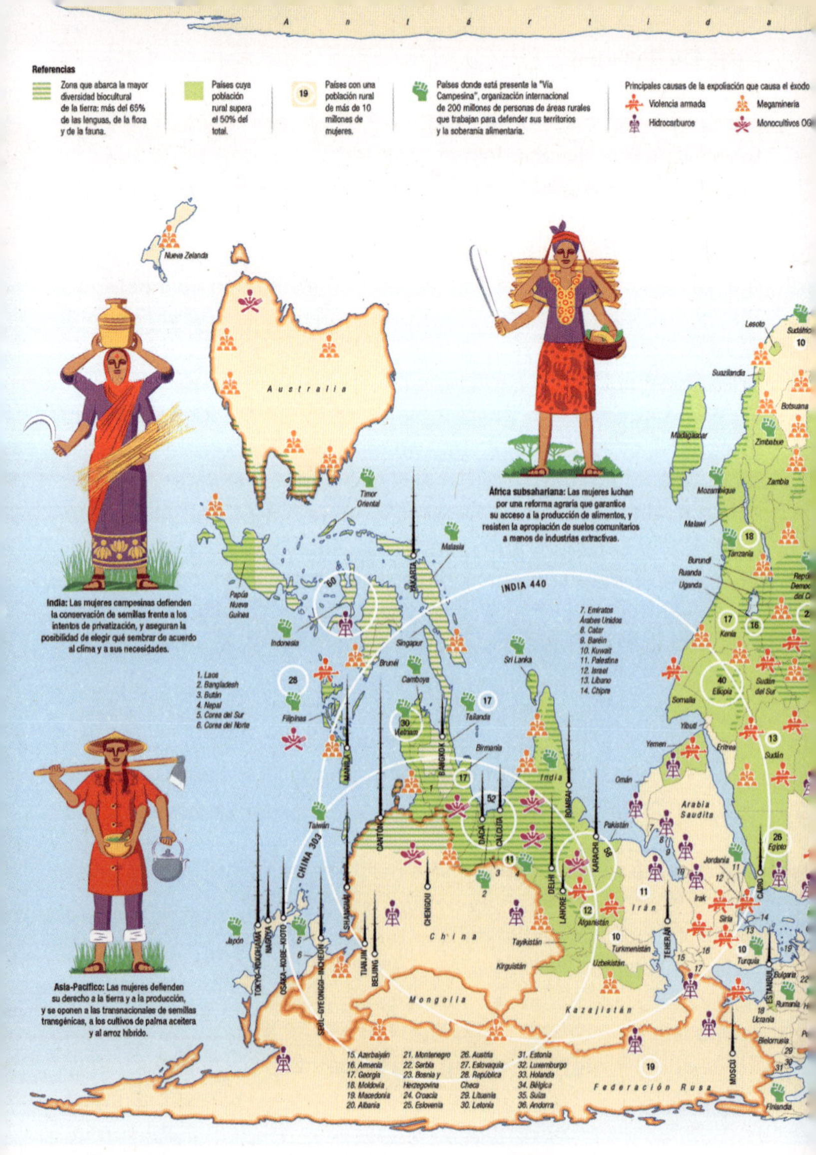

Referencias

- Zona que abarca la mayor diversidad biocultural de la tierra: más del 65% de las lenguas, de la flora y de la fauna.
- Países cuya población rural supera el 50% del total.
- **19** Países con una población rural de más de 10 millones de mujeres.
- Países donde está presente la "Vía Campesina", organización internacional de 200 millones de personas de áreas rurales que trabajan para defender sus territorios y la soberanía alimentaria.

Principales causas de la expoliación que causa el éxodo
- Violencia armada
- Hidrocarburos
- Megaminería
- Monocultivos OGM

India: Las mujeres campesinas defienden la conservación de semillas frente a los intentos de privatización, y aseguran la posibilidad de elegir qué sembrar de acuerdo al clima y a sus necesidades.

Asia-Pacífico: Las mujeres defienden su derecho a la tierra y a la producción, y se oponen a las transnacionales de semillas transgénicas, a los cultivos de palma aceitera y al arroz híbrido.

África subsahariana: Las mujeres luchan por una reforma agraria que garantice su acceso a la producción de alimentos, y resisten la apropiación de suelos comunitarios a manos de industrias extractivas.

1. Laos
2. Bangladesh
3. Bután
4. Nepal
5. Corea del Sur
6. Corea del Norte
7. Emiratos Árabes Unidos
8. Catar
9. Baréin
10. Kuwait
11. Palestina
12. Israel
13. Líbano
14. Chipre
15. Azerbaiyán
16. Armenia
17. Georgia
18. Moldavia
19. Macedonia
20. Albania
21. Montenegro
22. Serbia
23. Bosnia y Herzegovina
24. Croacia
25. Eslovenia
26. Austria
27. Eslovaquia
28. República Checa
29. Lituania
30. Letonia
31. Estonia
32. Luxemburgo
33. Holanda
34. Bélgica
35. Suiza
36. Andorra

En 2007, por primera vez en la historia, la población residente en ciudades es mayor a la población campesina. Aún así, en las zonas rurales viven unas 3.400 millones de personas que se dedican a producir alimentos y más de la mitad son mujeres. Ellas sostienen prácticas de reciprocidad, preservan las memorias y saberes ancestrales, trabajan y cultivan la tierra en equilibrio con los ciclos de la naturaleza; y aportan una solución a la crisis ecológica y a los desastres climáticos, cada vez más frecuentes en el mundo.

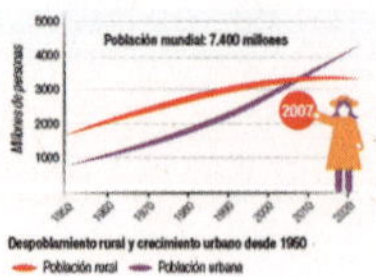

Trabajo rural y doméstico

Estas 1700 millones de mujeres representan un 25% de la población mundial, y alimentan a un 70% de los habitantes del planeta. Las mujeres rurales, además del cuidado de sembradíos, la obtención de agua y leña y la cría de animales; realizan un trabajo invisible y no remunerado: el doméstico, el cual incluye el cuidado de los hijos y de personas enfermas, la limpieza del hogar y la elaboración de alimentos, todas labores consideradas como una extensión (obligada) de sus tareas de reproducción biológica.

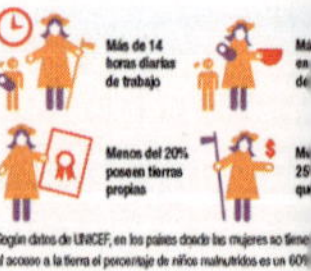

Según datos de UNICEF, en los países donde las mujeres no tienen acceso a la tierra el porcentaje de niños malnutridos es un 60%.

Iconoclasistas, To Whom Belongs the Land?, 2018.

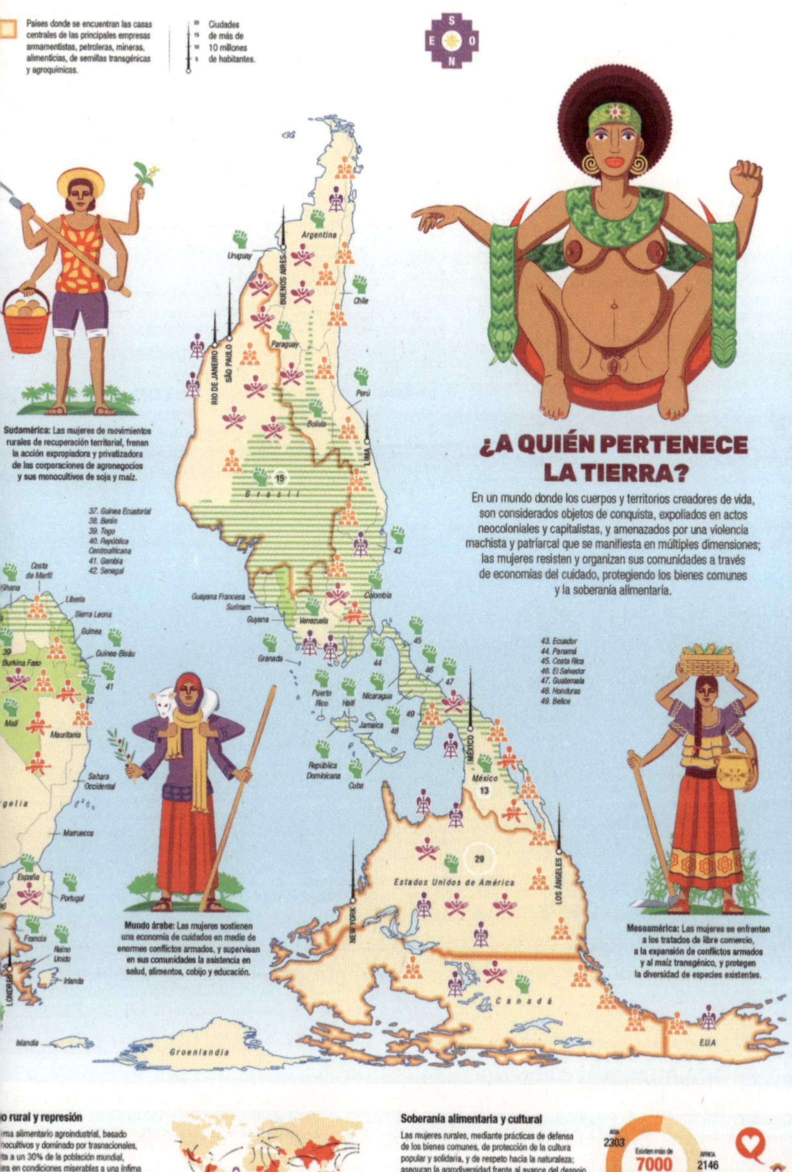

Países donde se encuentran las casas centrales de las principales empresas armamentistas, petroleras, mineras, alimenticias, de semillas transgénicas y agroquímicas.

20
15
10
Ciudades de más de 10 millones de habitantes.

S
E   O
N

Sudamérica: Las mujeres de movimientos rurales de recuperación territorial, frenan la acción expropiadora y privatizadora de las corporaciones de agronegocios y sus monocultivos de soja y maíz.

37. Guinea Ecuatorial
38. Benín
39. Togo
40. República Centroafricana
41. Gambia
42. Senegal

Mundo árabe: Las mujeres sostienen una economía de cuidados en medio de enormes conflictos armados, y supervisan en sus comunidades la asistencia en salud, alimentos, cobijo y educación.

¿A QUIÉN PERTENECE LA TIERRA?

En un mundo donde los cuerpos y territorios creadores de vida, son considerados objetos de conquista, expoliados en actos neocoloniales y capitalistas, y amenazados por una violencia machista y patriarcal que se manifiesta en múltiples dimensiones; las mujeres resisten y organizan sus comunidades a través de economías del cuidado, protegiendo los bienes comunes y la soberanía alimentaria.

43. Ecuador
44. Panamá
45. Costa Rica
46. El Salvador
47. Guatemala
48. Honduras
49. Belice

Mesoamérica: Las mujeres se enfrentan a los tratados de libre comercio, a la expansión de conflictos armados y al maíz transgénico, y protegen la diversidad de especies existentes.

Argentina
Uruguay
BUENOS AIRES
Chile
Paraguay
RIO DE JANEIRO
SÃO PAULO
Perú
Bolivia
Brasil
15
Guayana Francesa
Surinam
Guyana
Venezuela
Colombia
Granada
43
Puerto Rico
Haití
Nicaragua
Jamaica
República Dominicana
Cuba
44
45
46
47
49
48
MÉXICO
México
13
29
Estados Unidos de América
NEW YORK
LOS ÁNGELES
Canadá
E.U.A
Islandia
Groenlandia

Costa de Marfil
Ghana
Liberia
Sierra Leona
Guinea
Guinea-Bisáu
Burkina Faso
41
42
Malí
Mauritania
Sahara Occidental
Argelia
Marruecos
España
Portugal
Francia
Reino Unido
Irlanda
LONDRES

...o rural y represión
...ma alimentario agroindustrial, basado ...nocultivos y dominado por trasnacionales, ...ta un 30% de la población mundial, ...ea en condiciones miserables a una ínfima ...e los trabajadores rurales. Destruye el medio ...nte, empobrece y expulsa a los pobladores ...ios, mientras se expande a través de la ...zación y la represión, generando la pérdida ...erechos colectivos sobre los bienes naturales, ...formando lo común en propiedad privada.

48% de los migrantes son mujeres
Países con millones de desplazados por causas climáticas, económicas o violencia.
Algunas de las rutas de migraciones internacionales.

Soberanía alimentaria y cultural
Las mujeres rurales, mediante prácticas de defensa de los bienes comunes, de protección de la cultura popular y solidaria, y de respeto hacia la naturaleza; aseguran la agrodiversidad frente al avance del despojo neocolonial. Custodian, además, las más de 7 mil lenguas vivas en todo el mundo, cada una desarrollada durante siglos de costumbres y prácticas riquísimas, mayormente desconocidas, lo que las convierten guardianas de las memorias de la tierra.

Existen más de 7000 lenguas en el mundo
ASIA 2303
ÁFRICA 2146
OCEANÍA 1312
EUROPA 285
AMÉRICA 1060
Cantidad de lenguas madres por continente. Más del 50% de ellas está en peligro de desaparición.

Un proyecto de Iconoclasistas / Álbum-Deco con el apoyo de la Foundation for Arts Initiatives, 2018 acknowledge land ownership but see it as part of a larger ecology where they are simply stewards of the land on behalf of future generations.[46]

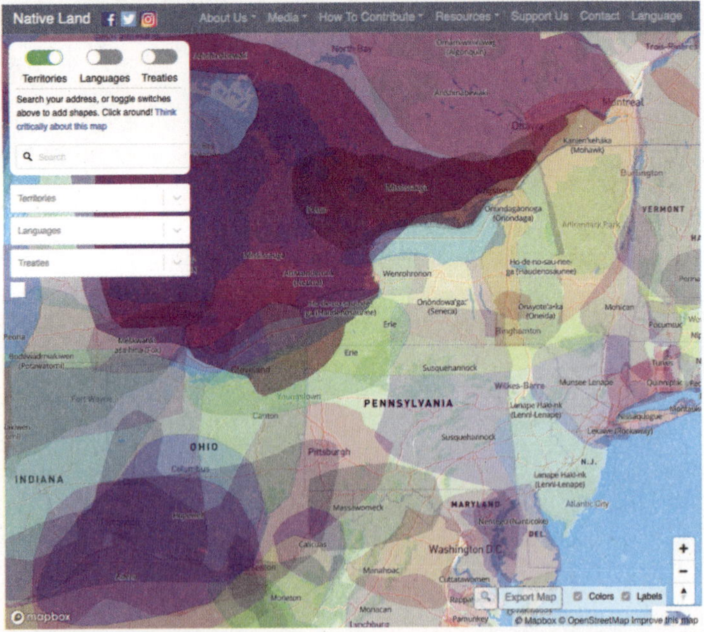

↑   Native land, nativeland.ca.

Iconoclasistas is a design collective from Argentina that uses collective mapping as a method to critically question the oppressive and capitalist nature of mapping. Founded in 2008, they see mapping as an 'organizational process' by way of 'collaborative work'. Another mapping project is Native Land, a collective of indigenous representatives in North America, who digitally and collectively map the lands, treaties, and languages of the tribes in North America. The website allows participation and adaptation with the help of users. Both Iconoclasistas and Native Land use European mapping as a starting point, but through a collective practice they challenge the idea that the viewpoint of a map is decided by one person. Conflicting and overlapping areas occur regularly and show mapping is also an act of collective world-making.

These counter mapping practices use mapping as a social process that is continuously questioned and subject to change in the form of a graphic dialogue. This follows from the famous quote 'a map is not the territory' by engineer and mathematician Alfred Korzybski. By this he meant that people often mistake a model of reality for reality itself. In other words, it is often assumed that maps offer a complete or at least sufficient representation of reality, while in fact they only show what the person who made it wants you to see. The advantage with maps for daily navigation is that

INDIAN LAND FOR SALE

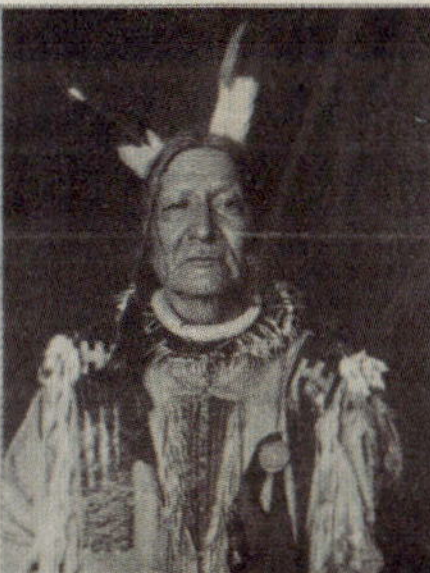

FINE LANDS IN THE WEST

IRRIGATED IRRIGABLE   GRAZING   AGRICULTURAL DRY FARMING

IN 1910 THE DEPARTMENT OF THE INTERIOR SOLD UNDER SEALED BIDS ALLOTTED INDIAN LAND AS FOLLOWS:

Location.	Acres.	Average Price per Acre.	Location.	Acres.	Average Price per Acre.
Colorado	5,211.21	$7.27	Oklahoma	34,664.00	$19.14
Idaho	17,013.00	24.85	Oregon	1,020.00	15.43
Kansas	1,684.50	33.45	South Dakota	120,445.00	16.53
Montana	11,034.00	9.86	Washington	4,879.00	41.37
Nebraska	5,641.00	36.65	Wisconsin	1,069.00	17.00
North Dakota	22,610.70	9.93	Wyoming	865.00	20.64

FOR THE YEAR 1911 IT IS ESTIMATED THAT 350,000 ACRES WILL BE OFFERED FOR SALE

For information as to the character of the land write for booklet, "INDIAN LANDS FOR SALE," to the Superintendent U. S. Indian School at any one of the following places:

CALIFORNIA:
  Hoopa.
COLORADO:
  Ignacio.
IDAHO:
  Lapwai.
KANSAS:
  Horton.
  Nadeau.

MINNESOTA:
  Onigum.
MONTANA:
  Crow Agency.
NEBRASKA:
  Macy.
  Santee.
  Winnebago.

NORTH DAKOTA:
  Fort Totten.
  Fort Yates.
OKLAHOMA:
  Anadarko.
  Cantonment.
  Colony.
  Darlington.
  Muskogee.
  Pawnee.

OKLAHOMA—Con.
  Sac and Fox Agency.
  Shawnee.
  Wyandotte.
OREGON:
  Klamath Agency.
  Pendleton.
  Roseburg.
  Siletz.

SOUTH DAKOTA:
  Cheyenne Agency.
  Crow Creek.
  Greenwood.
  Lower Brule.
  Pine Ridge.
  Rosebud.
  Sisseton.

WASHINGTON:
  Fort Simcoe.
  Fort Spokane.
  Tekoa.
  Tulalip.
WISCONSIN:
  Oneida.

WALTER L. FISHER,
Secretary of the Interior.

ROBERT G. VALENTINE,
Commissioner of Indian Affairs.

Advertisements for Native American land sale, United States Department of the Interior, 1911.

they are both ubiquitous and easy to access, so a decolonial and socially motivated mapping practice would therefore not have to replace existing maps, but can propose alternative ideas about how to understand land.

An office boy could figure out the number of square feet involved in a street opening or in a sale of land: even a lawyer's clerk could write a description of the necessary deed of sale, merely by filling in with the proper dimensions the standard document.

LEWIS MUMFORD, HISTORIAN

Visual Order vs. Working Order

The designer as engineer has translated the messy reality of human existence into manageable and legible forms. By creating categories, standards, and documents, the designer as engineer serves as an extension of the bureaucracy by which the nation state and market economies are governed. Inventions such as standardized forms, maps, and data visualizations helped to advance scientific research immensely. This has produced useful and successful tools, but the triumph of the Eurocentric scientific order also meant that a lot of knowledge was lost. A loss of vernacular practices that Scott has compared to the extinction of species.[47]

Capitalism has benefited greatly from standardization and simplification of the world order, which has made industrial production and trade more efficient. Professional standards within graphic design are highly uniform. Adobe, Javascript, Monotype, and Pantone are not only trademarks, they are also some of the necessary standards for efficient industrial production. As each item in industrial production needs to be identical to all the others, traces of labour, resource extraction, and human interaction are made invisible. Global industry standards have allowed global production cycles and outsourcing to take place. This has depleted the planet and alienated workers, with exploitation of labour and a climate crisis as a result. If we value the existence of our planet, our priority should be to produce less commodities and to produce more local and in a socially more meaningful manner.

The rational and scientific world view that this has created, is not only a capitalist phenomenon. Communist states such as Russia and China constructed their socialist politics on the same principles, with disastrous outcomes. Problems occur when the messy reality of human society is forced to conform to categories and standards that only serve the needs of a few. The point is that scientific thinking and rational ordering in society are necessary, as long as they don't forcefully dominate and suppress other perspectives.

There are reasons to be hopeful. In 1993 a stone with detailed carvings was found in the Navarra region in Spain. Scientists concluded this was in fact a map made 14,000 years ago, now known as the oldest map ever found. The carvings show mountains, rivers, ponds, and even routes.[48] That would suggest that early forms of graphic design such as sign making and mapmaking were around long before anything resembling capitalism existed. A graphic design that welcomes other forms of knowledge and perspectives that do not only have efficiency and profit as their goals. A socially aware graphic design should be able to look beyond industrial presets, and towards created shared social spaces of creativity and knowledge, accessible to everyone.

Digital technology has given designers more control over the production process, which opens up the possibility of bringing different forms of knowledge into graphic design. A move towards a non-capitalist practice of design will therefore have to question the very basics of how design is practiced, without going back to an eco-utopia of pre-industrial production. By starting small, in your own social circle and region, economies of reciprocity can create socially sensitive practices like the common lands did before capitalism. Searching for alternatives towards ways of working together that strengthen social bonds and relations, instead of breaking them.

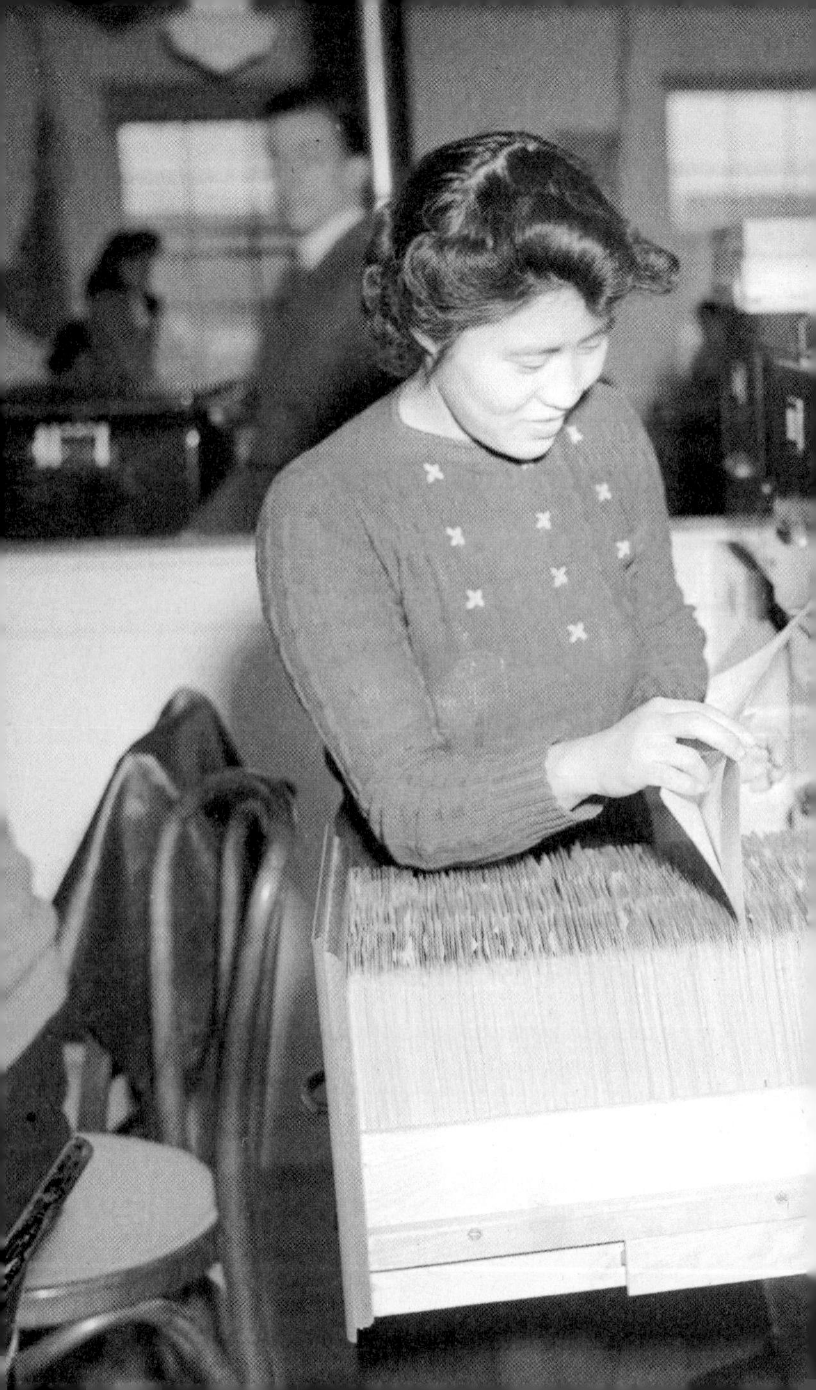

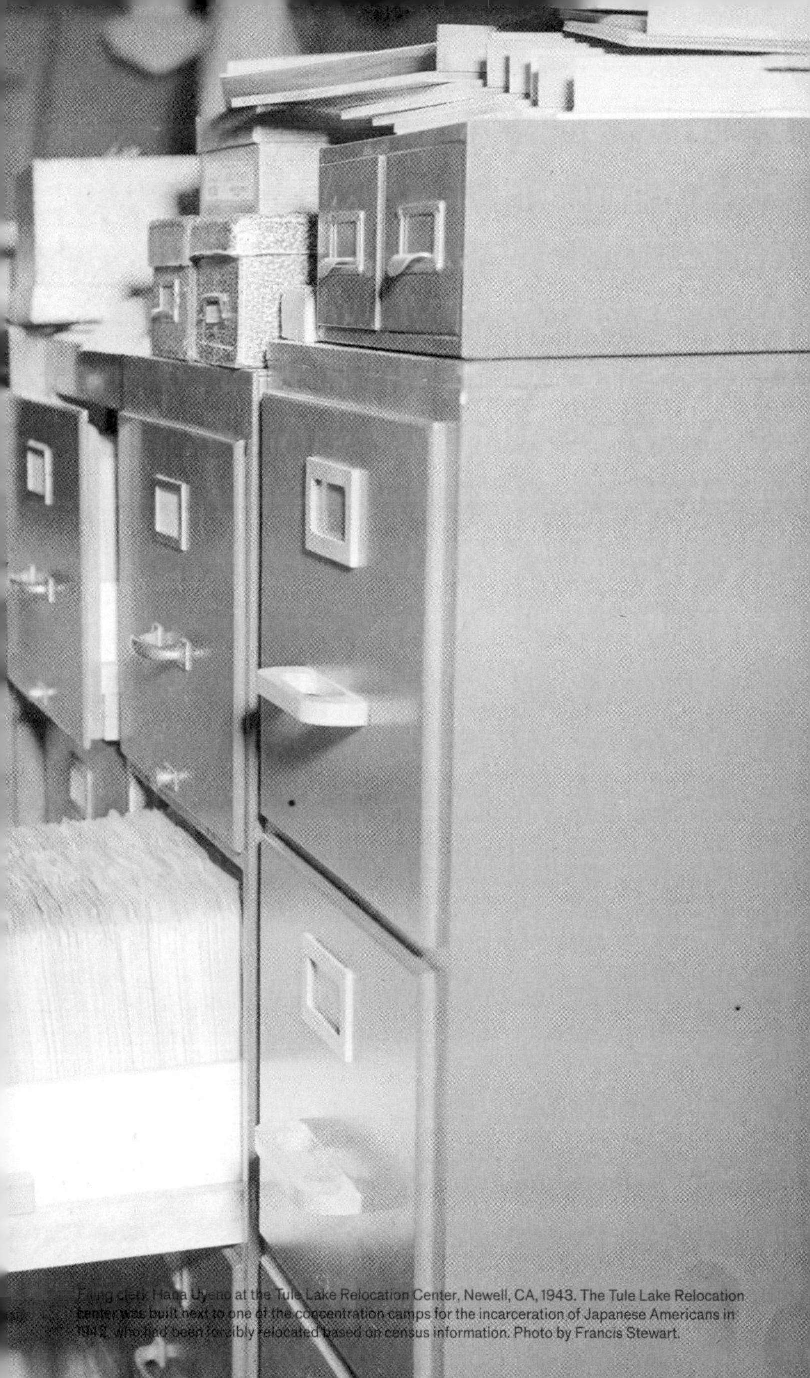

Filing clerk Hana Uyeno at the Tule Lake Relocation Center, Newell, CA, 1943. The Tule Lake Relocation Center was built next to one of the concentration camps for the incarceration of Japanese Americans in 1942, who had been forcibly relocated based on census information. Photo by Francis Stewart.

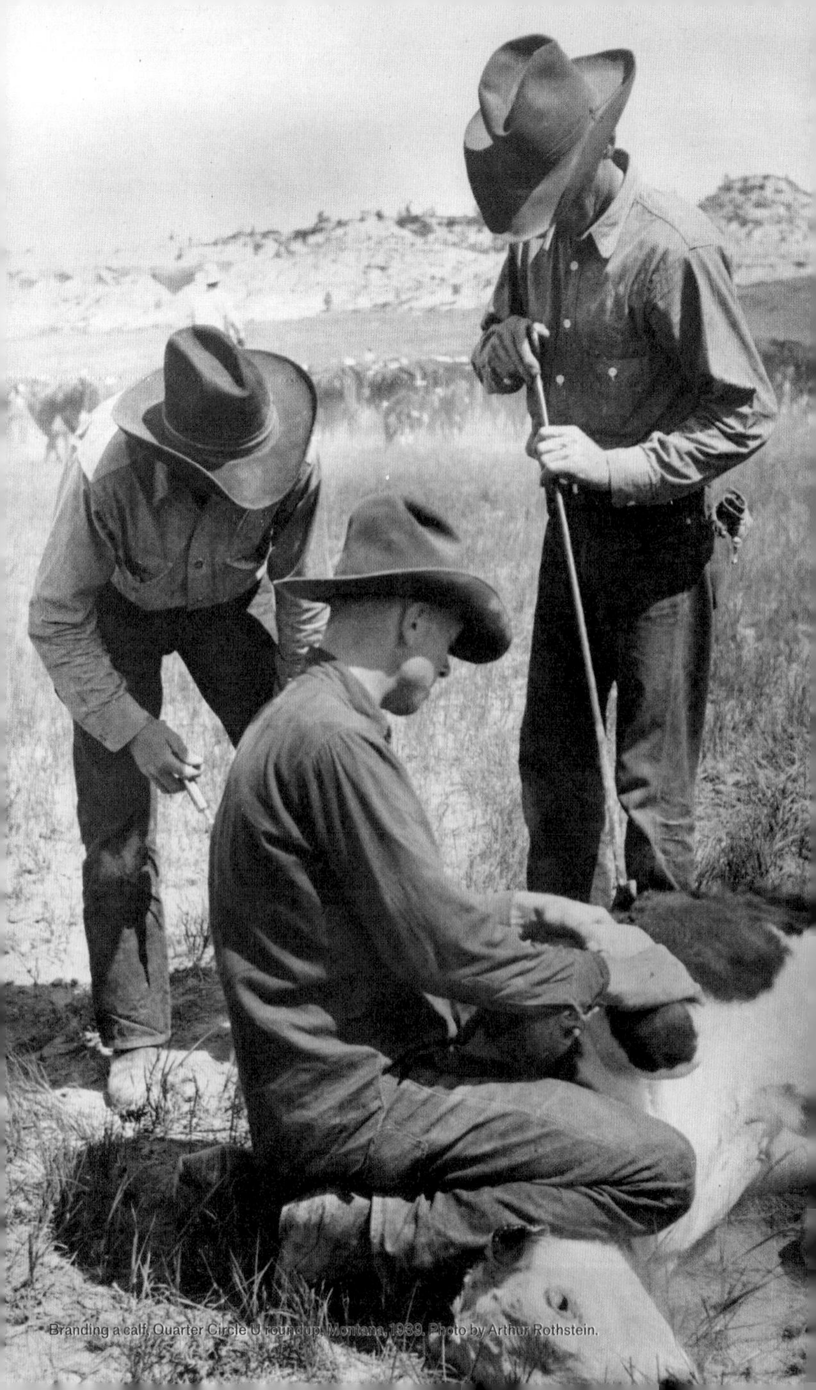

Branding a calf, Quarter Circle U roundup, Montana, 1939. Photo by Arthur Rothstein.

THE DESIGNER AS BRANDER

*The unveiling of a new brand identity
is an emotional opportunity to energize employees
around a new sense of purpose.*
RODNEY ABBOT

*There is much more to branding than a logo or style.
It is a manifestation of power.*
METAHAVEN

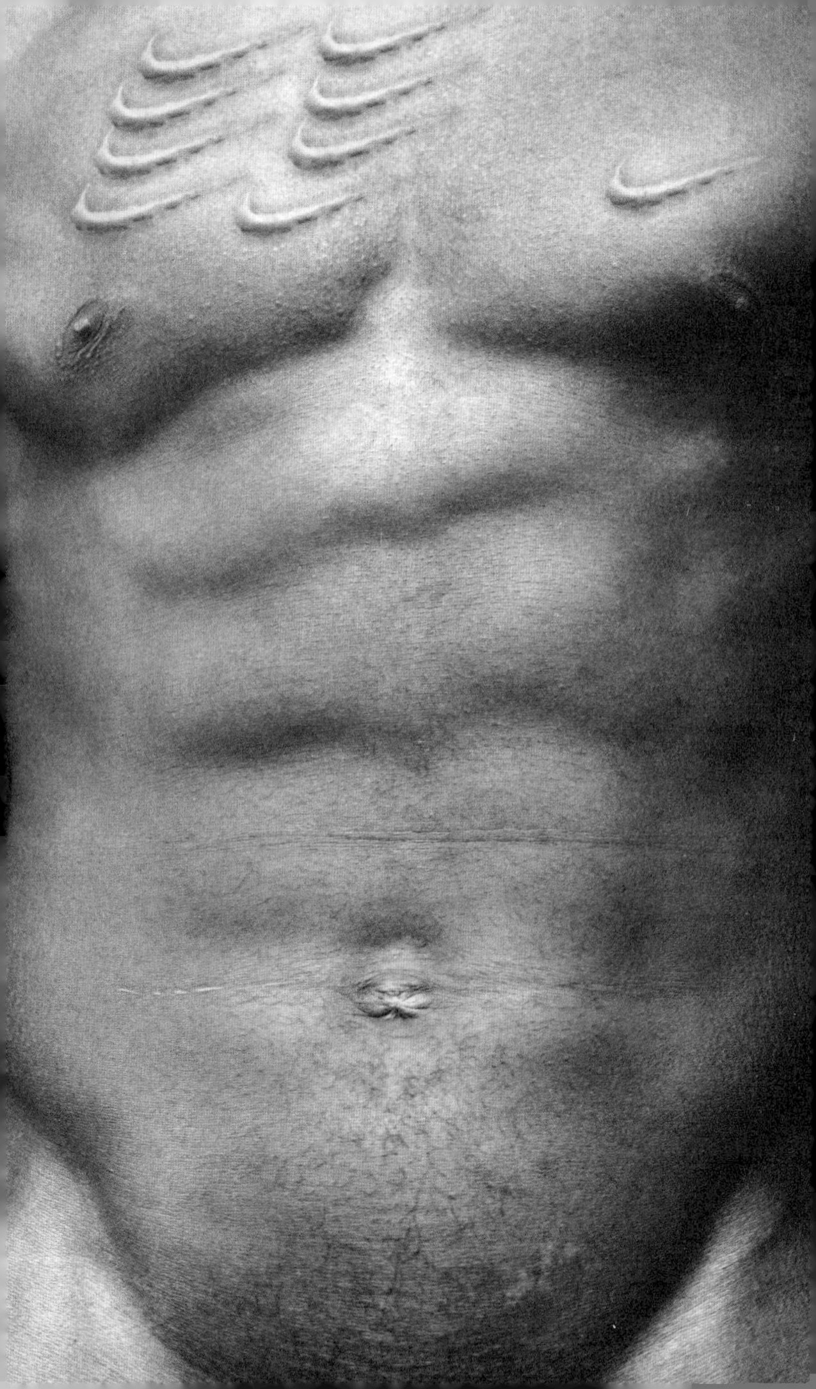

MAKING MARKS

From the Nike swoosh to the Christian cross, abstract symbols play an important role in human society. Elementary shapes such as the circle, square, triangle, the line, the arrow, and the cross have been found in 35,000-year-old cave drawings on different continents.[1] This would suggest that some symbols are universal, although their meaning is definitely not universally shared. Historian Yuval Noah Harari mentions sociological research that suggests groups of up to about 150 individuals can exist without symbolic representation. Once a group becomes larger, stories and myths are necessary to establish a social order. Harari cites religions, politics, professions, nation states, social classes, and corporations as examples of such myths.[2]

The subject of symbols is expansive, which is why this chapter limits itself to the use of symbols that mark products or services: *brands*. The designer as a brander could be a craftsman, an artist, or a designer, who creates symbols for products as a proof of quality, authenticity, identity, and promotion. People are naturally drawn to symbol making. Workmen in ancient Rome and Egypt left inscriptions of symbols and their initials at construction sites, discovered thousands of years later. Today the unheard and unseen use graffiti tags to leave their mark in public space.

Branding started with the marking of agricultural property. Brandings were a symbol of identification, but today they have become symbols for mass-produced products. With each step the maker of the product became further removed from the brand that it represented, until logotypes for businesses grew into graphic systems for multinational corporations known as corporate identities. Branding since then spread to include all aspects of life, with brands achieving an almost omnipresent and religious status. Nothing can escape 'branding'; cities, nations, water, air, even sand

←   Hank Willis Thomas, *Scarred Chest*, 2003.

can be branded. To find out which aspects of branding serve the capitalist system, this chapter retraces the designer as a brander, from its origins to the billion-dollar brands of today.

The Branding of Bodies

The word branding comes from the ancient Norse word *brandr*, meaning 'to burn'. One way of marking property was by burning a symbol into the hide of an animal, using a wooden torch called a brand. The word dates back to the early Middle Ages, but the Egyptians branded their livestock five thousand years ago. Livestock wasn't the only living form of property that was branded. David Graeber describes how in ancient Greece, slaves could be freed for a ransom, and they would be branded with the mark of their own currency.[3] Under Roman law, slaves were considered property. Runaway slaves were marked with the letters FGV for *fugitivus* (fugitive), while robbers were branded with FUR, for *fure* (thief) into the forehand, legs, and arms.[4]

Slavery took on an industrial scale during European colonialism, when labour was needed in the colonized territories. Enslaved peoples were branded with a hot iron on the forehead, breast, or arm. The horrifying act of burning an owner's logo into a person as branding is understood by author and educator Simone Browne as both a technology for marketing and for torture.[5]

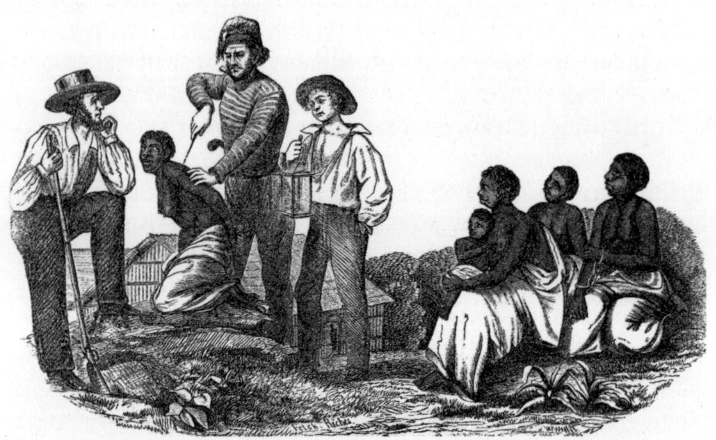
John H. Felch and William Riches, branding slaves, c. 1858.

Iron instruments fashioned into rather simple printed type became tools of torture.

SIMONE BROWNE, AUTHOR AND EDUCATOR

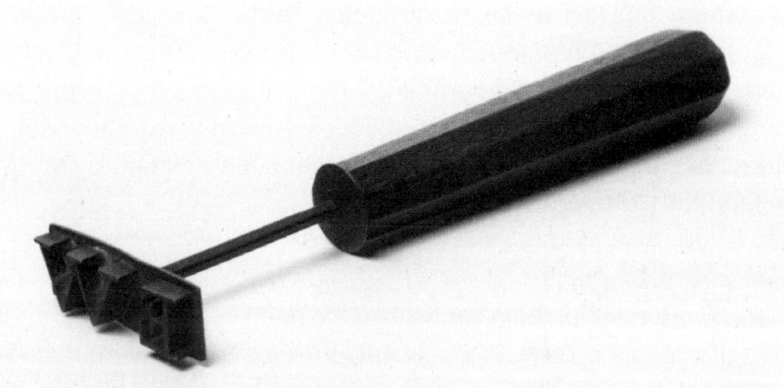

Branding iron with the letters 'E' and 'W', Latin America, 1877.

The branding of slaves was part of a designed cultural system of oppression and violence. When slaves from the Dutch West India Company (WIC) arrived on the Caribbean island of Curaçao they were branded before being sold. The WIC was one of the first corporations in the world, and already had 'brand' guidelines: 'as you purchase slaves you must mark them at the upper right arm with the silver marker CCN, which is sent along with you for that purpose', and then the method of branding itself,

> note the following when you do the branding: (1) the area of marking must first be rubbed with candle wax or oil; (2) The marker should only be as hot as when applied to paper, the paper gets red.[6]

The graphic systems for branding slaves signified locations, situations, or owners. Browne explains the branding system of the WIC after 1703:

> The company began to use alphabetic branding irons in an A–Z sequence, with the exception of the letters U and J so as not to be confused with the letters V and I, and the letter O was not used due to the iron being worn down.[7]

The Barbados Council branded the letter R on the forehead of slaves that set fire to sugarcane fields. In Brazil, runaway slaves were branded with the letter F.

It is important to understand this violent part of the history of branding not just as an exceptionally barbarous acts from long ago, but as a fundamental capitalist strategy. The transatlantic slave trade itself was a capitalist enterprise driven by profit that made industrial capitalism possible. Branding reveals the violent logic of capitalism's exploitation of people and planet, by turning everything into a commodity, even people.

Merchant Marks

The branding of objects came from the habit of craftsmen of marking their tools and creations. In ancient Egypt identity marks were found on the personal property used by workmen working on the pyramids. Identity marks could be derived from someone's name or initials, or a symbol related to the family name. A family symbol could even transfer from father to son.[8]

Before literacy became widespread, symbolic markings and colour schemes were necessary to identify friend or foe. Medieval knights who fought with closed visor needed shields with symbols and colours to distinguish one another on the battlefield. Heraldry books were produced with the graphic depictions of shields in order to assess the right amount of ransom money for captured

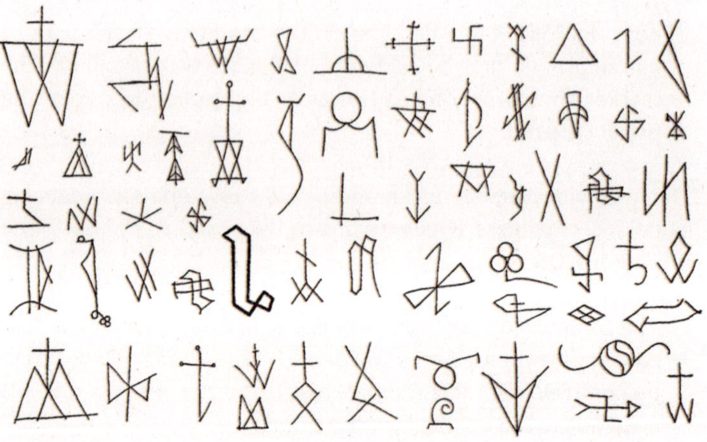

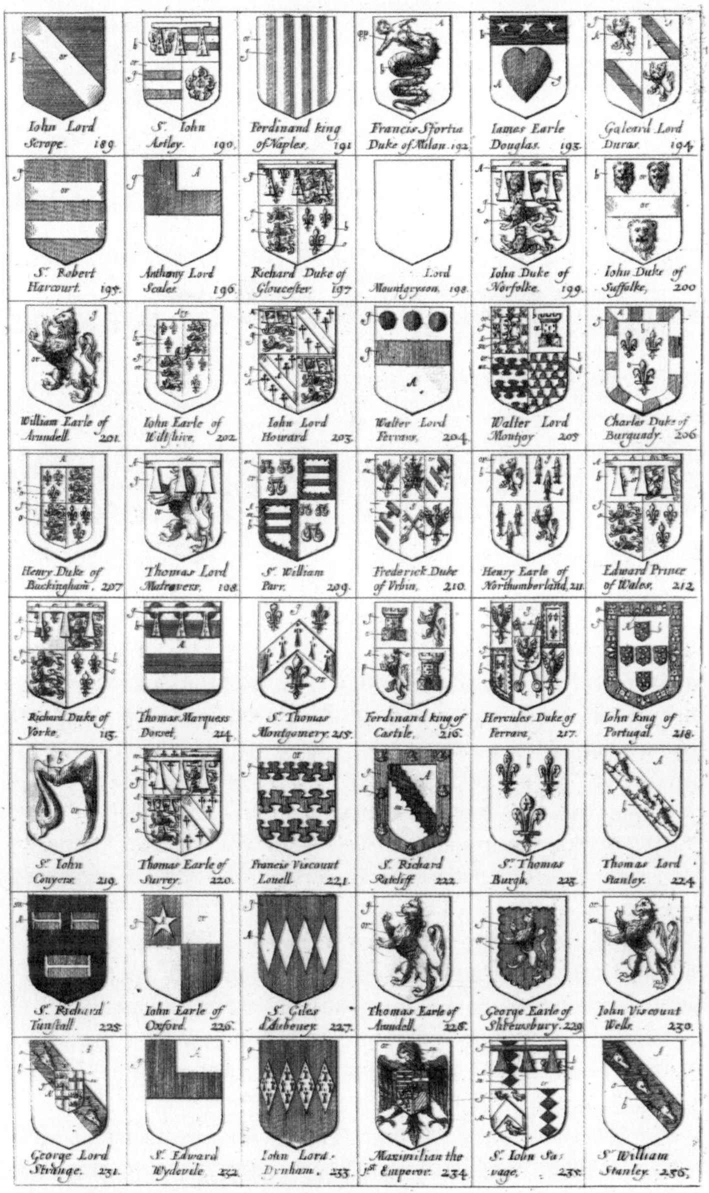

↑ Arms of Knights of the Garter, an order of knighthood in the British honours system, 1672–1677.

← Marks left by masons in King's College, thirteenth century, London.

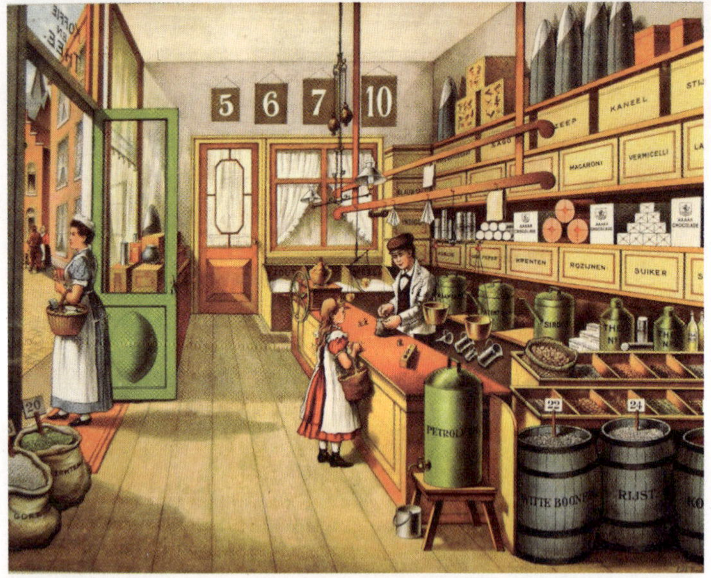

The grocer's, from a Dutch school teaching aid. Most items are sold brandless in bulk quantities.

knights. Shields were part of a visual identity, with symbolic imagery and specific colours that were used by aristocrat families for generations. The popularity of shields led European cities and towns to copy the custom and create their own shields as town symbols in the thirteenth century.

While towns and noblemen used shields, the guilds used merchant's marks. These were symbols used by the maker for manufactured goods. Merchant's marks were burned into wooden cases carrying products, or were pressed onto products themselves. In medieval Europe they were even compulsory.[9] Besides protecting the guilds, they were used to keep track of goods, to identify ownership, and thus became a sign of authentication and quality.

Crafts and specific regional production could be protected through brand names and symbols, which was essential for the guild's monopolies over manufacturing. These qualities can still be found in the use of some brands today. Merchant's marks were written or cut by hand, or stamped by the craftsman who made the product. Branding as a natural outcome of the production process itself would change with the industrial revolution.

Industrial Branding

In the craftsman's workshop, handmade products took great efforts, skills, and time to produce. The merchant's mark was a personal guarantee of quality by the workshop's master. The invention of the steam engine set in motion industrial production in the late eighteenth century, and the market would soon be flooded with identical mass-produced goods. These products were of much lower quality than the handmade products, and their form revealed little about the people who designed and produced them, and under which circumstances.

To compensate for the absent affinity that craftsmen instilled in their products, artists were hired to invent narratives, names, and symbols to replace the craftsmen's signature. These were always partly fictional, as the design of packaging and branding wasn't done on the factory floor where the objects were produced. One of the strategies to instil a familiar feeling onto lifeless industrial products was to invent fictional persons. Design theorists Ellen Lupton and J. Abbott Miller write that early industrial brands 'replaced the local shopkeeper as the interface between consumer and product'.[10] This is why the brands for generic foods were folksy and family-like: Campbell's Soup, Uncle Ben's, Aunt Jemima, and Quaker Oats. A lot of these early advertising ideas can still be found today, as brands create brand personalities as a substitute for human relationships. By using a consistent way of speaking, informal language, and friendly imagery, brands make us associate a product with a person. In her book *No Logo* (1999), Naomi Klein quotes a 1920s ad man working for General Electric, saying that GE is not an electric company but they are 'the initials of a friend'.[11]

The successful use of fiction to breathe life into products, taught early advertising professionals that they could sell anything by appealing to the customer's subconscious. Branding started to revolve around the creation of pleasant associations.

Filling the Void

The American Marketing Association defines a brand as a 'name, term, design, symbol, or any other feature that identifies one seller's good or service as distinct from those of other sellers'.[12] Undoubtedly brands can be symbols of quality and distinction, which have a genuine purpose. By creating marks that identify owners and makers of products, brands can even have a practical and cultural value.

Since the industrial revolution we have seen a very different function of brands. Overproduction under capitalism requires more aggressive methods to sell the surplus of products. Branding has become a promotional vehicle that disconnects the conditions of actual production, the workers, and the materials, from how products are sold. 'It has been the very business of the advertising industry to distance products from the factories that make them', writes Naomi Klein.[13]

To a large extent, the workers who actually assemble or make the products have no influence on how these are communicated and branded. This is done as far away as possible, to enable designers to develop fictional narratives for the purpose of selling the product independent of its material quality and origin. Copywriter Helen Woodward started her advertising career in 1907 and said: 'if you are advertising any product, never see the factory in which it was made.... Don't watch the people at work ... because, you see, when you know the truth about anything, the real inner truth—it is very hard to write the surface fluff which sells it.'[14]

Through the dogma of branding, graphic designers are learning to commodify all forms of information. Just as what goods signify matters more these days than their basic utility, so it goes that first, information must signify ownership and only secondly does it informs.

NICK BELL, DESIGNER

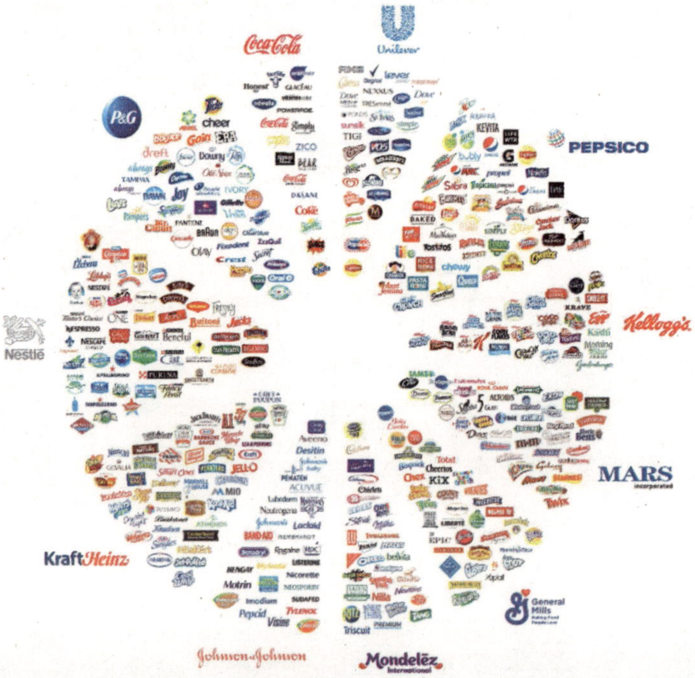

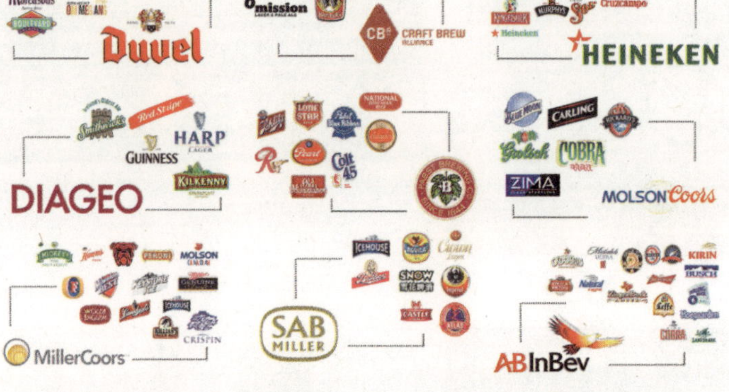

↑ The products in supermarkets give the perception of unlimited choice. But a closer look reveals most brands are owned by a eleven companies, who often compete with their own brands.

↑ Six largest beer companies in the world and their brands.

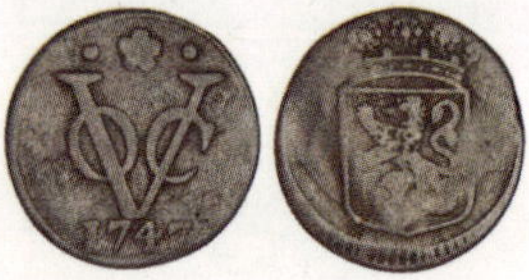

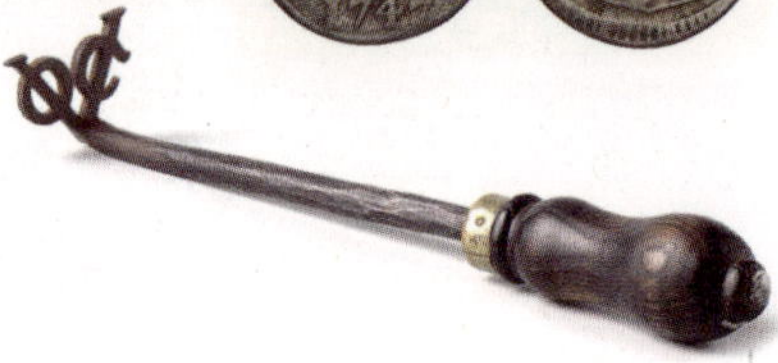

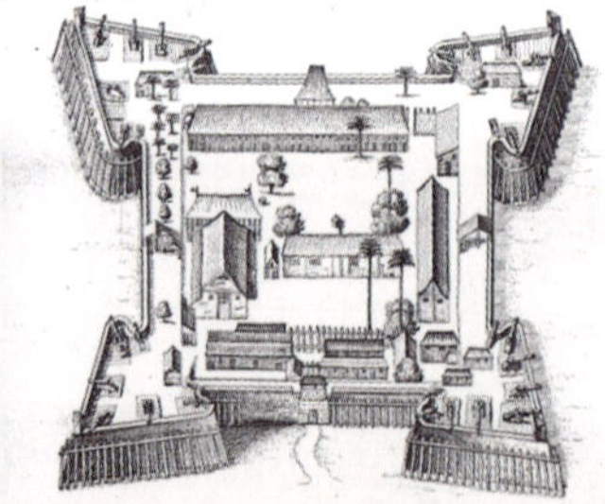

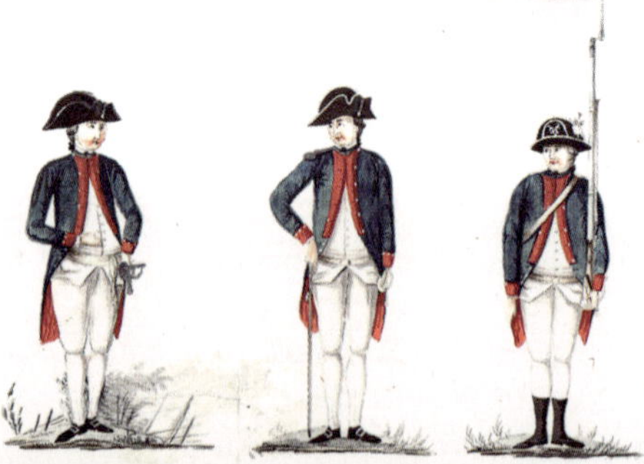

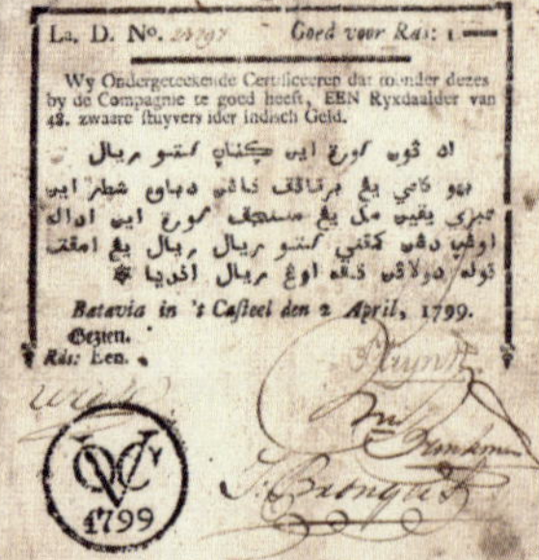

La. D. No. 28797. Goed voor Rds: 1

Wy Ondergeteekende Certificeeren dat wonder dezes by de Compagnie te goed heeft, EEN Ryxdaalder van 48. zwaare stuyvers ider indisch Geld.

اد قوب مورخ ايي حڤكناڤ كتتو مريال
ببو كامي يڠ مرتانل قاٸٮ دٻاو شطر ايٮ
تٮمرك بقيى مك يڠ مسجق مورخ ايٮ ادٱك
اوڤيٮ دٻٮ كتٮي كتتو مريال مريال يڠ امقت
ذوله دولاڤ ٮه اوڠ مريال أندٻيا

Batavia in 't Casteel den 2 April, 1799.
Gezien.
Rds: Een.

VOC 1799

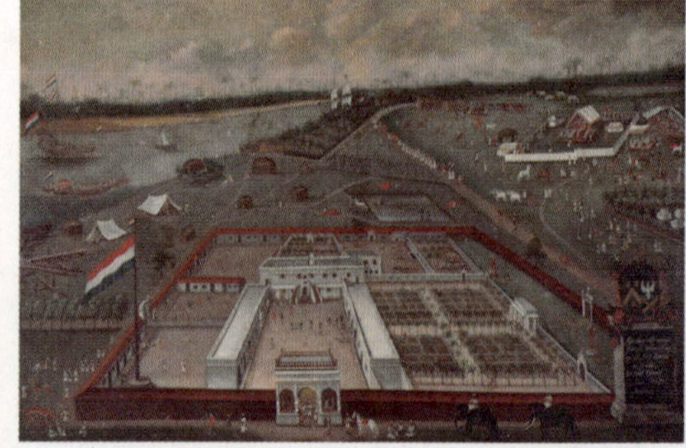

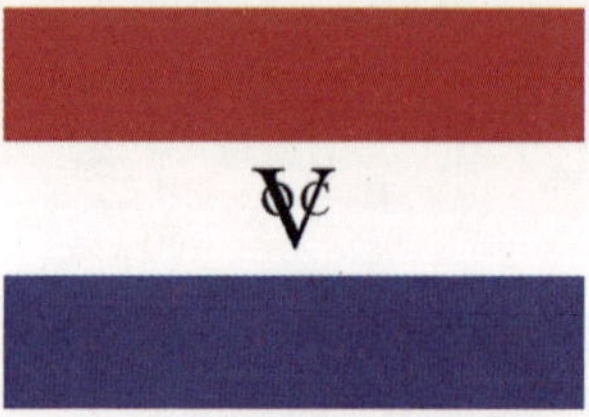

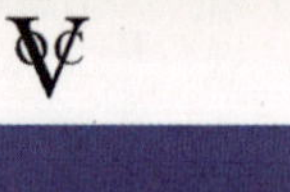

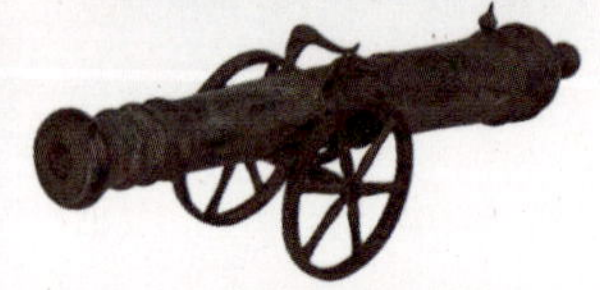

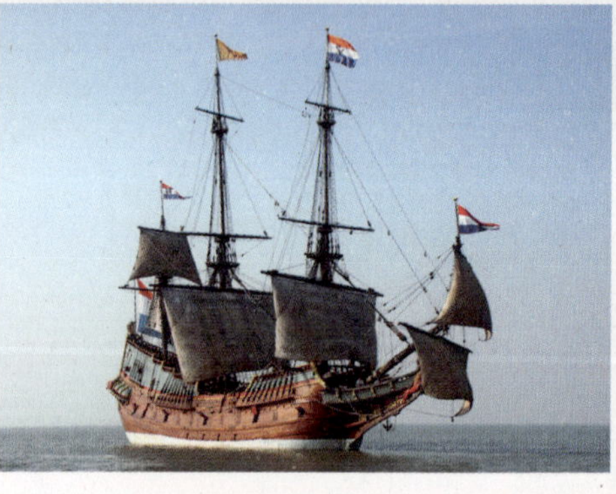

CORPORATE IDENTITY

Corporations are a legal form under which investors can pool funds together for a joint purpose. This is why they are also called joint-stock companies. We learned that merchant's marks expressed basic information about the maker and origin of handmade products. There was a clear relation between the symbol and the product. When companies grew larger and wanted to brand themselves instead of the product, this changed everything. Branding a group of investors joined together for a business interest, is an entirely different undertaking.

The first for-profit corporations were established in Europe during colonialism. Governments could not afford to back the risky, but highly profitable sea journeys, so they created join-stock companies that could attract money from investors. The enormous profits that were made in the slave trade and from colonial extraction and exploitation were the conditions under which the corporate form emerged. Among these first chartered multinational corporations were The Dutch East India Company, the Dutch West India Company, the British East India Company, and the Hudson's Bay Company.

The Dutch East India Company, *Vereenigde Oostindische Compagnie* (VOC), was one of the first corporations. It was founded in 1602 as a merger between competing shipping companies and it was decided that incorporating them would increase profits. The VOC had a fleet of 4,700 ships, its own army, fortresses, colonial settlements, and even minted its own coins. To communicate its power across continents, it created what might be the first corporate identity. VOC logos were emblazoned on stock, documents, books, maps, coins, flags, cannons, and even on branding irons used on slaves. The colonial armies of the VOC engaged in torture and terror, and for the indigenous populations the corporate identity

←   The first corporate identity and the first multinational, the Dutch East India Company, 1602–1799.

had 'become a sign of murder, torture and dispossession from their lands'.[15] For centuries, European colonial corporations reigned supreme, and the VOC is estimated to have been the most valuable company in history, with an estimated worth of $7.8 trillion today.[16]

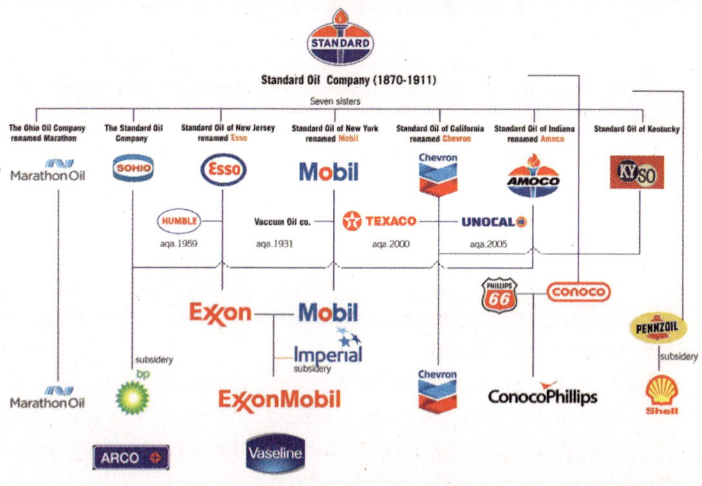

Capitalism naturally creates monopolies. John D. Rockefeller's Standard Oil was the biggest corporation before it was broken up because of anti-trust laws in the US in 1911.

Boom and Bust

Lucrative colonial endeavours created an investment hype in seventeenth-century Europe, that ultimately led to several financial crises. People who wanted a piece of the pie were prone to scams. Laws were set in place to strictly limit the setting up of corporations. The British Bubble Act of 1720 forbade the founding of any joint-stock companies, except for those approved by the crown.

With government regulations in place, many charter companies were disbanded and colonial territories became governed by the state. Corporations remained a relatively minor phenomenon until the railroad boom at the end of the 1800s, when laws in several states in the US made it easier to incorporate. Corporations such as Coca-Cola (1887), General Electric (1892), and US Steel (1901), were all established around this time.

Loosened regulations and the lack of a tax code in the US led to the famous 'robber barons' of the 1800s, such as John D.

Out of the desire within organisations and companies to fix or control their message came the principle of corporate identity.

NICK BELL, DESIGNER

Rockefeller, whose Standard Oil owned 90-95 percent of all oil refineries in the US and became one the wealthiest men in history. In 1911 monopolies such as Standard Oil and US Steel were forcefully broken up into smaller companies. Big companies were seen as exploitative giants, and widely criticized and ridiculed. During the Great Depression there was even a strong anti-advertising movement in the US.[17]

International Business Style

World War II had left Europe in ruins, but the US economy was still intact, and capitalism had come out victoriously. The Bretton Woods Agreement of 1944 established the US dollar as the world currency, and set the scene for an international financial market. Many designers from Germany had fled to the US, and now brought their modernist design aesthetics to corporations. The post-war design school in Ulm, Germany, responded to the horrors of the war by perfecting the modernist international style of graphic design for business applications. The idea was that by using elementary forms and sans-serif type a universal visual language would help bring peace and prosperity to all of humankind.

The growing post-war economies created a new wave of corporations that operated internationally. This required a consistent visual style, which was found in the assumed universal principles of modernist design. In the 1950s the first design studios in the US and Europe started to offer corporate branding to multinationals. Well-known examples are Unimark, Chermayeff & Geismar, and Paul Rand in the US, Total Design in the Netherlands, and Otl Aicher in Germany. These multidisciplinary design studios used modernist design principles to organize visual identity systems for virtually every corporation that mattered. Design studios themselves even adopted aspects of the corporate form, such as setting up offices worldwide, and working in large minimalist designed office spaces

Original tech company logos, 1998–2014.

Google

Spotify®

FACEBOOK

yahoo!

airbnb

Pinterest

Uber

Redesigned logos between 2014–2021.

Good graphic design is not tarnished by the greed or the illegal or other self-imploding acts of clients. We do not feel responsible for the character of those we work for.

while wearing suits, as opposed to the messy artist studios.

The design of these first corporate identities established many of the rules that are considered standard today, such as using grids and measurement systems, consistent colour use, and simple layout rules with simple and recognizable logotypes. Design theorist Philip Meggs writes how Unimark 'rejected individualistic design and believed that design could be a system, a basic structure set up so that other people could implement it effectively.'[18]

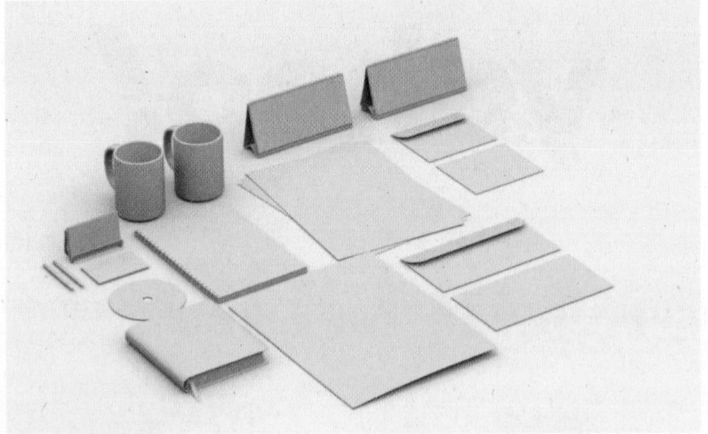

Identity design template.

Handwork and recognizable personal expression by the designer was considered inefficient and unwelcome for corporate design.[19] The systematic way of working led to the creation of the first identity manuals to ensure the design would be applied consistently across all continents.

Monocultural Branding

The large design studios from the 1950s and 1960s solidified the image of the corporate identity. Modernist design was a serious attempt to create a collective, universal style that was thought to last forever. The belief in the Swiss style of typography was so profound that Unimark studio saw it as their mission to propose the Helvetica typeface for any corporate identity. Total Design was criticized in the Netherlands for designing everything from phonebooks to corporate identities in the same style, flattening any cultural or historic differences and qualities in the name of technological progress and efficiency.

The modernist corporate identity form has claimed a universal design language, which was assumed to be the best form of communication for all countries and in any culture. This claim has been challenged by designers who point out that this is a very limited view of what design is, rooted in a Eurocentric modernist design culture. The corporate identity studios were also notably uncritical of capitalism and its worst excesses. Many designers sincerely believed that merely applying a modernist style was a radical act, while ignoring the actual political struggles of the time.

While designers compared logotypes, activists put the spotlights on corporations, revealing financial malpractice, labour exploitation, tax evasion, and the extraction of resources. In light of such a lack of morality, the professional modernist branding that designers provide has proven to successfully obfuscate corporate wrongdoings.

The partners of Chermayeff & Geismar—who branded oil companies, banks, and pharmaceutical companies—explain their view on corporate identity design as follows in *Printmag*: 'When we create a great logo for an environmental organization, we do not see ourselves as saving the planet. In the same way, we cannot take responsibility for the "evil" actions of corporations we brand'.[20]

Monopolies and Mergers

Whereas regulations of the post-war period prevented monopolies to be formed, deregulation in the 1980s paved the way for the mega-corporation. The ten largest mergers in US history happened during the presidency of Ronald Reagan (1980–1989).

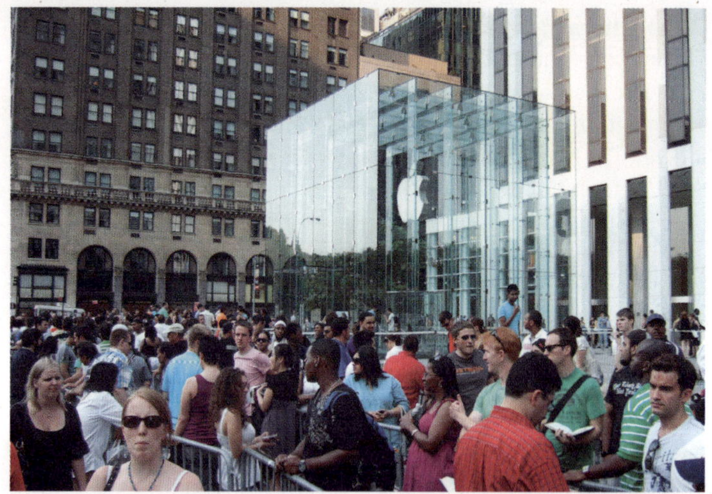

Waiting line at the Apple Store for the new iPhone, New York City, US. Photo by Rob DiCaterino, 2008.

The number of mergers and acquisitions led to a concentration of power around a handful of multinationals. Cheap overseas manufacturing and deregulation allowed corporations to bend the rules of law, maximizing profits without having to pay taxes or fair wages. Even though capitalism prides itself on being the system with the most choices, without regulation each sector naturally ends up being monopolized by a one or two companies. Some of these corporations have grown so big and powerful that they are no match for nation states. For example, Walmart has deeper pockets than Spain and Australia, and Royal Dutch Shell has more money than Saudi Arabia, Russia, or Mexico.[21]

In times of mergers and mega corporations, branding becomes part of a strategy to distance products from their holding companies. Tax havens and complicated financial constructions allow multinationals to pay little tax or none at all, while companies, brands, and holding companies create a legal maze of confusion. The largest beer company in the world is called Anheuser-Busch InBev SA/NV (shortened to AB InBev), and the merger between Glaxo Wellcome and SmithKline Beecham is called GlaxoSmithKline. This is not far removed from corporations in the science fiction novel *Super Sad True Love Story* by Gary Shteyngart where after decades of corporate mergers, the only remaining companies in

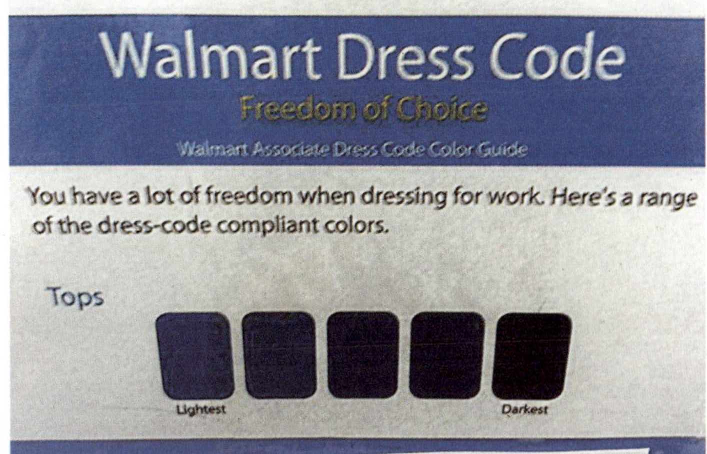

Walmart employee dress code.

the world are LandO'LakesGMFordCredit, AlliedWasteCVSCiti-groupCredit and ColgatePalmoliveYum!BrandsViacomCredit.[22]

An Identity for the Mind

In 2010 a US court ruled that corporations are persons by law, and have a right to free speech. Internet and social media platforms gave corporations new platforms to create personalized communication and services. On social media, corporations cultivate designed personalities, with clever jokes and witty replies to angry customers. Corporate identities have expanded to performative fields, extending brand guidelines to instructions for behaviour for 'staff on representative positions': what to wear, how to speak, what music to play in the store, and detailed scripts for how to deal with clients. For an employee being 'on brand' means to communicate all aspects of the brand at all times, whether or not they align with your mood, beliefs, interests, or talents. Brand personalities were created to fill the void of the absent craftsmen. Now those working for the brands have to hide their personality, in favour of adopting the artificial personality of the corporation.

Corporate identities were a response to a scaling of organizations, which required a clear and consistent communication strategy. Graphic systems allowed large groups of people to

PHILIPS

1920

PHILIPS

1968

PHILIPS

2008

PHILIPS

2013

Through the dogma of branding, graphic designers are learning to commodify all forms of information. Just as what goods signify matters more these days than their basic utility, so it goes that first, information must signify ownership and only secondly does it informs.

NICK BELL, DESIGNER

communicate and interact, and in that aspect the organizational part of the corporate identity design is not unlike wayfinding. But the success of the corporate identity has surpassed its functional use, and has become a dictatorship of professionalism that is intended to prevent creative expression from individuals within the corporate form.

Graphic designers should realize that their work on corporate identities can be used as a straitjacket by managers, to discipline their staff to stay 'on brand'. Designers aren't usually aware of the impact of corporate identities guidelines, as their work is finished when delivering the manual and the print-ready files. For those working within the corporation, especially in the lower echelons, it means a disciplining of behaviour for the sake of a designed image of consistency and efficiency. Why would corporations want to extinguish individual personalities in favour of a single dominating persona? Because the corporations are owned by the stockholders. They decide on the basis of their dividends, not on behalf of the well-being of people or the planet. Until that changes, the corporate identity will fulfil no other purpose than maximizing shareholder profit.

←   The Philips word mark has received periodic facelifts since the 1920s to make it appear the same but yet slightly updated, adapted to the fashion of the times.

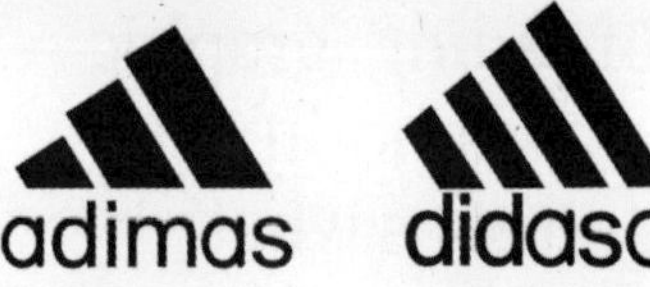

adimas

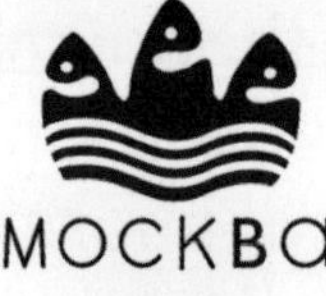

didasa

MOCKBA

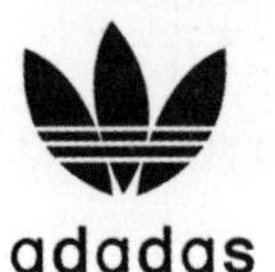

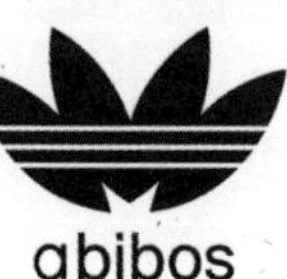

adadas

abibos

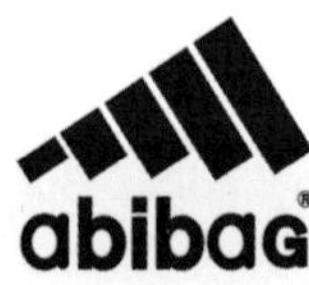

abibaG

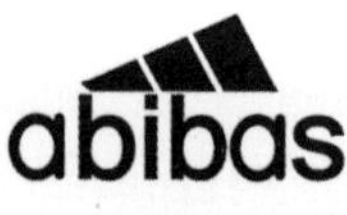

abibas

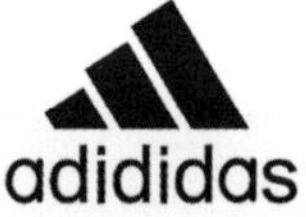

adididas

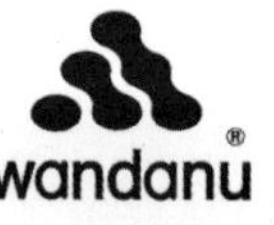

wandanu

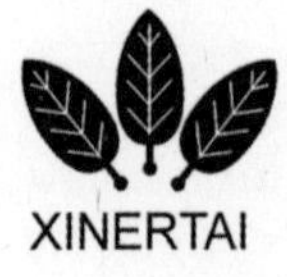

XINERTAI

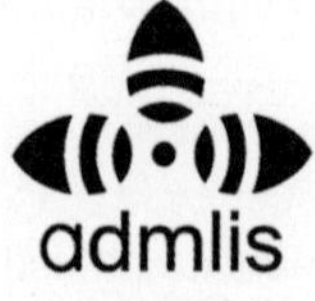

admlis

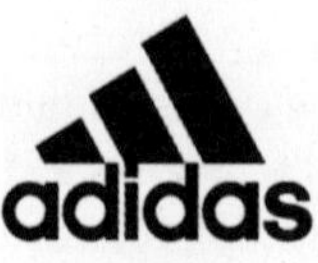

adidas

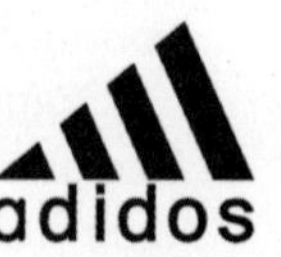

adidos

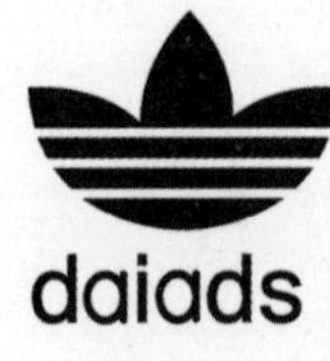

daiads

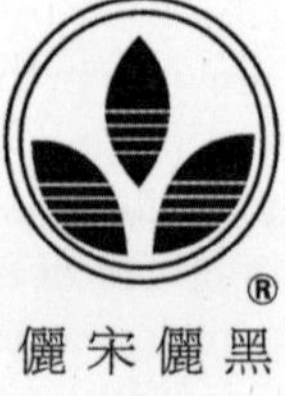

儷宋儷黑

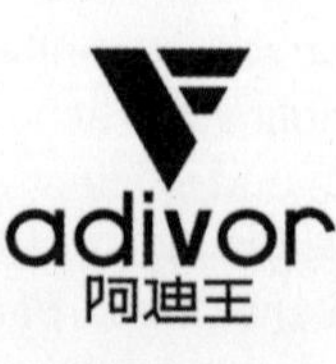

adivor
阿迪王

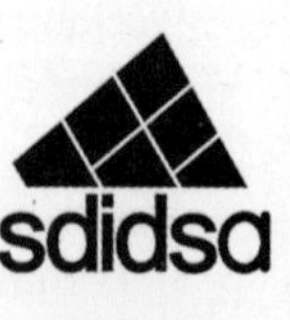

sdidsa

SPORTS

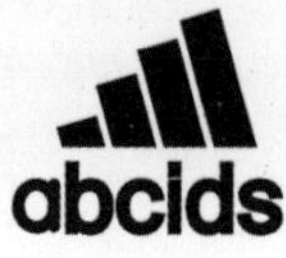

abcids

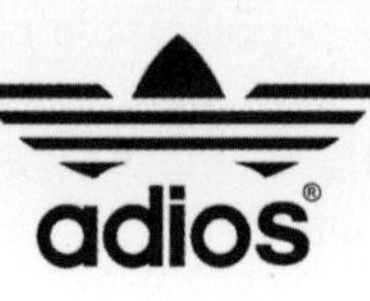

adios

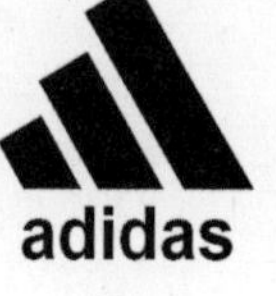

adidas

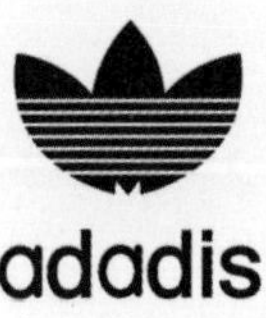

adadis

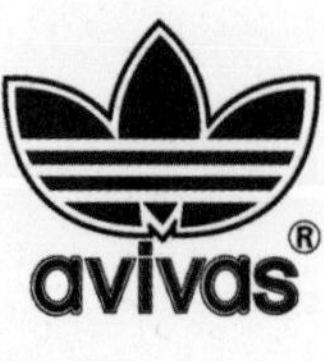

avivas

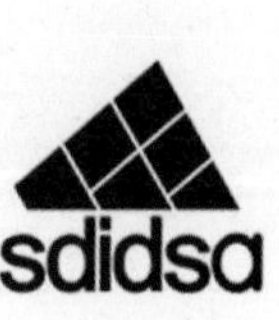

sdidsa

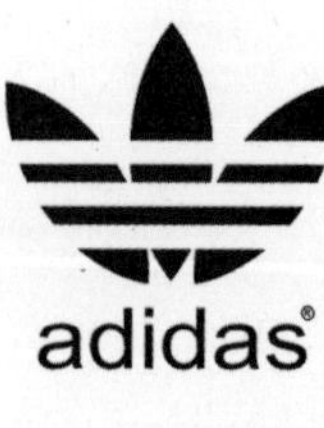

adidas

CONTRA-BRAND

Brands functioned as symbols of quality and authenticity, but today brands add value to generic products. Branded goods are often equated with expensive or high-quality goods. In fact, often simply slapping a known logo on a product can greatly increase its price. The high mark-ups that well-known brands use have lured counterfeiters into the world of branding.

According to the European Union, one of the most threatening phenomena to the safety and economic prosperity of the EU are fake brands. The value of traded counterfeit products is estimated between €600 billion and €1 trillion.[23] Five percent of goods imported into the EU are counterfeit or pirated. In an accountability test by the US government, two out of five brand name products bought online were fake. According to the OECD, 2.5 million jobs were lost worldwide to copyright infringement in 2015.[24] Fake Gucci bags, Nike shoes, iPhones, and DVDs mean lost revenue and taxes, and damage to a well-polished brand image.

Companies such as Alibaba, being a piracy super brand of sorts, offer identical-looking versions of branded goods for a fraction of the price. At the same time media companies are cracking down hard on the illegal downloads of books, films, and music. Governments launch campaigns to scare people away from buying fake brands, such as the EU webpage on counterfeiting that writes that fake items are hazardous and can cause safety risks, that 'counterfeit items are often produced in sweatshops or factories using child labour' and 'many of these groups are involved in extortion, prostitution, and terrorism'.[25]

Made in China

In the war that Europe has unleashed against fake brands, China is often portrayed as the culprit that cares little for copyrights. That narrative forgoes the historic role of manufacturing and branding.

When industrial production of branded goods was outsourced to China in the 1970s, much manufacturing knowledge was displaced as well. Chinese workers used their knowledge of brand products to produce counterfeit versions after hours, indistinguishable from the original. This created an entire industry called Shanzhai manufacturing. In counterfeit production every product is reverse-engineered, copied, and even improved, for example a iPhone copy that can carry two sim cards. Shanzhai manufacturing and other counterfeiting industries use well-known logos to charge higher prices. This has created an entire ecology of fake and hybrid brands, making use of people's inattentiveness with endless variations on brand names: Naik, Like, Kine, Mike, Nire, Hike, Nibe, Nkie, Niki, and Knie.

Creativity for Those Who Can Afford It

Luxury brands are not only counterfeited because the manufacturing knowledge became available through outsourcing. There is a demand for illegal copies because not everyone can afford the originals. The mark-up of luxury goods can exceed 400 percent, most of which goes to advertising and marketing budgets. In many countries, DVDs of Hollywood movies, Nike shoes, or iPhones, are simply unaffordable. People have to rely on counterfeited or illegal versions to have access to the brands they see advertised everywhere. In Cuba, which suffers from decades of a US trade embargo, movies from Hollywood studios are only available as bootlegs. Cuban artist Jota Izquierdo writes

> For the upper classes a connection to the Internet, to fashion, to what we call 'the first world' is easy. But for most of the population, piracy is a necessity; it means access to culture, development, and education, but most of all it's about the economy, a way of living, culture, and a way of consuming modernity.[26]

The difference between 'fake' and 'real' brands is often a matter of class. That means that the wealthiest of the world population experience the branded, HD, original versions, and the majority have to make do with the low-resolution, fake, pirated and dubbed versions of Western popular culture. The bootleg industry employs thousands of do-it-yourself designers who create custom artwork for pirated Hollywood movies and brand products. A section within the graphic design discipline that shows there is tremendous creativity in copying and pirating. Cuban designer Ernesto Oroza is one of them: 'I make most of the covers. There are designs, photos that I take from the original pictures. Most of them are in English, so I change them to Spanish. I do it myself or someone working with me does it'.[27]

Fake Fictions

Fake brands should not be dismissed as criminal acts that leech off the brand value of corporations. Counterfeit brands could be seen as an extension of the fictionalization of brands, which started with the industrial revolution. Now that production and branding no longer share a common reality, the fictionalized brands are easily transformed into formats that are even more disconnected from the product. Fake brands are in that sense a side effect of a global branding culture gone haywire, in the same way that Disney builds a 'world', Coca-Cola organizes festivals, and McDonald's makes reality TV. For corporations it should come as no surprise that moving manufacturing to low-wage countries, incentivizes underpaid workers to take this knowledge and, as good capitalists, invest it in their own business. Counterfeiting brand goods is therefore as capitalist as the outsourcing of production itself.

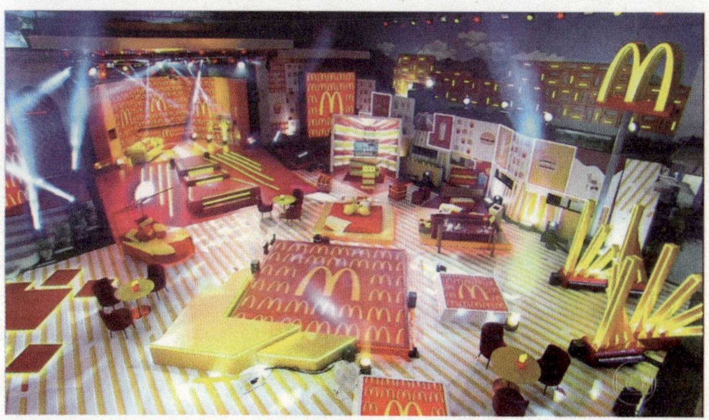

Big Brother Brazil creates a McDonald's episode of the reality TV show, 2021.

NUMAN TRADING LIMITED
VERDITE INVESTMENTS LTD.
MAJORCA ASSOCIATES, S. A.
NINGO CENTER LTD.
DOLMER PROPERTIES S.A.
STOGAN SERVICES CORP.
IMEXDA LTD.
STANDARD PACIFIC INC.
T.M.D. ENTERPRISES INC.
JUGAR OVERSEAS LTD.
TAWLER INTERNATIONAL INC.
ELLENTON COMPANY S.A.
GRENDEL PROPERTIES INC.
FANDEL HOLDINGS LIMITED
THRELKA INTERNATIONAL S.A.
WOODSPRING INDUSTRIES
TORRIJOS Y ASOCIADOS LTD.

STEALTH BRANDING

Brands usually increase the visibility of products and services, but branding can also be a way of hiding them. Logos on clothing used to be small and modestly placed so that they would only be visible to the trained eye. A subtle gesture to flaunt expensive clothes.[28] In the 1990s, the popularity of branding led companies to put huge logos on clothing. The logo itself became a symbol for capitalism, and a popular target for activists. *Adbusters* (1989) criticized the hypocrisy and unethical behaviour of brands, often by making variations on logos or ads. Naomi Klein comments how in the wake of her book *No Logo* some brands actually started to use a no logo-branding strategy. Starbucks opened an unbranded coffee shop in Seattle (known as stealth Starbucks) and Absolut Vodka launched an unbranded version of its liquor.[29]

When it comes to the branding of luxury goods, minimalist branding has been a strategy that caters to the tastes of the rich. Those who have money have the possibility of seeing fewer ads, especially as many free or cheap services have mandatory advertising. The designers from Metahaven write that abstaining from using logos is the way to attract the wealthiest of customers. They give the example of private banks in Geneva, where 'the absence of a name on the front door of a private bank implies confidentiality'.[30]

The Dirty Corners of Capitalism

The fierce competition that drives capitalism, has forced companies to cut costs wherever they can, in order to maximize profit. This creates scenarios where corporations scourge the edges of what is legal, stretching national borders and laws to their very limits. With the logos of large companies being under scrutiny, contractors with bland names and plain logos can be a way to not be noticed. Like shell companies with non-descriptive names are used to hide corporate profits and private wealth in tax havens.

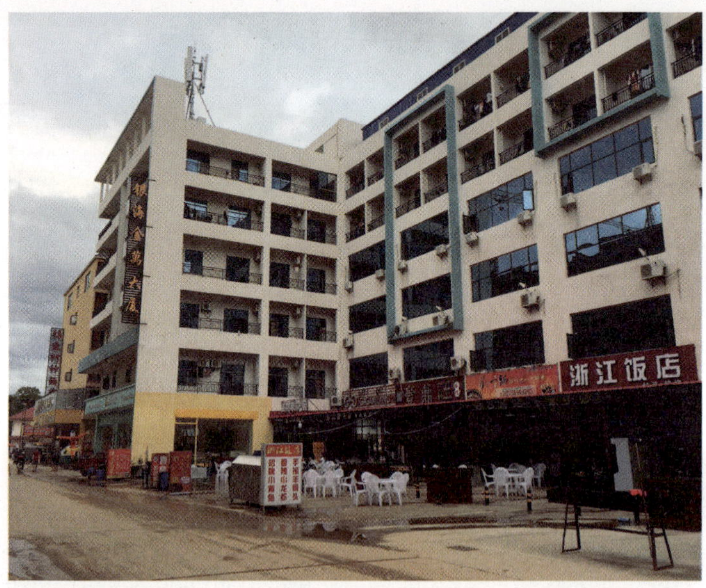

Lao-China Friendship Street in the Golden Triangle Special Economic Zone in Bokeo Province, Laos.

The cheap production of goods is partly a result of another state of exception, the Free Economic Zones, or Special Economic Zones. These are industrial areas with special legal regulations, such as low taxes and anti-union laws. The majority of industrial production in the world takes place in the 5,400 Free Economic Zones.[31] If companies move production to such a zone, they can receive 'tax holidays' which means they pay no income and property tax for five years. Inside these zones the world's manufacturing of branded goods takes place in indistinct locations.

Naomi Klein writes that the location of production is: 'a "trade secret" to be guarded at all costs'.[32] Companies prefer to hire contractors so they can avoid responsibility of paying fair wages or good working conditions. Brands often change contractors or offer new biddings to get better prices or a competitive advantage. These backstreets of capitalist production are often dirty in more than one way, and exposing too much of it could endanger the known brands connected to them.

War Branding

Knights used banners and shields to distinguish themselves on the battlefield. In contemporary warfare, intentionally not branding oneself can be a way of remaining unnoticed. The non-branding of military operations is something of a specialty for the US Central Intelligence Agency (CIA), who have created shell companies since the 1950s to carry out secret operations. During the Vietnam war, they used aircraft from CIA shell companies with names like Air America, Continental Air Services, Inc., and Civil Air Transport. Using bland corporate names and unmarked civilian aircraft, they carried out anti-terrorism and espionage operations in plain sight. Public scrutiny of covert operations by governments has increased the use of mercenaries or 'independent security contractors' for military operations. These private armies employ indistinct names and branding to avoid unwanted attention.

It's more of a philosophical point about how this war on terror has changed everyday life and insinuated itself into everyday life.

TREVOR PAGLEN, ARTIST AND GEOGRAPHER

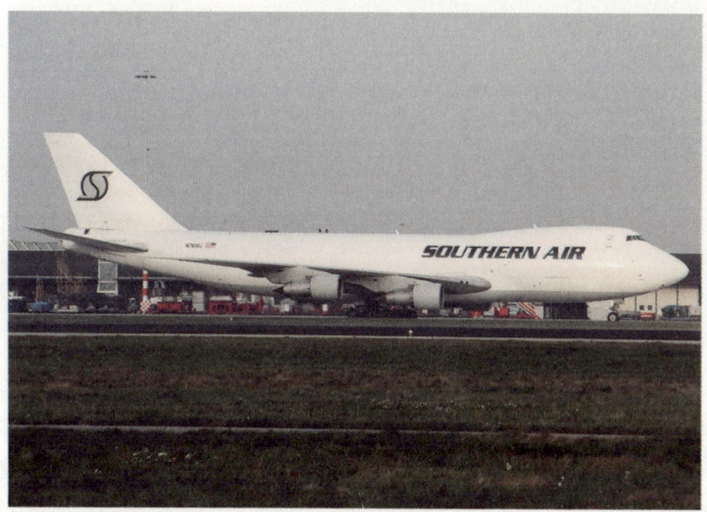

Aircraft of the Southern Air Transport, 1996, a front company for the CIA.

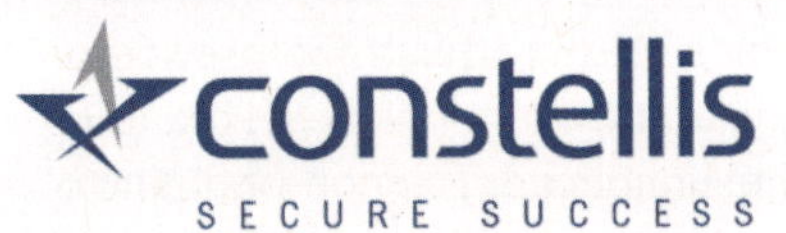

constellis
SECURE SUCCESS

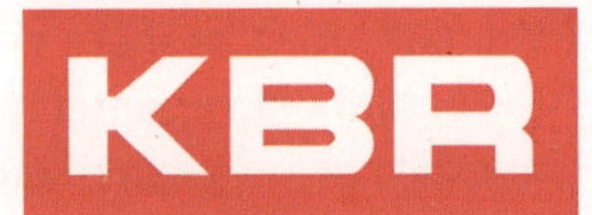

KBR

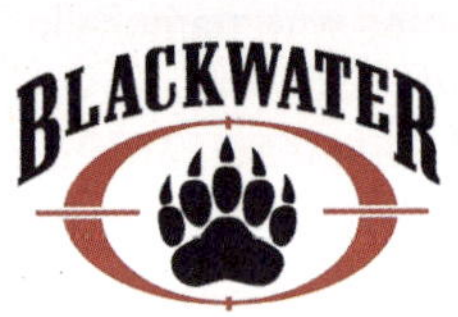

BLACKWATER

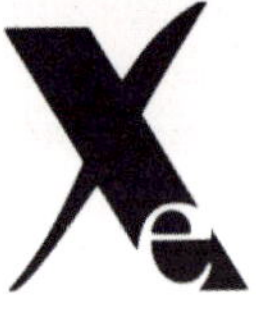

Xe

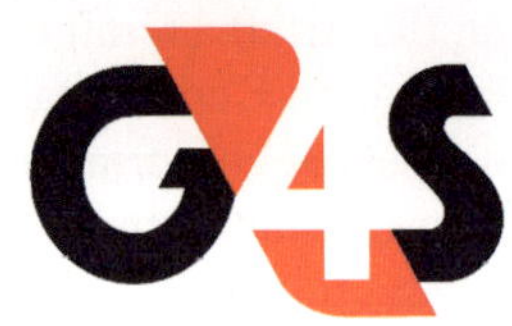

G4S

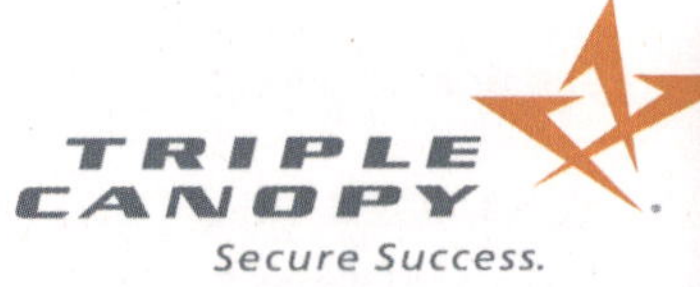

AEGIS

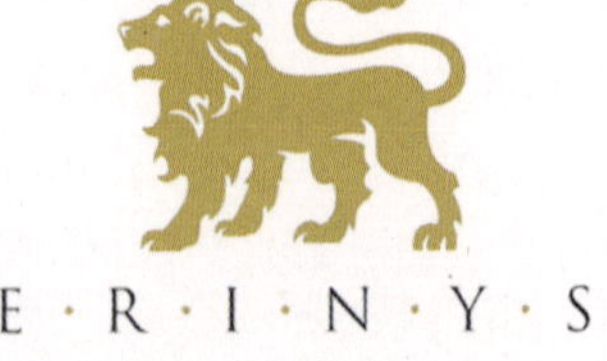

TRIPLE
CANOPY
Secure Success.

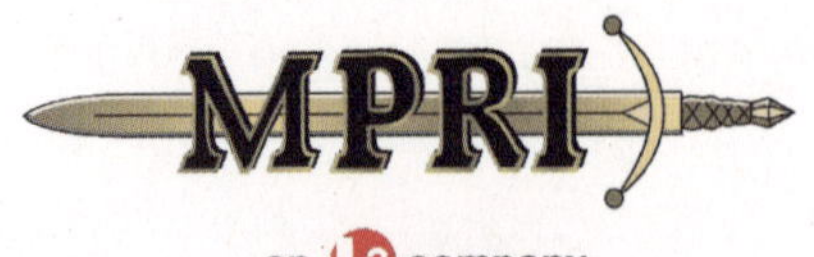

MPRI
an L3 company

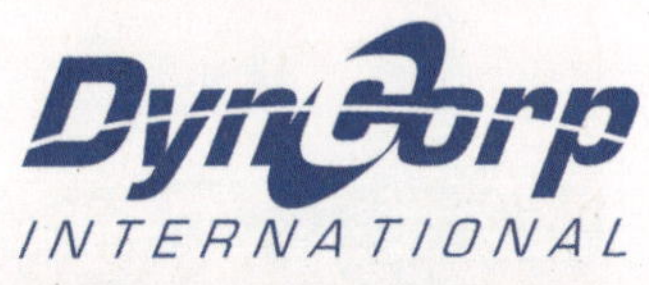

E · R · I · N · Y · S

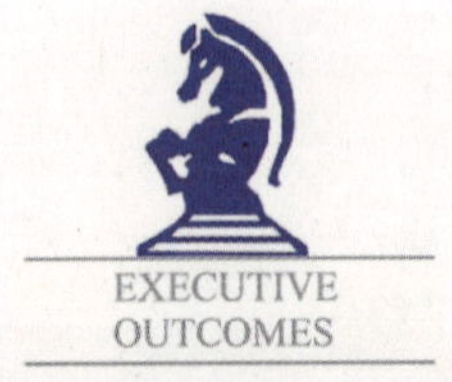

EXECUTIVE
OUTCOMES

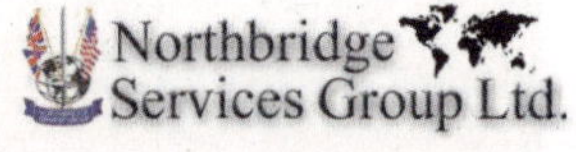

DynCorp
INTERNATIONAL

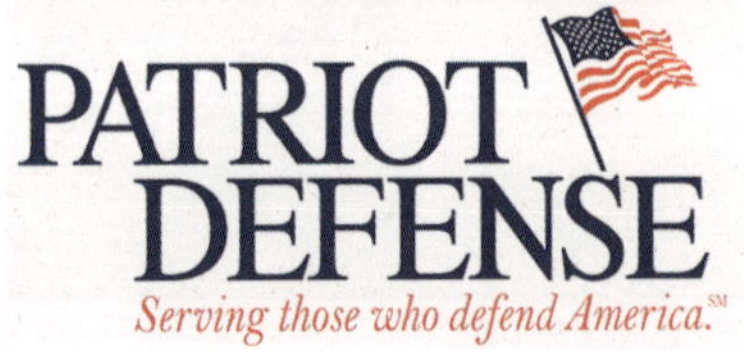

PATRIOT
DEFENSE
Serving those who defend America.

Northbridge
Services Group Ltd.

As recent as 2018, geographer and artist Trevor Paglen found that the CIA still uses shell companies to transport terrorism suspects. Prisoners were flown to illegal prisons with civilian aircraft, operated by companies such as Premier Executive Transport Services, and Aero Contractors Ltd.[33] These amateurishly branded companies were in fact purposefully non-branded to allow torture and violent interrogation to take place on illegal CIA prisons called 'black sites'. Torture and branding are still related, as it turns out.

Unbranding can be effective in creating confusion in a conflict situation, as the invasion of Crimea in 2014 illustrates. Russian special forces invaded and occupied the Ukrainian peninsula Crimea in 2014, wearing unmarked uniforms, stripped of any official identification. This allowed Russia to deny any involvement, claiming they were 'self-defence groups'. The Russian news media put a spin on the story by calling the troops 'polite men' or 'little green men'. Even in a time when the cameras are everywhere, the foreign media were forced to provide proof that these were, in fact, Russian special forces sent by the Russian government.

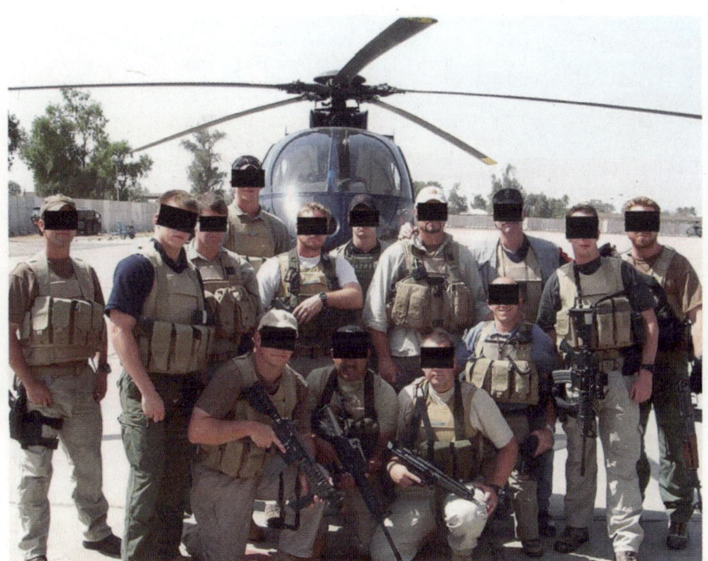

↑　Blackwater, the mercenary company founded in 1997 was rebranded after reports of wrongdoings in 2007, first Xe Services (2008), Academi (2011), and then Constellis Holdings (2014).

←　The branding of privatized warfare: mercenary companies logo.

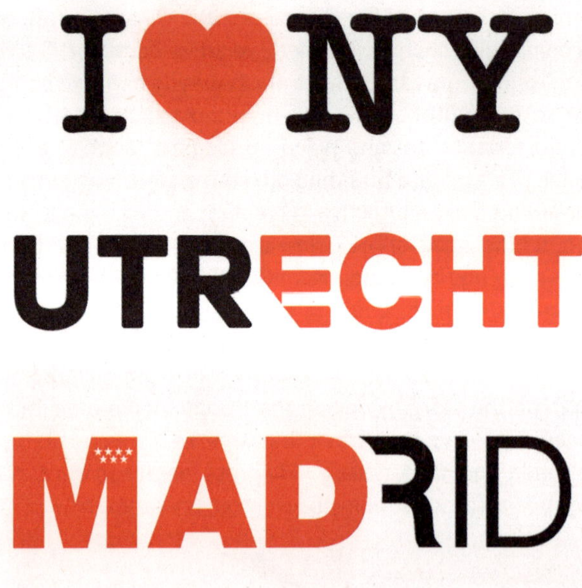

I ♥ NY
UTRECHT
MADRID

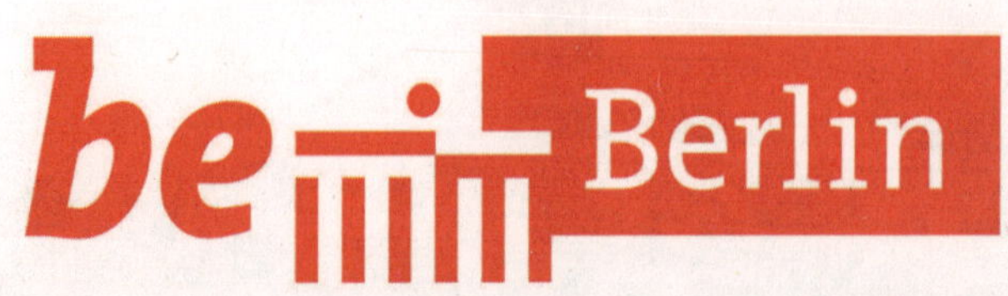

be Berlin
ONLY LYON
I amsterdam

SELLING THE CITY

Medieval cities in Europe had visual identifiers such as flags and coats of arms, which were inspired by the coats of arms of noble families. These were not created for the purpose of commerce, but to identify themselves among their rivals. Town guilds were likely to use the town coat of arms in their merchant's marks as a means of identification. The promotion of a town or city as a commodity, also known as place branding, is of a much more recent origin.

Place branding was introduced by marketeer Philip Kotler in the early 1990s, but its origins can be traced back to the 1970s. The cities in the Global North had grown because of manufacturing jobs, but now that manufacturing was being moved to low-wage countries they faced high unemployment. Cities such as Amsterdam and New York became unpopular and suffered from crashing real estate prices, loss in tax revenue, and rising crime rates. Cities that were in bad shape saw an opportunity with the growing tourism industry, which led cities to compete for investors and tourism dollars. In an effort to turn the economic tide, large corporations and banks persuaded cities to become centres for white-collar work, high-end entertainment, and tourism.

Branding cities went hand in hand with gentrification, which is the process of the influx of wealthier people in poorer neighbourhoods, leading to the displacement of lower-income residents. The bible of city branding is *The Rise of the Creative Class* by Richard Florida, in which he proposed that cities should focus on attracting creatives.[34] In his view, creative people attract businesses, which in turn leads to economic growth. His work was the foundation for policies of gentrification and city branding since the 2000s.

←   City brands: I Love NY by Milton Glaser, 1977; Utrecht by Koeweiden Postma, 2010; Madrid, 2008 by Cros & Machín, 2008; Be Berlin, 2008; Only Lyon, 2007; I Amsterdam, by KesselsKramer, 2004.

To Save the City We Had to Sell It

Perhaps the best-known city brand is 'I Love New York'. The famous logo was designed by Milton Glaser in 1977 for ad agency Wells Rich Greene. At the time, Glaser thought it was a short campaign and it wouldn't do much, and he didn't even receive any payment for his logo. As a native New Yorker, he saw the logo as his contribution to making the city a cleaner and safer place. In an interview from 2003, Glaser recalls the city at the time: 'You were just walking through all this dog shit day after day, in this filthy city, garbage, and so on.'[35]

By the end of World War II New York was a manufacturing city. In the decades that followed, jobs started disappearing when the garment industry began outsourcing to low-wage countries. Wealthy New Yorkers moved to the suburbs, and the mechanization of the cotton industry brought unemployed workers to the city.[36] With the rich leaving the city, tax revenues plummeted, and the city was struggling to make ends meet. New York saw crime figures rising and the subway was notoriously unsafe. At least, that is the narrative of the wealthy upper class, because although the city was struggling financially, it became the birthplace of an abundance of art and music movements. Hip Hop, Punk, Salsa Brava, and No Wave all started around this time, and New York was home to the most vibrant and diverse art and music scenes in the world up to the late 1980s.

Music and art didn't bring in enough taxes, however, and New York City almost went bankrupt in 1975. President Ford refused a federal bailout, which left the city with no other option than to ask the banks for help. The banks did not bend over so easily, and demanded that the city would impose austerity measures, meaning cut spending on public transport, healthcare, free university education, and social housing. The new policies were clearly aimed to stop people of colour from coming to New York. Housing administrator Roger Starr said 'Stop the Puerto Ricans and the rural blacks from living in the city ... reverse the role of the city ... it can no longer be the place of opportunity.'[37]

At the request of the banks, welfare programmes were cut, wages were frozen, and the free CUNY university introduced tuition fees.[38] 47,412 city employees were laid off, among whom

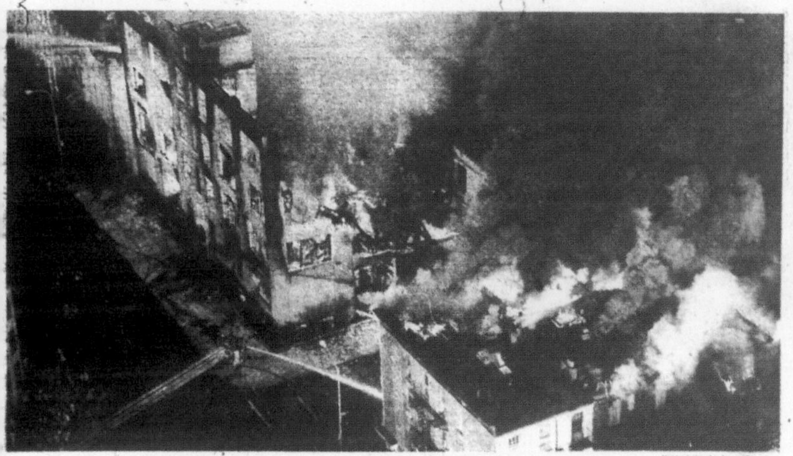

NY Daily News, 15 July 1977.

Stop the Puerto Ricans and the rural blacks from living in the city [...] reverse the role of the city [...] it can no longer be the place of opportunity.

19,000 teachers, 2,000 street sweepers and 20 percent of the police force.[39] Spending on public transport and hospitals was reduced. Instead, the city started handing out tax cuts for business-es to attract investment. $100 million in property tax breaks were given in 1980-81 to companies such as Philip Morris, AT&T, Chase Manhattan, and Lehman Brothers. By 1978, corporations paid only half of the tax rate compared to rates at the end of World War II.

What about the logo? On top of austerity measures and tax breaks, bankers insisted changing the image of the city. Instead of attracting struggling artists, the city needed to attract wealthy tourists to visit its theatres and museums to bring in money. The campaign with Milton Glaser's famous logo included commercials with Broadway actors, singers, and dancers performing the I Love New York theme song. It was a success. Hotel occupancy went up 20 percent, and more than 90,000 requests from the tourism branch came after the commercials aired.

But successful for whom? The city's new image made New Yorkers proud of their city, but it also came at a tremendous cost. Government workers that were laid off were predominantly black and Puerto Rican. Healthcare and university education was no longer free, public transport deteriorated (many wealthy New Yorkers did not use the subway) and the layoffs in the police force led to rising crime rates until 1990. Social geographer David Harvey writes that the power of the New York working class was undone in a few years.[40]

The design of a logo cannot be held responsible for the punitive measures that a city imposed on its lower-income residents under pressure from investment bankers. Milton Glaser (1929–2020) is remembered as a socially engaged graphic designer, who made AIDS posters for the World Health Organization, and co-edited

→   Souvenirs with Milton Glaser's I Love New York logo.

                    CAPS LOCK – Part 1

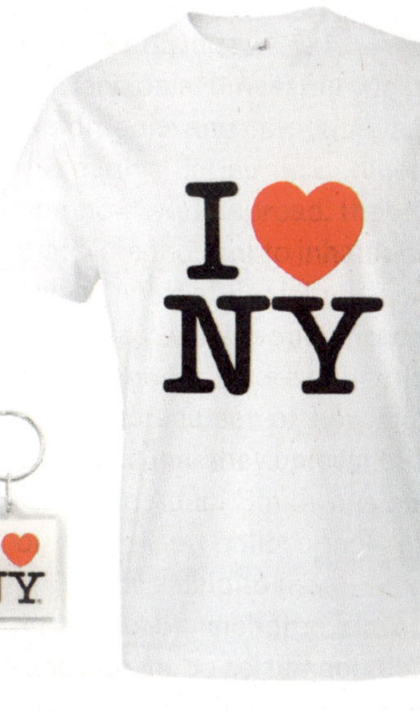

I ♥ NY

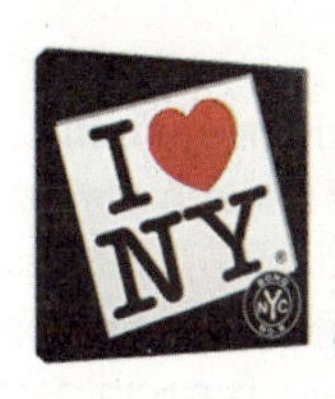

I ♥ NY

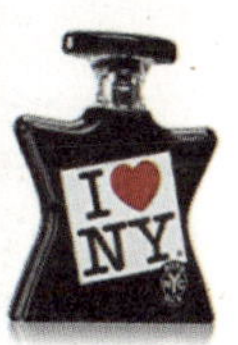

I ♥ NY

▲ DELTA
I ♥ NY

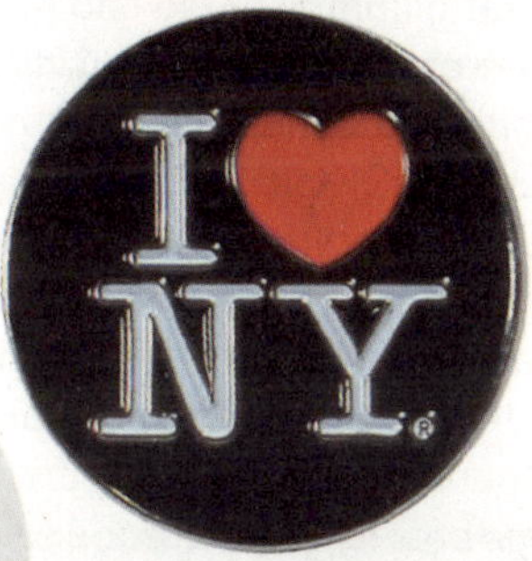

I ♥ NY

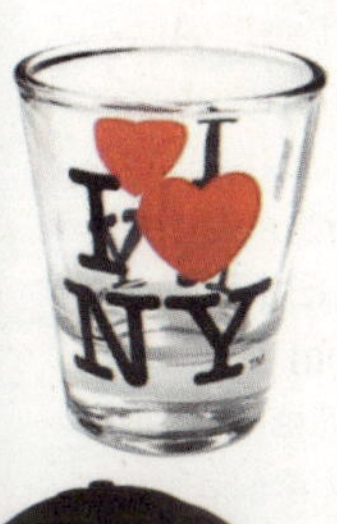

I ♥ NY

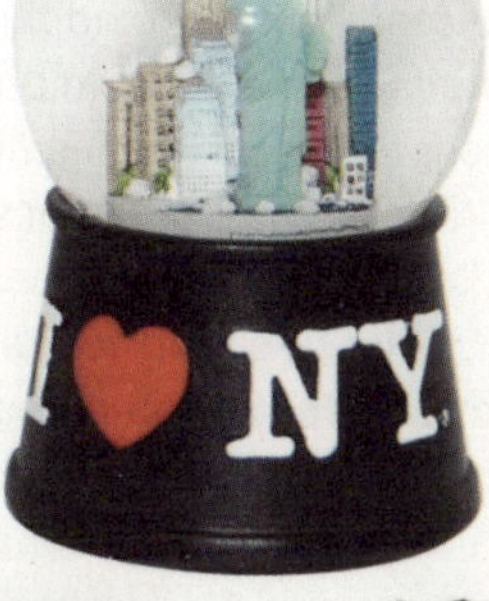

I ♥ NY

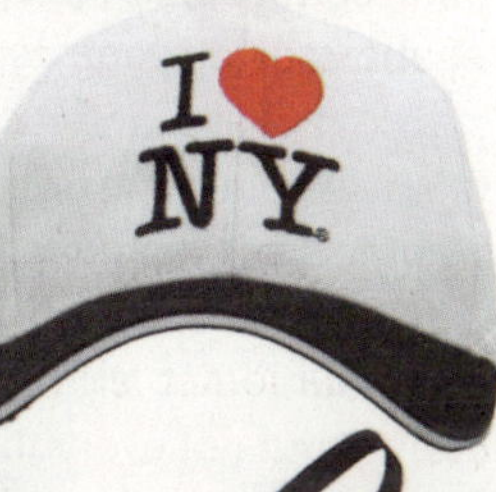

I ♥ NY

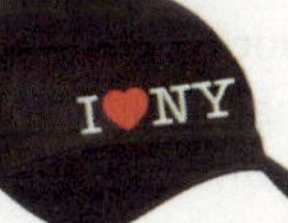

I ♥ NY

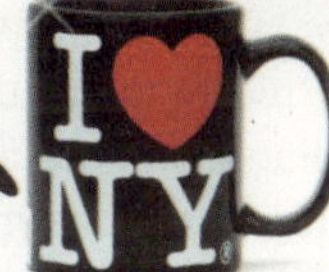

I ♥ NY

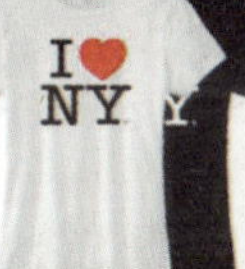

I ♥ NY

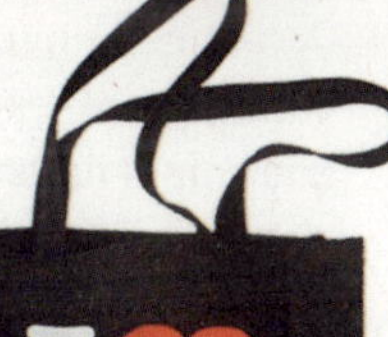

I ♥ NY

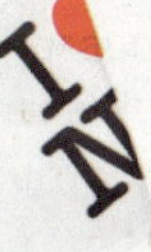

I ♥ NY

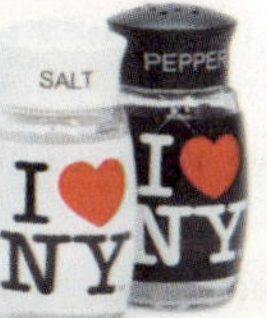

SALT
PEPPER
I ♥ NY
I ♥ NY

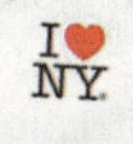

I ♥ NY

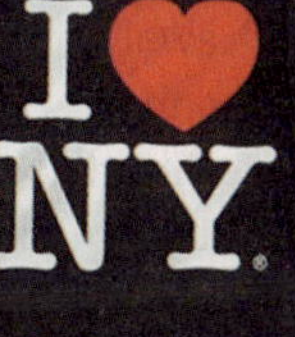

I ♥ NY

two books on political posters; *The Design of Dissent* (2005) and *The Design of Dissent* (2017). Glaser saw his I love New York logo as form of socially engaged design that helped improve the city he loved so dearly. When asked about his logo he said: 'I have to say that when you do something that you really feel is useful—when you have a positive social effect—it makes you feel great.'[41]

What this example shows is that even the work of socially engaged designers with good intentions can be used to drive gentrification. Glaser's successful city brand united people and made many New Yorkers proud, but it was also used to obfuscate the punishment of poor New Yorkers in favour of the wealthy.

Rise of the Real Estate Class
The New York City branding shows that successful city branding can have devastating consequences. Amsterdam is the city that I call home since 2003. With its 800,000 inhabitants it is a relatively small but comfortable city with a high standard of living. Tourists have always been drawn to Amsterdam's old centre with its liberal stance on soft drugs and prostitution. In 2004 the city decided they needed to attract a different kind of tourist. Less young scruffy types looking for weed, and more older tourists, families and organized tours with deeper pockets looking for culture and history.

Advertising agency KesselsKramer came up with the 'I Amsterdam' motto and logo to rebrand the city. A massive marketing offensive put 'I Amsterdam' logos on all communication in the city, websites, and campaigns, and placed a 23.5 metre wide 'I Amsterdam' logo in the museum district. By 2017 the number of tourists had doubled to eight million. The campaign brought in a lot of money, but not everyone profited.

Housing has always been scarce in the Netherlands, a country with one of the highest population densities in the world. The city of Amsterdam welcomed online platform Airbnb, which put pressure on the already tight housing market. The city of Amsterdam also actively promoted real estate to foreign investors. The I Amsterdam website boasts about 'Amsterdam's Unique Assets in High Demand' and 'Investors who have been sleeping for some years now, are waking up to the opportunities'.[42] The twelve

→ I Amsterdam logo on the Museumplein in Amsterdam, 2013. Photo by Kevin McGill.

 CAPS LOCK — Part 1

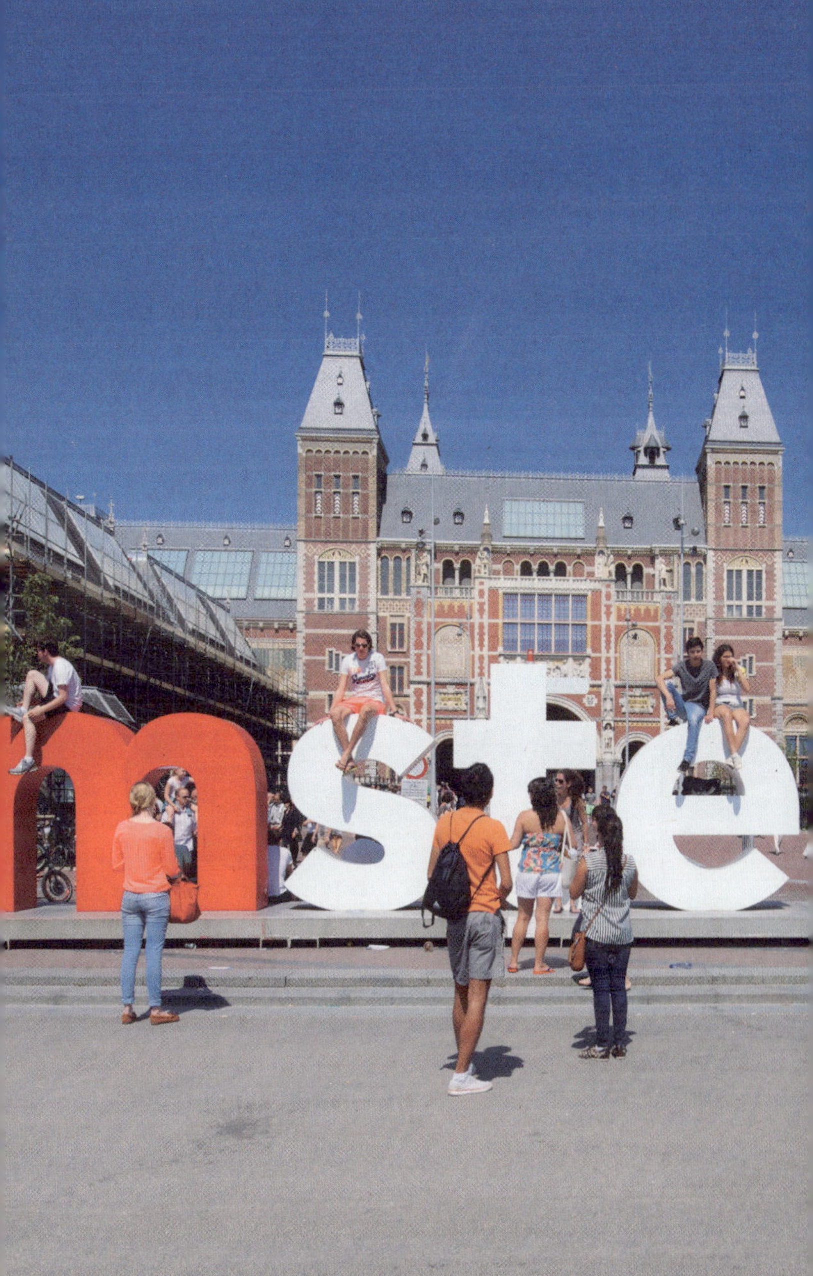

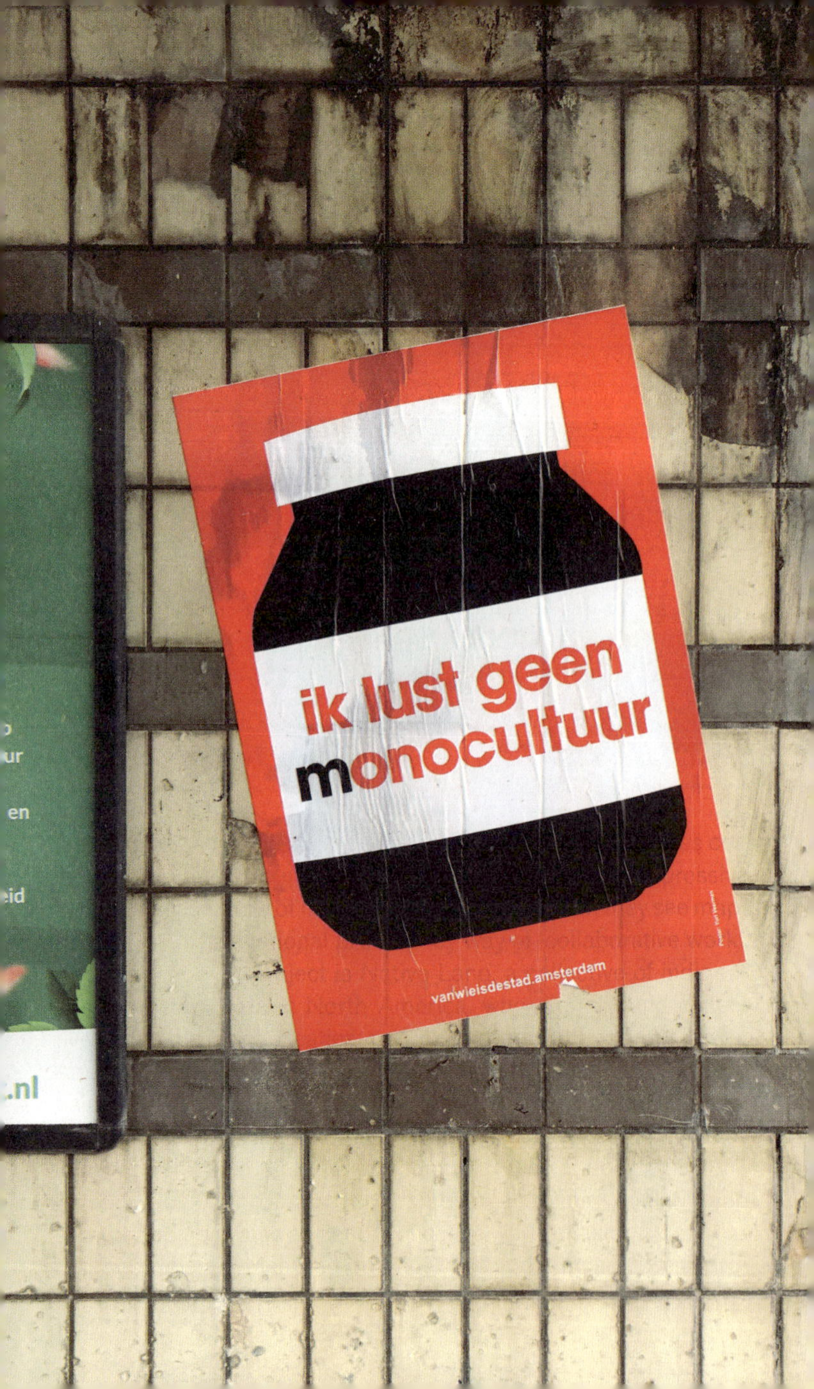

ik lust geen
monocultuur
vanwieisdestad.amsterdam

> For so long, people thought Airbnb was about renting houses. But really, we're about home. You see, a house is just a space, but a home is where you belong.
>
> BRIAN CHESKY, CEO OF AIRBNB

percent growth on real estate revenue has made investment so lucrative that one in four houses is bought in cash by investors, and many of these apartments are immediately put on the high-end rental market.

After the 2008 crisis, austerity measures had impacted the lower incomes more than average. Despite being one of the richest countries in the world, the number of homeless people in the city doubled in ten years. In 2016, one family was evicted from social housing on average every day, while in the same year 25,721 rooms were offered on Airbnb.[43] Home owners are benefiting from exorbitantly growing prices, while renters are faced with skyrocketing rents and stagnant wages. This has led to the 'rise of the real estate class' of families who own real estate and pass it down along family lines. Those who do not own real estate, will sooner or later have to leave the city because of its high rents.

In the 2018 municipal elections housing was one of the main topics. Myself and three other graphic designers created a series of posters to reclaim the city for all its inhabitants. Posted on a website, these could be downloaded for free and put up in front windows to show solidarity among residents in neighbourhoods. One group had downloaded the posters and pasted them all over the city.[44] Our campaign was not aimed at blaming Nutella stores or Airbnb for the city becoming unaffordable, as they are merely symbols of how the city council has allowed profitability to reign over liveability. City governments—like national governments—are representatives of the city's population, elected to decide what policies are in the best interest of all citizens. We have grown so accustomed to property ownership given priority over the right to housing, that a city like Amsterdam has a growing homeless population, while nine percent of the real estate stands vacant

← Yuri Veerman, poster for the Amsterdam elections, 2018. The text reads 'I don't eat monoculture'.

as investment, and 21,000 apartments are rented out via Airbnb. Amsterdam apartments rented to tourists were the most expensive in Europe in 2019.[45]

If cities are popular places to live, this will ultimately lead to rising real estate prices no matter what policies are in place. The point here is not that a city should close itself to tourism, or only cater to lower-income residents. But when public buildings and social housing are actively being sold off to become hotels or expensive apartments—as the city of Amsterdam has done— and subsequent rising real estate prices make the city unaffordable for everyone but the wealthiest, then the city is literally selling itself.

We Love Brands

This chapter started with the designer as a brander who creates signs of quality, authenticity, and identity for market goods. Part of the popularity of branding comes from the irresistible human urge to leave identity marks as a reminder of someone's existence. The expression of human identity through symbols can be found everywhere, from prehistoric cave paintings to graffiti tags. The love that we have for symbols and what they represent, has unfortunately been transformed into a brand universe, where all aspects of human life can be branded, and then sold as commodities.

Branding is one of graphic design's core functions, and a lot of design work is spent on designing identities, making style guides, and implementing corporate identities. Another part of branding is the brand image, created by graphic designers and advertisers with cool campaigns and attractive graphics to ensure the brand stays 'hip'. What seems like a good idea for the designer, will most likely end up as a memo to workers, dictating the clothing they can wear, or the language they can use, and how to properly use the new logo. In the enthusiasm of putting their mark on the world, the designers' ego can get in the way of understanding the social implications of their branding guidelines.

Most design studios advertise branding services on their websites saying something like 'We love brands'. But while many designers love brands, some feel uneasy about the relentless barrage of consumption messages that branding inevitably leads to. A discomfort that is no less part of the history of branding, at its most

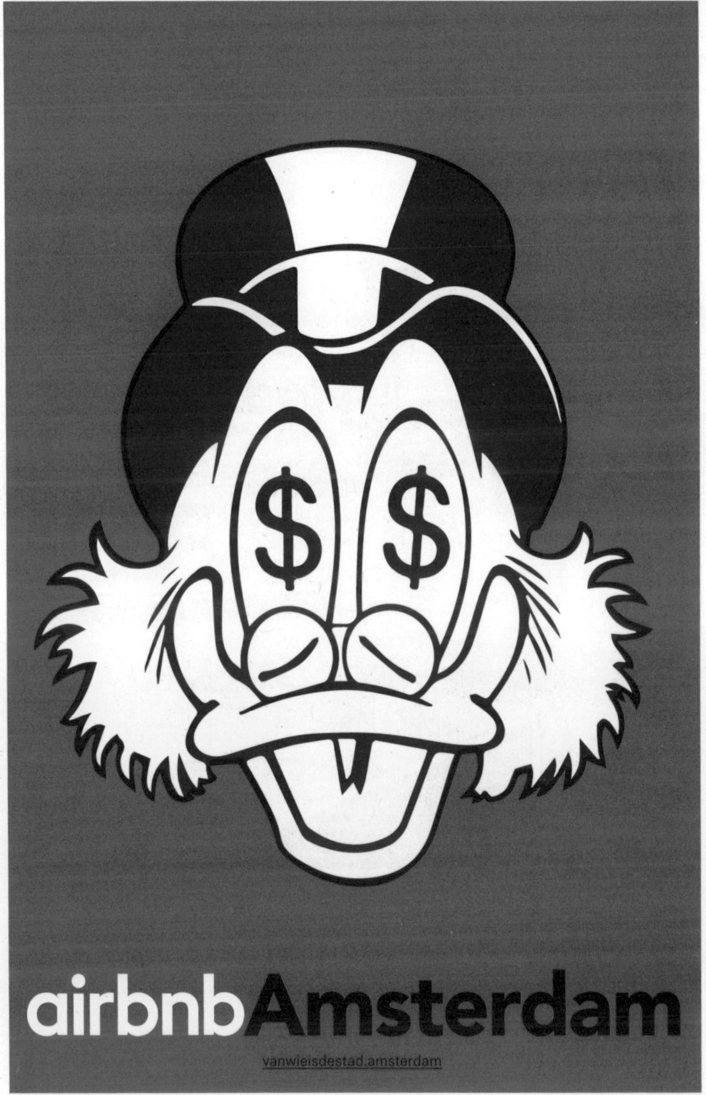

Ruben Pater, poster for the Amsterdam elections, 2018.

Honestly stop it with the logos. Stop making them and putting them on things.

WES ADAMS, DESIGNER

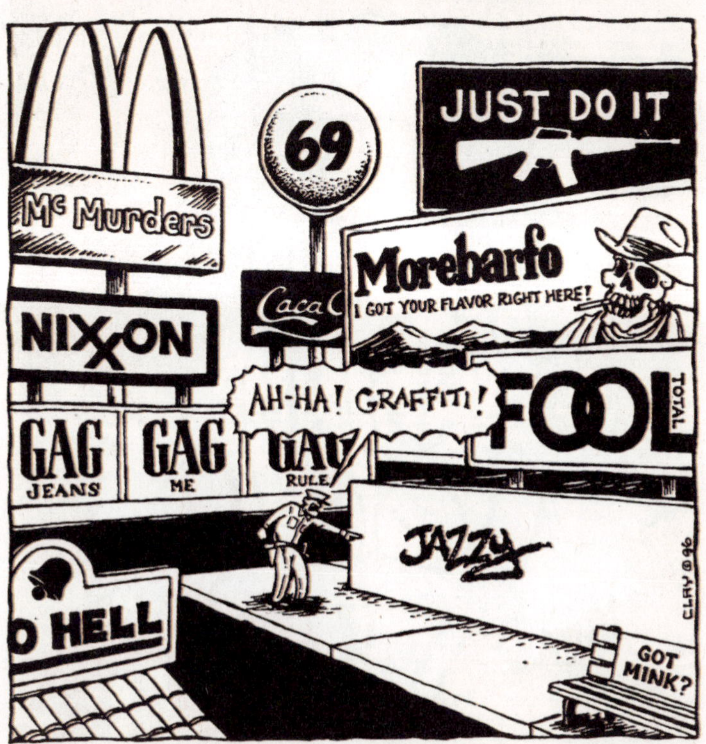

Clay Butler, 1996.

violent. Branding began literally as a weapon of torture, intended to dehumanize people by subjugating them into becoming objects for sale. We are also reminded of the uneasiness of advertisers during the industrial revolution, who did not want to see the horrible circumstances under which products were made, as it would make it impossible to write the copy to sell them. In efforts to brand all aspects of society, city branding has become a powerful tool in the hands of lawmakers for the gentrification of cities and the commodification of housing, which benefits the wealthy.

The redesign of corporate identities is a popular topic in the design press. Redesigns kickstart heated discussions on the Brand New website.[46] Discussing the logo design is perhaps amusing, but has little to do with the role that branding plays in our economic system. We cannot confuse a well-drawn logo with ethical ways of doing business. Designers cannot claim ignorance and externalize all ethics to the client. Brands are one of the ways in which designers fuel the continuous consumption of goods, and even a well-designed brand for a museum still uses the same logic of branding to sell more tickets, more merchandise, to increase visibility, to make more profit, perpetuating the narrative that everything needs branding.

Using symbols to signify a product's origin has its uses, as it has been done historically. Branding to simply mark a product or service is useful, but if we would limit branding to its functional qualities, the majority of brands would disappear instantly. The automatic response from designers is to simply put the logo on every imaginable product, and to see it as often and as big as possible. The process of enclosure of the commons in society, where shared spaces available to everyone that aren't privately owned are seized and sold off, from healthcare, to housing, to nature, often happens through branding.

There is an urban legend that people who live in cities recognize more logos than bird species. It could very well be true, as the average person is exposed to about 5,000 ads every day.[47] We should stop and think how graphic design has turned our streets into an architecture of billboards, and our media platforms into a banner paradise. Branding shows that capitalism sees everything as a product, and every social encounter as a sales opportunity. Graphic designers can play an important role in refusing that logic. To not treat every design job as a branding opportunity, and to take our responsibility to stop turning all aspects of our daily environment into products.

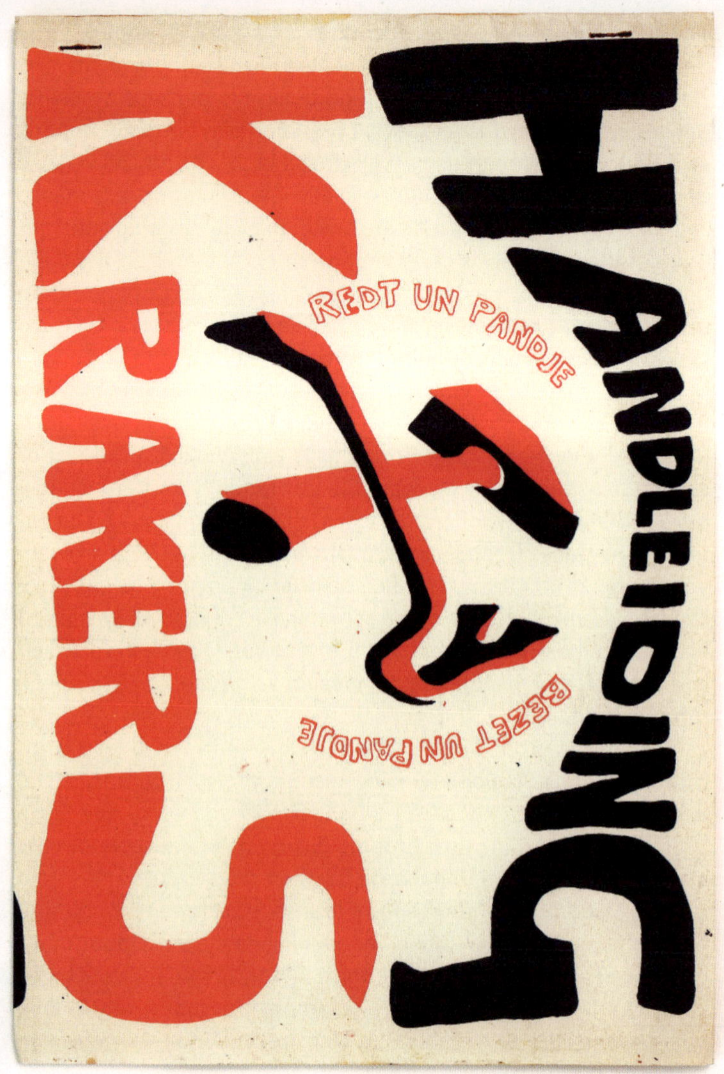

Squatting manual, May 1969. Published by Woningburo de Kraker, 1966. This cooperative to help and assist squatters emerged from the anarchist protest movement Provo in the 1960s, when housing was scarce in Amsterdam. *Kraken* is Dutch for squatting. The text reads: 'squatters' manual, save a house, squat a house'.

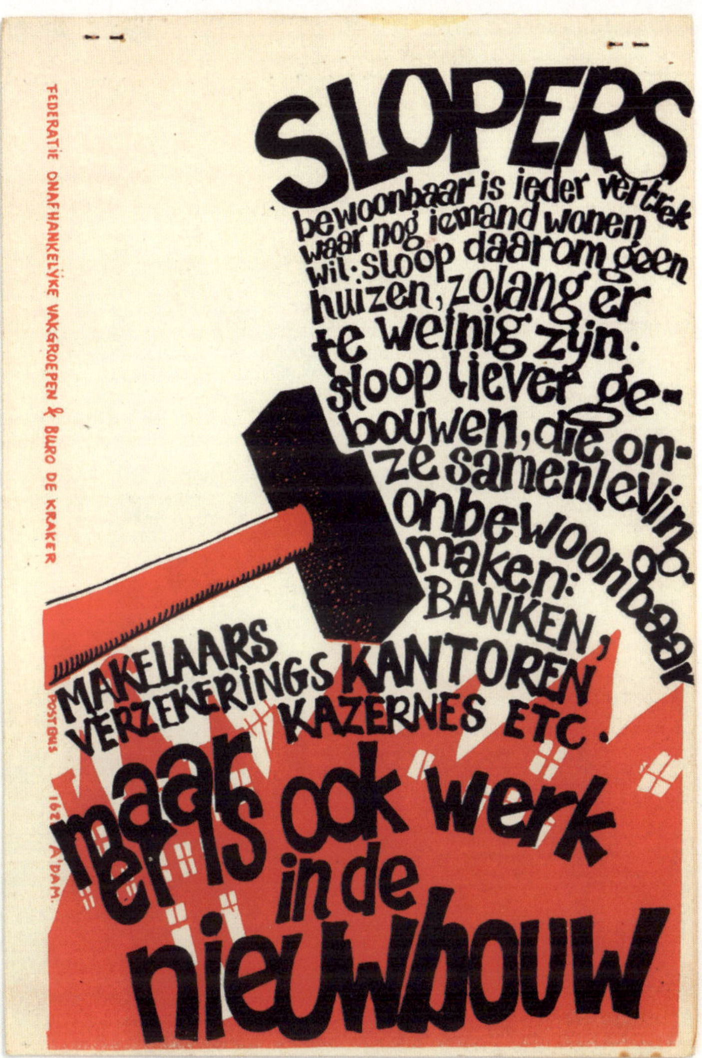

The text reads 'Demolishers: liveable is every quarters where someone wants to leave. Don't demolish houses as long as there are too few. Demolish buildings that make our society uninhabitable: banks, real-estate offices, insurance offices, army barracks. But there is also employment in new construction'.

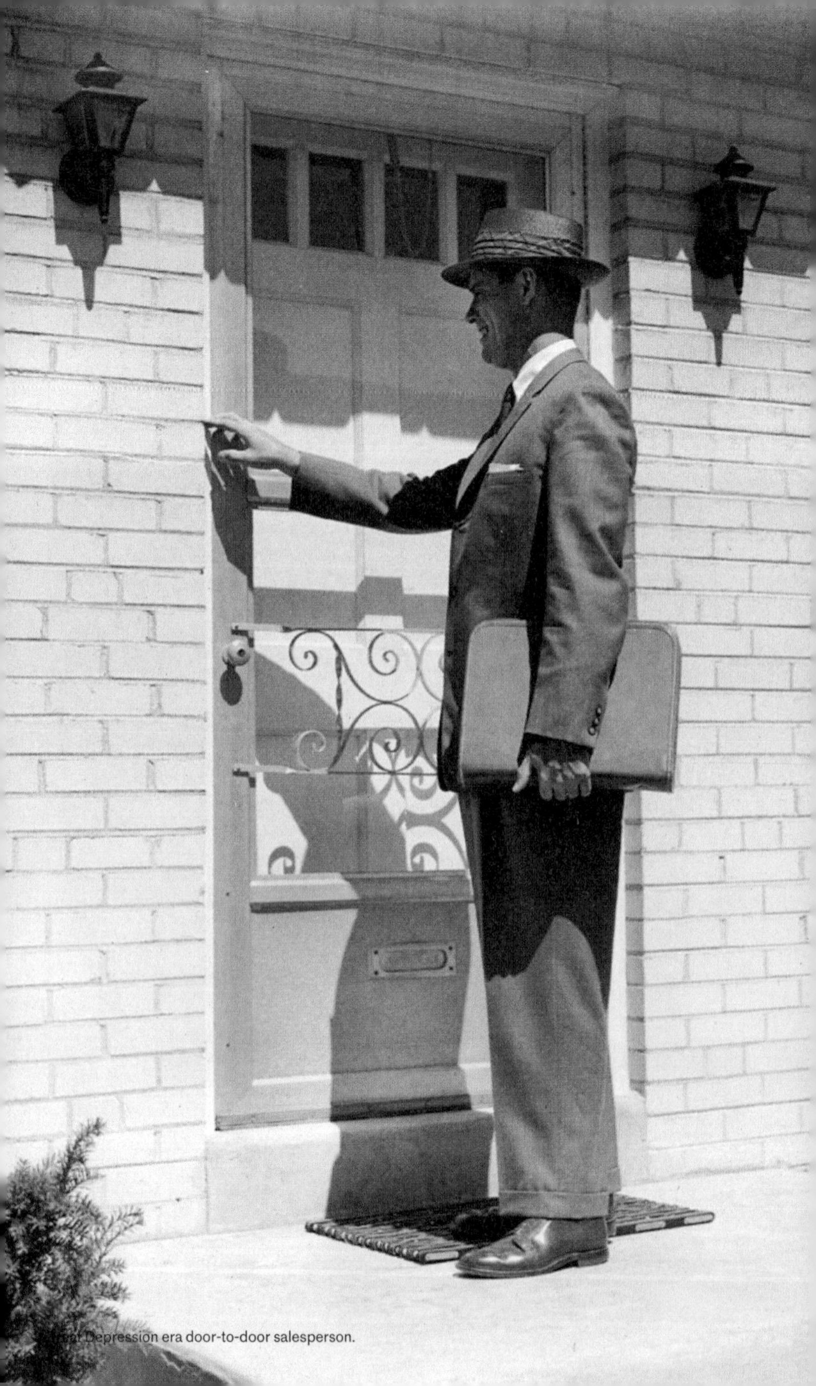

Great Depression era door-to-door salesperson.

THE DESIGNER AS SALES- PERSON

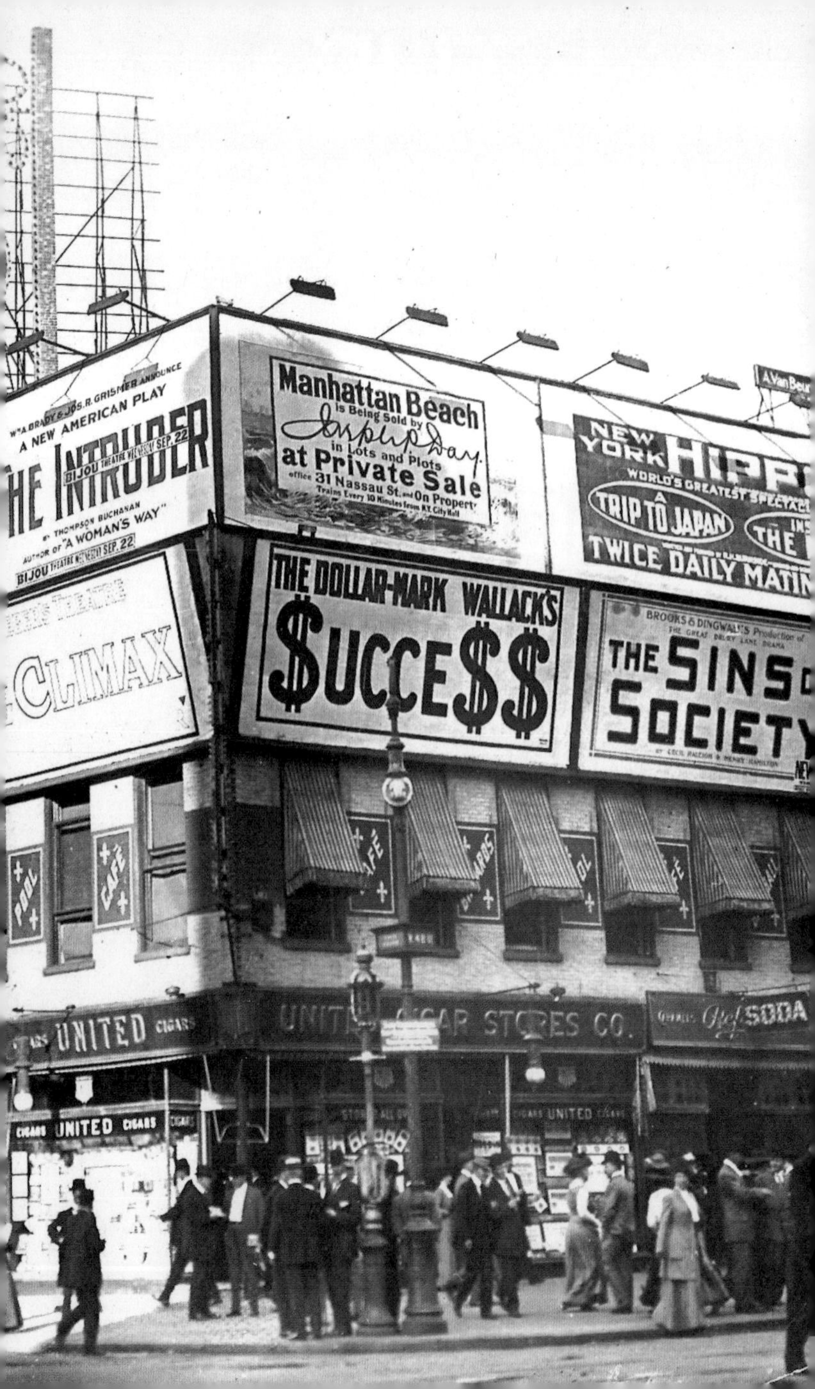
A NEW AMERICAN PLAY
WM A. BRADY & JOS. R. GRISMER ANNOUNCE
HE INTRUDER
BY THOMPSON BUCHANAN
AUTHOR OF "A WOMAN'S WAY"
BIJOU THEATRE WEDNESDAY SEP. 22
BIJOU THEATRE WEDNESDAY SEP. 22
CLIMAX
Manhattan Beach
is Being Sold by
Joseph Day.
in Lots and Plots
at Private Sale
office 31 Nassau St. and On Property
Trains Every 10 Minutes from N.Y. City Hall
THE DOLLAR-MARK WALLACK'S
$UCCE$$
NEW YORK HIPP
WORLD'S GREATEST SPECTACLE
A TRIP TO JAPAN THE
TWICE DAILY MATIN
BROOKS & DINGWALL'S Production of
THE GREAT DRURY LANE DRAMA
THE SINS OF
SOCIETY
BY CECIL RALEIGH & HENRY HAMILTON
POOL
CAFE
UNITED CIGARS
CIGARS UNITED CIGARS
UNITED CIGAR STORES CO.
SODA
CIGARS UNITED CIGARS

THE SALES CURSE

If you ask graphic designers if they work in advertising, they might raise an eyebrow. Many graphic designers don't have a very positive view of advertising, and prefer not to be associated with it. If graphic design is a skill that combines text and images for communication purposes, advertisers do the same for selling goods. Using design just to sell things is apparently not what graphic design is all about. In reality the two often merge, and in many countries the only jobs for graphic designers are in advertising. Much of the work that graphic designers do, such as branding or user experience design (UX design), is an extension of marketing strategies, and therefore directly or indirectly serves a sales purpose. The Designer as a Salesperson is therefore not limited to advertising, but includes all the ways in which graphic design is used to sell products and services.

Three hundred years of capitalism have blurred the distinction between communication and sales. Advertising is so omnipresent, especially after the privatization of public services such as healthcare and education, that we find the language of sales everywhere around us. Retirement homes refer to the elderly as 'clients', we describe nature as 'natural resources', and education is a way of 'investing' in our future. Socializing with our friends is 'networking'. With the enclosure of commons we are so conditioned to viewing the world as a marketplace that this logic has been largely copied in all areas of graphic design, including cultural institutions, public services, and non-profits.

The role of the salesperson is similar to that of the brander, in that they both create visibility for the purpose of promotion. While the brander uses logos, grids, images, and typography, the salesperson uses visual triggers, psychology, and other manipulative tactics of persuasion. The salesperson becomes an expert in making

←   Broadway Advertising on Times Square, 42nd St., New York City, 1909.

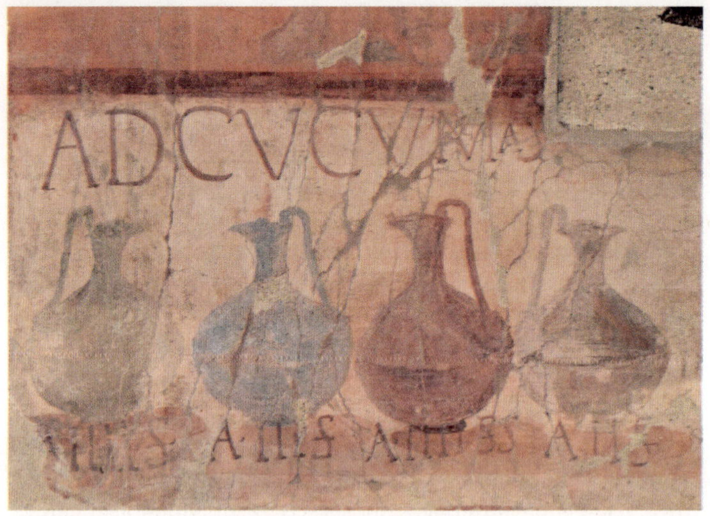

Ad Cucumas wine advertisement from 79 AD, found in Herculaneum, Italy.

consumers feel certain emotions or associations with a product, purely by appealing to their inner desires. The expert salesperson can make any product, however harmful or toxic, appear sympathetic. The complex role that advertising plays in capitalism is too broad a subject, so this chapter focuses on how graphic designers perform the role of salespersons, historically and today. Starting with the history of salesmanship itself.

The Men Who Sold the World

Oral salesmanship is the original form of advertising.[1] Promoting goods on a market using images or text has existed for thousands of years. Sellers who communicate the value and quality of their wares can still be found at any produce market. In principle little is wrong with that. Who doesn't appreciate a good performer or a skilfully hand-drawn sign?

Selling goods using promotion is inherent to trade. The Romans painted promotional messages by hand on walls, and one of the oldest printed advertisement found is for a needle shop in China during the Song Dynasty (960–1127 AD) using the slogan 'We buy high-quality steel rods and make quality fine needles, to be ready for use at home in no time.'[2]

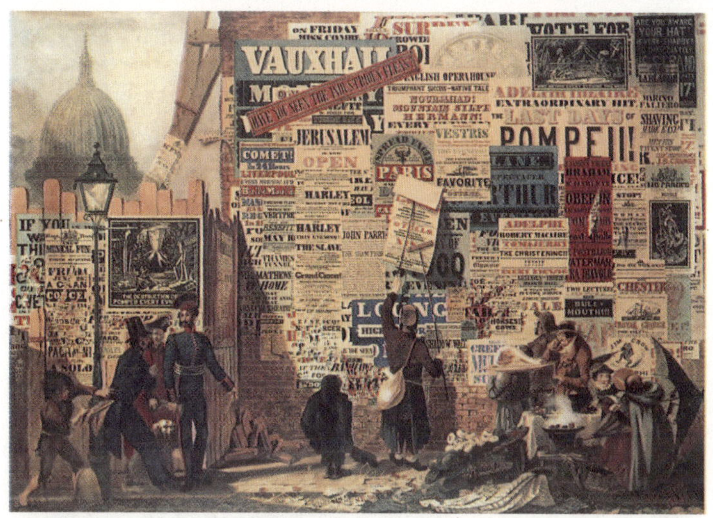

John Orlando Parry, pasted advertisements in public, London, 1835.

What changed under capitalism is the role of markets. Before capitalism, markets had a different function. Common lands under feudalism provided peasants with the means to survive. Markets provided goods that could not be made or grown in the community. Under capitalist land reform, common lands were enclosed and sold to the highest bidder. Farmers with no access to sustenance had to resort to wage labour to survive.[3] This was the first form of enclosure under capitalism, the privatization of lands that were accessible and could be used by peasant communities. Enclosure of the commons, meant that more and more people depended on markets for buying the means to survive. A central role of the market meant more products, more choices, and a more important role for the salesperson.

In Europe the industrial revolution flooded the market with mass-produced goods. Without consumer demand, goods would remain unsold. A sales strategy was necessary to boost the demand for overproduced goods, and the professional advertising discipline was born. We already read in the previous chapter how branding replaced the familiarity of the craftsman. Still, in the early nineteenth-century advertisements were rare, and of a more informative nature. Products were sold by appealing to novelty, explaining the products' features, by using handbills, posters, and small newspaper advertisements.[4] A turning point was the Great Exhibition of 1851, held in the Crystal Palace in London. Here at the heart of colonial and industrial power, the fruits of industrial production were celebrated through a spectacle of commodities, regarded by some as the birth of consumerism.[5]

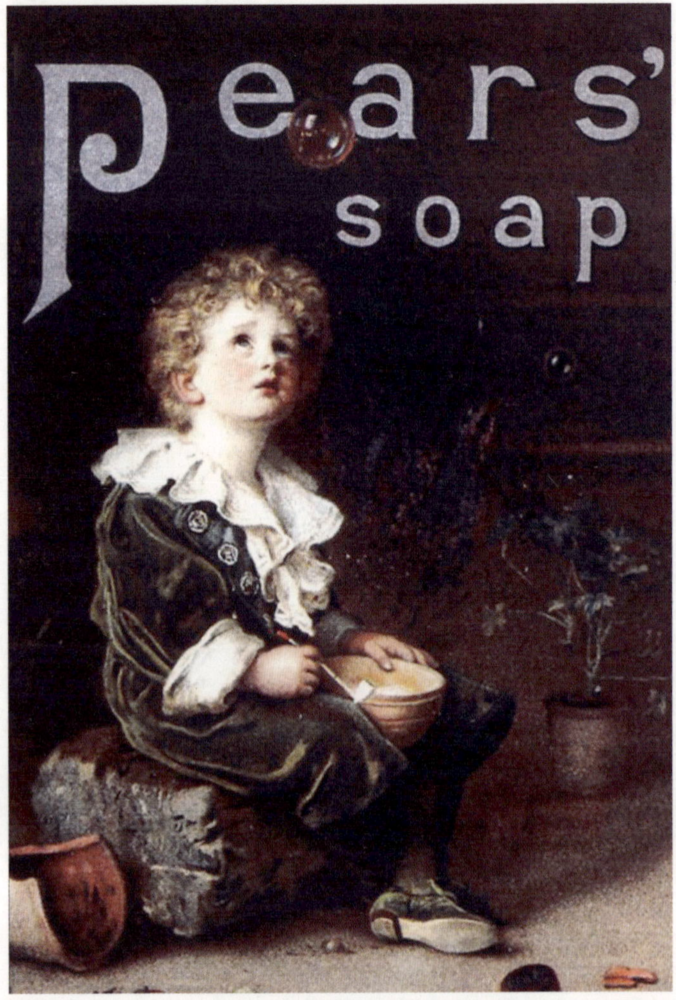

John Everett Millais and Pears' Soap, *Bubbles*, 1890.

Imperial Soap

Innovations in early advertising came from England during the second half of the nineteenth century. Feminist scholar Anne McClintock gives the example of Victorian soap advertisements in *Imperial Leather*.[6] Soap was first sold in unmarked bars, simply as 'soap', without any branding or advertising. International competition led British soap manufacturers to distinguish their soap by using advertising.

In 1886 the famous painter Sir John Everett Millais painted *Bubbles*, a work depicting a boy looking at a bubble. Chairman of Pears' Soap, Thomas J. Barrett, who became known as 'the father of advertising', came up with the idea to buy the painting and turn it into an advertisement for Pears' Soap by adding the logo.[7] The Bubbles advertisement was mass-produced and highly popular, even if it did not show the product itself. This idea broke new ground, and people realized effective advertising could be about much more than the product itself.

Another aspect that characterized early Victorian advertising, as McClintock points out, is the racism used to promote soap and other cleaning products. One Pears' Soap ad showed a black child being 'cleaned' using soap, making its skin white. Other soap ads used colonial racist tropes such as the monkey symbolizing the uncivilized and dirty 'other', and undomesticated tribes that needed

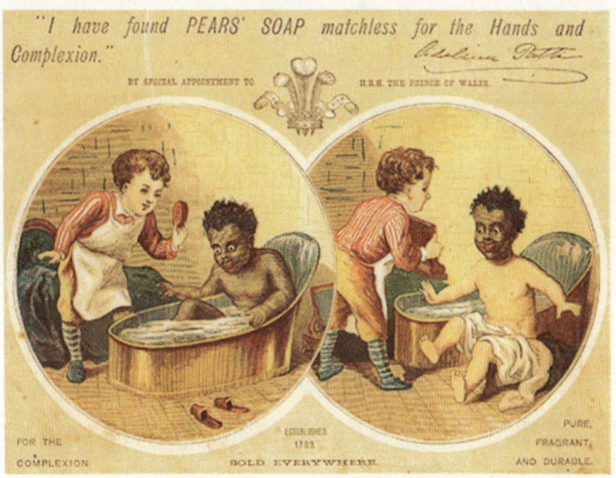

Pears' Soap magazine advertisement, Christmas 1884.

to be civilized. McClintock explains how soap production depended on cheap palm oil, coconut oil, and cottonseed oil, which came from slave plantations in the British empire. As soap itself was a product made from cheap resources and labour in the colonies, it is all the more bizarre that it was sold by equating a white skin with cleanliness and civilization, while a dark skin meant the opposite. Racism would continue to play an important role in promoting colonial products such as coffee, cacao, palm oil, and chocolate. McClintock shows how advertisements played a role in spreading racist ideas to a wider audience through what she calls 'commodity racism'.[8]

Victorian soap advertisements introduced the idea that artworks unrelated to the product itself could be used for effective advertising. The product gradually disappeared from advertisements by the end of the nineteenth century, making images and brands become more prominent.[9] Secondly, the popularity of racist imagery used by advertisers introduced ideas about white supremacy and racism among large groups in society. This period paved the way for more symbolic persuasion in advertising.

Consumer Engineering
While the potential power of branding and associative imagery began to sink in among manufacturers, psychology provided advertising with another tool to sell the excess of products. The theories of Sigmund Freud in the early 1900s put forward that people's behaviour is shaped by desires and forces in their subconscious. A nephew of Sigmund Freud, Edward Bernays, was a public relations expert who worked in the US. In his book *Propaganda* (1928) he wrote

It is chiefly the psychologists of the school of Freud who have pointed out that many of man's thoughts and actions are compensatory substitutes for desires which he has been obliged to suppress. A thing may be desired not for its intrinsic worth or usefulness, but because he has unconsciously come to see in it a symbol of something else, the desire for which he is ashamed to admit to himself.[10]

CAPS LOCK — Part 1

If we continue to allow business to replace civil society, advertising will replace cultural functions normally ascribed to writers, musicians and artists.

THOMAS FRANK, HISTORIAN

These radical insights quickly gained ground, and gave rise to focus group testing, and the use of psychological tricks to influence the subconscious of consumers. This became known as 'scientific advertising'. The public was largely unaware of the subliminal advertising techniques, until journalist Vance Packard published the bestseller *The Hidden Persuaders* (1957). The book gave a sensational insight in how psychology was used in advertising.

He showed how cigarettes and chewing gum were being marketed by appealing to 'oral comfort' from the mother's breast, a theory put forward by Freud. Packard describes how the design of supermarket packaging was based on 'eye movement' tests so it would have an impact during a quick glance, creating hypnotic effects that would put shoppers in a dream-like state.[11] In another

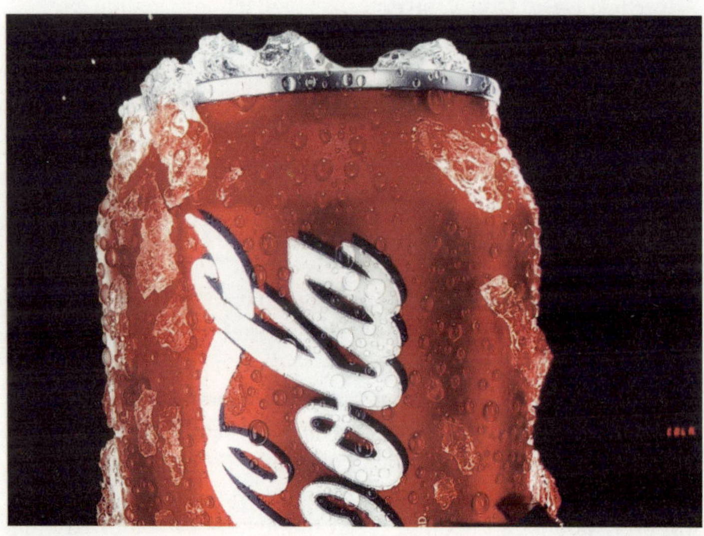

Subliminal advertising on a Coca-Cola vending machine. The ice on top of the can resembles the silhouette of a women lying down on her back. Coca-Cola, 2013.

> We have no proof that more material goods such as more cars or more gadgets has made anyone happier–in fact the evidence seems to point in the opposite direction.
>
> BERNICE ALLEN, OHIO UNIVERSITY

example he cites, Rorschach tests were used to predict which brand of cigarettes people would buy. Packard's findings did leave a somewhat exaggerated impression of the impact that psychology had on advertising, but at least people were aware there was a billion-dollar industry dedicated to find out how to make people buy more products.

Kings of Cool

The success of the scientific method had an adverse side-effect. Its rigid methods made advertising a conservative industry. Advertisements were 'engineered' based on focus group testing and psychological insights, following lists of requirements and findings. Advertiser David Ogilvy fervently believed in the scientific method. He even judged designs based on 'eleven commandments', and deducting points for sans-serif type, or the use of drawings instead of photographs.[12] It gave rise to a corporate business culture that avoided risk and creativity for fear of losing clients, producing a culture of men in grey flannel suits keeping clients happy with afternoon cocktails. The largest advertising company in 1957 was also the first advertising agency in the US and had been founded in 1896.

In *The Conquest of Cool* (1997), Thomas Frank writes how the 1960s counterculture changed the marketing and advertising industries. First the baby boom generation reached adolescence in the prosperous 1960s , which meant half of the population was young and had money to spend. The scientific method may have appealed to the consumer's subconscious, but it couldn't predict the subcultures that the young generation were forming. While the hip baby boomers began to resist the culture of conformity that had permeated the 1950s, young advertisers were fed up with

 CAPS LOCK – Part 1

making engineered, identical advertisements. Like the youth on the streets were wearing long hair and smoked marijuana to rebel against their parents' generation, young advertisers were rebelling against their older colleagues by using irony, self-mockery, and youth values such as freedom and anti-establishment. Conformity was replaced by individual expression through consumption.

The overwhelming success of 'hip' advertising in the 1960s solidified the idea that youth culture possessed the most valuable asset to a successful ad campaign: being cool. Whatever young people were thinking, it needed to be appropriated and capitalized on. If they loathed consumerism, advertising employed anti-advertising tactics. To keep up with the styles of the time 'typefaces and graphic design reflected new hallucinogenic styles as quickly as they could be invented', writes Frank.[13]

Since the 1960s, designers and advertisers are obsessed with selling 'cool'. Whoever finds the latest trend with accompanying styles, colours, and typefaces, will sell the most. Ad agencies prefer to hire the young and hip, who know how to tap into the ever-changing youth subcultures. Finding 'cool' has become equivalent of knowing what young people like, so advertisers go out of their way to scout upcoming and existing subcultures and appropriate their novel styles and ideas to sell products. Culture, even if created collectively, can be enclosed by capitalism and used for profit.

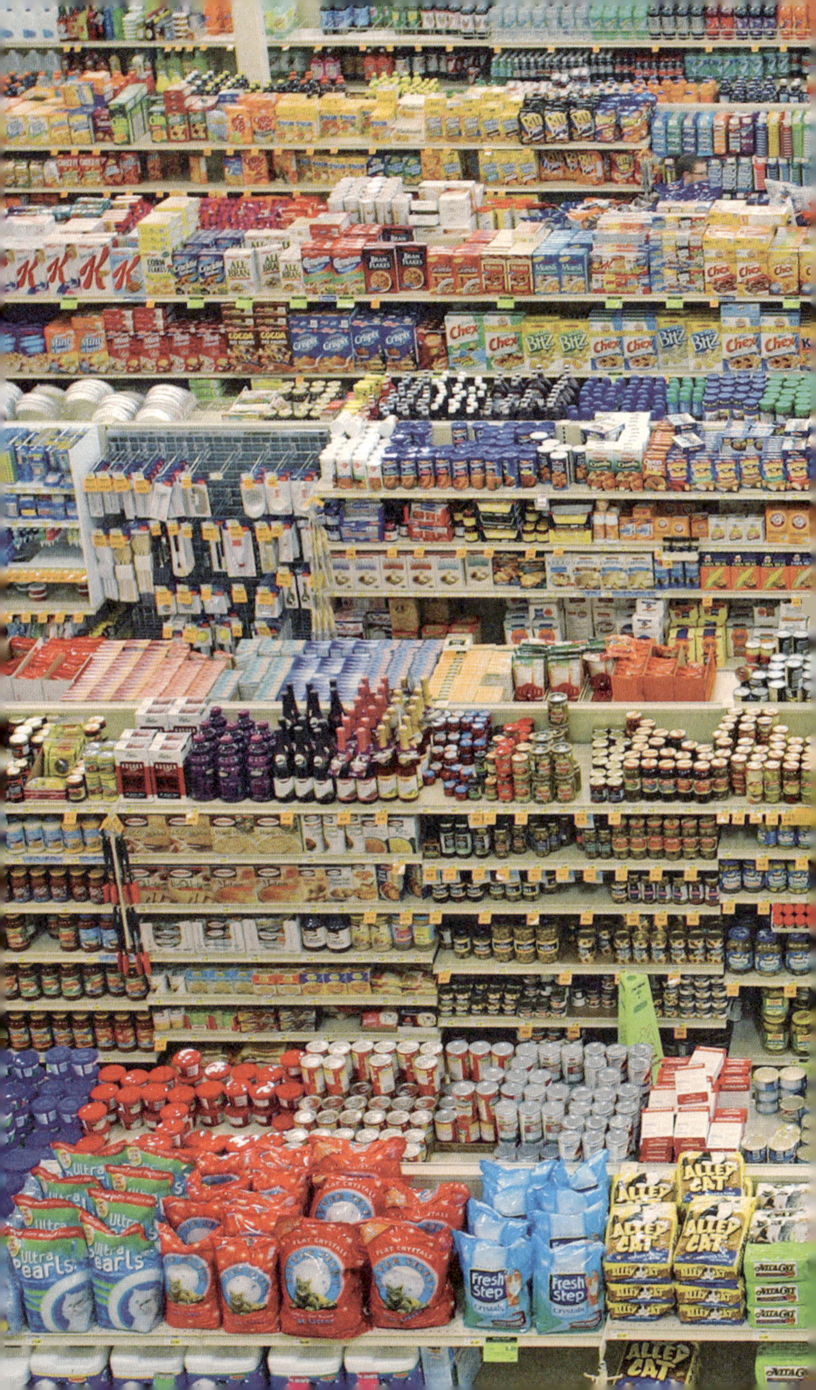

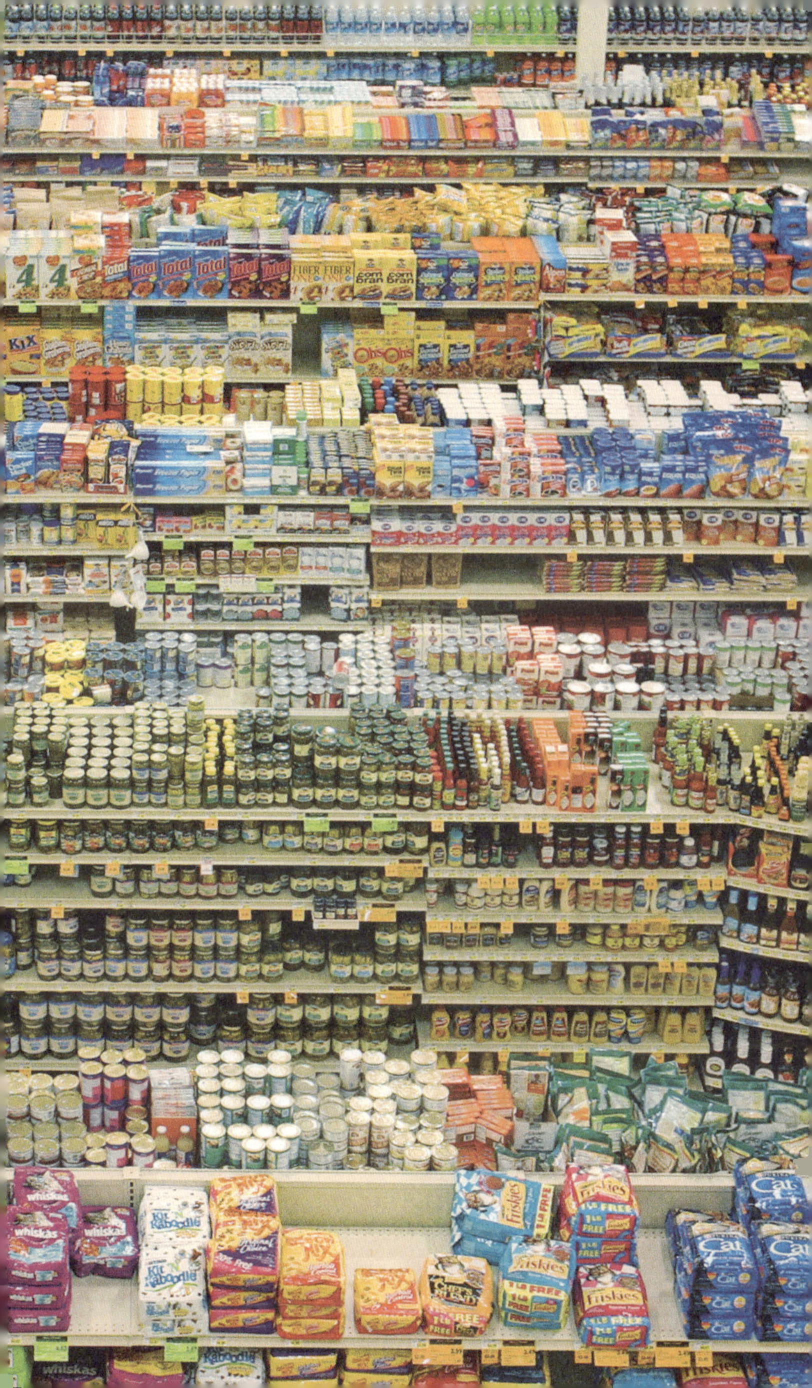

Tasting Images

After much of the manufacturing was outsourced to the Global South, the head offices of corporations became focused on management, logistics, and marketing. With the factories and blue-collar workers leaving, the last references to production were also gone, making room for a new wave of fiction. Companies realized they were not selling products but images, and advertising became even more important. Cheap production by workers in Asia, who were paid a fraction of what US workers had earned, freed up money and spending on advertising was doubled.[14] Companies such as Apple and Nike realized that advertising could do much more than sell products, and started constructing the first super brands. Phil Knight, the CEO of Nike said in 1992:

> For years we thought of ourselves as a production-oriented company, meaning we put all our emphasis on designing and manufacturing the product. But now we understand that the most important thing we do is market the product.[15]

Liberated from the burden of manufacturing, the possibilities in the marketing of companies were limitless. Brands created concept stores, movies, theme parks, and even entire towns. While the first super brands emerged, neoliberal policies of the 1980s pushed the privatization of almost all public services, leading to another form of enclosure of the commons. Suddenly everything could be sold as a product; healthcare, education, public transport, museums, low-income housing, and nature.

These newly privatized services all needed logos, branding, and advertising to compete with competitors in the market place. Even those institutions that were not yet privatized, such as the government and the military, increasingly turn to branding to 'stay with the times', as discussed in the chapter The Designer as a Brander. The money spent on advertising now 'outpaces the growth of the world economy by one-third'.[16]

Design and Destroy

Graphic design has profited enormously from the wave of privatization. Newly privatized services seek graphic designers to help them become competitive. Designers are happy to help, the idea being that 'they used to have an old-fashioned government look-and-feel, but this new design makes them contemporary and hip'. What is rarely mentioned in the design brief, is that privatization goes hand in hand with austerity measures. Job losses, pay cuts, and trimmed services, while graphic designers happily cash their cheques.

When the Dutch government privatized social care in 2014, it obfuscated an austerity operation, forcing a dramatic cut in the costs of services. So while all these services had to spend money on identities and promotional materials, the quality of care

When you package it effectively, you can even sell water expensively.

WALLY OLINS, BRANDING GURU

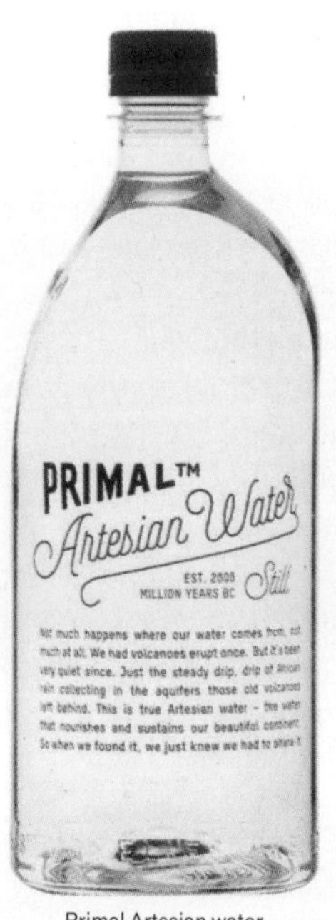

Primal Artesian water
€30 per 1 liter

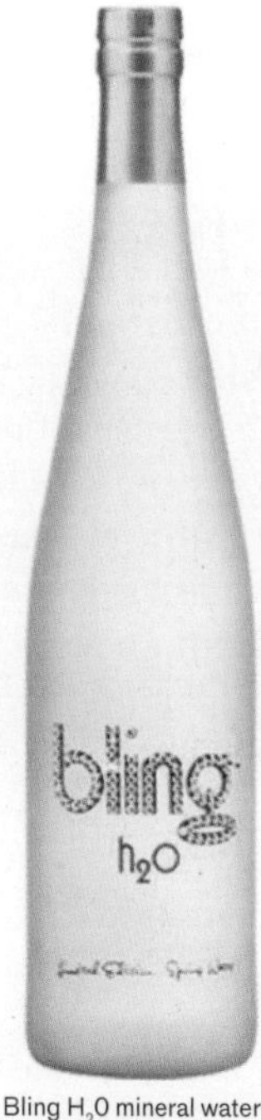

Bling H$_2$O mineral water
€75 per 750 ml

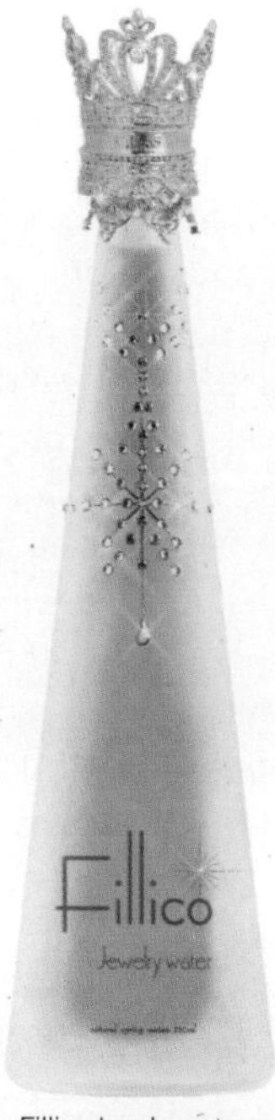

Fillico Jewelry water
€219 per 750 ml

deteriorated. Graphic designers are excellent at making services and products look appealing and desirable, but this becomes a curse when everyone does it. Designer Nick Bell gives the examples of art museums: 'I take issue with the heavy use of branding inside the exhibitions themselves. When I am already there, I don't need to be reminded of the fact all the time.'[17]

Graphic designers can be more critical of their role in how everyday life is enclosed and commodified for profit. What does it mean when museums are made to look the same as furniture brands? Government information leaflets that are indistinguishable from a tourism brochure? Services that provide low-income housing or healthcare look like start-ups? The role of the graphic designer as a salesperson has taken over many of the other roles.

How long can advertising keep up this seemingly endless pursuit of 'cool'? Is there a limit to how much of society, and life, can be marketed, branded, and sold? Social geographer David Harvey calls this 'creative destruction', a term from the 1950s coined by economist Joseph Schumpeter.[18] Creative destruction is the continuous capitalist process of destroying old structures, to make room for new, more profitable ones. Harvey notes that the fast production and consumption that came with the industrial revolution 'forced cultural producers into a market form of competition that was bound to reinforce processes of "creative destruction" within the aesthetic field itself'.[19]

In graphic design and advertising this means that when a typeface, a colour, a style, or a concept has been 'worn out' in the market, it has to be replaced with one that contradicts, responds, or mocks the previous one and thus creates value for products that appear 'different' but offer no new use value. Like a corporate identity that is redesigned after two years, just so the company can appear more current. Sometimes the metaphor becomes actual destruction, when large quantities of unsold clothes are burned because they have to make way for a new collection, or pallets of unused flyers and posters are thrown away because the company has rebranded itself again.

→   Bales of paper ready to ship from Waste Management's CID Recycling & Disposal
     operation on Chicago's far Southeast Side, 2015. Photo by Chris Bentley.
→   Paper crusher for paper downcycling, 2008. Photo by Matt Murphy.

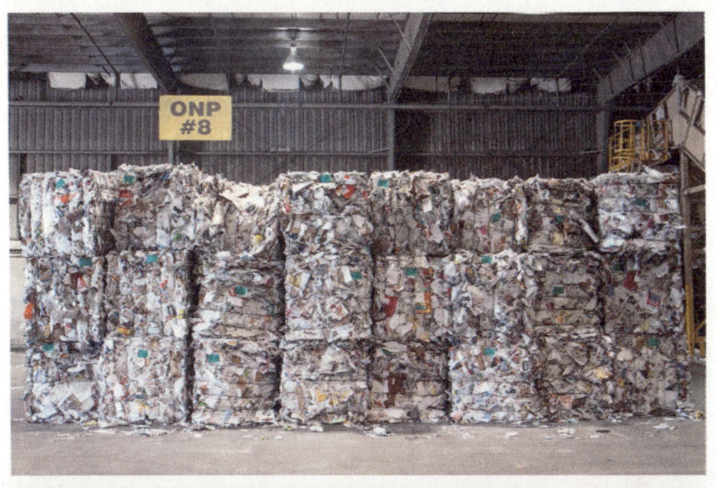

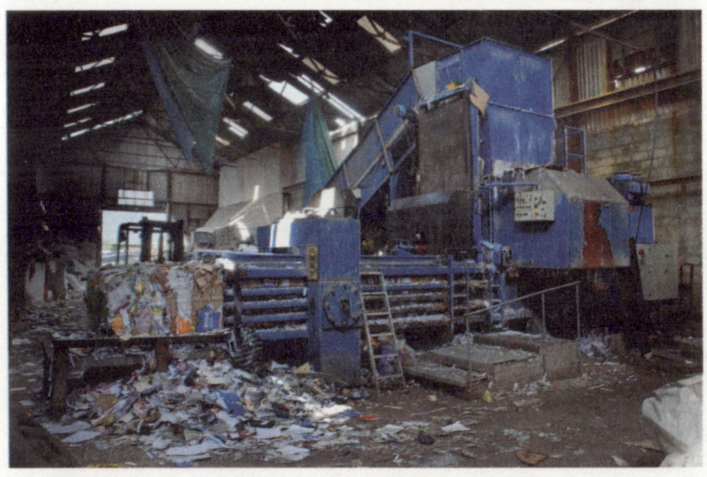

The design industry and the entire capitalist system depends on the ecological system for stability, raw materials and productive capacities society for stable markets.

JOANNA BOEHNERT, DESIGNER

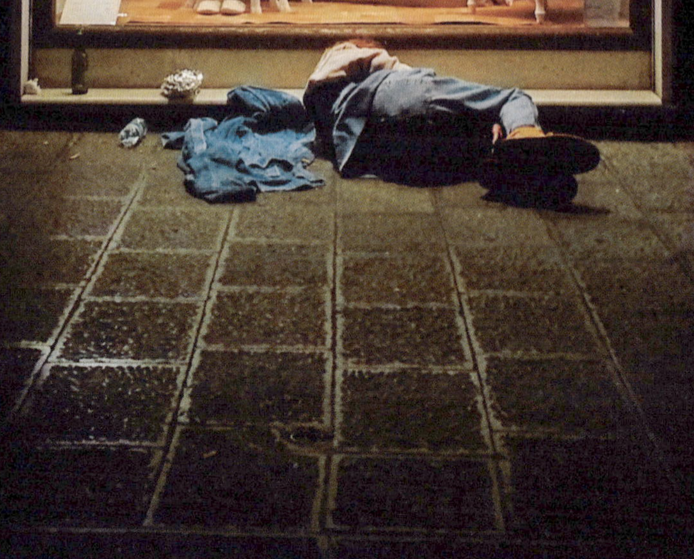

ZARA HOME
ZARA HOME

THE WORSHIP OF PRODUCTS

A spectre is haunting our society: it is the idolatry of products. We construct our identity through the clothes we wear, the cars we drive, our favourite beverages, and our beauty products. From an early age we are bombarded with advertising. The 5,000 commercial message we receive every day on average, have led us to believe that products make our lives meaningful.[20] No type of communication is so present as advertising, in all parts of society. There are almost no places left where advertising cannot reach us.

Advertising preys on basic human emotions, the existential feeling that we are not entirely happy about ourselves, that something is missing in our lives. If only there would be an easy way to unleash our inner potential, we would become truly happy. If we buy these products, we will be healthier, better looking, more desirable, and more successful. When we realize the promise fails, we feel even more empty, even miserable. Luckily there is always another product around the corner that once again promises us happiness.

Glow of Glamour
On the assembly line, mass-produced products don't present a very appealing narrative. A handmade shoe that is directly bought from the shoemaker has a clear value, as you know how much time, energy, and passion went into it, and advertising is not even needed. But a mass-produced shoe contains little or no information. Who assembled the shoe? Where do the leather and laces come from? Who designed it? Where was it made? What materials went into it? Were the workers paid well? We don't know, because this information is often inaccessible to the consumer. The social relations that constitute the capitalist economy are transformed into products (a shoe), which in turn are made up of smaller products (laces, leather, rubber).

← *Zara Home*, 2013. Photo by Rosaria Forcisi.

This brings us to what Karl Marx called 'commodity fetishism'. Marx developed this theory as one of the foundations of his critique of capitalism. He proposed that, contrary to the craftsman, the workers on the assembly line cannot become attached to the products they make. They are not supposed to think or be creative, nor are they allowed to put their mark on it. Their job is to make as many products as fast as possible. So even though the shoe went through the hands of many people, the traces of the people who made them remain invisible. The lost cognitive and creative potential of the worker is what he calls a 'fetishist' quality which is 'transferred' to products, when we start to believe that humanity's collective production power only consist of products.

The handmade shoe was valuable because the buyer was in direct contact with the producer and seller. Design and advertising replace the lost cognitive and creative potential with another type of fetishism, a desirable image that sells. David Harvey notes that branding and marketing have a very important function in hiding the complicated system of global production cycles, with its waste, exploitation, and profits. It also hides the social relations between the people that create, produce, and consume the products.[21] How else could you sell something for 150 dollars if the materials, wages, and production are only four dollars?

Marx goes even further to say that this fetishism makes us believe that all economic exchange in society is represented through the making and purchasing of products.[22] Any revolutionary ideas that challenge capitalism, notes David Harvey, should therefore find a different way to represent our collective power for production, without reducing everything to products.[23]

The state of being envied is what constitutes glamour. And publicity is the process of manufacturing glamour.

JOHN BERGER, WRITER AND ARTIST

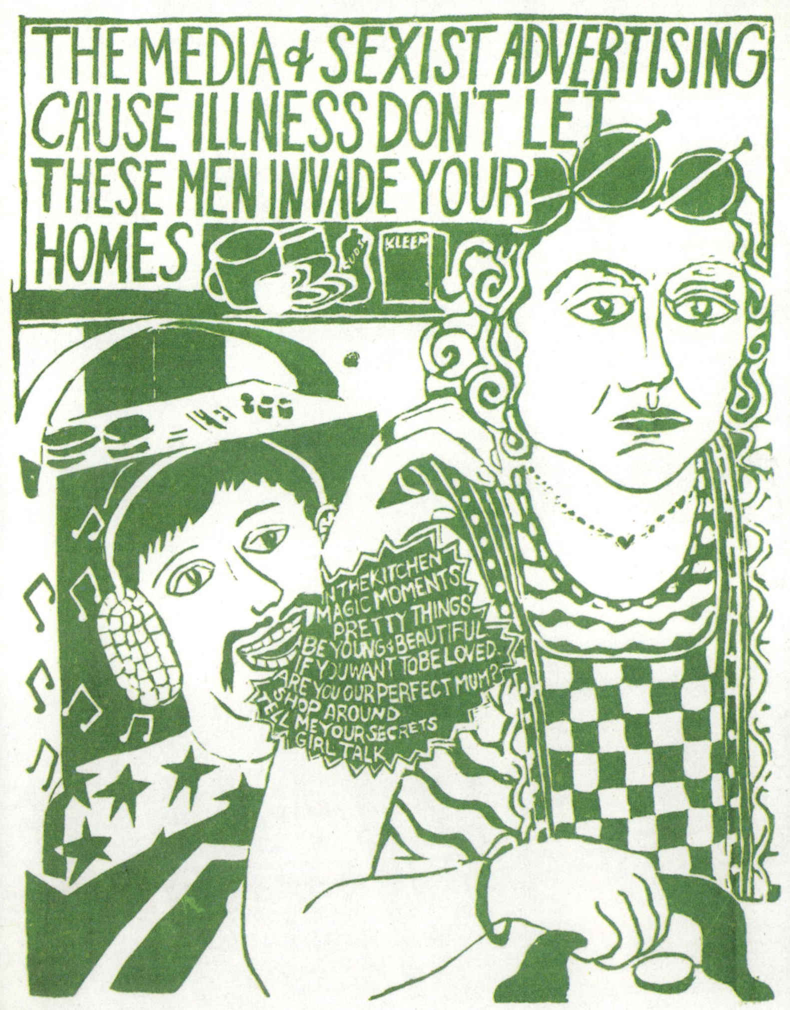

↑ See Red Women's Workshop, *Disc Jockey*, 1973.
→ Hedge trimmer advertisement, 1960s/1970s.

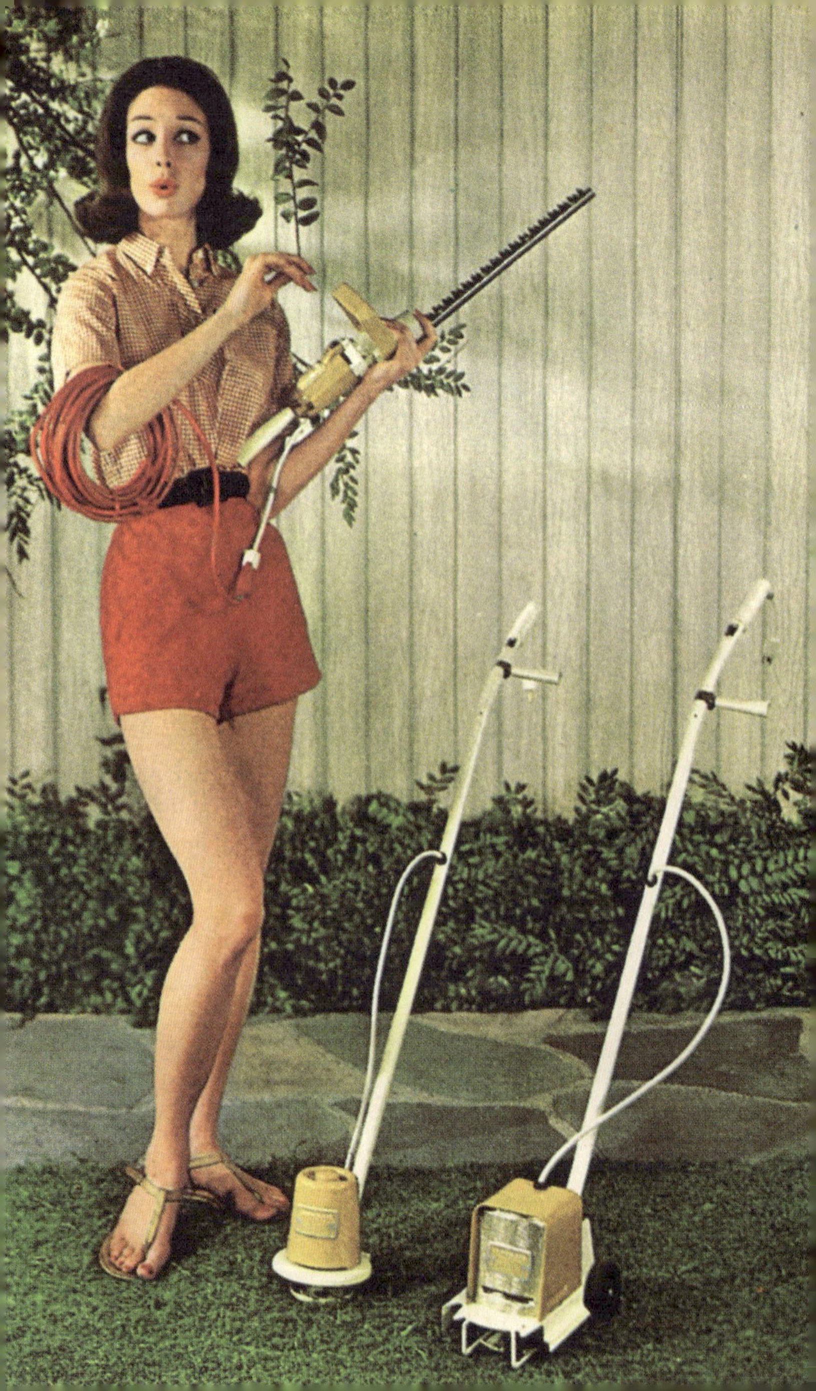

Value, therefore, does not have its description branded on its forehead–it rather transforms every product of labor into a social hieroglyphic. Later on, men try to decipher the hieroglyphic, to get behind the secret of their own social product.

KARL MARX, PHILOSOPHER

The Art of Envy

Commodity fetishism tells us that the influence of advertising is much more than just the way products are sold. It replaces social relations with images. John Berger wrote about this in *Ways of Seeing* (1972), wherein he proposes that advertising, just like the Pears' Soap ad, can never only be about the product itself. Ads are always about envying a happier, better self. Leading a meaningful life is not about who you are, but about what you possess. Think about how we treat people differently based on what they have. The wealthiest people are everywhere in the news and in the media. They are glamorized and adored, while those who have nothing are looked down upon, ridiculed, and criminalized. John Berger even argues that advertising is the very culture of today's society,[24] which ties in with the commodity fetishism that Marx spoke about.

If society is a series of social relations that are mediated through images, then advertising and graphic design shape the way society is organized. 'It is design that can serve to signal and reinforce the caste marks of a class system', notes designer Dejan Sudjic.[25] We are taught at a young age that our identity is what products we buy. This is why the promotion of products always makes us envious of those who have more. As Berger notes, 'The essence of glamour is being envied by others.'[26] The luxurious life that advertising promises us travels around the world via TV and the internet, reaching everyone including the poorest and most exploited. When the wealthiest 2,000 billionaires have more wealth than 60 percent of the world population combined,[27] it is no surprise that these images do not only create envy, but also anger.

DESIGN VS. ADVERTISING

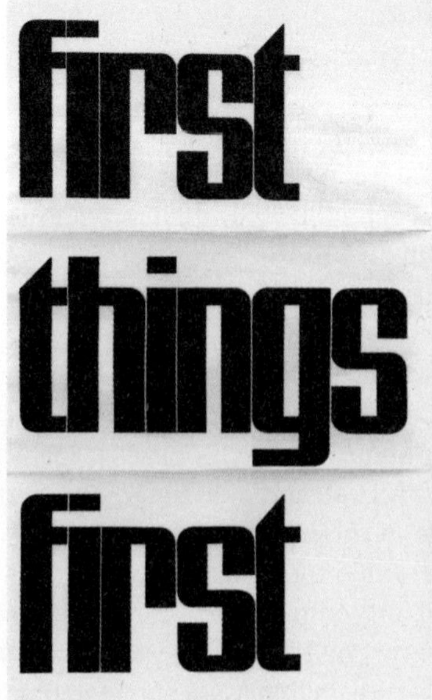

First Things First Manifesto

A manifesto

We, the undersigned, are graphic designers, photographers and students who have been brought up in a world in which the techniques and apparatus of advertising have persistently been presented to us as the most lucrative, effective and desirable means of using our talents. We have been bombarded with publications devoted to this belief, applauding the work of those who have flogged their skill and imagination to sell such things as:

cat food, stomach powders, detergent, hair restorer, striped toothpaste, aftershave lotion, beforeshave lotion, slimming diets, fattening diets, deodorants, fizzy water, cigarettes, roll-ons, pull-ons and slip-ons.

By far the greatest time and effort of those working in the advertising industry are wasted on these trivial purposes, which contribute little or nothing to our national prosperity.

In common with an increasing number of the general public, we have reached a saturation point at which the high pitched scream of consumer selling is no more than sheer noise. We think that there are other things more worth using our skill and experience on. There are signs for streets and buildings, books and periodicals, catalogues, instructional manuals, industrial photography, educational aids, films, television features, scientific and industrial publications and all the other media through which we promote our trade, our education, our culture and our greater awareness of the world.

We do not advocate the abolition of high pressure consumer advertising: this is not feasible. Nor do we want to take any of the fun out of life. But we are proposing a reversal of priorities in favour of the more useful and more lasting forms of communication. We hope that our society will tire of gimmick merchants, status salesmen and hidden persuaders, and that the prior call on our skills will be for worthwhile purposes. With this in mind, we propose to share our experience and opinions, and to make them available to colleagues, students and others who may be interested.

Edward Wright
Geoffrey White
William Slack
Caroline Rawlence
Ian McLaren
Sam Lambert
Ivor Kamlish
Gerald Jones
Bernard Higton
Brian Grimbly
John Garner
Ken Garland
Anthony Froshaug
Robin Fior
Germano Facetti
Ivan Dodd
Harriet Crowder
Anthony Clift
Gerry Cinamon
Robert Chapman
Ray Carpenter
Ken Briggs

Published by Ken Garland.
Printed by Goodwin Press Ltd. London N4

First Things First Manifesto, 1964.

It is evident how graphic designers deploy the role of the salesperson. On the one hand much of the graphic designer's income comes from advertising and branding, but on the other hand many graphic designers feel uneasy in performing the role of a salesperson. This is why graphic designers have often voiced their critique about advertising, as early as the 1880s. Almost every decade has brought forward prominent graphic design professionals who criticize advertising. One of the best-known examples is the *First Things First Manifesto* (1964), in which a group of graphic designers led by Ken Garland speak out against consumerism:

We have been bombarded with publications devoted to this belief, applauding the work of those who have flogged their skill
and imagination to sell such things as: cat food, stomach powders, detergent, hair restorer, striped toothpaste, aftershave
lotion, beforeshave lotion, slimming diets, fattening diets, deodorants, fizzy water, cigarettes, roll-ons, pull-ons and slip-ons.
By far the greatest effort of those working in the advertising
industry are wasted on these trivial purposes, which contribute
little or nothing to our national prosperity.[28]

The manifesto does not discount advertising completely, as it continues: 'We do not advocate the abolition of high-pressure consumer
advertising: this is not feasible.' Instead, the authors propose to
use the skills of designers for things more worthy, such as:

... signs for streets and buildings, books and periodicals, catalogues, instructional manuals, industrial photography, educational aids, films, television features, scientific and industrial
publications and all the other media through which we promote
our trade, our education, our culture and our greater awareness
of the world.[29]

It is admirable that graphic designers have been outspoken about
being complicit to capitalism. The *First Things First Manifesto* was
well received in the graphic design community, but some elementary questions remain unanswered, for example: how do we distinguish 'ethically good' from 'ethically bad' graphic design? Upon
closer inspection a division between 'worthy' and 'unworthy' design
doesn't hold up. Magazines are cited as 'good' examples, but don't
these often function as product catalogues with journalism in between? Books are also mentioned, but even a subversive art book
can catapult an artist's career, and create enormous value for the
work of the artist, 'creating demand' in its wake. Is a logo for a museum or an NGO also not a form of selling art or philanthropy?
     The manifesto asks graphic designers to stop selling products
and to put their skills and energy into 'charitable causes and social
marketing campaigns'. This is an admirable call for action, but how
realistic is this? The world's advertising budget was $563 billion

in 2017, while the total revenue of the eight largest NGOs com-bined was \$11.7 billion (in 2011).[30] If graphic designers really want to abandon commercial roles, then we will have to find other ways of creating value together without directly or indirectly fuelling capi-talism.

Creativity Drives Capitalism

If we look beyond the binary division between advertising and graphic design, we find its common economic signifier: the creative industries. The term is a recent invention that came about in the 1990s, after design aided the economic success of compan-ies like Nike and Apple. Branded as 'creative industries', design and advertising are now seen as the engine of economic develop-ment. TED talks, hackathons, and breakout sessions are organized to 'disrupt' industries and provide institutions with new ideas. As Joanna Boehnert writes: '… design is necessary for innovation and this inventive process is integral to capitalism, design and capital-ism have a cosy relationship.'[31]

In his influential book *The Rise of the Creative Class* (2002) Richard Florida argues that everyone can become part of the middle class if they make their work more creative. The book's influence is reflected by the inspirational quotes that litter social media platforms. 'Doing what you like is freedom, liking what you do is happiness.' Creativity was embraced by neoliberal econo-

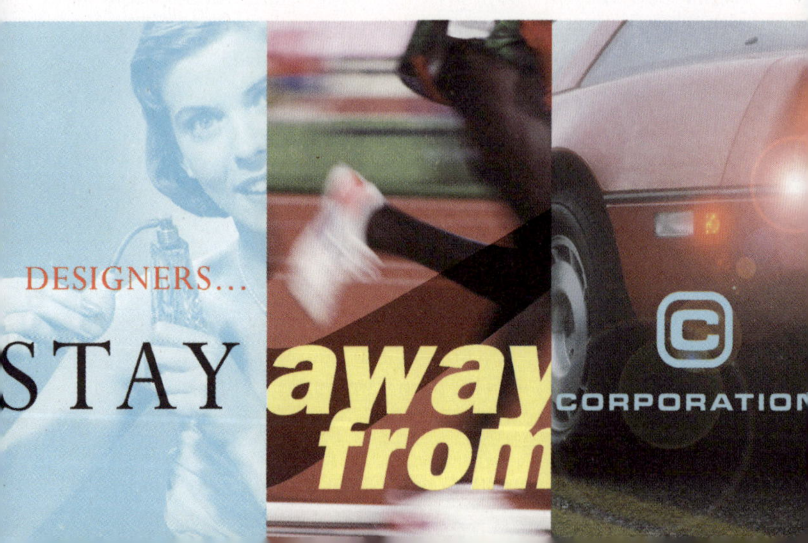

mists, arguing that the market is the most creative force of all. New products and ideas are created through a kind of 'natural selection' process. Neoliberal economic policies of the 1980s privatized public services, because these were considered 'uncreative', unable to adapt to competitive environments. In the eyes of these economists, more creativity means more economic growth.

In his book *Against Creativity* (2018), Oli Mould explains how creativity that only serves economic growth, can never be truly creative.[32] Ideas that challenge the economic model are either appropriated for profit, or discarded if too radical. The push towards more creativity in society has simply meant more strain on people's daily lives. We are expected 'to be creative' while serving coffee, or selling clothes for minimum wage. We are expected to see our home as our office, mixing work and free time, and change our life schedule at the whim of our bosses and clients. We are expected to always be available, on call, at a keyboard to answer e-mails or messages in a flexible creative economy. That is not creativity but an attempt to squeeze more and more value out of people without granting them the benefits of permanent contracts and higher wages.

Poster for the launch of *First Things First Manifesto* for *Adbusters*, Jonathan Barnbrook, 2000.

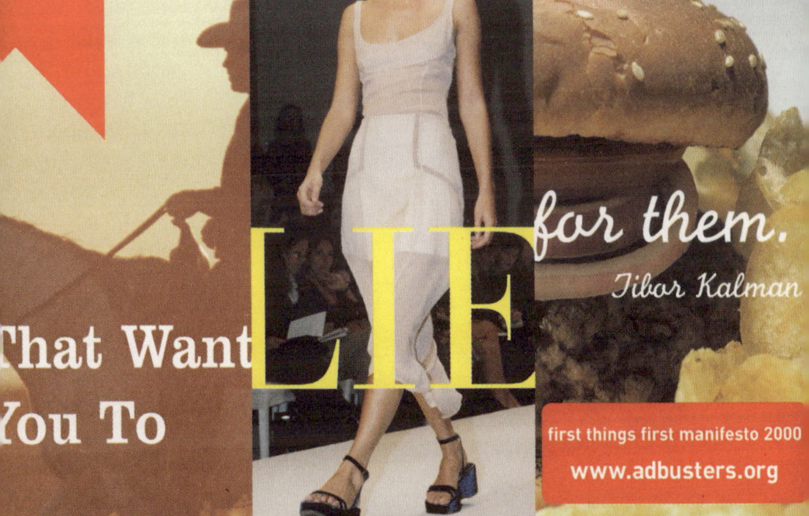

Cynical Cycle

Being at the centre of the sales curve, it is logical that many graphic designers develop a 'cynical relationship to both consumerism and capitalism', writes Boehnert.[33] Designers are frustrated with the discipline, but see no other ways of making money. Even in the *First Things First Manifesto*, authors express their ambivalence:

> Commercial work has always paid the bills, but many graphic designers have now let it become, in large measure, what graphic designers do. ... Consumerism is running uncontested; it must be challenged by other perspectives expressed, in part, through the visual languages and resources of design.[34]

As part of the creative industries, graphic design is at the centre of economic growth. A museum, a homeless shelter, a hospital, even social housing must be branded and sold using design. It's not just that only some graphic design serves the market, it is almost impossible to practice graphic design today without turning everything into a desirable product. Daniel van der Velden calls this 'the problem of luxury'. In our late capitalist society graphic design can no longer claim neutrality and be used for 'pure and objective' communication. He says: 'The hope that some designers still cherish, of being commissioned to work from the perspective of objective need, is in vain. Design only generates longing.'[35]

When all forms of creativity are enclosed by capitalism, we have to find other ways to defend creativity from continuous appropriation so that creative work can benefit the public and not just serve for profit. That means designers will make less money, and will have to find alternative ways of creating value. But by working more collectively, organizing in union-like ways,[36] creating commons and setting up new earning models, designers can spend less energy and resources competing with each other and instead work collectively to find new ways of working without continuing to be the grease of capitalism's gears.

→ Adbusters was founded in 1989 by former advertiser Kalle Lasn, as a collective of activists, designers and media activists against advertising and capitalism. They are known for *jamming* advertisements, created critical versions of existing ads in the 1990s and 2000s.

The hope that some designers still cherish, of being commissioned to work from the perspective of objective need, is in vain. Design only generates longing.

DANIEL VAN DER VELDEN, DESIGNER

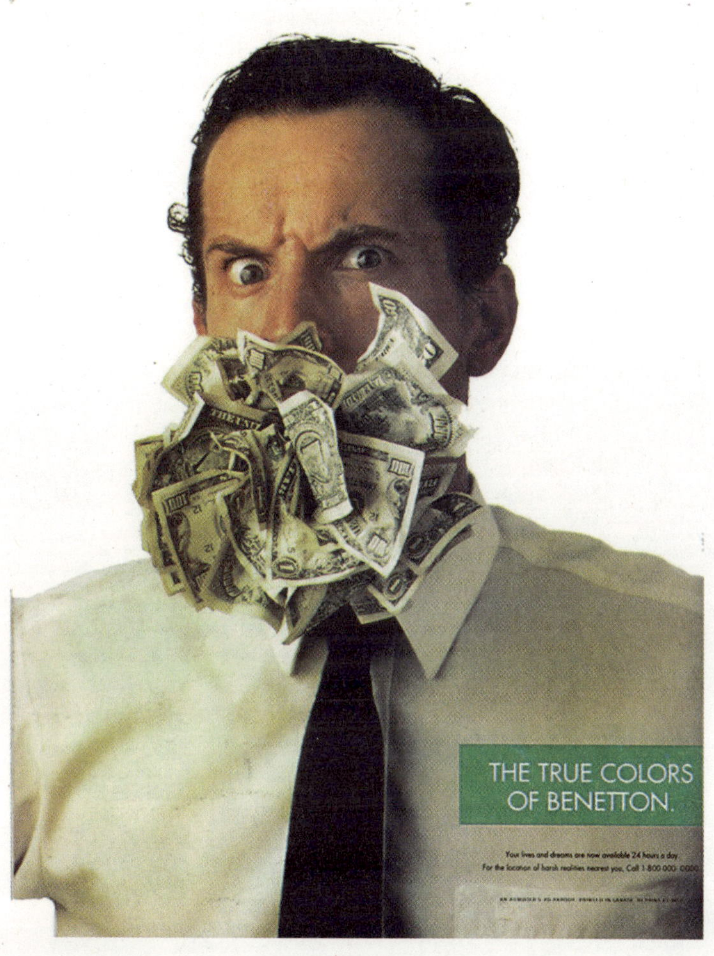

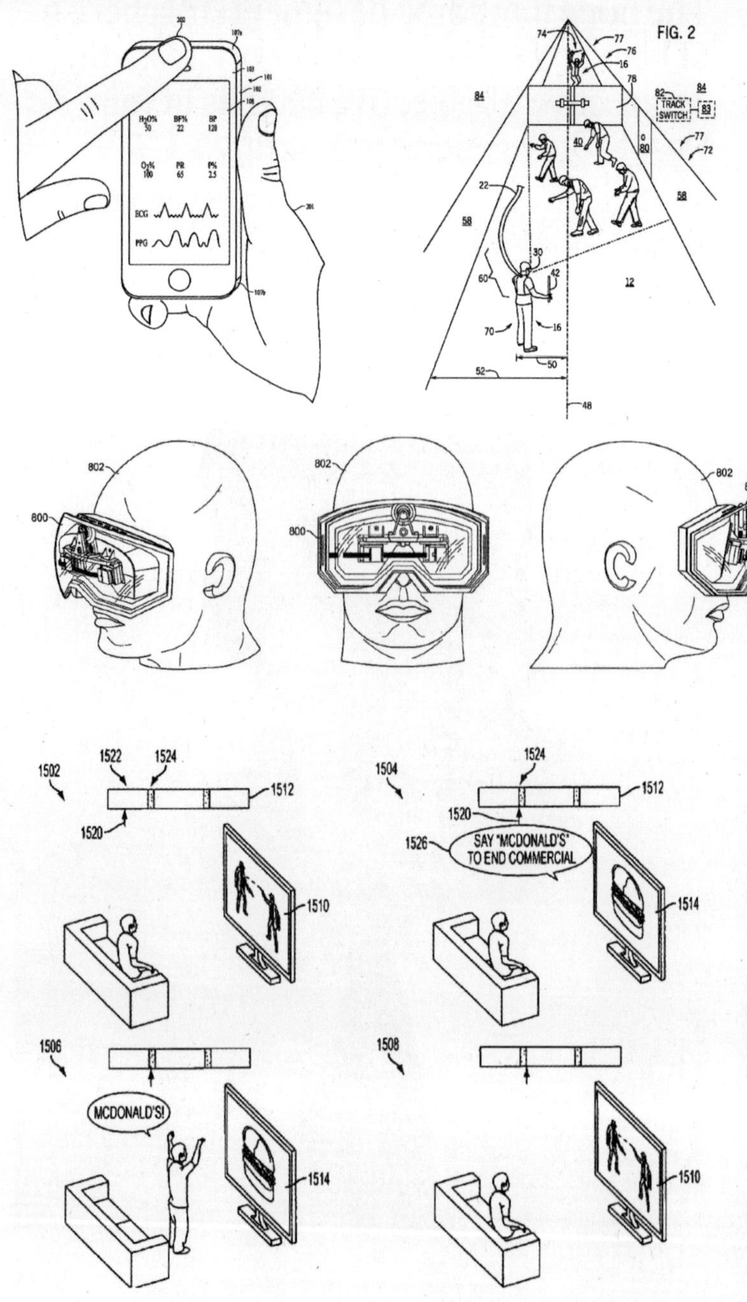
FIG. 2
H2O%
50
BF%
22
BP
120
O2%
100
PR
65
P%
25
ECG
PPG
TRACK SWITCH
SAY "MCDONALD'S" TO END COMMERCIAL
MCDONALD'S!
1502
1504
1506
1508
1510
1512
1514
1520
1522
1524
1526
800
802

QUANTIFIED EVERYTHING

Measuring the effects of campaigns is standard practice in advertising. Everything from focus groups and questionnaires to hidden cameras is used, so that copy, typography, photography, and colours can be optimized for maximum sales impact. In the role of the salesperson, design decisions are never about just the aesthetics and ideas. David Ogilvy quotes adman Rosser Reeves saying: 'Do you want fine writing? Do you want masterpieces? Or do you want to see the goddamned sales curve start moving up?'[37]

The fixation on commensurability can be challenging for graphic designers, who are usually more inspired by the artistic and creative aspects of the work. Advertising that only responds to market testing will not likely yield creative results; every product will end up looking the same, which—if you go to any supermarket or most corporate websites—already is more or less of the reality. The claim that only free market competition leads to true innovation stands in stark contrast to the lack of variety in much design and advertising.

Automated Salespersons

Quantification reaches new altitudes through the use of data. Only a few decades ago the newspaper was the most important news source. Today only one in a hundred people under 24 reads a physical newspaper in the Netherlands. The fast changing of media has changed the advertising landscape. In 2016 the online advertising market overtook television advertising in size, and the largest advertising platforms are not the printed media or TV anymore, but tech companies. Google is known for its search engine and email services, but 89 percent of its money is made from advertising. Social media platform Facebook earns 96.6 percent of its turnover from advertisements.[38]

← Illustrations from US patents by Apple and Facebook.

The best minds of my generation are thinking about how to make people click ads.

JEFF HAMMERBACHER, FORMER FACEBOOK EMPLOYEE

The internet has opened up new possibilities for measuring the effects of design. Online behaviour can be tracked in real time: what pages are accessed, how quickly people scroll, finger and eye movements can be tracked on the latest smartphones using face recognition and other sensors. Especially in user experience (UX) design, metrics are part of almost every design decision. Various ways of testing, such as A/B testing are standard procedures when designing user interfaces. A/B testing works as follows; you present a user with different designs at random (design A or design B). The system then looks which version of the design is more effective, in other words which one yields more sales, clicks, or likes. A/B tested designs will look the same at a first glance, but with tiny changes; a different colour underline, a different photo, a different shade of blue, a variation on the same typeface.

Say fifteen variations are presented randomly to users, and after testing those for weeks the metrics of all versions are compared. Google famously tested 41 shades of blue using A/B testing to decide on the colours for the Gmail interface design.[39] If you feel that the interfaces of your favourite websites tend to look more and more the same, it might have to do with obsessive testing. This is the culmination of the designer as a salesperson, when every minor design decision is optimized and scrutinized until the maximum of profit can be extracted.

Surveillance Advertising

In 1996 the early version of the web was meant to democratize the sharing and publishing of information, a digital commons of knowledge. Fifteen years later that potential has almost evaporated, as companies such as Facebook and Google have monopolized most online platforms. In her book *Surveillance Capitalism* (2019), Shoshana Zuboff describes how Google and Facebook use their monopolies to make a profit off our data. Our browsing behaviour is tracked, packaged, and sold as data profiles for personalized

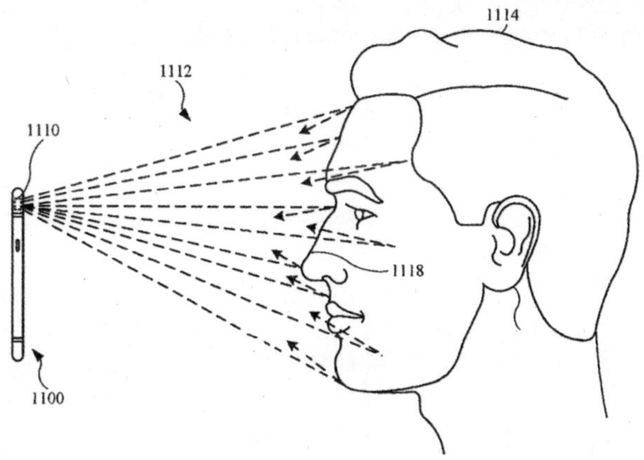

Illustration from US patent 2019/0045094 A1 filed by Apple, 2019.

ads. This is an automated process that happens in fractions of a second. These online auctions sell ad space based on data profiles to the highest bidder. Today's online advertising is no longer dictated by art directors, but by people with a PhD in mathematics and data science who spend all day thinking how to make people click on ads.

The holy grail of advertising is microtargeting, an automated personalized ad where images, text, and graphic design are generated based on individual tastes and needs. It will be able to present a product you didn't know you needed, until you saw it. Advertisers can read a user's emotions with their phone's camera, which can tell if you are feeling happy, sad, curious, or excited. Facebook applied for an emotion detection patent as early as 2014.[40]

If you think using an Adblocker plugin, and refraining from social media will save you from being targeted, you are mistaken. Online advertising and user tracking is making its way into physical space. Video screens placed in the city of Amsterdam are using built-in cameras to record how long and where people look at which advertisements to optimize the advertisement design and display time.

If you played the game Pokémon Go! you may have been targeted for a new kind of advertising in public space. Zuboff writes how this popular game was developed by the Google Maps team in 2016 with the intent of developing new ways of advertising.

In the game, people use their smartphone camera to find virtual Pokémon creatures in real life locations, a town square, a forest, or a mall. Soon after launch, deals were made with franchises like McDonald's and Starbucks for sponsored locations, luring players into stores.[41] By strategically placing game objectives, players were seduced to make real live purchases, while playing a game on smartphones.

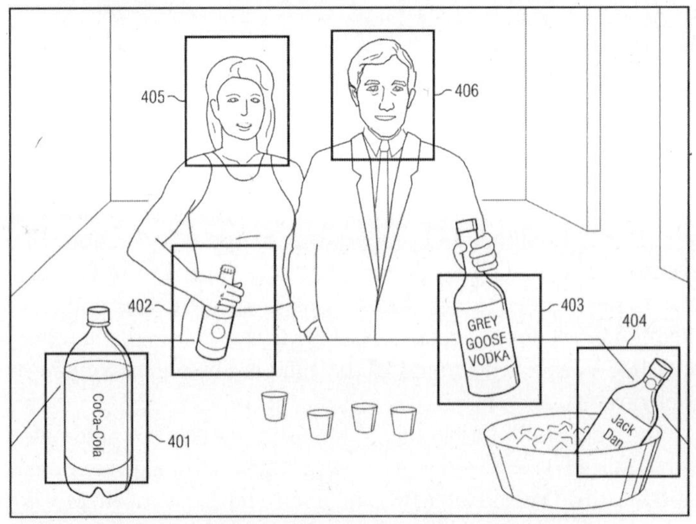

Illustration from Facebook patent 10257293 B2 for using user photos for advertising, 2019.

Advertising works most effectively when it's in line with what people are already trying to do. And people are trying to communicate in a certain way on Facebook, so there's really a whole new opportunity for a new type of advertising model within that.

MARK ZUCKERBERG, FACEBOOK

Invasive Instagram Design

Online advertising is developing smarter and more invasive methods, but so far, its effects have had mixed results. A third of the internet users are using ad blockers, and a research done by Dutch online journalistic platform *De Correspondent* in 2017 showed that the effects of much online advertising are based on corrupt or fraudulent data.[42] One of the largest advertisers in the world, Proctor & Gamble, was so fed up that they decreased their online advertising by $200 million in 2017, and their sales did not decrease, but actually increased by two percent.[43] The overrated impact of online advertising puts even more pressure on using influencers.

How is graphic design responding to the race towards automated salesmanship? On the one hand, graphic design is becoming increasingly automated itself. Internet banners and interface designs are already 'assembled' automatically based on different spaces and user data. A/B testing can update and optimize font styles, colours, and images. If your data profile says you are conservative, perhaps the system chooses the Trajan typeface. In this scenario many graphic design jobs could become obsolete within two decades.

On the other hand, graphic designers embrace the possibilities of outdoor screens, by experimenting with 'interactive posters' or 'moving screens'. Creating mesmerizing visual effects using bright colours and quick movements to attract the eye of the viewer, in a busy urban landscape. The increasing importance of Instagram for design portfolios has transformed the screen aesthetic, resorting to bright colours and animation, to stand out in the cacophony of the infinite scroll. We see the same high-impact psycho-aesthetics return in experiments for moving posters.

Advertising is most welcoming to this creativity, as this is the breeding ground for a new generation of high impact video ads. We should ask ourselves: if we are already so bombarded with advertisements and popups on our smartphones, why would anyone like to have moving video ads on their phones and in public space? Graphic designers should perhaps not try to outrun the inevitable automation of design tasks by resorting to high impact design. Instead, graphic designers can question, subvert, and even hack automated online advertising towards other benefits. Use their skills to look at real-life social relations instead of seeing users as clients and their behaviour as data profiles.[44]

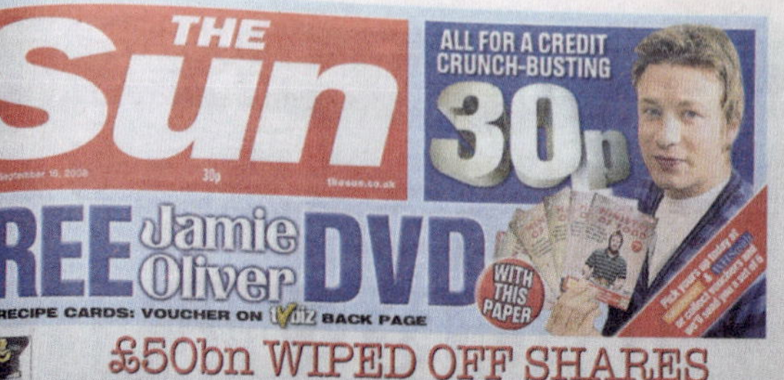

Guardian

Stock markets in biggest fall since 2008 as virus fears trigger panic selling

Woman 'felt hunted' by Salmond, sex offence trial hears

The New York Times

VOL.CXXXVII...No. 47,298   NEW YORK, TUESDAY, OCTOBER 20, 1987   30 CENTS

STOCKS PLUNGE 508 POINTS, A DROP OF 22.6%; 604 MILLION VOLUME NEARLY DOUBLES RECORD

U.S. Ships Shell Iran Installation

A Huge Blow to the Five-Year Bull Market

WORLDWIDE IMPAC

BROOKLYN DAILY EAGLE

And Complete Long Island News

th YEAR—No. 295.   ★ NEW YORK CITY, THURSDAY, OCTOBER 24, 1929. ★   32 PAGES

LATE
WALL STREET
1:15 PRICES
THRE

WALL ST. IN PANIC AS STOCKS CRAS

Attempt Made to Kill Italy's Crown Prince

STOCKS CR
IN RUSH T
BILLION

Duty Group
e $700,000 to
olidge Drive

Morgan, Mitch
Stocks in
Check Rush

FOR MORE LOBBYISTS

---

re Record

OCTOBER 29, 1929—THIRTY-TWO PAGES

SE ON STOC

VALUES SUFFER S
EVER EXPERIENC

GIRL WHO WON SUIT AGAINST THAW DELUGE

Bankers Will
Enter Market

Bond Market
Is Irregular

CRASH SALE

The sales curve is dictated by seasons and cycles. Colours and styles periodically resuscitate the consumer's appetite for new products. The same economic system is also subject to the cycles of boom and bust. Capitalism was intended as a system where supply and demand create a natural equilibrium. In reality there have been six recessions since 1973.[45]

Some economists believe that the reoccurrence of crises is only temporary and can one day be solved if only the right policy is in place—although this is usually said during the upward curve. In 2003, economist Robert Lucas declared that the problem of economic crisis had finally been solved. Five years later a major financial crisis hit. The 2008 crisis was caused by speculative finance, which was valued at over three times the GDP, which is the worth of actual services and goods produced.[46] Twelve years after the crisis that speculation has not been reigned in but is even a larger part of the economy than it was in 2007.

Crisis Design

Karl Marx wrote that crises in capitalism were not coincidental, but a natural result of the capitalist system. He predicted that crises would worsen, and ultimately bring the whole system down. The only reason that capitalism has been able to avoid a total meltdown so far, is its use of harsh methods such as austerity, outsourcing, new managerial techniques, lay-offs, and even warfare to bring the system back to life. A time of crisis requires radical reorganization of capitalism, and design plays an important role. For example, when manufacturers in the early twentieth century found that their products were no longer being bought, they decided to give them shorter life-spans, or stylistic makeovers.

A light bulb from 1901 hangs in a fire station in Livermore,

← Newspaper headlines of the stock market crashes of 1929, 1987, and 2008.

California. After more than a hundred years it still works. The first light bulbs had a much longer life span, but when manufacturers realized they could sell more of them if the bulbs were intentionally made of lower quality. This strategy is called 'planned obsolescence'; the practice of intentionally designing products of lesser quality, or with a built-in a limited life span, so that consumers will have to buy them more often. Planned obsolescence is especially popular in electronics where software updates make older hardware artificially slow,[47] or printers that stop working after a fixed number of prints.

Another form of crisis design in the twenties was copied from the fashion industry; styling, or streamlining. It started with the automobile industry, which saw a decline in sales during the Great Depression. To create demand in times of crisis, cars were given

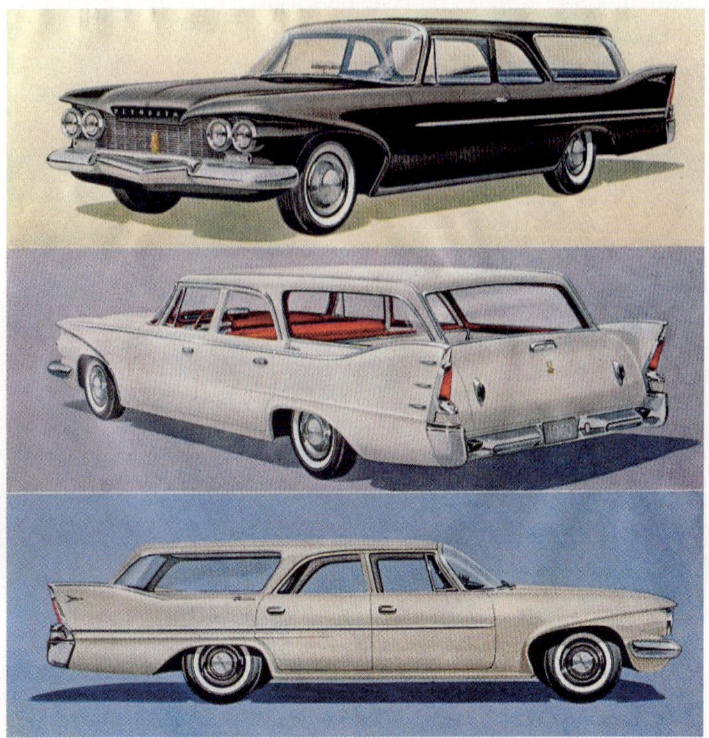

Brochure for the Plymouth station wagon, 1960s.

     CAPS LOCK – Part 1

Styling is so much part of our culture and of the job of many a designer that we perceive it as a given. It is something that implies progress, novelty, and sophistication, highly valued qualities in our society.

MARJANNE VAN HELVERT, DESIGNER

new exteriors, making them seem like new models while in fact they were the same underneath. People would simply buy a new car because the old one was 'out of style'. Designers like Raymond Loewy became famous for streamlining old products into new ones. Design theorist Marjanne van Helvert writes that while planned obsolescence is criticized today for wasting resources, during the crisis it was seen as a positive invention, a 'necessary and successful interference with declining sales'.[48]

In crisis design, graphic design plays its part in marketing these products. Even more, the restyling of logos and corporate identities can reinvigorate sales for services and products that are exactly the same. A new logo is often the result of a company wanting to appear 'new'.

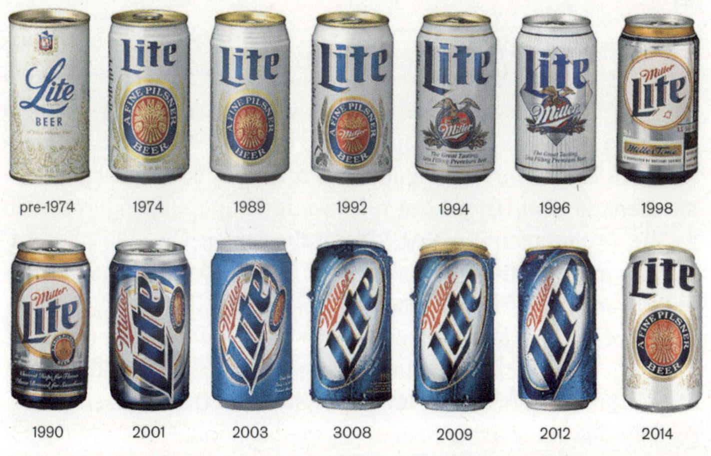

Product styling, packaging of Miller Lite beer 1974–2014.

The predatory cycle of boom and bust requires design and advertising, to periodically kickstart the engine of economic growth.

Shock Jocks
When a US drone strike killed a high-ranking Iranian general on 3 January, 2020, the frightening news of a looming war between the US and Iran was good news for defence companies. The stock of Northrop Grumman jumped by 5.4 percent and the stock of Lockheed Martin, the largest arms manufacturer in the world, went up 3.6 percent. Wars, disasters, and climate change have deadly and devastating consequences for people and planet, but for certain people they can be profitable. This is because capitalism's growth runs into obstacles; unions, environmental regulations, and governments that resist privatization. To remove these obstacles to an otherwise 'perfect system', neoliberal economist Milton Friedman advocated to make use of crises. In his view, only a crisis creates the conditions to completely overhaul any system to replace it with a 'pure' form of capitalism called neoliberalism. He saw no issue in working with Chilean dictator Pinochet, and his policies were also applied in the aftermath of the second Iraq War and hurricane Katrina. In both situations, terror and disorder were used to privatize public facilities and implement neoliberal austerity policies. Naomi Klein calls this 'disaster capitalism' in her book *The Shock Doctrine*.[49]

For some corporations a bad crisis is good business. Public relations are effective tools at the disposal of corporations, as a new logo or a good story spin can sway the public opinion from outcry to empathy. One of the world's biggest PR firms is Burston Cohn & Wolfe (formerly Burston-Marsteller) specializing in crisis management. They have represented unpopular figures such as the Argentinian dictator Videla, the Union Carbide corporation during the chemical gas leak at Bhopal, India,[50] the nuclear meltdown at the Three Mile Island plant, and the tobacco industry for which they spread doubt about the scientific evidence of its cancerous effects.[51] Sometimes a rebranding can be the go-to strategy in times of crisis. News Corp is one of the largest news organizations in the world, owned by media mogul Rupert Murdoch whose net worth is estimated at $13 billion. *News of the World* is

                    CAPS LOCK – Part 1

one of his British tabloids, which became known for hacking the phone of the Royal family and bribing police officers. Murdoch responded adequately with rebranding. Parent company News International was renamed News UK, and the holding company News International was renamed News Corp, with a redesign of its identity two years later. The old logo featured a blue globe with centred serif type, reminiscent of the 1930s. The website 'Brand New' where rebrands are discussed among designers, described the old identity as 'a prop for a villain in a Hollywood movie'.[52] To rid the company of evil-empire associations, the designers chose to use Murdoch's handwriting himself, a more 'human' gesture from a wealthy businessman who is known to use fear and intimidation to influence politics.

Only a crisis—actual or perceived— produces real change. When that crisis occurs, the actions that are taken depend on the ideas that are lying around.

MILTON FRIEDMAN, ECONOMIST

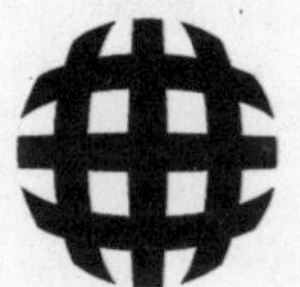

News Corporation

1923

2013

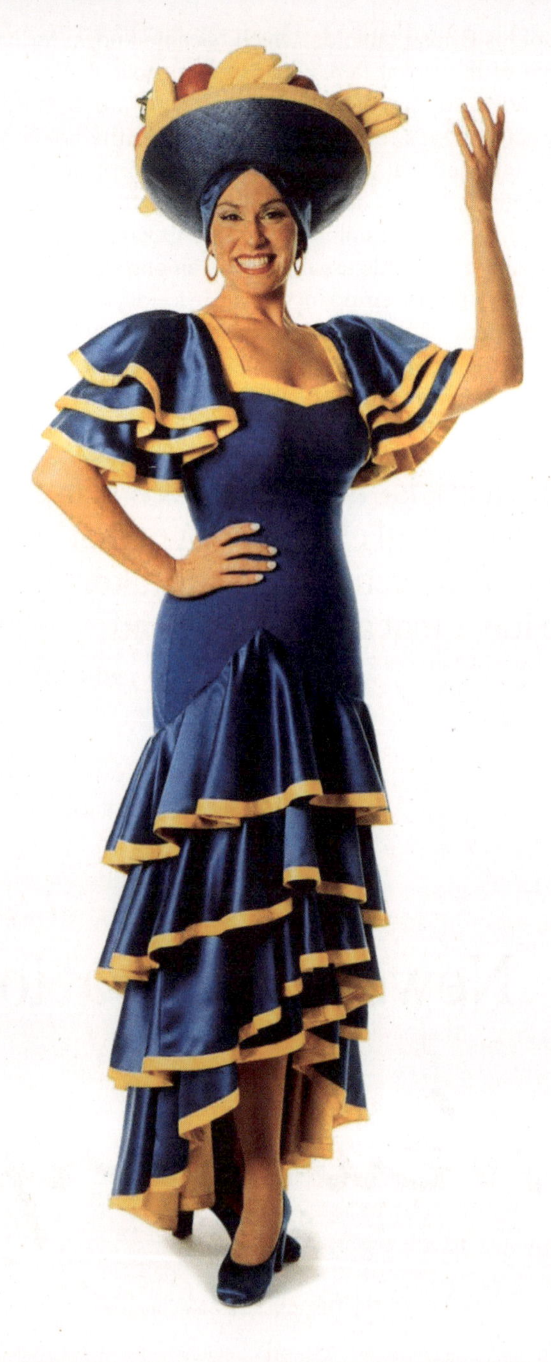

BANANA REPUBLIC

Advertising has the power to turn every crisis into a sales opportunity, but advertising is also useful for hiding violence, murder, and exploitation in pursuit of profit. A case in point is the story of Chiquita bananas. The banana was a rare fruit, until the United Fruit Company from the US popularized it using the brand name Chiquita. With the recognizable blue sticker adorning 'Miss Chiquita', the company has used advertising and public relations to successfully introduce the banana everywhere in the world.

The banana may be associated with Latin America, but the fruit is native to New Guinea and Malaysia. It was introduced in the Americas by Portuguese colonizers, and in the 1870s it was the New Yorker Minor Cooper Keith who introduced bananas in the United States. This turned out to be a lucrative decision, and he soon controlled the banana trade in Central America and Colombia. In 1899 a merger with the Boston Fruit Company created the United Fruit Company, controlling 80 percent of all banana imports in the US.

Señorita Chiquita

Because the banana was unknown in the United States, advertising needed to persuade people to make it part of their daily diet. Marketing created educational materials for schools and United Fruit paired up with cereal company Kellogg to introduce the banana as a breakfast food. It was a great success. Public relations expert Edward Bernays used his psychological persuasion methods to create a female banana character called Señorita Chiquita Banana in 1944, inspired by Brazilian actress Carmen Miranda. Wearing a fruit hat and a Latin American dress, she was featured in an animated advertisement created by Disney with the hit song *I'm Chiquita banana*.

← Miss Chiquita Banana, 1980s.

Miss Chiquita has become an advertising icon, now in use for over seventy years to promote bananas. A sexualized image of a Latina woman who always smiles, and wears a hat of fruit while dancing salsa. The surrounding advertising and design perpetuate the idea that 'the tropics are a place of simplicity and abundance, and her characterization as fun and carefree is particularly insulting considering the realities of banana production', writes the Food Empowerment project.[53] The sexualized images used to sell bananas stand in stark contrast to the Latin American women who work in the banana industry under horrible conditions, and often fall ill from pesticides used on plantations.

El Pulpo

In efforts to acquire arable land for the banana plantations in the first half of the twentieth century, United Fruit soon became the largest landowner in Central America, and was nicknamed *el pulpo* (the octopus) by Latin American journalists. In Guatemala the company wasn't just the largest landowner, it also controlled the post, the radio, and the telegraph. A United Fruit executive explained why the country was selected for banana plantations:

> Guatemala was chosen as the site for the company's earliest development activities ... because at the time we entered Central America, Guatemala's government was the region's weakest, most corrupt and most pliable.[54]

In Honduras, a US-backed president kicked indigenous people off their communal lands, so it could be sold to United Fruit. The tentacles of the octopus reached deep. US secretary of state John Foster Dulles had worked for United Fruit as a lawyer. His brother Allen Dulles was head of the CIA and a board member of United Fruit. President Eisenhower's personal secretary was married to United Fruit's PR man, and the ambassador to the UN owned a large amount of United Fruit stock.

When the Guatemalans democratically elected Jacobo Árbenz, a politician who challenged United Fruit's land use with land reforms, the company intervened. Edward Bernays was hired to

→   Map by the United Fruit Company, 1909.

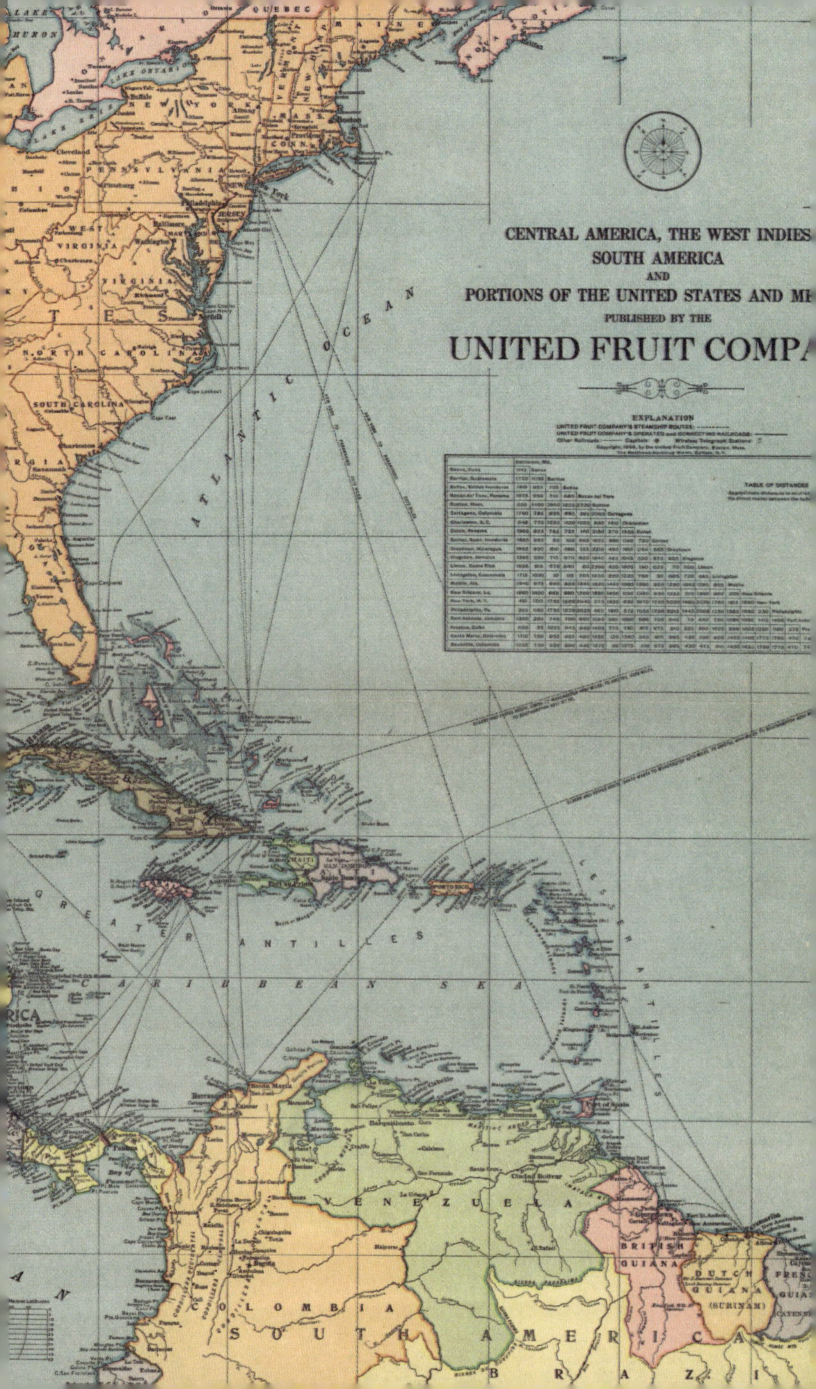

CENTRAL AMERICA, THE WEST INDIES
SOUTH AMERICA
AND
PORTIONS OF THE UNITED STATES AND ME
PUBLISHED BY THE
UNITED FRUIT COMPA
EXPLANATION
UNITED FRUIT COMPANY'S STEAMSHIP ROUTES:
UNITED FRUIT COMPANY'S OPERATED and CONNECTING RAILROADS:
Other Railroads: Capitals: Wireless Telegraph Stations:
Copyright, 1909, by the United Fruit Company, Boston, Mass.
The Matthews-Northrup Works, Buffalo, N.Y.
TABLE OF DISTANCES
ATLANTIC OCEAN
QUEBEC
NOVA SCOTIA
MAINE
PENNSYLVANIA
NEW YORK
NEW JERSEY
WEST VIRGINIA
VIRGINIA
NORTH CAROLINA
SOUTH CAROLINA
FLORIDA
GREATER ANTILLES
LESSER ANTILLES
CARIBBEAN SEA
HAITI
SAN DOMINGO
PORTO RICO
VENEZUELA
COLOMBIA
BRITISH GUIANA
DUTCH GUIANA (SURINAM)
FRENCH GUIANA (CAYENNE)
SOUTH AMERICA
BRAZIL

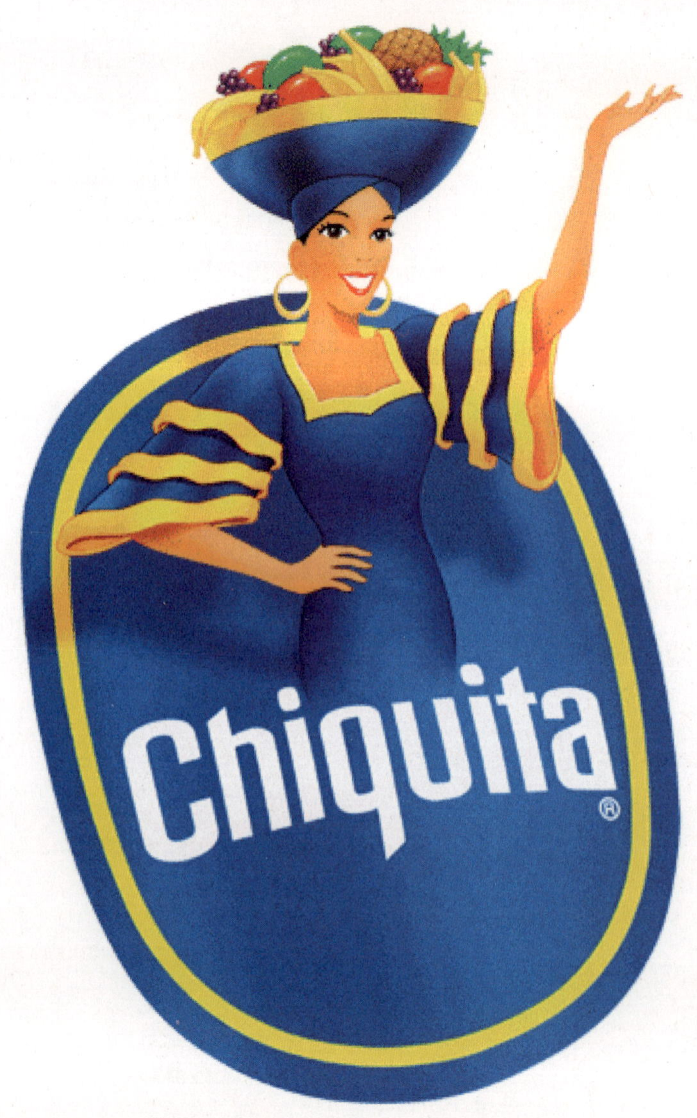

Miss Chiquita banana, 2000s.

Chiquita banana presents sexualized and exoticized visions of Latin American women, and perpetuates stereotypical images of Latin America and the people who live there.

THE FOOD EMPOWERMENT PROJECT

launch a PR offensive to paint the newly elected leader as a communist, and United Fruit pressured the US government to organize a coup. In 1954 a CIA-backed coup overthrew Árbenz and instated a pro-US military dictator in Guatemala. What the US claimed as a 'success' against communism, led to more than thirty years of military rule and violence. In 1959 a similar fate threatened Cuba when Fidel Castro nationalized the assets of the United Fruit Company. In 1961 President Kennedy ordered an invasion to put a pro-US government in power. The continuous attempts by United Fruit to bribe and topple governments in Central America with help from the US government led to the term 'banana republic'.

The Banana Massacre
The conditions on the plantations of United Fruit were deplorable. Workers were not paid in money but in vouchers, which they had to spend in shops owned by United Fruit. Workers went on strike regularly. In Colombia, 32,000 banana workers went on strike in 1928, to demand a six-day work week, the abolition of voucher payments, and a pay raise. United Fruit demanded that the Colombian government end the strike, and the US government threatened Colombia with an invasion if they would not act soon.

On 5 December 1928, the Colombian military opened fire on striking banana workers in the central square of Ciénaga, a day known as the banana massacre. The exact number of casualties is disputed, but a cable from the US embassy to the Secretary of State in 1929 said: 'I have the honour to report that the Bogotá representative of the United Fruit Company told me yesterday that the total number of strikers killed by the Colombian military exceeded one thousand.'[55]

Local testimonies usually put the number of casualties at three thousand.[56]

We're the leader in banana leadership. Because we have pushed the boundaries of the industry for decades, our brand is iconic and known the world over. We honor this heritage not by playing defense, but by continuing to bravely go where other banana brands wouldn't dare go.

CHIQUITA INTERNATIONAL CORPORATE STATEMENT, 2019

Banana Power

United Fruit used advertising and graphic design to persuade millions of people to use bananas as a regular part of their diet, while covering up their political interference and violence to gain a business advantage. Using narratives and media to influence politics through public relations is known as 'soft power'. Design and advertising for companies such as Nike and Coca-Cola, but also Hollywood cinema, are ways to advance the interests of the United States abroad by portraying a positive image of the country and its culture.[57]

The conditions under which bananas are produced today are still highly problematic. The branding of Chiquita has successfully kept this out of sight, promoting the banana as a healthy and fun product. Although the horrible history of Chiquita is well documented, bananas are still the best-selling fruit in the supermarket. Its low price does not represent the environmental impact, the water scarcity, and the exploitation of labour. Child labour still exists on plantations, and a Swiss magazine exposed 12-hour work days on Chiquita plantations in Ecuador.[58] Chiquita controlled 90 percent of the market until 1970, and together with Dole they are the two top banana companies in the US.

→   Banana workers, Costa Rica, 1908.

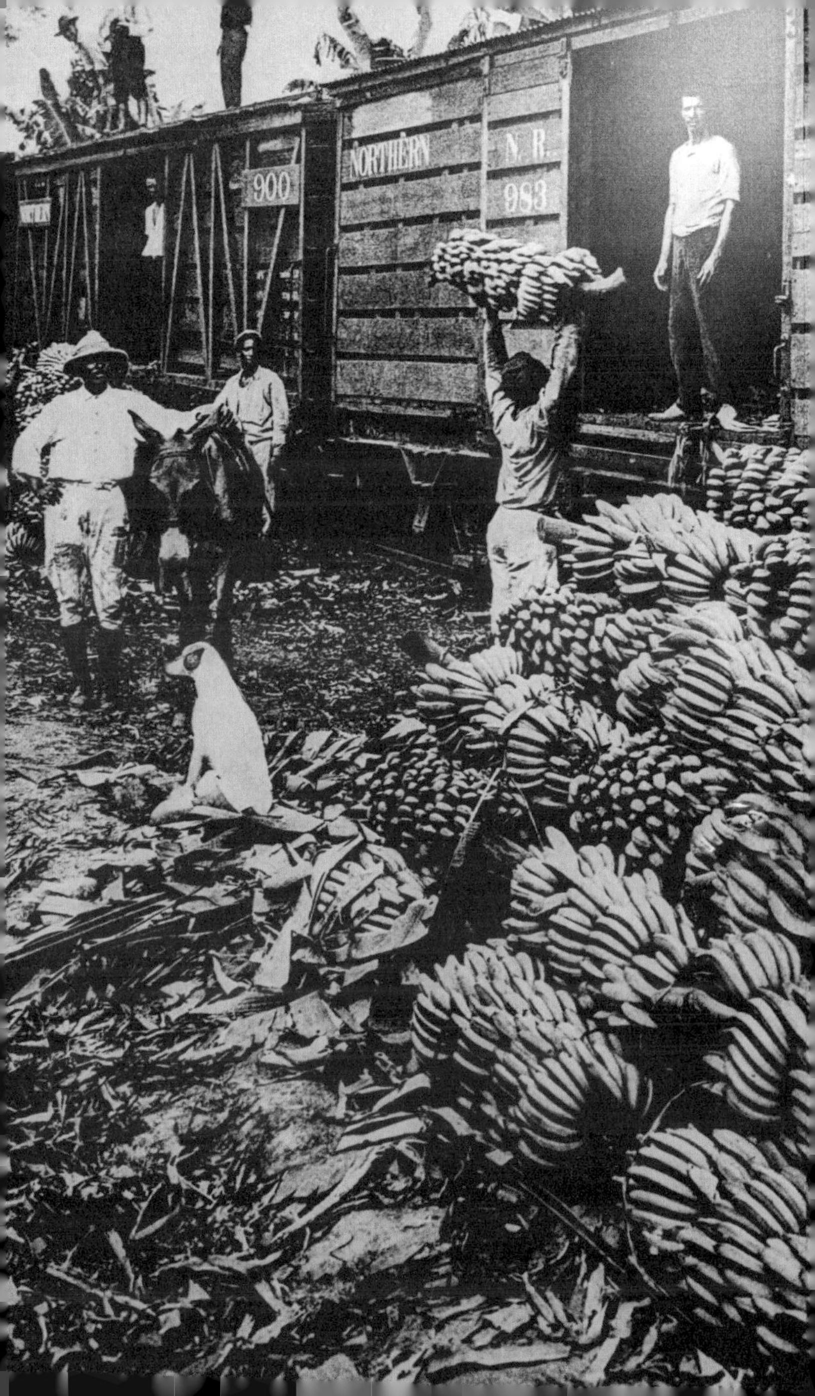
900
NORTHERN
N. R.
983

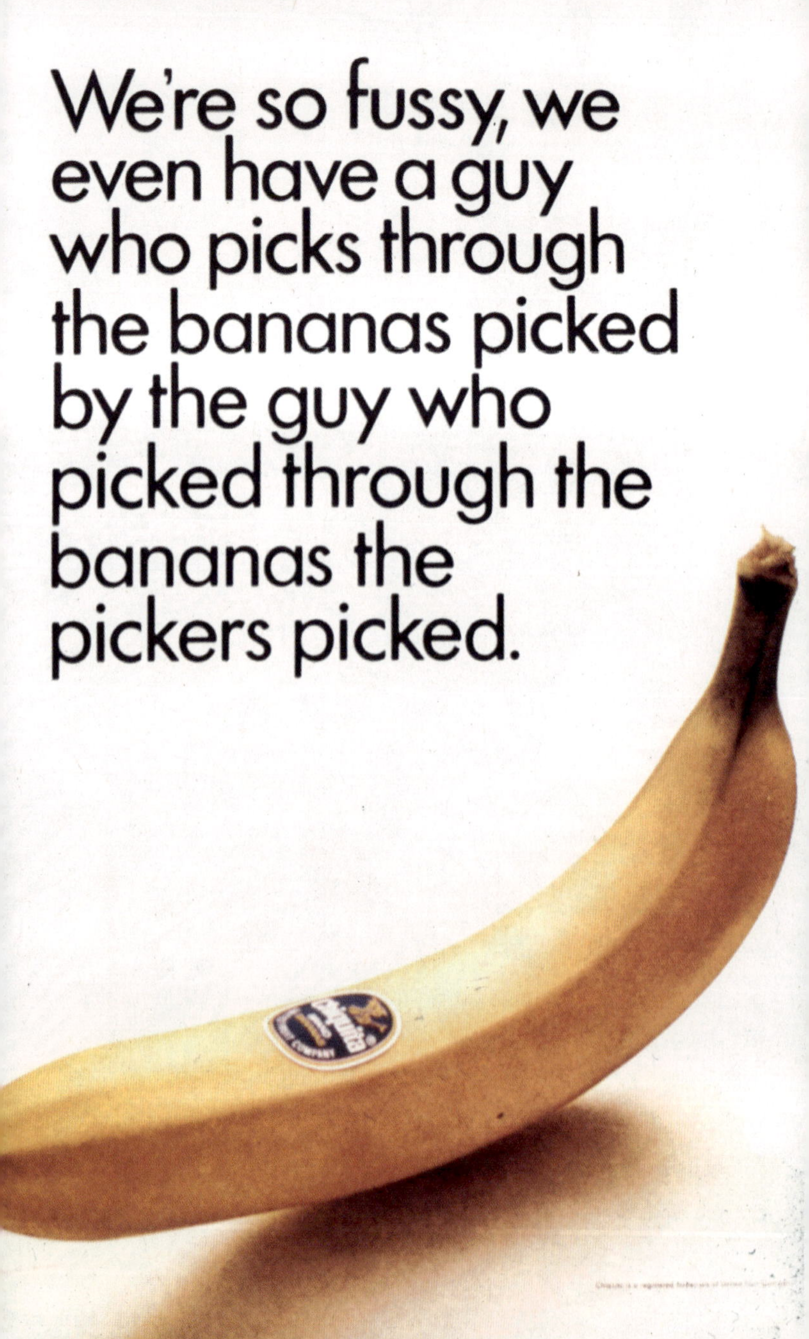
We're so fussy, we even have a guy who picks through the bananas picked by the guy who picked through the bananas the pickers picked.

The political involvement of US fruit companies in Latin America has led to decades of unstable governments and armed violence in Guatemala, Honduras, and Colombia. Guatemala suffered the most, and is still one of the most violent countries in Latin America. Between 2011–2012, seven banana union members were murdered in Guatemala. Colombia has been scarred by violence for decades, and scandals still surround the activities of United Fruit Company, now rebranded as Chiquita International. In 2007 they admitted paying $1.7 million to death squads in Colombia, to silence union organizers and intimidate farmers.

The example of United Fruit illustrates that cheap products cannot be produced ethically under capitalism, but require aggressive advertising, political meddling, dispossession of common lands, exploitation, and violence. Advertisements for Chiquita bananas have won many awards, and the company has managed to keep a pristine image, despite decades of violence and wrongdoings. In 2020 it was the 40th most popular food and snack brand.[59] The image is what protects Chiquita banana.

The End of Advertising

We began this chapter with the uneasy relation that many graphic designers have with advertising. It's not just designers. Many people don't like advertising. Many of us install Adblockers, we switch the channel, or look away or mute the sound when we see ads. Billboards are defaced and *jammed* regularly, by collectives such as Brandalism. Even advertising legend David Ogilvy wrote that he hated billboards, and he even swore he would start chopping them down after his retirement.[60] So why don't we just ban advertising altogether?

In 2007, São Paulo became the first city to ban all outdoor advertising. 15,000 billboards were taken down, and 300,000 storefront signs. Some billboards were replaced with street art, as part of the new policy *Cidada Limpa* (clean city) which was supported by 70 percent of the residents.[61] Two years later Chennai in India followed by banning billboards, and in 2014 the French city Grenoble was the first European city to ban all outdoor advertising. The more than three hundred advertising signs in Grenoble

← Chiquita banana advertisement, 1970s.

were replaced with trees and community noticeboards.[62]

If advertising would be banned from public space everywhere, it would certainly be a blow to a system of consumption that relies on constant seduction. But ads would still be on our phones, on websites, on the radio, and on TV. Advertisers would find new channels and new ways to reach us. The truth is that many cities depend on the revenue from advertising, especially since neoliberal policies dictate that government services have to be financially profitable. Five years after the ban, São Paulo has gradually introduced controlled forms of advertising again.

This chapter offers a bleak view of how, in a timespan of two centuries, society has been commodified bit by bit through enclosure of free and public spaces. Young people nowadays welcome personal advertising as a way of earning money by becoming influencers. A recent study shows that for children in the UK between 11 and 16, social media influencer was the second most popular profession.[63] It's no surprise that in our current media environment, young people aspire to be famous and wealthy, even if that means selling out. The constant pressure of advertising messages is like a mandatory form of commercial entertainment that we have to endure to keep a high standard of living. Because it is not just about ads or where we see them, but how human language and behaviour itself are changed because of capitalism.

The question is if the wealthy want to give up luxury in exchange for less commercials. The richest 20 percent has grown accustomed to luxuries and a high standard of living, which can only be artificially kept in place by commercializing all aspects of life. Advertising is the very foundation of an economic system that seeks to expand until it has absorbed everything in its path. If advertising is the culture of society itself, as John Berger wrote,[64] than limiting advertising is not enough. We have to change society.

The history of critique from graphic designers against advertising is admirable, and shows that there is support to change the system. But so far complaints have only led to more commercialization, and graphic design has become a lot more, not less, commercial since 1964. It is clear that if designers choose to do less work for marketing and advertising, it will not likely have structural effects. Especially as the logic of the salesperson can now be found in the branding of all parts of society, after the enclosure of commons such as healthcare, welfare, education, and other public services.

On the positive side, designers still have free will. We can find different ways to mediate social relations when value is created. Rather than distinguishing between advertising and graphic design, a question that all designers could ask themselves is, how do I question commercialization in my personal role as consumer and producer in the economy?

The role of the salesperson is not only harmful. People have always been selling and promoting wares, but the problem is that capitalism has created a force of consumerism that only serves to generate profit, and commercialization is no longer proportional to our basic needs. The culture of consumption has almost obliterated other societal forms, for example those based on trust, reciprocity, and solidarity.

At the moment, design 'destroys the visibility of other possibilities'[65] writes Boehnert. Possibilities about a different way of visual communication in society, possibilities of other ways to create and measure value. Possibilities that are about strengthening local bonds, local economies, and focusing on 'needs rather than wants'[66] as Victor Papanek wrote. A socially aware design could be a valuable tool to create economies of solidarity, based on the well-being of all living beings.

There are professions more harmful than industrial design, but only a very few of them. And possibly only one profession is phonier. Advertising design.

VICTOR PAPANEK, DESIGNER

→ *American way of life*, 1937. Queue of black residents of Louisville, KY, waiting for relief supplies during the Ohio River flood, US, 1937. Photo by Margaret Bourke-White.

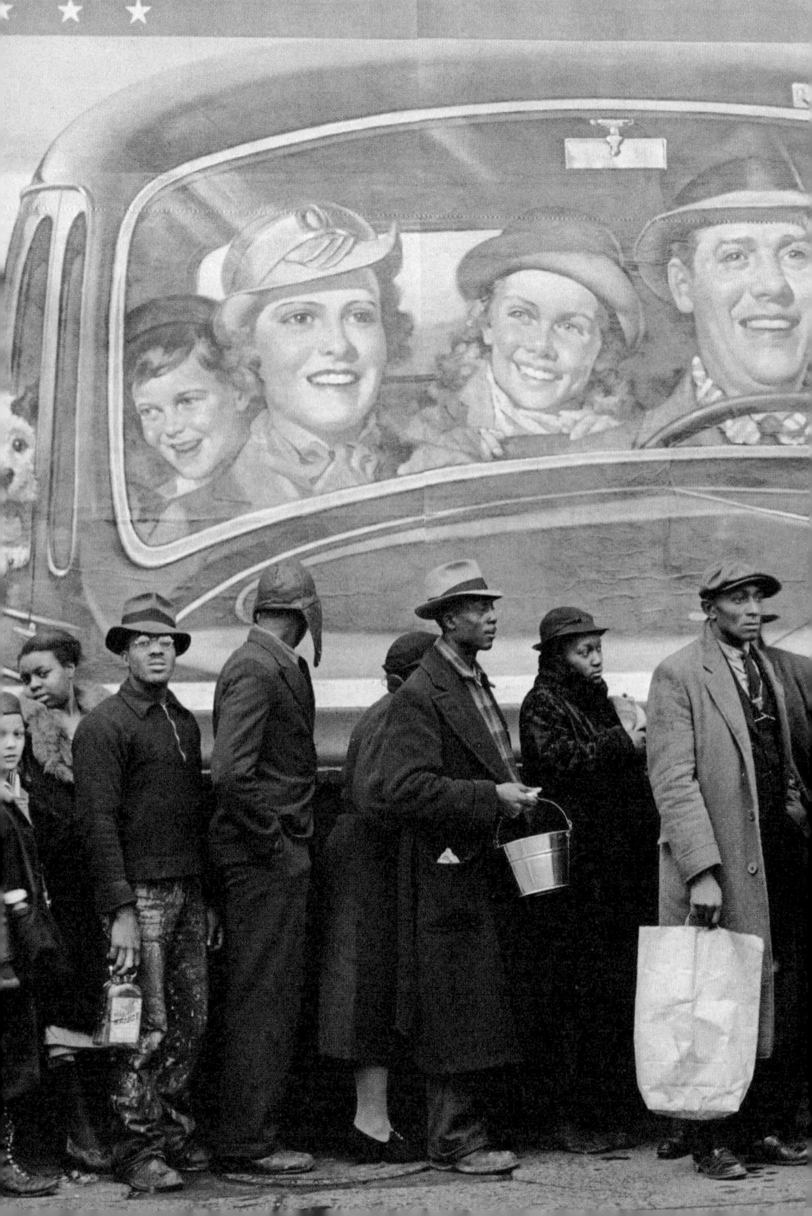

WORLD'S HIGHEST S

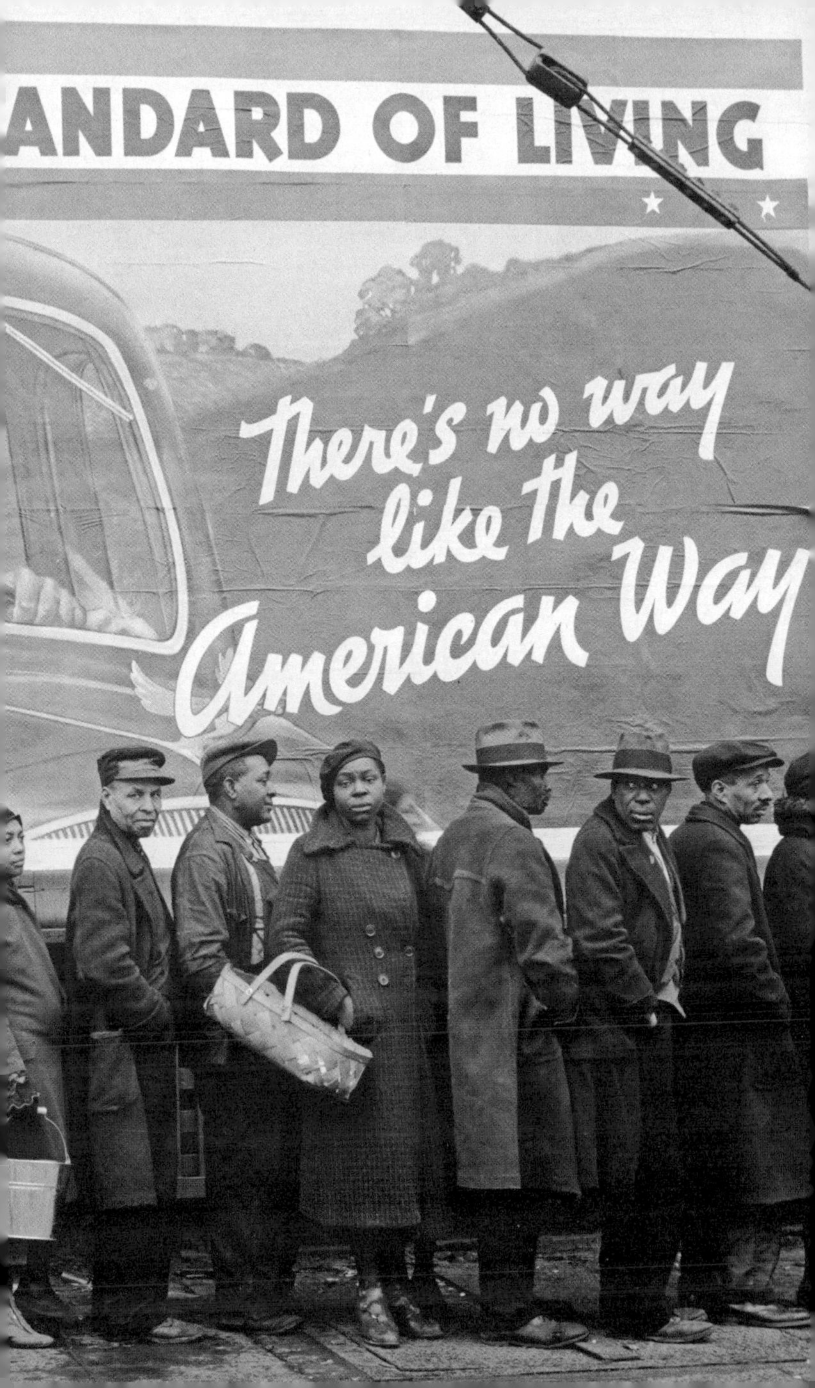

ANDARD OF LIVING
There's no way
like the
American Way

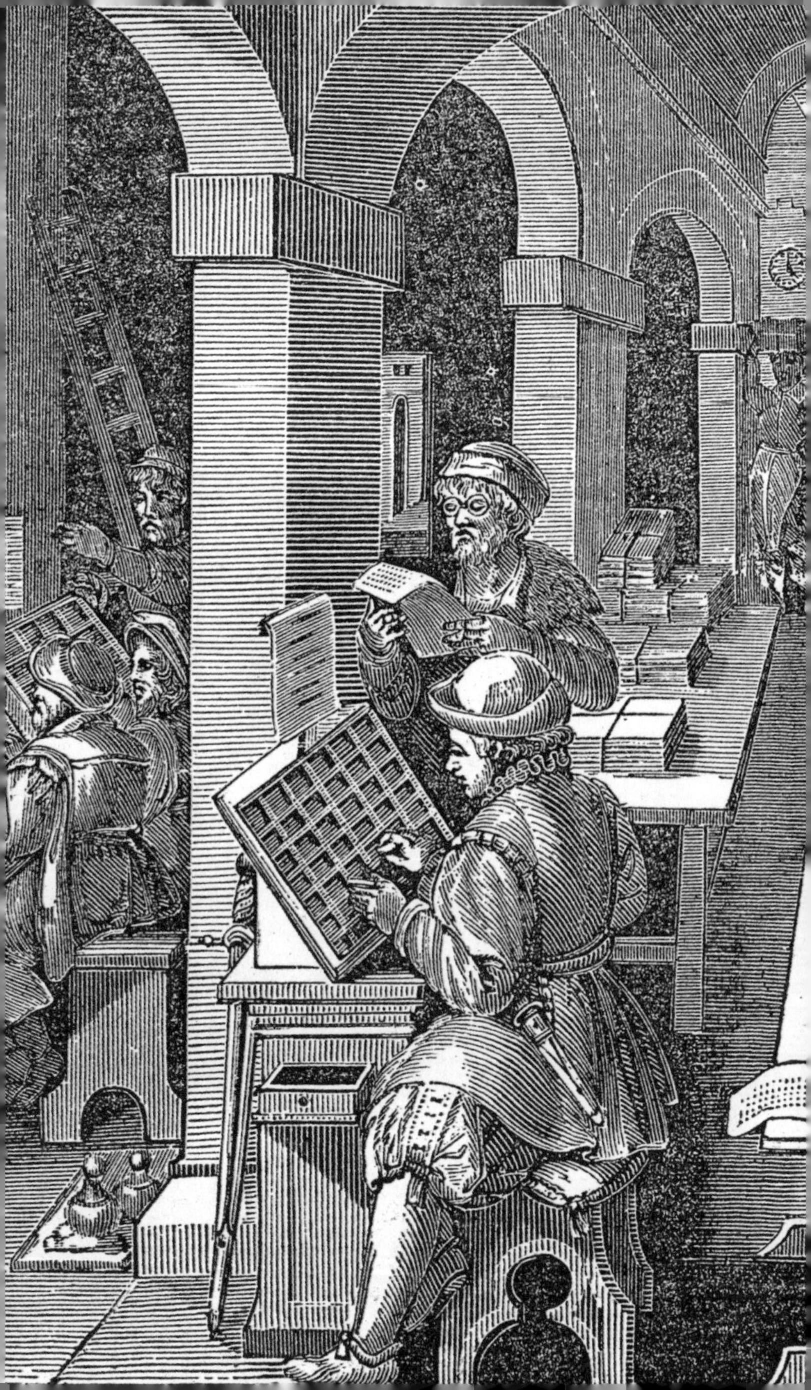

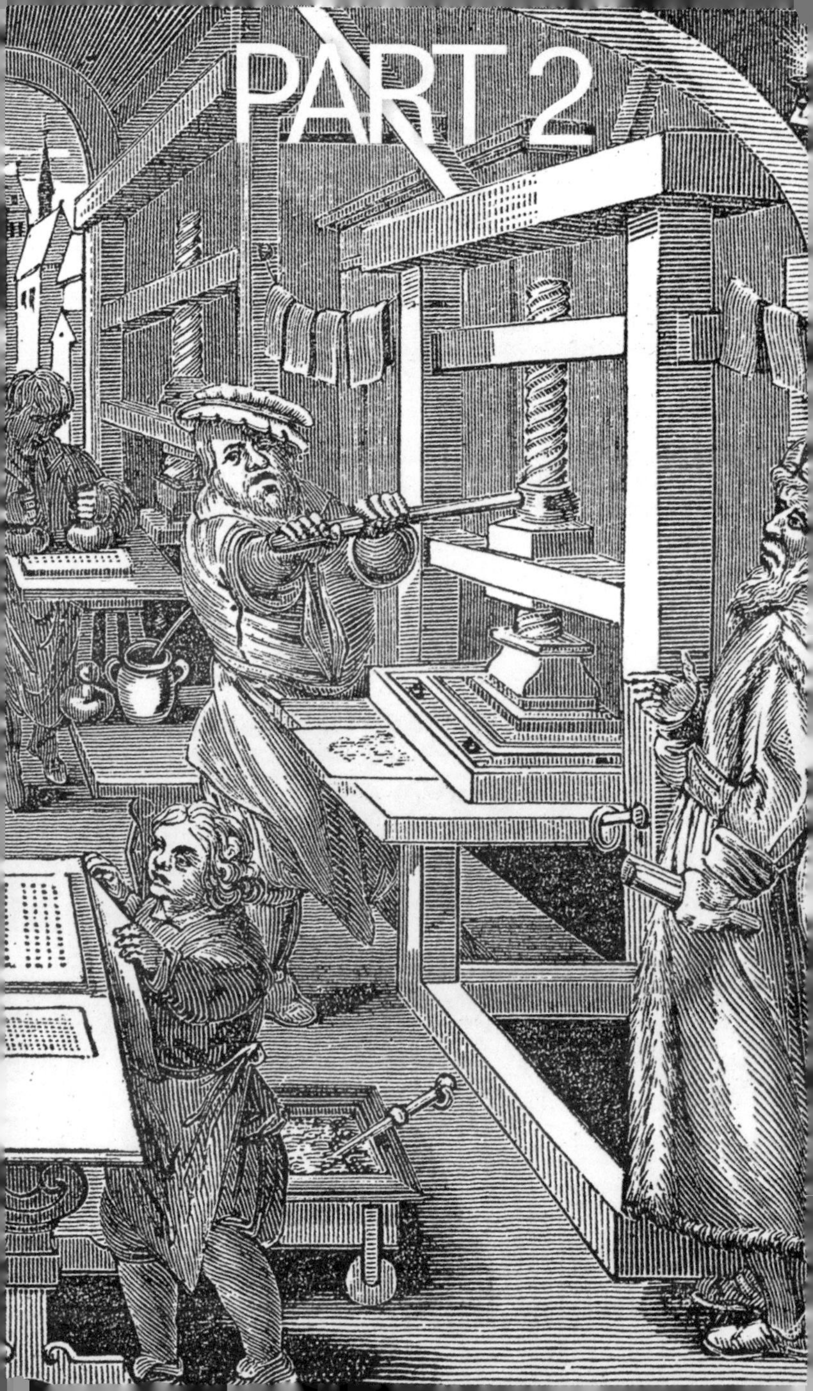
PART 2

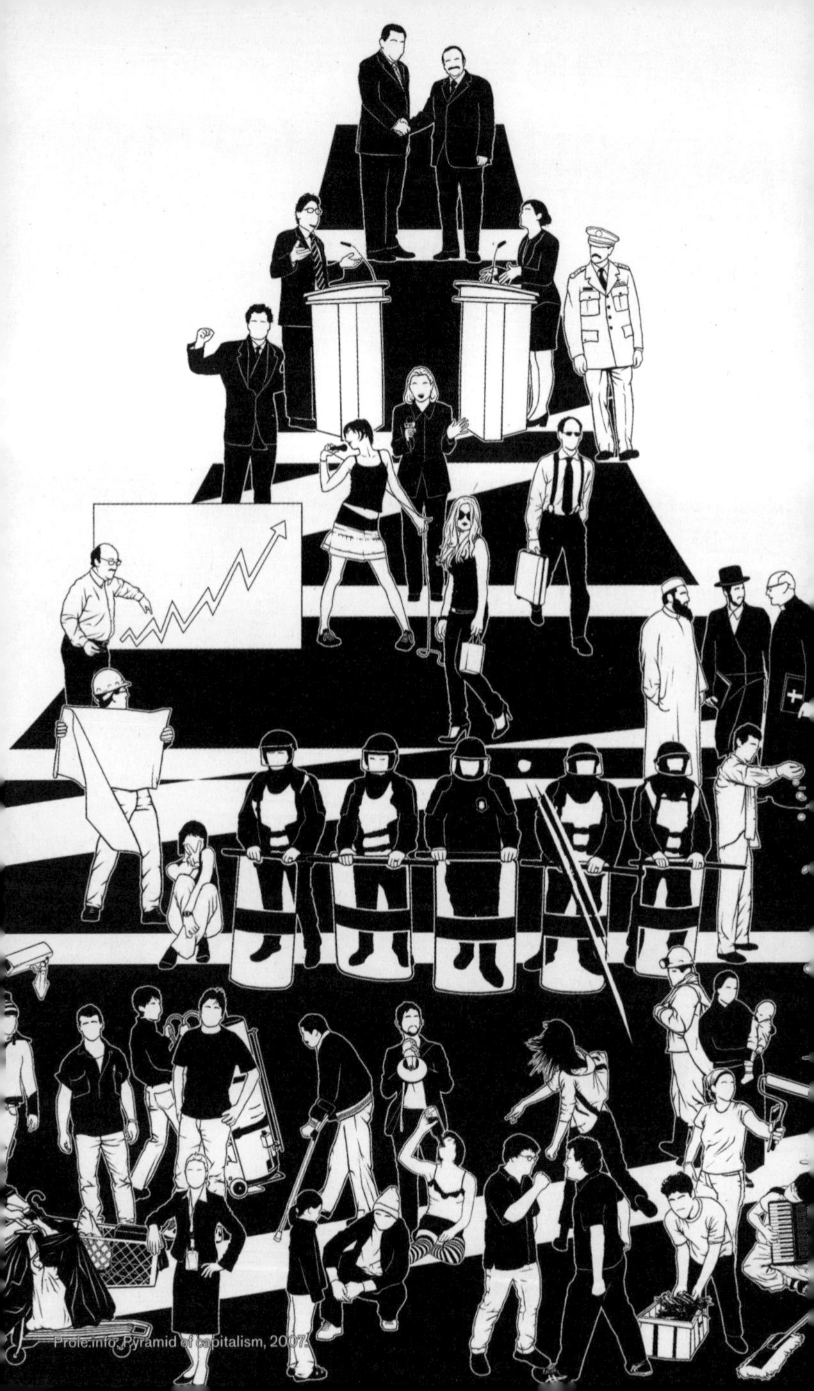

Prole.info, Pyramid of capitalism, 2007.

THE DESIGNER AS WORKER

It is not an accident that most men start thinking of getting married as soon as they get their first job.

This is not only because now they can afford it, but because having somebody at home who takes care of you is the only condition not to go crazy after a day spent on an assembly line or at a desk.
SILVIA FEDERICI

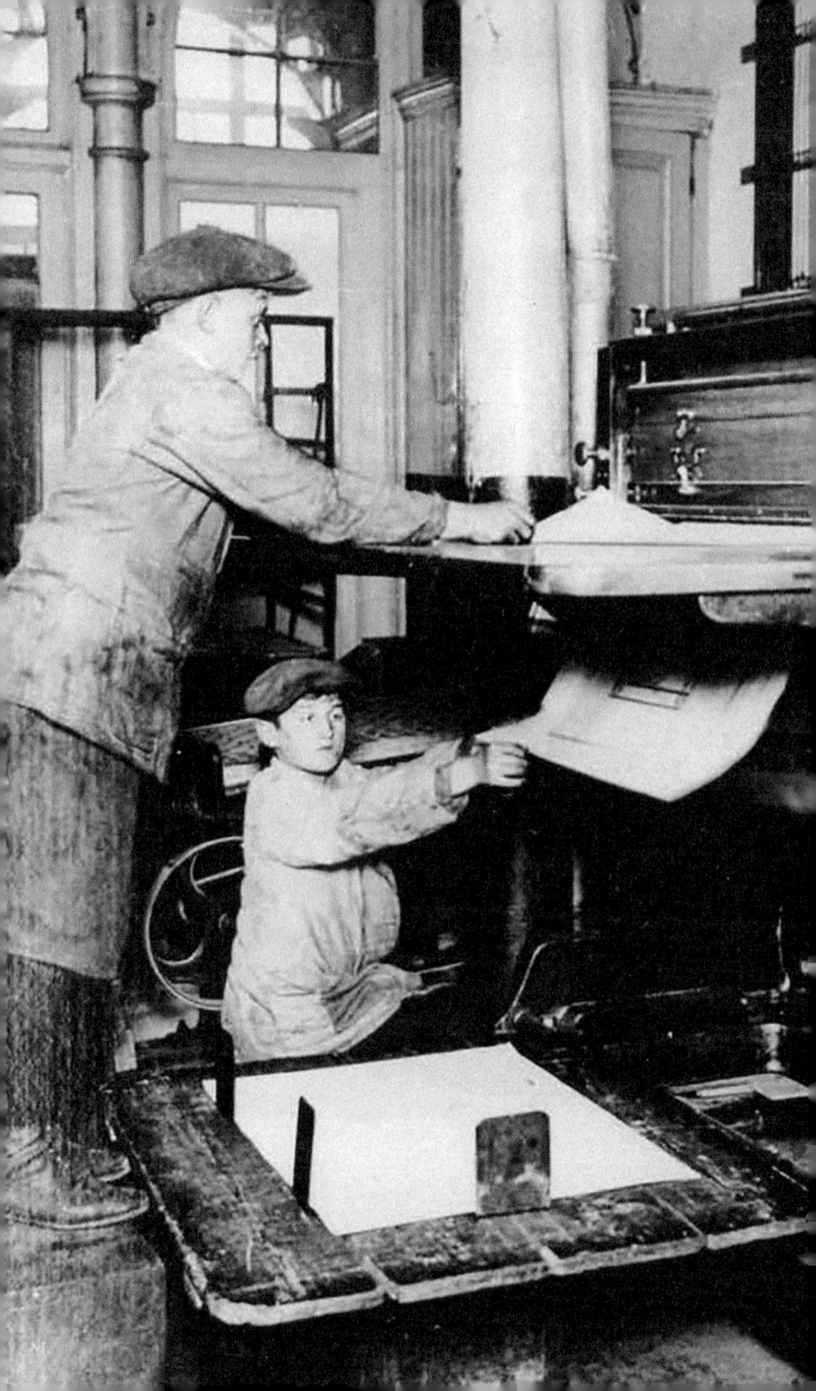

A HISTORY OF WORK

Our lives revolve around work. We spend most of our time working, training for work, looking for work, or recovering from it. Education and healthcare prepare people for work. Sleep, family time, exercise, study, and leisure, are needed to be productive at work. Work is not only necessary for our basic needs: food, clothing, and shelter, it also structures our lives and indicates our status in society.

The social significance of work is remarkable, because many people don't particularly like their work. A 2019 Gallup survey shows that 45 percent of employees in the US are unhappy with their jobs.[1] Job satisfaction among graphic designers is a bit higher, with 35 percent of designers being unsatisfied with their work.[2] Even so, many view creative work and design as a privilege: a way to 'turn your hobby into a job', or even as a passion, to quote a popular meme.

The previous chapters discussed how the work of designers bolsters capitalism. Graphic designers create forms, such as bank notes, contracts, maps, passports, documents, and financial statements that provide proof of property and economic transactions. By branding and advertising products and services, designers play an important role in boosting consumerism. The images and ideas designers produce, and even the laptops and software that designers use for their work, play a role in creating consumer demand.

The following chapters shift the focus from what designers make, to how they work. Designers that take on the role of workers, bosses, freelancers, teachers, non-professionals, or the unemployed. The Designer as Worker touches the core of the economic role that designers play in society. It also offers practical ideas for how design work can be done differently, by looking at what unions, cooperatives, and solidarity networks have to offer.

← Child working in a print shop, the Netherlands, c. 1900.

Perhaps you are eager to understand if you're being exploited, if your workday is too long, if you can avoid freelancing for bottom rates, or doing unpaid design work. But before we go into the specifics, we need to cover some basic ground about work itself. Did people always work this hard? How do we work today, and how is it different from centuries ago? How was the length of the working day decided, and can we work less?

A short summary of the history of work will help to contextualize the social and economic role of work—including design work—in society. This offers the opportunity to organize a different work environment for designers, both individually and collectively.

Work Before the Industrial Revolution

What do we mean by work? The Western conception of work today is very different from what it was before the industrial revolution. We consider work as an activity that generates income, usually in a space outside of the home. Or as the *Oxford Dictionary* describes it: 'a mental or physical activity as a means of earning income'. This definition excludes a whole range of activities that are essential to society. Think of caring, raising children, cleaning, cooking, volunteer work, political and social organizing, informal work in black and grey markets, and farming for sustenance. All of which make up a sizable portion of our economic activities, but are all unpaid and undervalued reproductive labour. These activities are ignored by most economists, even though society would collapse without them.

This strict separation between work and non-work did not exist in medieval Europe. Most people grew their own food, produced their own clothing, and made household items.[3] Farm work revolved around the seasons, where harvest time was the busiest, while in winter people worked less. Contrary to the image of the toiling peasant, the medieval work day was slow, even leisurely, compared to work after the industrial revolution.[4] There was no distinction between items sold at markets and those used for own consumption.[5] Feminist scholar Silvia Federici writes that within a peasant household, both women and men were expected to share the work. Land was given by a feudal lord to a family unit, and it was not unusual for women to manage it in their name. She notes

CAPS LOCK — Part 2

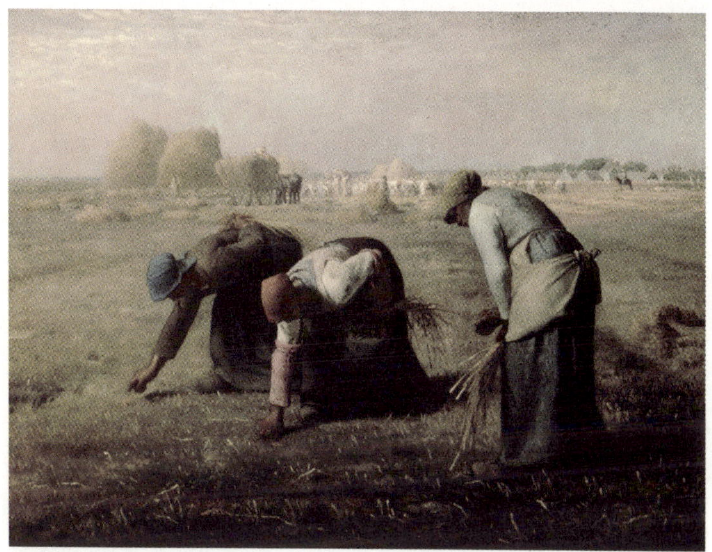

Jean-François Millet, *The Gleaners*, 1857.

The reciprocal, the immediate and the gratuitous were pushed out of the economic sphere, devalued and banned from economic statistics so that their continued existence went unnoticed.

ANDREA KOMLOSY, HISTORIAN

that 'the sexual division of labor in it was less pronounced and less discriminating than in a capitalist farm'.[6]

Colonialism brought economic expansion to Europe, and its wealth created a thriving merchant class. This challenged the divine order of birth right on which the power of feudal lords depended. Enclosure laws and the subsequent dispossession of farmers, slowly transformed manors into capitalist agriculture businesses. Common lands on which peasants depended, literally replacing people with sheep and crops. The productivity of the land rose, but many lost their means to survive.[7] People had to resort to wage labour, a form of work which was relatively uncommon before the 1700s. It was looked down upon, and seen as a form of slavery.[8]

Industrialization throughout the eighteenth and nineteenth century eventually made wage labour the dominant form of work. Work moved from the house to the factory, in shifts based on hourly rates in wage contracts. The modernization of work eliminated other forms that used to be prevalent in European societies, as Andrea Komlosy writes: 'The reciprocal, the immediate and the gratuitous were pushed out of the economic sphere, devalued and banned from economic statistics so that their continued existence went unnoticed.'[9] Colonization would further export this European idea of work across the globe, doing away with other ideas about work.

The Protestant Work Ethic

'There is nothing better for a person than to enjoy their work, because that is their lot.'[10] This quote from Ecclesiastes 3:22 is a testimony of how the European view of work was largely shaped by Christianity. Religious doctrine held that work was a blessing, and repetitive or heavy labour—like that of monks who meticulously copied manuscripts—was seen as a service to God. Sociologist and philosopher Max Weber wrote about this in his book *The Protestant Ethic and the Spirit of Capitalism* (1905). In this influential work he proposed that there was such a thing as a capitalist work ethic, which sprung directly from the Protestant values of work, which were punctuality and frugality. At the heart of Weber's argument is the term 'calling' (*Beruf* in German), a term that did not exist prior to Protestantism. 'One's calling' (from God) meant that hard work was the highest duty in society, 'which man has to accept as a divine ordinance, to which he must adapt himself.'[11] Work was not just an economic necessity, it became a 'moral practice and collective ethical obligation', as Kathi Weeks writes in *The Problems with Work.*[12]

The factory owners embraced the Protestant work ethic, preaching hard work as a moral, individual duty that benefited society as a whole. This religious foundation still shapes the moral dedication towards work under capitalism. The Protestant work ethic is heralded as the origin of high productivity and wealth in the Anglo-Saxon and Northern European countries, even though this ignores the role of slavery, resource extraction, and unpaid reproductive labour without which capitalism could not exist.

Blessings and Burdens of the Industrial Revolution

The steam-powered machines of the industrial revolution needed to run day and night, and so it came to be that the factory clock replaced the sun as the rhythm of work. Work no longer followed the sun and the seasons, but the strokes of the factory clock.

Factories resembled prisons with in-house dormitories and continuous surveillance. Workplace regulations did not exist in the beginning of the industrial revolution, and workers had to put in 80 hours a week or more in dangerous and unhealthy conditions. Accidents were the order of the day, and life expectancy of workers actually went down in industrial areas. In 1840 a farm worker in England had a life-expectancy of thirty-eight, while a factory worker in Liverpool did not live longer than fifteen years on average.[13] Children as young as eight were employed, working shifts of fourteen hours a day. Deaths from overwork as befell seamstress Mary Anne Walkley, who died after working a thirty-hour shift, were not uncommon. These brutal conditions persisted because the

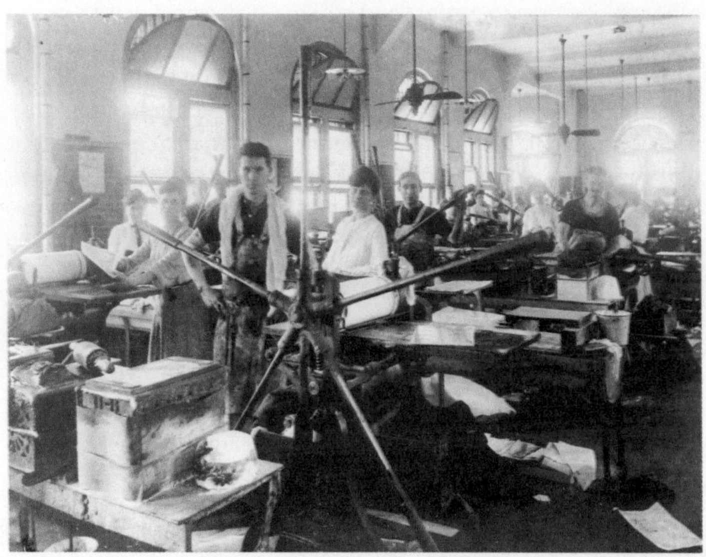

Employees at the Bureau of Engraving and Printing, US, 1904. Photo by Waldon Fawcett.

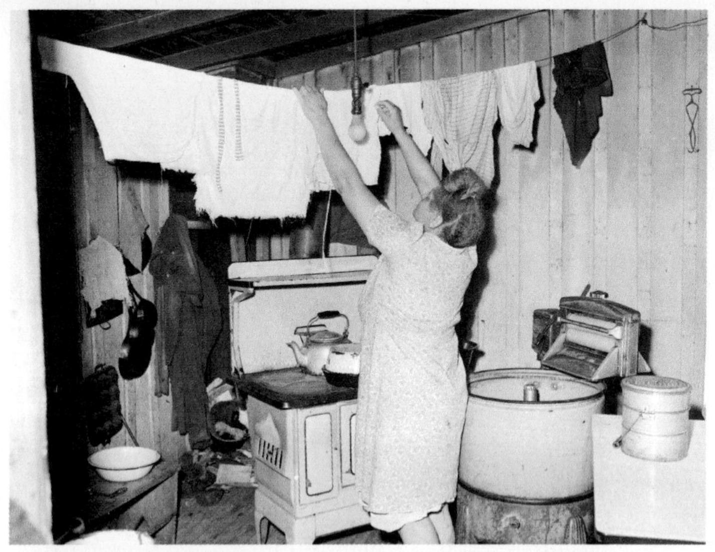

Mrs. Furman Currington, the wife of a miner, hangs up laundry, Harlan County, KY, US, 1946.

majority of people were not allowed to vote, and those who were welcomed mass profits. For disgruntled workers there was no other choice than to protest and strike, which was met with police or military force.

Despite the horrible conditions of early industrial production, wage labour and factory work provided a way out of another oppressive system: feudalism. Freedom from feudal control meant that any individual could find employment, and escape domination by patriarchs or feudal lords. Wages for factory work were ridiculously meagre, but it meant workers did have their own money, which meant more freedom of movement and individual choices than farm life could offer.

By the turn of the century, worker strikes and protests finally convinced governments to implement safety and work regulations, for example limiting child labour and introducing the eleven-hour work day. Workers were no longer forbidden to organize, which paved the way for the first unions. In 1855, the UK labour movement began a campaign for the eight-hour work day: eight hours labour, eight hours recreation, and eight hours of rest; a goal that wasn't achieved until 1919.

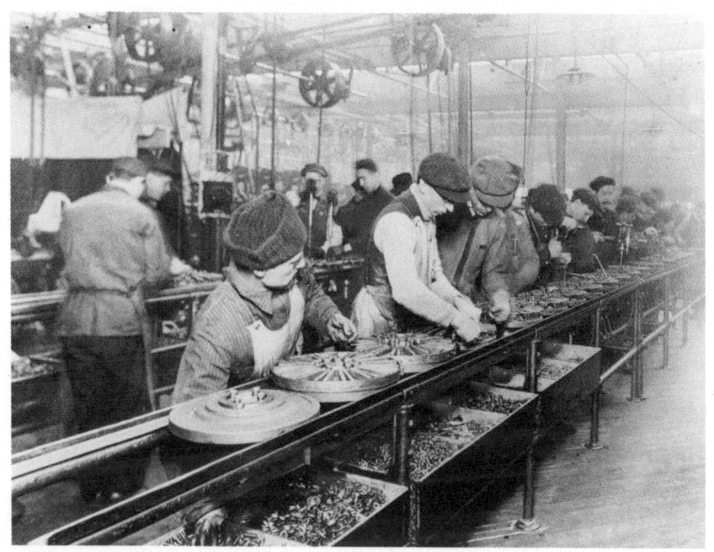

Ford workers on the first moving assembly line, Highland Park, MI, US, 1913.

Mass Production and Mass Consumption

In the early twentieth century the situation of workers improved thanks to the hard struggle of the labour movement, with shorter working days, safer work environments, and more pay. Although factory owners first resisted these measures, they quickly realized the benefits. The low life-expectancy and low wages of workers hadn't created the consumer class that was needed to purchase all those mass-produced products.

US industrialist Henry Ford understood that production and consumption were two sides of the same coin. In his car factory he doubled the industry-standard wage to $5 a day, just so his work-ers could afford to buy the cars that they themselves produced. He also closed the factories on Saturdays and Sundays, which meant more leisure time in which to consume. This period of capitalism is known as Fordism, and lasted roughly until the 1970s. More leisure time and better pay did not mean that working in Ford's factories was gratifying. The technologically advanced River Rouge plant was so efficient that skilled metal workers were expected to simply execute the repetitive tasks dictated by the assembly line. James C. Scott notes that a metal worker in the River Rouge plant could have worked there for five or ten years without learning a single thing.[14]

Under Fordism, the factory floor workers were strictly separated from managers and technicians, who relied on paper bureaucracy for communication. A military-style, top-down hierarchy was introduced using communication technologies. This so-called 'scientific management', was invented by engineer Frederick Taylor (1865–1915). His method monitored every activity on the work floor, to see how it could be done faster and more efficiently. He subdivided the work into different tasks, and with his stopwatch measured the time it took the fastest worker to complete them. He then suggested factories should pay workers by piece rather than by the hour, rewarding the fastest and punishing the slowest. His scientific method increased productivity manifold but he was intensely hated by workers, for obvious reasons.

Fordism is sometimes called the 'golden age of capitalism', now admired for its lifelong job contracts, strong unions, and good salaries. What appeared to be a more socialist capitalism was only possible because of the availability of cheap raw materials from (former) colonies, the exploitation of workers of colour, and the unpaid domestic work by women. Employers strongly advocated the male breadwinner model, which meant women were expected

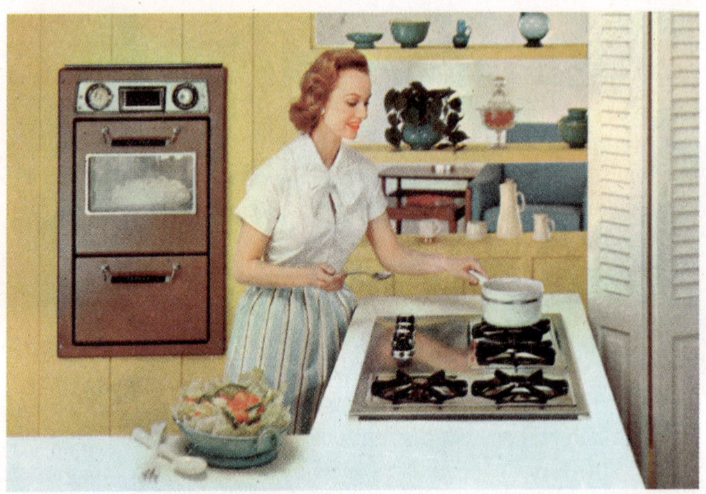

Advertising image of a kitchen in the 1950s and 1960s

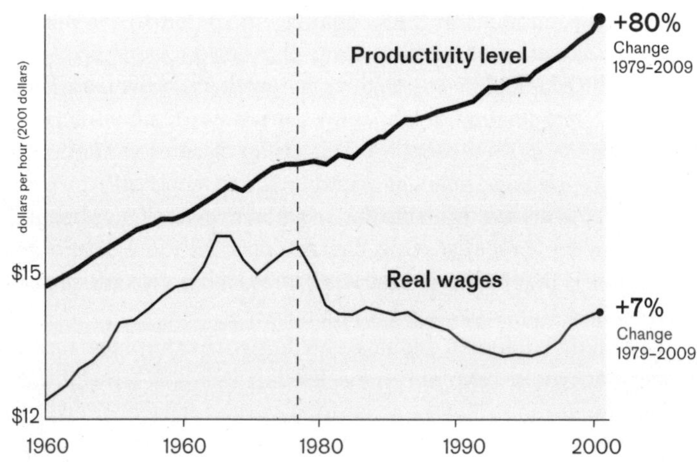

to stay at home and do unpaid domestic work including raising children, caring, cleaning, cooking, and organizing the household. The nuclear family was actively promoted by lawmakers, politicians, employers, and religious leaders as a crucial part of the work discipline.[15] The male labour contract forged gender relations in work, as Kathi Weeks points out. The model of the nuclear family served capitalism by providing unpaid reproductive labour to keep male workers productive.

Minimum Job Security, Maximum Oversight

Halfway through the 1970s the higher oil price, cheap credit, and advances in information and communication technologies led corporations to move manufacturing to low-wage countries. Lifelong loyalty of workers under Fordism didn't stop corporations from laying off thousands of workers. Child labour and sixteen-hour work days were illegal in Europe and the US, but those laws didn't always apply in the Free Economic Zones in the Global South. Multinationals pressured subcontractors for bottom prices, which led to the exploitation of industrial workers, much in the same way as workers had been exploited in Europe in the nineteenth century.

Figures from the International Labour Organization show that 40 million people in the world today are still coerced into forced labour.[16]

As the economies in the Global North shifted to the service economy, areas such as marketing and design expanded. This shift from blue-collar to white-collar work is known as Post-Fordism. Deregulation of labour laws made flexible contracts the rule rather than the exception. This rising class of workers with flexible contracts, permanent uncertainty, and faced with the pressure of being always available and promoting oneself, has become known as the precariat. One characteristic of the Post-Fordist work ethic is that it demands all workers to be creative and flexible beyond their formal work requirements.

Digital technologies enabled new forms of workplace surveillance that would have surprised Frederick Taylor himself. Employee monitoring software in use today divides the work into strict deadlines which have to be met. Journalist Emily Guendelsberger worked at an Amazon warehouse as an order picker and has described her work process. She was issued a digital controller that told her the next order to pick, with a status bar that would give her the time allocated for the task counting down the seconds. Taking longer than the allocated time would generate warnings. She explains how Amazon uses clocks and metrics to 'constrain the inefficiencies of human workers so they act more like robots'.[17] At her McDonald's job, each task was optimized to the second. Target sandwich assembly time: twenty-two seconds. Target sandwich wrapping time: fourteen seconds. Being late one minute would generate an alarm with the manager and would mean she would be yelled at for being late.

For designers, Post-Fordism ushered in a golden age. The growing emphasis on marketing, public relations, and management consultancy led to an increased demand for designers in the 1980s, as Guy Julier points out.[18] Today, designers are seen as the ideal Post-Fordist workers, because they work almost exclusively on intellectual property and immaterial products, and they embrace creativity and individuality. Sooner or later, designers too will be challenged by the same forces of global competition that laid off industrial workers. With the rise of algorithmically produced design, and online job platforms for design services such as Fiverr and a growing designer class, the question is not if design will remain a viable profession in post-industrial societies under capitalism, but for how long.

As a young designer, I believe that over-working is almost essential for success. A 9–5 job is not always enough time to learn or experiment with our practice, so I would almost argue that the hours after work can be vital in working towards 'success', especially within the creative industries.

DUNCAN BRAZZIL, DESIGNER

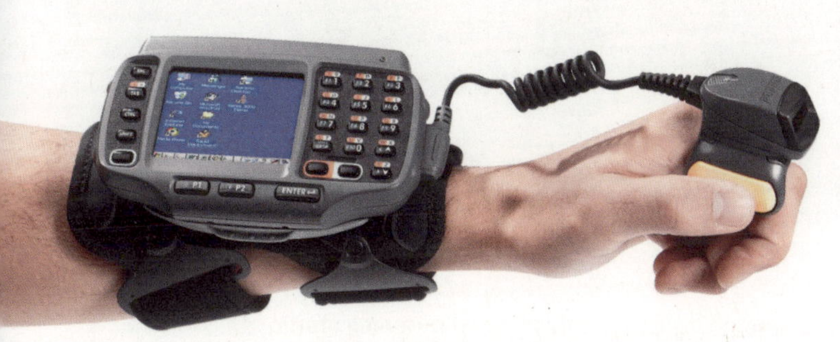

Motorola WT4090 Wearable Mobile Computer, used in Amazon fulfilment centres.

MY WORK IS MY PASSION

To other white-collar workers, the working conditions of graphic designers may appear comfortable. Designers are asked to do creative work and are paid for it. No work uniforms, staring at spreadsheets, or working in grey cubicles: designers work in a 'studio'. They are surrounded by posters and artworks and are casually dressed. Can designers complain about horrible bosses, long hours, stress, and low pay, without sounding pitiful?

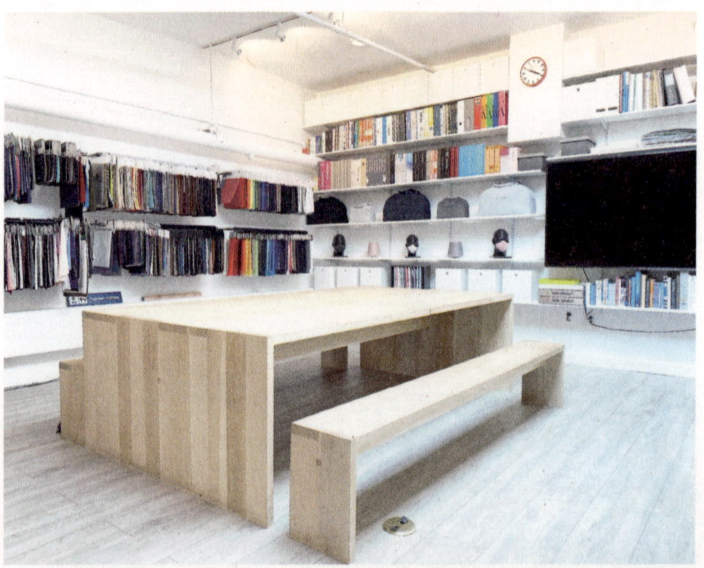

Bilio design studio, Oakland, US.

Some designers are lucky to enjoy a nice studio atmosphere, nice clients, and the occasional creative brief to sink their teeth in. But the reality is that most graphic design work is nothing like the romantic image of the creative genius. Most design work is a daily grind of marketing and communication maintenance for corporations:

designing log-in screens for corporate intranets, typesetting legal product disclaimers, retooling advertisements for social media formats, and optimizing corporate logos with by-lines. Routine design jobs which have to be carried out according to strict brand guidelines dictated by other designers.[19]

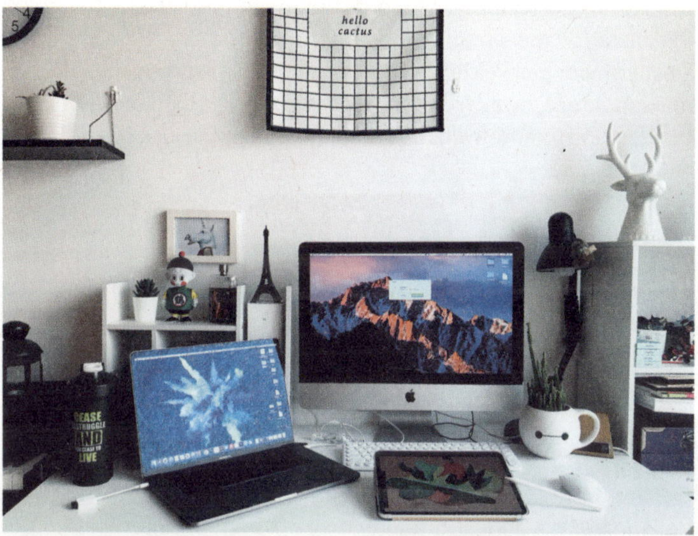

Home studio of a designer.

It is great to be passionate about being a designer, but beware that making your hobby into a job has become a strategy for clients and employers to demand work situations that would be unacceptable elsewhere: unpaid internships, pulling all-nighters, working week-ends, and unpaid designs competitions. These are all common practices in design because there are more designers than jobs (more about that later), and secondly, people assume that because designers do what they love, they will happily accept any working condition no matter how problematic.

What doesn't help is that this work culture is promoted, even celebrated by designers themselves. In the well-known book for beginning designers *How to be a graphic designer, without losing your soul*, designer and writer Adrian Shaughnessy kicks off by saying 'always remember there are millions of people who'd swap jobs with you if they could'.[20] He continues with 'Design is about commitment: if you want to have a nine-to-five existence, go and get a job in a government tax office'.[21]

Passion is what makes designers the ideal workers in this stage of capitalism. Designers are flexible, always available, dress up, don't strike, don't unionize, and are inspired on demand. Designer Daniel van der Velden warned designers not to become the working class of the creative industry. In his article 'Research and Destroy' Van der Velden quotes a Dutch politician saying: 'We are making a turn, away from the assembly line to the laboratory and the design studios, from the working class to the creative class.'[22]

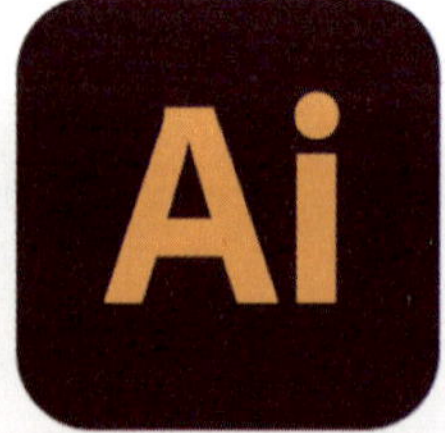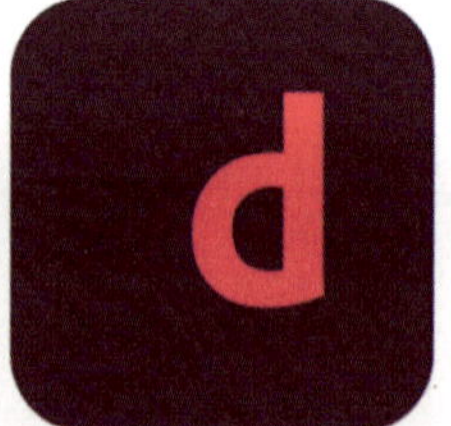

Alex Medina, 2021.

Getting Paid
Let's imagine you just graduated as a designer and ready to get that first job to repay those student loans. How much money can you expect to make? Unfortunately, salaries are not standardized for graphic designers, and can show huge differences per country, per discipline, even within a studio. Some graphic design jobs might not even pay the rent, while others allow you to live comfortably. A junior designer will be modestly paid and usually once you become more experienced you will likely get a raise. Until a certain point, because the upper echelons of the design industry, where the highest salaries are earned, are largely the domain of those with a background in business or marketing.

When it comes to studio work, the unwritten rule is, 'the more money a client spends the less freedom they permit', Shaughnessy admits.[23] Designers who work for corporate clients are likely to earn more, while designers working in the cultural field or for non-profits often make less. Salary not only depends on the type of clients and the studio, they are still subject to outdated power structures.

I have a beast of a project going to the printer on Sunday night, I've been working on it nights & weekends for 4 weeks, along with all my other regular freelance and my full time job.

ANONYMOUS DESIGNER

This is most visible in the wage gap between women and men, and between different ethnicities. Women in the US earn on average 79 percent of what their male colleagues make. For women of colour the pay gap is even greater, with 64 percent for African American women and 56 percent for Latina women, compared to white men in the same job.[24] Although this issue is increasingly being brought forward, much work is still to be done to achieve equal pay.

Exploitation at Work

According to the *Oxford Dictionary*, exploitation is 'the action or fact of treating someone unfairly in order to benefit from their work', The most obvious example of exploitation is when the employer or client takes advantage of designers by demanding unpaid work, unpaid overtime, or working nights or weekends. A survey from 2013 by Brave New Alps among graphic designers in Italy found that 56 percent of overtime was not paid or paid only occasionally.[25] It is problematic for many reasons if designers need to rely on financial support from family or friends to survive, which suggests only people from affluent backgrounds can practice design. One of the reasons why graphic designers are perhaps less aware of exploitation, is that they are passionate about what they do. 'Designers also feel very grateful to be within the so-called creative class, which can easily lead to people being taken advantage of,' writes Christopher Lacy from the Evening Class collective.[26]

The truth is, exploitation at work is not just about unpaid work and working overtime. One of the ways designers, and other workers are exploited is by wages. You would think that signing a labour contract is a free choice. After all you are free to choose to sign the contract or not. But is it really a free choice if we have to choose between work and starvation? That is why wage labour was also called wage slavery in efforts to mobilize people against it, without comparing it to the conditions of slavery. Wage slavery is a more hidden form of exploitation, which comes from the unequal relationship between employer and employee. As Shaugnessy points out, 'The art colleges are producing record numbers of graduates and this means there is unlikely a shortage of talent—in fact, there's a glut.'[27] Employers can demand certain wages and work conditions, if there are plenty of others who would take the job instead. What seems like a choice made from our free will, is in fact a system of exploitation that few can escape from.

Marx put forward another theory of exploitation, which also discusses the nature of the wage itself: surplus value. Let's go back to the medieval workshop, where the shoemaker calculates the

The art colleges are producing record numbers of graduates and this means there is unlikely a shortage of talent—in fact, there's a glut.

ADRIAN SHAUGNESSY, DESIGNER

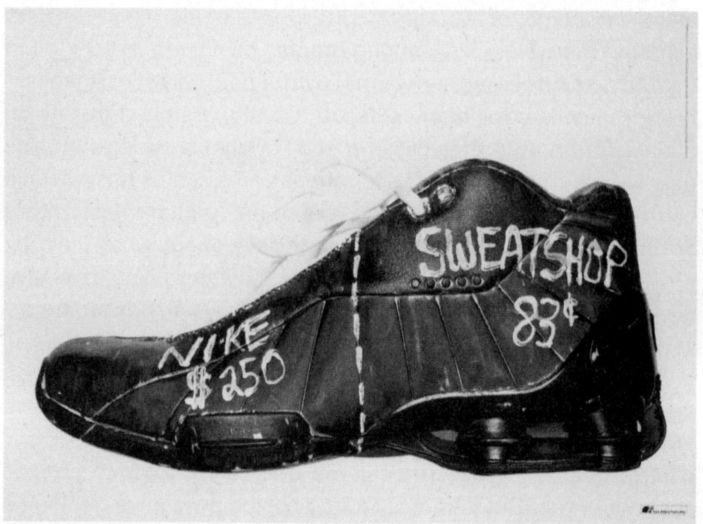

Chris Gergley, Maquila Solidarity Network, *Adbusters*, 2005.

price of the shoe based on the hours spent and the materials used. Income and costs are transparent, because designer, producer, and salesperson all work under the same roof. With the capitalist division of labour, the relation between the price of the shoe and the wages of the maker of the shoe is a lot murkier. Let's say a pair of sneakers costs $100 in the store, but the worker who made them gets paid 75 cents.[28] So while the worker receives less than one percent of the sales price, most of the profit goes to marketing and retail, the CEO's annual $13.9 million salary, and the shareholders.

In this form of exploitation, the employer or seller siphons off most of the value that the worker creates, and uses it to their benefit. Going back to design, if you make $25 an hour, and your boss sells your labour to the client for $60, you are being exploited because your boss pockets the difference. Whether he uses that money to invest it in new computers or to buy a new sports car is irrelevant. He does it with value that you created, not him. That difference between the value the worker creates and the selling price of the product is surplus value.[29] Another way surplus value is created, is by fluctuating value in the market place, by for example speculation or increased demand. While the worker who made the sneaker is paid the same, a high demand for a rare sneaker could inflate the price allowing sellers or investors to profit a lot more from the sneaker than the worker who made it.

The neoclassical economists don't agree. Nobel Memorial Prize winner economist Gary Becker explained the unequal wage system as a consequence of human capital. These are the economically relevant qualities of workers, such as education, IQ, dexterity, experience, and personality.[30] In other words, if workers want to be paid better, they should seek extra schooling, get training, or take better care of their bodies. The theory of human capital aims to improve productivity by dehumanizing workers, reducing them to their economic qualities. Corporate human resources departments are set up to do exactly that, increasing human capital within the capitalist enterprise.

While the reigning economic perspective places the responsibility for better wages on the workers' ability to improve mental and physical qualities, the shareholders who reap the profits stay out of the picture. Surplus value and profits are so important to capitalism because companies can only grow and make a profit by maximizing what they can take from each worker. This way every boss is inclined to pay their employees as little as possible, and sell their labour to the client at the highest possible price, just in the case of the sneaker where only one percent of the price is labour costs. Even if a benevolent employer would refuse to exploit workers, the company would go under from the pressure of others who don't mind paying lower wages. This is how capitalism nudges employers to partake in exploitative behaviour even if it goes against their own beliefs.

Capitalists argue that surplus value is necessary to make the company grow, which in turn would hire more workers, and lead to higher standard of living for everyone, also known as trickle-down economics. In reality most of the wealth tends to pile up at the top with a small percentage of business owners. A UN report showed that inequality has increased in most developed countries since 1990,[31] and the world's richest one percent have now twice as much wealth as 6.9 billion people combined.[32] The CEOs of the most valuable US companies made 312 times more than the average worker in 2018, while in 1965 the salary of a CEO was 20 times the average worker salary, and 41 times in 1983.[33] The next time you cash your pay check, think about how much of the value you created went to your bosses' pockets.

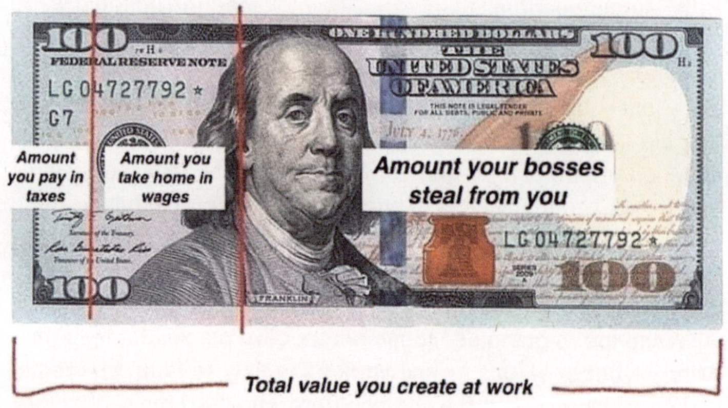

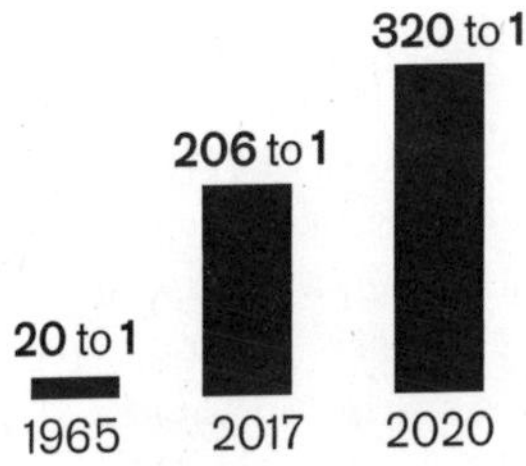

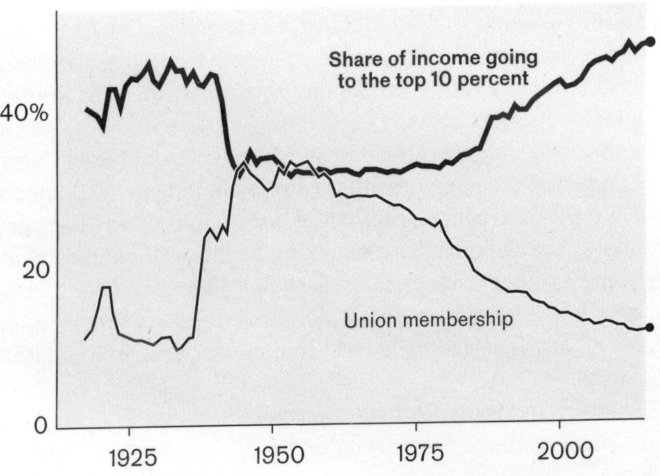

Unpaid Internships

The first work experience of a graphic designer is often an internship. In most design schools, students do a three- to six-month internship at the end of their study, which is usually paid, but also often unpaid. The reality is that some studios, especially those doing cultural or pro bono work, can only remain financially solvent by having multiple unpaid interns at all times employed at the studio.

I know many designers who justify unpaid internships because they themselves had one. Rather than perpetuating this practice, we should normalize paid internship labour.

AGGIE TOPPINS, DESIGNER

'Graphic design volunteer wanted', read a 2017 job posting by the South Australian Health and Medical Research Institute (SAHMRI). Or in their words: 'A great opportunity for a Graphic Design student who wishes to gain some great experience and start an exciting portfolio of their work.' There are even auctions for high value internships, where students pay money for an internship; a six-week internship at the UN was sold for $22,000. These are some of the examples of exploitative practices mentioned by the Precarious Workers Brigade, a UK collective that wrote *Training for Exploitation?*, a guide for art and design teachers to inform students about exploitation.[34]

There are no statistics about unpaid internships, but Brave New Alps conducted a survey among designers in Italy in 2013 which found that 55.6 percent of internships were unpaid, and 40.6 percent of graphic design interns could not survive without receiving help from parents or friends to cover their living costs. In attempts to shame and blame those who still offer unpaid internships, a number of surveys have been held that collect data from interns themselves.

Payinterns.nyc is a website that list design studios that pay their interns more than the NYC living wage, and others have helped to increase the pressure on studios to stop unpaid internships. Designer, writer, and teacher Aggie Toppins wrote a passionate plea to designers in 2018: 'I know many designers who justify unpaid internships because they themselves had one. Rather than perpetuating this practice, we should normalize paid internship labour.' She points out that unpaid internships shift the burden of living costs to family and friends, which means only the more affluent students can afford it. If entry-level positions in design are only available to the privileged few, design as a discipline will become

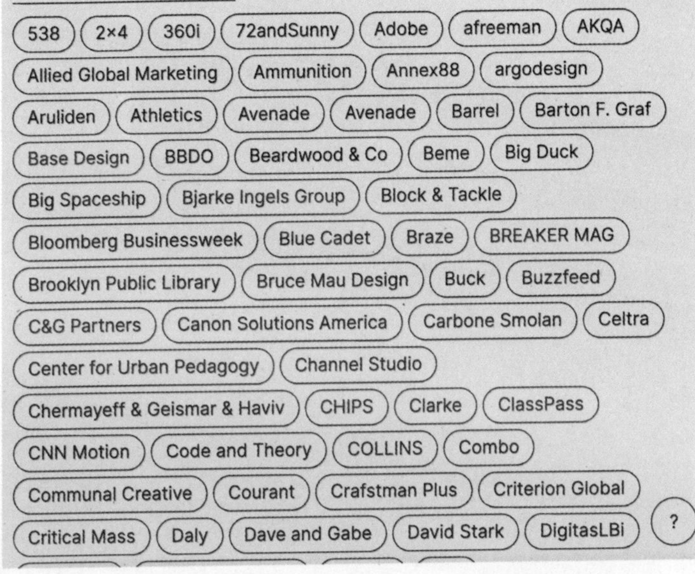

Website payinterns.nyc

more inaccessible to those with a working-class background.[35]

Unpaid internships are unethical, but we should be careful to see salary as the only factor of exploitative internships. Some are paid, but are forced to work a lot of overtime, perform tasks that are not design-related such as cleaning and cooking, or are subjected to other forms of exploitation such as abuse, intimidation, or bullying. Unpaid internships should be outlawed, but other types of exploitation should be reported and dealt with similarly.

Salary Transparency and Collective Bargaining

After your internship you manage to get a job interview. However, the salary is not listed on the application. What do you do? You will have to bargain with your future employer about the starting salary, even though you—recent graduate, no job experience—have no

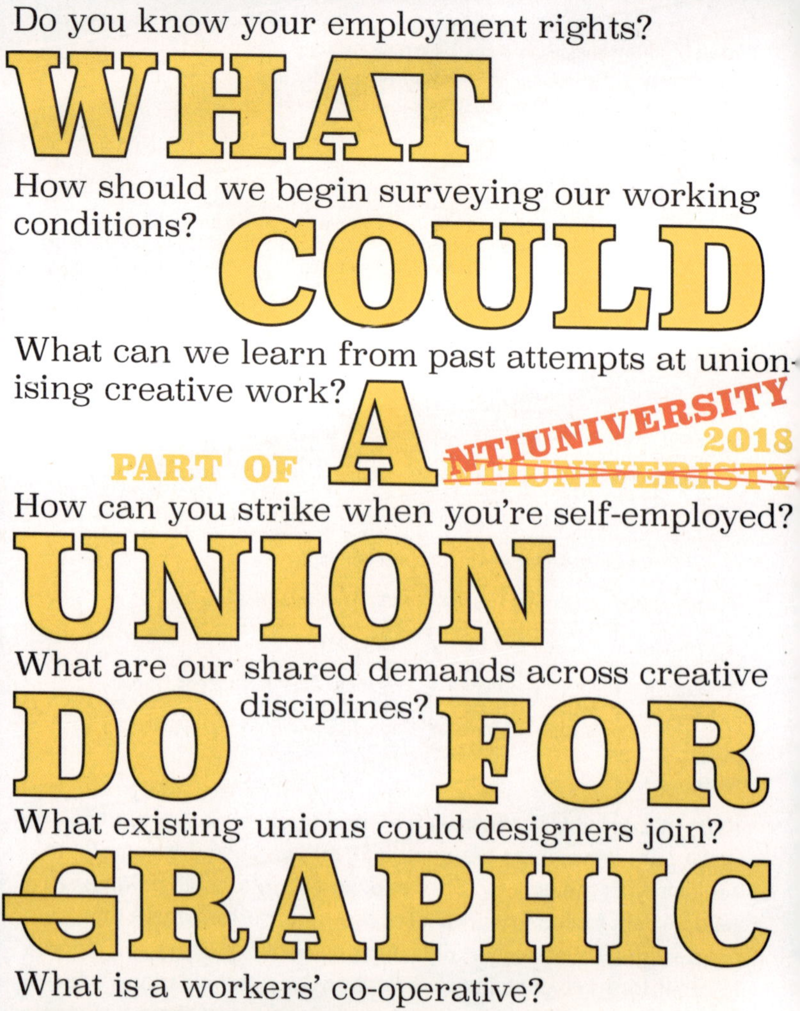

Do you know your employment rights?

WHAT

How should we begin surveying our working conditions?

COULD

What can we learn from past attempts at unionising creative work?

A

ANTIUNIVERSITY 2018

How can you strike when you're self-employed?

UNION

What are our shared demands across creative disciplines?

DO   FOR

What existing unions could designers join?

GRAPHIC

What is a workers' co-operative?

DESIGN?

Thursday 14th June, 7.00—9.30pm
Evening Class: 48 Aberfeldy St, London E14 0NU

Poster by Evening Class, 2018.

idea how much you can ask. Speaking from experience, bargaining for a salary can be pretty intimidating.

Undisclosed salaries, or salary cloaking as it is called, is the practice of not listing salaries in job applications. Employers do have a number in mind, but not disclosing it gives them the advantage to bargain for lower salaries. Research has shown that negotiating salaries disadvantages women, people of colour, and people with families to support.[36] Collectives such as Evening Class in the UK have demanded the ending of undisclosed salaries, as they write in their open letter against the practice:

> Graduates just out of university should not be expected to be experienced enough to be able to 'negotiate' a fair wage. The possibility of being listened to, or being successful when negotiating, is…subject to gender, race, and class privileges—particularly when there is no initial figure to negotiate with.[37]

The only way to arm yourself against this is to speak to other workers and come to collective agreements. You can begin by asking your friends or colleagues how much they are paid, or ask your employer to disclose salaries. If you are looking to find out if you are paid fairly, you can start by looking up average salaries for designers in your country. Many trade organizations have guidelines for salaries, which employers can abide by but are not required to do so.

Knowing that you have been exploited by employers at some point in your life might come as a bit of a shock. If we need to work to survive, how can we possibly have any influence on how we work and how we are paid? There are different ways, ranging from easy to more advanced: getting together with colleagues, organizing in cooperatives, unionizing, refusing work, strikes, and so on. Strategies and ideas to circumvent or resist the exploitative effects of capitalism as a designer will be discussed at the end of this chapter.

WORK IT HARDER DO IT FASTER

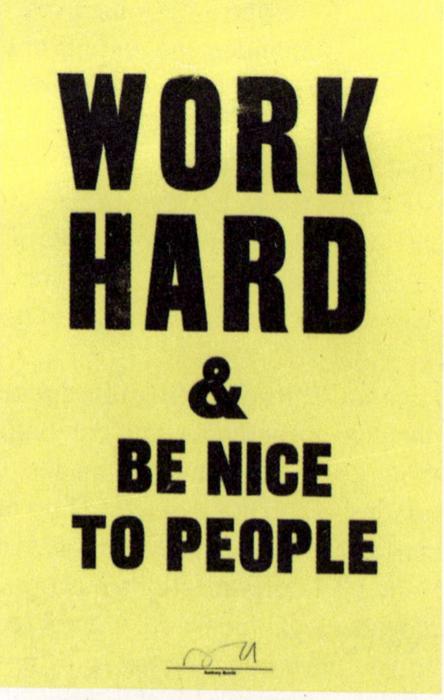

Poster by Anthony Burrill.

In a supermarket, graphic designer Anthony Burrill overheard an old lady sharing her secret to a happy life with the young woman at the checkout: 'Work hard and be nice to people.'[38] This inspired him to make hand-printed posters with the same slogan, which became a genuine graphic design bestseller. Similar inspirational quotes about working hard now adorn many walls at co-working spaces and start-ups. Facebook employees receive a 'Little Red Book', in which one of the spread reads 'The Quick Shall Inherit the Earth' in capital letters. Graphic designer Ben Barry produced inspirational posters that read 'Work it Harder' and 'Do It Faster', which hang in Facebook's offices.[39]

These motivational slogans are not just hollow rhetoric. According to the statistics, graphic designers are hard workers. 58 percent of graphic designers work more than fifty hours a week in the UK, even though a work week cannot legally be longer than forty-eight hours.[40] 53 percent of designers work forty hours or more in the Netherlands,[41] and in the US more than a third of designers work forty to fifty hours a week, and eight percent up to sixty hours.[42] Evening Class even speaks about a culture of overwork that permeates the design industry.

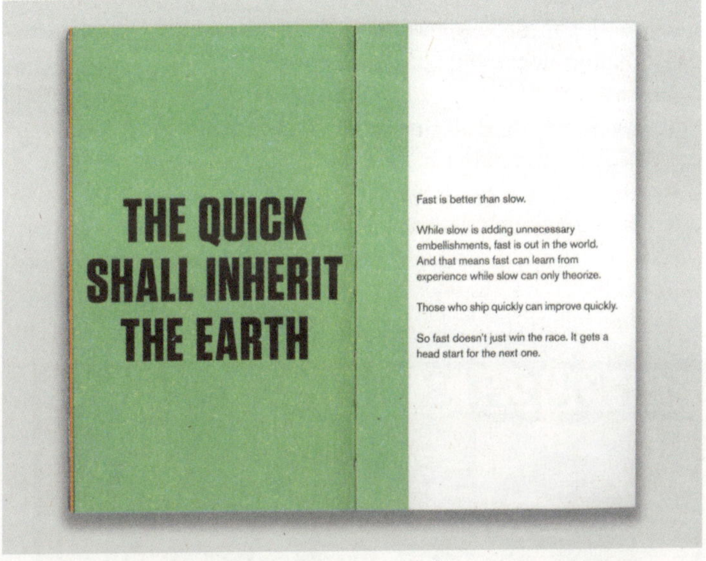

Booklet for Facebook employees, by Ben Barry.

Why do designers work so hard? First of all, the design community prides itself on hard work. Experienced designers often boast in interviews about pulling all-nighters and working non-stop. For young designers this comes as a warning that working hard is not only expected, it is essential to advance your career. Designer Duncan Brazzil said

As a young designer, I believe that overworking is almost essential for success. A 9-5 job is not always enough time to learn or experiment with our practice, so I would almost argue that the hours after work can be vital in working towards 'success', especially within the creative industries.[43]

The persistent claim that hard work is a cultural phenomenon of design culture, is affirmed by Shaughnessy: 'If you were to try and take those long hours away from them, they would resist. It's part of the joy of doing something that they love.'[44]

An excess of designers graduating and entering the job market has created an even more pressing culture of competition. Some offices promote in-house competitions by letting designers compete for jobs, leading to situations where designers steal the presentation documents of their colleagues, presenting them as if they were their own. Toxic cultures of mistrust and envy among employees are the stuff that burnouts are made of. Coaches and psychologist are called in to help, and otherwise meditation or yoga are popular ways to relieve stress. Others resort to time management techniques such as the Pomodoro Technique to increase productivity. These coping mechanisms do not address the root of the problem, but view psychological pressures at work as a form of individual failure.

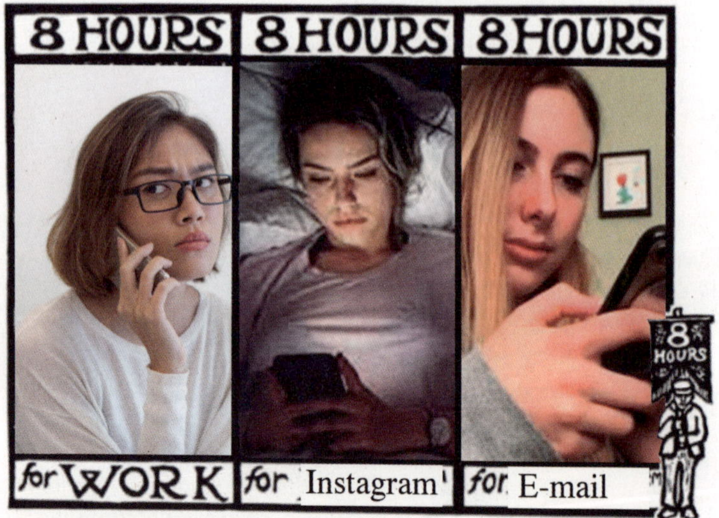

↑   Meme by Ruben Pater, 2020.
→   Google Calendar.

I feel my body and mind deteriorating from the stress, the unfair wages and overall unethical practices they participate in. It's taking a toll. Can anyone else relate?

ANONYMOUS DESIGNER

Micromanagement

'Moments are the elements of profit' wrote Marx. Since the dawn of capitalism, employers have tried everything to make workers work as long and as hard as possible. When watches were still uncommon, some factory clocks in the UK were 'adjusted' to run slower on purpose to steal time from workers. The invention of the assembly line quickly exposed individuals who worked too slow, as the line would be held up and work would pile up. The speed of the production line now dictated the work pace.

Time has always been subject to manipulation and control to optimize it for capitalism. For example, the invention of time zones in 1884 enabled an efficient international trade system, and daylight saving time was enacted in 1916 in the US after intense corporate lobbying. One extra hour of sunlight meant more time to shop, and more time to play golf.[45] Today, employers can monitor workers by the millisecond. Popular software among employers

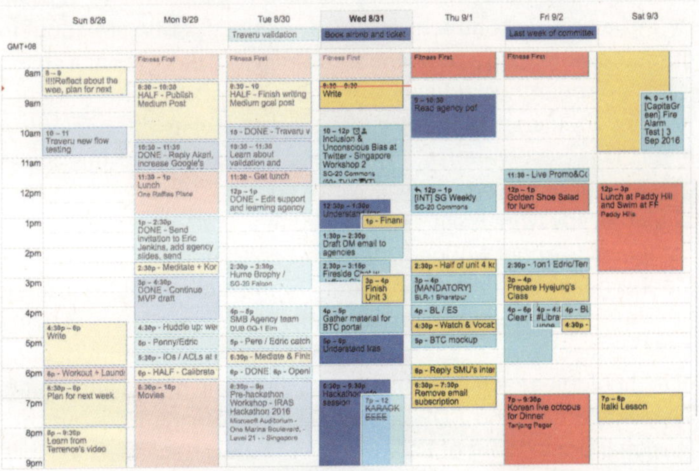

are dashboards that monitor tasks and work speed and efficiency, ranking employees and sending warnings if they miss targets or deadlines.

The economist John Maynard Keynes predicted in 1930 that his grandchildren would only work 15 hours a week, thanks to technological developments. We have seen tremendous technological innovation, but many designers are still working about forty hours a week on average. Actually, productivity has steadily increased since the 1970s. Statistics show that an average worker in the US produces $40 more value per hour than in 1970, even after adjustment for inflation.[46] Compare that to the work ethic of the pre-industrial foraging societies like the Ju/'houansi from eastern Namibia. Anthropologists observed these hunter-gatherers in 1966, and found they spend only 15 hours a week finding food,[47] using the rest of the time for rest, or leisure. Similar anthropological research shows that hunter-gatherers worked a lot less than the average person today.

A Job is Better Than No Job

Have you ever been laid off or afraid of losing your job? You are not the only one. According to the 2019 AIGA survey, 56 percent of graphic designers are a little concerned about losing their job, and 16 percent are very concerned.[48] Permanent contracts in design are becoming rarer, ever since neoliberal politics have pushed for more flexible contracts. For many designers who are about to graduate, obtaining a permanent contract as a designer at a studio is in some countries as likely as winning the lottery.

Early industrial capitalism was already faced with unemployment. This 'reserve army' of workers, as Marx called them, was essential to keep wages down. With a pool of unemployed workers available, any worker can be replaced at a whiff, whether they are complaining about working conditions or asking for higher wages. Marx argues that this reserve army of unemployed is necessary, otherwise wages would rise and profits would drop.[49]

Most layoffs in design have been the result of the introduction of technologies such as desktop publishing and digital publishing. The web, email, and PDF communication formats have put professional printers out of business over the last decade. Of course,

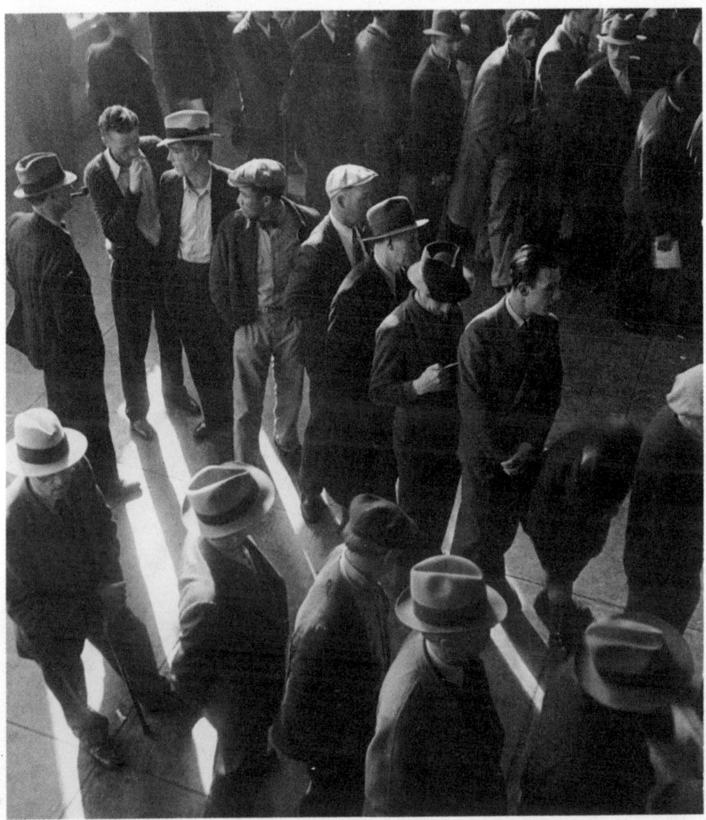

Jobless men lined up to file claims for unemployment compensation, 1939–1946. Photo by Dorothea Lange.

these technologies make design also more competitive, but for how long? Many miners were laid off in Northern Europe in the 1980s, but that didn't mean coal production stopped, it was just moved to low-wage countries. 'The competitive advantage', writes Daniel van der Velden, 'will quickly become a thing of the past, if holding a mouse proves cheaper in Beijing than in the west of Holland'.[50]

On a psychological level being laid off is a traumatic experience, especially because today's neoliberal society has disciplined us to blame ourselves. 'I was fired', is now interpreted as 'I faced a crisis and I had a decision to make', writes sociologist Richard Sennett.[51] This view is common among designers as well. 'If your search for a job is going badly, you must urgently reassess. You must search for ways of refining your presentation,'[52] says Shaughnessy. In other words, we internalize a structural lack of jobs as a personal failure, and we'll do anything, learn coding, learn new software, improve our portfolio, optimizing and questioning all aspects of our personality in the hope that our luck will turn. Design students at Kingston University in London can even take classes in which they learn to modify their 'body language to not only appeal more to an employer, but to increase [their] confidence too!'[53]

The Happy Show
Design is obsessed with positivity. A big part of graphic design is making companies, events, and objects appear more joyful using positive associations. Design studios are the example of 'fun' workplaces with football tables, colourful knickknacks, and inspirational posters. Designers are also expected to project a sense of happiness themselves at all times. 'Niceness' is considered a necessary quality in the creative industries today, as Silvio Lorusso comments.[54] In order to find work, designers are expected to keep developing, improving and optimizing personal and professional profiles. To stay hireable and competitive, designers have to exhibit positivity and personal growth using frequent social media updates and networking events. Forcing oneself to exhibit positivity and success for long periods of time takes its toll. In the UK depression is now the most treated condition by the NHS.[55] The Designers' Inquiry by Brave New Alps from 2013 among Italian designers mentions that 44 percent experienced stress, 30 percent had anxiety or panic attacks, and 73 percent suffered from depression. A survey of 767 designers is not representative for the entire design discipline, but the rates are still alarmingly high.[56]

The philosopher Mark Fisher pointed out that the rise in mental health issues is a result of capitalism's demand for workers to continually self-improve. He observed 'that only the affluent are winners and that access to the top is open to anyone willing to work hard enough', and 'if you do not succeed, there is only one person to blame'.[57] Mental health programmes at work are mostly focused on alcohol and drug addiction, and are only focused on employees' individual mental health as long as it boosts their productivity.[58]

The individual is supposed to cope with the stress in a labour market where flexibility and confidence are seen as necessary qualities.

Unattainable productivity benchmarks have created a culture of efficiency aimed at economic growth at the expense of the well-being of workers. With smartphones the concept of downtime is disappearing. We are expected to always be available for employers or clients. As a Dutch business expert boasted: 'Stress is not a matter of not having enough time, it is a matter of prioritizing.' The design world should be more alert and responsible about rising mental health issues, as they remain largely undiscussed. After the barrage of criticism presented in this chapter on the working conditions of designers, it's about time we take a step back and keep in mind that work in its current structure is not likely to disappear overnight.

44 percent of designers had experienced stress, 30 percent had experienced anxiety or panic attacks, and 73 percent suffered from depression.

BRAVE NEW ALPS SURVEY

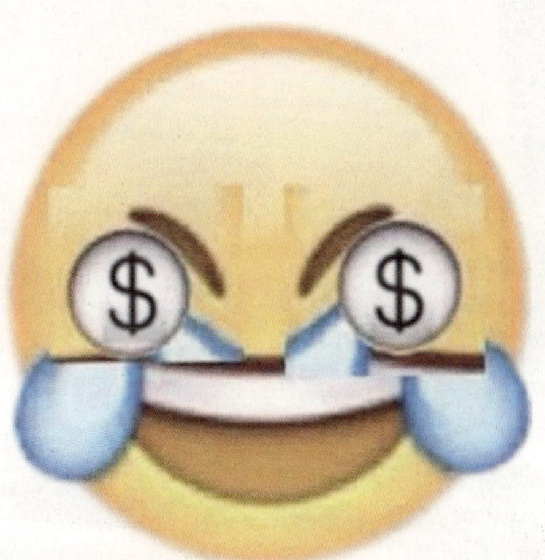

↑   Variant of the cursed emoji meme by Ruben Pater, 2021.
→   See Red Women's Workshop, 'Capitalism also depends on domestic labour', 1975.

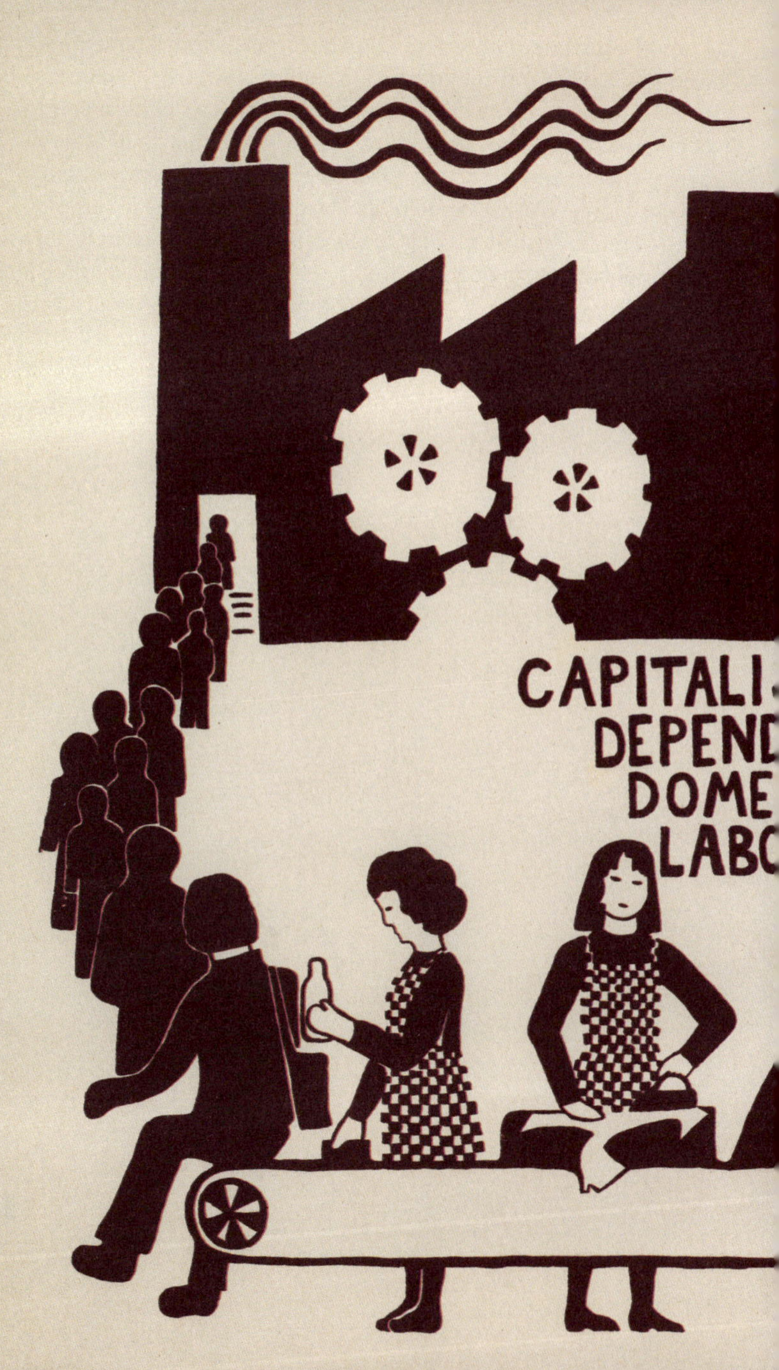
CAPITALI...
DEPEND...
DOME...
LABO...

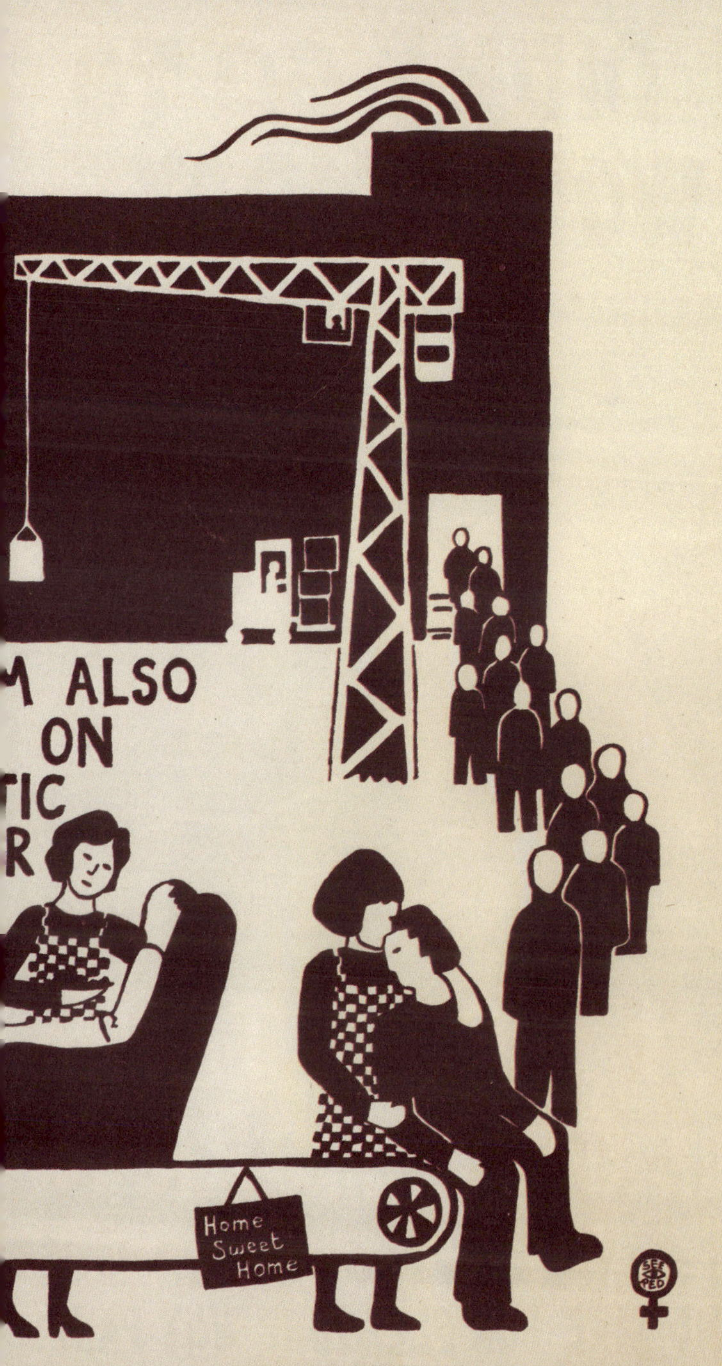
M ALSO
ON
TIC
R
Home
Sweet
Home

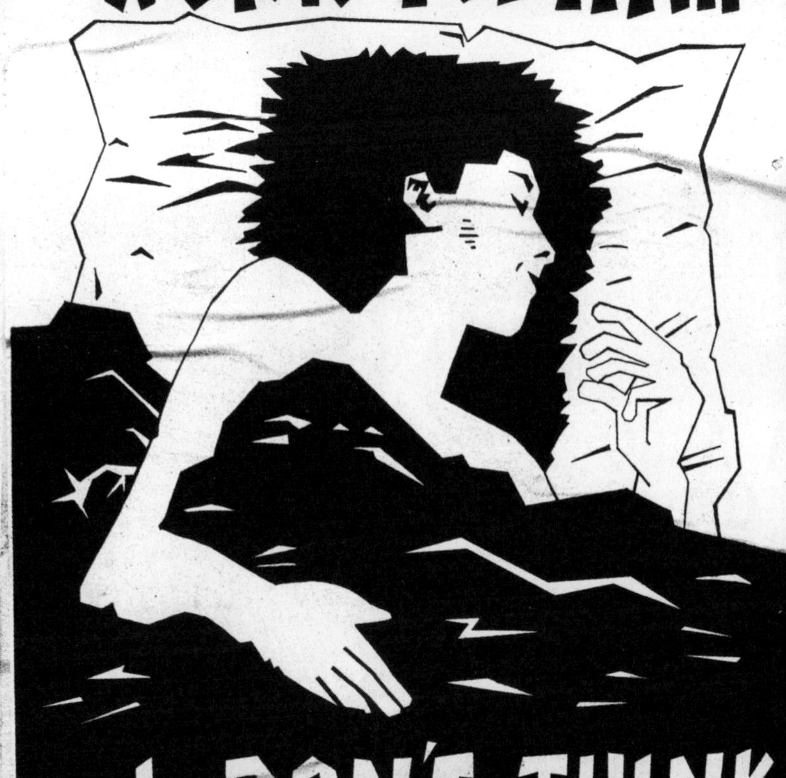

I DIDN'T GO TO WORK TODAY...
... I DON'T THINK I'LL GO TOMORROW
LET'S TAKE CONTROL OF OUR LIVES
AND LIVE FOR PLEASURE NOT PAIN

THE END OF WORK

In 1953 the artist Guy Debord painted the text 'Ne travaillez jamais' (never work) on a wall on the Rue de Seine in Paris. In a letter he explained the graffiti by saying 'the great majority of people work, and that said work is, despite the strongest repulsion, imposed on the near totality of workers by a crushing constraint'.[59] Work has always been part of human existence, and unequal power structures have inevitably led to bad working conditions. This has been the case under feudalism, capitalism, and communism. In its present form, the capitalist exploitation at work is not likely to disappear soon. Everyone has to survive, so ideas about non-exploitative forms of work are desperately needed. Here we will look into some strategies and alternatives that have been imagined.

The Right to Be Lazy

In a world focused on efficiency and productivity, the most radical form of political action is maybe doing nothing at all. History is full of example of laziness in response to strict work ethics, in what Kathi Weeks adequately calls 'a parallel history' of work.[60] Bums, beatniks, slackers, or hippies, invented their own acts of anti-work resistance in their small but important ways. There is nothing more frustrating to those in power than people who have no demands, no alternatives, and simply do nothing.

In ancient Greece, idleness was appreciated for its creative potential. Manual labour was something for women, peasants, and slaves. A citizen—which meant a wealthy man—would engage in something called *praxis*: stimulating activities such as education, philosophy, and political life. Even though the Greeks' distaste for work could only exist by virtue of the exploitation of others, it has inspired many thinkers to denounce the morality of hard work, and to make a plea for laziness or hedonism. Paul Lafargue, who was

← Poster by Ekomedia for *Fifth Estate* magazine, 1987.

Karl Marx' son-in-law, even wrote a book about it called *The Right to Be Lazy* (1880), in which he argued for laziness as a prerequisite for progress. He suggested to limit work to three hours a day.[61]

The utopia of a world without work, such as the Greeks and Lafargue envisioned, sounds very tempting. There is a surging movement for a universal basic income (UBI), an unconditional income for everyone, so at least basic needs are met. People would still work, but not just to survive, but mostly because they want to, which changes the conditions of work entirely. The issue around the UBI is complicated, but what it does at least, is to affirm that everyone contributes to society, unrelated to someone's employment, gender, or social status.

The only problem is that these ideas come from a European perspective, built on the exploitation of colonized peoples and lands. A future high-tech utopia might make a three-hour work day possible for a privileged few (with or without a basic income), but it will most likely not be a utopia for all. Fantasizing about a world without work while unfair and exploitative labour conditions are still rampant, is highly Eurocentric, writes Andrea Komlosy.[62] That doesn't mean the UBI or forms of more equal taxation won't work. But unless these are implemented worldwide, people in the Global South will continue to be exploited for cheap manufacturing.

A more ethical approach would be to resist the culture of productivity and efficiency as a goal in itself. What we can learn from the bums, hippies, and dropouts before us is that we, in Lafargue's words, have a right to not to be productive. In graphic design everyone seems busy with the next big thing. Designers are expected to have new work to show, new lectures to finish, more Instagram posts, or attend to that new client's work, feeding this unsatiable hunger of novelty which only leads to more work, feelings of anxiety and stress. Acknowledging that this is not a possibility for many designers, if our work situation permits us to do less, we could choose to be less focused on work and more on creating other forms of value for ourselves and our communities.

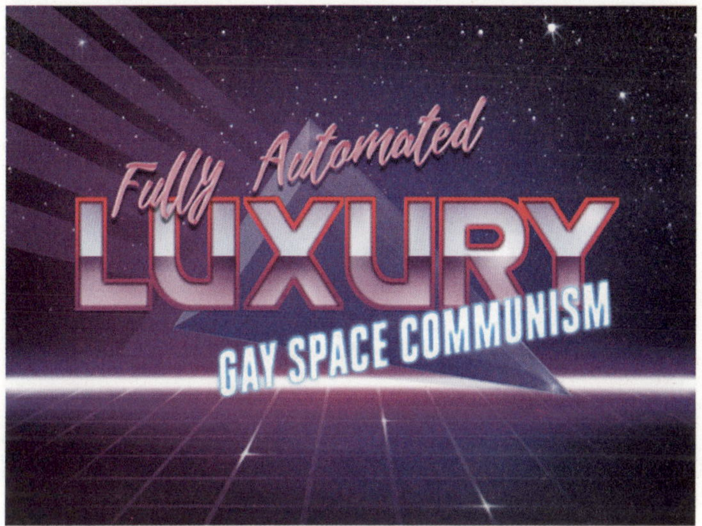

Fully Automated Luxury Gay Space Communism meme, 2017.

The refusal of work is a refusal of the ideology of work as highest calling and moral duty, a refusal of work as the necessary center of social life and means of access to the rights and claims of citizenship, and a refusal of the necessity of capitalist control of production.

KATHI WEEKS, THEORIST

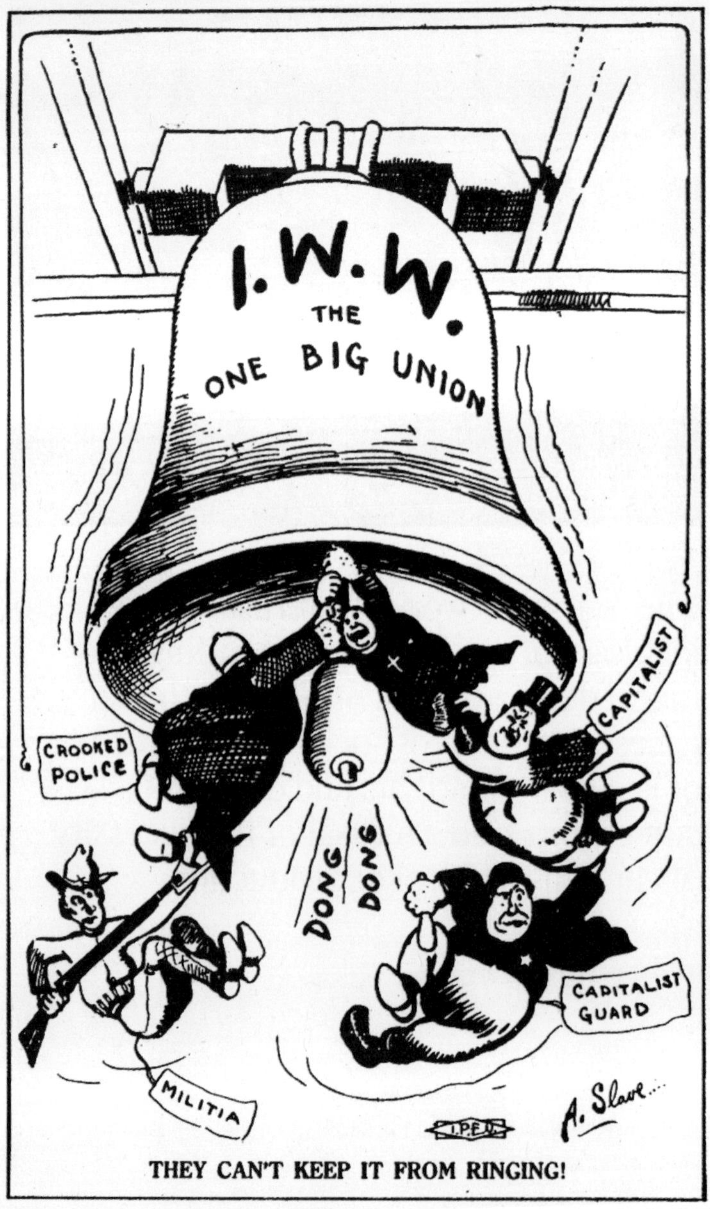

Cartoon from the Industrial Worker by A. Slave, 1912.

SHOWING SOLIDARITY

Until alternative structures are realized, there are practical actions that can improve conditions in the workplace in the meantime. This starts by showing solidarity with co-workers. Solidarity as a term might sound abstract and isn't heard that much anymore today. The Precarious Workers Brigade writes: 'To re-introduce solidarity into educational conversations about work is to offer an alternative that does not otherwise seem to exist. Under the neoliberal logic, anyone you meet, including a co-worker, is largely understood as another networking opportunity.'[63]

In other words, capitalism has tried very hard for people in the workplace to see each other as competitors instead of allies. While we are pushed on the work floor to strive for individual achievement (a pay raise, a better position), we are too busy with ourselves to think about organizing and collectively improving working conditions, which would benefit everyone. Worker solidarity means taking the responsibility to talk to your co-workers or fellow freelancers about getting paid, overwork, work conflicts, and other forms of exploitation. It is easier to demand better wages or less overtime if you speak on behalf of a group.[64]

Set Personal Work Rules and Boundaries
Compared to a few decades ago, work has seeped into our leisure time. Many employees are expected to be available and answer phone and email after work hours. Setting boundaries for your employer is necessary to maintain a good personal mental health. Evening Class suggests to make a list of rules for work for yourself. For example, to only check emails at certain times, to not work on weekends, to remove email notifications from your phone, to take enough holiday.

The only ones who will ever stand up for workers are other workers. Stand together and unionize.

MIKE MONTEIRO, DESIGNER

Set up a Worker Inquiry
Little or no information existed about the working lives of ordinary people until labour organizations started to collect the information themselves. Without solid understanding of working conditions, it is more difficult to demand changes. The simple act of organizing discussions, setting up surveys, questionnaires, or online forms, can help to lay bare the issues faced by workers. There is little information about how long graphic designers work, what kind of exploitation they are faced with, and what abuse and conditions exist, simply because it hasn't been documented. Recently, design collectives such as Brave New Alps in Italy and Evening Class in the UK have begun to collect information amongst designers, which has led to critical debate in the field of graphic design.[65] Professional organizations such as the AIGA are beginning to collect some data on how designers work, but we need more.

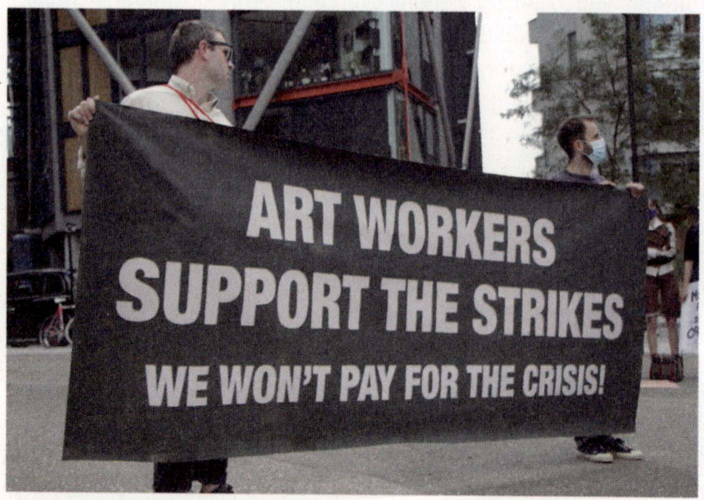

Tate workers on strike, 2020, Tate Modern, London.

Organize a Strike

Nothing makes an employer feel the power of employees like a strike. If nobody shows up for work, you'll have your boss' attention. Ultimately a strike is a stand-off: will the company go bankrupt before the strikers give up? That's why ideally in a successful strike every worker needs to be involved. Traditionally it is unions that organize strikes, because they have the funds to support workers and their families. Striking might not be effective in a small graphic design studio, as a few employees could be temporarily replaced by freelancers. For in-house designers at larger companies, or at institutions such as universities or museums, it may prove to be worthwhile. Strikes may seem old fashioned, but they do still exist! On 1 November 2018, more than 20,000 Google employees organized a worldwide walkout in a collective effort to end forced arbitration, inequality in pay, and demanding transparency about sexual harassment cases within the company.[66] In 2016, a group of Deliveroo riders in the UK went on strike for six days, to protest the company's new payment policies.[67]

Organize Solidarity Networks

A solidarity network is an organized group of people that can raise money, picket, or do other actions to assist workers in conflicts with their employer. The more people are on your side, the stronger you stand. This is helpful when you are being fired for the wrong reasons, if you did not receive a pay check, or if you are a freelancer with a client who did not pay. Workers are protected by labour laws, but the legal system is so expensive and complicated that an individual worker has little chance of success in pursuing legal action against their employer. Solidarity networks can drum up a crowd of people that can pressure employers more effectively. *Vloerwerk* in Amsterdam is a solidarity network that helps employees or freelancers in work conflicts by using direct action, and is very successfully in reclaiming unpaid wages or demanding pay for freelancers, or getting people their jobs back if they were wrongfully dismissed.[68] Just by organizing a group of six or seven people, they have managed to put enough pressure on employers to be successful.

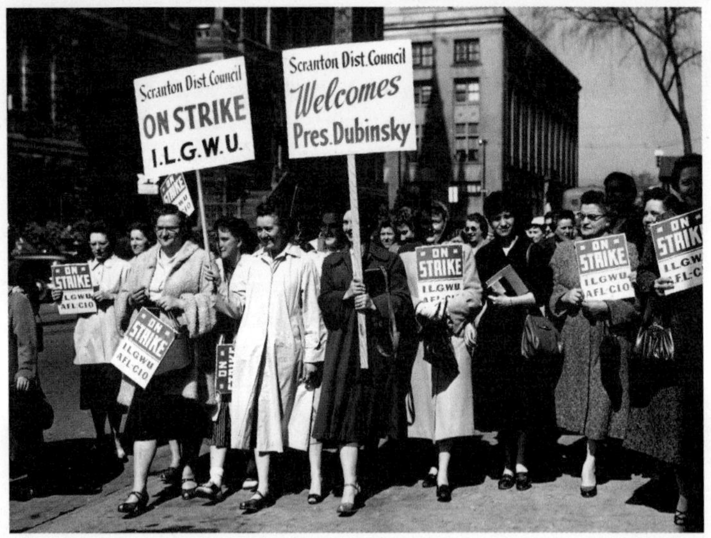

↑   International Ladies Garment Workers Union on strike, 1958.
→   Union 'bug' from the Detroit Printing Co-op.

Join a Union

Labour unions have a bad rep these days, but without them we wouldn't have weekends, pensions, company health care, or the eight-hour work day. There is a reason why unions were illegal for a long time, and why employers aren't fans of unions. In the UK, unions had to operate illegally until 1872, when they were legalized. By organizing in unions, individual workers can negotiate labour contracts or better working conditions. It was thanks to unions that blue-collar workers in the North Atlantic nations had relative good salaries and benefits until the 1980s.

When you join a union, you pay them a percentage of your salary, so they can bargain for better wages, hours, and working conditions on your behalf. There are also unions who serve freelance workers or those with flexible contracts. There are few graphic designers organized in unions today, precisely because the individual creativity and competition is seen as so central to design. Bargaining for collective hourly rates or salaries seems difficult when everyone is each other's competitor, and work conditions are so varied as in design. With online design market websites such as

Fiverr, minimal prices have plummeted and the lack of collective organization is now back to haunt graphic design.

Historically, printers and typographers were well organized in strong unions, such as the International Typographical Union (1852–1986). The ITU is the oldest labour organization in the US and secured an eight-hour work day in 1906, after spending $4 million on strike support. In 1964 the ITU counted 121,858 members in the US alone. Print work produced in unionized print shops would carry a 'union bug', a small graphic element that showed the work had been done in unionized printshops. Unions are a powerful force to help workers, but unions did not always extend their solidarity to all workers. In the nineteenth century, for example, many unions excluded women and people of colour.

If you are a designer and thinking about joining a union, or if you are interested in starting one, you can find more information at the United Voices of the World in the UK,[69] and the *Eye on Design* blog has two articles by Perrin Drumm on the subject.[70] An often heard complaint is that unions were useful for large companies and industrial manufacturing, and they no longer respond effectively to the current flexible, global, and dispersed labour market. However, several groups of creative workers and designers are setting up new unions that can assist freelance designers or those working under flexible contracts.

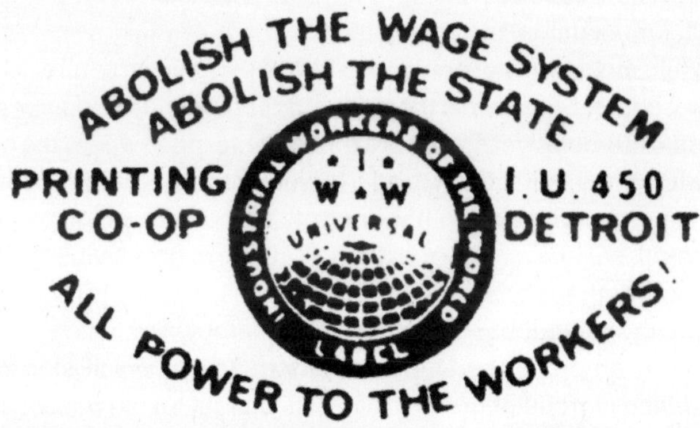

Unions also offer legal support and funding, which can serve both designers working freelance or wage labourers. In the UK, the UVW's designers + cultural workers have organized workers across the creative industries. The UVW-DCW say on their website they are: '...taking action against exploitative practices including; unfair wages, salary cloaking, unpaid overtime, illegal unpaid internships, work-related stress and burnout, and precarious freelance and temporary work'.[71]

One of the things I love about being in a co-op is having complete control over my own time.

GEMMA COPELAND, DESIGNER

Start a Business without Bosses

So far, this chapter has discussed the origins of work, the culture of design work, how designers are exploited, and how designers can improve their own work situation. At times, the writing may suggest the world is divided into workers and bosses, but that is certainly not the intention. Employers can exert power over employees through the wage system, which creates the class society as Marx described it. But there are also examples of design businesses who work without hierarchy, and manage to run a successful business based on equal relations, without exploitation. For example, the cooperative.

While most forms of enterprise have a pyramid structure, where a few people, bosses, partners, or shareholders have power over others, a cooperative (co-op) is a form of enterprise where the company is owned collectively, and everyone has equal voting power. Each member of the coop has one vote, so no one person can own the co-op, sell the co-op, or extract profit from its activities.[72] If it's run according to the seven co-op principles, a co-op is essentially a company without bosses and without hierchy.[73]

One example is the Detroit Printing Co-op, which started in 1969 when a group of political activists bought an old offset press. In their printshop anyone could use the press, but you would have to operate and fix it yourself, and not use it for profit.[74] Co-ops like the Detroit Printing Co-op were small, but co-ops can be big as well. Mondragon is a federation of worker co-ops in the Spanish Basque country, working in finance, retail, and other areas. The company is owned collectively by its 81,000 workers. One of the rules in Mondragon is that managers cannot be paid more than five times the minimum wage in their co-op. There are many co-ops that are very successful, including graphic design co-ops. The French studio Grapus was comprised of three co-ops, Design Action and the Red Sun Press in the US are co-ops, and a recent one is Common Knowledge in the UK.[75]

Co-ops are not some magic cure that will solve all possible forms of exploitation or toxic working conditions. Just as in any group of people, abuse of power can occur in many ways. It is important to point out that joining a union or setting up a cooperative also take a lot of time. Paradoxically, finding better working conditions could end up leading to more work in the short term. If every decision has to be made with consensus from all participants, the process could end up taking too much of everyone's time, which was one of the criticisms on the Occupy movement.[76] There are different strategies to overcome this, one of which is consent decision-making, used by the Common Knowledge co-op.[77] In the last chapter you can read more about practical experiences in horizontal decision-making.

The advantage of the co-op is that power is equally distributed, which makes it more difficult for one person to dominate others. A business without hierarchy can have different legal forms, and some design studios prefer a foundation, or another form, depending on the country. Setting up a co-op might sound abstract, as any organizational form tends to be. That is why the last chapter of this book features interviews with six design collectives from Europe, Latin America, and the US, who all have managed to organize a design business in more egalitarian and ethical ways.[78] Don't take my word for it, take theirs.

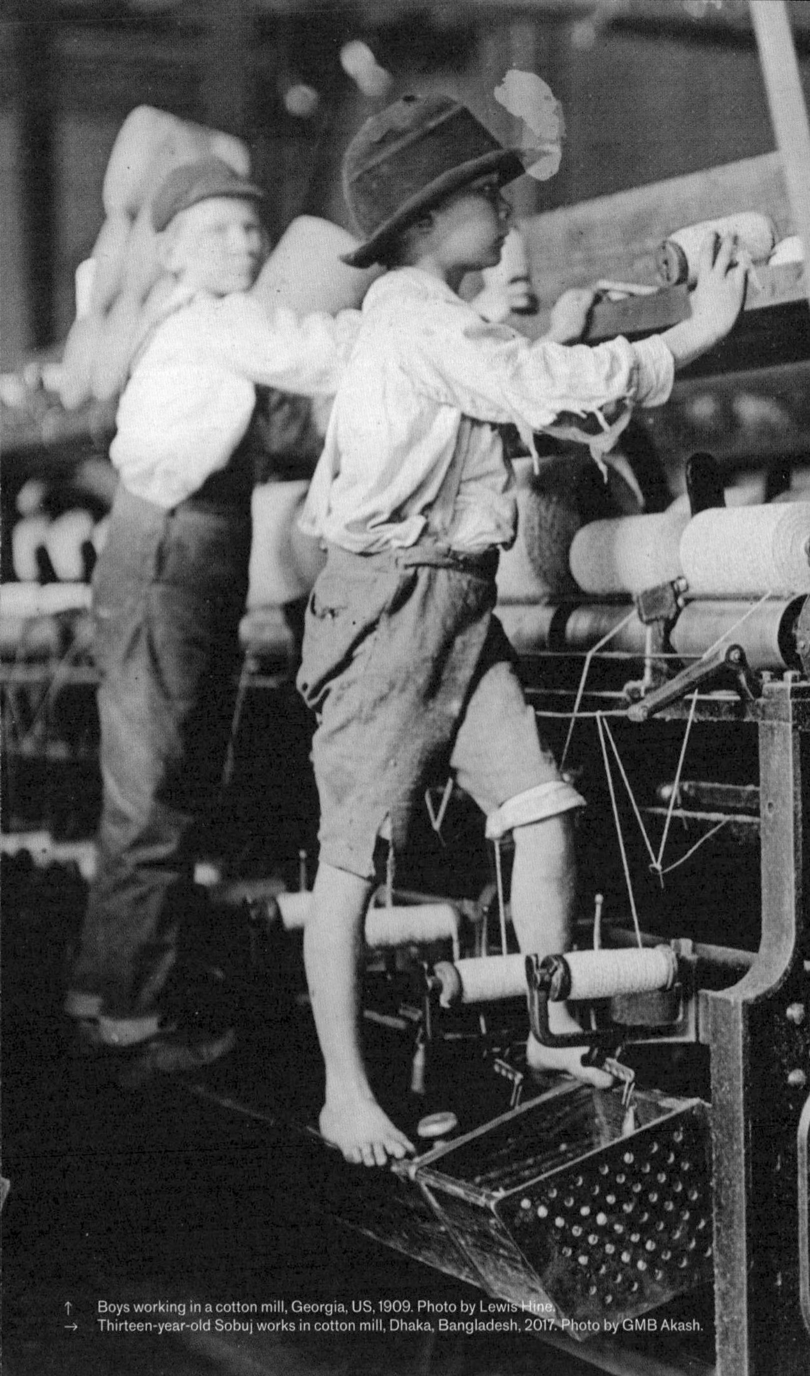

↑ Boys working in a cotton mill, Georgia, US, 1909. Photo by Lewis Hine.
→ Thirteen-year-old Sobuj works in cotton mill, Dhaka, Bangladesh, 2017. Photo by GMB Akash.

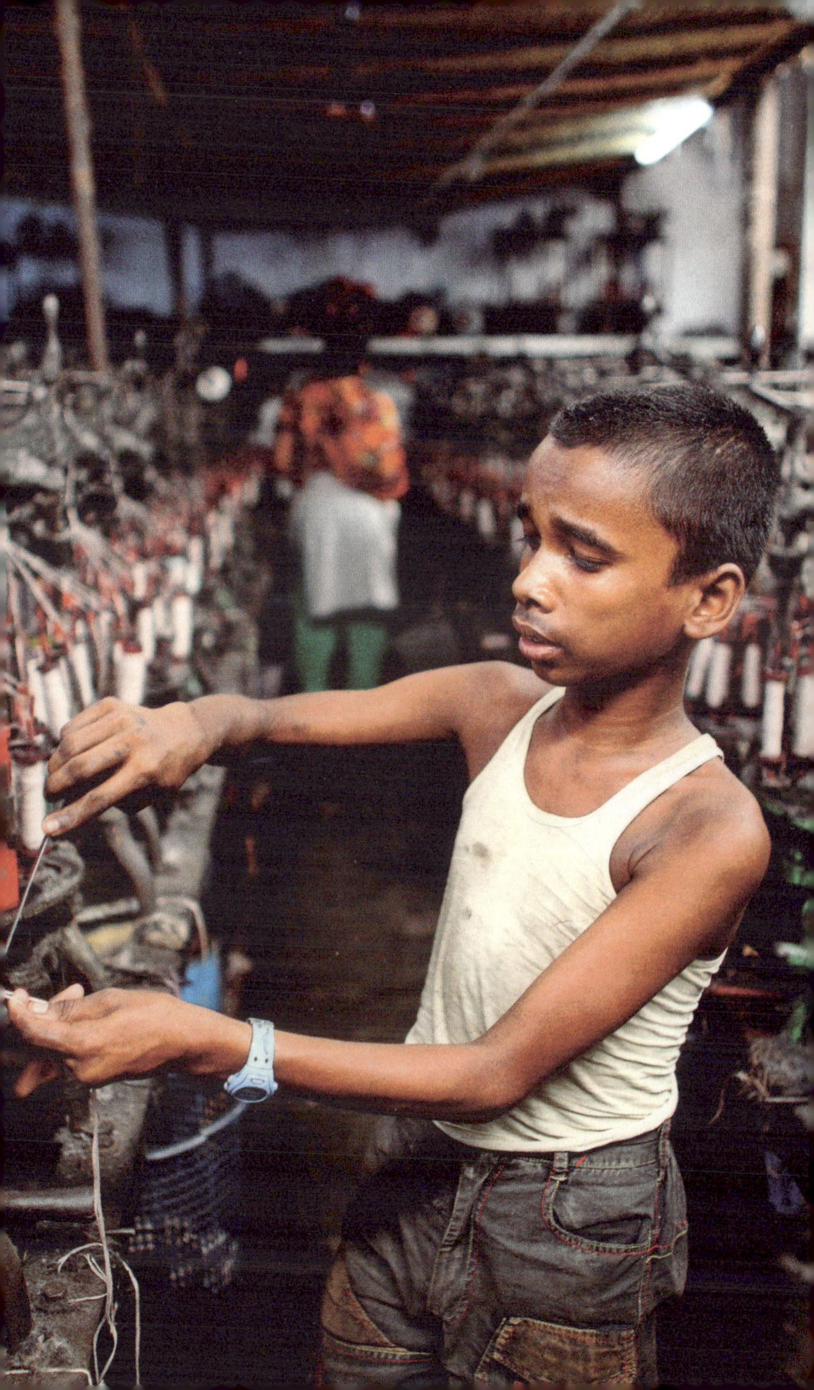

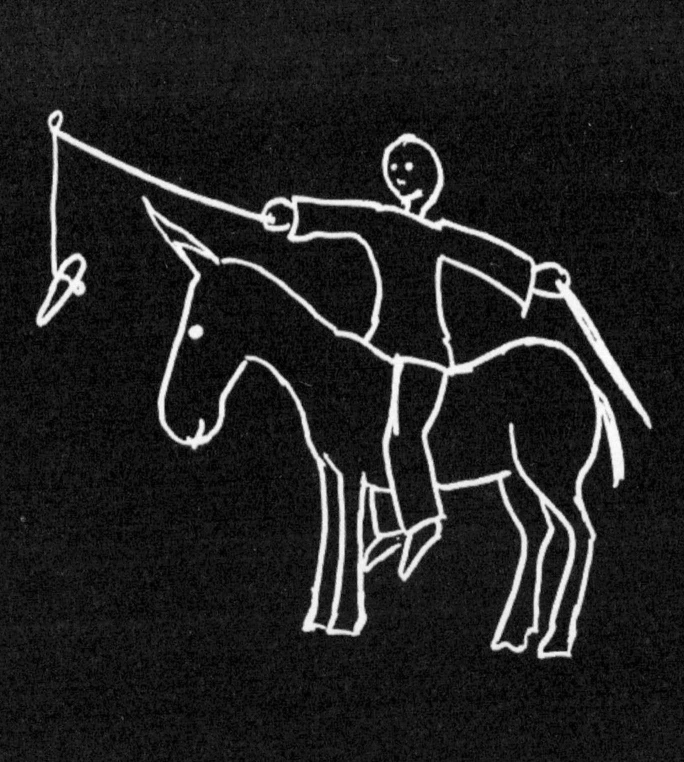

THE DESIGNER AS ENTRE- PRENEUR

You have to be burning with an idea, or a problem, or a wrong that you want to right. If you're not passionate enough from the start, you'll never stick it out.

STEVE JOBS

I am burned out and I keep getting up every morning and doing the same thing and pulling off another win working weekends but at what cost?

ANONYMOUS DESIGNER

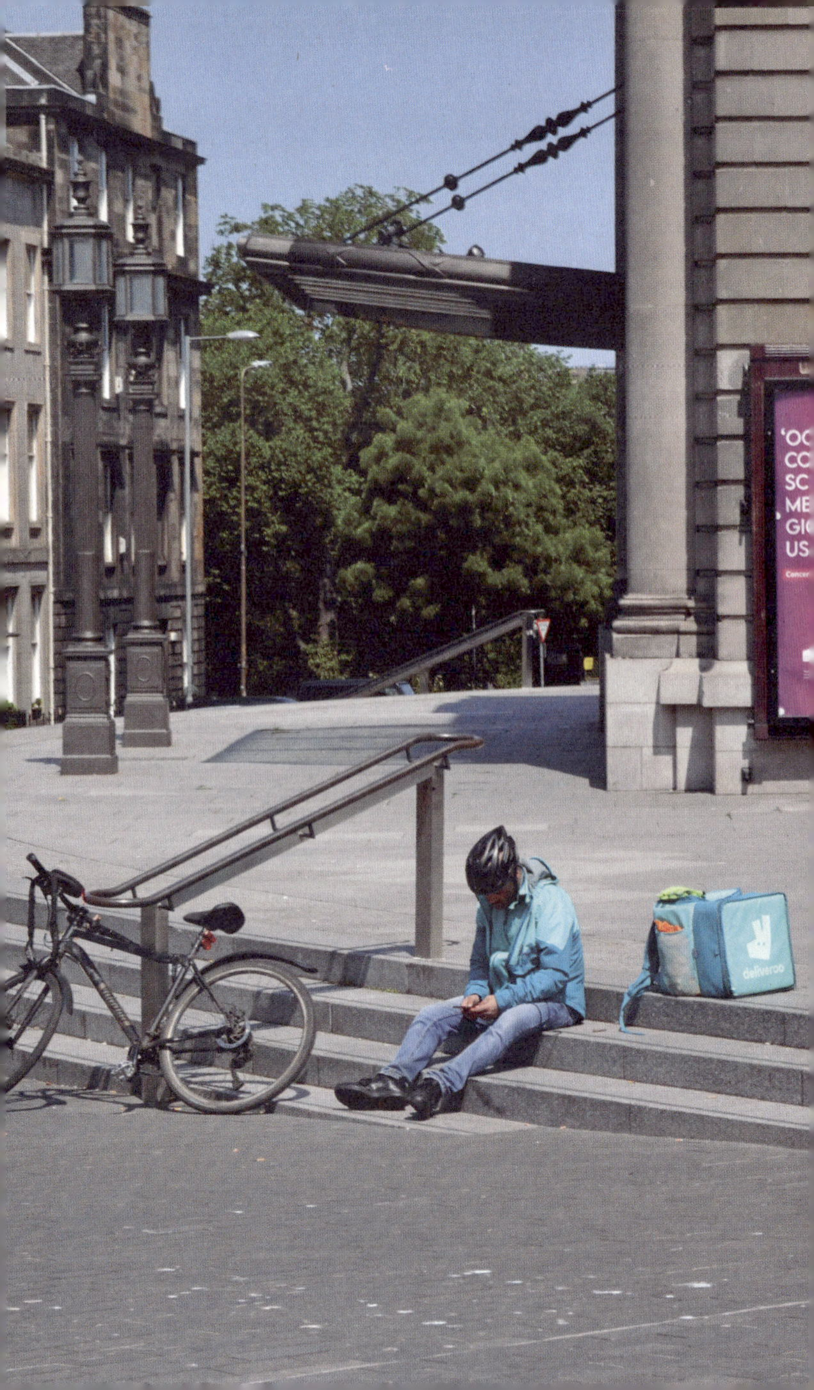
'OC
CO
SC
ME
GIO
US
Concer
deliveroo

LIKE A BOSS

The previous chapter was all about working for a boss, and this chapter is about becoming your own boss. There are different reasons why designers start a business. Some are simply fed up working for others, for others freelancing is the only option. There are fewer long-term jobs available in print-oriented graphic design studios, and even design jobs that were known for stability, such as in-house design, teaching at design schools, or designing for public services, are increasingly done by freelancers.

The entrepreneur is 'a person who sets up a business or businesses, taking on financial risks in the hope of profit', says the *Oxford Dictionary*. The term is often used to portray risk-taking individuals who try their luck in starting businesses, hoping one of them will turn a mighty profit. Similarly, the term 'design entrepreneur' is used to denote designers who create and sell their own products, as in the book *The Design Entrepreneur* by Steven Heller and Lita Talarico.[1] Although designers launching their own products can be great, these various forms of entrepreneurship should mainly be seen as a response to the precarious situation that many designers find themselves in today. Freelancing, launching your own products, hustling small jobs, even becoming investors,[2] are not really core qualities of designers. They are part of a survival mechanism in a society where income from design jobs is increasingly uncertain and temporary.

Neoliberal economic policies of the past forty years have made entrepreneurship the role model to aspire to. The narrative that is put forward is that citizens are no longer passively waiting for the state, but are encouraged to take financial risks and set up businesses themselves, even though 20 percent of businesses fail in the first year, and 45 percent in the second year.[3] Through debts and entrepreneurship, we are all expected to share the risks of an

← Deliveroo rider, Scotland, 2020.

economy based on financial speculation.[4] We should therefore, under neoliberal capitalism, understand the term entrepreneur as an ideology that interprets uncertainty as opportunity. This chapter looks at the designer as an entrepreneur, who by choice or by necessity, starts his or her own business to survive. By looking closely at the narratives around entrepreneurship, we can hopefully be better prepared for self-employment, and find alternative ways to show support and solidarity instead of competing with one another.

The Age of the Entrepreneur

Folk tales of yore may feature kings, princesses, or knights. In the stories about capitalism, the entrepreneur is the hero. The self-made woman or man who achieves status and wealth by working hard and making smart business decisions on their own account. The highest in public office are often entrepreneurs recruited from business, to bring their knack for innovation and agility to the government. At the top of the food chain are the Silicon Valley billionaires, who have succeeded in becoming the richest men on the planet, often before the age of 30.

It's one of the foundational stories of capitalism; a person of simple upbringing who overcomes hardships against all odds,

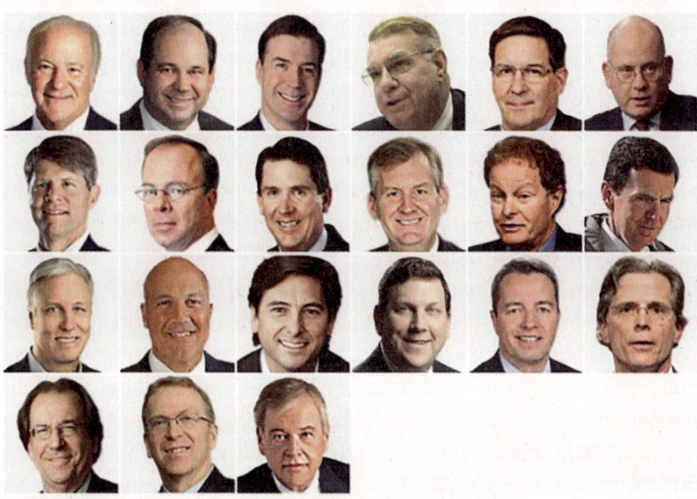

There are almost as many CEOs named John, as there are female CEOs, in the 2018 Fortune 500.

CAPS LOCK — Part 2

and succeeds admirably, thanks to hard work and entrepreneurial skills. Contemporary rags-to-riches stories are enjoyable but they are also myths. What is presented as a meritocracy is in fact more about who your family is and whom you know. Wealthy parents send their children to elite universities and schools, to help them establish business networks at a young age. Through select schools and political influence, elites use their wealth and networks to maintain their status for future generations, otherwise known as the 'old boys network'.

The second myth is that individual entrepreneurs are successful because of individual achievements. 'Apple's success is supposedly built upon the genius of Steve Jobs, not the army of Chinese workers in Foxconn, the children mining the raw materials in the DRC, or the innovation in glass-toughness technology by Gorilla Glass', writes Oli Mould in *Against Creativity* (2018).[5] Tech companies like Google and Facebook wouldn't exist without government funding, as President Obama said in April 2012. Investments from the US military and NASA developed the technologies on which the tech industry is based. The internet itself was a project by the US defence research department DARPA[6] and so were Apple's Siri, face recognition, and other GPS-enabled services.[7]

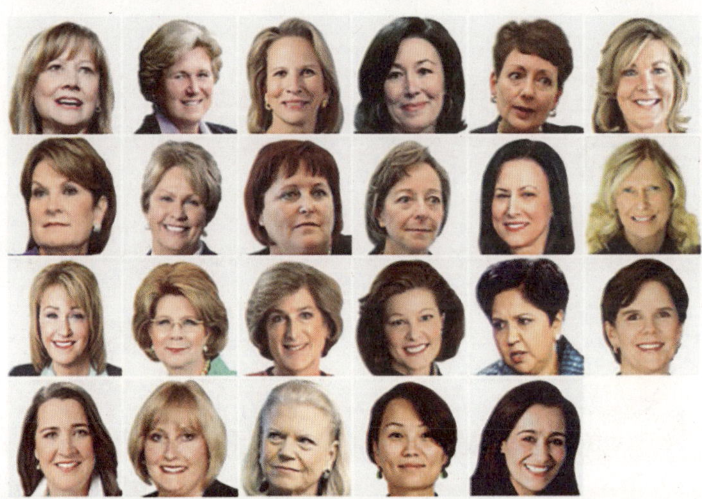

Source: *The New York Times.*

Lastly, if everyone truly has an equal opportunity to become a successful entrepreneur, why are there only five black CEOs, and only twenty-five female CEOs in the Fortune 500? The culture in graphic design is slightly better, but still far from equal. 61 percent of graphic designers in the US are women, but only 29 percent of creative directors in the US are women.[8] At graphic design conferences in the US 60 percent of speakers are men.[9] In a questionnaire from the UK, women were more likely to suggest that whom you know is more important to advance one's career in graphic design.[10]

Designers who are not 'born' into a network, will have to work harder to get clients, receive visibility and recognition. Those from lower-income backgrounds are less likely to be able to afford a degree from a prestigious design school, have less access to the

I am more than old enough to understand than no job is a dream but design takes this notion to a level unparalleled with low pay, ridiculously unfair scrutiny and competition that never reaches a point of stability.

ANONYMOUS DESIGNER

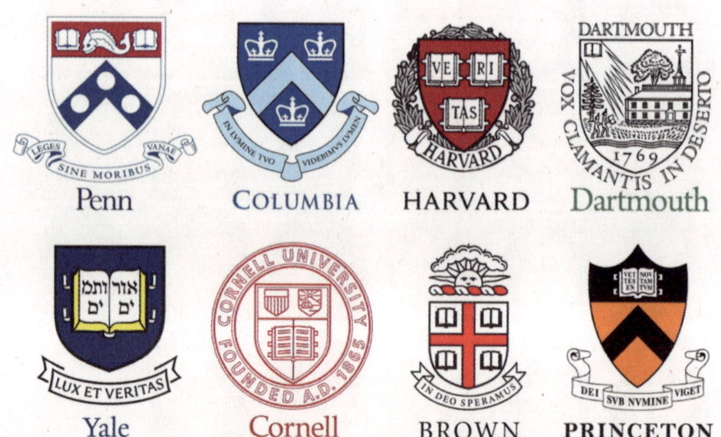

The prestigious Ivy League universities in the US, also known as the 'ancient eight'.

pricy hardware and graphics software, and are less likely to accept unpaid internships or underpaid positions to build their CVs. The narrative of entrepreneurism as a goal in itself has created a false image of boundless individual potential, where any designer can reach stardom if only they work hard enough and pursue business opportunities.

The language of entrepreneurship has invaded our language: education is 'investing' in your children, recipients of unemployed benefits are offered entrepreneurial skill trainings: we are all expected to be risk-takers and investors.[11] This false idol of success pits designers against each other in a constant cut-throat competition, which will ultimately not lead to better working conditions. It will more likely increase inequality, as the influence of class, race, and gender are too often ignored. This 'unhealthy competition' has led to a culture of overwork, rising rates of depression and burn-outs among designers.[12]

Don't Believe the Hype

If you start your own business, you'll be expected to promote it to get your first job. It might appear that designers are naturally gifted to do this, but the statistics tell a different story. A survey among graphic designers in the UK found that 42 percent of women and 34 percent of men were 'very or fairly comfortable' with promoting their work.[13] For many designers, chatting up clients and selling their work are seen as unwelcome chores. As one designer wrote about freelance work: 'I get way too stressed about these things in ways that rarely bother me at my day job when I'm just one part of a larger operation.'[14]

Under neoliberalism 'we are each increasingly expected to generate our own hype', writes Max Haiven.[15] Receiving recognition is constructing a successful image of hype-ness. For example, regularly posting work on social media that isn't visible anywhere else, self-publishing books and magazines, getting booked for conferences, working for high profile clients, or winning design awards.

Design awards are a particular kind of hype flavour. Anyone who has ever submitted work to a competition, knows that awards are more about admission fees than the quality of the work. Some of them guarantee a win if you'll just spend enough money.

Admittedly, there are still designs awards that are determined to set high quality standards and serve both as merit and a critique of the industry, but the vast majority of them are based on business models that profit from the designers' desire to be recognized.

A high-profile client can also create hype. Acquiring these design jobs often means doing free pitches, or unpaid speculative work. This occurs when a client asks a shortlist of design studios to submit creative proposals, with only the winning proposal receiving paid work. In a 2016 survey 70 percent of graphic designers condemned unpaid pitches.[16] For designer Sarah Boris, one in four jobs she received were unpaid pitches.[17] She writes that this practice is exploitative both on the end of the designer and the client. Pitches are costly procedures that can take a lot of time, so while on paper the client receives free work, in practice a lot of time goes into communication, reviewing results, and negotiating conditions. Graphic design trade organizations have tried to outlaw unpaid pitches, but this is hindered by legislation, such as the EU regulations that demand 'healthy competition'.[18]

These examples are not meant to suggest that the designer's desire to be recognized is inherently wrong or inviting exploitation. Distinguishing oneself through exhibiting personal talents is one of the things that can make working in design rewarding. But signature work alone is rarely enough to get clients, and not every designer has the money and time to invest in awards and unpaid pitches, or the stamina to go out and sell themselves.

That's why pro bono work is great. You choose to do it, and if you're choosing to do it to grow your own work, your deal is essentially that you're not going to collaborate. You're going to do the job the way you think the job is gonna be done— and they're gonna use it. That's a power thing. That's not a victim thing.

PAULA SCHER, DESIGNER

Ultimately hype is focused around recognizable individuals, while design work is almost always done collectively, taking production and clients into account. Perhaps competition doesn't have to be the decisive feature in graphic designers. Working collaboratively or working uncredited are now rare sights among professional graphic designers, but they could mean a change of scenery that is urgently needed to create a healthier working environment.

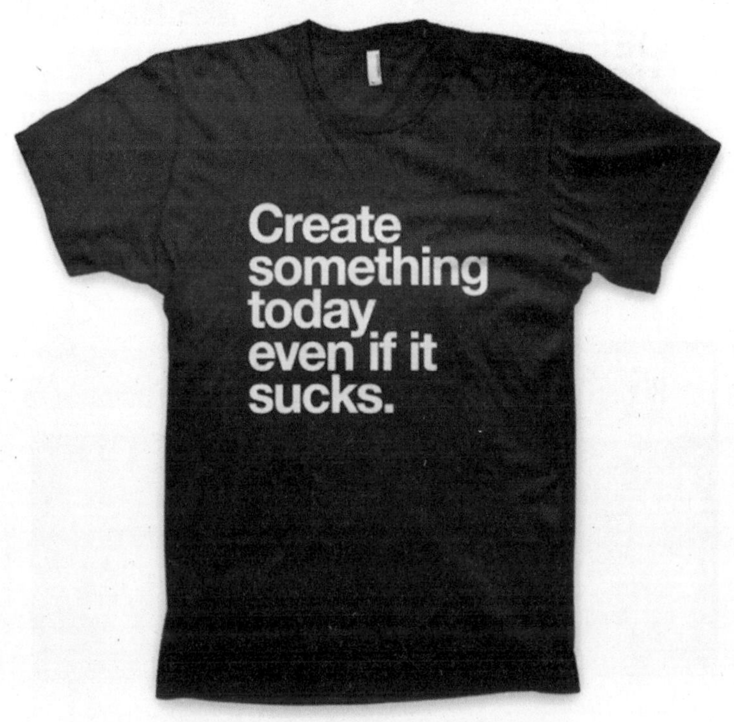

Create Something Today T-shirt, Mu Mu's store, 2017.

Don't Get a Job …
Make a Job
How to make it as
a creative graduate
Gem Barton

Propaganda / Put yourself out there / Release early, release often / Going Mobile / Go guerrilla / Bend the rules / Don't reinvent the wheel / Specialism vs Diversity / Learn from your idols / Swim against the tide / Question everything / Tough Calls / Trust your instincts / Move mountains / Imagine best-case scenarios / Going it Alone vs Teaming up / Don't run before you can walk / Exploit your interests / Feel your way / Be true to yourself / Push, pull, tear, tear / Gusto / Reinvent yourself / Create positive change / Keep on learning /

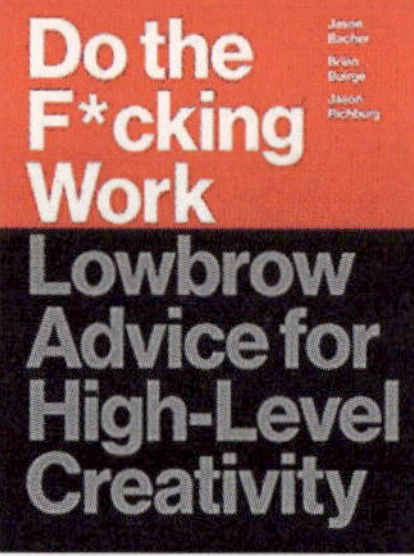

Jason
Bacher
Brian
Buirge
Jason
Richburg
Do the
F*cking
Work
Lowbrow
Advice for
High-Level
Creativity

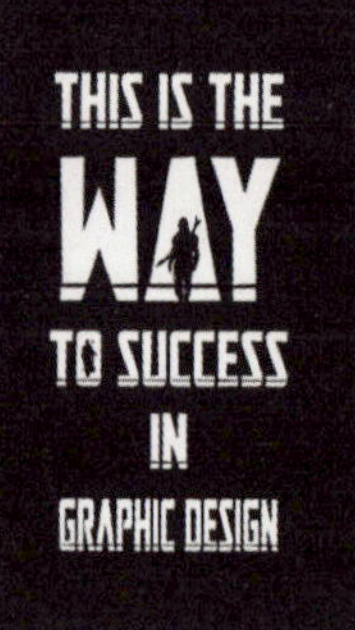

THIS IS THE
WAY
TO SUCCESS
IN
GRAPHIC DESIGN

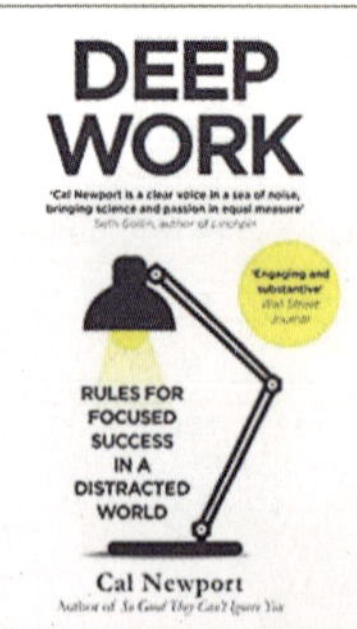

DEEP
WORK
'Cal Newport is a clear voice in a sea of noise, bringing science and passion in equal measure'
Seth Godin, author of Linchpin
'Engaging and substantive'
Wall Street Journal
RULES FOR
FOCUSED
SUCCESS
IN A
DISTRACTED
WORLD
Cal Newport
Author of So Good They Can't Ignore You

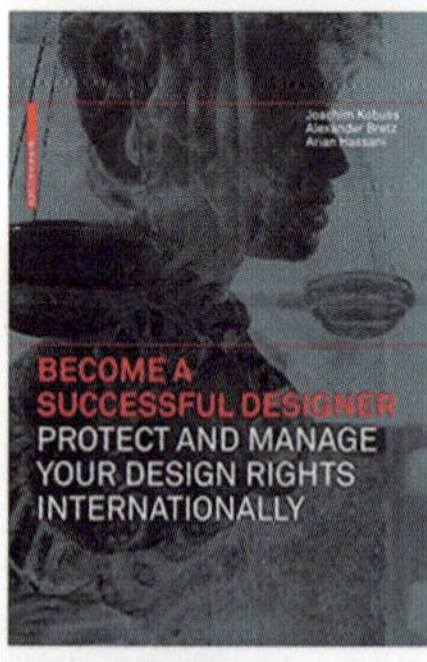

Joachim Kobuss
Alexander Bretz
Arian Hassani
BECOME A
SUCCESSFUL DESIGNER
PROTECT AND MANAGE
YOUR DESIGN RIGHTS
INTERNATIONALLY

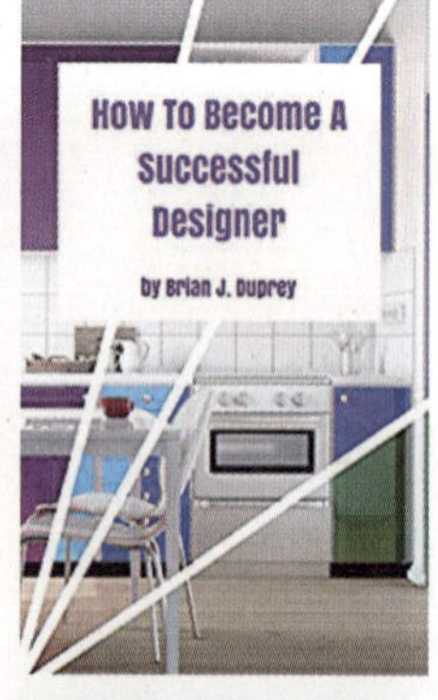

HOW TO Become A
Successful
Designer
by Brian J. Duprey

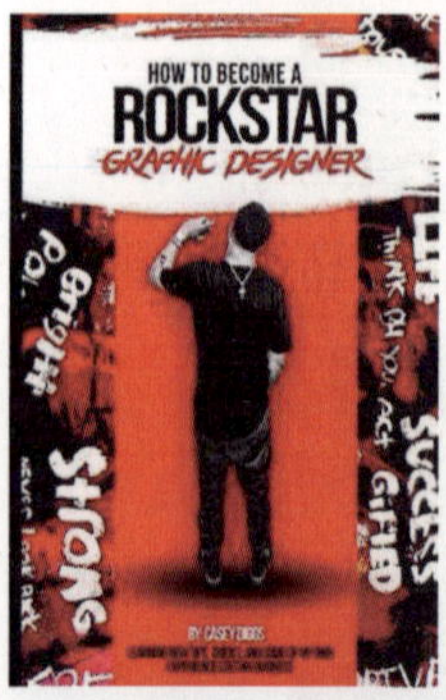

HOW TO BECOME A
ROCKSTAR
GRAPHIC DESIGNER
BY CASEY DOSS

WORK
FOR
MONEY,
DESIGN
FOR
LOVE
Answers to the Most Frequently Asked Questions About
Starting and Running a Successful Design Business
By David Airey and The Design Community

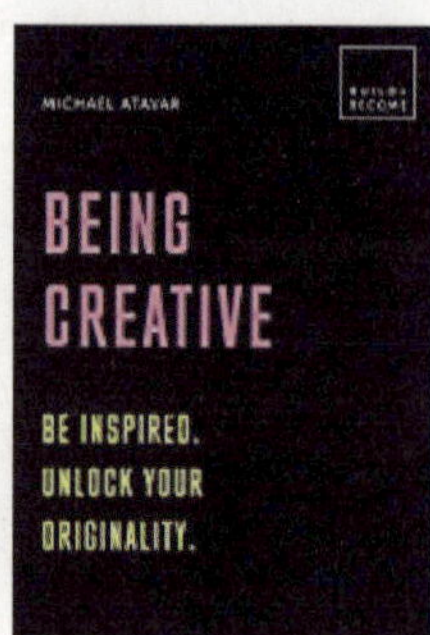

MICHAEL ATAVAR
BUILD
BECOME
BEING
CREATIVE
BE INSPIRED.
UNLOCK YOUR
ORIGINALITY.

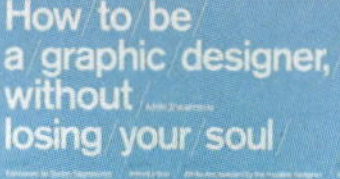

How to be
a graphic designer,
without
losing your soul

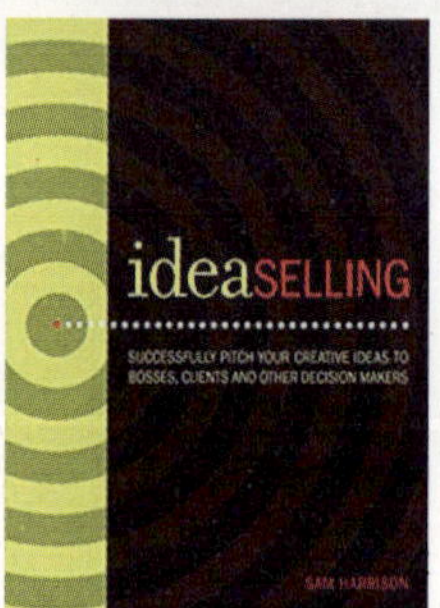

ideaSELLING
SUCCESSFULLY PITCH YOUR CREATIVE IDEAS TO
BOSSES, CLIENTS AND OTHER DECISION MAKERS
SAM HARRISON

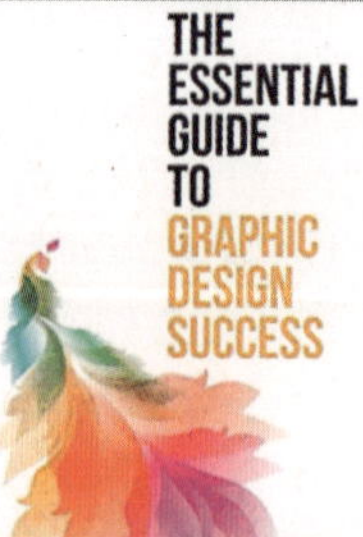

THE
ESSENTIAL
GUIDE
TO
GRAPHIC
DESIGN
SUCCESS

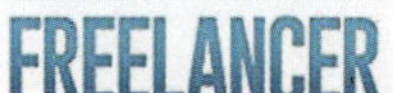

FREELANCER

THE STAR DESIGNER

Entrepreneurship aligns closely with originality. 'The need to find the new is what generates all entrepreneurial spirit and makes it such a challenging field' Heller and Talarico write in *The Design Entrepreneur*.[19] Starting a design company means differentiating yourself among those thousands of other designers, with an original name, portfolio, and a personal branding. Authorship is a condition for economic success in the creative industries. Stories in the design press overflow with 'star designers', revealing what secrets lie behind the work and what drives these geniuses. Following the rags-to-riches myth of capitalism, the design press suggests that originality, talent, and work hard, can turn everyone into a star designer.

Printers and engravers in the medieval workshop did not entertain such thoughts. In the workshop, work was collective and anonymous, in service of higher powers such as family, the guild, and religion. The apprentice learned by copying others, while the journeymen used their skills to travel around and find work, hoping to eventually start their own shop.[20] They were definitely entrepreneurial,[21] but not aspiring to become original artists.

During the Renaissance the 'creative genius' first appeared in fine arts, but it wasn't until the nineteenth century that ideas of originality became common in design. Slowly aided by the success of multinational corporations and their marketing strategies, graphic design in Europe and the US grew into a fashionable line of work, with the first prominent graphic designers becoming well-known in the second half of the twentieth century.

The shift from manufacturing to immaterial products around the 1980s also meant the production of culture became integrated with production itself—in what theorist Fredric Jameson calls: 'an increasingly essential structural function to aesthetic innovation

← Covers of books that promise a successful career in graphic design.

and experimentation' to bring, 'fresh waves of even more novel seeming goods'.[22] In other words, the super brands of the 1990s relied heavily on star designers to create the language of the 'new cool'. In the 2000s designers began to issue books with their own work, which were often promotional vehicles filled with spectacular imagery, lacking any serious criticism or self-reflection.[23] The culture of producing monographs is described by Evening Class as: designers who try 'inserting themselves into the canon'.[24]

Celebrity culture in design is perhaps related to the phenomenon of brand equity, or brand value. Design can boost a company's value, with exemplary companies like Apple that went from a $100 million market value in 1980, to $2 trillion today, in large part because of the work of design.[25] Nike was a minor shoe company in the 1970s, worth about $300,000, and after rebranding itself as a design-oriented company, reached $400 million value in 1990, to $194 billion today. When designers realized that a clearly authored visual language adds market value, fashionable design such as record covers, music videos, expressive typography, and other signature work was brought to the centre of graphic design.

In an op-ed for *Eye on Design*, Aggie Toppins points out that the 'cult of hero worship' is in fact a flawed interpretation of design history. Designers such as William Morris, and Ray and Charles Eames, worked with large teams of designers, interns, printers, and production assistants. While assistants and support staff were mostly left out of the history books, the work of so-called 'design heroes' is celebrated. She proposes a more realistic and social perspective on design authorship, as she points out; design has 'always been collaborative'.[26]

Toxicity at Work

'Companies only have two gears, forward and reverse, and standing still is the same as going backwards', says Adrian Shaughnessy on a studio's hiring policy.[27] As the previous chapter pointed out, there is no fair labour market in graphic design. Since there are more designers than jobs, an employer can pretty much choose the conditions. Unpaid overtime? Sure. Hiring graduated designers as interns? There is always someone who will do it.

The work relation in the pre-industrial printing workshop cen-

Individual creators are, to no small extent, historical fabrications. Let's suspend the cult of hero worship to reflect on this myth.

AGGIE TOPPINS, DESIGNER

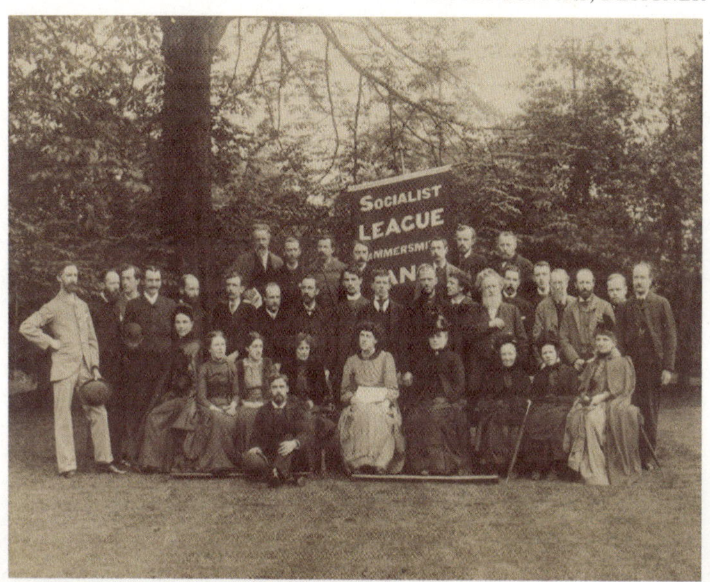

William Morris and the staff of the Kelmscott Press, c. 1884.

tred around family and community life, where care and trust were necessary for survival. That brought about its own flavour of toxicity, as the unquestioned dominion of the workshop master easily led to exploitative or abusive working conditions from which it was difficult to escape. With the increased scale and individualism in the market economy, the trust between the employer and employee was replaced by contracts and the pay check. These were formal arrangements that protected the worker from harmful community or family structures, but also created a less trusting workplace and this can lead to a situation where employees will try do as little as possible, while employers will try to pay as little as possible.

When hiring designers, smaller studios can spend time to build a relation of trust with new employees. Larger design firms on the other hand, outsource the trust to human resources personnel, who have their quantitative methods. For example, reading personnel email or using software that monitors workers' behaviour and productivity.

One way for design businesses to build trust among co-workers is by eliminating all forms of hierarchy. Examples are the cooperatives mentioned in the previous chapter, or other businesses that employ a horizontal structure.[28] Such a structure can still have leadership roles: some people are simply more skilled at type design or client presentations and some are naturally better at leading. Some cooperatives change leadership roles periodically. The benefit of a cooperative is that you don't have to decide things yourself, but you can discuss them collectively, in order to achieve the best conditions for work on equal footing. Although it might mean you will spend more time on making decisions.

If you choose to start a business and hire staff—including freelancers—it is important to respect work relations as you would respect any other close social relations. We spend more waking time with our colleagues than with our families, so a healthy and trusting work relation benefits everyone. Hiring someone means they rely on your money to survive, to feed their families, to pay the rent, have social and economic security. That is why paying fair wages should be the starting point, and not the legal minimum wage.

If you are in need of extra help but the future of the work relation is uncertain, be up front about the temporality. Design studios often hire troves of designers in times of growth, and when the work dries up, lay them off just as easily. People may have uprooted their lives just for that job. If you offer someone a job, understand that they assume they can stay for a longer period of time. Why not foster long-term work relations based on trust, solidarity, and reciprocity?

I worked for a company that tracked everything designers were doing. It felt like working at a factory. But the agency was very productive. Not very good for fostering creativity. They used Robohead software to track workers. You would get an average of many hours a logo takes, how much time a brochure takes, etc.

ANONYMOUS DESIGNER

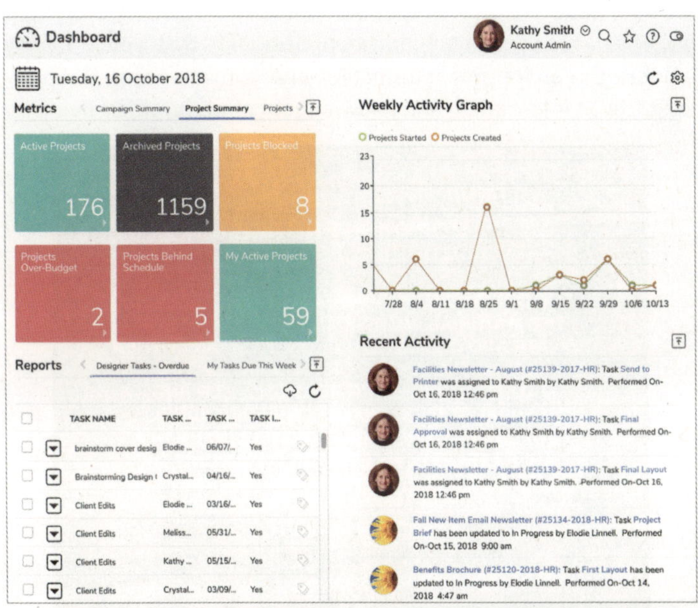

Robohead software, a management tool for monitoring the creative and marketing work process, 2021.

INTELLECTUAL PROPERTY

Books on graphic design ethics use a lot of paper explaining the protection of intellectual property. Nothing is more sacred for designers than the right to originality, and nothing makes them angrier than others copying their work. Well-known designers employ lawyers to track down cases of copyright infringement.

This fixation on intellectual property is somewhat understandable as the work of graphic designers today is mostly immaterial and produces value through ideas, images, and concepts, which can be easily copied in digital form. Copyright law in itself seems benevolent, if it would protect the author against someone profiting from stealing ideas. There is nothing ethical about someone stealing another's work and profiting from it. However, copyright law doesn't really protect individual designers that well. It mostly hinders the sharing of information and blocks access to knowledge, even information and knowledge that was created publicly.

DreamWorks home entertainment copyright notice, 2001.

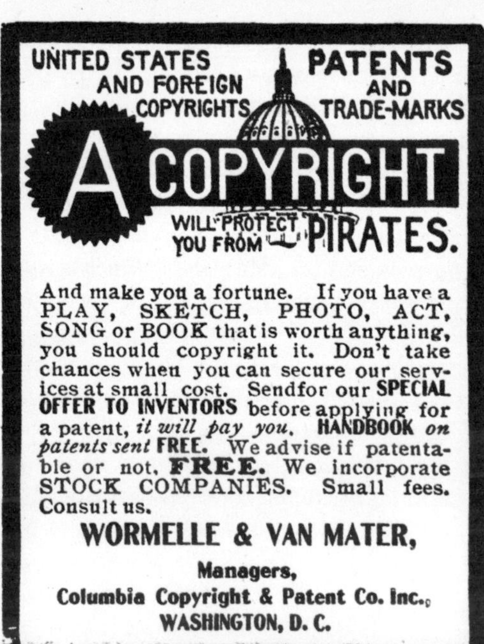

Copyright notice by Columbia.

In the end copyright law does little for the majority of designers if they cannot afford lawyers. Companies such as H&M and Urban Outfitters have made it their business model to steal from other designers, aided by armies of lawyers who will see to it that they can get away with it in some form. Tech companies spend a lot of time patenting every idea, to maintain monopolies over potential future products. Because filing patents and hiring copyright lawyers is pricy, copyright law ends up serving corporations and slowing down innovation, instead of protecting individual creatives. A case in point are companies that patent words and colours, allowing them exclusive use. The company T-Mobile bought the rights to the colour magenta in 2008, a primary colour for the printing industry. They sued other companies over using a colour they claim as their own.[29]

Culture and knowledge are collectively created and publicly funded, by systems of education, scientific research, collective historical efforts, publicly run archives, and study centres, which is why they have been called 'intellectual commons'. Like the common lands that offered a collective space for collective making of community and resources, knowledge and culture are created collectively, and are collectively improved by discourse and innovation. Copyright law is a way of privatizing collective knowledge, and limiting access to that knowledge for the purposes of profit, a process not unlike the enclosure of the common lands that expelled peasants from publicly accessible lands. Which is why Max Haiven calls this process of limiting access to knowledge and culture 'enclosure 2.0'.[30]

While capitalism is celebrated for its innovative qualities, patents actively restrict innovation by privatizing and therefore limiting the access to culture and knowledge.[31] By its fixation on copyrights, the graphic design industry is defining culture and knowledge as forms of property that have to be bought and traded. Designers should profit from the works they create, but the current

Dear friends at Linotype!

THIS is indeed an embarrassing SITUATION. To our knowledge the site you refer to **AND** the **activities** taking place there does **NOT** violate **Swedish** law. As a matter of fact I'm quite sure u doesn't even **violate GERMAN** law. You should also be pleased to notice that **SWEDISH law**, as far as one can tell, conforms to **the** specifications of the harmonisation directive **2001/29/EC.**

But lets cut to **core** of the problem. The **Pirate BAY** does not in anyway handle your intellectual property or any of **the** data contained in the designs, nor do we **RELAY** such **data**.

The site, and the tracker, is merely **a way** of connecting people; kind of like what **NOKIA** does. The actual data **IS** stored on the individual users' **computers;** if horrible crimes of bloody **MURDER** and such are being committed, **AS we** speak, it is them who are the **criminals.** One would not **prosecute** Nokia just because terrorists use **THEIR** phones.

However; this activity is not **illegal** in **SWEDEN**. There are some more or less relevant cases from the Swedish Supreme **COURT**, but I doubt that they would be much to you. **CONSIDERING** the current situation we feel that we are **obliged** to leave the torrent on the site until the Swedish law is changed or the Supreme Court rules that what we do is illegal.

Best wishes!

/JUDAS, on the behalf of The **Pirate** Bay

The Pirate Bay letter to Linotype, 2006.

copyright system does not live up to its claim that it serves everyone equally.

There are good alternatives to copyright that believe in the protection and care for intellectual commons. One of these is Creative Commons, a non-profit that offers various systems of open access to knowledge, promoting collaboration and creativity while protecting the creative's right to profit.[32] Another one is Copyleft, a reciprocal license from the software community that looks more at culture and knowledge in the long run. If you license a work as Copyleft, it should be publicly available and everyone is allowed to modify and adapt it, as long as any derivate is also licensed as Copyleft, which means all adaptations are also freely available, and no version can ever be restricted.[33]

OSP calls for a generous artistic practice that recognizes that culture is above all based on the circulation of ideas, and on the fact that any work is derivative by nature, in the sense that it is informed by preceding works.

OPEN SOURCE PUBLISHING

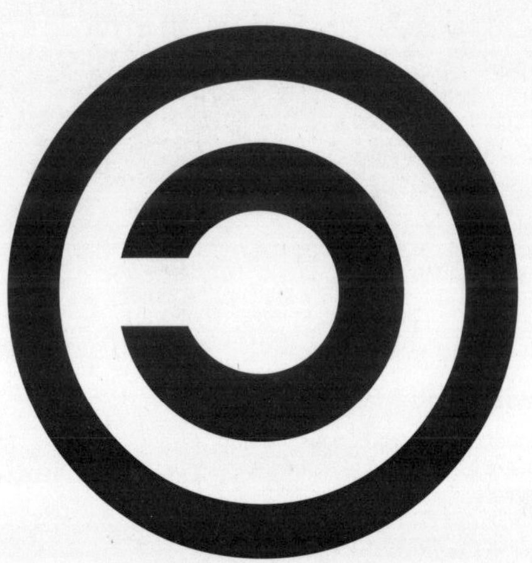

Copyleft logo.

Micro-Entrepreneur

We know an entrepreneur is a risk-taker who starts a business. But are you still an entrepreneur when you deliver meals on a bicycle? Are you an entrepreneur if you do online gigs for less than five dollars? The division between entrepreneurs and employees used to be a lot clearer. You were either working for someone, or someone was working for you. Now almost every economic sector, from construction workers, creative workers, food deliverers, taxi drivers to education is switching to freelancers. Journalist Sarah Grey writes that an industry like journalism has completely restructured in a short time. Entire newspapers and magazines are run on a 'skeleton crew' without journalists or editors—surrounded by hundreds of freelancers.[34]

Self-employment is also rising among creatives. In 2008 in the Netherlands 24 percent of creative workers were self-employed, and in ten years this almost doubled to 46 percent. In the UK one

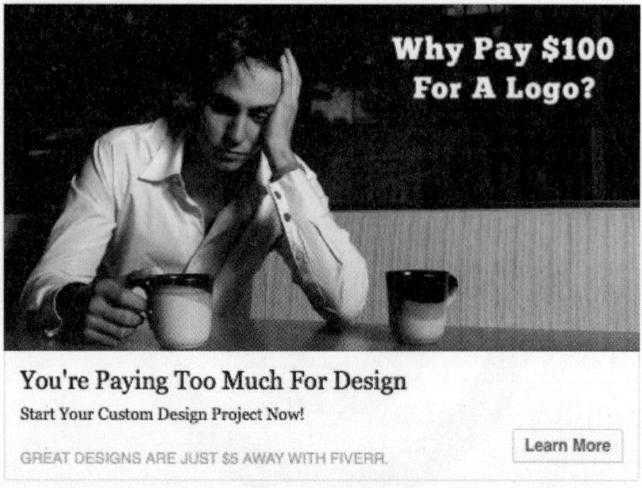

Facebook advertisement for Fiverr.

in four creative workers are freelancers, and according to the US Bureau of Labor Statistics, 21 percent of graphic designers in the US are self-employed.[35] Many people at first welcome freelance work. You can choose your own hours, and there is always a glimmer of hope that your business is destined to become economically successful. What starting freelancers often don't fully realize is that they are responsible for pension, taxes, health care and other benefits that employers usually take care of.[36]

In 2015 a freelance graphic designer from the Netherlands had an accident while mountain-biking and suffered a spinal cord injury. Like most freelancers, he did not have a disability insurance, so it was upon his friends and family to raise the €300,000 needed to pay for his medical bills and expenses.[37] In a British survey amongst graphic designers in 2015, 62 percent of those between twenty and thirty years old did not have a pension plan, and of those between thirty and forty years old, 43 percent had no pension plan. In the US, many freelancers have to use crowdfunding platforms like gofund.me to pay for medical bills.[38]

One out of three freelancers in the Netherlands has an income below the subsistence minimum.[39] Desperate for work, freelancers start giving courses to other freelancers how to become successful, thus reaching another level of exploiting each other's precarity. Winners of this race to the bottom are the companies who hire freelancers, who pay less employment benefits, and low freelance rates. It is even legal for companies like Deliveroo and Uber to pay freelancers below minimum wage.[40] This growing class of entrepreneurs consists of a growing group of people who are exploited through constant competition, who lack a steady income, or steady working hours, and don't have any social benefits. Lorusso argues that this new class is the entreprecariat, a combination of entrepreneur, precarious (lacking in stability and security) and proletariat (the poorest class of working people).

Sell yourself as if you're a Rolls Royce even though you know you're a Fiat Panda.

MIGUEL DIAS, DESIGNER

For freelance designers, online market places are the next battle-ground. On websites like Fiverr you can post jobs for graphic design, writing, 3D graphics, and other creative services. The name comes from a five-dollar bill, a reference to the low prices people offer their skills for. An army of so-called micro-entrepreneurs make a living on these platforms, while Fiverr takes a 20 percent cut.[41] Silvio Lorusso writes that undercutting professional rates is part of its appeal. Fiverr even advertises saying: 'why pay $100 for a logo?' Websites that offer cheap graphic design were around before, but until recently, the lack of quality didn't seriously threaten the rest of the graphic design industry. That is beginning to change. Lorusso continues to say that Fiverr had 600,000 jobs posted on the site by 2012, and that there are now more than a hundred sites like it. The question is for how long designers can keep their hourly rates, if the same services can be bought for a fraction of the price.

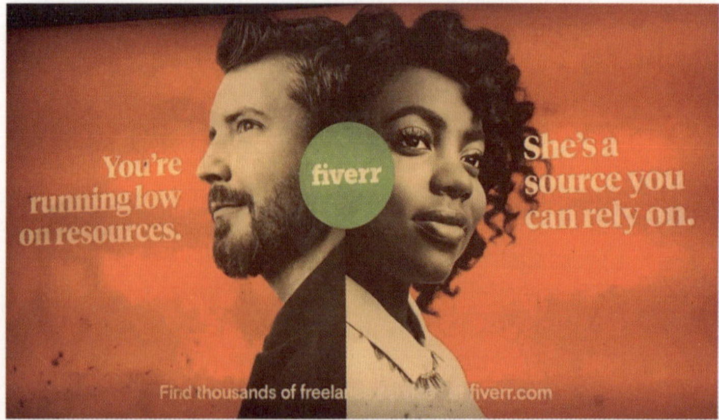

A Fiverr ad campaign, criticized for exploiting women of colour, 2019.

Care, not Competition

Designers are caught between a rock—being exploited by a boss—and a hard place—being exploited by clients. On top of that, many designers also want to use their work for something meaning-ful, such as helping a friendly business, promoting social issues, or supporting political causes. Elzenbaumer points out that it is 'hard for most to survive, let alone to produce work that is socially

I think the way you recession-proof yourself is that you understand that your design skills can apply in a multitude of situations.

JASON SCHUPBACH, DEAN AT A DESIGN COLLEGE

meaningful outside the scope of the market'.[42] How to earn your living with individual creative skills, and still show solidarity, is one of the most pressing question for designers today.

First, we can rethink the role of competition in design, which is now geared towards replacing outdated design work, rather than building a foundation for future visual communication. 'Newness' in design is celebrated as its highest virtue by both the design press, design museums, and many of its practitioners. Sasha Costanza-Chock writes that in a society dominated by capitalism and patriarchy, 'new' is in higher regard in a design than repairing, maintaining, and caring for something to keep it intact.[43] Looking at graphic design as a way of 'caring' for communication rather than continuously searching for the next trend, without context or knowledge of history, requires long-term processes that are collaborative, more interdisciplinary, and less about individual achievement.

A shift from competition to care also actively challenges the underlying economic model. Sociologist Richard Sennett has studied in detail how people worked over the last decades, and observes that a short-term economy is incompatible with the long-term goals of society. He has witnessed first-hand that steady social work relations have been replaced by flexible ones, while uprooting families by forcing them to move looking for work. Qualities like 'detachment and superficial cooperativeness' are considered better for the precarious work situations of today.[44]

There is a tenacious assumption among designers, that design exists only by virtue of the market. 'In the way that we conduct ourselves as designers, we are as free as the marketplace allows us to be.'[45] writes Shaugnessy. Why wouldn't graphic design be able to exist outside of capitalism? Early forms of graphic design were practiced long before capitalism existed, in service of many different human needs. That doesn't mean design activities should be not exchanged for some kind of value. Value exchange exists in all types of economies, but that is not the same as saying design can only be measured by the yardstick of market value.

Graphic designers are increasingly voicing their discontent with the current economic system, and are coming up with ideas that promote collaboration and the free exchange of knowledge. They are starting cooperatives, designing typefaces, and doing open-source work that others can share, modify, download, or 'fork'.[46] For example, the French type foundry Velvetyn offers high-quality open-source fonts, and writes: 'We believe that not all graphic or typographic creations should be part of a market economy and we support the freedom to subvert its rules.'[47] The creation of design commons can be a useful strategy, which will be explained further in the final chapter.

Freelance designers were not represented by unions until now, but that is changing. In the UK designers and art workers were inspired by a new union for people working for Deliveroo and Uber called the Independent Workers of Great Britain (IWGB), to start the UWV designers+cultural workers union for freelance and regular employed designers.[48] Practical organization of freelance workers is desperately needed, but Bianca Elzenbaumer also reminds us that designers should 'let go of an individualistic and competitive approach, in favour of an experimentation with collective forms of making and producing that challenge the procedures of precarisation'.[49]

There is no necessity for a strict divide between entrepreneurs and workers if better working conditions for designers are to be realized. It is both the designer as worker, and the designer as entrepreneur who are faced with the same challenges: unbridled competition and toxic work relations in a blind pursuit of individual celebrity status, until there is no other mutual understanding left than pay checks and (temporary) contracts. Rather than leaving the others to their own demise, it is only in solidarity among each other that better and less work can be realized.

→   A website that shows how long it take Jeff Bezos, former CEO of Amazon, to earn your salary.
      kisbridgingloans.co.uk/finance-news/how-long-will-it-take-jeff-bezos-to-earn-your-salary.

                    CAPS LOCK — Part 2

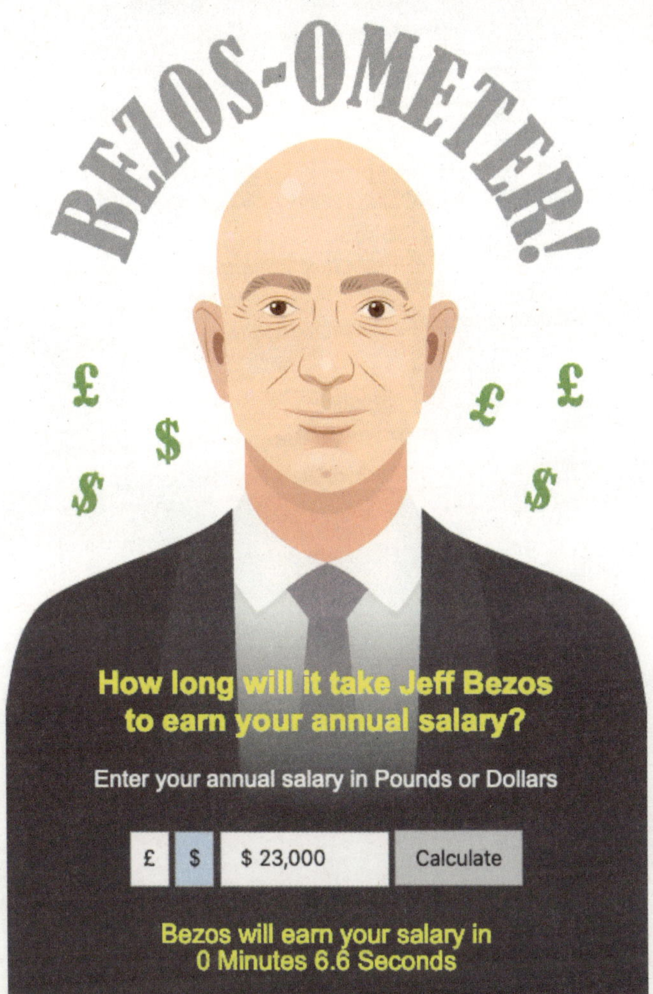

BEZOS-OMETER!
£ $
$ £
$ £
How long will it take Jeff Bezos to earn your annual salary?
Enter your annual salary in Pounds or Dollars
£
$
$ 23,000
Calculate
Bezos will earn your salary in
0 Minutes 6.6 Seconds
You have been on this page for
0 Minutes 40 Seconds
In that time, Jeff Bezos has earnt
£ 106,840.00
$ 139,240.00

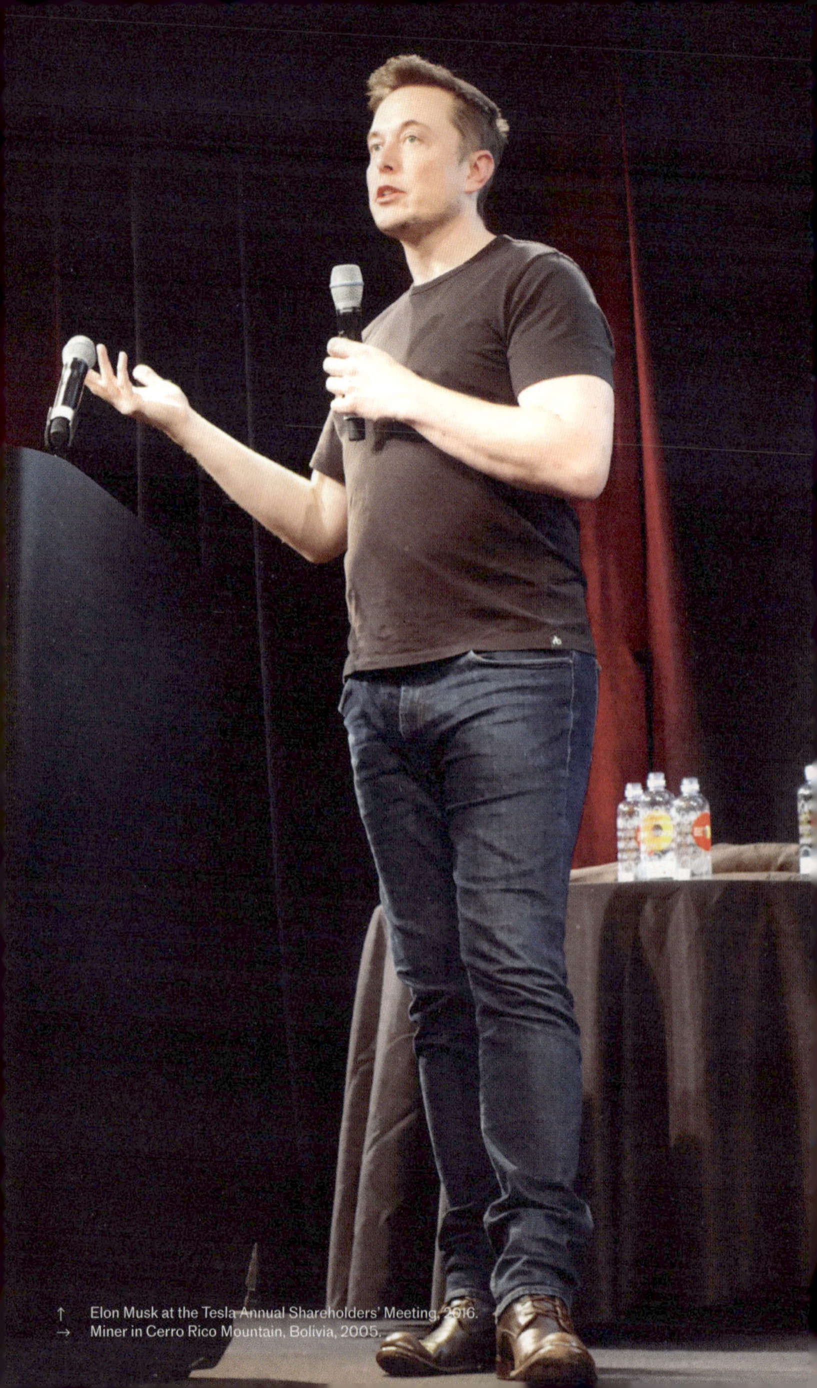

↑   Elon Musk at the Tesla Annual Shareholders' Meeting, 2016.
→   Miner in Cerro Rico Mountain, Bolivia, 2005.

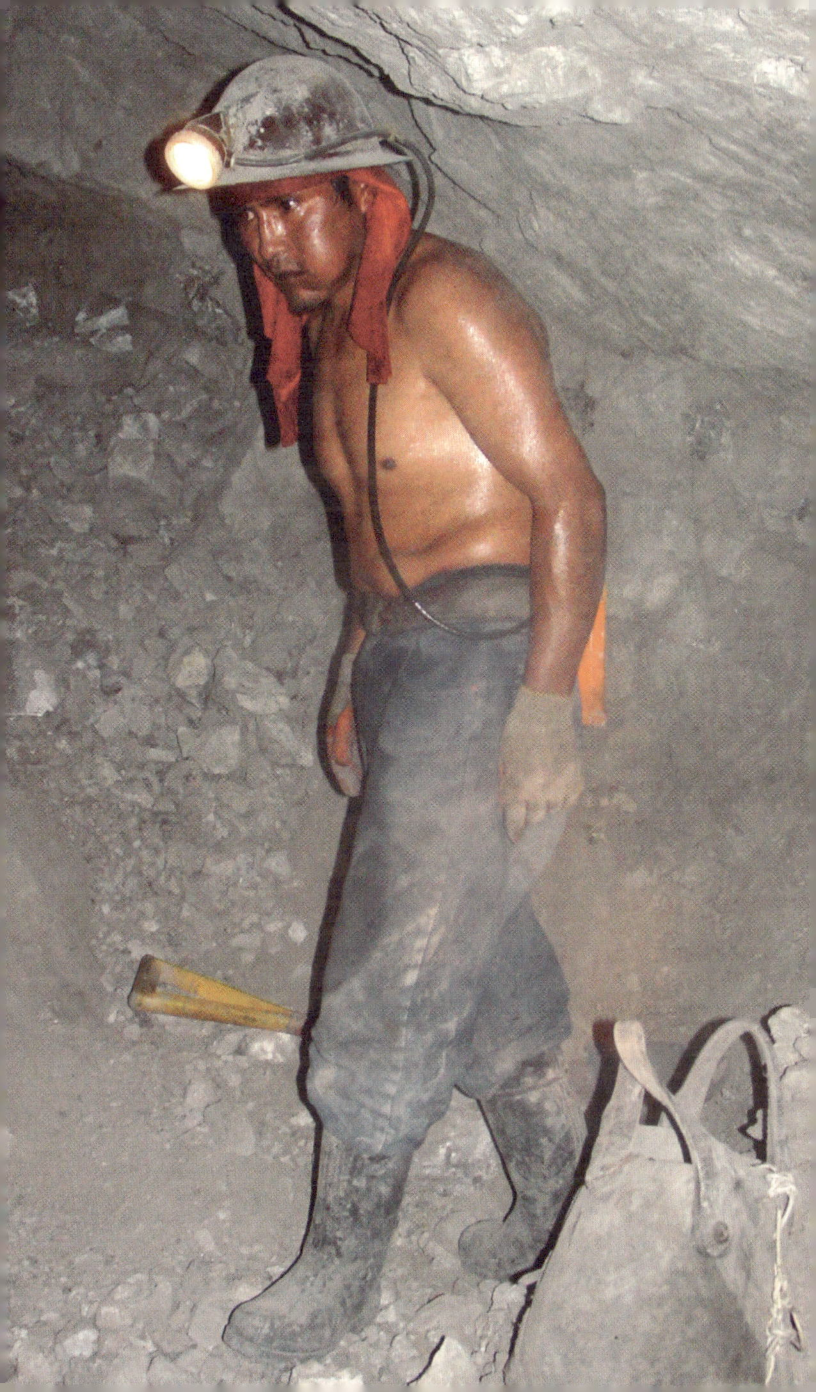

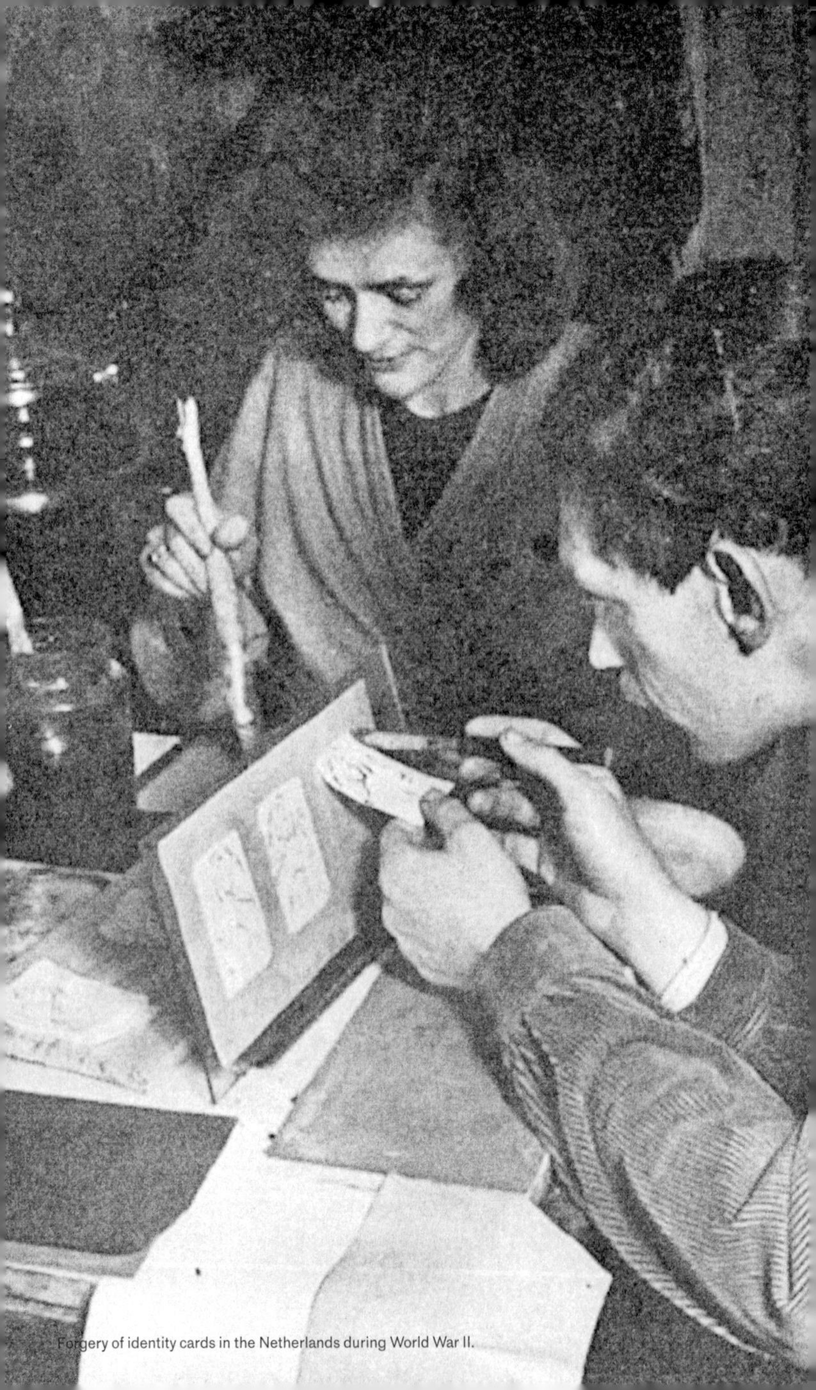

Forgery of identity cards in the Netherlands during World War II.

THE DESIGNER AS AMATEUR

> *I like democracy as much as the next person, but because of new technologies, the definition of 'amateur' in fields like graphic design, photography, film and music, is being redefined with everything so democratic, we can lose the elite status that gives us credibility.*
>
> STEVEN HELLER

> *We might be better off if we jettison the idea of a singular definition of what design should be, and perhaps a single organization for all graphic designers.*
>
> MICHAEL ROCK

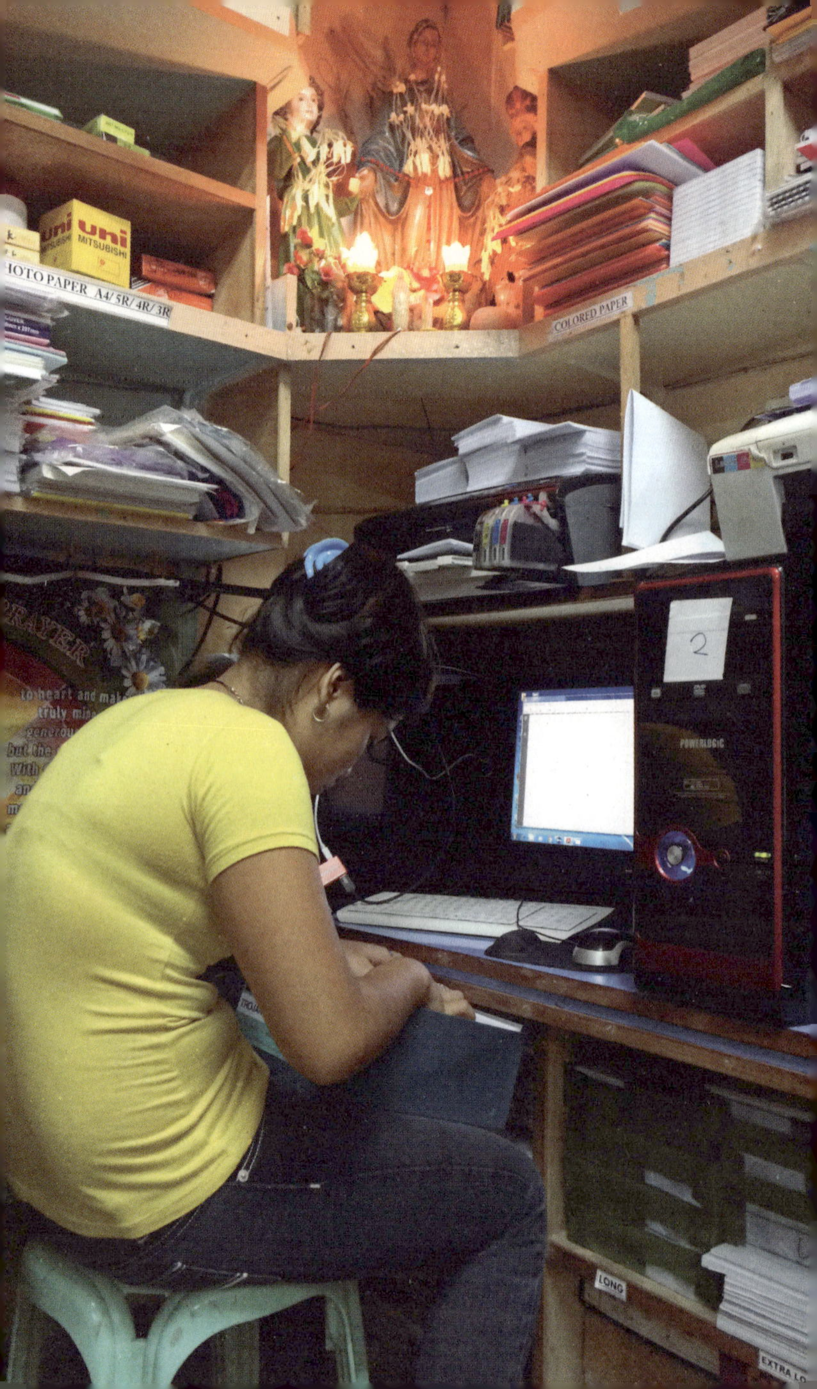

uni MITSUBISHI
uni MITSUBISHI
PHOTO PAPER A4/ 5R/ 4R/ 3R
COLORED PAPER
PRAYER
POWERLOGIC
2
LONG
EXTRA L

WHO IS A DESIGNER?

What makes someone a graphic designer? Is it the quality of the work, is it about having a design degree, or is it just what you call yourself? And who decides what a designer is? This third chapter on the working conditions of designers, is about the difference between amateur and professional designers. It looks at how professional standards and trade organizations came into being, and how professionalism has led to the exclusion of people from graphic design.

Compared to architecture, engineering, and law, you don't need a license to practice graphic design. The title 'designer' isn't protected, it doesn't require an educational background, or a formal code of conduct. Some even say that everyone is a designer, and design is 'basic to all human activity', as Victor Papanek put forward.[1] Just like the majority of houses in the world are not designed by architects, most visual communication is probably not designed by professional graphic designers.

If we look at the graphic design work that is featured in the design press and conferences, it almost exclusively features work for well-known cultural or commercial clients by professional graphic designers. Awards and conferences are sponsored by multinationals and foster tight connections with the industry. At these events, non-professional or amateur designers are hardly featured. To understand why some people get the credits and pay-ment for doing design, and others don't, we look back and find out how the distinction between the professional and the amateur came into being.

For the Love of Design

The word amateur is often used pejoratively in design. For in-stance, when design work lacks a certain quality or longevity. The word amateur comes from the Latin *amator,* which means lover. These passionate roots reveal that amateurs are individuals who enjoy what they do, whether they are being paid or not.

Most design historians agree that humans have always practiced some form of design. Design theory books start with showing cave paintings and stone tools as examples of the earliest forms of design. 'We are all designers', says design theorist Tony Fry. Design theorist and writer Anne-Marie Willis calls design 'fundamental to being human—we design, that is to say, we deliberate, plan and scheme in ways which prefigure our actions and makings.'[2] The interest in design for everyday use is as relevant in urban societies, as it is for hunter-gatherers. As Papanek explains, 'design is also cleaning and reorganizing a desk drawer, pulling an impacted tooth, baking an apple pie, choosing sides for a back-lot baseball game, and educating a child.'[3]

If design is done by everyone, then why are only some rewarded for it? Writer Sasha Costanza-Chock points at 'the political economy of design',[4] and the fact that the 'access to design work is deeply unequal and is shaped by the matrix of domination'.[5] In other words, the access to paid design work is only granted to those in privileged positions, which relies on ties with industry, education, and the design institutions. Professional design organizations have a firm hand in deciding what design is, by maintaining quality standards for membership using norms derived from industrial production. The matrix of domination that Costanza-Chock describes, leads to a situation where positions of power in the professional design world aren't as accessible as design makes it seem. We will see how the notion of the professional designer is in large part based on a capitalism, colonialism, and patriarchy.

The Rise of Professionalism

It wasn't until the sixteenth century that the first professionals emerged in the fields of law, medicine, and theology. A 'profession' was the name of the vow that had to be taken before entering these occupations.[6] Only the upper classes could enter these professions, after they had received education in the first universities, which were founded by the Catholic Church. Fields like engineering and pharmacy followed suit, and the first contours of

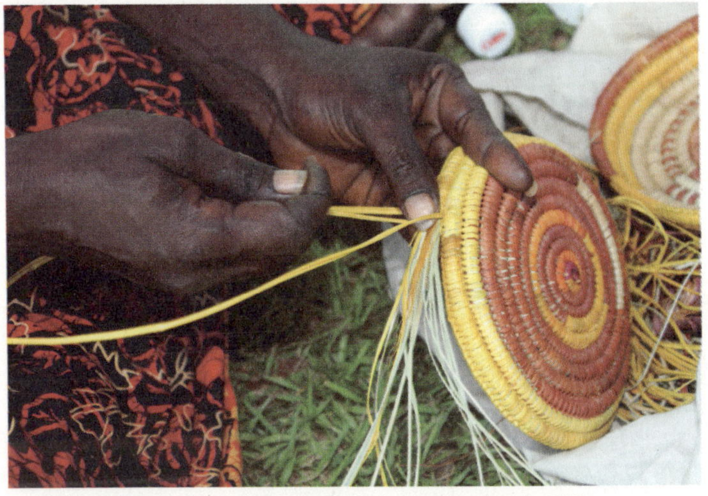

Christine Owney from the Jawoyn tribe weaving a basket from tree roots, Australia, 2006.

professionalism were a few highly protected disciplines, restricted to a small elite.

Graphic design wasn't a separate discipline yet and early design activities such as printing, etching, and typesetting were practiced on workshop floors and considered working class jobs.[7]

Workshops were often family-owned, and usually led by the head of the household. Guilds united workshops in one town or region, and exerted control over who could carry out the craft to protect the interests of the local trade, as Richard Sennett explains in *The Craftsman*.[8] They had their own mechanism of exclusion, and were not very accessible for outsiders without family connections, or a without a journeymen's license.

Industrialization brought about the necessity for professionalization in design. The workshop model could not meet the requirements of the scale of mass production, which required specialized tasks. Advertising became one the earliest professionalized disciplines, with the Outdoor Advertising Association lobbying group being founded in 1891. Advertising journal *Printers Ink* was launched in 1888.[9] In the UK, the first design associations and specialized design schools appeared by the end of the nineteenth century, born from the Arts and Crafts movement. This vibrant birth of the design discipline saw the foundation of many

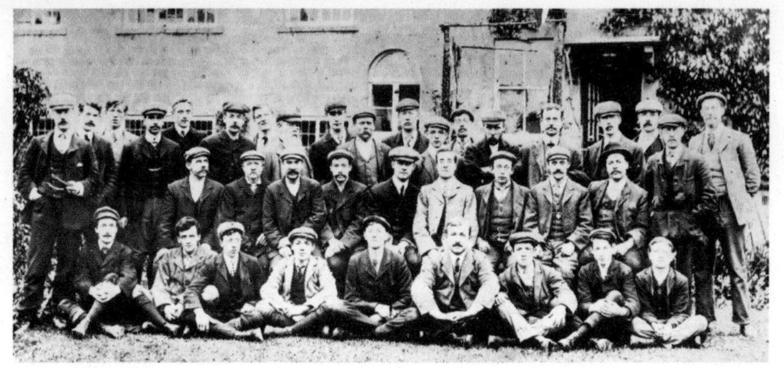

The Guild of Handicraft, 1906.

professional organizations such as the Art Workers' Guild, the Guild of Handicraft, and the Century Guild.

Arts & Crafts was a movement that argued for a return to a more craft-based approach to design, in response to the loss of quality in mass produced goods. With its socialist leanings it wished to improve the horrible working conditions of industrial workers. In doing so, it shaped design into the professional practice it is today. Following the Arts & Crafts movement in the UK, similar arts and design organizations sprung up around Europe, such as the German *Werkbund* and the Dutch *De Stijl*, which played an important role in bringing emerging forms of modernism in design to the foreground.

By the 1920s new revolutionary design schools in Europe, in particular the Bauhaus in Germany and VKhUTEMAS in Russia, sought a unity between art and industry, emphasizing the social importance of industrial mass production. The Bauhaus were open to anyone regardless of age or sex, but female students were highly encouraged to focus on so-called women's work like weaving and textiles. The VKhUTEMAS in Moscow aimed to have a representative student body, specifically recruiting students from worker and farmer backgrounds. In the UK, female designers

All men are designers. All that we do, almost all the time, is design, for design is basic to all human activity.

VICTOR PAPANEK, DESIGNER

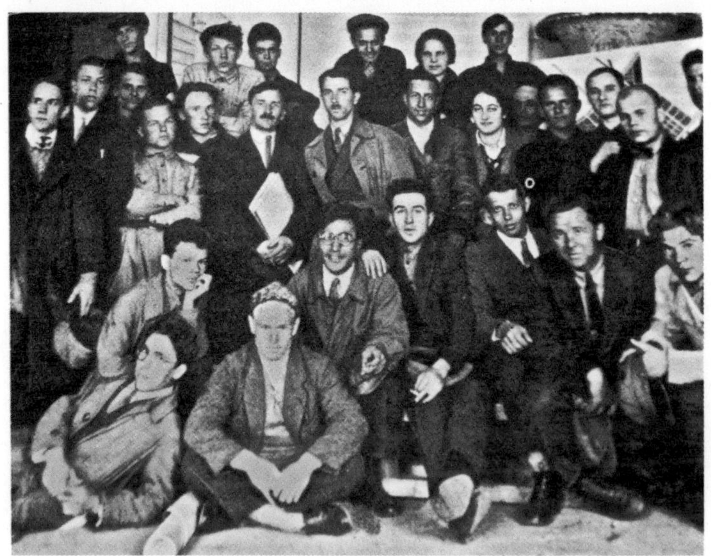

VKhUTEMAS students, 1927.

were encouraged to work in the domestic sphere, and were not welcome in the upper echelons of British design associations until after the 1950s.[10]

Within a century, professionalism in design has turned into a complex network of institutions, trade associations, academic degrees, and industry sponsorship. The connections create an infrastructure that legitimizes graphic design by the virtue of certain industry standards of quality and originality. A membership of a professional association can mean a higher chance of winning awards or commissions, or being invited to deliver a keynote at a conference. In design education, some institutions require tutors to have MA or PhD degrees, making it difficult, or even impossible for self-taught designers to enter these institutions. As positions at the top of these institutions are still dominated by privileged groups in society, designers from marginalized backgrounds are underrepresented in both trade organizations and design school faculties.[11]

If You Don't Get Paid, it's Not Work
What distinguishes a professional from an amateur? A designer

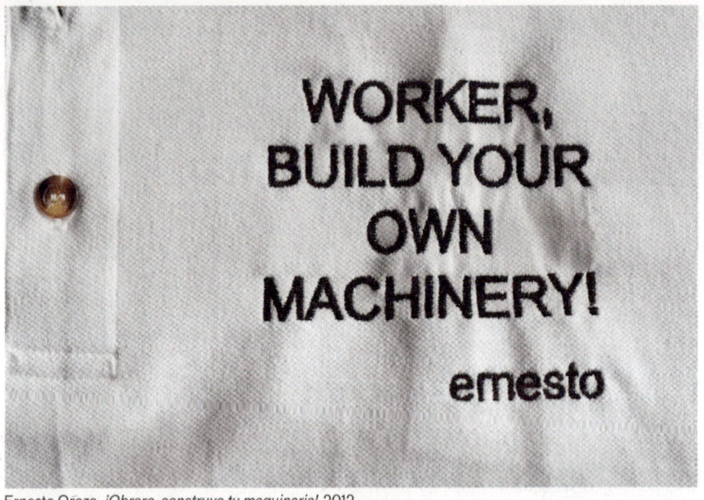

Ernesto Oroza, *¡Obrero, construye tu maquinaria!*, 2012.

who doesn't make money with designs, is less likely to be considered a professional. That seems obvious enough, but the capitalist idea of work has led to the exclusion of many activities from the economy. Consider the fact that some of the most vital work is unpaid and not considered work at all. Domestic work and informal house work like raising children, cleaning, cooking, fixing, and taking care of sick or aging family members. Because it is not valued as 'real' work, this predominantly female workforce does not get paid, cannot put it on their CVs, or receive welfare or benefits based on this working history. The fact that one of the highest paid 'creative' jobs is that of marketing consultant, and that parents teaching their children to draw is not considered work at all, says plenty about how creative work is valued in capitalism.

When designer Michel Rock visited his first national design conference in 1994, he wrote: 'Ray Gun is hobnobbing with Emigre, Aldus is eyeing Adobe across the room, a Benetton magazine is whispering in the corner with a corporate annual report, Yale disses Cranbrook over cocktails. With that many graphic designers in a single room, you cannot help pondering issues of professional association.'[12]

Design professionalism thrives on a cosy mingling of design celebrities and industry. Design conferences and awards will devote little attention to handwritten signs for a corner bodega or quilts made by domestic workers, unless they are curated by a design professional and officially selected as 'design'. Costanza-Chock explains that many designers thus appropriate and build on the unpaid design work done by amateurs.[13]

The emphasis on industry involvement and monetary value does not suggest that design can be judged regardless of its economic and social context. Some design is simply more impactful or useful for a wider audience. Like any creative work, it is important to reward those who excel, which is after all at the heart of learning, sharing, and enjoying creativity. One of the better qualities of the design industry is that it is still acceptable for graphic designers to be self-taught.

A Matter of Taste

Amateur or vernacular design is all about taste. What is beautiful or not has been the subject of many philosophical debates. For centuries aesthetics was discussed as something pure, with an inherent personal or natural quality. In the 1960s the French sociologist Pierre Bourdieu took a different approach to aesthetics, and surveyed the cultural preferences of various French households. From his detailed findings, he concluded that 'good taste' is often the taste of the ruling class, and each social group is recognizable by their own aesthetic codes, separating one class from another. The status of each class depends on social capital, which consists

There is so much incredible, insanely beautiful design in South America, made by people that Design would not call designers. Historically, it has not been considered Design; it was labeled as craft or some other elitist term Designers came up with to denigrate and devalue many peoples' traditions and narratives.

RAMON TEJADA, DESIGNER

of social qualities passed on through education and upbringing. Bourdieu showed that taste is not merely a qualitative matter, but a social orientation that is decided by social factors such as family, education, and wealth.[14]

The awareness of different cultural codes between classes started to appear in graphic design in the 1980s. Tibor Kalman, a self-taught graphic designer, saw an emancipatory potential in work made by non-designers; roadside sign paintings, shopfront lettering, and shop sale posters. His studio M&Co became well-known with work inspired by vernacular designs. 'I guess I got sick of beauty. And then I got very interested in what is mundane and ordinary and things like that, and then even more interested in like, what a shack looks like In the Caribbean.'[15] Kalman favoured this 'anti-design' because of its cultural diversity and authenticity, which inspired his later work for Benetton's magazine *Colors*.

Years later the vernacular style had become trendy among designers in the US. Design writer Rick Poynor suggested that its success had to do with its nostalgic quality, which 'triggers reassuring emotion in consumers'.[16] Celebrating vernacular design was perhaps once motivated by class consciousness, but it was easily appropriated by capitalism's search for new aesthetics. Others disliked low-brow aesthetics, and believed designers should be the harbingers of good taste, as Mr. Keedy's wrote in an essay in *Emigre* in 2004: 'Although they are unlikely to admit it, designers are implicit stylists and tastemakers. ... Culture is expressed and understood through style, which is mostly created and evaluated by designers.'[17]

Today, the appropriations of vernacular and non-professional aesthetics are plentiful, but graphic design still harbours a sense of entitlement as the sole proprietors of 'good taste'. Professionalism can have its blind spots, as Pentagram's 2015 identity for Hillary Clinton's presidential campaign demonstrates. The design featured the capital letter 'H' with a rightward pointing arrow. The design for Trump's campaign was a red baseball cap with a plagiarized slogan, typeset in all caps serifs. Despite its amateurism, the baseball cap design ended up being one of the most famous and most copied US election items ever. After the election, designer Michael Bierut from Pentagram admitted that the professionalism

                    CAPS LOCK — Part 2

Isn't style too important to be left in the hands of amateurs?

MR. KEEDY, DESIGNER

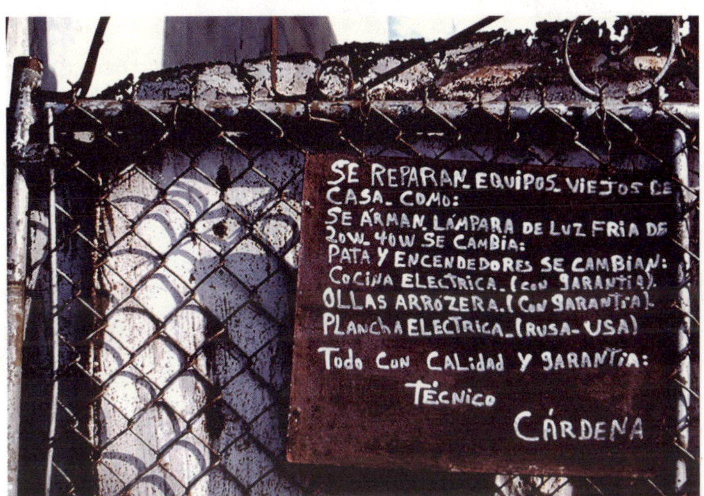

Penelope De Bozzi and Ernesto Oroza, Repair shop in Cuba, 1999.

of the design could have 'reinforced the establishment status'[18] that Hillary Clinton was criticized for.

There is much less of a clear divide between vernacular and professional design today, but that doesn't mean class divisions have disappeared. A Dutch government report from 2014 mentioned that after decades of diminished differences between social groups, the gap is widening again.[19] The highest educated in society rarely socialize with the lowest educated. Visual languages are still coded to appeal to certain social groups, which are increasingly divided along the lines of education and income. Graphic designers have to master the visual language that speaks to their respective audiences, which means that the majority of professional graphic designers are fluent in addressing those who have the most money to spend; the higher educated, the urban situated, and privileged classes. When other groups in society are addressed, designers can be confronted with the shortcomings of their own educational and social background.

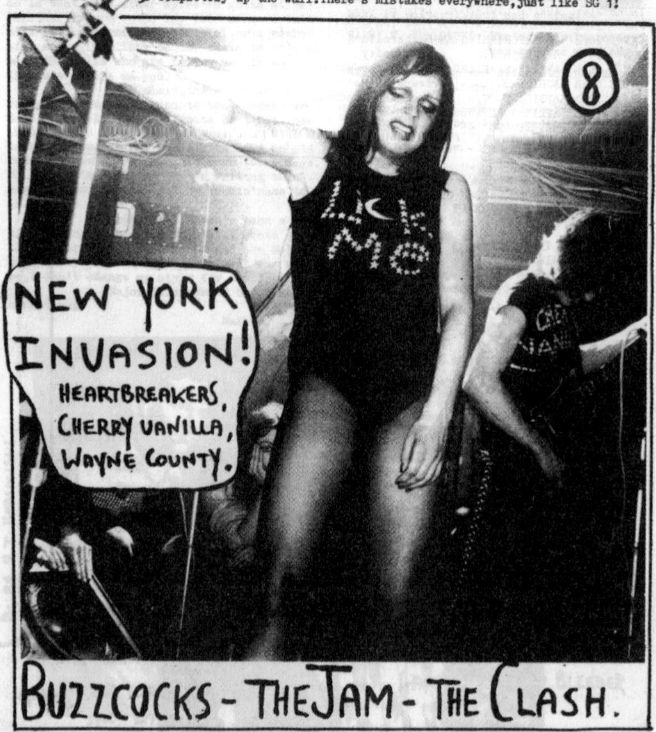

Mark Perry, *Sniffin' Glue*, March 1977.

Everyone Can be a Designer

Printers maintained a monopoly on mass-produced visual communication for centuries. This made it easier for authorities to control the distribution of information. In the nineteenth century, cheaper printing presses gave rise to an amateur printing culture. In the US at the time, 50,000 different newspapers were made by amateur printers, much to the outrage of the trade press, as Lisa Gitelman notes.[20] The mimeograph became available in the 1900s, making it somewhat easier and less expensive to own printing equipment. Mimeography was known as stencil printing or Risograph, a technique favoured by political groups to print political leaflets or underground newspapers that needed fast and cheap reproduction.

Do-it-yourself (DIY) culture emerged from home improvement in the 1950s, when construction materials became available to common households. The first appearance of ready-mixed paint was resisted by the oil and colour business that feared the end of their monopoly.[21] The invention of the commercial photocopier in 1959 opened up mass media production for a larger audience, and created a new wave of DIY graphic design. Handmade magazines in punk culture created an underground culture of media circulation made by fans with access to photocopiers in the late 1970s. These were no minor operations, for instance the punk zine *Sniffin' Glue* (1976–1977) by Mark Perry was produced in a print run of 10,000 copies.[22] The punk DIY culture valued self-sufficiency and challenged communication monopolies by media companies. Design theorist Paul Atkinson calls DIY therefore a 'leveller of class' and a 'political force' by which personal messages could reach a wider audience.[23]

Desktop computers and graphic design software changed the access to graphic design production completely in the 1990s. Even though computers and printers were expensive at first, soon every person with a computer and (bootlegged) graphic software could achieve the same technical quality as professionals, much to the dismay of many designers who feared to lose their status and livelihood. 'By making our work so easy to do, we are devaluing our profession', warned design historian Steven Heller. 'With everything so democratic, we can lose the elite status that gives us credibility.'[24] That hasn't been the case, as Ellen Lupton points out in her book on DIY design, seeing that 'the field got bigger rather than smaller'.[25] The democratization of graphic design, print production, and online publishing has allowed people without prior access to media to claim their space in the production of knowledge and culture. These examples of DIY culture are from

Europe and the US, but DIY culture should be understood as culturally diverse as other cultural forms, and each region has its own DIY with its cultural specificities.

The broader accessibility of graphic design tools is a positive development, but that doesn't mean there aren't any risks. Websites such as Fiverr and TaskRabbit facilitate a new online gig economy for cultural services like graphic design.[26] Anyone can simply post a job, for example the design of a logo or an infographic, and designers are set to pit against each other to deliver the best results for the lowest price. If graphic designers aren't able to organize themselves in solidarity, tech companies can easily monopolize the link between client and designers as they have done in other sectors. A new interpretation of trade organizations should not exclude people from design, or exist to merely protect professional standards but to establish bargaining power for designers, for more collectively organized and less toxic design work.

Professional Neutrality

As the chapter 'The Designer as a Scribe' demonstrated, graphic designers possess technical skills that are needed to prevent counterfeiting, and guarantee the authenticity of valuable graphic documents such as currencies, birth certificates, drivers licenses, degrees, and so forth.[27] Professionality goes hand in hand with accountability. Having knowledge of how to reproduce documents gives graphic designers a position of 'document power'. An unwritten rule in graphic design ethics is that these powers are not abused in any way.

Gitelman recounts the early days of job printers in the late 1800s, when job printers provided businesses with basic administrative documents: ledgers, bill-books, chequebooks, cash books, orders, worker's time schedules, etc. Printer Oscar Harpel, famous for his sample book *Typograph* (1871), was arrested in Cincinnati for counterfeiting meal tickets and using them at a local restaurant.[28] Today, security measures against counterfeiting are even hardcoded in programmes such as Adobe Photoshop, as anyone who has tried to scan or edit an image of a banknote will quickly learn.

We believe that everyone is an expert based on their own lived experience, and that we all have unique and brilliant contributions to bring to a design process.

SASHA COSTANZA-CHOCK, DESIGNER

Desperate times call for desperate measures, and under certain circumstances graphic designers will have to choose whether to abide by their professionality or defy authority. Knowledge of documents and reproduction techniques can be reappropriated by graphic designers in times of need. During World War II, printers, artists, and graphic designers in the Netherlands used their skills of reproduction in the resistance against the German occupation. One of the leading figures was Gerrit van der Veen, a sculptor who had previously designed banknotes for the Dutch mint. This acquainted him with technical knowledge on watermarks and banknotes. Van der Veen founded an underground counterfeiting agency that produced illegal documents in large numbers, working together with artists and printers. The agency employed hundreds of people, producing over 65,000 false IDs and 75,000 food stamps. In 1944 he was executed after a failed attack on a jailhouse in Amsterdam, the night after he and other resistance fighters had successfully stolen 10,000 blank IDs from the state printer's offices.

Practicing a profession with certain quality standards is not the same as showing solidarity in times of repression. Dutch graphic designers were asked during World War II by the German authorities to pledge allegiance if they wanted to keep getting commissions. Some refused and went underground to assist in counterfeiting activities, but many also signed the pledge, afraid to lose work or becoming suspect themselves, even though their Jewish colleagues had already been arrested and deported in large numbers. It is under these circumstances that professionality and economic dependency are questioned at its very core.

Informal Economies

The analysis of professional design thus far has been limited to a Western perspective. However, in many countries, studying design, and studying in general, is only available to a few. We should also keep in mind that the informal economy is the still the largest employer worldwide. Informal jobs account for 60 percent of all jobs, and in Sub-Saharan Africa for as much as 75 percent.[29] The term 'informal' has a negative connotation, which is why journalist Robert Neuwirth prefers the term 'System D', which comes from the French *débrouillard*, meaning resourceful. The term provides a different way of looking at the informal economy, one that is successful not despite of, but thanks to, the lack of official infrastructures.

Design work in the informal economy is relevant because it responds to local demands, rather than being a product of 'global' campaigns directed from afar. The limited availability of materials and a lack of infrastructure has given rise to rich design cultures, often by people who don't call themselves designers at all. Media consumption in the Global South depends on informal channels, because foreign music, books, software, and movies are simple unaffordable for most. For those practicing graphic design, acquiring legal software and font licenses is not always an option. A subscription to Adobe Creative Cloud is $79 a month, and typeface licenses can run up to a $100 per weight.

Brazilian author Andrea Bandoni calls System D design a 'survival strategy', an 'expression of a collective improvisational spirit', filling 'a niche in the local non-official economic system'.[31] Some of this 'unlicensed' creativity was born out of necessity under colonialism, as Neuwirth points out. Slaves and serfs were often excluded from the official economy: 'System D was their system, and potentially their liberation.'[32]

In contrast to the Western professional design culture, which is built around institutions and primarily focuses on luxurious products or global campaigns, System D design is small-scale, and responds to local conditions using local production qualities. Global advertising campaigns that try to blend in with local contexts can end up making cultural mistakes that are misguided, or worse, offensive.[33]

                    CAPS LOCK – Part 2

Many a respectable American citizen of today got his education, and many a legitimate and constructive enterprise got its initial capital, from peddling, piracy, smuggling, and illegality.

JANE JACOBS, SOCIOLOGIST

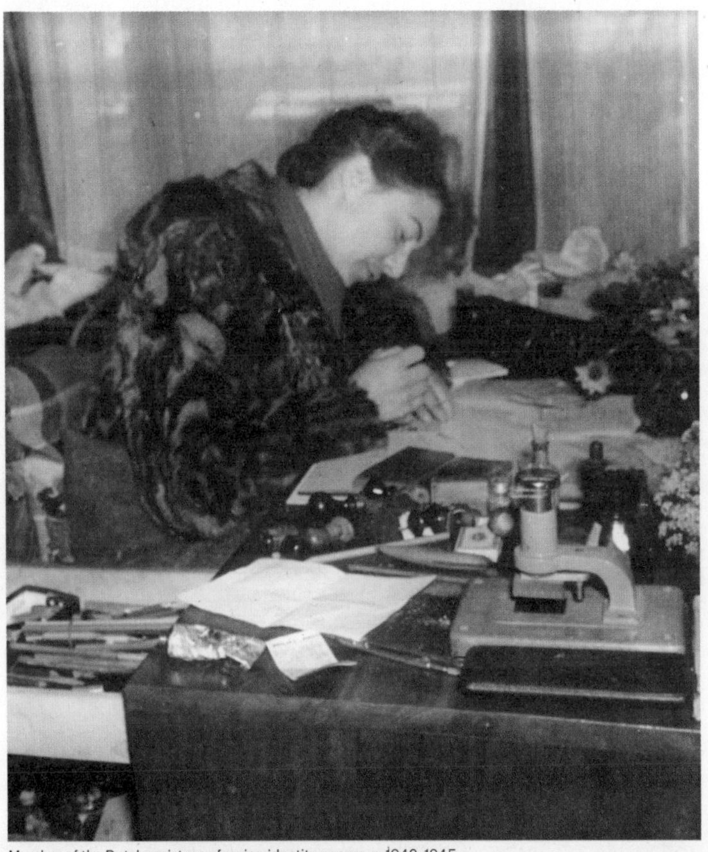

Member of the Dutch resistance forging identity papers, c. 1942–1945.

Just as the vernacular design of 1980s New York was an inspiration to professional designers, discoloured paper, bad printing, or hand-drawn typefaces produced in the informal economy are sometimes glorified by Western designers. Romanticizing aesthetics that are born from poverty and scarcity should be avoided, as Cuban designer Ernesto Oroza points out.[34] Rather than fixating on the aesthetics, System D design can provide more socially aware communication tactics and strategies that are better situated in communities. In *Design Justice* (2020), Sasha Costanza-Chock suggests that keeping design work invisible or hidden from the official economy can even be a strategy to 'avoid incorporation and appropriation'.[35] A System D approach to design can be a way to survive for communities that face repression, or those involved in resistance.

Hardworking Goodlooking is a graphic design and publishing collective based in the Philippines, the US, and the Netherlands. Vernacular and DIY from the Philippines is their natural habitat, but rather than appropriating or copying styles, they are 'interested in decolonization of cultural labor, parlance in the vernacular, and the value of what has been invisible'.[36] In other words they explore the edges of unofficial cultural production by carefully documenting vernacular aesthetics, valuing it by producing new work with local producers, and forging collaboration with local artists on equal footing.

Gatekeepers

By questioning the nature of professionalism this chapter has tried to shed a light on the way amateurs operate in the field of graphic design. The themes discussed in this chapter come together in the underlying economic power structures that have shaped the design 'professionals' as we know them today, and keep shaping both education and practice.

By retracing the origin of the design professional to its earliest appearances, we find that the profession is a form of protection and exclusion, limiting the access to knowledge, the access to the means of production, and the influence over discourse. This was the case for the medieval guilds as well as for the design schools and professional organizations that followed. By the 1900s the

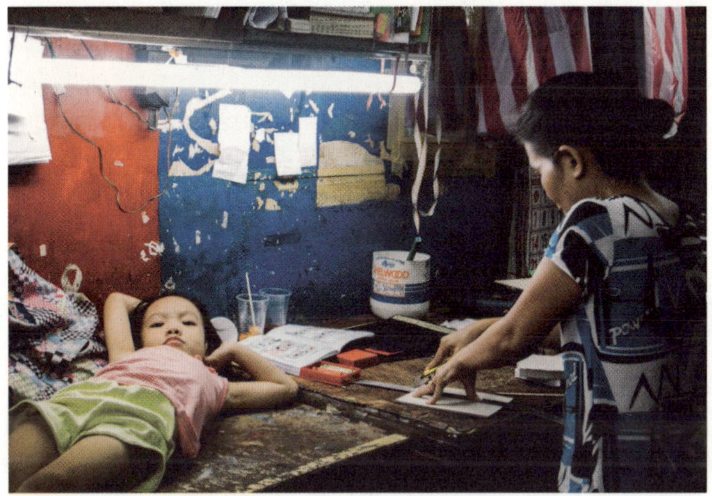

Ma'am Ateng of Tito Aquino Noscal Printing Services in Manila, and her daughter, the Philippines, 2015.

role of European design professional was reserved for a privileged class of mostly men, who relied on access to industry and mass production.

For the majority of society, including women, the working class, the uneducated, and the marginalized, design could only be practiced informally as unpaid amateur work. We see the same inequality in access to the professional design world with the overrepresentation of Western designers in international design organizations such as ICOGRADA or AGI today. By measures of equality, these bodies do not represent the variety of design culture in the world, but are dominated by a Eurocentric and capitalist interpretation of design.

It would be a mistake to discount or discredit professional design organizations by their historic power structures alone. A certain degree of 'professionality' in design can safeguard qualities, for example in sustainability, durability, and safety. We should not underestimate the value of designers using accessibility standards like W3C[37] so the colour blind can use websites, and designers using durable binding so that books can have long lives. Those standards, even though some are more important than others,[38] are well-served to live within design schools and design associations. However, associations and design schools have gained tremendous influence by judging portfolios and catering to the needs of industry.

How can this change? Design organizations can pivot to play more of a social function, by organizing designers locally, discussing issues in the field in collective ways, and by collective lobbying or bargaining. Trade organizations already help freelancers in legal conflicts, and make sure employed designers receive better pay.[39] The social aspects of professional design that come closest to the role of unions and the organization of intellectual commons, remain urgently needed to achieve better work conditions for designers, and to create alternative economic models.

'We might be better off if we jettison the idea of a singular definition of what design should be, and perhaps a single organization for all graphic designers', said Michael Rock in his essay on professionalism.[40] How do we keep what is good about professionalism, and improve the parts that are harmful? A more inclusive definition of design can indeed open design to non-professional knowledge, differences in education, and diverse cultural and social backgrounds.

The Design Justice network tries to be an inclusive organization for designers, and lists a series of principles on their website, one of which reads: 'We believe that everyone is an expert based on their own lived experience, and that we all have unique and brilliant contributions to bring to a design process.'[41] Sasha Costanza-Chock references feminist standpoint theory in this context which: 'recognizes that all knowledge is situated in a particular embodied experience of the knower'.[42] There is much more to learn from this rich insight, but in the case of the amateur and the professional it can help to understand that design knowledge is not limited to professionals, but spread out over many types of people and interests, the majority of which are unrecognized, uncredited or left without compensation for their contributions.

A more ethical sharing of knowledge and resources in design begins with the realization that the majority of design in the world is done by those who do not call themselves designers. Following the principle of situated knowledge, this means that those who harbour design knowledge should be recognized and become part of the value exchange in the professional sphere, by receiving

visibility, recognition, and compensation through a radical redistribution of the benefits of design. Hopefully the distinction between
the professional and the amateur will then become something of
the past.

We might be better off if we jettison
the idea of a singular definition of what
design should be, and perhaps a single
organization for all graphic designers.

MICHAEL ROCK, DESIGNER

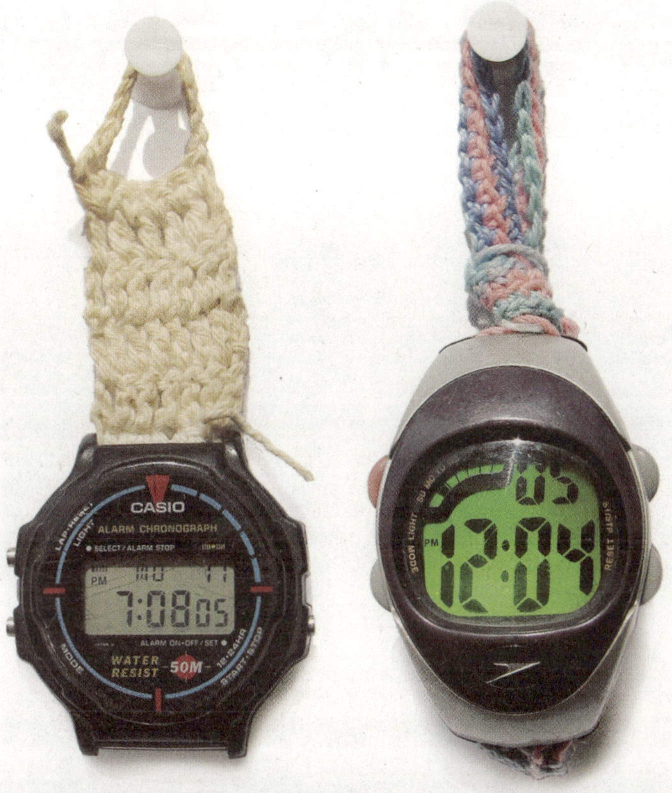

Ernesto Oroza, *Two Wall Clocks*, 2016.

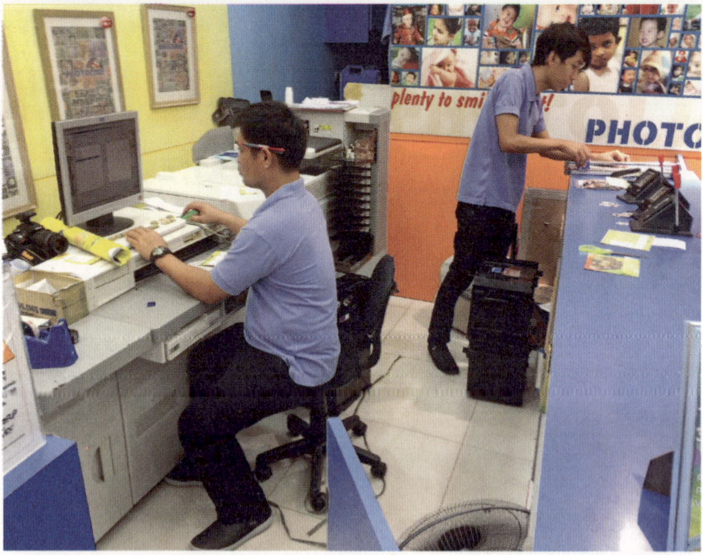

plenty to smi
PHOTO

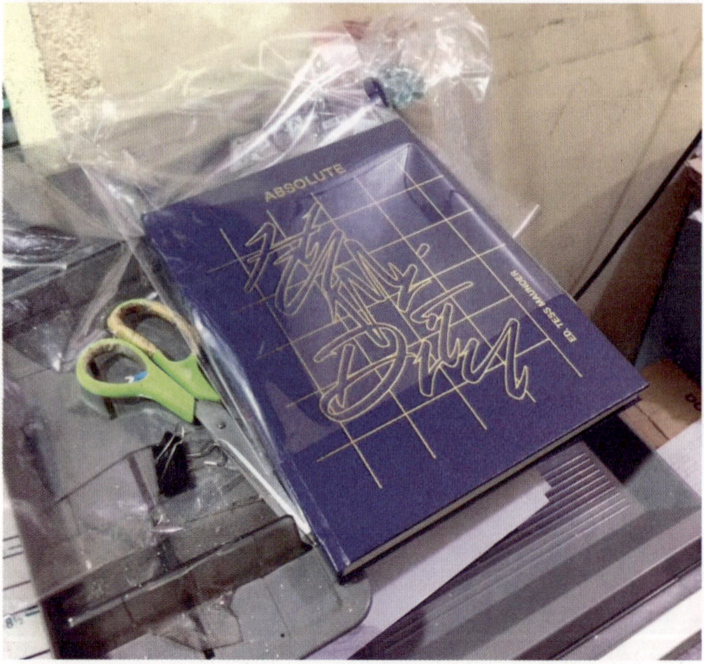

ABSOLUTE
ED TESS MAINOCR

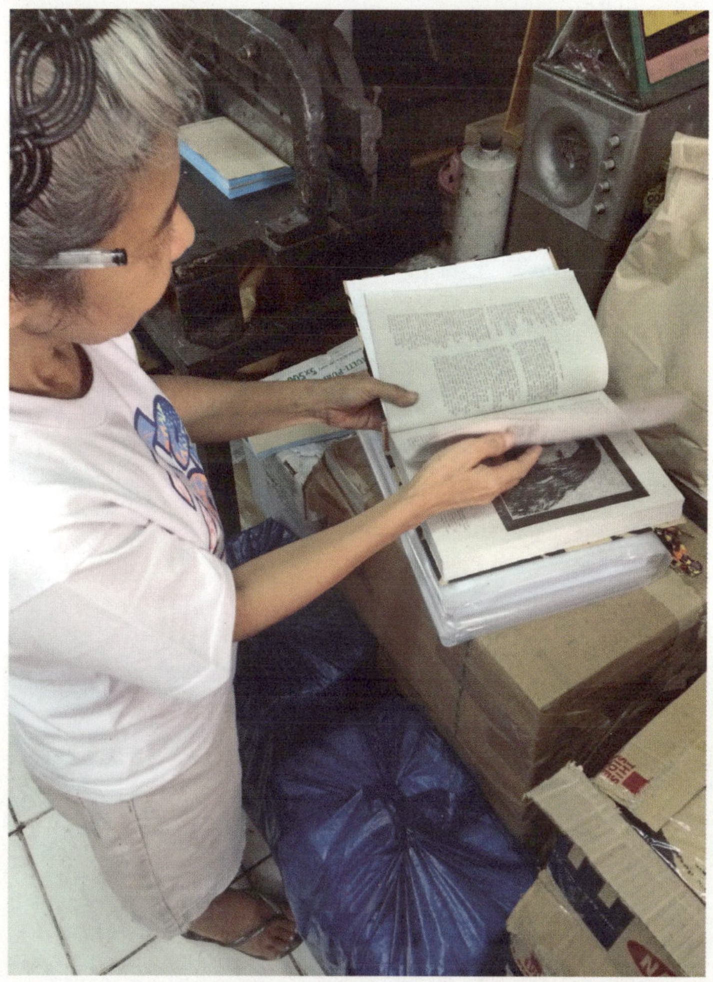

↑   Quality control of *In Darkness*, a publication by Kristian and Kevin Henson, published by
     Hardworking Goodlooking. All three editions were printed at Cute Bookstore on Recto Avenue,
     a cottage industry print hotspot in Manila, underneath the LRT (Light Rail Transit) overpass.
←↑   Photoline is a photo shop at SM City Sucat in Parañaque City. On a supply run for AFOU (Association
     for the Filling of Every Container Until it Leaks), an illustration portfolio and quixotic office giveaway
     collection by artists Ines Agathe Maud and Paul Guian.
←   Pick up day for *Absolute Humidity* at Tito Aquino Noscal Printing Services, Hardworking
     Goodlooking's preferred Recto printers. This book, edited by Tess Maunder, contains essays and
     interviews about the cultural and other weathers of the Asia Pacific region. All photos by Hardworking
     Goodlooking.

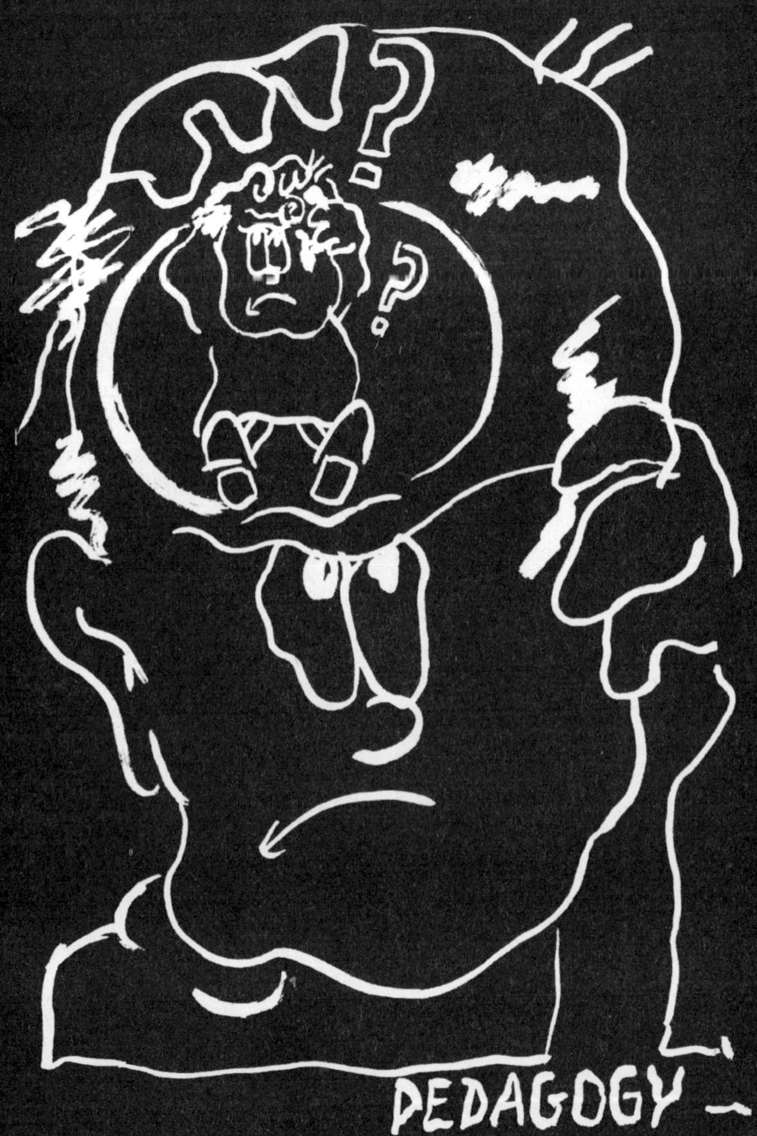

Illustration by Blandine Molin, 2021.

THE DESIGNER AS EDUCATOR

School is the advertising agency which makes you believe that you need the society as it is.
IVAN ILLICH

The classroom remains the most radical space of possibility in the academy.
BELL HOOKS

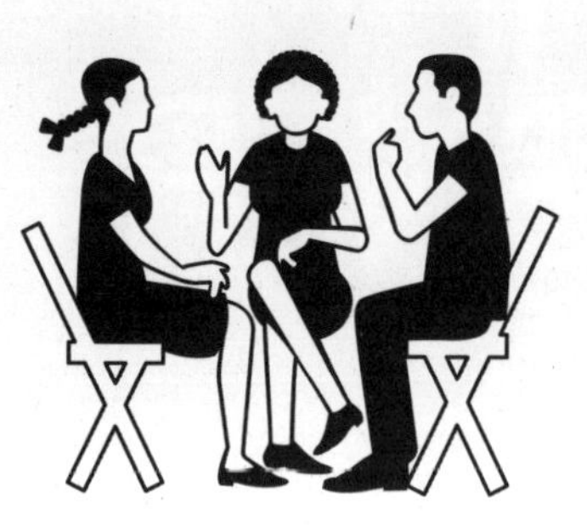

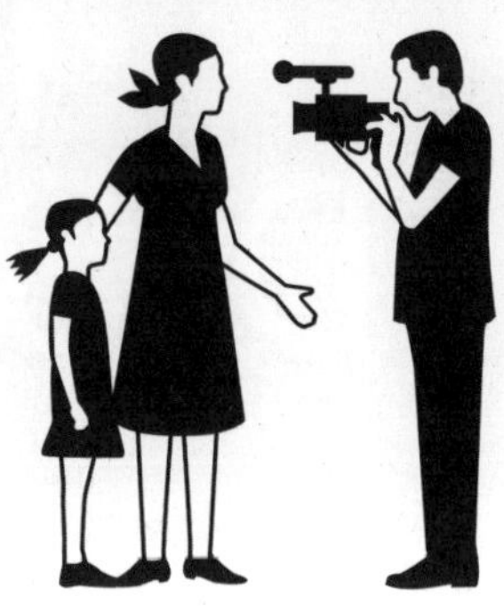

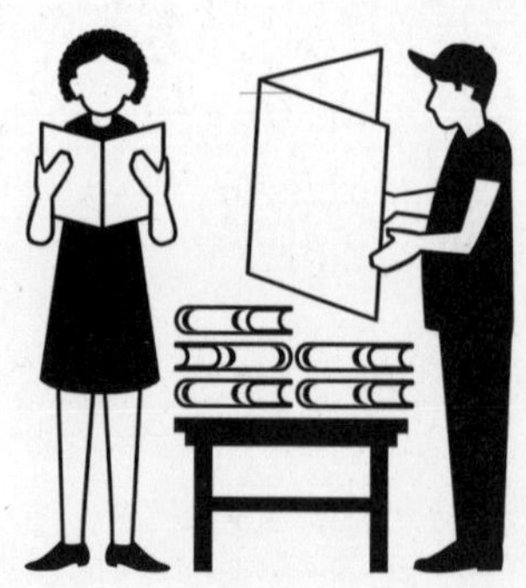

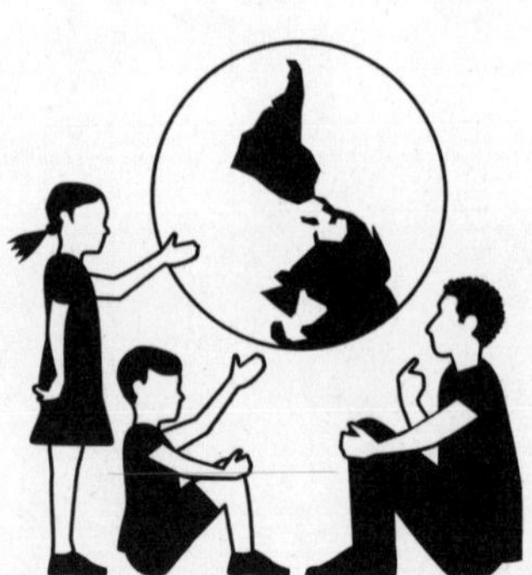

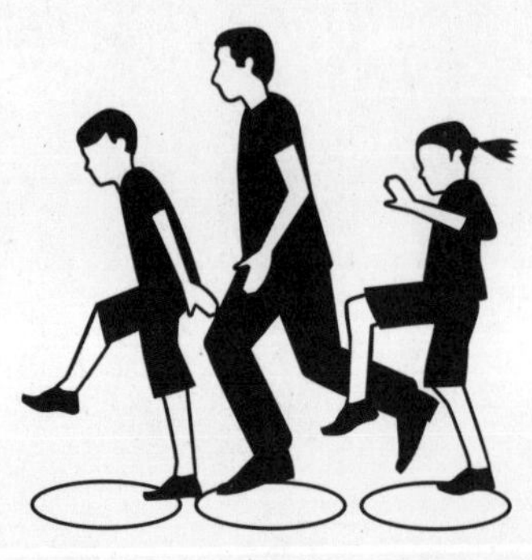

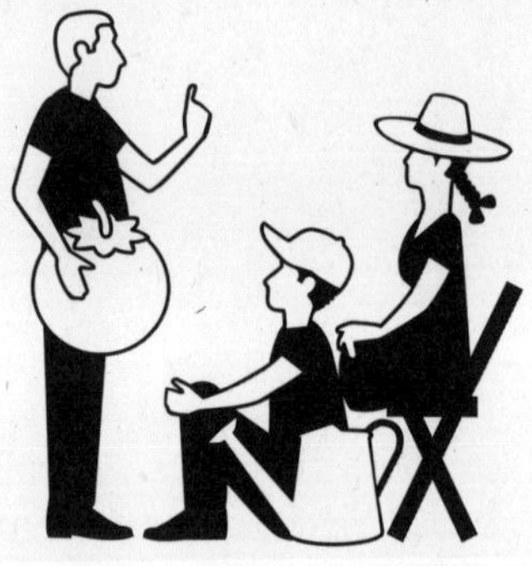

TEACHING DESIGN

How do you learn graphic design? Less than a 150 years ago, graphic design was a practice-skilled job. The first design schools were founded in the early twentieth century and within a century design education had become an entire industry. Today, graphic design education is provided as summer schools, vocational courses, bachelor degrees, master degrees, and PhD programmes. A design education is not the only thing that can nourish the talent and skills needed to practice design. Graphic design still exhibits some characteristics of a craft-based discipline, which can be learned in practice rather than from theory.

We've read about graphic designers as workers, entrepreneurs, and amateurs. In the last chapter of this section, we shift the focus to the history of education, and how economic conditions have shaped graphic design education. It is hardly surprising that design education is geared towards the needs of the industry. Professional graphic design evolved from the needs of industrial production, and education should be able to provide designers with skills that can pay the rent. But there has been a shift over the last three decades. Design education has become more costly and privatized, with a lot more graphic designers graduating than there are jobs available. With some graphic design degrees costing up to $50,000 a year, a student debt is about the only guarantee a design degree can give you.

Design graduates have become products themselves, produced by schools that resemble 'designer factories'. As such, design education has succumbed to criticism. Practitioners, students, and teachers have voiced their concerns that education should be less focused on quantity, and that the social aspects of learning are getting lost in the pressure of earning educational commodities, also known as study credits. Alternatives for graphic design education

← Icons by Iconoclasistas, 2015.

are popping up, challenging conservative teaching methods and earning models. By beginning with the history of graphic design education itself, we will work our way towards finding alternatives.

A Short History of Education

Education is an important activity for young people to become members of society. Young children and/or parents may not always realize the benefit of education, which is why compulsory primary education can provide some equal grounding. Teachers are placed in a position of authority to instil order and discipline for the learning to take place. Not complying with the rules of the teacher and the school will inevitably lead to punishment

Learning wasn't always like this. Hunter-gatherers did not distinguish learning from play or work, and education was much more integrated in daily social life. Children learned through play and exploration alongside adults, without a strict hierarchy between students and teachers. These learning/playing activities were self-chosen and intrinsically motivated, which is different from how education is viewed today.[1]

The first agricultural societies in the Middle East changed the idea of education. These societies were much more hierarchical, with emperors and landowners ruling over a mass of slaves and workers. There were schools that trained scribes, a pre-modern form of the administrator/printer/typographer, which were accessible for boys from the upper classes.[2] Most children had to work, just like their parents, and the most important lesson to be learned was that masters and elders had to be obeyed.

Literacy in ancient civilizations was extremely limited, and access to written knowledge was aligned with positions of power. By reserving education for the upper classes, this knowledge was kept within an elite circle. There were exceptions, for example in ancient Greece where literacy was widespread among male citizens.[3] Sparta even provided public schooling. In Athens the upper classes could follow secondary education at the lyceum, or at Plato's Academy, a school which took place in a park.

Until the Renaissance, the Catholic Church had a monopoly on education and knowledge production in Europe. In the Middle Ages, literacy rates dropped considerably compared to the Greek

CAPS LOCK — Part 2

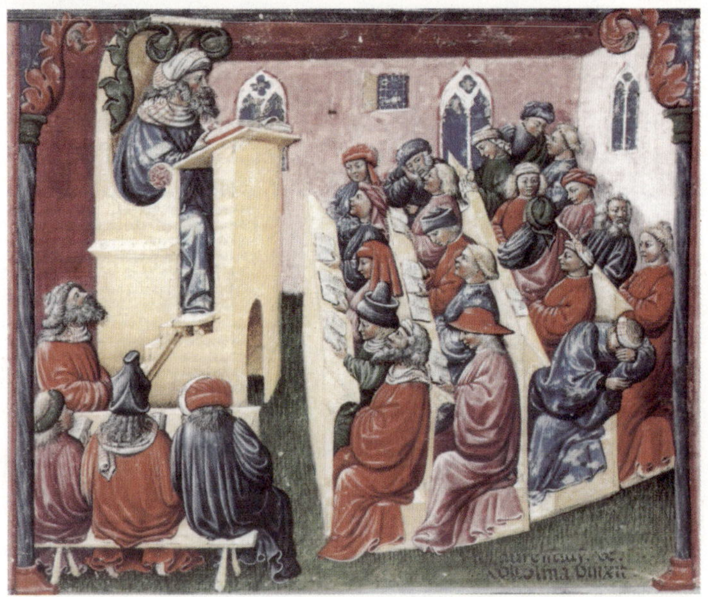

The first universities. Henricus de Alemannia with his students, University of Bologna, fourteenth century.

city states. The only schools were Cathedral or Monastic schools where the nobility and clergy received their education. These eventually became the first European universities in cities such as Bologna, Paris, and Oxford from the eleventh and twelfth century onwards, which taught law, theology, and medicine to the upper classes.

Gutenberg's invention of the printing press in Europe was a turning point for literacy numbers, as books could be printed in languages other than Latin. A vibrant print culture and an increasing number of religious schools pushed literacy in the UK between 1550–1750 from 20 to 54 percent.[4] Enlightenment thinkers wrote extensively on the importance of education, and the first nation states saw public education as a way to educate and shape their citizens.

The Workshop and the Studio

Until the end of the nineteenth century, graphic design in Europe was taught on the workshop floor. Printing shops were often family businesses, and would double as a family home. In the workshop, apprentices and journeymen worked under a master who dictated standards and quality.[5] An apprenticeship took five to ten years, and it would take about the same time to become a journeyman. A journeyman could submit his 'masterpiece' at the end of his learning period and try to become a master himself. Owning a workshop depended on whether your family had the financial resources, since ownership was often passed on within a family.[6] Without the capital to set up shop, journeymen would have to travel around, selling their labour, not unlike the freelance graphic designers of today.[7]

A shift took place in Italy during the Renaissance, when artists were sponsored by wealthy merchants, like the Medici family. Sennett shows how the Renaissance artist became focused on individual creativity, giving rise to a split between the artist and the craftsman.[8] While printers were craftsmen that worked collectively and for whom originality was less important, the Renaissance artist embraced autonomous creativity, and promoted a unique style to find work. These Italian artists founded the first art schools in the sixteenth and seventeenth century called *Accademia*, the model for modern art schools. The academy only accepted establish artists, and its role was to elevate their influence in society, ensuring important commissions would go to its prestigious members.[9]

The School as a Factory
It wasn't until the end of the nineteenth century that education became compulsory in Europe. Children under the age of nine were still legally employed in factories until 1883, and factory owners even lobbied to have children considered adults at the age of ten or eleven to keep them working longer.[10] The struggle of the labour movement eventually led to universal education, and a ban on child labour. Education finished by the age of twelve or thirteen, and most children would start working anyway. This turned out to be a positive development for factory owners. Children learned how to read and write, and they learned discipline and punctuality, making them better workers.

The French philosopher Michel Foucault saw the societies of eighteenth- and nineteenth-century Europe as disciplinary societies. Foucault observed how a person moves from one controlled

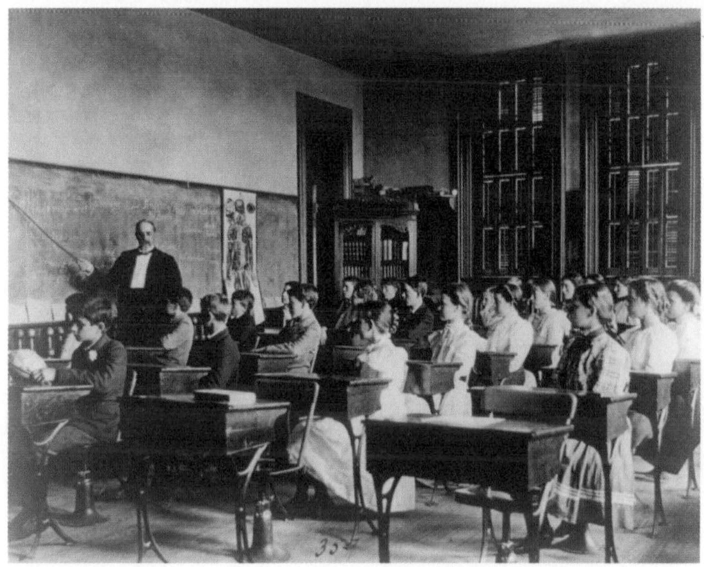

School children studying anatomy or health, Washington DC, US, 1899. Photo by F.B. Johnston.

environment to the next: the family, the school, the army, the factory, and in between the hospital or the prison.[11] Each environment was organized through strict hierarchy and with its own disciplinary measures. The nineteenth-century educator Ellwood Patterson said: 'Our schools are, in a sense, factories, in which the raw products (children) are to be shaped and fashioned into products to meet the various demands of life.'[12]

Schools created better workers, but education also taught ideas about society itself. Ivan Illich argued in *Deschooling Society* (1968) that the main purpose of schools is to prepare children for a society where everything is measured and ranked by the system of grades, credits, and diplomas. These 'educational commodities' are necessary to prove one has 'gained' the knowledge that can be used for employment. Illich writes how these ideas are not explicitly taught, but part of an 'hidden curriculum', the unspoken rules of education.[13] Illich notes that most learning isn't done in schools anyway, since people's most valuable life lessons are learned outside of school; through friends, family, and play.[14]

Disciplining citizens is still central to education. 'A large part of education is geared towards insisting people stick to given time-

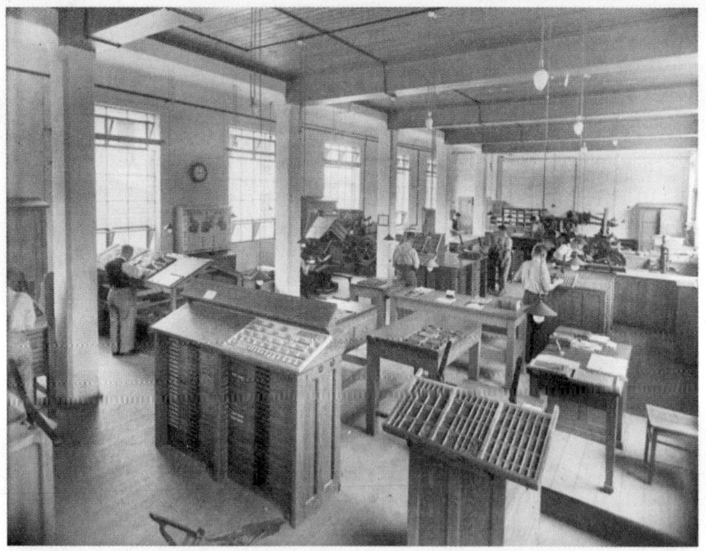

Students working in a printers trade school workshop, Australia, 1935.

frames, work within deadlines, and measure activities to a clock and a calendar respectively', writes designer Bianca Elzenbaumer.[15] As employability became the goal of education, the industry dictated the curriculum. The Precarious Workers Brigade notes how the capitalist idea of education leaves little room for 'critical thinking and the development of alternatives'.[16] As such educational institutions will always reproduce the same society they were built in, and will not likely produce ideas that are radical or revolutionary.

The Birth of Design Education

The industrial revolution ushered in the need for the first formal design schools. The skills of designers had to be redirected towards mass production. Commercial arts such as advertising and packaging responded first, and trade schools started teaching illustration for reproduction. Journalism studies first started courses in marketing and advertising in the US in 1893. Art schools still refused to teach design courses, which led to complaints from designers. In an article from 1887, designer Selwyn Image sneered at the Royal Academy of Art that it should change its name to the 'Royal Academy of Oil Painting'.[17]

A large part of education is geared towards insisting people stick to given timeframes, work within deadlines, and measure activities to a clock and a calendar respectively.

BIANCA ELZENBAUMER, DESIGNER

At the height of industrialization, designers in the UK organized themselves in various professional bodies. The intent was 'to render all branches of art the sphere, no longer of the tradesman, but of the artist'.[18] These guilds were the foundation of the influential Arts and Crafts movement and led to the first design schools in Europe, such as the Glasgow School of Art, the Vienna School of Applied Arts, and the Central School of Art and Design in London (now Central Saint Martins).

Design schools did not replace traditional craft, but their aim was to teach skills needed for industrial production that could not be acquired in the workshop.[19] The influence of the Arts and Crafts movement in design education also brought a social awareness to design education. Arts and Crafts wanted to bring design (art) and production (craft) together again, referring to a glorified notion of work during medieval times, to improve the lives of workers, and create design objects of better and more durable quality. Arts and Crafts strengthened the idea that design was a vocation, and that being a designer was considered a valued profession. The paradox of the Arts and Crafts was that some of the handmade products turned out to be so expensive to produce, they became collectors' items for the wealthy.[20]

Art into Industry

An historic overview of European design education isn't complete without a reference to the German Bauhaus (1919–1933), considered the benchmark for Western design education. The Bauhaus was an arts and design school with socialist ideals, but unlike the Arts and Crafts movement, founder Walter Gropius believed socialism was better achieved through industrial mass production. Gropius believed a socialist consumer aesthetic could transform society: 'the more their class pride grows, the more the people will despise imitating the rich and independently invent their own style of living'.[21]

Design education at the Bauhaus was based on the pre-industrial workshop model, and divided along lines of materials such as stone, wood, metal, textile, clay, and glass. Each workshop was fitted with the latest industrial machines, so students could become acquainted with industrial production techniques. In these workshops the school would 'create a new guild of craftsmen'.[22] Its foundational text sneered at fine art (*beaux arts*) schools who had been incapable of bringing arts and crafts together, only catering to the taste of the upper classes. The Bauhaus wanted to get rid of the 'classist' division between the arts and crafts, but this time with the most modern techniques available, using the slogan 'Art into Industry'.

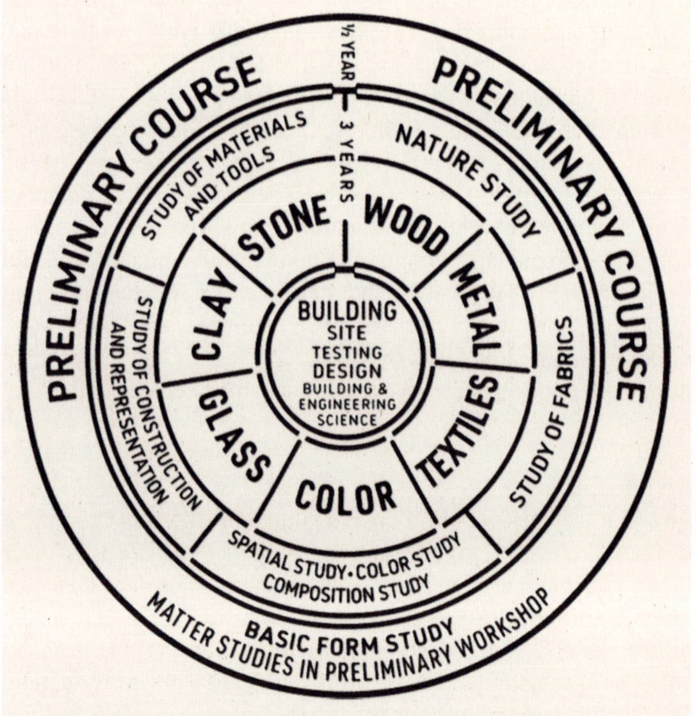

↑ Walter Gropius, Bauhaus curriculum, 1922.
→ Students in the course by Buckminster Fuller at Black Mountain College, summer 1949.

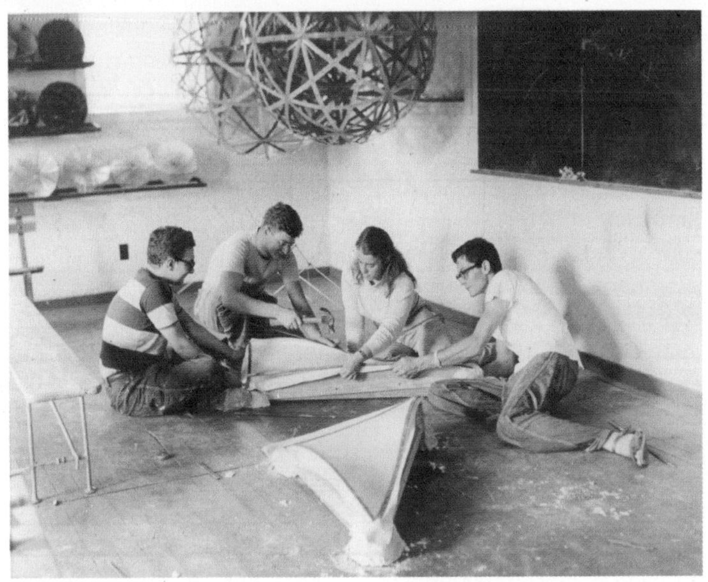

The pedagogy of the Bauhaus was influenced by the new education movement in Europe. Educators such as Maria Montessori and Rudolf Steiner believed that children's development would benefit from more freedom. They integrated arts, gardening, games, and gymnastics in education, while discouraging standardized textbooks and strict attendance. The Bauhaus extended this more holistic vision to higher education, with the belief that every human is talented, and talent could be applied to all disciplines. Following the new educational principles, gymnastics and theatre were integrated in the Bauhaus curriculum.

Despite its socialist ideals, politics at the Bauhaus would not get in the way of individual artistic expression. Gropius and many teachers were careful not to be overtly political. Only under director Hannes Meyer the Bauhaus briefly turned 'red'. After three years he was fired, and commented: 'A training centre for socialist architecture is impossible under capitalist conditions.'[23] His successor Ludwig Mies van der Rohe shied away from politics, and right before the Nazis closed the school, Gropius defended the school's existence by claiming there was no subversive political intent at the Bauhaus.

During the existence of the Bauhaus, few of its designs were mass-produced. Partly because of the technological limitations of the time, but also because the working class wasn't very enthusiastic about the aesthetic that was envisioned for them. Bauhaus had its biggest impact after it closed. Bauhaus professors Herbert Bayer, László Moholy-Nagy, and Mies van de Rohe fled to the US, and found employment at corporations. Thanks to post-war US economic and political influence, the modernist Bauhaus aesthetic spread across the globe, albeit mostly stripped of its socialist ideals.

In search of a more socialist role for design, the Bauhaus found an effective way to merge art and industry. This in turn created the blueprint for a design method that flawlessly connects with the needs of industrial production. With its emphasis that politics should not get in the way of creativity, its apolitical appearance has made the Bauhaus the ideal model for design schools for industrial production in capitalism. Precisely because it centralizes objects and production, and not the social relations under which they are created.

The Creative Curriculum
Over the course of the twentieth century, design education became a worldwide network of thousands of design schools, colleges, and universities. A shortage of highly qualified personnel after World War II convinced governments to provide scholarships to those from lower income groups. US veterans could study for free thanks to the G.I. Bill, although Afro-American veterans were notably excluded. Secondary education became affordable in Europe, and many families were able to send one of their children to university for the first time. The membership of the US association of graphic designers (AIGA) went from 500 in 1920 to 10,000 in 1997.[24]

By the 1970s the shortage of qualified personnel had been solved, and a series of recessions heralded in neoliberal politics. Government services were privatized to become 'cost-efficient', and the accessibility of secondary education was partly reversed. The benefits of education were increasingly being weighed against the costs. Design education, which had enjoyed a relative autonomy, had to start monitoring its financial solvency and quantifying its output. Secondary education in Europe was standardized with the Bologna accord of 1999, which created a system for study credits and degrees.

While design education was losing its relative autonomy, 'creativity' was becoming the new buzzword, thanks to Richard Florida's mantra 'everyone is creative'. Under influence of Florida, politicians began to rebrand art and design as 'creative industries'. Pioneered in the UK under Tony Blair in 1998, the creative potential

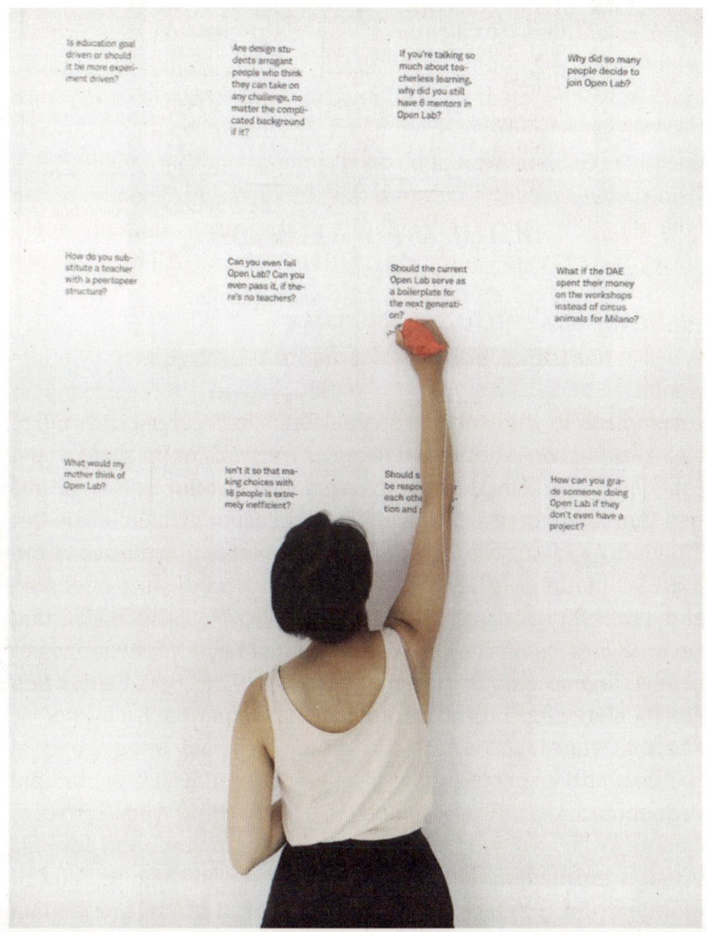

OpenLAB is a department run by students at the Design Academy, Eindhoven 2016. Photo by Alvin Arthur.

of the arts was redirected to fit the needs of industry. Design schools were encouraged to partner with corporations, and more autonomous or speculative projects should be directed to 'solving' issues in society, much like tech companies try to 'solve' socio-economic issues such as homelessness or poverty with websites and apps.[25] The Decolonizing Design collective writes how this process allows no time for research or insights in its 'historic and conditional complexity',[26] and this can only yield unrealistic and problematic ideas masking as solutions.

The long-term influence of Florida's ideas should not be underestimated, as Oli Mould explains. Terms like the 'the creative industries', the 'creative economy', and the 'creative class', have become synonymous with economic growth.[27] This retools art and design as an extension of business innovation. Extrapolating this vision would mean to cut all public funding, and finance design education through business partnerships. Design students would act as part of the research and development arm of industry.

Who Even Has $50,850?

When a fourteen-year-old boy named Arthur Frederick Wingate wanted to become a sign writer in 1930, he was offered a two-year scholarship to study at Wimbledon Technical School of Art. But as his family could not afford two more years of extra study or the school uniform, Wingate had to turn down the offer.[28]

Education can be expensive. Not just because of tuition costs, but students need to pay for study materials, housing, food, and clothing. Even if tuition is free, most design education is time-intensive, and not every student can combine studying with a job that covers living expenses. Students will either have to loan money or receive financial aid from family or friends. The cost of education and the dependency on external financial aid has made it harder for students from lower income backgrounds to study design.

Graphic design education is free in some countries, for example Argentina, India, Russia, Taiwan, Cuba, Norway, and Germany. Countries like France and Belgium, where education is paid for through taxation, have very low tuition fees. On the other end of the spectrum, graphic design is also offered at private universities where one year of Bachelor studies costs between $30,000–

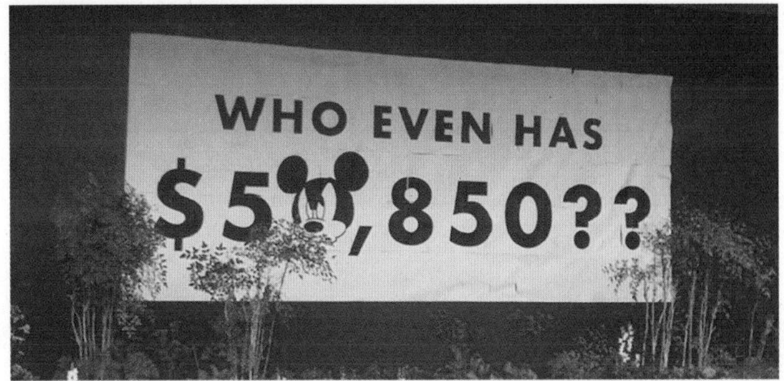

Student protest banner against tuition raise, CalArts, 2019. Photo by Fernanda Haiabe.

Made the mistake of going to art school (and racking up $95k in student debt) instead of teaching myself because I thought a degree was required.

ANONYMOUS DESIGNER

$50,000. Studying graphic design can mean having parents that can cough up 200 K, or taking out loans, which will leave students with huge debts. Guy Standing writes how both rankings and credits systems have made education into an industry that produces graduates as commodities.[29] First students pay high fees in exchange for a diploma, then the debts students have racked up can be invested and traded as financial commodities, serving two economic purposes at once.

In 2019 the California-based private art school CalArts, founded by Walt Disney, reported that it would raise its tuition with 4.5 percent to $50,850 a year.[30] If one includes housing, food, and other costs, the annual sum required would be closer to $78,000. Students protested with a banner that said 'Who even has $50,850?' featuring Mickey Mouse. The price of education is remarkable as CalArts talks about 'thriving on the diversity of its artists' on their website.[31] Given the high cost of education, some argue that education can't be free for everyone. On the other hands, all kinds of public institutions are expensive, like the military, for example. The US spends 686 billion on its military every year, and 59.9

billion on education. The cost of education is a political choice, not just a financial one.

The problem with unaffordable education is that voices from lower income communities are less represented in society. The voice of the uneducated, the poor, and the marginalized are mostly absent from history books, for this very reason. An expensive design education could lead to a wealthy class of designers who assume their audience is also well-off, which can obfuscate some of the most important social issues in society such as inequality and privilege.

We cannot go beyond the consumer society unless we first understand that obligatory public schools inevitably reproduce such a society.

IVAN ILLICH, PHILOSOPHER

Design school rankings 2019	Tuition*	Tuition**
1 RCA, UK	$12,183	$36,239
2 Parsons, US	$24,380	$24,380
3 RISD, US	$52,860	$52,860
4 MIT, US	$53,450	$53,450
5 Politecnico di Milano, IT	$3,952	$4,404
6 UAL, UK	$11,249	$19,936
7 Pratt, US	$51,870	$51,870
8 Art Intitute of Chicago, US	$49,310	$49,310
9 Aalto University, FI	$0	$13,549
10 Stanford University, US	$51,354	$51,354
| |	|	|
18 Tongji University, CN	$5,000	$5,000
18 University of Buenos Aires, AR	$0	$0
24 Design Academy, NL	$2,419	$11,178

↑ Highest ranked design schools and their tuition for domestic* and for foreign students**. Statistics from topuniversities.com/university-rankings/university-subject-rankings/2020/art-design. 2019 tuition fees from each institution's website.
→ Illustration by Blandine Molin, 2021.

Viewing education as a monetary exchange overlooks the possibility that education is perhaps not only about preparing for work. The German word for education is *Bildung*. It means a process of personal and cultural maturation, both in a philosophical and educational sense. If we see education not merely as a commodity but as a familiarization with public culture and knowledge, then it is logical that everyone should have access to it. Education is therefore also a commons, a public source of knowledge exchange which has become more and more enclosed by capitalism for the purposes of profit.

Towards a Radical Pedagogy

Curricula and school structures has been largely shaped by those who supply its funding, which is why we are faced with an educational system today that mostly serves the needs of capitalism. Fortunately, there is no lack in ideas about alternative education, which can provide useful perspectives for a different kind of graphic design education.

One of the pioneers of alternative education was the Brazilian educator and philosopher Paulo Freire, author of *Pedagogy of the Oppressed* (1968). Written during the military dictatorship, Freire found that existing educational forms were unable to empower those who were oppressed. The problem with education is that it does not invite critical thinking. Students are simply asked to copy and memorize the knowledge of the teacher without question, which he called 'the banking model' of education. Instead,

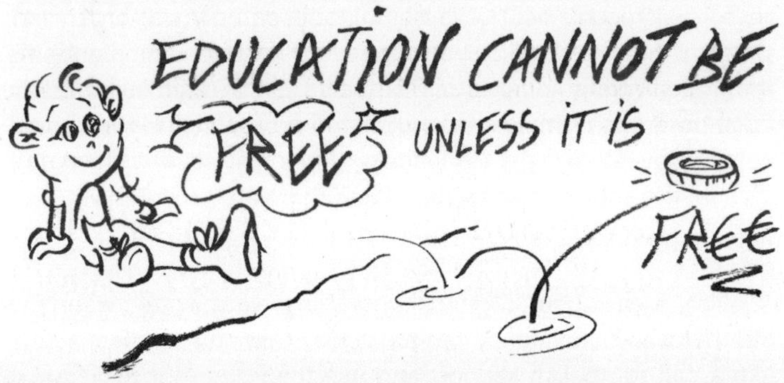

he proposed a 'problem-posing' method of education, where the teacher is no longer dictating but exchanging knowledge with the students. The teacher presents the material and the students critically reflect, allowing them to challenge the ideas of the teacher. While the banking model becomes a form of indoctrination, the problem-posing model invites critical consciousness. He argues that an oppressive regime will never allow problem-posing education, because the very foundations of the regime would be questioned.[32]

Ivan Illich was a contemporary of Freire, and introduced the idea of the 'hidden curriculum' mentioned earlier. As an alternative he suggests that everyone should be a student *and* a teacher. Radical pedagogy should not limit the education to teachers, or limit the spaces of learning to classrooms. He proposed that all knowledge should be accessible, and every space, every factory and institution should be a space of learning. It would certainly be a radical idea that anyone can walk into a hospital, a space engineering lab, a farm, or an artist studio and learn all there is to know without restrictions.

The 1970s brought some interesting ideas to design education, for example the arts and design education at the Feminist Studio Workshop led by artist Judy Chicago and graphic designer Sheila Levrant de Bretteville. As part of the Woman's Building (1973–1991) in Los Angeles, design and art education was integrated with the women's rights movement and students and staff were often involved in public performances as part of queer and women's activism.[33] The Antiuniversity (1968) in London was a school with no formal requirements, no tuition, and entirely self-organized. Cultural theorists Stuart Hall taught courses, and in three months the Antiuniversity counted 300 students and 50 staff members. In 2015 the Antiuniversity was resurrected in response to the budget cuts on education in the UK in the previous year. Its website states: 'Events are entirely free to attend and there are no criteria to take part. Everyone's a teacher, everyone's a student, everyone's welcome.'[34]

Illich' ideas about 'deschooling society' were written when the internet was in its infancy, but today his ideas could almost sound like a call to abolish schools and use the internet to facilitate a

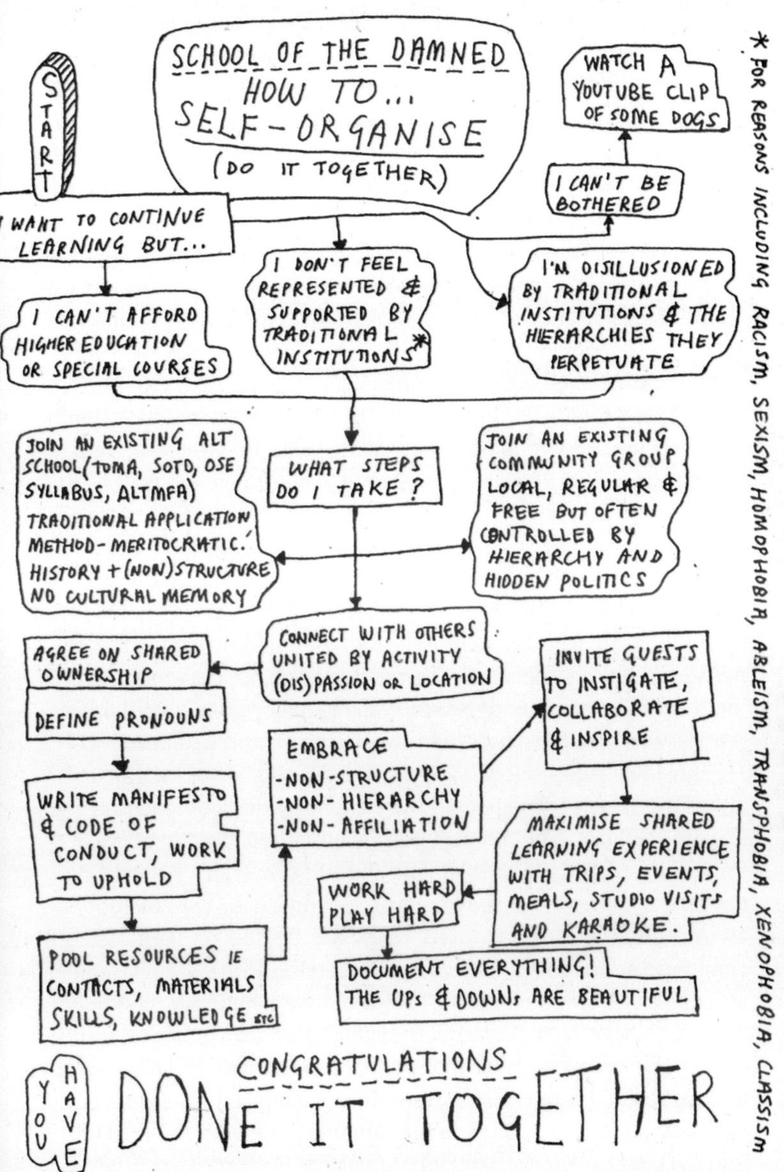

School of the Damned, class of 2018. schoolofthedamnedarchive.tumblr.com libertarian form of education. This would sound like music in the ears of Silicon Valley tech companies, who aim to 'disrupt' the often state-controlled education market by further privatizing education and who would benefit from facilitating courses via digital platforms. In her article about remote teaching during the Covid-19 pandemic, Naomi Klein writes that this would worsen education for children who are in abusive, crowded, or noisy homes, with limited or no access to internet.[35] This would not mean a democratization of knowledge, but a total enclosure of education as a commons, ensuring that tech companies can profit from education.

The Design Schools of the Future
As we have read, there are many reasons to be unsatisfied with design education in its current form. In response to the privatization of education, there have been many alternative ideas to transform design education from different sides. On one side there are those who are tired of design education being expensive and business-oriented, and wish to change it towards a more affordable, inclusive, and socially oriented education. On the opposite side we find educators who are pushing for more collaboration with businesses to ensure more employment options for designers. More focus on UX design and design thinking, where design education tends more towards a hybrid between design and business.

The first, more social view of design education has brought an abundance of small-scale educational initiatives such as the Parallel School, The Ventriloquist Summerschool, A School, A Park, School of the Damned, and the Antiuniversity. At the Alternative Art School Fair in New York City in 2016, 50 educational alternatives were represented. Many are free to participate, and challenge educational models by not working with a strict teacher-student hierarchy, decentring Western design histories, and being multi-disciplinary. In *Extra-Curricular* (2018), designer and writer Jacob Lindgren discusses many of these initiatives, but also warns the reader that 'after school' alternatives should not remain supplements, and we should still fundamentally challenge the institutions to change 'models and ideologies'.[36]

The second, more market-oriented view on design education comes from the notion that design education is not preparing

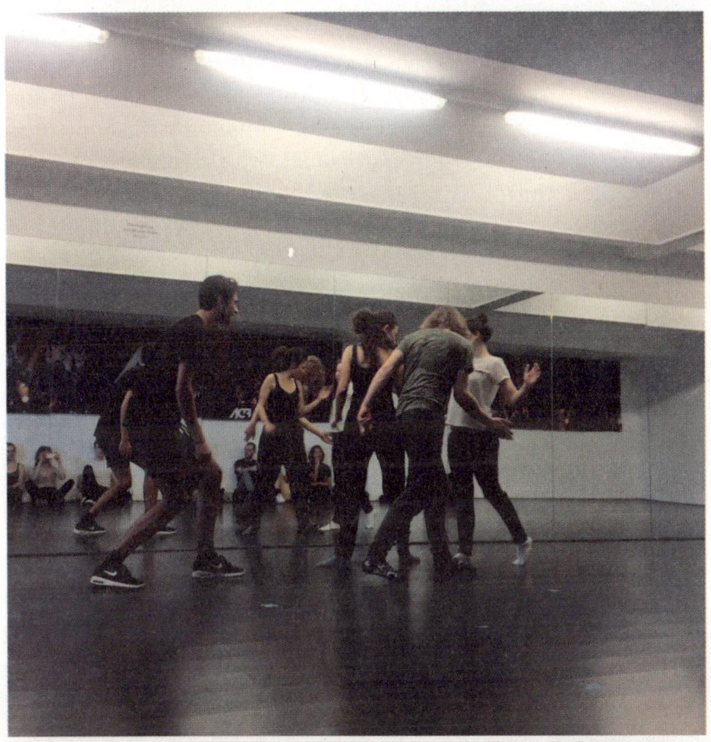

Body motion class taught by students, OpenLAB, Design Academy, 2016. Photo by Jim Brady.

There is no such thing as a neutral education process. It either conforms students to the logic of the dominant system or becomes the practice of freedom, working towards the transformation of society.

PAULO FREIRE, EDUCATOR

students enough for market demand. The rising market value of subdisciplines such as UX design, design thinking, and service design are still underrepresented in many design schools. There is the 'Future of Design Education', a recent call to change design education to better face the problems of the twenty-first century.[37]

Design theorist Cameron Tonkinwise points out that its founders are from multinationals such as IBM, Proctor & Gamble, Philips, and JP Morgan Chase, which begs the question which 'twenty-first century problems' they have in mind.[38] Another development is the business-meets-design curriculum, which can be found at Arizona State University's Design School. The Master programme Science, Innovation and Venture Development, is an attempt to make design education 'recession proof' by folding it into business studies. The programme will be 'less interested in narrow disciplines like pure graphic design, and more concerned with developing entrepreneurial and transferable skills like problem solving, languages, and public speaking'.[39]

With these developments in play, what can we expect for the future of design education? The model of the European design school, which originated in the 1900s, is still firmly in place but under increasing pressure from neoliberal economic thinking and a diversifying discipline. Debates about the future of education mostly focus on what designers should be learning, rather than how and where. What the radical pedagogies by Freire, Illich, and bell hooks in *Teaching to Transgress* (1994) reveal, is that capitalist education is not just about training people for work; it is the system of learning itself, the disciplining structure, power structures, and the student-teacher relation that block radical changes in society.

If graphic design refuses to only serve the interest of capitalism, a radical transformation of design education is necessary that questions the very nature of how knowledge is produced and commodified in society. That means abandoning the idea that graphic design can only be taught in school, and acknowledging that everyone can be a teacher, everyone can be a student, and the classroom can be everywhere. It would be wrong to interpret this as a call for a 'flexible desk university'. Nomadic universities have been around, but inevitably lead to a socially alienated form of education with high carbon emissions.

Meaningful design work exists by the virtue of strong social relations that are locally rooted. Colleges and universities can play an important role in fostering social relations and preserving local cultural specifics. Institutions also harbour a lot of knowledge and have important public facilities such as workshops, libraries, and lecture halls. But institutions need to be subjected to far-reaching forms of democratization and de-financialization. Education needs to avoid spending its time and energy on disciplining students into embodying capitalist values of efficiency, productivity, and obedience. If we regard education as a fundamental public service that should be accessible to everyone, education is a commons. As any other commons, education should be protected and defended against the pressures of capitalism to privatize, own, or influence the exchange of knowledge in society.

'We cannot go beyond the consumer society unless we first understand that obligatory public schools inevitably reproduce such a society', said Ivan Illich.[40] A design education that wants to produce creative and critical thinkers should start by listening to the needs of people, rather than the needs of industry.

> Home was the place where I was forced to conform to someone else's image of who and what I should be. School was the place where I could forget that self and, through ideas, reinvent myself.
>
> BELL HOOKS, EDUCATOR AND ACTIVIST

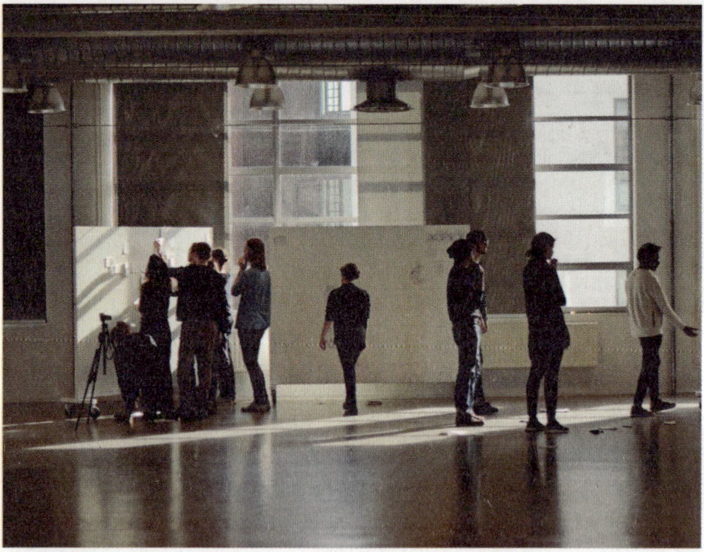

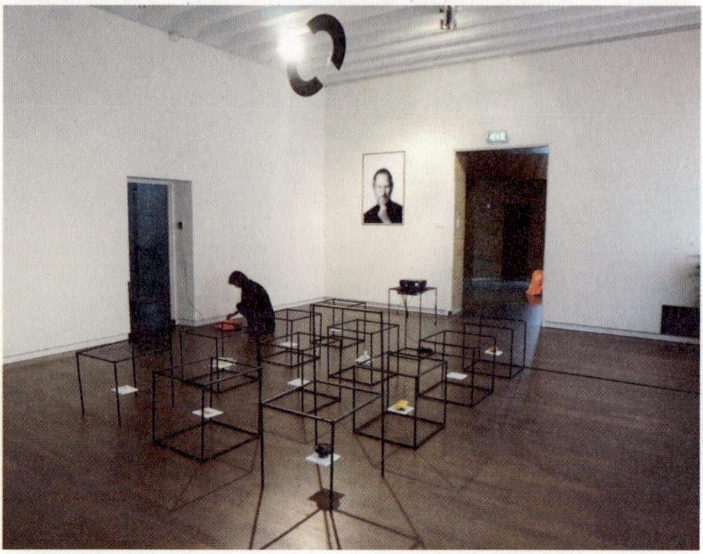

↑ OpenLAB organisation workshop, Design Academy, 2016. Photo by Arvid Jense.
↑ OpenLAB end of the year exhibition, Design Academy, 2016. Photo by Alvin Arthur.

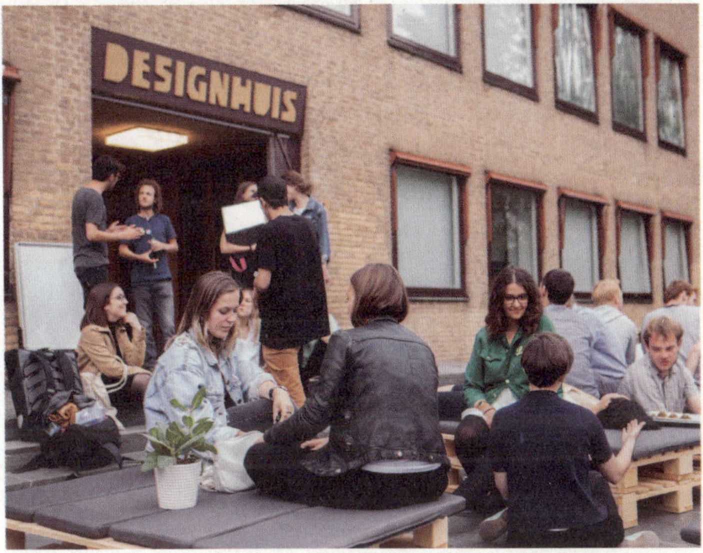

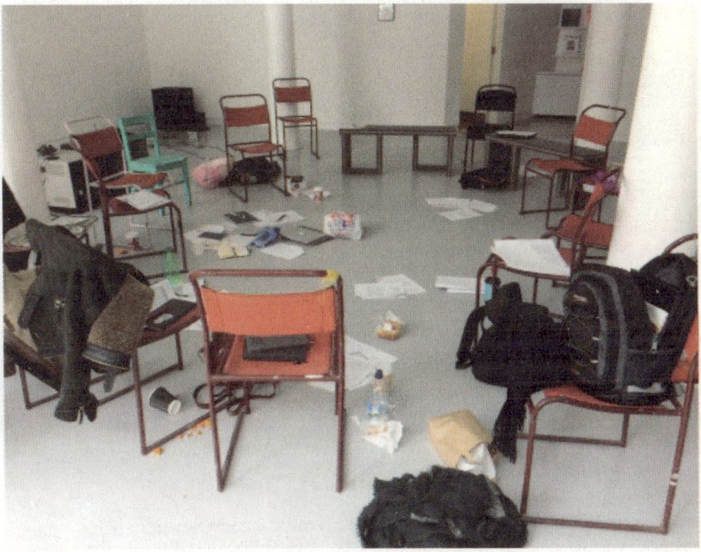

↑   OpenLAB end of the year exhibition, Design Academy, 2016. Photo by Jim Brady.
↑   School of the Damned, London. schoolofthedamnedarchive.tumblr.com

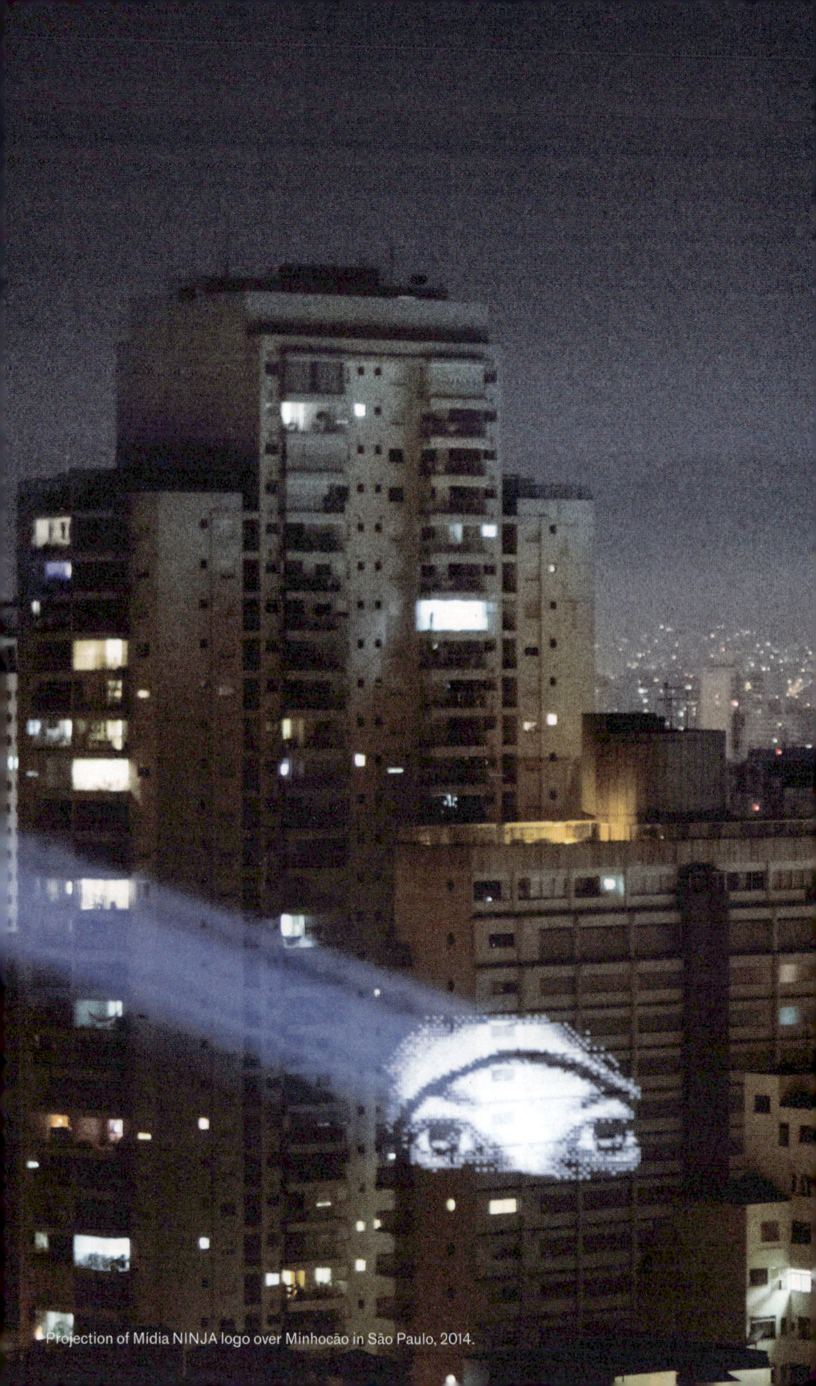

Projection of Mídia NINJA logo over Minhocão in São Paulo, 2014.

PART 3

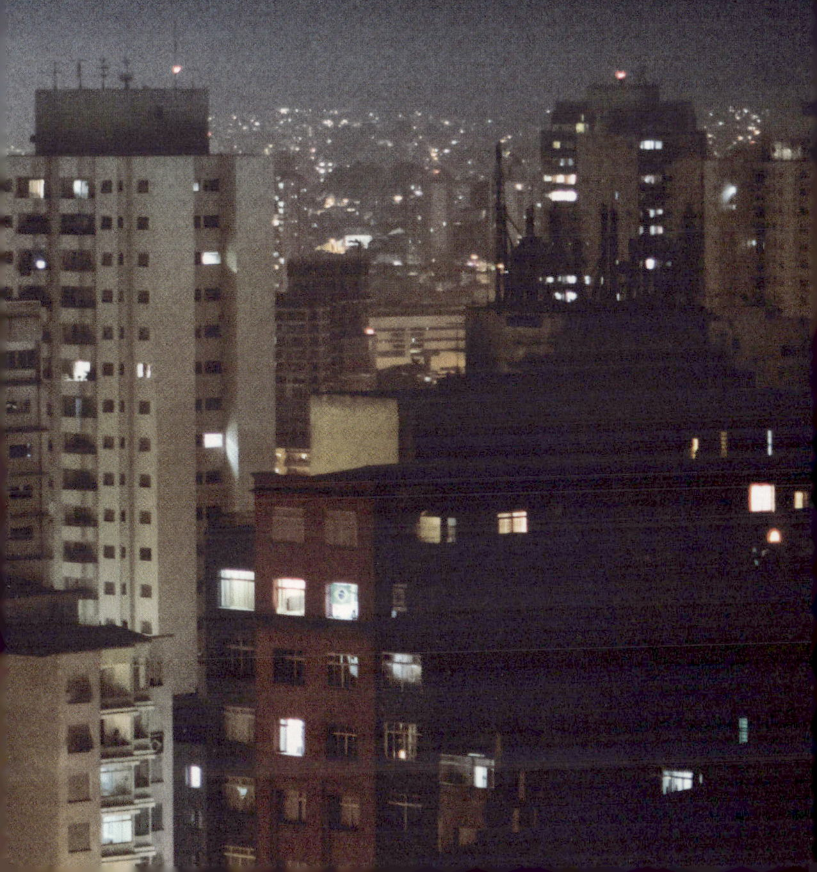

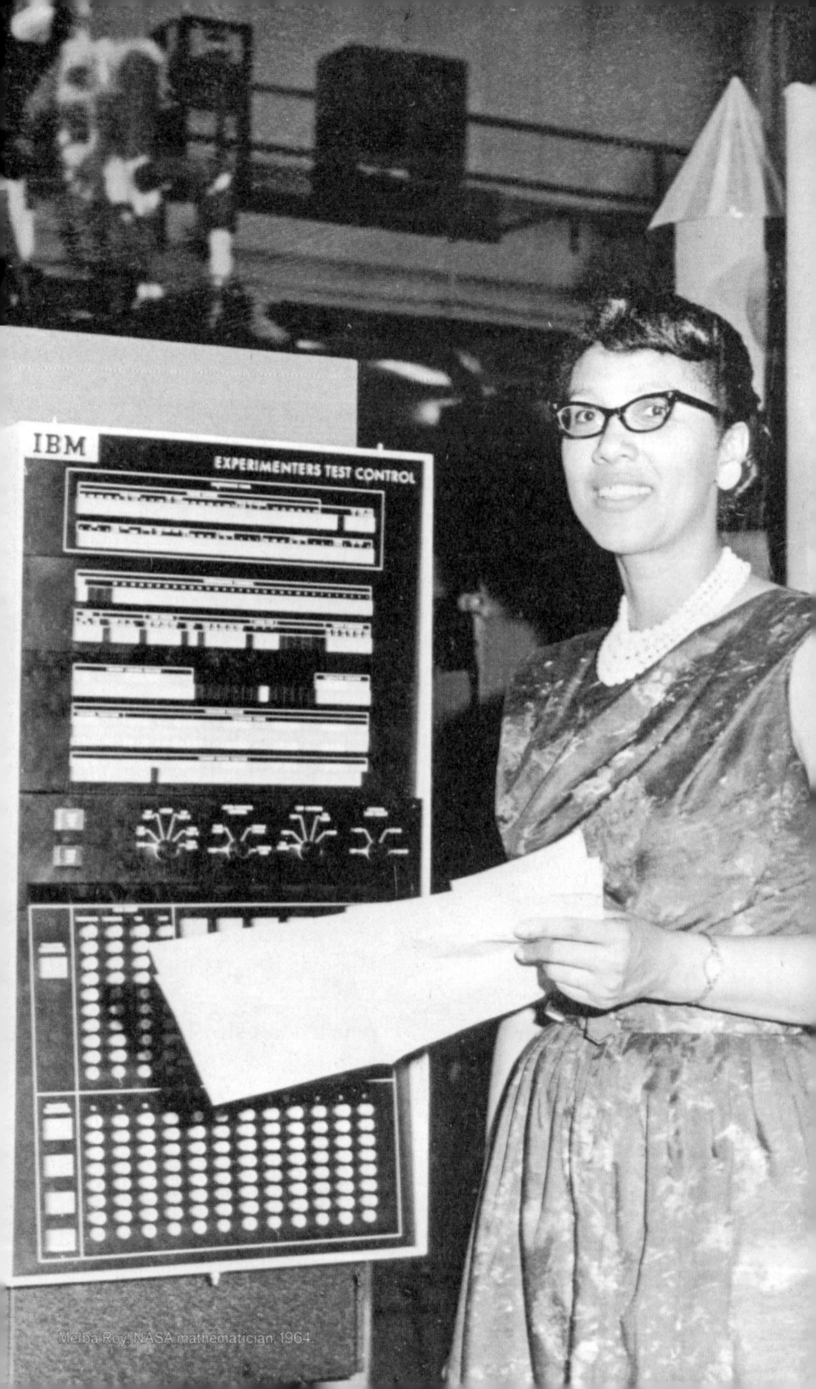

Melba Roy, NASA mathematician, 1964.

THE DESIGNER AS HACKER

*Steve Jobs promised us computers as bicycles for the mind
what we got instead are assembly lines for the spirit.*
EVGENY MOROZOV

Don't hate the media, become the media
JELLO BIAFRA

THE AGE OF DATA

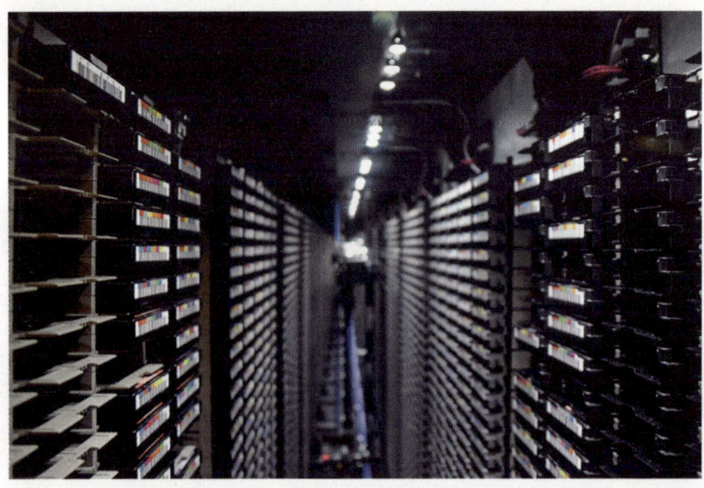

Every society is shaped by its raw materials. The industrial revolution ushered in the age of coal with its factory fumes and railroad tycoons. What followed was the age of petroleum, with traffic jams and oil barons. Today, the age of data is characterized by e-waste and tech billionaires. But unlike oil and coal, data cannot be seen, touched, or smelled. Still, it manages to fuel economies, sway elections, and earn advertising dollars.

Before the age of data, graphic designers needed access to photo type equipment and printing presses. The means of production of graphic design were owned by companies and rarely by individuals. The arrival of the first personal computers—in the early 1980s—meant designers could be involved with all stages of production. Forty years later, everyone with a computer has access to the same quality of digital media production as professionals.

The shift from analogue to digital design goes beyond the production process. Earlier industrial processes required specialists from different fields to develop, maintain, and customize technology. Material craftmanship has been largely replaced by an 'upgrade addiction' for graphic design software and hardware, as Drucker and McVarish point out.[1]

The first four chapters of this book looked at how the work of graphic designers serves capitalist production; as scribes, engineers, branders, and salespersons. The next four chapters discussed how designers participate in the economy as workers, entrepreneurs, amateurs, and educators. Now we arrive at the last section of this book. The Designer as a Hacker is the first of four chapters that look at possible strategies that have surfaced to challenge the current economic conditions within design. The hacker can provide a perspective to understand culture and knowledge production that comes from the emerging digital technologies of the twentieth century.

As the production and infrastructure of publishing has radically changed, the designer as a hacker offers potential new roles for designers. The role of a hacker is not just about learning to code or tinker with technology, it is a mentality towards a more ethical digital production. That power is harder and harder to secure, as the online publishing and production platforms are now effectively governed by a handful of billion-dollar companies. This chapter

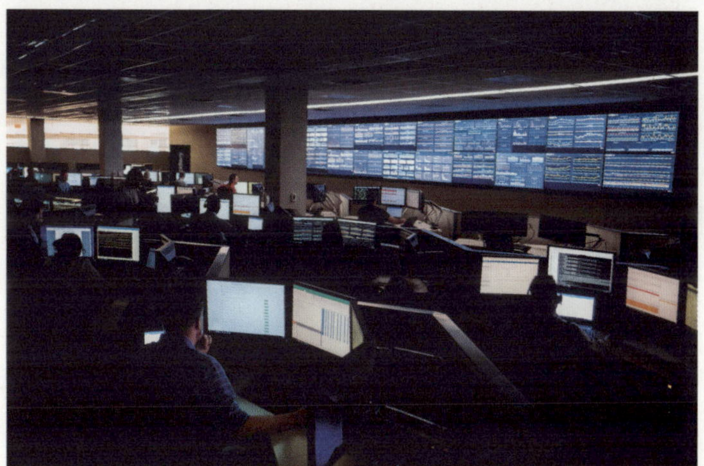

↑ Blackberry network operation center, Waterloo, Canada.
← CERN Computer Center, Meyrin, Switzerland, 2014.

takes the hacker as an exemplary role of someone who uses technology for the benefit of society, rather than for profit.

What is a Hacker?
A hacker is often thought of as someone who breaks into computer networks with malicious intent. Even the *Oxford Dictionary* defines a hacker as a person who gains unauthorized access to data. This negative frame—sadly brought on by news media in the 1980s—has tainted the original meaning of the term. A 1984 glossary for computer programmers explains that a hacker is 'a person who enjoys exploring the details of programmable systems and how to stretch their capabilities, as opposed to most users, who prefer to learn only the minimum necessary.'[2] Of course there are hackers who break into computer networks and/or engage in cybercrime, but those are called 'crackers', or 'black-hat hackers'.

The term hacker emerged in the sixties at the MIT AI Lab in the US. The term was used for students who messed around (hacked) with the switching networks for model trains. Hackers were interested in building their own computing systems by exchanging expertise and ideas amongst each other. As such, hacking is not limited to computing. A hacker is merely 'an expert or enthusiast of any kind', wrote tech journalist Steven Levy.[3]

Early hackers were Steve Wozniak, who hand-built the Apple I personal computer in 1976, and Richard Stallman, who developed GNU/Linux in 1983 while at MIT AI Lab. Steve Wozniak shared the blueprints and the source code of his Apple I for free, so others could improve and build on it. In turn, his computer could not have been built without the information shared by others at the Homebrew Computer Club in California, of which he was a member. Without hackers experimenting, sharing, and tinkering with technology, we would not have had the computers, smartphones, and the networks we use today.

Now that digital networks are critical infrastructures, the role of the hacker re-emerges at the centre of society. Graphic designers can share their skills across digital networks that are global and real-time. As many of these networks were imagined and built by hackers, they can provide designers with useful strategies and critical insights.

CAPS LOCK – Part 3

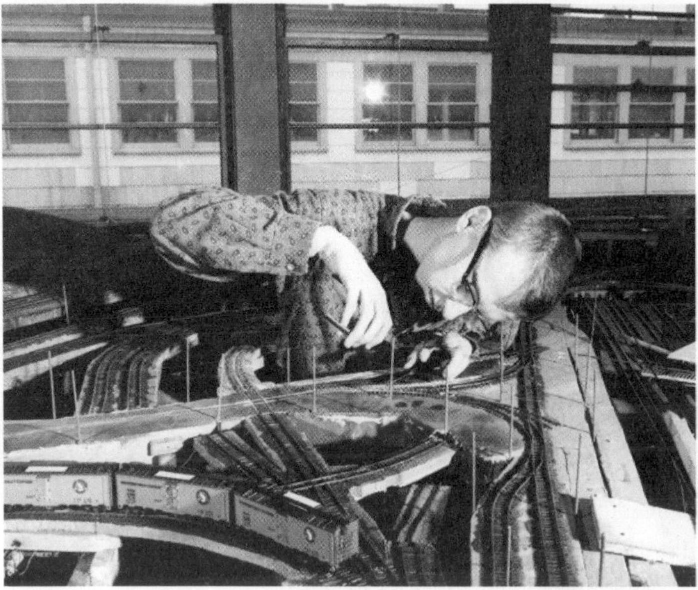

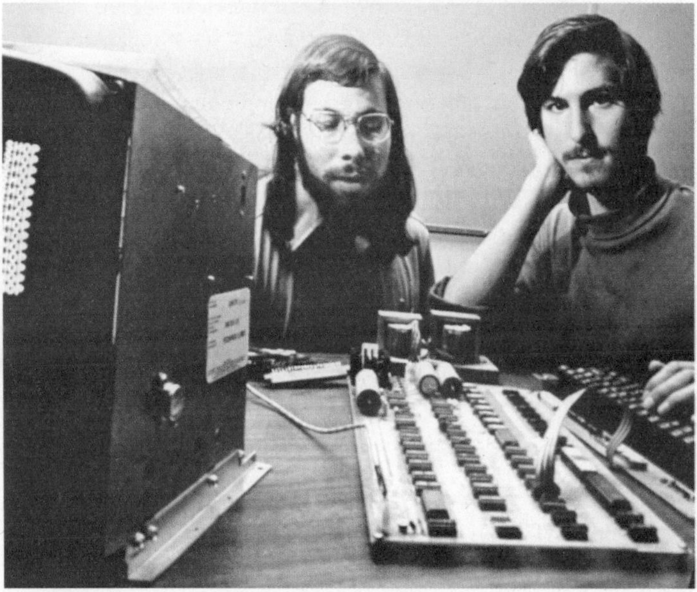

↑ The Tech Model Railroad Club, MIT, 1960s.
↑ Steve Wozniak and Steve Jobs with the Apple I, 1976.

The Designer as Hacker

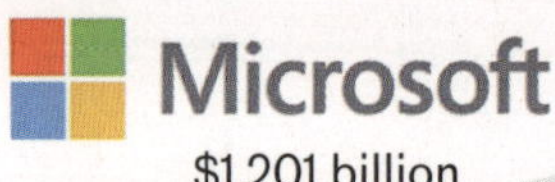

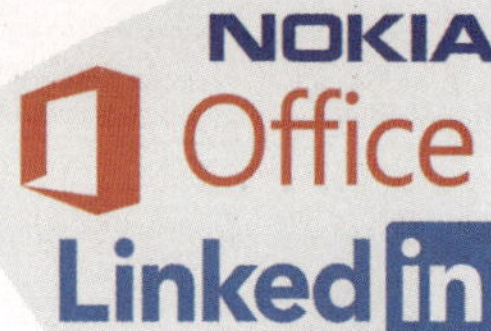

VIACOMCBS
$25 billion

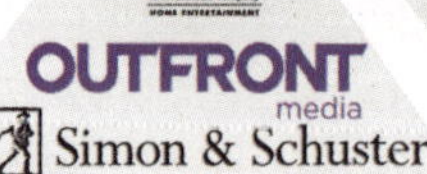
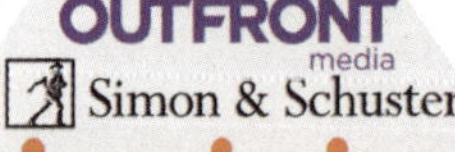

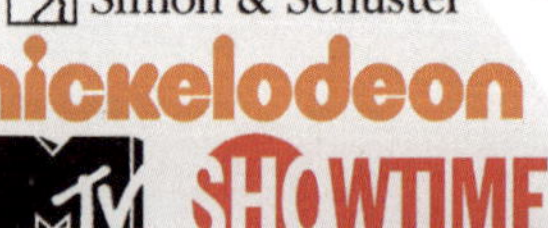
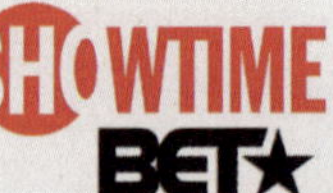
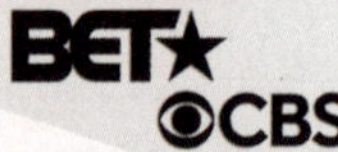

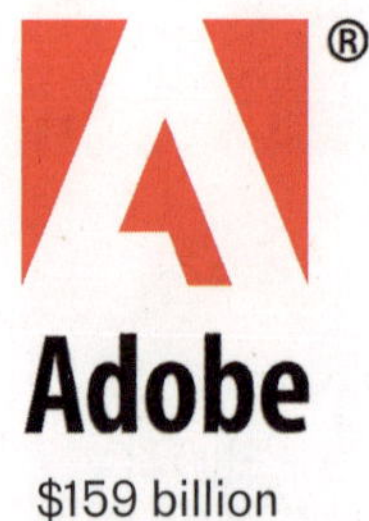

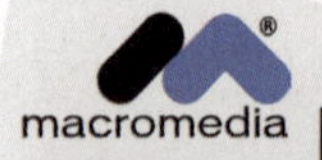
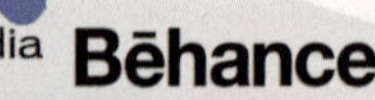

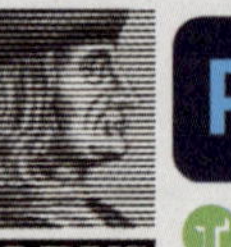
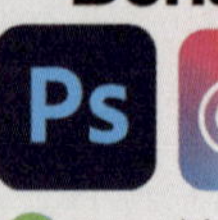

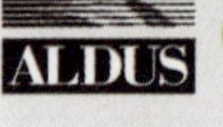
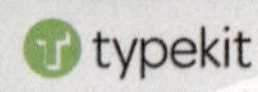

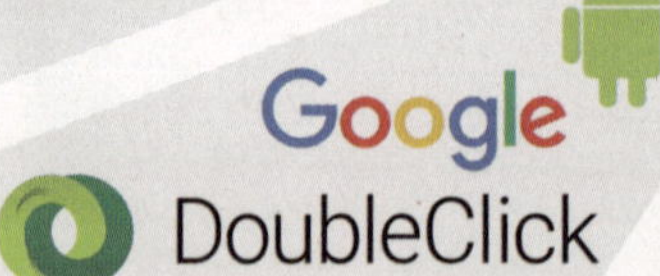

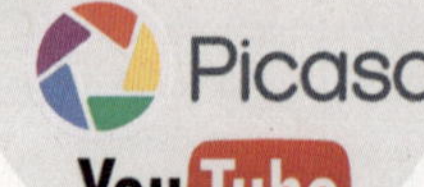
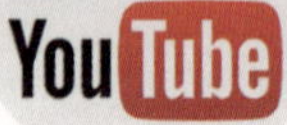

Alphabet
$920 billion

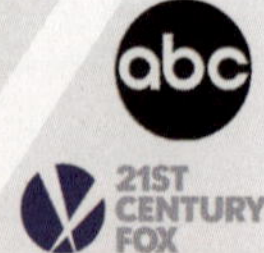

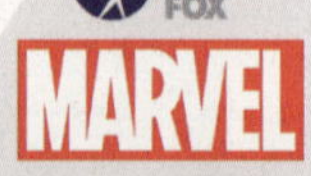

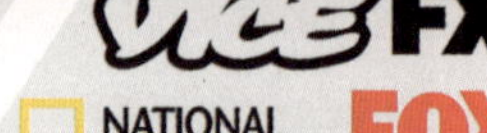
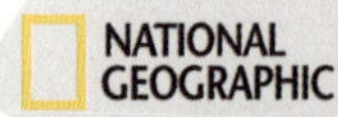
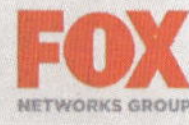

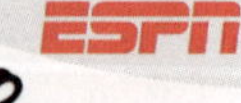

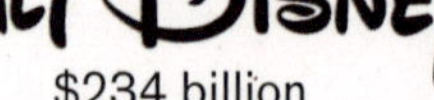

Figures are the company's market value in December 2019.
Infographic by Ruben Pater, 2021.

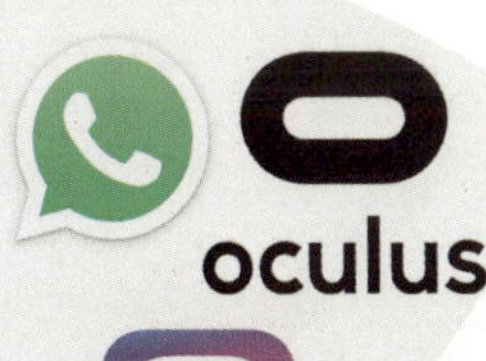
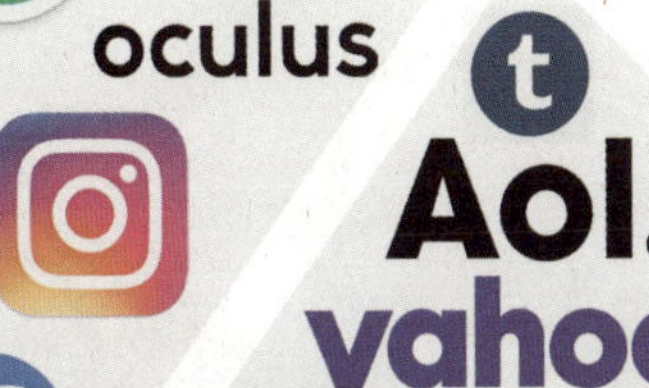
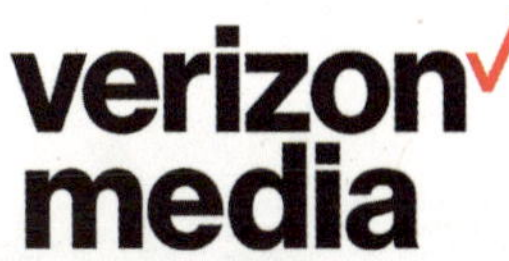

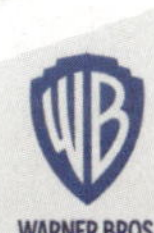
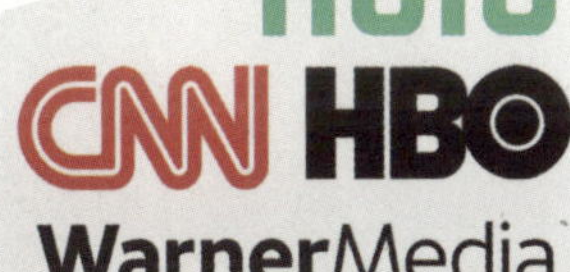
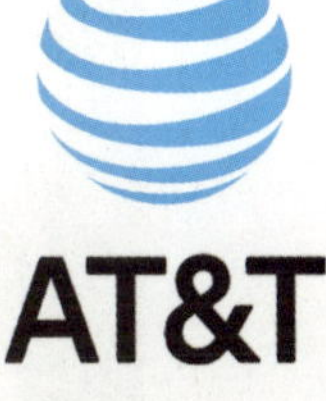

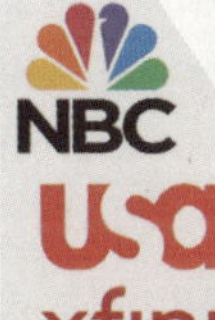
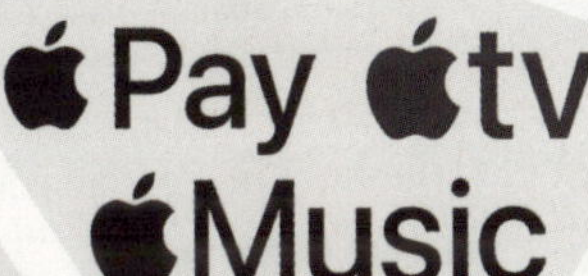
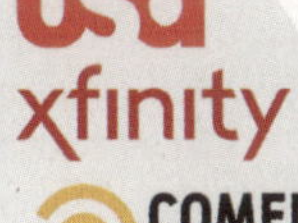

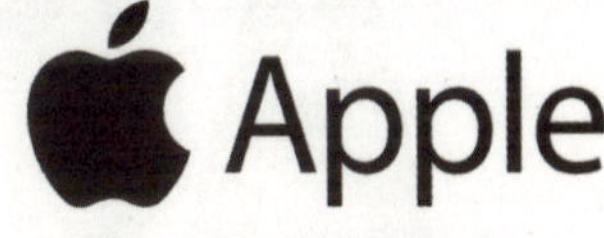
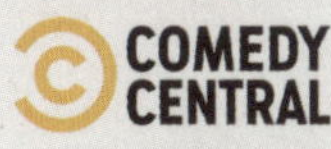
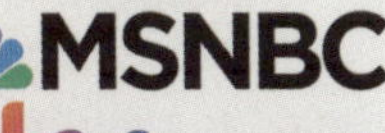
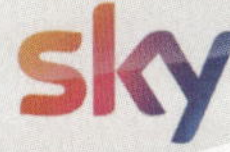
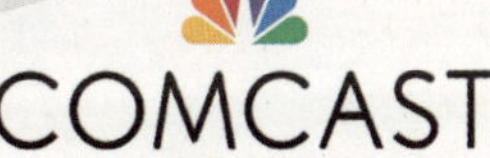

FACEBOOK
$585 billion
oculus

Aol.
yahoo!
TechCrunch
verizon

verizon media
$253 billion

hulu
CNN HBO
WarnerMedia
WARNER BROS.
DC

AT&T
$283 billion

SHAZAM
Pay tv
Music

NBC
USA
xfinity
COMEDY CENTRAL
MSNBC
sky

Apple
$1.263 billion

COMCAST
$205 billion

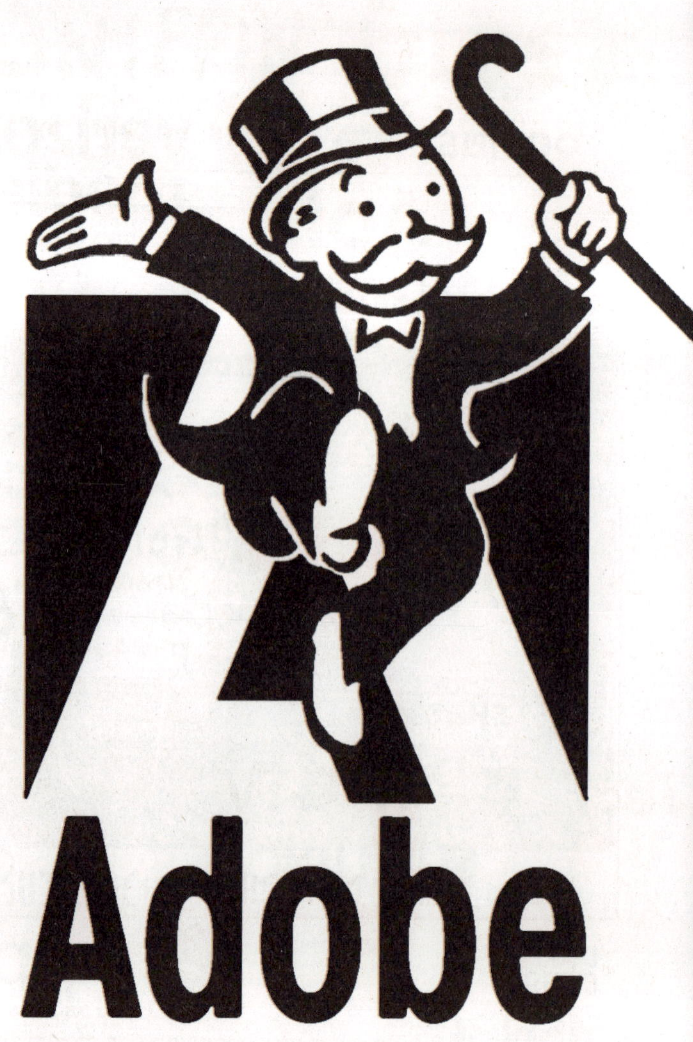

Illustration by Ruben Pater, 2020.

          CAPS LOCK — Part 3

Who Owns the Network

The internet was developed during the cold war by the US military as a communication network that could withstand a nuclear war. Until the 1990s its function was limited to military and scientific purposes. That changed with the invention of the web by British scientist Tim Berners-Lee in 1989. He also invented HTML and the HTTP protocol, and he built the first web browser. Berners-Lee refused commercial offers and convinced the scientific institution to make the code freely available. Initially, as a space for the free exchange of knowledge, the internet was regarded as a commons. Just as the common lands that were accessible for peasants in seventeenth-century England, the internet offered a similar potential for the free access and exchange of information.[4]

The potential for free exchange did not last long. After US congress passed a law in 1992, the internet was opened up for commercial use. Companies rushed in to own parts of the web, sparking the first dot-com boom. Between 1995 and 2004 a digital gold rush colonized the network, changing the internet from a digital commons into a privatized digital space.[5] The extent to which this changed the world economy becomes clear when we compare the wealthiest companies at the time. In 1980 the top ten most valuable companies were large manufacturing corporations such as IBM, Exxon, Shell Oil, Toyota, and General Electric. Ten years later the first tech companies appeared in the list, and today the five most valuable companies in the world are Google, Facebook, Amazon, and Microsoft.[6] Almost all tech companies that produce mostly digital products and services.

These handful of tech companies do not only own most online platforms, but also much of the physical infrastructure that the internet is built on. 95 percent of the world's internet traffic moves through underwater cables connecting the continents. More than half of this infrastructure is owned by Google, Facebook, Amazon and Microsoft. If you compare the map of today's underwater internet cables, they closely resemble the map of the transatlantic telegraph cables dating back from the 1850s. Internet follows a nineteenth-century infrastructure, which puts the power over networks firmly in the hands of former colonial powers. As James Bridle points out: Latin America's undersea internet cables are

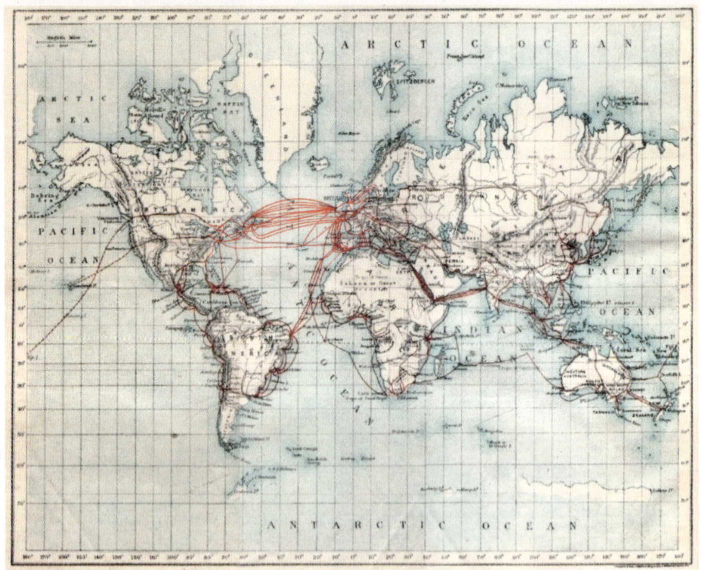

Chart of submarine telegraph cable routes, The Eastern Telegraph Co., 1901.

owned by Spanish companies, and 'the fastest data routes to West Africa still run through London'.[7]

How does the infrastructure of the internet influence graphic design? Perhaps the computers that designers use are made by Apple, their design software by Adobe, their files are stored on Amazon webservers, using Google's internet cables, sent via cell phone towers owned by AT&T, and published on Instagram, ViacomCBS, or WarnerMedia. The production of visual communication today is almost impossible without using the platforms, products, or services of these media conglomerates.

The power that tech corporations wield over visual communication becomes clear with the example of *emoji*, a visual language of more than 1,000 characters used by billions of people worldwide. Like all other digital alphabets, emoji are governed by the non-profit Unicode consortium, which is based in the US. Adding new emoji is voted on by members of the consortium. Its full members communicate in English, and the majority are employees of Adobe, Apple, Google, IBM, Microsoft, Oracle, and Yahoo. What appears to be an international visual language, is in fact decided

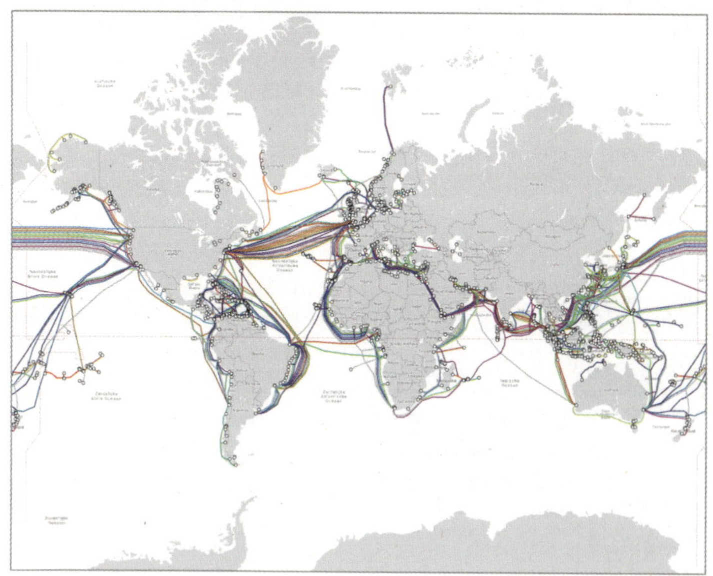

Submarine Cable Map of the internet, 2021.

by a small group from the US tech industry, as Aditya Mukerjee explains.[8] Their privilege may be reflected in the lack of emoji for illness, poverty, hunger, and war. Keith Spencer points out in an article that emoji has plenty of options for foods, objects and products: '...they perfectly resemble the market economy that created them, and which has turned everything it can into a commodity. The market has come at last to commodify our feelings'.[9]

The Network Society

'Societies have always been shaped more by the nature of the media by which men communicate than by the content of the communication', wrote Marshall McLuhan.[10] The same could be said about the networks that distribute communication. Less than two centuries ago, visual communication was mostly conceived, produced, and distributed locally. Visual communication was bound by the speed of horses or boats. In the second half of the nineteenth century the telegraph, the telephone, and the radio were invented, all using electricity that allowed communication at the speed of light. Culminating in television and the internet, this realized a 'a dialogue on a global scale'.[11]

While people need sleep and crops need sun, information never rests and isn't limited by geographical boundaries. The society that emerged with electronic communication is what sociologist Manuel Castells calls the network society. A world economy based on information can stretch time and space to serve the needs of capitalism. In his trilogy *The Information Age: Economy, Society and Culture* (1998), Castells explains that the network society has made time zones and borders almost irrelevant, as flows of capital and information can simply ignore them; spaceless flows and timeless time. In the network society everything is on-demand and real-time; from working and shopping to finance.[12] He believes that inequality will revolve around access to information and technology. A digital divide between those inside and outside the network.

4.5 billion people connected to one network offer a tremendous marketing potential. Any promotional message can potentially be viewed by billions, if the message can survive the daily barrage of visual stimulation. To stand out in the crowd, visual communication in the network relies more and more on exploiting our psychological instincts using algorithms. In the ocean of websites, luring a user to a site is akin to setting a trap. Once you take the bait, the clock starts ticking. The longer we spent on digital platforms, the more ads we see, the more likely we are to make a purchase. UX designers deploy legions of tricks to keep users on websites as long as possible. Infinite scrolling, dark patterns, bright and noisy notifications, intentionally confusing navigation, and auto-play, are some of the tactics that designers have copied from the gambling industry to keep us hooked to our screens.

The possibilities of the network can also be emancipating. So much information and connections makes it more difficult to keep secrets. 'Leaks' by various whistle-blowers have exposed large surveillance schemes, tax evasion by the rich, and fraud by corporations. Some designers, like Rogier Klomp, use the availability of connections and information to address state corruption. In his work *Big data: the Shell search* (2013), made with Shuchen Tan, they collected LinkedIn profiles of people who worked both at the

→   Dennis de Bel and Roel Roscam Abbing, *Packet Radio*, 2014. A zine how to turn a cheap walkie-talkie into an internet device can be downloaded on dennisdebel.nl.

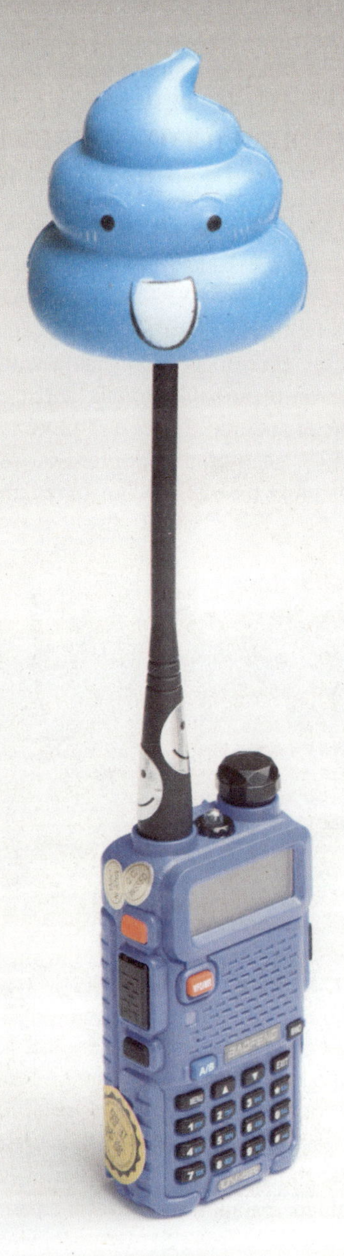

Dutch government and Royal Dutch Shell. Their research revealed a revolving door system where the border between the interests of fossil fuel industry and the Dutch state are heavily intertwined. Such 'hacks' show that relatively simple searches on social media platforms, by their sheer volume, can lead to effective narratives.[13]

Merchants of Data

If data is the most valuable raw material, then how is it mined? How is it sold? Google was one of the first who pioneered the gathering and monetizing of data in the early 2000s. The first Google search engine used people's input to optimize search results. Individual data profiles were later used to present users with tailor-made advertisements. Reading a person's emails and tracking movements with free services such as Gmail and Google Maps could produce even more precise profiles. 'Content-targeted advertising' had made Google more than $10 million in revenue by 2004.[14]

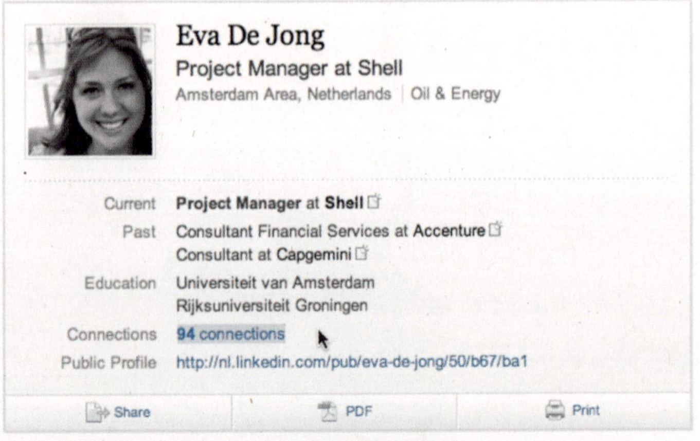

LinkedIn account of a fake Shell employee for Big Data: The Shell Search, 2013. klomp.tv

Companies that profit from people's data engage in what social psychologist Shoshana Zuboff calls 'surveillance capitalism'. Contrary to the saying: 'If you're not paying for the product, you are the product', Zuboff suggests that our data profiles are the products, not us. People supply the data—the raw material—which is then refined into data profiles. Detailed data profiles can predict what

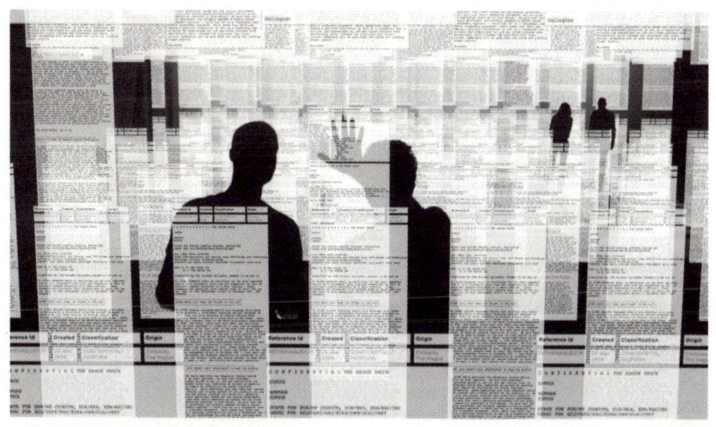

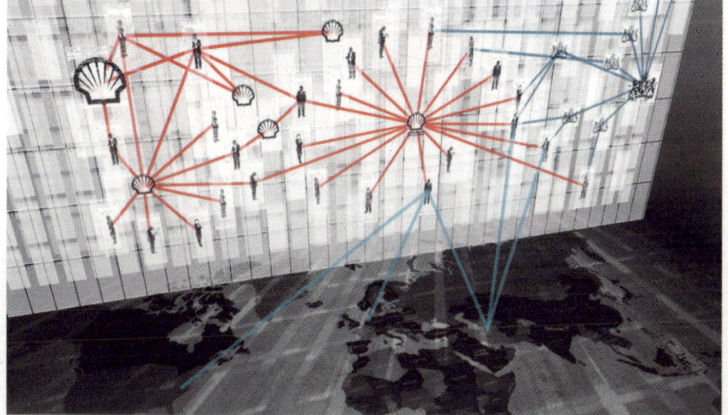

Rogier Klomp and Shuchen Tan, Big Data: The Shell Search, 2013. klomp.tv

you desire, but also what you will desire in the future. It doesn't just show better ads, it can also nudge people into certain behaviour and predict financial markets through understanding collective behaviour.

The company Cambridge Analytica became notorious by their attempts to persuade people to vote, based on their Facebook profiles. They were hired by Donald Trump for his election campaign, and by the Brexit Leave campaign. Cambridge Analytica gained illegal access to millions of Facebook users' data, and used them to design psychographics: microtargeted ads that manipulate people's behaviour by customizing design and content based

This counter-profiling data will be continuously released on a dedicated platform as
notifications, optimized for social media
sharing by each visitor. This will result in a
distributed counter-propaganda campaign,
eventually polluting the social feeds of big
tech companies.

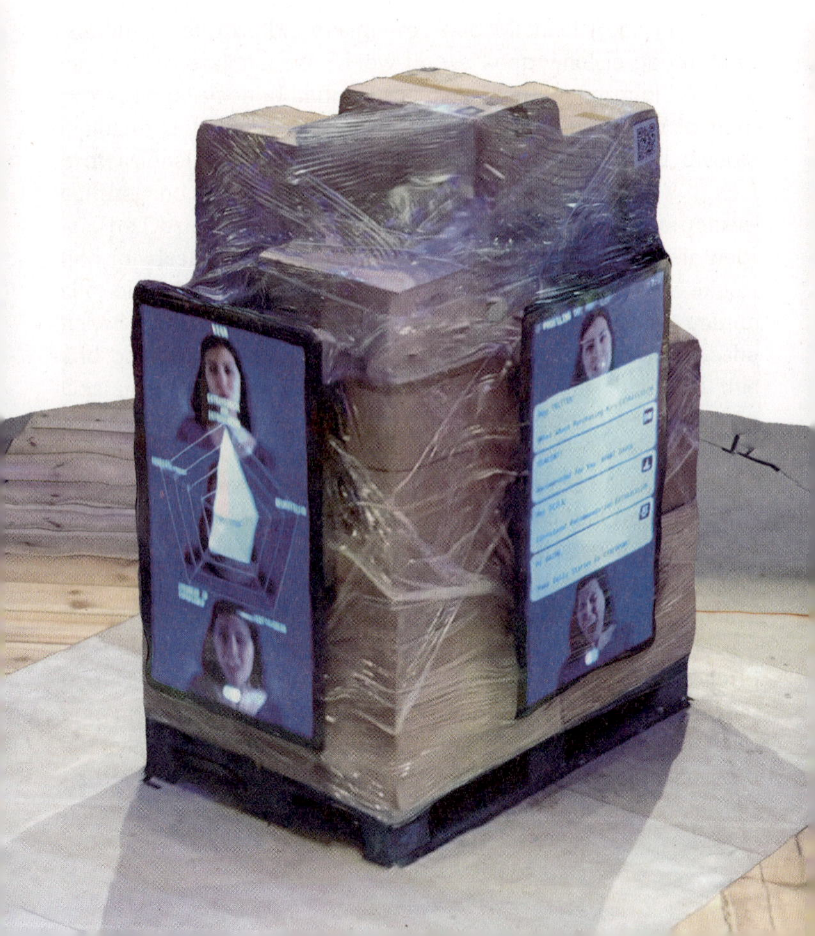

on Facebook profiles. With the right amount of personal data, the graphic designer as a hacker becomes the engineer of psychological warfare. Author James Bridle notes that Cambridge Analytica also employed military personnel, one of whom was the former director of psychological operations in Afghanistan for the British military.[15] Cambridge Analytica's clients Trump and the 'Leave' campaign won, although experts doubt if their targeted ads played a significant role. Vote Leave director Dominic Cummings said about Cambridge Analytica: 'We couldn't have done it without them.'[16]

The whistle-blower who exposed the Cambridge Analytica scandal now works for the Forum for Information and Democracy, an independent organization dedicated to 'promote democratic principles in the global information and communication space'. Their 2020 report included 250 recommendations on how to stop false or manipulated information. The most important advice is to 'implement "circuit breakers" for social media so that new viral content is temporarily stopped from spreading before it is fact-checked'. Others are 'limiting the use of micro-targeting advertising messages', and 'banning the use of so-called dark patterns—user interfaces designed to confuse or frustrate the user, such as making it intentionally difficult to delete your account'.[18]

Could the power dynamic of data profiling be reversed? In their 2018 work 'Profiling the Profilers', art and design collective Disnovation did exactly that. Based on scientific research of private data profiles, the collective decided to make psychological, cultural, and political data profiles of big tech companies. They worked together with data scientists using Wikipedia articles to analyse political orientation, ethical orientation, propaganda techniques, biases and addictions of companies such as Google, Amazon, and Facebook. The work was exhibited as an installation together with a website that shows the entire research process.[19]

Pixel Engineers and Time Thieves
Designing user interfaces used to be a subdiscipline of graphic design. Now rebranded as UX design, the discipline is rapidly taking the lead. Contrary to print design, the effects of user inter-

← Disnovation.org, Profiling the Profilers, 2018–2019.

face design can be measured immediately and in great detail, as we read in the chapter 'The Design as Salesperson'. Programmes such as trackers and cookies collect data about user behaviour. As ecommerce keeps growing—worldwide online sales have almost doubled between 2017 and 2020—each design decision has the potential to be monetized. That makes it difficult for UX designers to resist design tactics engineered to increase sales, or 'conversion rates' on ethical grounds.

In the experience economy, every business must be a digital busines

ADOBE SYSTEMS

A/B testing and programmatic recommendations can create a perfectly engineered interface design that yields the highest profits. UX designer Matthew Strom explains that for a company like Amazon, moving the checkout button on their website could mean losing 'millions of dollars in a single minute'.[20] With that amount of money involved, there is little wiggle room for a debate about the morality or aesthetics of consumer-engineered interfaces. Engineered interfaces have led to a Darwinist devolution of aesthetics, where only the design elements that yield profits survive, leading to an aesthetic of risk-aversion and sameness.

Design ethicist Tristan Harris wrote how UX design has learned how to make people addicted to their smartphones, and that by intentionally confusing users, using addictive stimuli, and limitations, users can be manipulated into spending more and more time on websites. Real-time communication accelerates the speed of production, with little time to reflect ethically. Harris gives designers the advice that our time is scarce, and should be 'protected with the same rigor as privacy and other digital rights'.[21] Philosopher Franco 'Bifo' Berardi echoes his sentiment: 'Do not forget that your brain functions in time, and needs time in order to give attention and understanding. But attention cannot be infinitely accelerated.'[22]

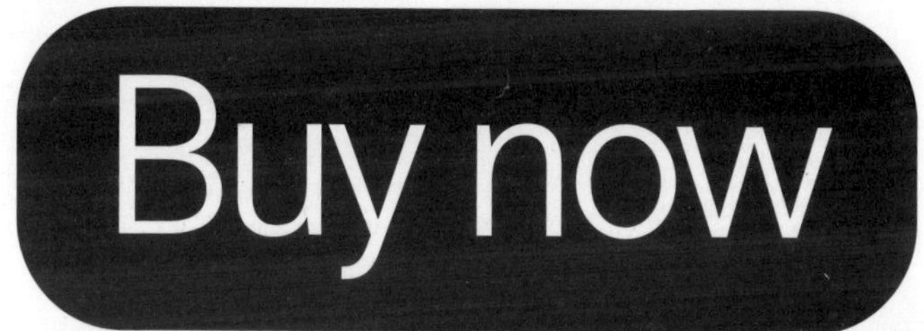

Offer expires in 23 seconds

Stupid Artificial Intelligence

Another quality that separates data from other raw materials, is its abundance. The amount of data is so enormous that it cannot possibly be processed manually. This is why tech companies need to use artificial intelligent (AI) software to process data. Machine learning is a form of AI, where software learns autonomously by using large sets of training data. For example, Google translate was developed by using the transcripts of the United Nations and the European Parliament.[23] Large image sets are used to 'train' programs to recognize images, or create new ones. Xerox developed the Pretty Image algorithm (2011), which curates the most beautiful images from your camera photos, so that you never have to select your own photographs anymore.[24]

Visual AI went from being a scientific field to consumer-ready software, as 'neural filters' are now incorporated in the 2020

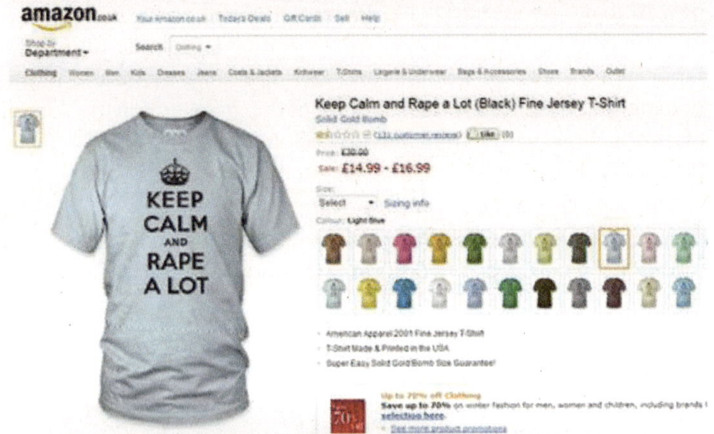

Automated designed T-shirts design for sale on Amazon, 2013.

version of Adobe Photoshop. Its 'Smart Portrait filter' can alter the facial expression of an existing person's portrait: '...generating happiness, surprise, anger, or aging any portrait'.[25] Although marketed for personal use, it is clear how such computing power can also be used for manipulation or a culture of visual fake. A *New York Post* article interviewed influencers who said: 'Everyone's editing their photos', adding that being natural on the popular app: '...isn't always financially rewarding'.[26] This pushes visual culture towards an algorithmic capitalist aesthetic; a world of digital fakes and post-truth images, engineered to maximize likes, clicks, and advertising profits.

In 2017, Adobe estimated that almost one-third of all internet traffic is non-human.[27] Those are automatic programs called 'bots' that crawl the internet, luring humans to their generated web shops. Whatever term you search for, you will find T-shirts, mugs, and other results generated for you. An entire production chain of design, production, and shipping automated and without human intervention. These artificial intelligence systems sometimes reveal their true stupidity, like in 2013 when Amazon sold T-shirts that carried the text 'Keep Calm and Rape A Lot', and 'Keep Calm and Knife Her'. It turned out these designs, based on the famous 'Keep Calm and Carry On' design from 1939, were generated with-

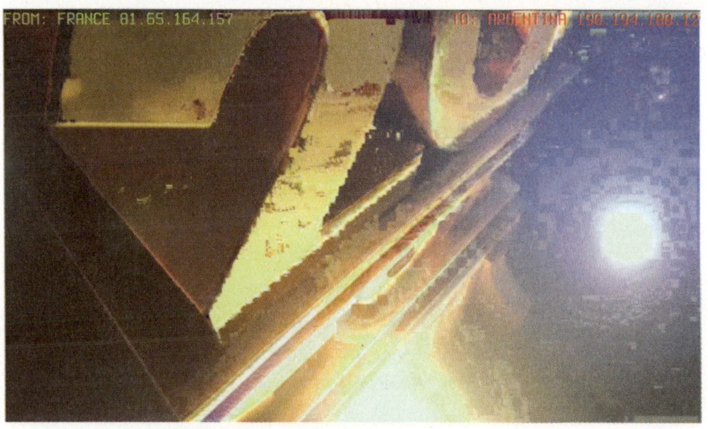

Disnovation.org, Pirate Cinema, still from pirated Hollywood video, 2013.

out any human oversight, and Amazon retracted the items.[28]

Contrary to the promise that capitalism creates an abundance of choice, the aesthetics of automation have evolved into a more uniform visual culture. On top of that, access to technology is distributed very unequally worldwide. High-bandwidth internet is limited to urban areas, primarily in wealthy countries. One in four people in the world does not have access to internet, and 60 percent doesn't have a smartphone.[29] Large parts of the world population have to make do with low-resolution images, pixelated cinema, or no digital communication at all. In an essay from 2012, artist and writer Hito Steyerl speaks of a 'class of images', where HD, 4K, and rich visual media are available to those with access to technology and the money to pay for copyrights, while the rest of world is left with visual debris, the so-called 'poor images'. Understanding images as an expression of inequality, reveals the ownership and production standards of images. Steyerl also finds an empowering potential within the poor image: 'The economy of poor images', she says, 'enables the participation of a much larger group of producers than ever before'.[30]

The Hacker Ethic

The data economy has proven to be just as exploitative and proprietary as the manufacturing economy that preceded it. The more digital the work of graphic designers is becoming, the more the privately owned infrastructure will influence the production process and the aesthetics. The tools that graphic designers use are owned by companies that answer to shareholders: Adobe, Apple, Google, Facebook, and Linotype. They create the code, standards, platforms, colours, and filters that shape a lot of graphic design.

What designers can learn from hackers is that in order to use tools critically, they need to be understood, adapted, and customized. 'Designers need to learn how to write, read, and fix code. They need to get literate before they can call themselves hackers', says Anja Groten from Hackers & Designers.[31] This is why more and more design schools teach coding, so that designers can create their own tools and filters in order to customize their designed output. This makes designers less dependent on preformatted tools from media companies.

Some argue that designers don't need to learn to code in order to understand the tools they use. In his book *New Dark Age*, James Bridle warns that good programmers can be just as uncritical of the economic and social context of technology and that it is more about learning a critical understanding of technology than the skill of coding itself.[32] A good example is the traffic jam that artist Simon Weckert created in March 2020. He noticed that Google Maps uses location data from users to warn for traffic jams. Weckert put 99 smartphones with location tracking in a hand barrow, and walked with it through Berlin. This tricked Google Maps into thinking large buses were jamming the traffic, while there was in fact very little traffic. No matter how 'smart' technology is, a good idea can still outsmart it.[33]

Open Source

The digital technology available today was developed by sharing source codes and hardware blueprints. Artist and developer Roel Roscam Abbing points out that early social media platforms were developed together with users, such as Twitter where the @ and the # were proposed by users before they became recognizable features.[34] Early computer users were also actively building and programming the platforms. The process of peer production is a form of collective making that is also used for websites like Wikipedia.

Richard Stallman echoes Bridle's concern that it's not about

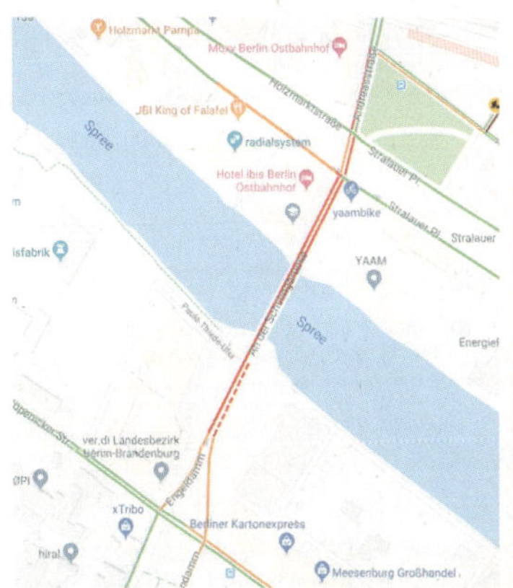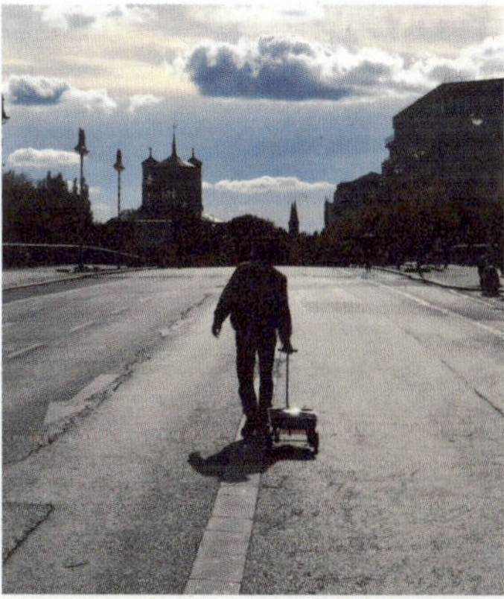
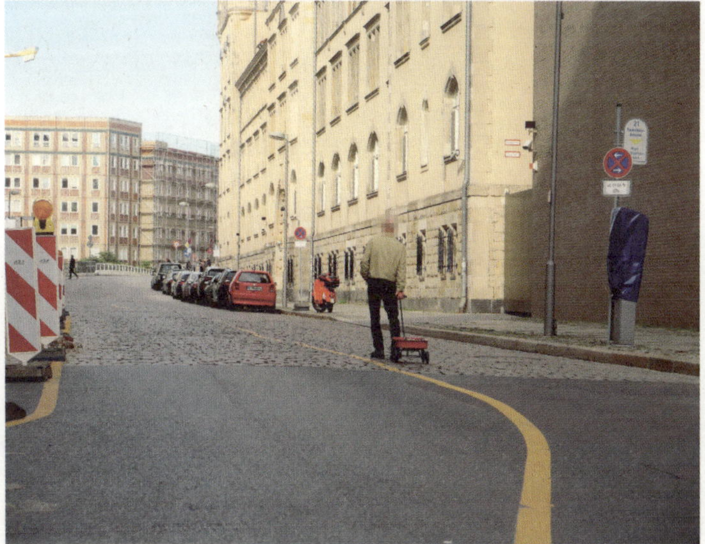

Simon Weckert, Google Maps Hacks, 2020. Image via simonweckert.com/googlemapshacks.html

teaching everyone to code, but about open collaboration. 'Either the users control the program, or the program controls the users.' Free/Libre, or open-source software (FLOSS) can do just that. The source code of FLOSS is freely available so others can modify, improve, and redistribute it. Open source doesn't mean that all software should be free, or that the work of programmers has no value. Stallman explains that this is about software 'that respects

Every non-free program is an injustice

RICHARD STALLMAN, DEVELOPER

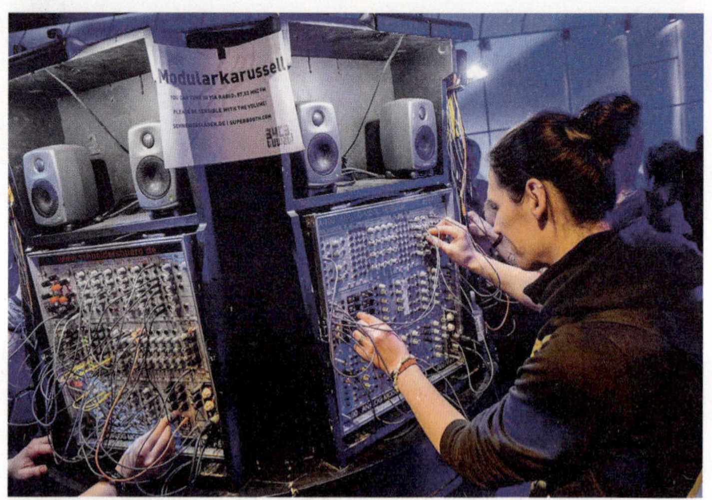

Chaos Communication Congress, Leipzig, Germany, 2017.

users' freedom and community'.[35] More and more designers bring the hacker mentality into graphic design, for instance Open Source Publishing (OSP) from Brussels, Belgium. This graphic design collective only uses free and open-source software. One of their activities is designing typefaces with open-source tools, which are released as Libre fonts, 'meaning they are released under libre software licenses that allow modification, re-distribution and use'.[36] In the last chapter you can read more about how OSP makes graphic design using open-source software.

Activism surrounding open-source software reminds us that a reciprocal exchange of knowledge is not a given, but must be defended against continuous attempts at enclosure by capitalism.[37] The software and hardware that is now sold, was in large part collectively built using open-source software, by exchanging ideas and blueprints. Tech companies have understood well how collective sources can be enclosed and exploited. Platforms such as Airbnb and Uber have successfully appropriated resources that were first for free social use, like letting someone use your spare room, or giving someone a ride, and have turned it into the 'sharing economy'. These companies effectively have used a visual language that appears social and community-like, while in fact they are robbing us of our few remaining social potential spaces that we have for equal exchange, while profiting from it. A process that Max Haiven calls 'enclosure 3.0'.[38] This goes to show that these 'commons' where social exchange is possible outside the market, even if it is sharing a room or giving someone a ride, need to be defended against enclosure if we appreciate their social value.

Ethical Digital Design

As we have seen, hacker culture provides a valuable guideline for all critical makers—including designers—in the form of what is known as the hacker ethic. Although not limited to one manifesto or text, it is helpful to quote some of the texts associated with it. First the seminal book *Hackers* (1984), in which Steven Levy says: 'Access to computers should be unlimited and total', and that the hacking ethic is about 'all information should be free', and hackers 'should be judged by their skills, not by their background, ethnicity, gender, position, or education.'[39] The second one is from digital activist and designer Aral Balkan, who co-wrote an ethical design manifesto in 2017:

> Technology that respects human rights is decentralised, peer-to-peer, zero-knowledge, end-to-end encrypted, free and open source, interoperable, accessible, and sustainable. It respects and protects your civil liberties, reduces inequality, and benefits democracy. Technology that respects human effort is functional, convenient, and reliable. It is thoughtful and accommodating; not arrogant or demanding. It understands that you might be distracted or differently-abled. It respects the limited time you have on this planet.[40]

The Dutch collective Hackers & Designers brings together disciplines for hybrid experiments. Anja Groten is one of the founders, and writes: 'Hacking is not discipline-specific.' She sees hacking first and foremost as a social activity. 'The technologies we are building and using are created by a vast number of other people.'[41] Hackers & Designers invite both creatives and developers to

Hacking is a way to emancipate users of technology from being passive consumers to becoming critical makers.

ANJA GROTEN, DESIGNER

experiment in workshops with critical making: a way of engaging with design and technology in a playful manner that challenges ownership of the network. Certain aspects of the hacker have already been appropriated by tech companies and used for profit motives. It is essential that the hacker ethic is not just practiced, but its values should also continuously be defended and propagated.

Designers who are intrigued by the hacking mentality, but don't know where to start: it's a good thing that hackers embrace the digital commons and often share their knowledge. Documentation, tutorials, and instructional videos can be found everywhere on the web for free. A good start are the annual hacker conferences such as Chaos Computer Congress in Germany, and Defcon in the US. All lectures can be viewed for free online at media.ccc.de and media.defcon.org. Artists and designers are regular visitors and speakers, and although some lectures are technically challenging, they often are practical. One of the lectures at Defcon 16 in 2013 explains in detail how to hack outdoor digital billboards.[42] What does the hackers mentality have to offer? Anja Groten from Hackers & Designers sums it up: 'Hacking is a way to emancipate users of technology from being passive consumers to becoming critical makers.'[43]

→ Disnovation.org, Profiling the Profilers, 2018–2019.

"

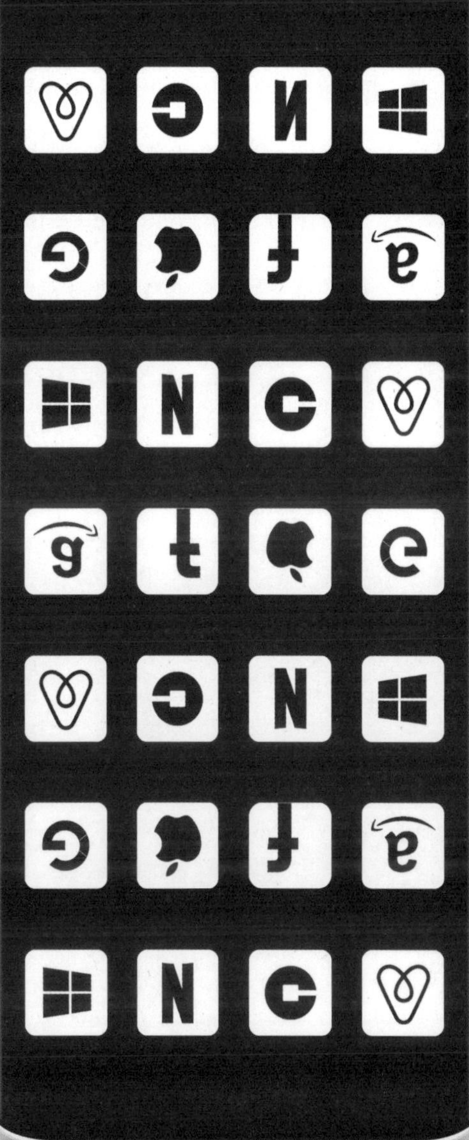

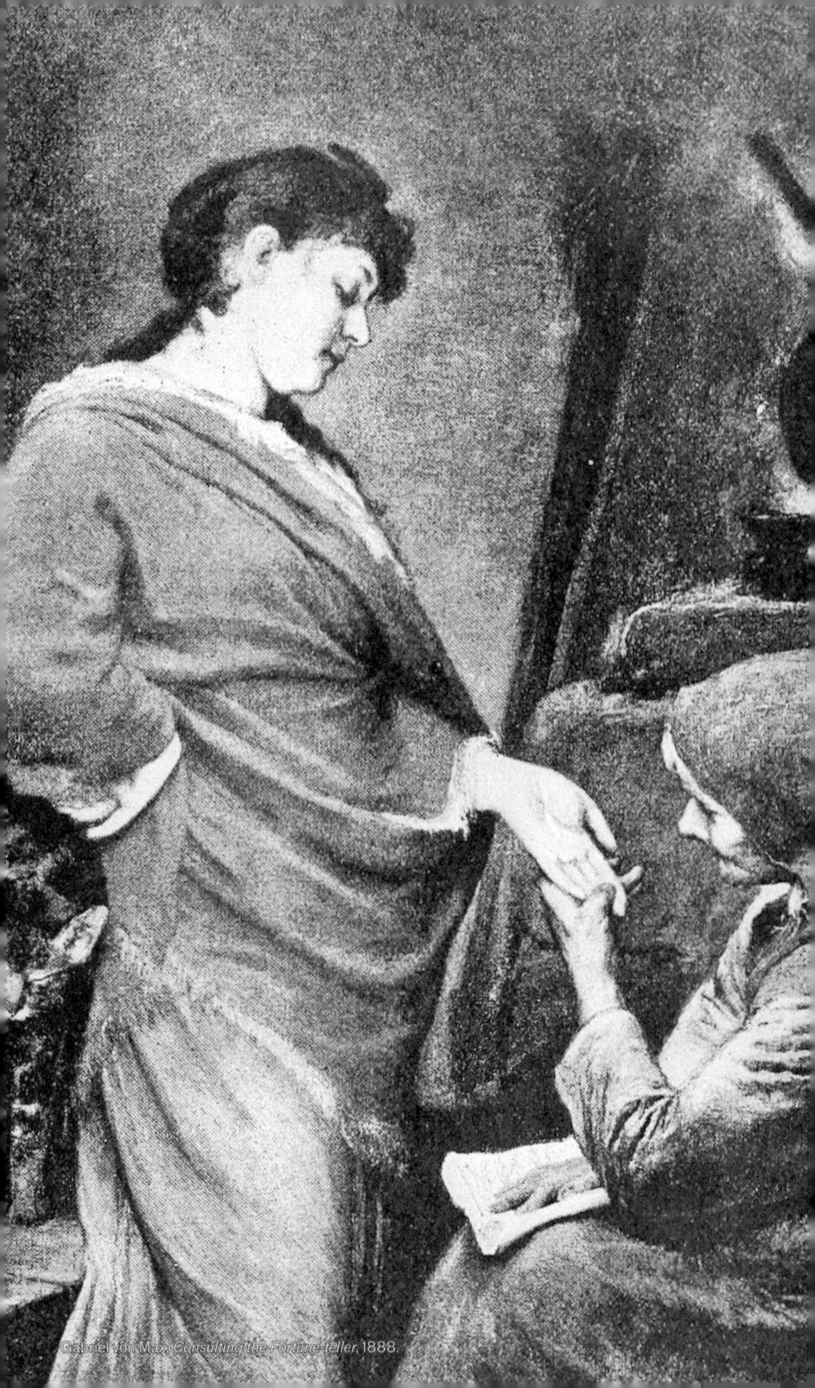

Gabriel von Max. *Consulting the Fortune-teller,* 1888.

THE DESIGNER AS FUTURIST

*Speculative design is the most feasible
way out and way forward.*
BENJAMIN BRATTON

Your dystopia is happening to us, right now.
LUIZA PRADO AND PEDRO OLIVEIRA

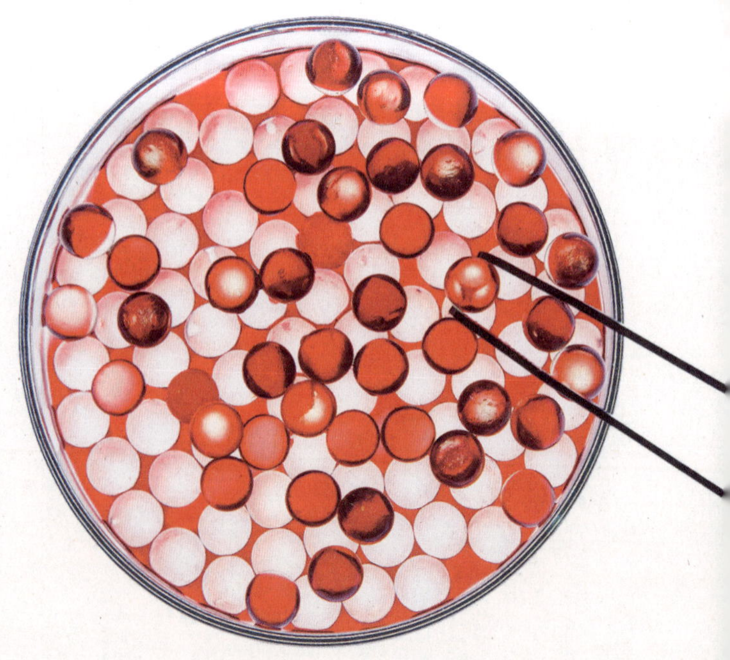

Next Nature, *The InVitro Meat Cookbook* on laboratory grown meat, 2014. Next Nature invited designers to imagine using speculative imagery what lab-grown meat products would look like.

THE SPECTRE OF SPECULATIVE DESIGN

The future is fertile ground for creativity, in the form of dreams, oracles, horoscopes, or science-fiction movies; humanity is always eager to find new ways to anticipate its fate. The future is a way for designers to imagine fantastic worlds and float ideas that are not yet feasible. In that sense the future can be a space for experimentation but also an escape hatch from the constraints of reality. The logic being, that if designers only respond to briefs, there is little room to think about a different future society.

Speculative design and design fiction are some of the design methods that imagine future products and services, often in relation to new technologies. Inspired by futurology and science fiction, speculative designers imagine and visualize future scenarios that do not produce new products or tangible results, but act as discussion pieces to help long-term strategic decision-making.

This chapter is the second of four strategies that have emerged from the design discipline in response to capitalism. The designer as a futurist argues that design's impact on the environment, politics, and society can only be addressed by going beyond what is currently possible. By only responding to demands from the industry, criticality in design has been hindered by the limits of production cycles. Future thinking can come in useful if designers don't want to repeat the mistakes of the past, like the abundance of plastics based on fossil fuel extraction, or low-quality products that serve planned obsolescence.

Distinguishing design from speculative design can be difficult, as some designers argue that all design is speculative by nature.[1] However, we can objectively argue there is a fundamental difference between a design that is produced for immediate use value with unknown variables (will people buy it, can this product still be used in five years), and design in which the entire context is based on conditions that do not yet exist (space colonies, unlimited energy sources, or genetically altered human DNA).

Creative and conceptual imaginations are design's core strengths, but unfortunately these qualities have been appropriated by capitalism to yield financial profits rather than to improve the lives of most people. This chapter tries to specify how speculative design can embrace long-term thinking as a transformative potential, rather than using speculation as a driver for financial profits.

Priests and Prophets

Predicting the future used to be the domain of religious leaders and fortune tellers. Knowing the future was either a form of fraud or wisdom. Futurology appeared as a field of study at the end of World War II. It was used by the RAND corporation to predict the chances of a nuclear war. RAND (an acronym for Research and Development) was a think-tank for the US military and specialized in 'anticipating risks and opportunities'[2] by producing written reports and processing large amounts of data. The same future models that were developed to calculate the risk of mass annihilation would later be helpful to predict economic behaviour, among other things.

Today, futurology is known as future studies or strategic foresight. Scientific methods that use mathematics to calculate the probability of future economic and geopolitical scenarios. Strategic foresight relies on a technical approach that involves mathematicians, economists who produce models of risk management for insurance models and stock markets. By quantifying the certainty or uncertainty of future events, its risks can be measured, packaged, and traded as financial commodities. As the authors of *Speculate This!* comment, now even the chances of terrorist attacks or a financial meltdown can be quantified using risk assessment.[3]

Prediction methods are based on data from the present and the past, which can be useful if the conditions remain the same. Sudden changes, however, are notoriously unpredictable. That's why futurologists use something called the futures cone.

The Futures Cone

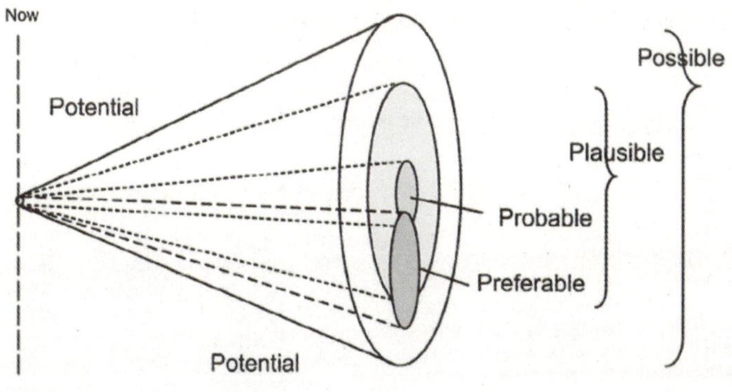

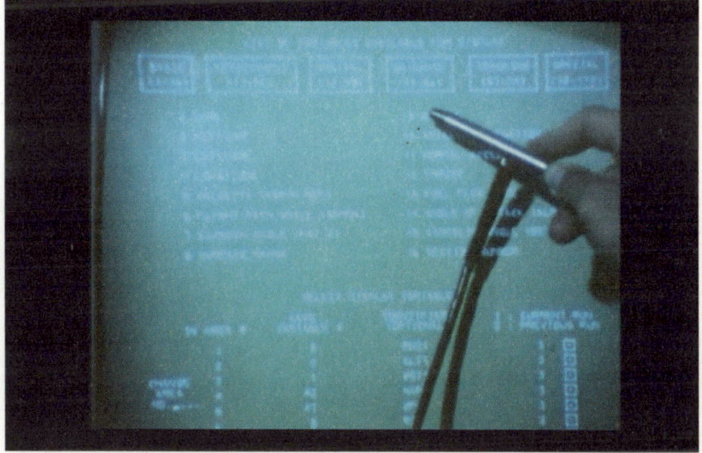

↑   Joseph Voros, Futures Cone, 2000.
↑   The RAND Corporation presents Graphic Rocket, movie, 1966.

The futures cone is a diagram developed by physicist Joseph Voros that classifies three kinds of futures: possible, probable, and preferable. The model does not predict the future, but rather maps out possibilities in order to better anticipate coming events. The futures cone was featured in the book *Speculative Everything* by designers Anthony Dunne and Fiona Raby, and is considered an essential part of the speculative design method.[4]

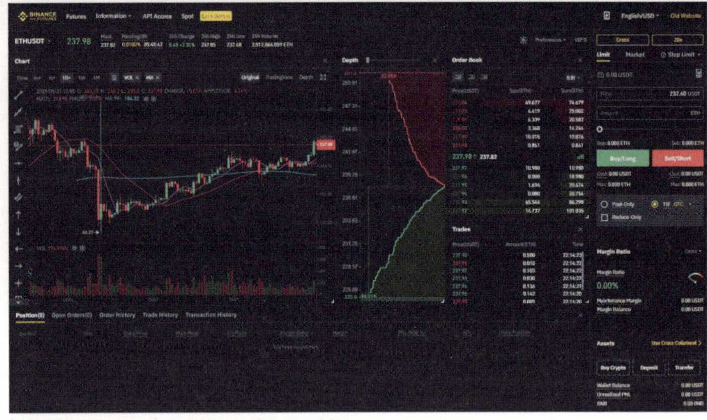

Binance Futures trading Exchange mobile app, 2021.

The Prediction Economy

Speculation is at the very core of the financial system. The natural tendency of capitalism is to grow, which happens through investment based on expected profits. Real estate and the stock market are the most obvious examples of financial speculation, but there is also an entire sphere within the economy called speculative finance.

The beginning of speculative finance can be traced back to 1971, with the decoupling of the US dollar from the gold standard.[5] Accompanied with deregulation of the financial system, this paved the way for a growing financial sector, which by the late 1980s overtook the manufacturing sector in size in the US. The advantage of speculative finance over the 'real' economy is that it is not bound by any rules. Right before the 2008 crisis, speculative finance had grown to three times the world GDP, the production of all goods and services in the 'real' economy.[6]

One of these speculative financial instruments is the derivative. Derivative trading, or futures trading, places a bet on the future value of a commodity or stock. Derivatives cannot avert future catastrophes, but they can insure the owner against the risk of future catastrophes and profit from it. Derivatives or futures can also be traded as commodities themselves. This 'futures trading' now comprises 85 percent of all global trade.[7] A form of futures trading and one of the causes of the 2008 financial crash were

Credit Default Swaps (CDS), a financial product that has been referred to as a 'financial weapon of mass destruction'.[8]

The growth of speculative finance seemed infinite, until the financial system crashed. Three million people lost their homes in the US, and banks had to be bailed out with half of the world's GDP. Due to the deregulation of the financial sector speculative finance had come to dominate the world economy. Speculation does have its limits, but more than a decade after the financial crash the speculative economy has not been reigned in, but is even bigger than it was in 2007. With no more territories to colonize and no more bodies to exploit, capitalism has begun to enclose the future.

Ubiquitous access to data has created the illusion that it is possible to quantify the future. Technology companies use immense amounts of behavioural data and refine them into 'prediction products'.[9] This term is brought forward by Shoshana Zuboff, who argues that online advertising is moving towards what she calls 'behavioral futures markets'.[10] Data collection, whether accurate or not, provides the material base for the mathematical models that drive financial speculation.

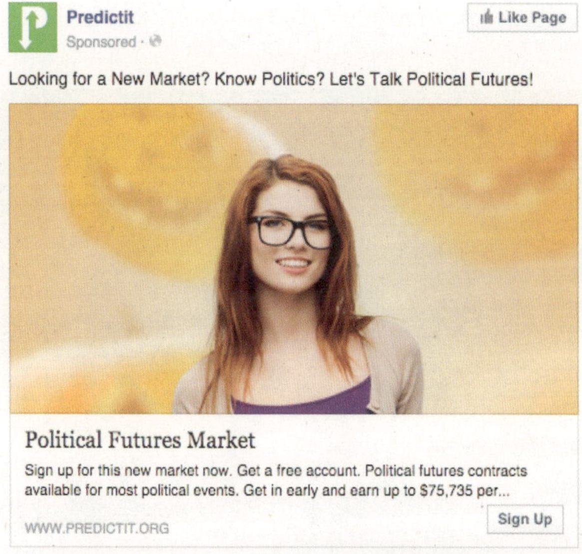

Facebook advertisement from the now defunct prediction market Predictit.

Design and the Future

Speculative designers are usually motivated by the possibilities of new technologies. Consumer products outfitted with the latest technologies are introduced at such a fast pace that there is little time to reflect on long-term impact. Speculative designers create design briefs for themselves that question the use of technology. What will a city full of drones look like? What if all energy was renewable, free, and abundant? What if entire countries would flood due to climate change?

More speculatively, asteroid mining–whose technical barriers are presently being surmounted–could provide us with not only more energy than we can ever imagine but also more iron, gold, platinum and nickel. Resource scarcity would be a thing of the past.

AARON BASTANI, WRITER AND JOURNALIST

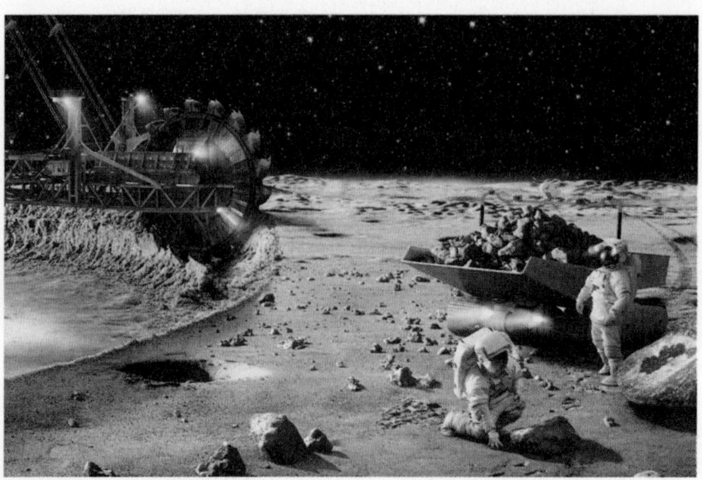

Dassault Systemes, asteroid mining, 2014.

Speculative forms of art and design have always existed, but as a distinct discipline speculative design emerged in the 1960s and 1970s, with conceptual architects such as Superstudio and Archizoom. Breaking with the modernist paradigm, these architects worked on critical and speculative visions for the future. The term wasn't coined until 1999, when British designer Anthony Dunne published *Hertzian Tales*, in which he wrote,

> The challenge is to blur the boundaries between the real and the fictional, so that the visionary becomes more real and the real is seen as just one limited possibility, a product of ideology maintained through the uncritical design of a surfeit of consumer goods.[11]

As pioneers of the speculative design method, Dunne and Fiona Raby saw it as a way to design for preferable futures by avoiding the pressure of market demands and criticizing the designers' slavish relation to capitalism. Their book lays out the potential of speculative design as a critique:

> Triggered by the financial crash of 2008, there has been a new wave of interest in thinking about alternatives to the current system. And although no new forms of capitalism have emerged yet, there is a growing desire for other ways of managing our economic lives and the relationship among state, market, citizen, and consumer.[12]

Early speculative design was done by students of The Royal College of Art in London where Dunne and Raby taught, and made its way to galleries and museums. In these environments designs could ignite debates about political or social issues. It did not take long before Silicon Valley companies noticed the potential of speculative design, and adopted its methods to imagine new markets and float ideas for future products under the name 'design fiction'.[13] While early speculative design came from architecture and product design, the field later also included graphic design. 'All Possible Futures' was a 2014 exhibition curated by graphic designer Jon Sueda[14] that explored speculative work by graphic designers.

Trading Futures

Speculative design is closely related to science fiction. Movies such as *2001: A Space Odyssey* (1968), *Minority Report* (2002), *Wall-E* (2008), and the television series *Black Mirror* (2011–present) are often cited by speculative designers as examples. Science fiction is a narrative genre that was born out of artists' imaginations of how technology could influence society. The early industrial revolution inspired the first science-fiction novels such as *Frankenstein* (1818) by Mary Shelley and the work of H.G. Wells and Jules Verne.

As a creative medium, science fiction has been used to serve every purpose imaginable. Many science-fiction works have developed parallel to, or in response to capitalism. *Star Trek*'s motto 'To boldly go where no man has gone before', embodies a form of space colonization that aligns with capitalist ideas of unlimited expansion. On the other hand, novels by authors such as Octavia Butler, Ursula K. Le Guin, and the Black Quantum Futurism collective imagine futures that are feminist, anti-racist, and anti-capitalist. Science-fiction offers inspiration and guidance for moral questions by using the future as a mirror for the present. As an art form, science fiction is first and foremost a form of entertainment. Design on the other hand, creates products or services that have use value. A recurring question in debates on speculative design, is whether it has use value like other forms of design, or is it art or entertainment like science fiction?

If speculative design is like science fiction, then what purpose does it serve? Fredric Jameson wrote: 'It is easier to imagine the end of the world than to imagine the end of capitalism'.[15] Philosopher Mark Fisher wrote that anti-capitalist futures: '...performs our anti-capitalism for us ... Allowing us to consume with impunity.'[16] 'The fantasy being that Western consumerism, far from being intrinsically implicated in systemic global inequalities, could itself solve them. All we have to do is buy the right products.'[17]

Science-fiction movies that warn against climate change and foresee the end of the world are more popular than ever, but that hasn't stopped the climate crisis from happening. Series such as *Black Mirror* and *Years and Years* show the possible future impact

→　AKQA, Blockchain Banking Engineer 2030, advertisement for MiSK Global Forum, 2018.

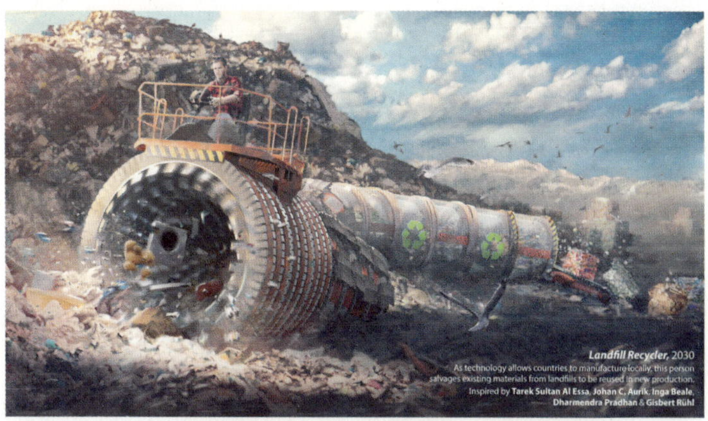

Landfill Recycler, 2030
As technology allows countries to manufacture locally, this person salvages existing materials from landfills to be reused in new production.
Inspired by **Tarek Sultan Al Essa, Johan C. Aurik, Inga Beale, Dharmendra Pradhan** & **Gisbert Rühl**

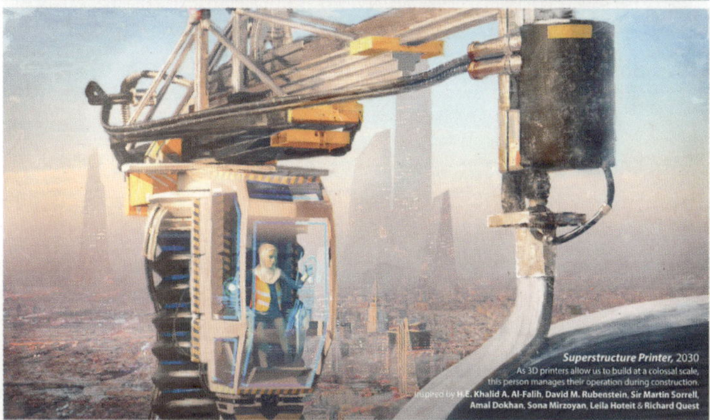

Superstructure Printer, 2030
As 3D printers allow us to build at a colossal scale, this person manages their operation during construction.
Inspired by **H.E. Khalid A. Al-Falih, David M. Rubenstein, Sir Martin Sorrell, Amal Dokhan, Sona Mirzoyan, Leila Hoteit** & **Richard Quest**

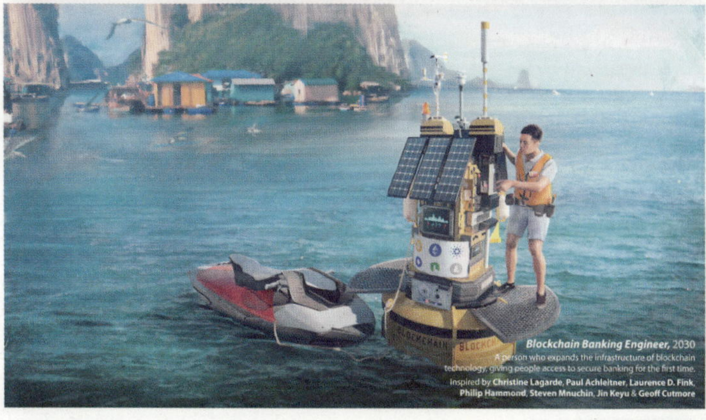

Blockchain Banking Engineer, 2030
A person who expands the infrastructure of blockchain technology, giving people access to secure banking for the first time.
Inspired by **Christine Lagarde, Paul Achleitner, Laurence D. Fink, Philip Hammond, Steven Mnuchin, Jin Keyu** & **Geoff Cutmore**

The fantasy being that Western consumerism, far from being intrinsically implicated in systemic global inequalities, could itself solve them. All we have to do is buy the right products.

MARK FISHER, PHILOSOPHER

of social media in our lives, but that hasn't led to stricter policies for tech companies. A risk is that even critical and dystopian futures can end up creating economic value in the form of traded futures. Fictional scenarios can be critical and clever, but in the end merely serve as artistic commodities. This is how critical forms of speculative design can become a capitalist tool to profit from the future, without taking responsibility for the present.

Commodification of the Future

Digital tools like computer graphics and 3D prototyping have made it easier for designers to visualize future scenarios convincingly. The largest companies in the world are financial and technology firms, and their immaterial commodities need to be visualized: apps, websites, 3D environments, animations, games, digital finances, and so on. Just as the manufacturing industry of the twentieth century needed designers to style products, speculative design is perfectly equipped to visualize the immaterial commodities that are being produced today.

Speculative design also serves tech companies such as Google, Facebook, Samsung, Microsoft, and Uber to materialize their innovative claims. We tend to view these companies as innovative businesses that work on free internet access in remote areas, or ending poverty with microloans, or eradicating disease using 'disruptive' technology. The economic reality is that Google and Facebook make most of their money from advertising.[18]

Digital visualizations are an attractive way to spin positive press for companies to obfuscate their harmful business models. The oil company Saudi Aramco and the United Arab Emirates both commissioned speculative designers to imagine post-energy

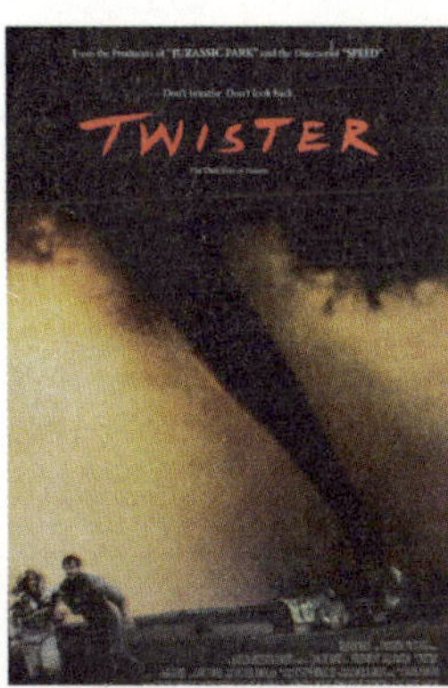

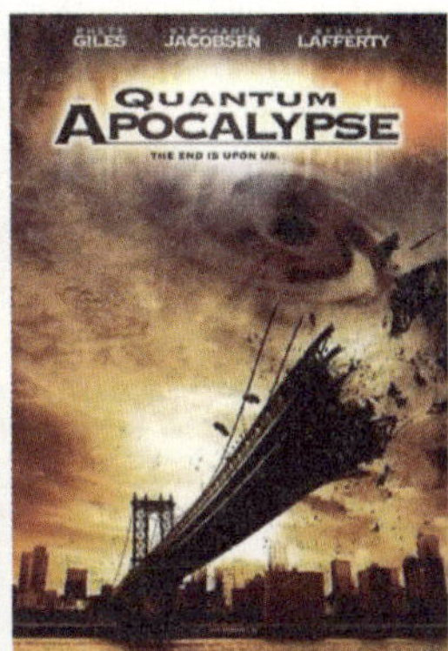

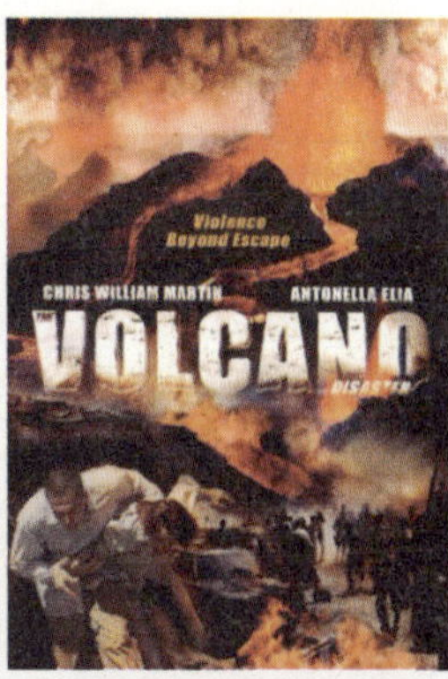

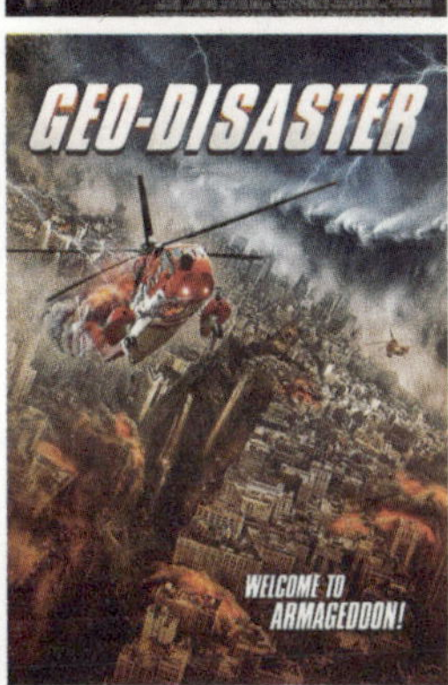

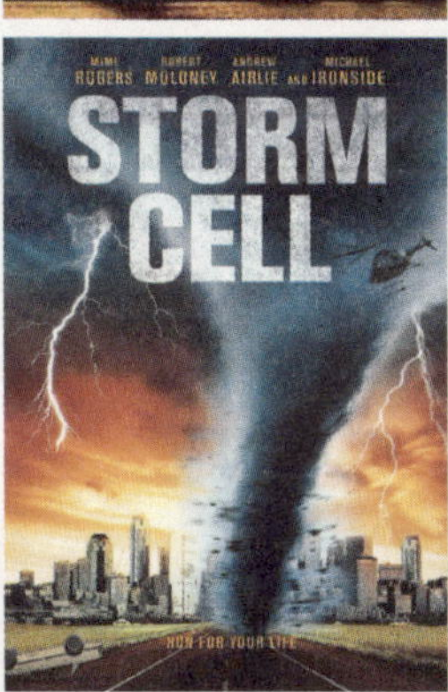

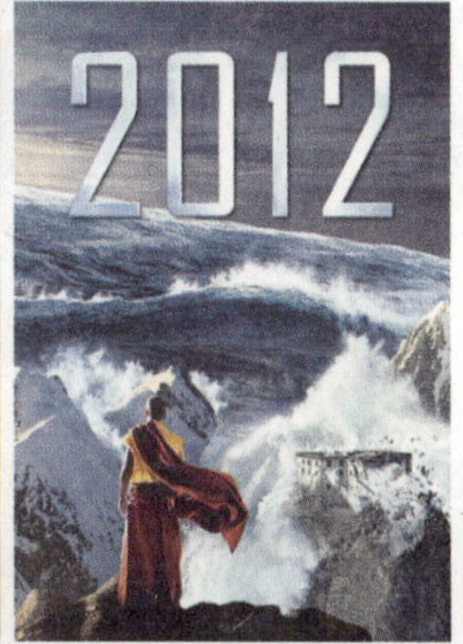

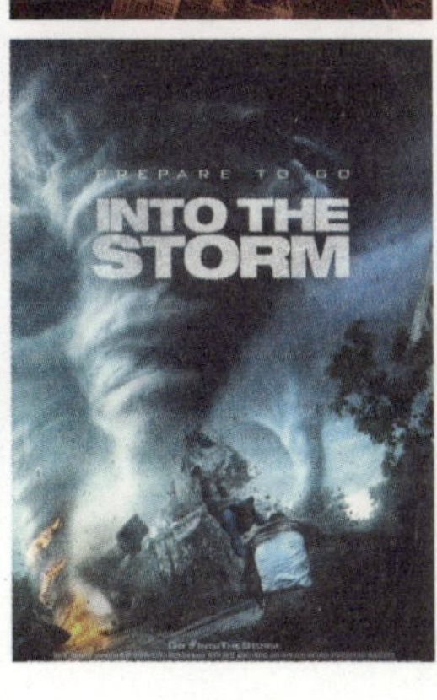

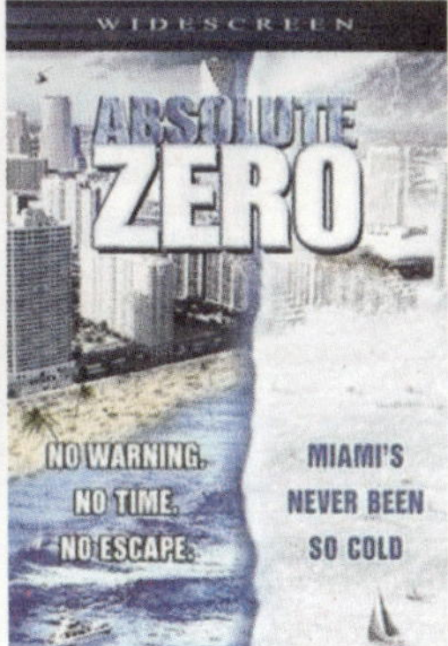

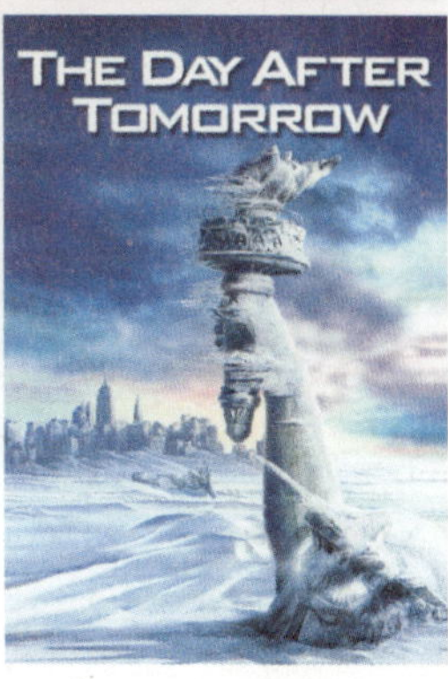

Disaster movies: *Twister* (1996), *Quantum Apocalypse* (2010), *Volcano* (2005), *Geo-Disaster* (2017), *Storm Cell* (2008), *2012* (2009), *Into The Storm* (2014), *Absolute Zero* (2006), *The Day After Tomorrow* (2004).

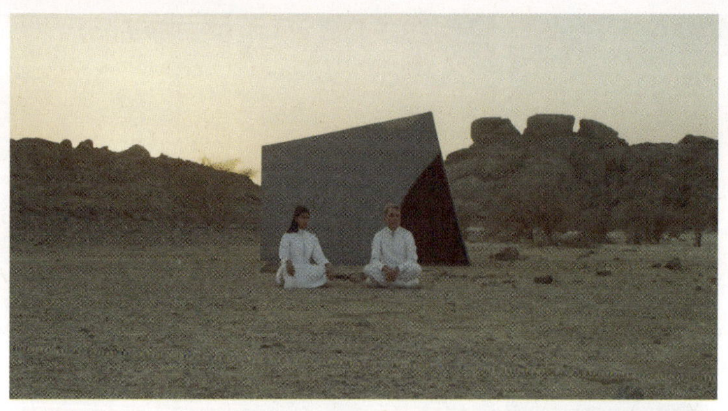

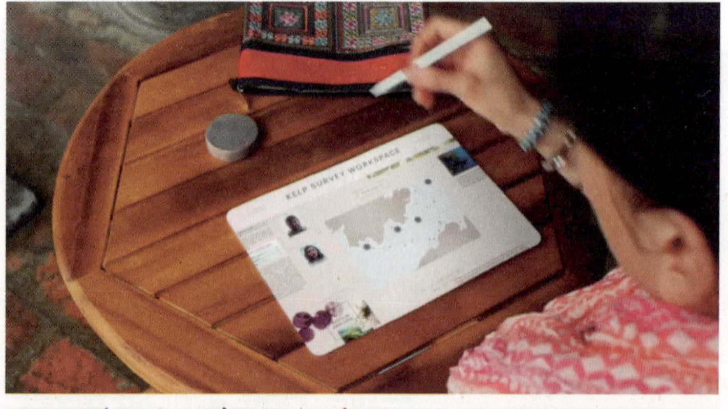

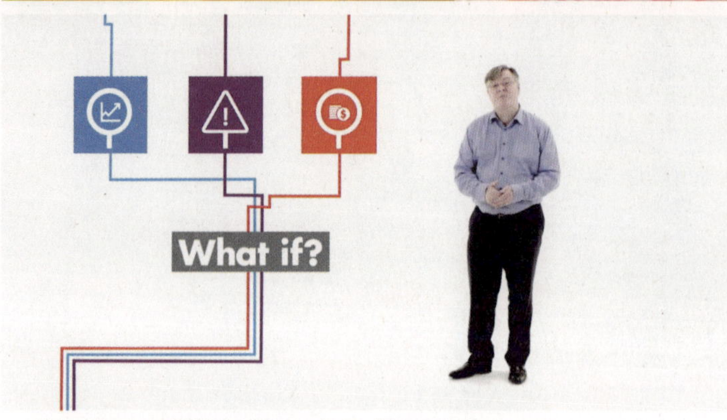

↑   Michael Mogensen, NIUN, *Saudi Futures*, for Saudi Aramco, 2018.
↑   Microsoft, Productivity Future Vision, 2015.
↑   Royal Dutch Shell, Future Studies video, 2017.

futures,[19] which conveniently allows them to shift the conversation away from the damaging effects of fossil fuel industry on which their business model depends. Either as fantasy or as prototype, speculative design helps to raise stock value and keep an appearance of competitiveness. Speculative design is able to create value without selling products or services, independent of whether these speculative scenarios are actually realized.

Design consultants and trendwatchers use speculative design to provide their multinational retail clients with ideas for new products and markets. Scenarios, for example those envisioned by consultants such as Future Laboratory invariably depict wealthy households using expensive products.[20] A future productivity vision by Microsoft show how their products can be integrated in the workflow of 2040.[21] All sleekly designed gadgets and invisible screens in the video that plays in South-East Asia, without any mention of climate change, waste, or scarcity. Uber used a speculative design scenario to envision UberAir, 'the future of urban mobility'. A futuristic system of electric private taxi jets taking off from skyscrapers, that would certainly only serve the top one percent earners to escape the realities of congested city traffic.[22]

Even future scenarios that are not utilized for product development can be a useful instrument for backing up corporate restructuring or mass lay-offs, under the cloak of 'innovation'. Other industries, such as the much-criticized energy companies, use speculative design to paint pictures of green growth future that cannot be further apart from their actual strategies.[23] Deliberately using speculative design as a way to obfuscate the realities of the climate crisis is perhaps the most unethical outcome of the use of design fiction.

Design Derivatives

Faced with the dilemmas of a pandemic, an impending environmental crisis, and rising inequality, it is logical that designers resort to speculation to avoid facing the complexity of society's problems. Especially considering design's involvement in the current production cycle, which has produced so much exploitation, waste, and carbon emissions. It is design's imperative to come up with products or services, so logically speculative design results in new (speculative) products. Perhaps it is this tendency of thinking in new marketable products that design must resist, and which have clouded possible futures of de-growth and climate justice. Speculative design should stop imagining luxury fantasies for the one percent, whether it is the form of lab-grown meat, extra-planetary colonization, or augmented interfaces for consumer electronics. As Françoise Vergès pointed out, a new green and sustainable world 'rarely addresses who will do the work of post-disaster cleanup'.[24] The only ethical future imagines a world that protects and respects the life of all living beings.

That doesn't mean speculative design doesn't have a role to play. We need to imagine societies with less products and better social relations. Where fixing, mending, and social organization can be part of a thriving society, which is more inclusive and less servient to profits. A useful reference is the 'Cheat Sheet for a Non- (or Less-) Colonialist Speculative Design',[25] written by designers Pedro Oliveira and Luiza Prado in response to an online debate following the MoMA exhibition 'Design and Violence' in 2013.[26]

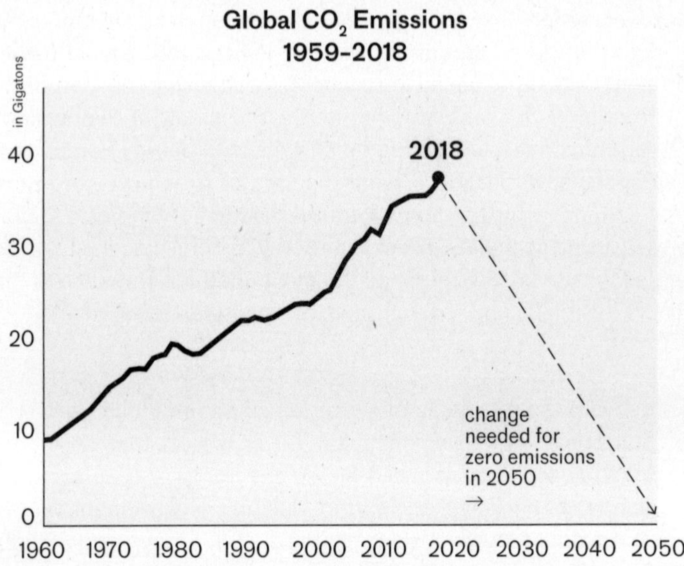

→   Earthrise, the photo of the Earth taken from Apollo 8, 1968. Photo by Bill Anders.

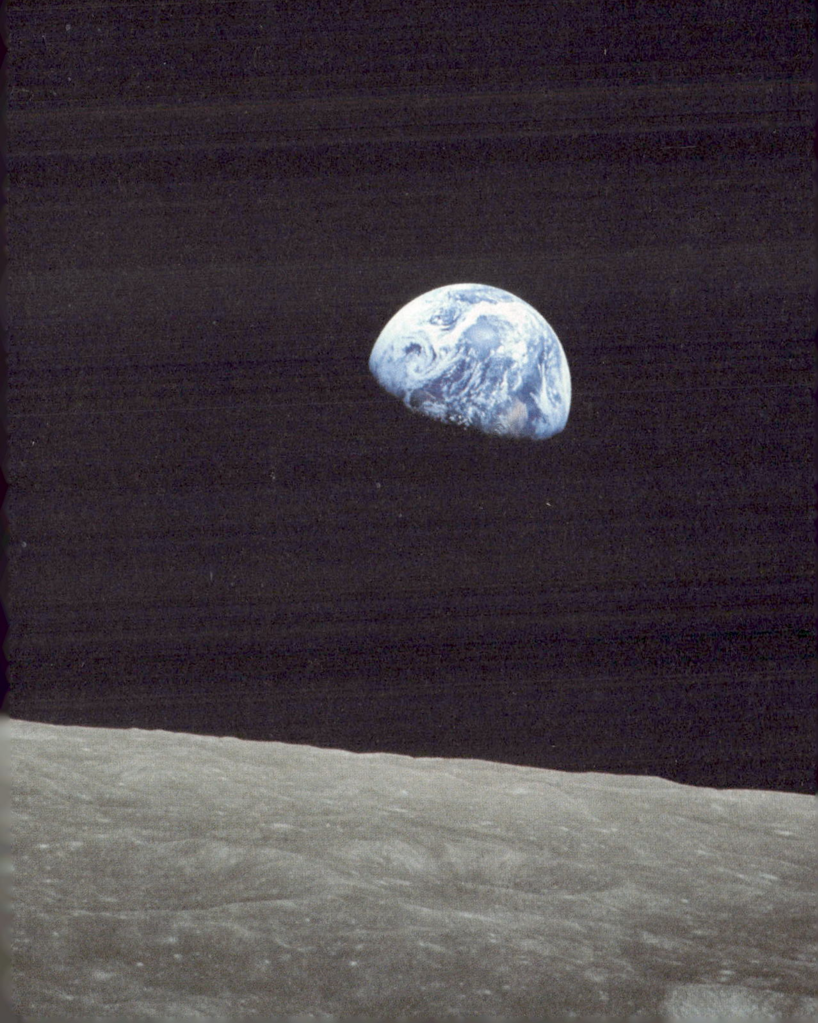

The assumption is that it is not politically acceptable to question economic growth and that no nation would voluntary limit growth in the name of the climate or environment; therefore green growth must be true, since the alternative is disaster.

JASON HICKEL AND GIORGIO KALLIS, SCIENTISTS

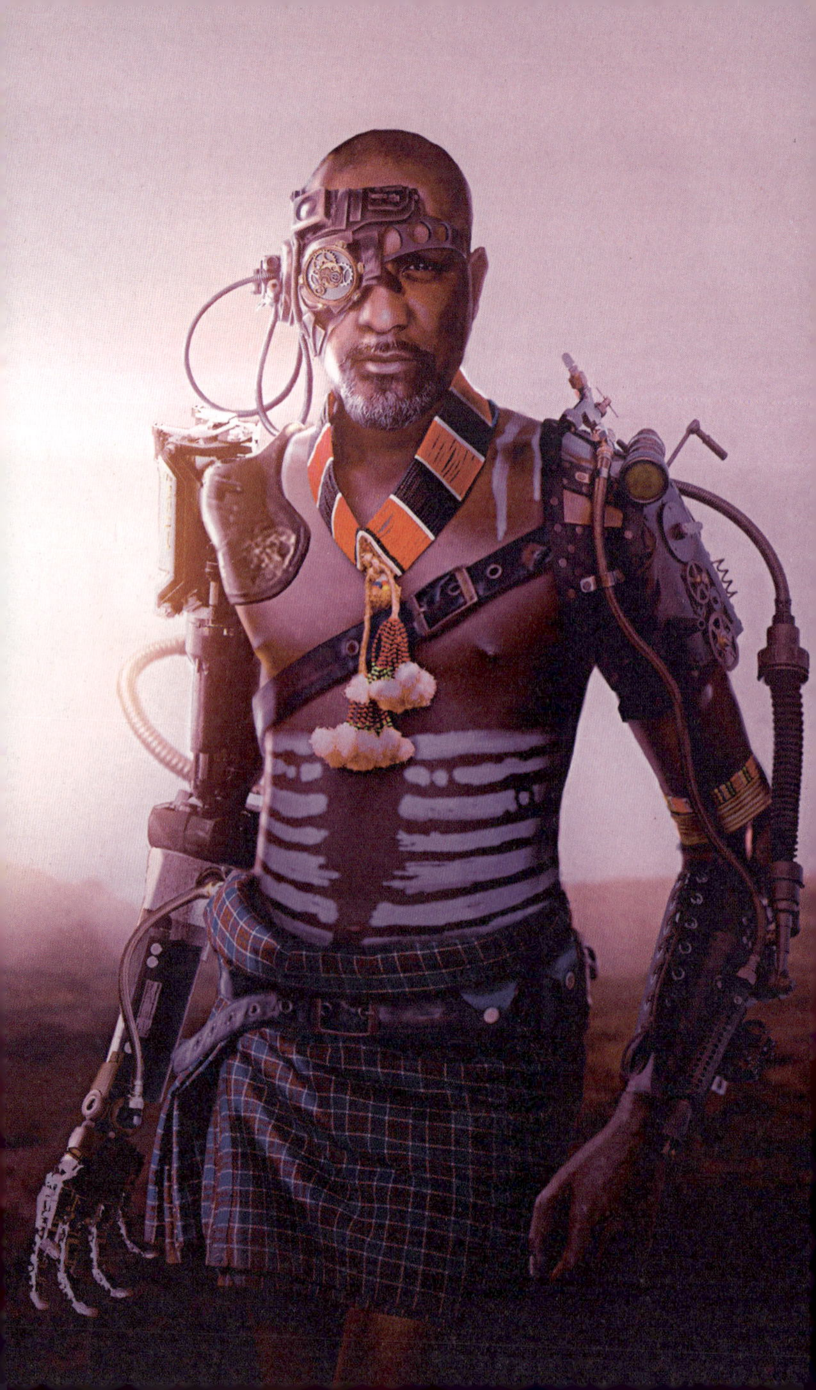

The MoMA exhibition spawned an online discussion about the privilege of many speculative designers, who are often based in the Global North, using grant money or subsidies to imagine futures of starvation, scarcity, or climate disasters. Speculative situations which are a reality in many parts of the world. The cheat sheet aims to confront designers with their own position and privilege in relation to the fictional world they are envisioning.

The paradox of speculative design is that designers can avoid taking responsibility for a future by imagining it outside of their own social context. A lack of intergenerational thinking is a typically Western phenomenon, according to philosopher Roman Krznaric.[27] The risk is that futures are imagined that are seen as separate from bodies and communities. In contrast to certain indigenous cultures that focus on long-term responsibility. The Haudenosaunee and Dakota in the US use the Seventh Generation Principle, a philosophy that any decision of today should create a sustainable world for seven future generations to come.[28] *Whakapapa* is a principle from Māori culture in which the present is always connected to past and future generations. This means that choices that are made now will have to face responsibilities for the future they invariably create or envision because that future is inhabited.

If speculative design wants to play a role in imagining better societies, designers should assume responsibility for the current crises and understand their own role in them. By embracing the emancipatory potential of the future and resisting the enclosure of the future by capitalism. If not, the future will only exist as commodities for entertainment or financial speculation. We should imagine futures built on notions of solidarity, justice, and equality that can be used to solve today's crises as well. They might not look as sexy, and not as flawless as the futures we are used to seeing. But at least they will be futures for the many, not for the few.

← Solen Feyissa, Serengeti Cyborg, 2020.
→ Rick Guidice, Visualization for a fictional donut-shaped space colony, NASA, 1970s.

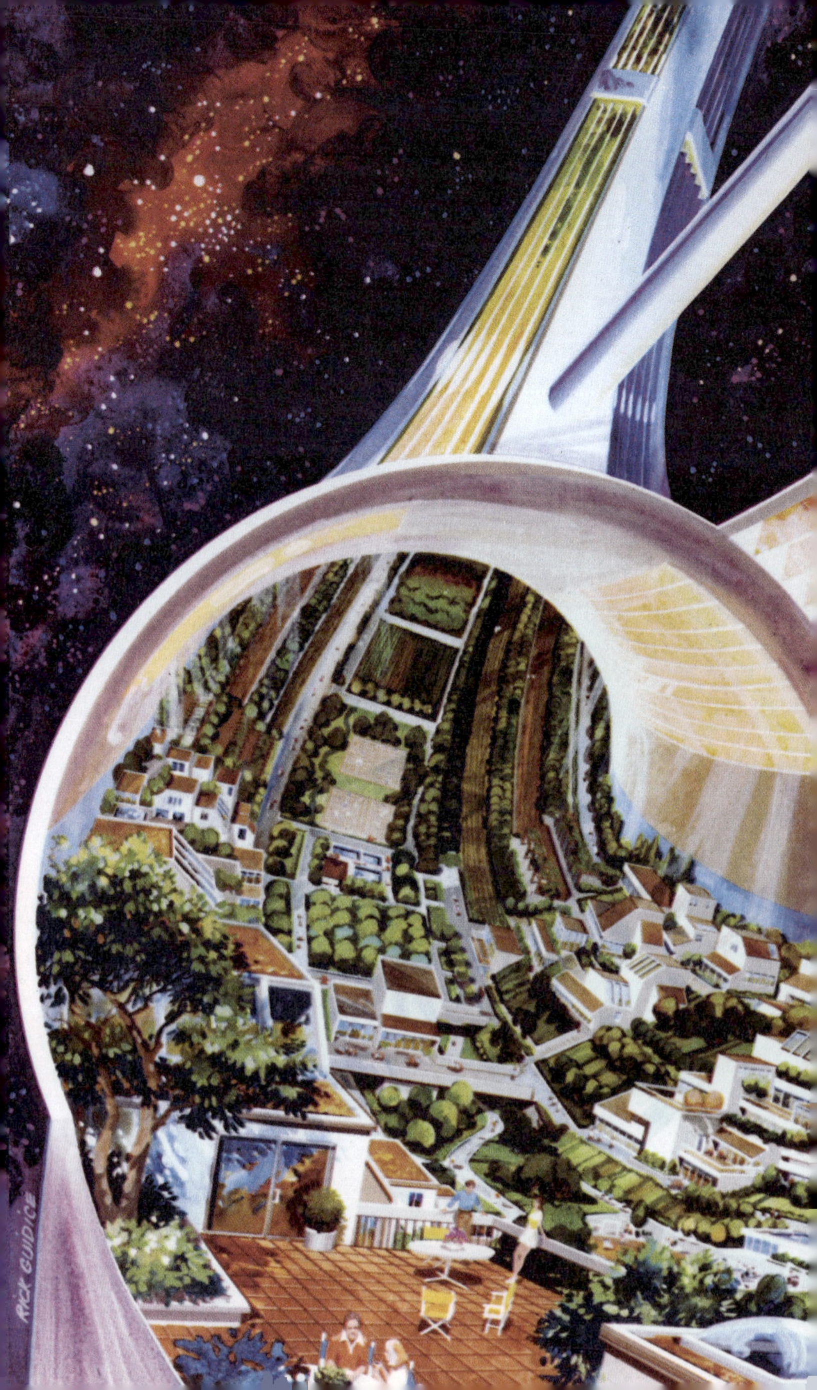

RICK GUIDICE

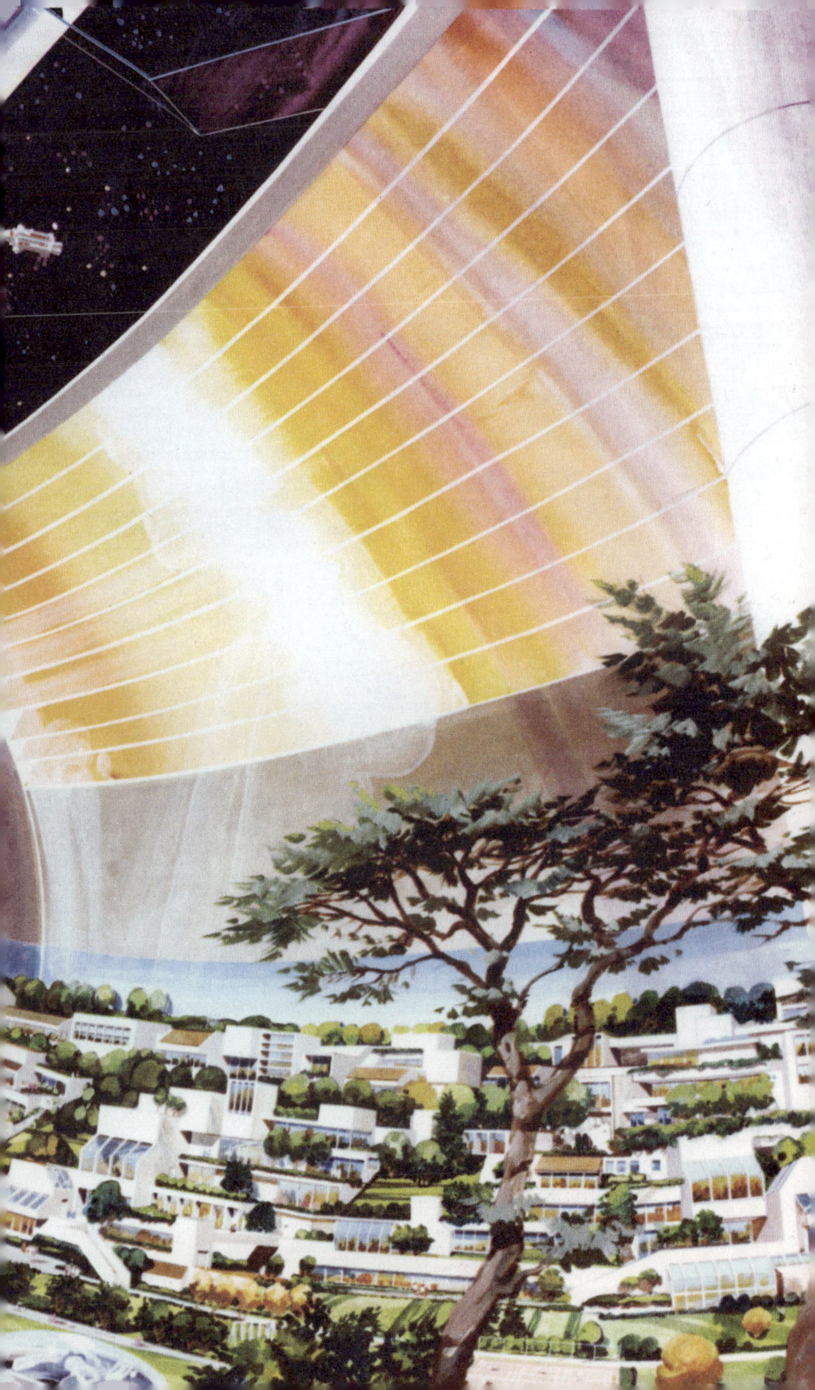

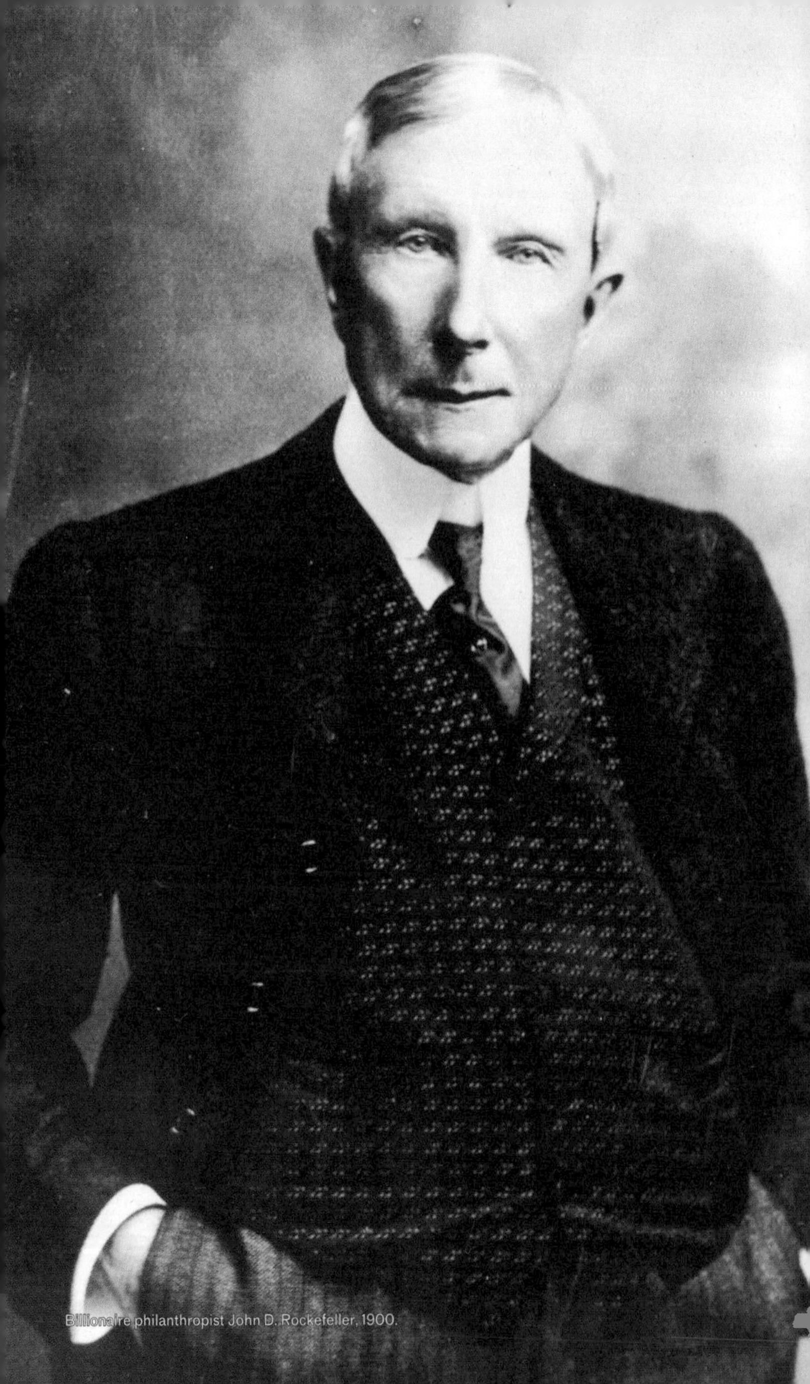

Billionaire philanthropist John D. Rockefeller, 1900.

THE DESIGNER AS PHILAN- THROPIST

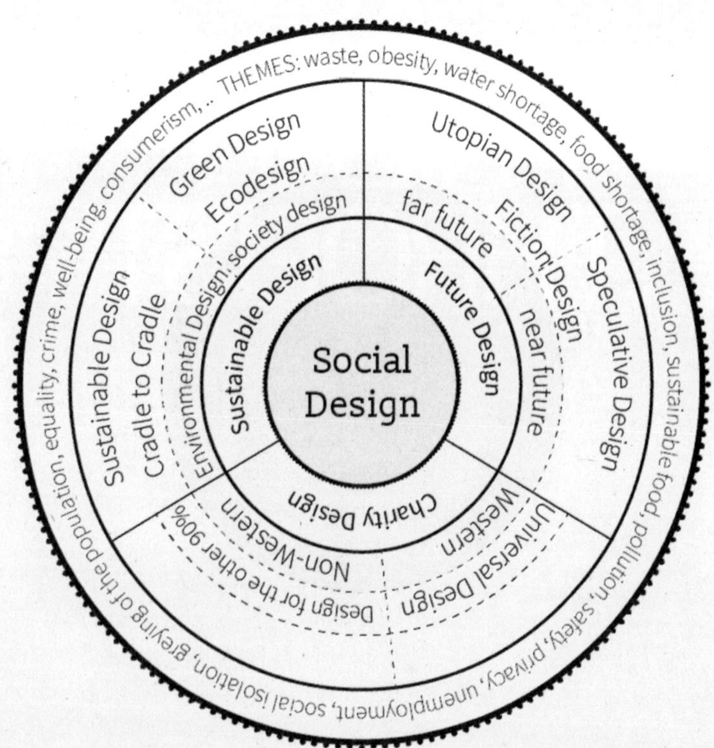

Madelaine Berlis, Social design graph, 2015.

CHANGE MAKERS

How can designers help others? It can be disappointing for designers to learn that their work is merely used to sell products, or ends up as luxury items on the shelves of the rich. A growing movement of designers is strongly motivated to use their skills for the benefit of the public good, instead of serving capitalism.

This section discusses some of the strategies that designers can employ to avoid getting locked in the cycle of capitalist production. The philanthropist is born from the realization that designers are partly responsible for waste, the extraction of resources, and the climate crisis. The designer as philanthropist donates time and skills to address social issues that benefit the public good, instead of selling more products.

Victor Papanek (1923–1998) more or less pioneered social design. He wanted designers to work with NGOs rather than for the industry. He also suggested that designers shouldn't wait for clients, but 'be more sensitive in realising what problems exist'.[1] That alludes to a prevailing idea at the time, that design is a problem-solving activity. Especially during the late modernism of the 1970s and 1980s, this idea that design could solve problems picked up steam. An engineering view on design was common, and many designers, such as Paul Rand, believed designers should not get involved in social issues at all.[2]

Following the Silicon Valley mantra to 'move fast and break things', the problem-solving capacities that are attributed to design today are considerable.[3] Poverty, climate change, racial injustice, deforestation. No problem is too big, too controversial, or too political, to be 'solved' through design. Hackathons, design challenges, and conferences use design to address social, political, or environmental issues. Design has come from a position of being humble, to one of hubris. Confident that design can do what is considered 'too big for governments and NGOs alone'.[4]

In this chapter we will see to what extent design can contribute to 'a better society' when designers become philanthropists and donate their time and resources to social causes. Can design 'solve' problems at all, and in what ways has design's fixation for solutionism clouded its self-image? As the saying goes, the road to hell is paved with good intentions, and we shall see how design's intentions to do good play out in the real world.

Philantrocapitalism

Giving is universal. Whether it is gifting, tribute, charity, or philanthropy. Upon closer inspection there is a fundamental difference between reciprocal giving, and philanthropy or charity. Philanthropists are persons of means, who choose to spend their wealth for the purpose of helping the less fortunate. This may appear like a selfless act of kindness, but it is always a 'competitive and strategic' act, writes political scientist Rob Reich.[5] In other words, the wealthy usually don't just give their money away without expecting anything in return. Philanthropy has historically been used by the rich to increase political power, spread religion, improve a public image, or divert attention from less admirable activities.

In colonial times, European philanthropy in the colonies went hand in hand with violence to 'civilize' indigenous peoples, and philanthropy has been shaped by these policies ever since. Christian missions used education, medicine, and hunger relief as an instrument to 'help' those who were regarded as 'backward' by Europeans. The tremendous wealth that Europeans hoarded by exploiting the colonized was defensible by those in power because of its good intentions. The violence and exploitation under colonialism was rationalized with ideas such as 'the white man's burden'; a phrase coined by British novelist Rudyard Kipling, meaning white Europeans were morally obliged to civilize non-white peoples, to encourage their 'progress', in European terms.[6]

Before the twentieth century, the absence of state welfare provided a way for wealthy merchants and industrialists to gain political power by donating to the poor, founding schools and hospitals. Excluded from political participation by the aristocratic elite, the new wealthy class used philanthropy to successfully build a

→ S. Broder and the US. Office of War Information, 1942.

Next to money and guns, the third largest North American export is the U.S. idealist, who turns up in every theatre of the world: the teacher, the volunteer, the missioner, the community organizer, the economic developer, and the vacationing do-gooder.

IVAN ILLICH, PHILOSOPHER

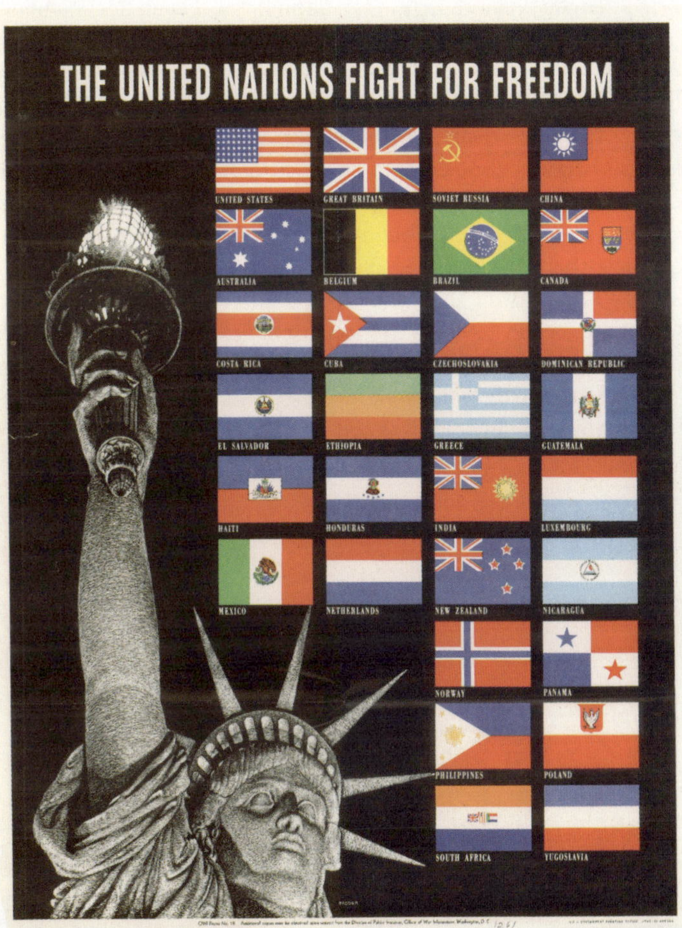

political powerbase. Even 'robber barons' such as Andrew Carnegie and John D. Rockefeller are remembered for their philanthropy, even though their fortunes were amassed through unbridled exploitation of people and planet.

The belief that capitalism is better at social emancipation and the redistribution of wealth than the state, is what historian Mikkel Thorup calls 'philanthrocapitalism'.[7] Lavish donations to social causes is a way for corporations to be seen as benevolent, without damaging their business model by changing unethical practices. As philanthropy is tax deductible, it is also a financially attractive strategy. In his book *Just Giving: Why Philanthropy Is Failing Democracy and How It Can Do Better*, Reich estimates that tax subsidies for philanthropy cost the US taxpayer $50 billion each year.[8] For example, the Chan and Zuckerberg initiative, founded by Facebook's former CEO Mark Zuckerberg and his partner Priscilla Chan, is a fund that has pledged almost 45 billion dollars in Facebook shares to cure all diseases by 2100. In light of Zuckerberg's 'pledge' to fix health care,[9] a recent BBC article speaks about how Facebook, Google and Microsoft have evaded to pay $3 billion in taxes in the Global South, which could have been spent on fighting the Covid-19 pandemic.[10]

In his book Reich shows how both philanthropy and inequality have grown immensely over the last decades, and he considers them two sides of the same coin. As the tax rate for the wealthiest

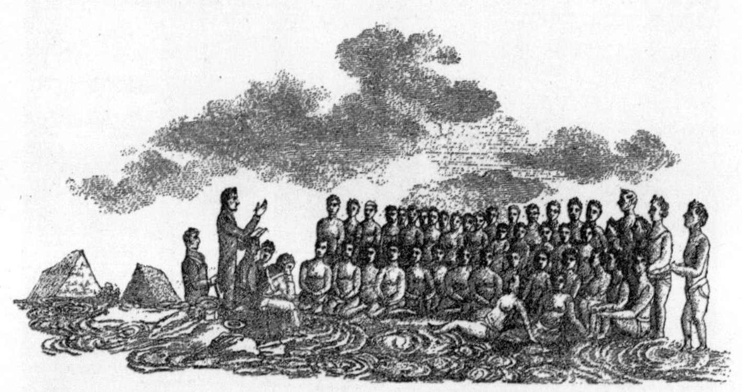

William Ellis, *A Missionary Preaching to Natives, Kokukano, Hawaii,* 1822.-1823.

CAPS LOCK – Part 3

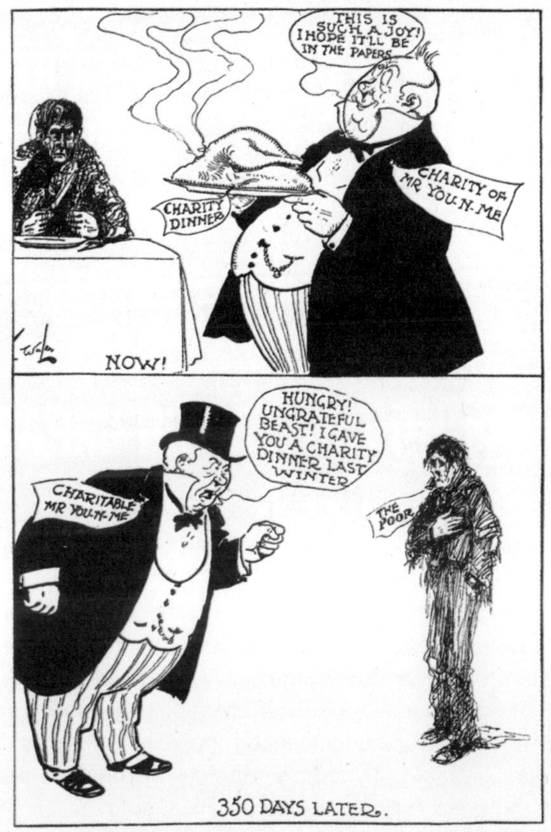

Ryan Walker, Cartoon in *Arena Magazine* volume 35, 1906.

was diminished from 70 to 28 percent under the Reagan administration, funding of welfare and social services was severely cut. During the World Economic Forum in Davos in 2019, US congressperson Alexandria Ocasio-Cortez proposed reinstating the 70 percent tax on those earning over 10 million a year. Her proposal was received with ridicule by CEO Michael Dell, who responded that the wealthy are much better at solving the world's problems than governments are.[11] Trans activist, author, and teacher Dean Spade remarks in his book *Mutual Aid* that the charity model reinforces the idea that 'rich people are inherently better and more moral than poor people, which is why they deserve to be on top'.[12]

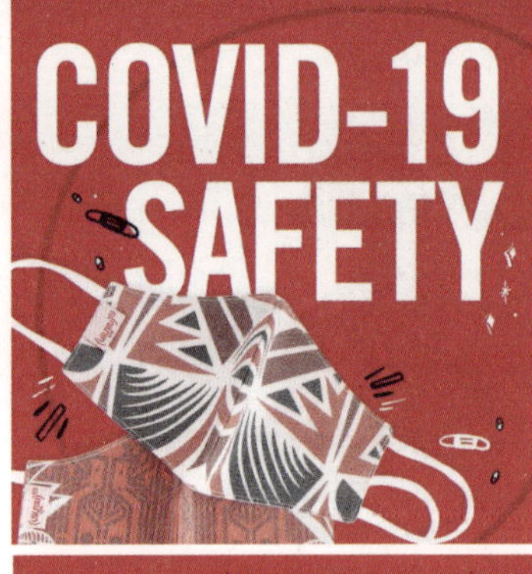

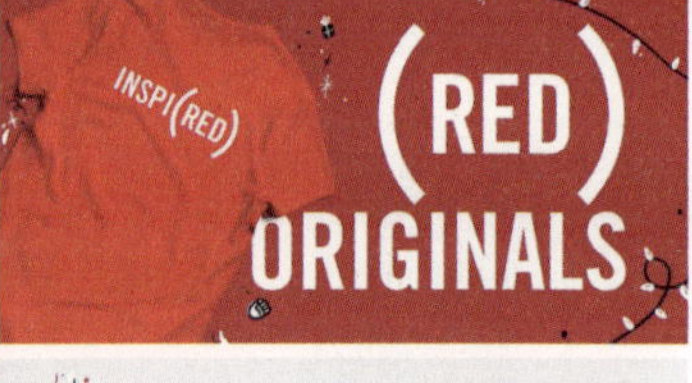

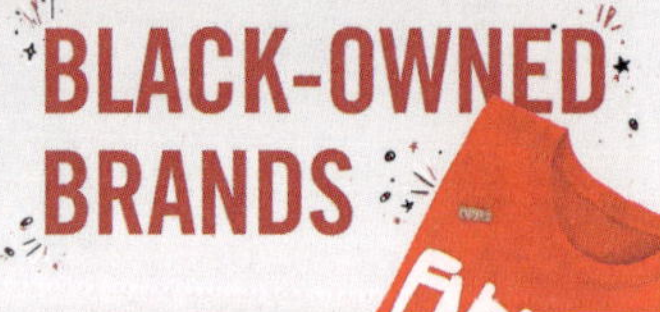

Banners from the website of (RED), 2020, red.org.

Secondly, philanthrocapitalism packages social solidarity in the form of products that can be purchased, like the One Laptop Per Child, Bono's RED product range, and other 'socially responsible' brands. Philosopher Mark Fisher mentions that this commodification of solidarity has convinced individuals they can 'solve' the world's problems by simply purchasing different products, 'without the need for any kind of political solution or systemic reorganization'.[13] The structure of philanthropy undermines community-based solidarity and state welfare services. A small group of ultra-rich individuals can decide how money should be redistributed. It is hardly surprising that they choose forms of spending that best serve their own interests.

The reason this chapter looks into the origins of philanthropy, is that 'design for good' projects from the Global North follow the same logic. Both are based on ideas about 'development' and 'doing good' and the benevolence of the rich, such as helping the 'poor' or 'marginalized' peoples in the Global South, or local communities that are seen as 'other'. Both design-for-good and philanthropy tend to prefer short-term, commodified solutions: projects, challenges, apps: products that can be quickly developed and

In order to work more intelligently, the whole practice of design has to be turned around. Designers can no longer be the employees of corporations, but rather must work directly for the client group—that is, the people who are in need of a product.

VICTOR PAPANEK, DESIGNER

distributed immediately. Products that look good in the media on photos and videos, instead of facing the complex messy reality that a structural approach would entail.

Design for Good

Designers that choose to work for the benefit of social causes, are neither a recent phenomenon, nor a Western one. Especially design work in the non-professional sphere is often done for the benefit of the community. People who make their own clothes, tools, and build their own houses is how design started in the first place. The fact that the beginning of social design is usually placed in the 1970s with the work of Victor Papanek, is because he wrote about it, practiced it, and taught it in a professional context.

Papanek's work was seen as radical at the time, but it did fit the post-war emergence of organizations such as the IMF (1944), the World Bank (1944), and the United Nations (1945). These Western organizations were founded to prevent future conflicts, promote world trade, and improve the conditions in former colonies, some- times with the ulterior motive to block communist expansion. Important environmental studies such as Rachel Carson's *Silent Spring* (1962) and *The Limits to Growth* report (1972), exposed the threats of pollution and climate change and led to the foundation of many environmental groups such as Greenpeace (1971). It is from these surroundings of post-war economic prosperity, cold war pol- itics, and a Western missionary zeal that design for good emerged.

In his book *Design for the Real World*, Papanek emphasized that design 'operates mainly as a marketing tool of big business',[14] while 75 percent of the world population at the time lived in

It is not about being hip or cool, nor is it about being seen as creative or being a problem-solver. It is not about the objects and images associated with one's name nor about having articles written about oneself in glossy magazines. Rather it is about something profoundly unfashionable. It's about being serious.

TONY FRY, PHILOSOPHER

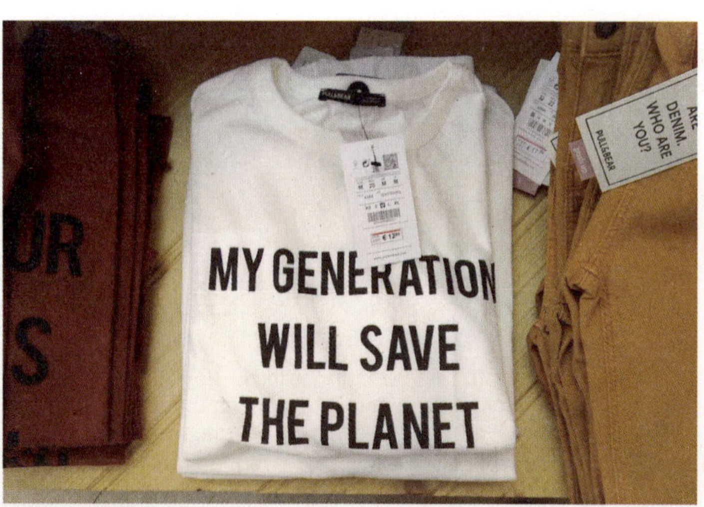

T-shirt from Pull&Bear, via Boring Dystopia, 2019.

abject poverty. He suggested that if every designer could allocate one-tenth of the working time: '...designing for many instead of designing for money',[15] that would add up to an enormous effort to help the developing world. The industrial designers did not appreciate his critique, and he was kicked out of industrial design trade organizations in the US.[16] He continued working with his students on humanitarian projects for non-profits.

From Papanek's call to action, a series of terms have emerged with a philanthropic attitude towards design, such as design for development, social design, and design thinking. Especially social design has flourished since the 1990s, with books, conferences, and academic programmes. Its popularity proves that many designers do not adhere to the modernist interpretation of the designer who should stay out of politics. Accumulating crises of climate change, racism, gender issues, fascist politics, and a massive rise in inequality demands designers to actively scrutinize their own responsibilities within these crises.

But there is another, more opportunistic reason at play. In an article about social design, co-written by Dung-Sheng Chen,[17] the authors point out that the diminished welfare state in Europe has created new markets in social areas, which were previously under stewardship of the state. Elderly care, health care, and housing are now partly or entirely privatized markets, as part of the enclosure by capitalism of social commons. As the 2008 financial crisis has dried up a lot of traditional design work, in order to survive designers are seeking to profit from these new social markets, or starting their own social projects with state or private funding.

Here is where the good intentions of the designer collide with the economic logic of the design industry. If social designers seek to 'improve' areas that are poor or struggling, designer and researcher Danah Abdulla remarks, how does that rhyme with social design programmes for which students pay $30,000 per year?[18] This shows the gap between those who design, and those who are 'to be designed'. This highly unequal relationship becomes apparent in that many prominent social designers are from more affluent backgrounds in the Global North. Abdulla brings forward the 'Design Ignites Change' awards,[19] where 'an overwhelming number of projects [are] targeting communities in Asia, Africa, and South America',[20] while most of the designers are from the Global North. The consequence is that designers 'tend to focus on communities with the following criteria: run down, poor, and the furthest away from their own personal experience.' She calls this problematic relation 'design imperialism'.[21]

As we have observed, the role of the designer as a philanthropist is a profound ambiguous one. Certainly, it provides ways for designers to get involved in work that benefits a larger public. The fact that so many designers are willing to donate time and resources

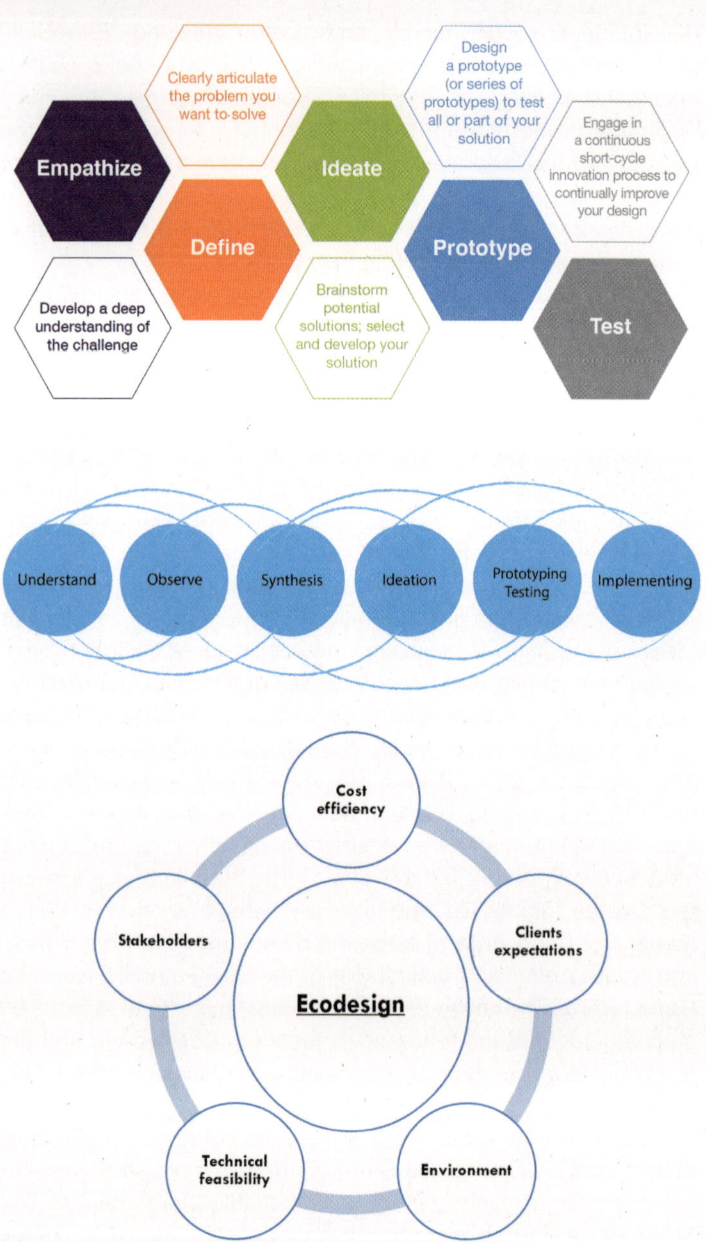

Empathize
Clearly articulate the problem you want to solve
Ideate
Design a prototype (or series of prototypes) to test all or part of your solution
Engage in a continuous short-cycle innovation process to continually improve your design
Define
Prototype
Develop a deep understanding of the challenge
Brainstorm potential solutions; select and develop your solution
Test
Understand
Observe
Synthesis
Ideation
Prototyping Testing
Implementing
Cost efficiency
Stakeholders
Clients expectations
Ecodesign
Technical feasibility
Environment

for a public cause is admirable. On the other hand, overconfidence in design's abilities, and unchecked privilege on the part of the designer can lead to an unequal power dynamic.

Design Thinking

Social design is no longer something practiced by just a few rebellious designers, it has become big business. Design thinking is a subdiscipline of design, mostly found in business and management contexts. It is perhaps at once the most successful and the most hated form of design, as the popularity of Natasha Jen's article 'Why Design Thinking is Bullshit' illustrates.[22] Coining the term design thinking is credited to the multinational IDEO, a design consultancy company in Silicon Valley. According to CEO Tim Brown, 'Design thinking is a human-centered approach to innovation that draws from the designer's toolkit to integrate the needs of people, the possibilities of technology, and the requirements for business success.'[23]

In the world of Design Thinking, all aspects of society are privatized and 'solved' by design consultants. This is the design version of what technology writer Evgeny Morozov calls 'solutionism': 'The idea that given the right code, algorithms and robots, technology can solve all of mankind's problems, effectively making life "frictionless" and trouble-free.'[24] The danger of solutionism is that we trust private companies in the hope that they can solve complex issue that are social, political, and collective in nature, such as poverty, housing, or health care.

Its practitioners often call design thinking 'human centred', and emphasize its ability for social innovation, while in fact applying a 'dumbed-down version' to the world of business, of what designers always have been doing.[25] The famous Design Thinking model consist of five hexagons which read 'Empathize', 'Define', 'Ideate', 'Prototype', and 'Test'. Design thinking has been able to profit from its own promotion, as designer Darin Buzon observes. IDEO offers a five-week 'Insights for innovation' course for $499, and a four-day Design Thinking bootcamp from Stanford university costs $12,600.[26] Upon closer inspection, Design Thinking is a different form of management and business administration, that further

← Diagrams of Social Design and Design Thinking methods.

entrenches design ideas within capitalist enterprise.

Designer and cultural historian Maggie Gram gives examples of how design thinking is applied to 'social issues'. She recounts how IDEO was hired to improve the community of Gainsville in the US, a community where 57 percent of resident 'struggle to meet basic needs'.[27] The town's mayor was convinced this was due to a lack of competitiveness and he hired IDEO. After eight weeks of research and hundreds of interviews, IDEO concluded that Gainsville needed to be more 'design minded'. A new logo and a tagline was developed, and workshops on design thinking were given to people on the city commission. The new design mentality led to the firing of long-time public administrators while young people from outside of the community were hired. Gram notes that IDEO's intervention did nothing about affordable housing, food prices, or the lacks in education in this community, because these are caused by 'poverty, income disparity, structural racism, environmental injustice, unregulated market capitalism', as Gram writes, and not a lack in competitiveness. One resident whom she quotes, sums it up: 'Gainesville is not a Silicon Valley start-up.'

Design Like You Give a Damn

Another example of social design is the annual Dutch design conference What Design Can Do (WDCD). In 2013, millions of displaced people made their way to Europe to find a life of safety flee-

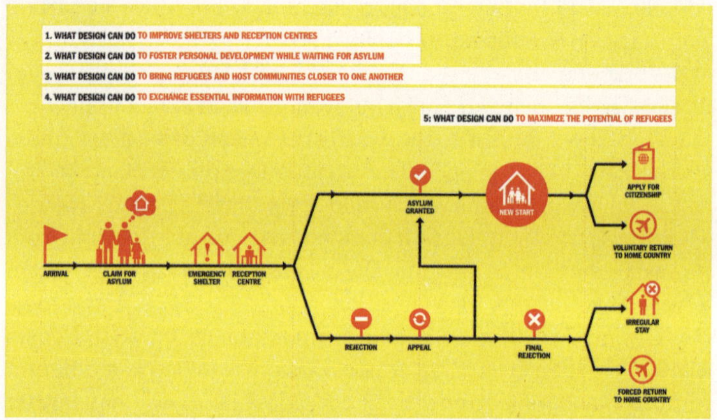

What Design Can Do Refugee Challenge briefing, 2014.

ing a civil war in Syria. In the midst of this political turmoil, WDCD —a conference that introduces itself on the website with 'design like you give a damn—decided to organize a 'Refugee design challenge' together with UNICEF and IKEA, in which designers were asked to come up with 'bold ideas' for a crisis of 'biblical proportions'.[28]

The briefing invited designers from around the world to design shelters, clothing, apps, and PR campaigns to help improve the situation of refugees. Designers had to pitch their ideas in a one-minute video, which would enter a start-up incubator process. Five finalists would receive €10,000 to fund their ideas. The open call was announced with a lot of media attention, appealing to the humanitarian side of designers calling them 'game-changers', with slogans like: 'participating in this contest will make you feel good!'[29]

Following the announcement, three articles publicly criticized

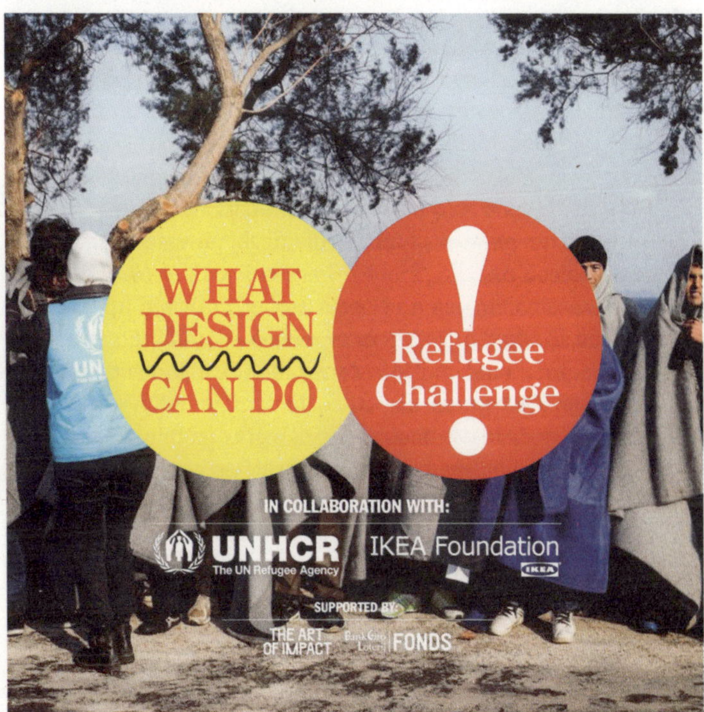

What Design Can Do Refugee Challenge announcement, 2014.

the What Design Can Do (WDCD) Refugee Challenge, one of which was written by myself.[30] The articles did not question the good intentions of the Refugee Challenge, but rather focused on how it was defined as a design problem. It reduced the complex issue of migration into designed objects like shelters, apps, campaigns, and wearables—while leaving out all the political conditions that influence migration: famine, war, inequality, colonialism, and foreign aid. The suggestion that individual designers can provide solutions that are 'too big for NGOs and governments',[31] ignores the fact that European governments have been using design very effectively to keep people from entering Europe. The EU has erected double-tier fences, designed electronic passport systems, border security sensors, and uses drone surveillance. The budgets for which dwarf the funding of the Refugee Challenge.[32]

Months after the open call, a total of 631 design proposals from 70 countries were submitted, out of which 25 projects were nominated and five were selected as finalists. One nominee was an architect, who proposed to combine the shelter of refugees with another pressing issue, the desertification of Southern Europe. The idea was to have the refugees work the land to make it arable again, after which it could be sold to European citizens for farming, while the refugees would move to work in the next barren desert. The question is how work camps in the desert are meant to benefit refugees themselves.

Another nominee was a collective who proposed a reality TV show called *Refugees Got Talent*.[33] By having refugees sing and dance for a TV audience they hope to create a positive image of the refugees themselves. Besides the problematic assumption that refugees want to do this, instead of work or study, the question is why they would not be allowed in the already existing TV show *Holland's Got Talent*.

Some projects were more nuanced and considerate towards the needs of refugees. One of the winners was MakersUnite, a start-up by European designers who train refugees as creative makers and let them participate to make a series of products, many of which are made out of life vests.[34] Given the urgent need to find training for newcomers, this project at least provides a practical service. But saying a start-up like Makersunite offers solutions to a

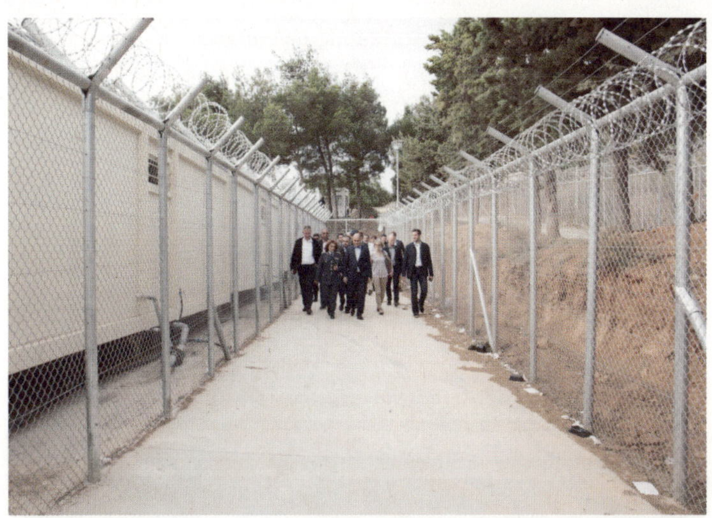

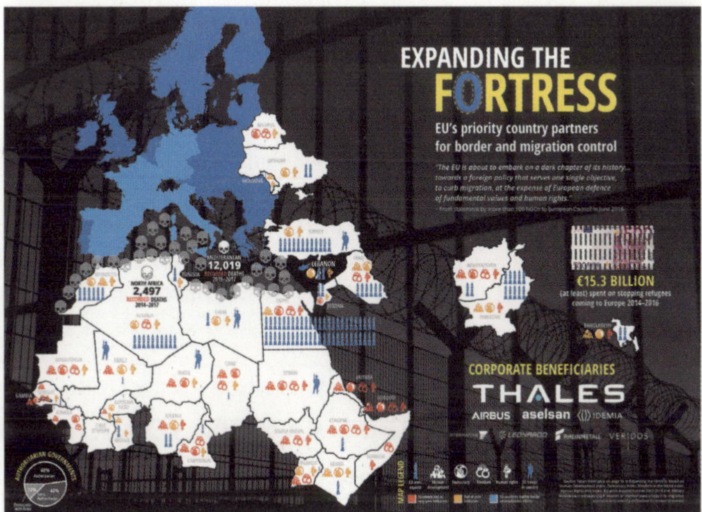

↑   Refugee reception centre, Kos, Greece, 2017. EU reception centres are dangerously overcrowded.
↑   Expanding the Fortress, EU defence's industry's involvement, TNI, 2018.

'refugee crises' would be overstating its impact.

Perhaps it seems petty to criticize designers who have given their time and resources for the well-being of others, which is something that should be applauded instead of discouraged. The good intentions and hard work of designers are not in question here, but design should be subjected to critique, whether its intentions are honourable or not. With the history of Western philanthropy in mind, doing good cannot be separated from the political and economic context that makes it possible in the first place.

The reason why people make the dangerous sea journey across the Mediterranean is because the EU doesn't allow people without a visa to enter the continent via airplane. This law has contributed to the deaths of 33,000 refugees who have died trying to cross the Mediterranean, making the EU border the deadliest in the world.[35] Instead of simply allowing such a safer form of travel, the WDCD conference is used to serve as a sympathetic gesture to hide what is essentially a politics of violence. The WDCD Refugee Challenge is precisely how neoliberal politics uses design to avoid taking responsibility for the political situation it is part of. While structural funding to address the issue is lacking, designers step in to provide quick and cheap 'solutions' for social issues that look good in the media, so that governments have proof they are doing 'something'. Many projects that came out of the Refugee Challenge are undoubtedly sympathetic and well-intended, but the designs will live on mostly as prototypes in portfolios and conference presentations.

You can be sure that help like that is not designed to get to the root causes of poverty and violence. It is designed to help improve the image of the elites who are funding it and put a tiny, inadequate Band-Aid on the massive social wound that their greed creates.

DEAN SPADE, TRANS ACTIVIST

The White Saviour Industrial Complex

From colonial pillaging, Christian missions, adventurous tourism, to TED talks and sustainable development goals, the long history of NGOs and Western countries helping the Global South is still on-going. It now continues on the same footing under the pretence of philanthropy. Ivan Illich spoke at a conference for US volunteers in 1968: 'Next to money and guns, the third largest North American export is the US idealist, who turns up in every theatre of the world: the teacher, the volunteer, the missionary, the community organizer, the economic developer, and the vacationing do-gooder.'[36] The popularity of terms such as 'design for good' or 'design for positive change' reveal that the intentions of designers are more important than the needs of those who are being helped. What is less evident with those good intentions is the position of privilege of the designer, which often remains unacknowledged. The person who helps, whether it is the billionaire philanthropist or the social designer from far away, has the time or resources available that the persons who are being 'helped' do not have. This creates an unequal power relation. Writer and photographer Teju Cole wrote

> Africa has provided a space onto which white egos can conveniently be projected. It is a liberated space in which the usual rules do not apply: a nobody from America or Europe can go to Africa and become a godlike saviour or, at the very least, have his or her emotional needs satisfied. Many have done it under the banner of 'making a difference'.[37]

What Cole aptly calls the White Saviour Industrial Complex, has become 'the fastest growing industry'.[38] Cole points out that we all need to examine our privileges in this global relation of inequality. Our phones use coltan from mines in the Congo, and are made in China under exploitative practices, as he comments, 'I don't fool myself that I am not implicated in these transnational networks of oppressive practices.'[39]

The privileges mentioned above, fall under what Sasha Costanza-Chock calls the matrix of domination: 'white supremacy, heteropatriarchy, capitalism, ableism, settler colonialism, and other forms of structural inequality'.[40] To prevent repeating the same domination within all design practices, she brings forward a concept called Design Justice: 'a framework for analysis of how design distributes benefits and burdens between various groups of people'. One of the strategies that design justice employs is that designers and the community work together in 'meaningful participation in designer decisions', so that community-based knowledge is recognized and not subjected to a cultural domination by an outside design intervention.[41]

Mutual Aid

Social design and design for good have thus far proven to be mostly unable to escape domination by capitalist and neo-colonial power structures. The underlying problem is that designers sometimes see their work as being separate from their personal circumstances and privilege. It doesn't mean that individual designers cannot make a small but important contribution in the form of a poster or in support of a cause, as long as designers acknowledge their privilege, and do not confuse 'designing for' with participatory forms of design or solving social issues using design. If designers choose to work with a community, being or becoming part of that community is necessary to engage with reciprocal forms of aid.

A useful concept how to be part of a community without domination is mutual aid. According to the *Oxford Dictionary*, mutual aid is support or assistance given and reciprocated, especially as a social or political mechanism. This basically means 'we help each other', rather than 'I help you'. Mutual aid is an ancient idea, it is how societies have helped each other to survive for thousands of years. Using it as a political strategy was popularized by anarchist philosopher Peter Kropotkin in 1902, and is more relevant than ever.[42] Charity by states, billionaires, and NGOs is so normalized, that many can simply not imagine that in big crisis situations citizens are able to help each other.

Dean Spade explains in 'Solidarity Not Charity' that charity and philanthropy are never free, and often come with disciplinary and stigmatizing conditions. For example, to be eligible for financial aid you often have to be looking for work, you have to be sober, participate in trainings, or subject yourself to other moralistic conditions.[43] Mutual aid groups are horizontally organized aid

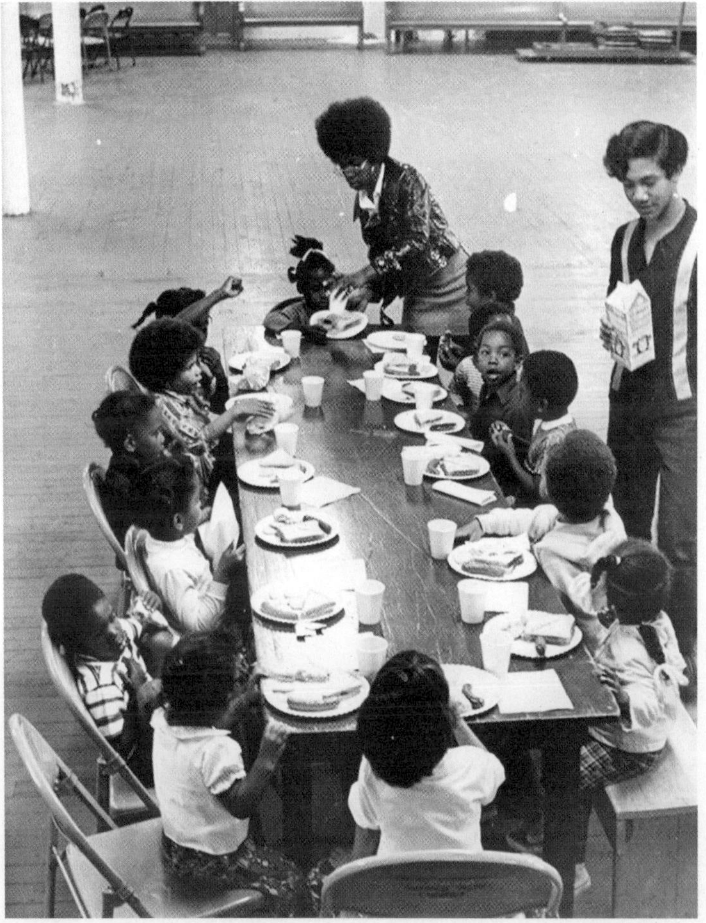

Black Panthers serving children free breakfast, Sacred Heart Church, San Francisco. Photo by Ducho Dennis.

collectives, often based on consensus-based decision-making.[44] A famous example of mutual aid are the social programmes by the Black Panther Party.

As the US state failed to provide black communities with proper health care and food services, the Black Panther Party organized a free breakfast programme, a free ambulance programme and free medical clinics in their own communities. The free breakfast programme from 1969 was so popular that at one point it was

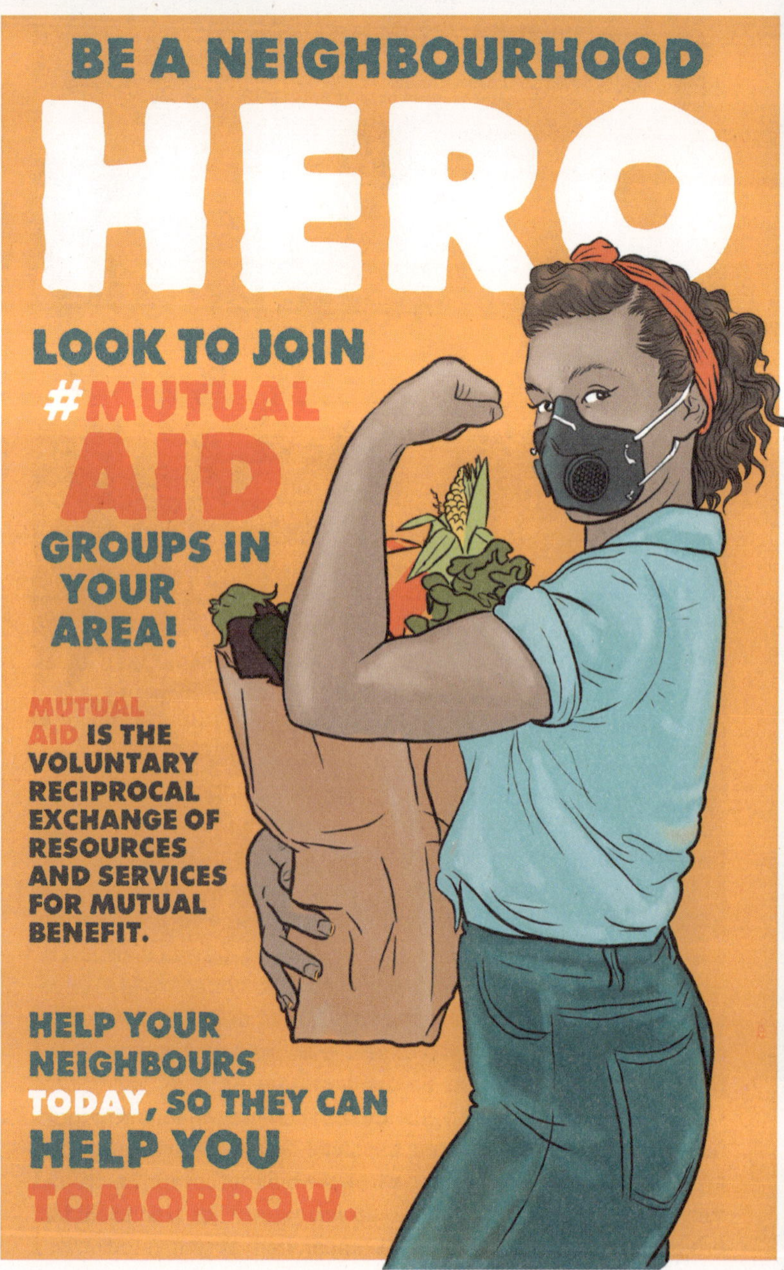

BE A NEIGHBOURHOOD
HERO
LOOK TO JOIN
#MUTUAL
AID
GROUPS IN
YOUR
AREA!
MUTUAL AID IS THE VOLUNTARY RECIPROCAL EXCHANGE OF RESOURCES AND SERVICES FOR MUTUAL BENEFIT.
HELP YOUR NEIGHBOURS TODAY, SO THEY CAN HELP YOU TOMORROW.

feeding 10,000 children every day.[45] A more recent example is the Mutual Disaster Relief, which began as a grass-roots organization in New Orleans, a few days after hurricane Katrina in 2005. The collective provides disaster relief funds and resources in community-based aid programmes.[46] During the Covid-19 pandemic many neighbourhoods set up forms of mutual aid, pasting posters or setting up chat groups offering to do groceries for people, basic care, helping with paying rent, or organizing rent-strikes in solidarity with people who cannot afford to pay their rent.

If designers, or any person for that matter, want to use their skills for the benefit of public good, they should be encouraged to do so. But not in the way that a complex issue somewhere in the world, can be randomly selected and 'solved' with a new design, an object, a video, or a workshop. Any socially engaged form of design has to be grounded in a designer's own personal environment and social circumstances. To effectively and ethically help others, only locally informed and reciprocal forms of aid can truly avoid power domination.

When offering to help others, it is always better to start with the people you know before getting involved in faraway situations, or remote areas, in situations that are nearly impossible to understand from a distance. Designers can become involved in mutual aid organizations, or think about how design can help mutual aid projects to be effective. Freelance designers who have no access to pensions or disability insurance have formed groups to build up collective funds to help those in case a critical health situation occurs. Mutual aid offers a practical framework to redirect 'design for good' and 'social design' projects in more ethical and reciprocal ways.

←   Poster by Nicole Marie Burton, 2020. nicolemariecomix.wordpress.com

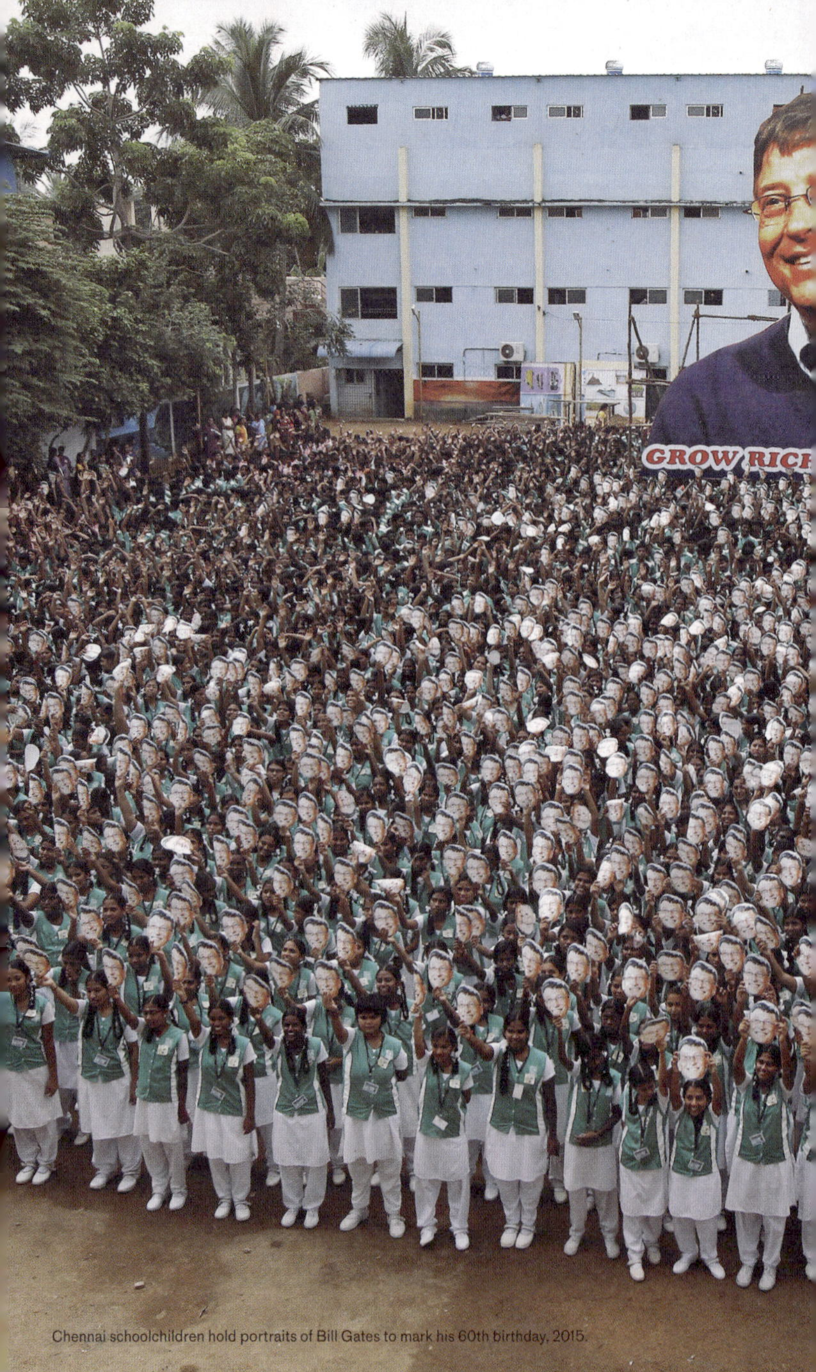

Chennai schoolchildren hold portraits of Bill Gates to mark his 60th birthday, 2015.

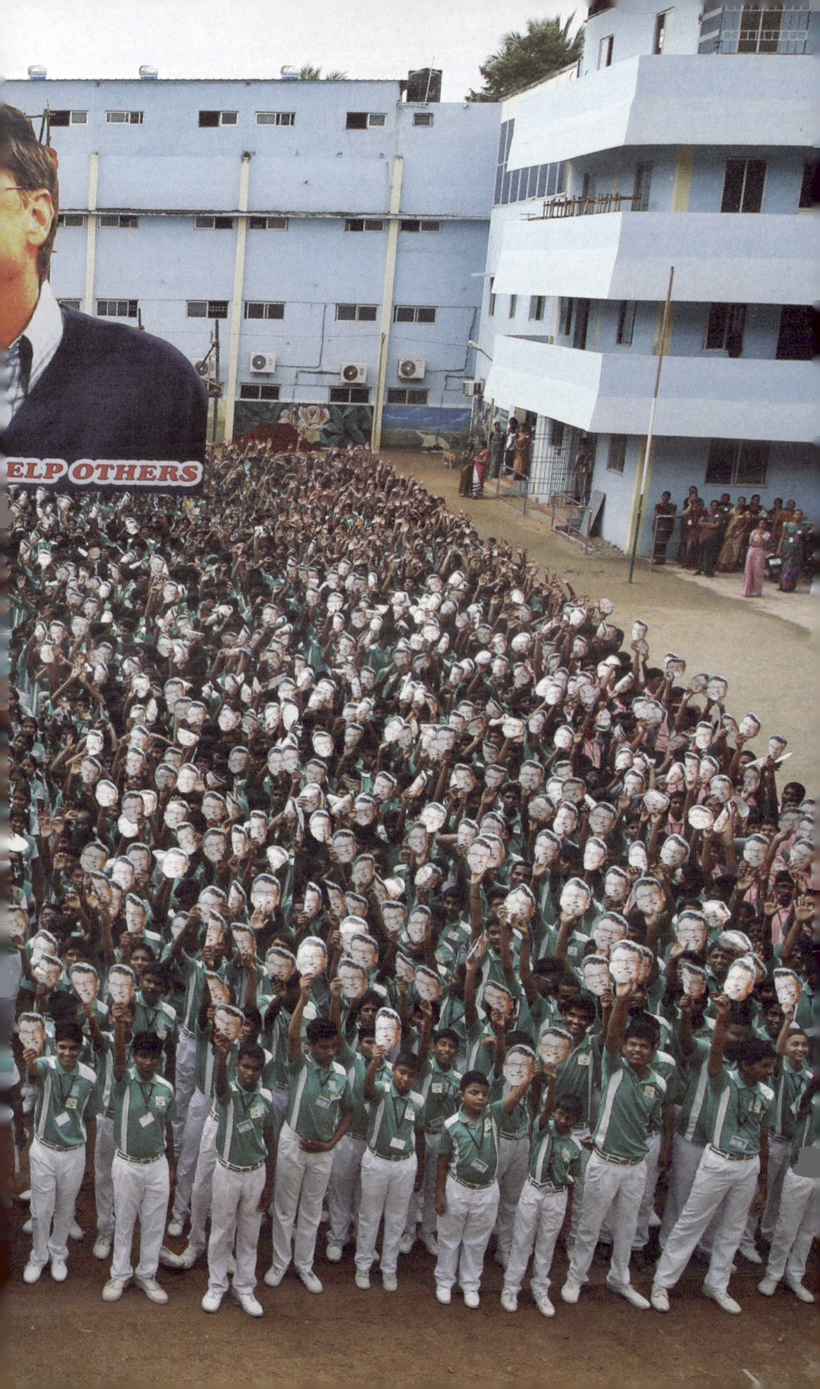
ELP OTHERS

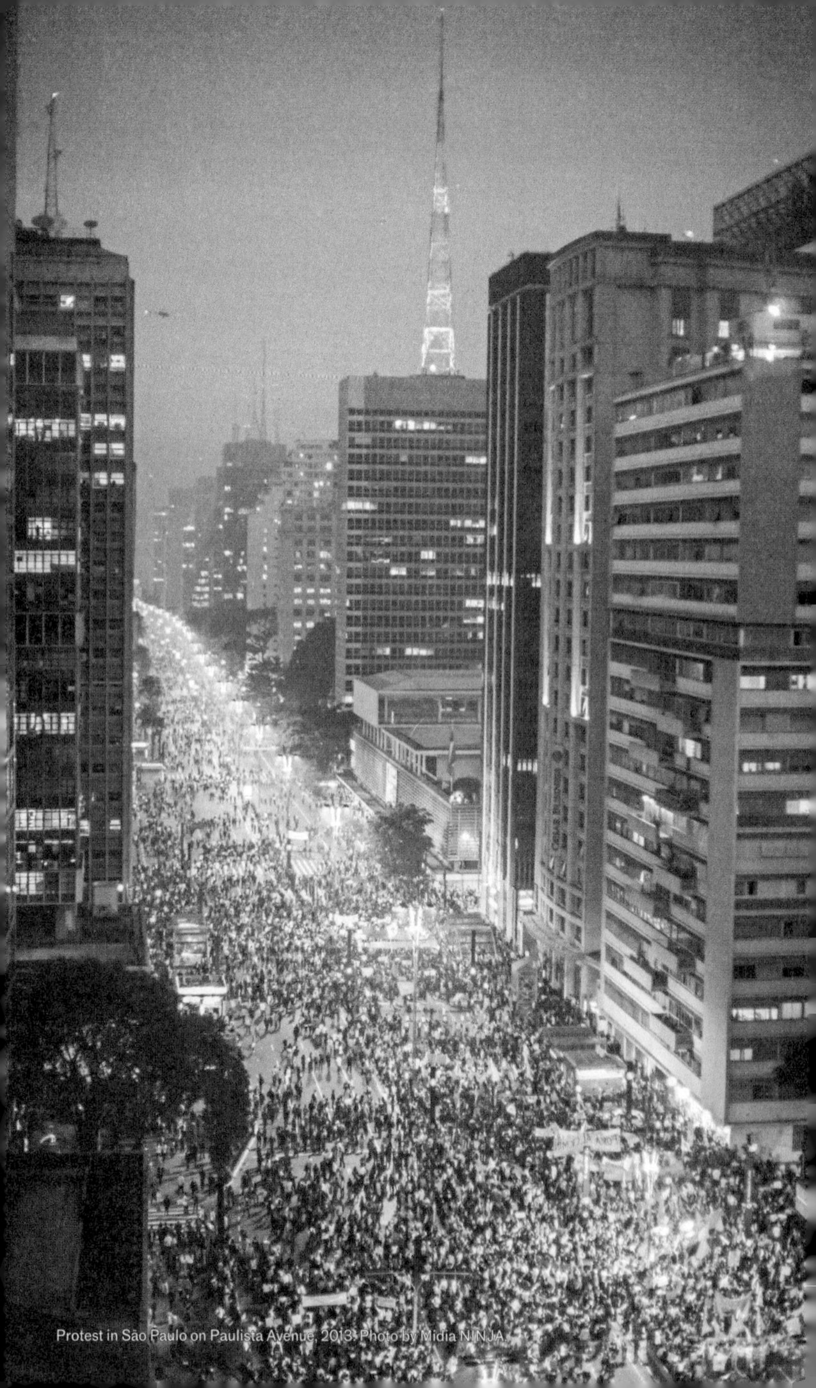

Protest in São Paulo on Paulista Avenue, 2013. Photo by Mídia NINJA

THE
DESIGNER
AS
ACTIVIST

Prodigy is, at its essence, adaptability and persistent, positive obsession. Without persistence, what remains is an enthusiasm of the moment. Without adaptability, what remains may be channeled into destructive fanaticism. Without positive obsession, there is nothing at all.

OCTAVIA E. BUTLER

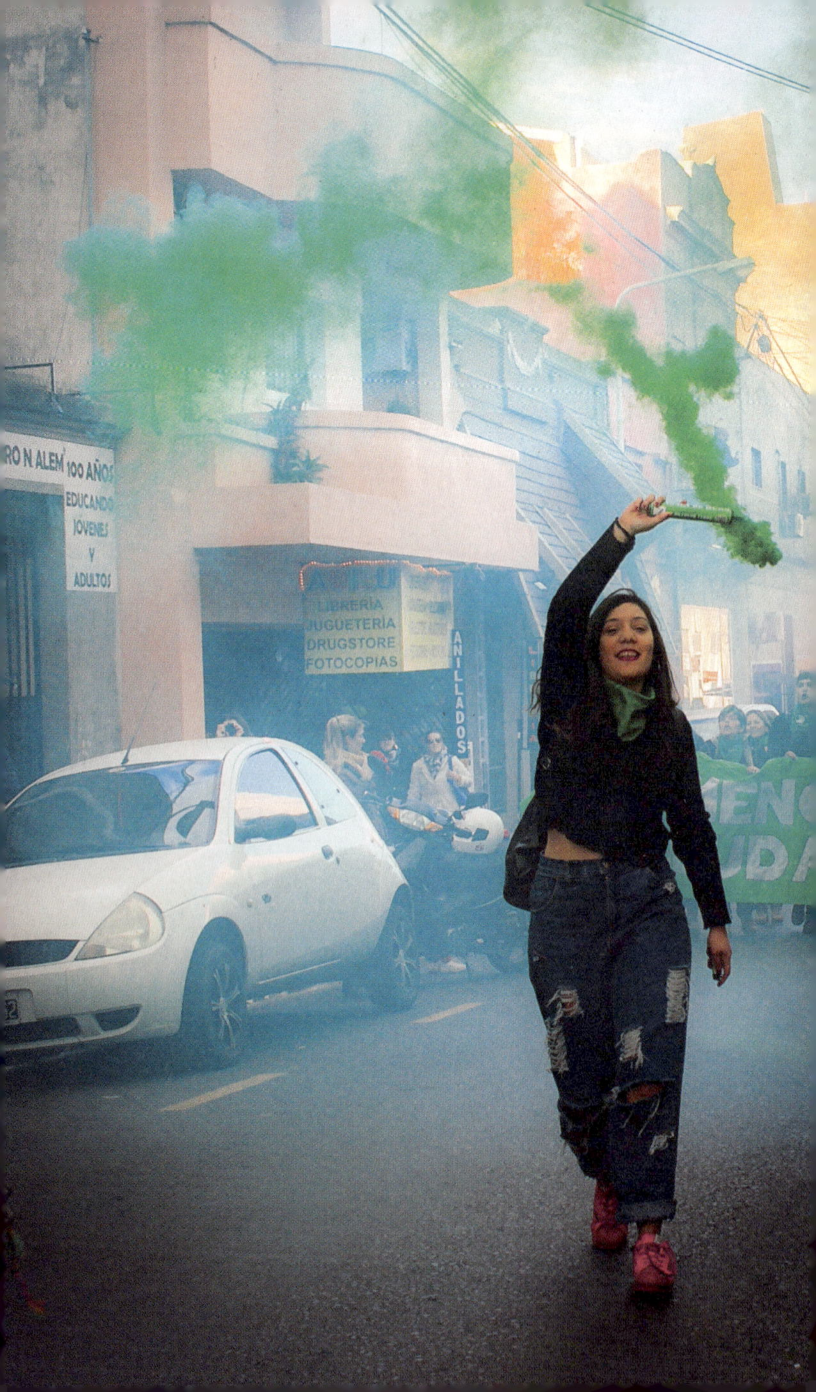
RO N. ALEM 100 AÑOS
EDUCANDO
JOVENES
Y
ADULTOS
LIBRERIA
JUGUETERIA
DRUGSTORE
FOTOCOPIAS
ANILLADOS

WHAT IS ACTIVISM?

This part has shown some of the ways in which designers have attempted to resist the grip of capitalism in recent decades. By taking on roles as hackers, futurists, and philanthropists, the idea was to escape from being a cog in the machine of capitalist production. These roles may have appeared to have offered a way out, but turned out to be just as easily appropriated by the forces of capitalism. It has become clear throughout this book how, historically, capitalism has been able to enclose different forms of resistance by designers. Each era saw a different generation, using tactics such as writing manifests, designing anti-capitalist campaigns, and political organizing. This takes us to the last role in this book: the designer as an activist.

The Oxford Dictionary calls activism 'the policy or action of using vigorous campaigning to bring about political or social change'.[1] That leads to the question which political and social change is intended? Activism often implies social or progressive ideals, but capitalists and fascists also want political and social change, although in an entirely different direction. What constitutes 'change'? Is it enough to design a poster for the Black Lives Matter movement and posting it on social media? Or does it mean risking your life by printing anti-government newspapers under a dictatorship? How do we know what amount of 'change' is enough for activism?

The designer as an activist is not easily defined, and can be misinterpreted. That is why design theorists have put forward terms and definitions to solve this paradox. Design theorist Ann Thorpe introduces four criteria for design activism: framing/revealing/challenging an issue, making a claim for change on that issue, working on behalf of a neglected, excluded, or disadvantaged

← Ni Una Menos protest, Argentina, 2018. Green symbolizes reproductive rights and the pro-abortion movement. Abortion was legalized in Argentina in January 2021. Photo by Paula Kindsvater.

group, and disrupting routine practices or systems of authority outside traditional channels of change.[1] Some examples she cites are a post-tsunami housing in Sri Lanka designed by MIT Senseable City Lab, and a design for a US courthouse that 'reveals openness and fairness'. They fit the criteria, but are they really different from a 'normal' design brief? Instead of building a more open courthouse, what about advocating for the abolition of prisons and imagining more community-driven forms of justice? Post-tsunami housing is important, but why are designers from the US designing housing for Sri Lanka, when funds could be used to set up reciprocal and long-term forms of mutual aid within the community? When design activism is so loosely defined, it may only produce a less harmful version of design.

Design activist Uday Dandavate defines activism as participating 'in some form of action for social change'.[2] In his view design activism is best achieved within corporations, where designers can have a stronger impact and 'serve as the conscience'.[3] This interpretation of design activism serves Dandavate's clientele, which includes Microsoft, Google, and Ford.[4] A third interpretation is from designer and writer Carl DiSalvo. He coined 'adversarial design', which he defines as design that is 'evoking and engaging political issues'. His book of the same title shows designed objects that challenge or provoke existing power structures, like counter-surveillance objects. A useful perspective, but this still revolves around designed objects and their intended activist or adversarial effect, but does not question how these objects are designed or produced, and the economy that surrounds them.[5]

These examples of design activism do not directly critique capitalism itself, and can easily be appropriated by capitalism's appetite for growth. We have seen this happen in the form of 'causewashing', a term that describes businesses that use activist or social causes for the purposes of positive PR.[6] Examples are corporations that promote breast cancer awareness through brand activism, even though they sell products that cause cancer.[7] Or corporations that publicly support Black Lives Matter, without addressing structural racism and inequality within their own companies.[8] Anything can be now branded as activism, from banks using cryptocurrencies to oil companies doing clean energy workshops.

Twitter Surveys ✔
@TwitterSurveys

Twitter would like your feedback.

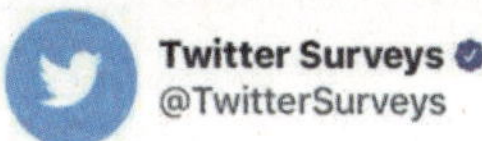

16:14 · 2/15/19 · Twitter Web Client

Promoted

Two examples of causewashing:
↑   LQBTQI+ rights branding for Royal Dutch Shell.
↑   Advertising poll on Twitter.

How is this contradiction resolved? Further on in this chapter six design collectives are featured that mostly work for and with social movements for progressive political goals, while keeping in mind the power structures and privileges that surround design work. But before we look into their practices, first we need to better understand how work and life are both subjected to capitalism.

The Personal is Political
The ways in which graphic designers respond to capitalism show a recurring pattern: time and resources are donated for a social cause. Victor Papanek illustrates this with the example of the tithe from medieval times. The tithe were the crops that peasants would set aside to feed the poor. In this line of thinking Papanek suggest 'Being designers, we can pay by giving ten percent of our crop of ideas and talents to the seventy-five percent of mankind in need.'[9] Designers do this by donating a small amount of their time and resources to non-profits, social causes, or activist purposes, in trying to do their part in changing the world.

The logic is, that a donation of time and resources is seen as a 'solution' for social causes, while the power structures stay in place. Peasants who share some crops with the poor help to keep people alive, but this does not address the underlying reasons for poverty (feudalism). Similarly, designers who spend a few hours a week making posters for social causes, do not resist the underlying power structure (capitalism), especially when the rest of their week is spent working for corporations. Activism for social change is reduced to a task that is scheduled in for a few hours a week. Undoubtedly, these are generous and admirable gestures, but that's what they are: gestures. They give the appearance of benevolence while keeping the status quo firmly in place. What we have learned about capitalism and graphic design, is that this relationship doesn't limit itself to a critique of consumerism or advertising. All aspects of life—including the role of design education, competition and overwork, unpaid domestic work, and caring for children—support capitalism in its current structures. If anti-capitalist activism is reduced to statements alone, other aspects such as working and living conditions are not addressed.

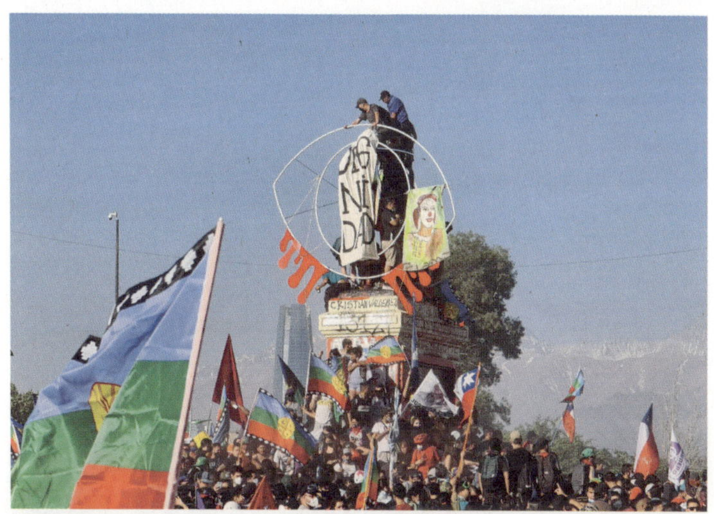

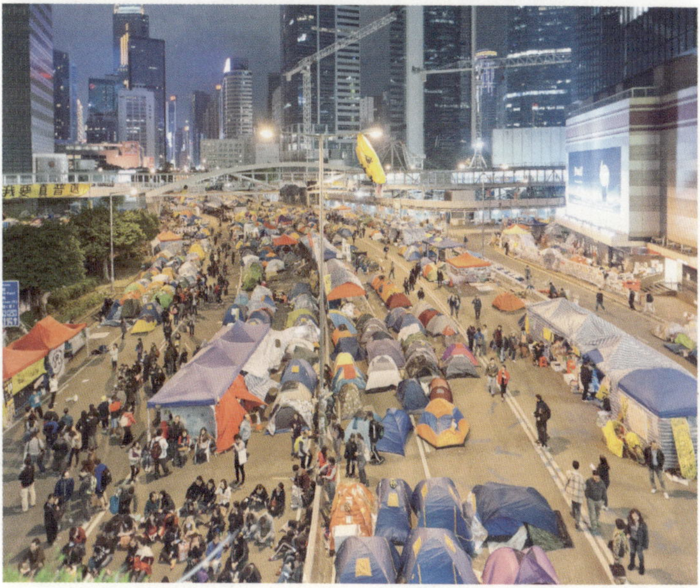

↑ Artistic intervention in Chile, 2020, during protests against corruption, inequality and privatization. The flag of Chile as well as the indigenous Mapuche flag can be seen. Photo by Javier Collao.

↑ Hong Kong protest camp, 2014. The sit-in protests called the Umbrella Revolution, was directed against the electoral reforms by the Chinese government. Photo by Ken Ohyama.

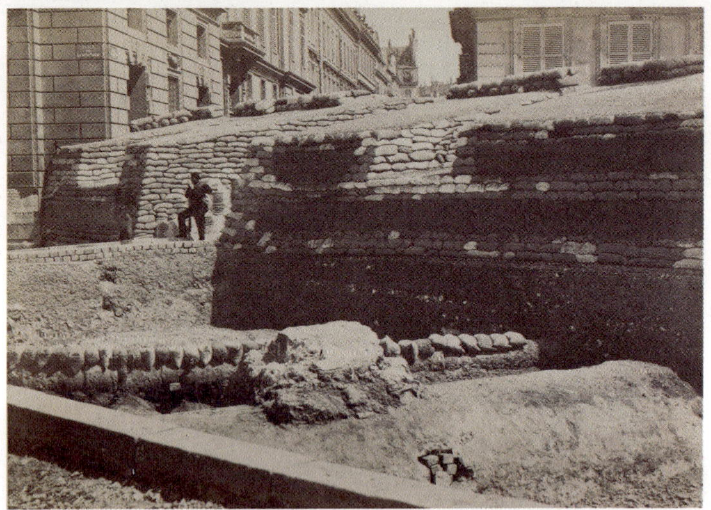

↑ Paris Commune barricade at Place de la Concorde, 1871. Shoemaker Napoléon Gaillard showed a talent for such constructions and designed them. Photo by Augustin-Hippolyte Collard.

The design collectives featured in this chapter understand that critiquing capitalism involves both work and non-work. This doesn't mean work and life are interchangeable (as capitalism would prefer), but that working ethically and living ethically go hand in hand. This is why the collectives in this chapter not only discuss design aesthetics and typefaces, but also parental leave, their communities, collaborators, and families. Any serious attempt to see design as ethical must also look at how designers work, how they treat/ pay their co-workers and interns, how they function in the community, and scrutinize their personal privilege and positions of power.

The Design Commons

We have read how the origins of capitalism are historically placed at the enclosure of the commons. Under feudalism these were lands that were accessible to the peasant community, and crucial for sustaining and developing a collective social life. Capitalism started by seizing these commons by kicking peasants off the land, and using it for capitalist agriculture. The same enclosure process occurred later with the enclosure of knowledge using patents and copyrights, with the enclosure of public services by privatizing health care and welfare, and lastly with the sharing economy.[10] The way branding has been used to turn everything from air to health care into commodities is an example of how design aids the enclosure of commons. Capitalism's logic has been, and still is, to find the last remaining spaces of equal exchange and open access, and privatize those spaces for profit.

Graphic design is a creative process. Designers continuously create new ideas, objects, spaces, and forms of knowledge that are shared with the world. Some of these designs are made outside of capitalism (without profit motive) and can be accessed and used by everyone, in which case they could be part of a commons. However, capitalism needs to grow, and in order to do so it will try to enclose these ideas and spaces by finding ways to make a profit of them, as we have seen in the previous chapters. The paradoxical question then becomes: how can you practice design outside of capitalism, when capitalism itself will do everything to try to appropriate anti-capitalist ideas or practices for its benefit? Commoning, which is the process of creating and defending commons, has proven to be a useful strategy for designers to avoid their work being appropriated by capitalism. This strategy will be further explored in the Outro, but for now let's see how these six collectives have developed practices that try to escape from capitalism.

What follows are interviews with six design collectives from different continents. Design collectives that all work in service of social movements and progressive political goals, while also running an ethical practice, keeping in mind the power structures and privileges that surround design work. By creating design work outside of capitalism, they all aim to contribute to the commons in their own way. Using simple and practical ideas, they share how they work hard to practice more ethical and anti-capitalist design, instead of describing it in theory. How do you make money? How does a design studio without bosses make decisions? Can you survive making work for activist movements? A series of interviews and documentation from these design collectives gives us a glimpse of how other design practices are possible.

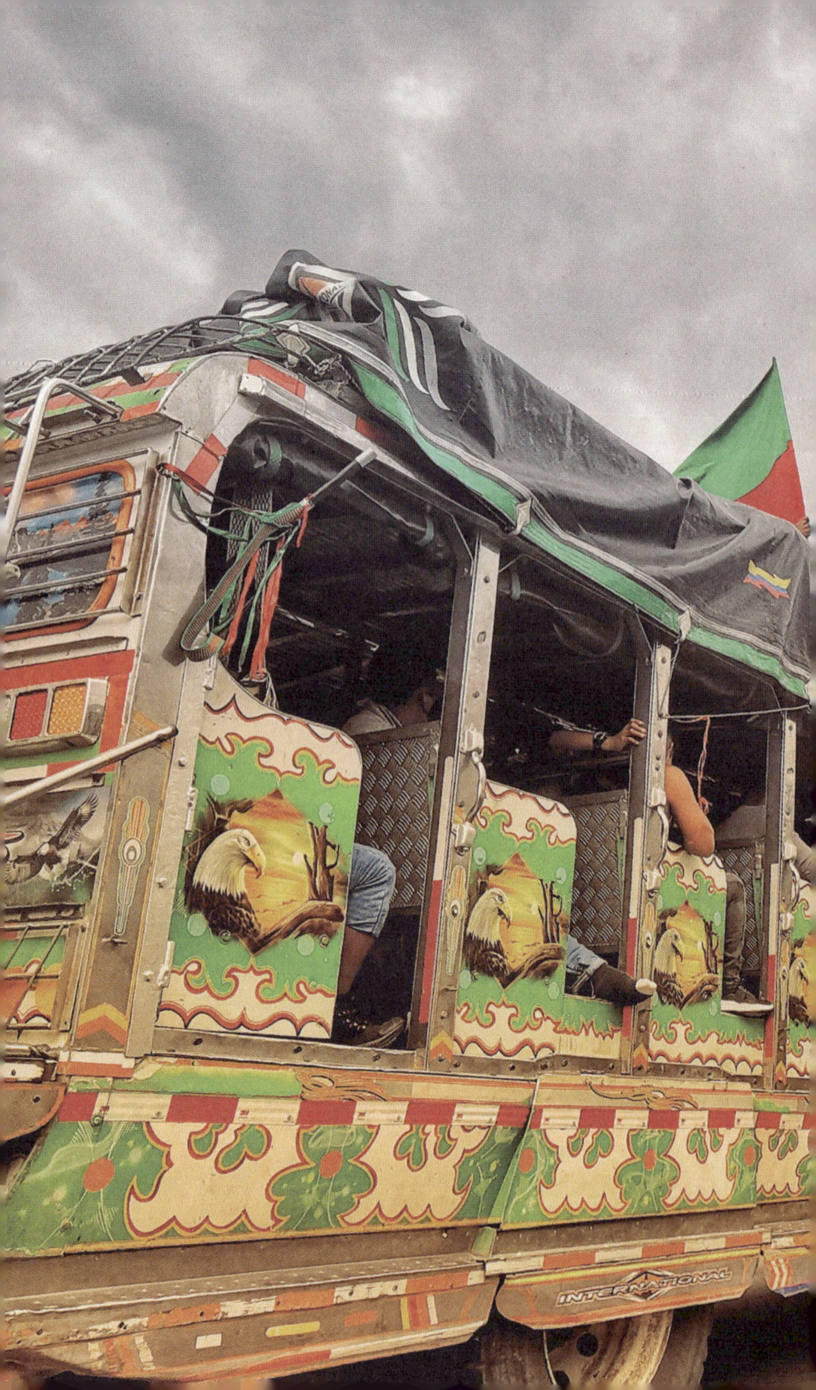

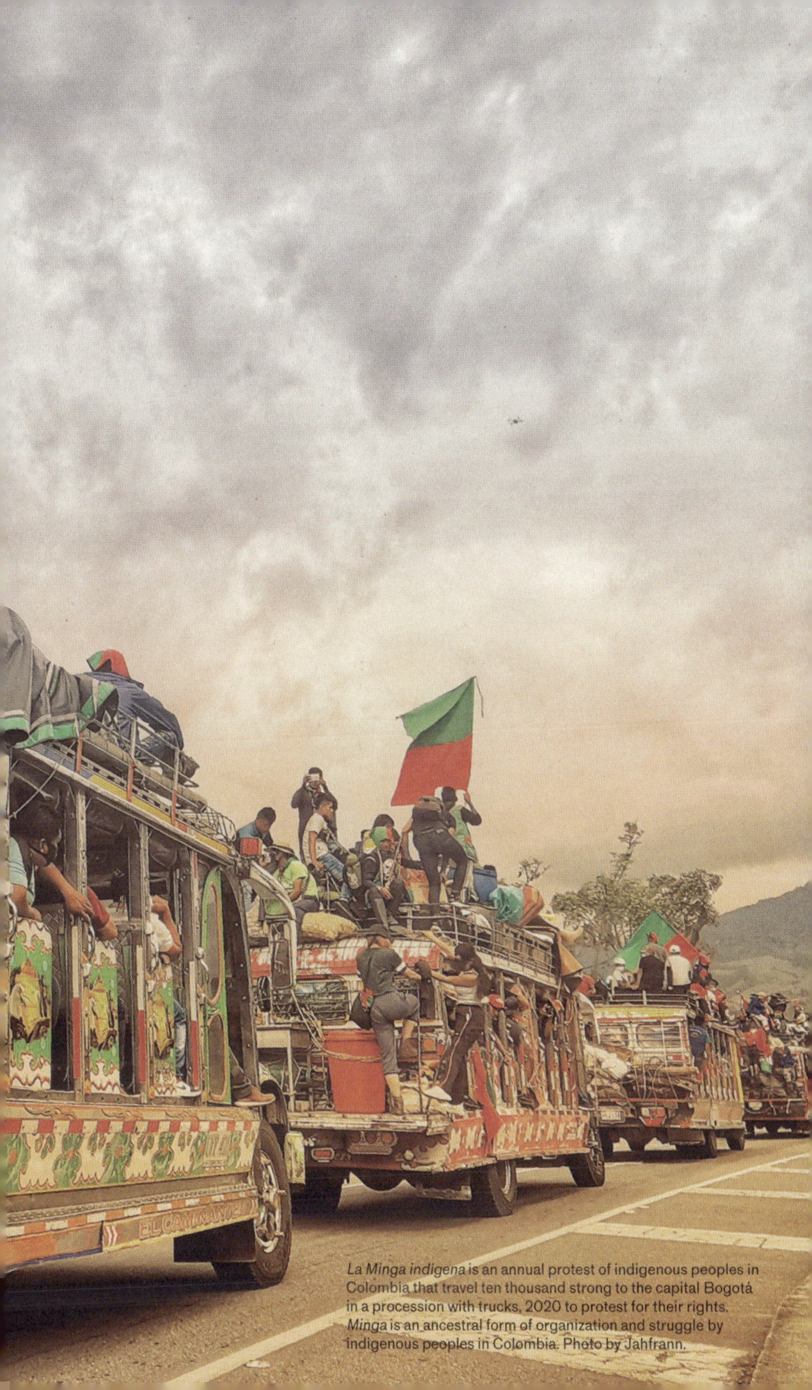

La Minga indigena is an annual protest of indigenous peoples in Colombia that travel ten thousand strong to the capital Bogotá in a procession with trucks, 2020 to protest for their rights. *Minga* is an ancestral form of organization and struggle by indigenous peoples in Colombia. Photo by Jahfrann.

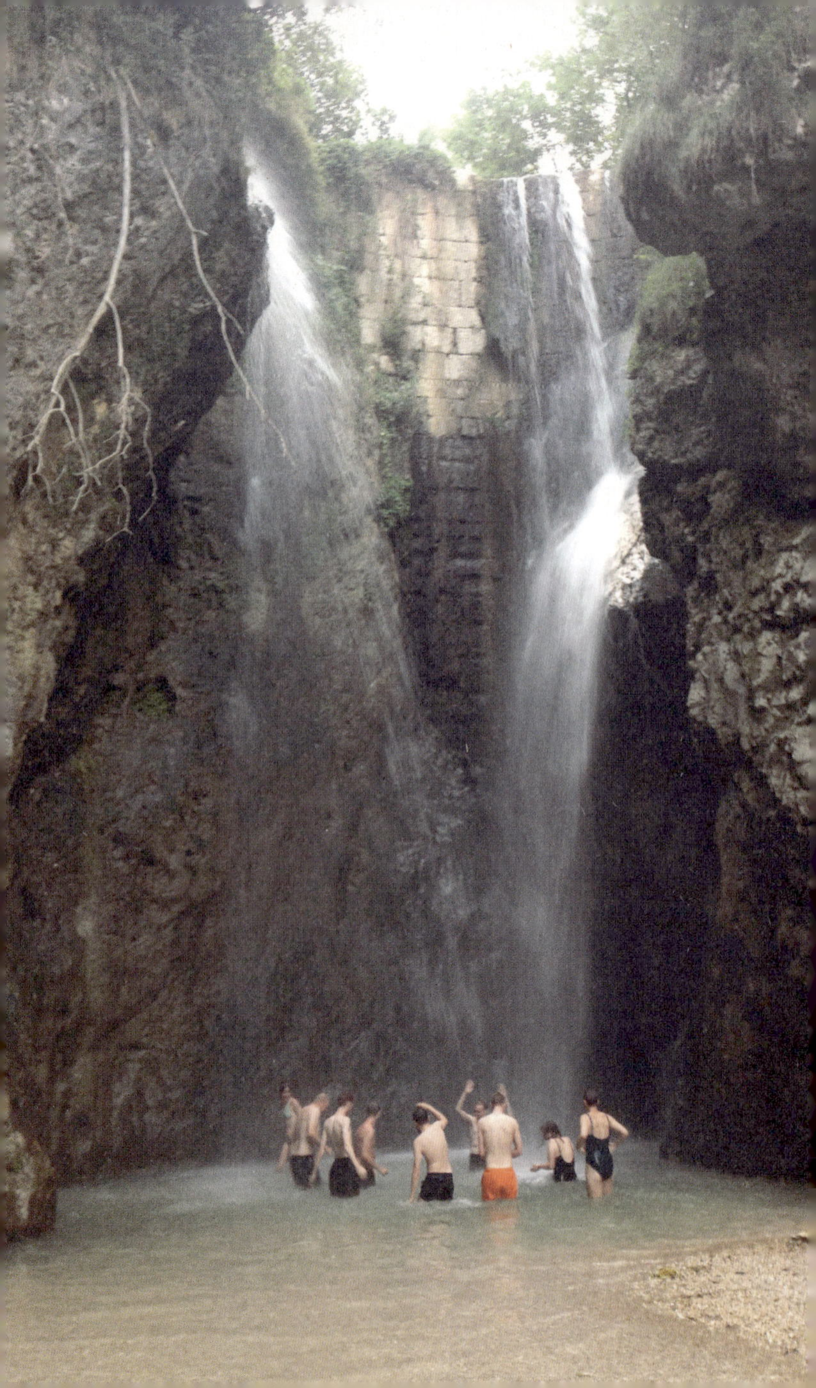

BRAVE NEW ALPS

Situated in the Vallagarina valley in the Italian alps, Brave New Alps is an eco-friendly and radical design collective that has been organizing community projects in the region. The collective began as a collaboration between Bianca Elzenbaumer and Fabio Franz in 2005, after they had finished their BA studies in graphic design in London. Photos on their website show many gatherings of people, eating, discussing, and working together against the backdrop of the Italian alps. In their own words they 'combine design research methods with radical pedagogy, feral approaches to community economies and lots of DIY making and organizing'.[11] Their work is incredibly diverse, from workshops, conferences, organizing spaces, writing, and commoning to community-building processes, construction, and printing.

At the time of writing there are twelve Brave New Alpinists: designers, web programmers, two agro-ecologists, a farmer, and art therapists, about half of whom work outside of the Valley.

What do they do on a day-to-day basis?
Caring for, creating, and defending communal and community economies is what Brave New Alps have set out to do. La Foresta is a community academy at a local train station; Comunità Frizzante is a local drinks project; and the Alpine Community Economies Lab is an EU-funded research project. These community projects require good listening skills and patience, which is contrary to how many designers work. Bianca recounts that a lot of their everyday activities are facilitating: writing grants, having meetings, having coffee, doing co-design workshops, going on walks, and cooking together. These activities are not just a necessary administrative step before designing, they *are* the design process. For Brave New Alps every activity no matter how small can be

←   Brave New Alps taking Evening Class for a swim close to their home, 2018.

radical. They consider even financial administration to be 'a space for radical action', or 'radmin' as they call it. Their design work is not strictly separated from other social activities, as they say 'life and work continually blend'. Fixing bikes, taking care of their four-year-old son, reading, and studying are as much part of their activities as design. Which is what makes working for them meaningful and pleasurable.

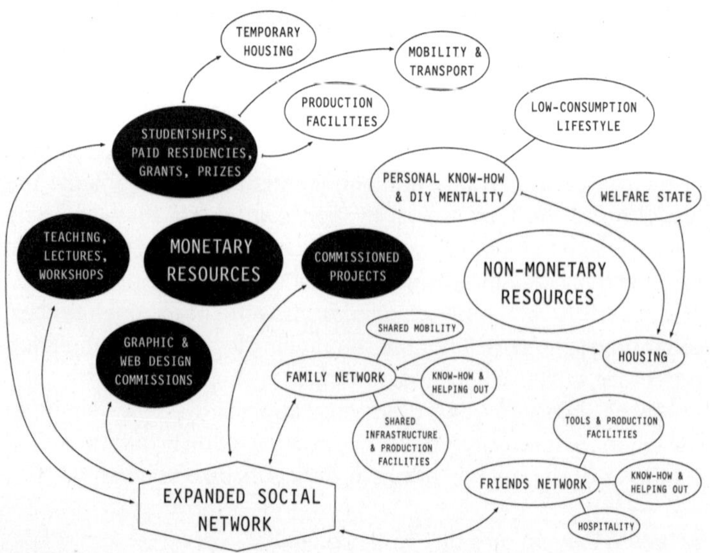

Where do they get money?

The activities of Brave New Alps are sustained by a mixed income of local development project funds, grants, research projects, and civil service funds. Graphic design, exhibitions, or lecturing actually contribute very little to their income, which currently sustains six salaries. Bianca emphasizes this is only possible because they have modest lifestyles. Fabio and Bianca live on the top floor of Fabio's parents' house, and Bianca's mum donated her old car to the collective. If the founders would still be living in London, they could not have afforded to run such a practice, as they say themselves. But being locally rooted is not only a cost issue, it is de-precarizing, in their words. The community provides access to fruit and vegetable

gardens, sharing resources, and the community's existing support networks and vice versa. For example, when they received
a donation of power tools for their maker space, community
members were invited to make use of them.

How are they structured?

From the start the duo wanted to create some sort of collective but,
they 'did not manage—probably because we were still too much
linked to the idea of the designer genius, individual visibility', which
is what designers are taught. A key moment was the founding
of a cultural association in 2012, a legal form that allows them to
engage in collaborations and have access to funding. A cultural
association can link up with local administrations, foundations,
and takes them into the higher echelons of funding that long-term
projects require. All their work is credited collectively but individuals can and do take credit, depending on who is involved. Their
work is freely available through the Copyleft licensing, a reciprocal
from of licensing compared to copyright, which is about protecting
intellectual property.

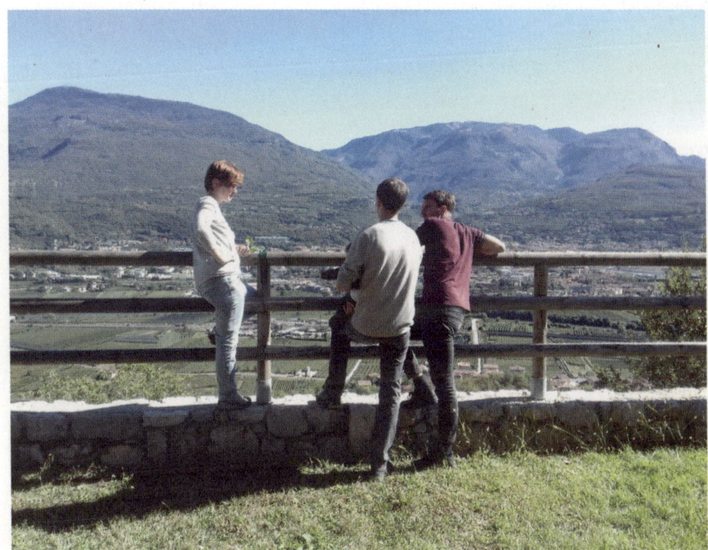

↑   Brave New Alps looking out over de Vallagarina valley with Hannes Langguth, 2016.
←   Map of the economy of the Brave New Alps, 2020.

What is their role in the design community?
Brave New Alps have been not just working as designers, they are also adamant on sharing and collecting examples of other designers that experiment with alternative models. The lack of research into the economic conditions of designers led them to start the 'Designers Inquiry', an effort to collect statistics about working conditions of designers. More than 750 designers working and living in Italy answered the questionnaire, relating to working hours, wages, and their personal social and economic situations. Another research project in labour conditions of designers is 'Precarity Pilot', a website that helps designers to learn how to set up alternative practices, coordinate, redefine career models and organize one's time and money. Between 2015 and 2019 the website collected many references, and includes interviews with twelve design collectives. In doing so, Brave New Alps does not just try to experiment with new models on a practical level, but also shares its finding and resources along the way. This is because they understand economy not as something abstract that is expressed in mathematics, but as social relations that are created on a small scale. This is why they make an effort to write reference letters, supervise MA students (although they don't teach), offer residencies, and support others with micro-loans between €100–300 to start a study or buy equipment to start a practice.

How do they run a practice with long-term projects?
One of the strong points of the design practice of the Brave New Alps is that they are valued greatly in their community, because they organize people and get things done. While perhaps for the traditional graphic design community their work is not understood as design ('not enough style, not enough coolness, not enough authorship') they are less interested in professional approval than in making a difference locally. However, community projects can take long and are not easily 'finished', with some of their projects taking up to nine years. At this point they cannot take on more work for this reason, but the positive side of this is that others join the project and can take over part of the responsibilities so that work becomes more collective. While some designers may abhor such long processes, Brave New Alps has learned to embrace them.

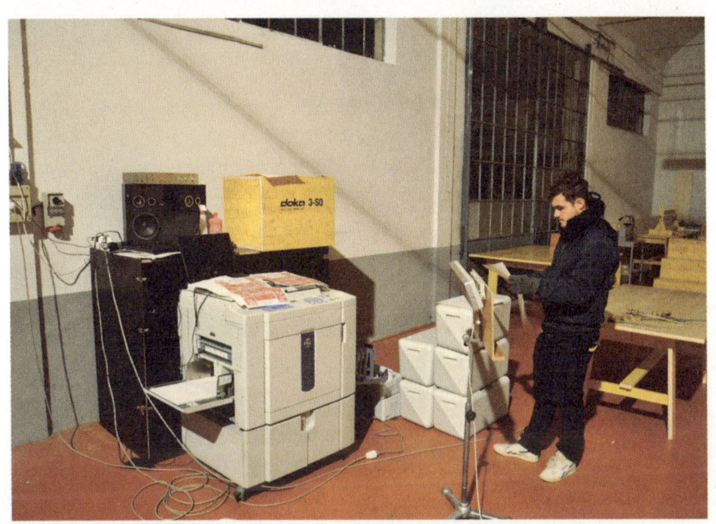

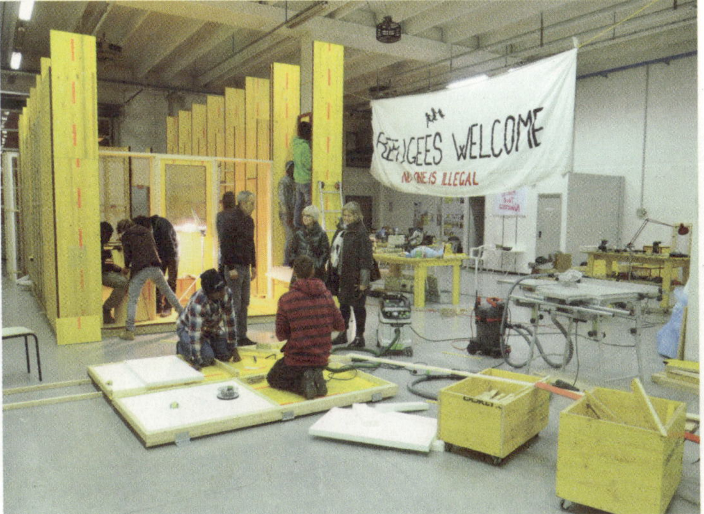

↑ Mobile woodworking workshop, 2017.
↑ Risograph printing, 2016.

They see a future where 'We see ourselves as embarked on a 40-year project for the creation of commons (so at least up to our mid-70s) and so everything we can do that supports others to create commons is worthwhile.'[12]

What's their advice to designers who are looking to change their practice?

First, they write, choose one thing that is meaningful to you and that you want to hold onto (a place, a topic, a pilot flame), and stay with it. This can protect you from 'the demand of hyper-flexibility' that so many designers are subjected to, constantly switching and responding to outside stimuli. This pilot flame will help focus and stay centred.

Their second piece of advice is to realize that it is not 'your individual genius' that makes a solid design practice, but the social bonds around you. This is a very underappreciated aspect of design. If you appreciate that the people around you are central to your work, they will support you in return. After all the rich and their 'old-boys network' work like this, so why shouldn't designers be able to build stronger bonds?

brave-new-alps.com

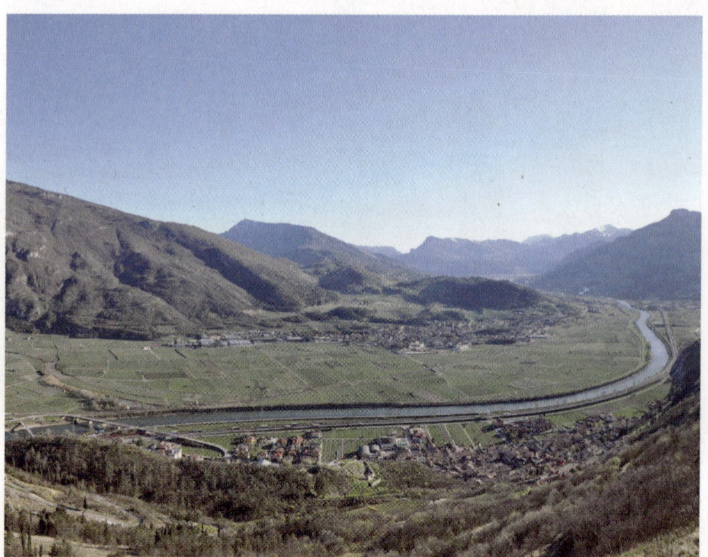

↑   View on the Vallagarina valley from the Brave New Alps office, 2016.
→   Drinks production, 2020.

                    CAPS LOCK — Part 3

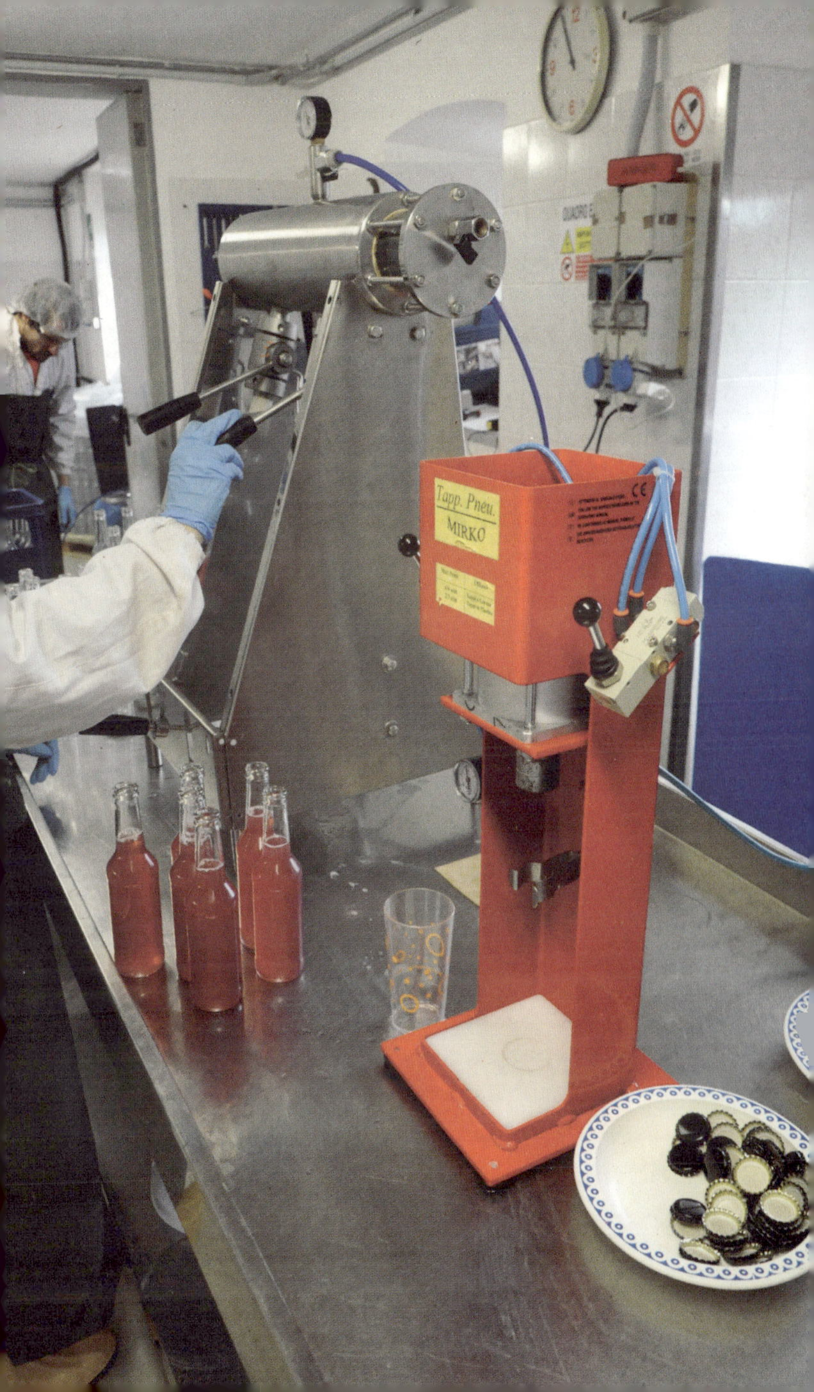
Tapp. Pnéu.
MIRKO
CE

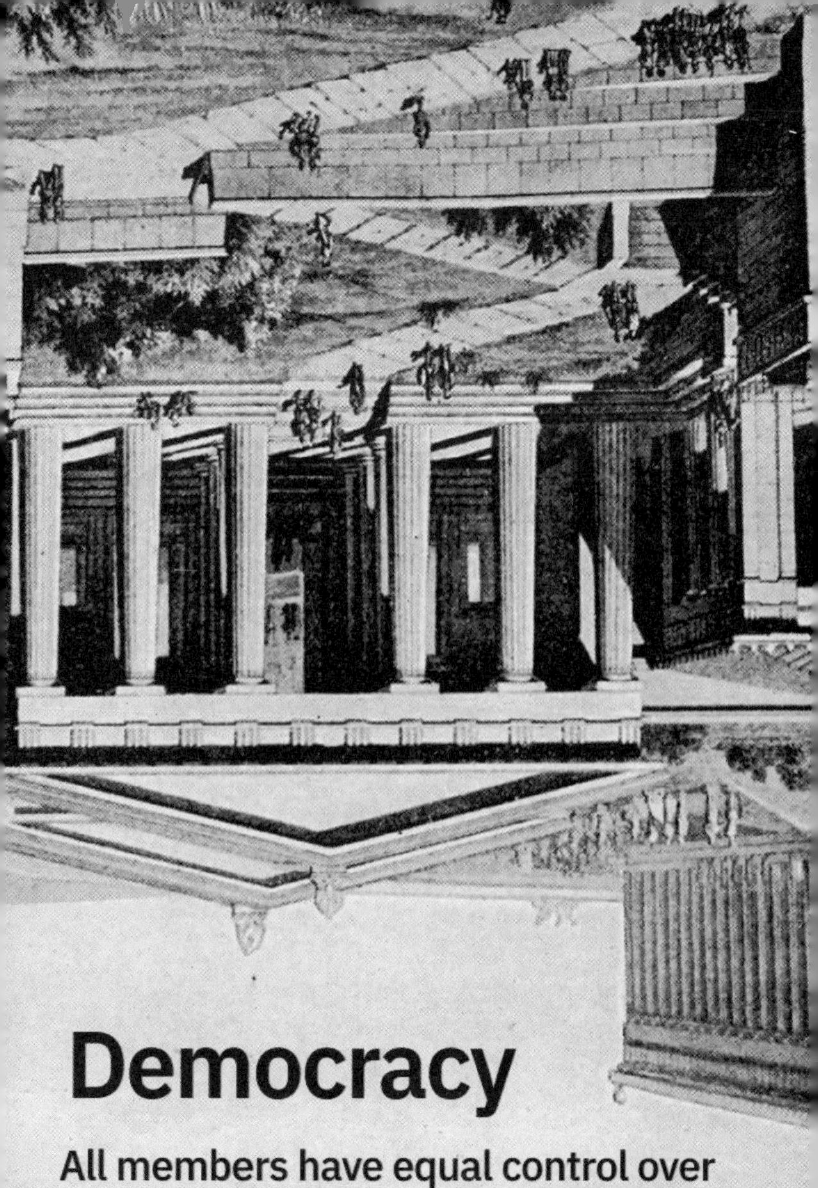

Democracy

All members have equal control over the co-op.

One member, one vote.

COMMON KNOWLEDGE

Common Knowledge is a worker cooperative (co-op) from the UK, that creates digital tools for direct action and grassroots organizing. What makes their work particularly interesting, is how they use technology in a collaborative and ethical way to support radical politics. UX design and the development of digital platforms are notorious for being subjected to surveillance capitalism.[13] Common Knowledge started in 2018 in search of how digital tools can help activist organizations. A reoccurring problem of activist organizations is that many people want to get involved, but don't know how. Common Knowledge has worked hard to use the social potential of the internet and the availability of digital tools to help expand the reach of grassroots activists. In a period of a few years, the collective has built digital tools for organizations such as Nurses United, Progressive International, London Renters Union, and the union United Voices of the World.

What do they do on a day-to-day basis?
The co-op consists of five members working on strategy, user research, facilitation, design, and software engineering. Besides working on commissioned and self-initiated projects, they also organize trainings and workshops for activist organizations. They teach activists how to use their digital profile more effectively. Common Knowledge also advocates for the cooperative form by being spokespersons, and by giving advice on how to run a cooperative.

Where do they get money and how do they share income?
The income of the co-op comes from client work, grants, and consultancy work for organizations that align with their values. The cooperative is not-for-profit, and its articles of institution prescribe that members cannot earn dividends. Salaries are the same for all

members, and any financial surplus goes into maintaining the co-op, or to solidarity work for underfunded groups. All grants they receive are listed on the co-op's website, and they strive to make all their finances public. In an interview with designer Gemma Copeland, who is one of the co-op's members, she emphasizes that an important part of being a co-op is openly discussing finances among members, and collectively decide how to protect each other from financial precarity.

How are they structured?
As a worker cooperative, Common Knowledge is democratically owned and adheres to the seven cooperative principles.[14] Its legal structure is a limited company by guarantee of which all members are directors. The articles of association are informed by the co-operative principles, which is what makes it a co-op rather than a regular limited company. The daily work of running the co-op and making decisions are based on sociocracy, a form of govern-ance based on consent rather than consensus. This is how it works: any member can propose something to the rest of the group, but instead of voting or reaching consensus, other members can decide to either give their consent or block the proposal. The criteria for consenting to a proposal is that it's 'good enough for now and safe enough to try'.[15] The model of consent is based on mutual trust rather than consensus, and the co-op found it to be more practical in day-to-day decision-making. The cooperative form also allows greater freedom for members in their work environ-ment. Gemma Copeland writes 'One of the things I love about being in a co-op is having complete control over my own time',[16] which allows her to pursue different ideas.

> I also love not being restricted to one role, or being defined as only a 'designer'. I can try out whatever interests me and learn more through the process. This feels much more fitting to what it actually means to be a person.[17]

How do they collaborate with clients?
The collective uses two practical frameworks to collaborate with clients in a non-hierarchical way: sociocracy and scrum.

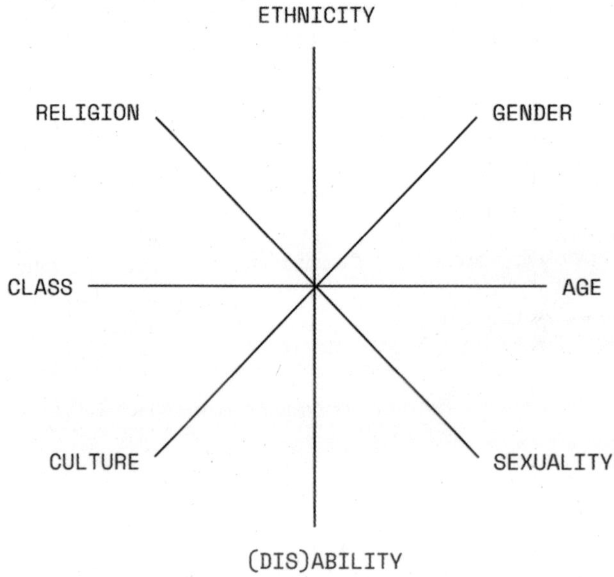

↑   Diagram of intersectional analysis.
↑   Diagram of organisation types.

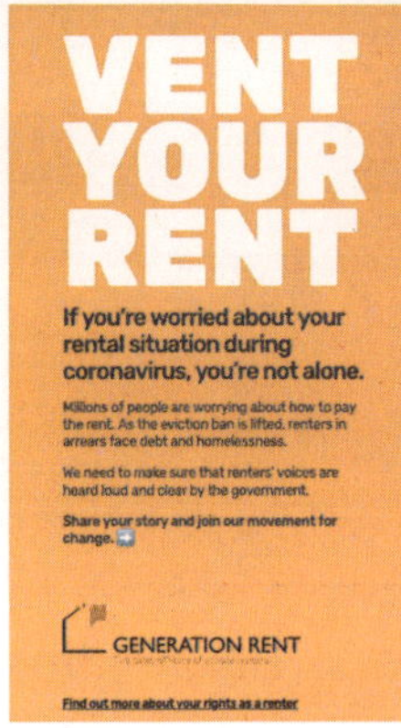

VENT YOUR RENT

If you're worried about your rental situation during coronavirus, you're not alone.

Millions of people are worrying about how to pay the rent. As the eviction ban is lifted, renters in arrears face debt and homelessness.

We need to make sure that renters' voices are heard loud and clear by the government.

Share your story and join our movement for change.

GENERATION RENT

Find out more about your rights as a renter

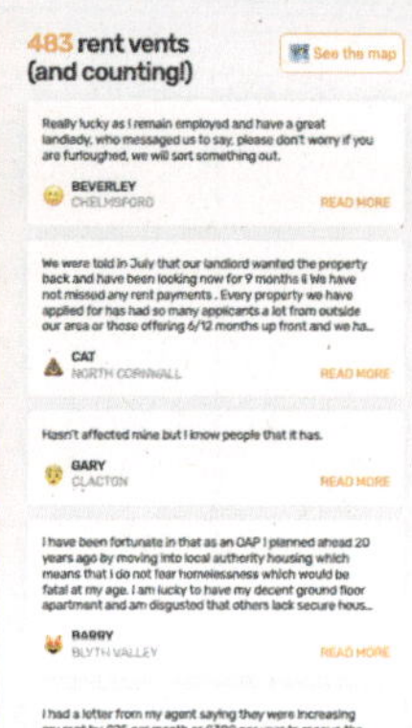

483 rent vents (and counting!)

See the map

Really lucky as I remain employed and have a great landlady, who messaged us to say, please don't worry if you are furloughed, we will sort something out.

BEVERLEY
CHELMSFORD
READ MORE

We were told in July that our landlord wanted the property back and have been looking now for 9 months & We have not missed any rent payments . Every property we have applied for has had so many applicants a lot from outside our area or those offering 6/12 months up front and we ha...

CAT
NORTH CORNWALL
READ MORE

Hasn't affected mine but I know people that it has.

GARY
CLACTON
READ MORE

I have been fortunate in that as an OAP I planned ahead 20 years ago by moving into local authority housing which means that I do not fear homelessness which would be fatal at my age. I am lucky to have my decent ground floor apartment and am disgusted that others lack secure hous...

BARRY
BLYTH VALLEY
READ MORE

I had a letter from my agent saying they were increasing my rent by £25 per month or £300 per year to recoup the cost of the new government legislation regarding the

Now, add your story

How has coronavirus affected your rental situation?

Your renter experience

We'll moderate then post your story + first name + rough location publicly alongside others. Or click here to share privately.

Pick an emoji for your rent vent story

or   Pick random

First name   Last name

Email

Postcode

Your rental situation
Select all that apply

How has coronavirus impacted your finances?
I am still on full pay
My income has fallen but I'm receiving support
I am not eligible for Universal Credit
I am not eligible to have 80% of my income paid by

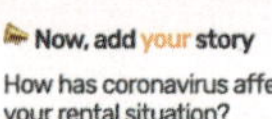

AIRSIFT

DUSTBOXES   OBSERVATIONS   ANALYSIS   STORIES   ABOUT   SIGN IN

Air pollution is a planetary health emergency. Air quality monitors are not always located where air pollution is occurring, and citizens might have many reasons to gather data to document and analyze air quality.

Airsift brings together information for you to set up a citizen-led monitoring project to keep track of air quality in your area.

DUSTBOXES
Review Dustbox data on particulate matter levels and check air quality measurements.

OBSERVATIONS
Gather and browse evidence that might indicate pollution or other activity is occuring.

ANALYSIS
Explore Dustbox data, create plots and identify air pollution problems.

STORIES
Draw together different kinds of

PM2.5 (MG/M3) CONCENTRATION
N/A   0-5   5-10   10-25   25-50   50+

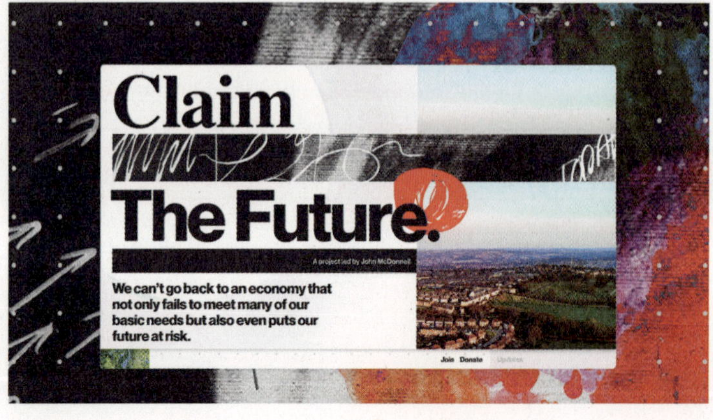

Claim
The Future.

A project led by John McDonnell

We can't go back to an economy that not only fails to meet many of our basic needs but also even puts our future at risk.

Join Donate   Updates

My advice? Join a union, start a co-op

GEMMA COPELAND, DESIGNER

Sociocracy uses consent-based decision-making to optimize organization efficiency, while ensuring that everyone's voice is heard. Scrum is ubiquitous in the world of software development and prioritizes horizontal collaboration and iteration over formal processes and structures. In terms of software, Common Knowledge uses Notion for building knowledge databases and Loomio for implementing sociocracy. Loomio is a tool developed during Occupy Wall Street for practical decision-making in horizontally structured collectives. Copeland explains that Loomio was built by a co-op, and that co-founder Richard Bartlett envisions technology in such a way 'that multiple small teams can work together and share knowledge directly, rather than to build huge co-ops. These teams can then connect and work in solidarity with a wider network.'[18]

How can technology help activist groups?
Despite the fact that the design of many internet platforms is driven by profits, digital technology is actually well placed to facilitate distributed self-organization, says Copeland. It is ubiquitous and distributed, which makes it easier to scale up your organizing and reach a huge number of people. In their few years of existence, Common Knowledge has noticed that many grassroots campaigns rely on a range of consumer technologies, usually linked together by volunteers doing, what she calls 'repetitive, mind-numbing tasks'.[19] A lot of these can be automated or at least improved, which leaves people with more time to actually do the organizing they set out to do. The usability testing part of the digital design process is a way to directly talk to community members and see how they interact with the digital tools. User-centred design often has a strong research component. This can, of course, be done in an extractive way, where people are just seen as a resource to be harvested for insights. However, it can also be done in a way that

←   Website for the Vent Your Rent, 2020.
←   Website for the Airsift, 2021.
←   Website for Claim the Future, 2020. In collaboration with Michael Oswell and Ilyanna Kerr.

truly engages a community, where they can not only share their lived experience, but also help make decisions and steer the direction of a design process.

Copeland gives the example of Telegram groups in the Hong Kong protest movement with tens of thousands of people, that use polls to collectively decide where to go next, whether they should assemble somewhere or disperse. Activists using Airdrop to create ad hoc peer-to-peer networks where they can share instructions. These types of communication tools have a huge importance within activist organizations. Activists often use off-the-shelf tools because they're free and ubiquitous, but there are really big security concerns when using Google and Facebook. These companies have so much unfair advantage, because they can offer products for free, which they pay for from their advertising revenues. There are more and more free, open-source, well-designed tools available these days (e.g., NextCloud, Signal) that focus on security and encryption, so it would be much better if people moved their organizing towards these platforms.

What's their advice to designers who are looking to change their practice?
I think there are some aspects of design as a mindset that afford the kind of radical, systemic change that we need. For example, design is an iterative process—it's about following continuous cycles of reflection and action. Design is, by definition, always in the future, always about imagining. It is also inherently relational and social: it only exists in conversation with other people, clients, or groups. Copeland is clear about her advice to designers. 'Join a union, start a co-op.'[20] She remembers her first involvement in designing for activists,

One of the key things I learned was that it was about being humble: approaching the organisations you want to help and asking what you can do, rather than just creating a poster. Socially engaged work might sometimes means not doing something, or contributing to something that already exists.[21]

commonknowledge.coop

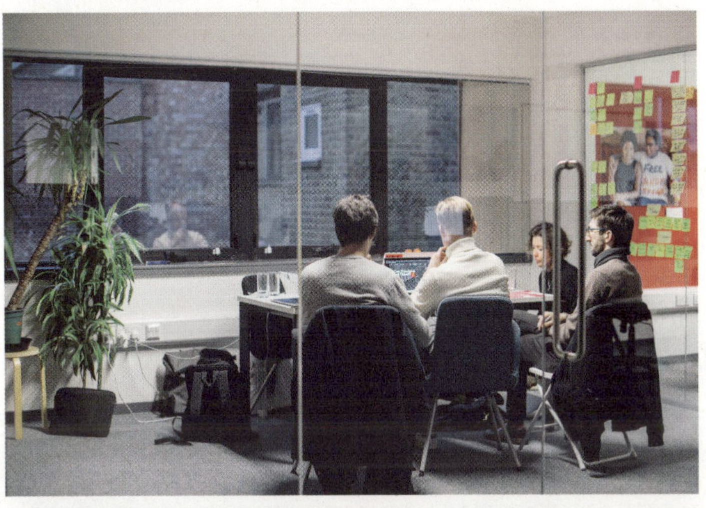

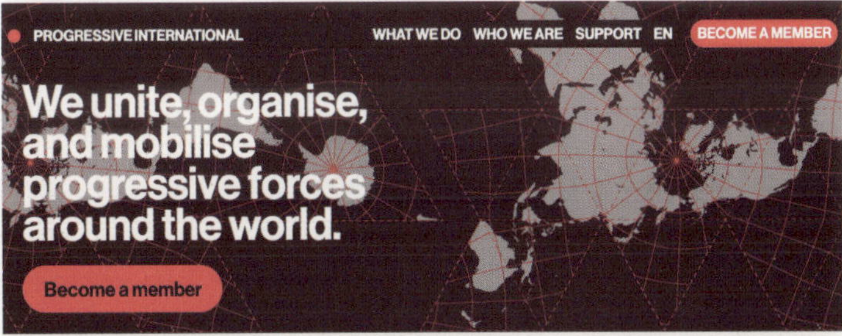

Wire

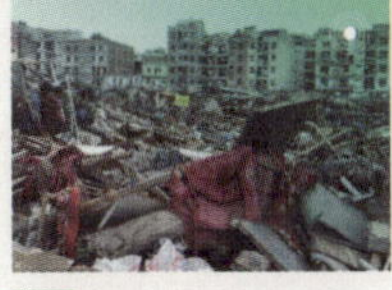

The Pandemic Paradox: Welfare Measures and Forced Evictions for Delhi's Marginal Urban Dwellers

Despite the pandemic, the question for Delhi's slum dwellers is still what welfare means if the right to housing is breached.

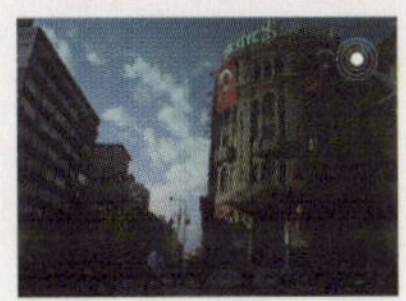

Democracy is on trial in Turkey. We are mobilizing to defend it.

The PI delegation arrives to Turkey to witness the historic trial of the "Kobani case."

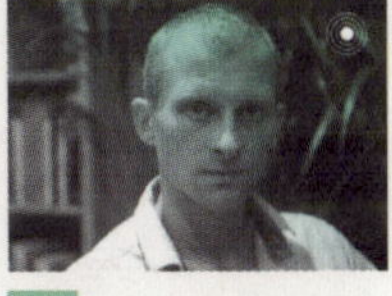

Sakhnin: The February Theses — The Left and the Political Crisis in Russia

PI Council member Alexey Sakhnin sets out his perspective on the protests that swept Russia in February 2021 — and charts a way forward for the Russian left.

↑ Workshop Common Knowledge with Progressive International, 2019.
↑ Website for Progressive International, 2021.

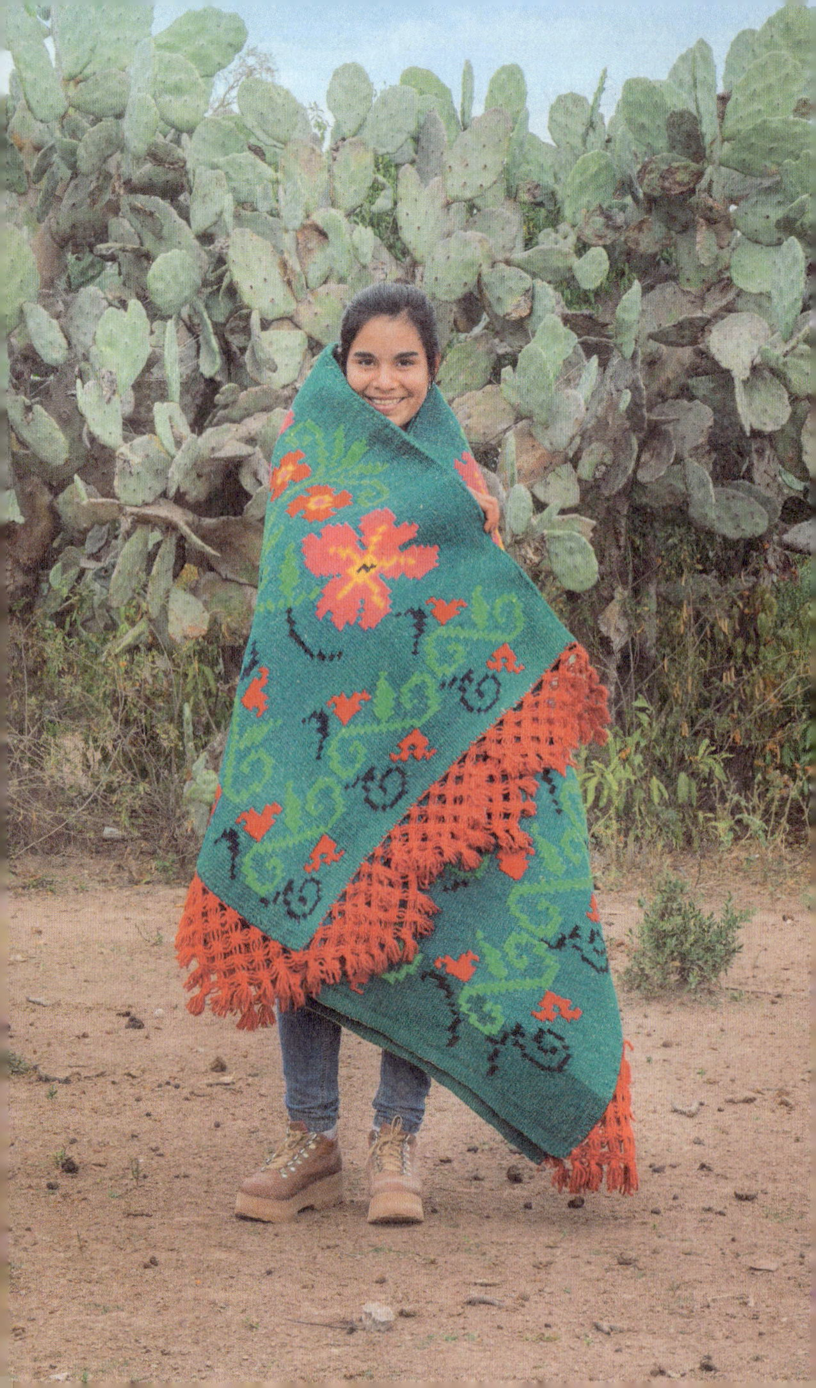

COOPERATIVA DE DISEÑO

In a huge factory building in the Almagro barrio in Argentina's capital Buenos Aires, a group of six women run Cooperativa de Diseño, or 'the design cooperative'. The studio was founded in 2011 when seven women designers wanted their work to engage with the social and political situation in Latin America. Some were already working in 'regular' design jobs, but they missed working together on social engagement. When founding a collective, the idea was to use the form of the horizontal cooperative in the spirit of the worker cooperatives that took over factories in Argentina in the wake of the 1997 economic crisis. One of those factories is the IMPA, a plastics and metal factory that went bankrupt and was taken over—quite successfully—by the workers. The Cooperativa de Diseño is located within the factory building, in one of the spaces in what was later transformed into a cultural centre. The IMPA also includes a high school, a workers' university, a radio and TV station, a community centre and a theatre. Today the IMPA is still a worker-owned factory that still produces aluminium packaging and plastic trays for airplane food.

What do they do on a day-to-day basis?
Cooperativa de Diseño is a multidisciplinary design studio. Its members have backgrounds in graphic design, audio-visual production, and product design, so they cover a lot of potential design work that social movements may require. Not unlike commercial design studios, their output consists of branding, product design, websites, film, and workshops. More important is for *who* they work. The main purpose of the Cooperativa is to put design tools in the hands of social movements, which in Latin America often do not have the resources or the network to use such tools effectively. The Cooperativa is clear that they intend to 'run a practice that

←   Photography and communication for the Atamisqui community, 2019.

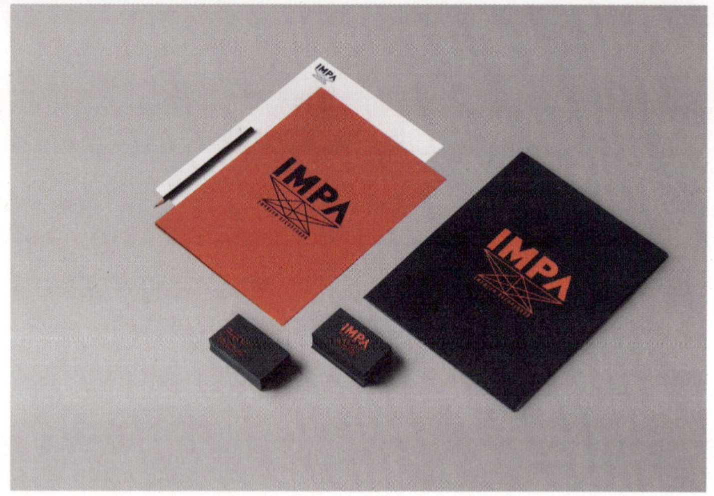

Identity design for the IMPA cooperative, 2012.

questions capitalist practices', linking with other co-ops and trans-forming ideas about how we work and how we create value. Their clients include indigenous artisans, NGOs, collectives, workers' cooperatives, queer and women's movements. All their design work is credited collectively, simply 'because that's the way we work'.

How are they structured?

The cooperative organizational structure (or co-op) is based on the seven cooperative principles. The difference with a regular company is that in a horizontal organizational form everyone is valued the same, whether you are a filmmaker or a cleaner. Some co-ops do this by a one-person, one-vote policy. Cooperativa de Diseño doesn't use the voting system, but makes decisions by discussing and reaching consensus. Horizontal decision-making—or *horizontalidad* in Spanish—is more about having no strict hierarchy. For example, if one person in the collective has more knowledge about a topic, their voice carries more weight than that of others. But when big decisions are taken in this collective, everyone's opinion counts equally. Practicing *horizontalidad* is not easy, it is about rethinking structures and building trust and commitment. Otherwise, it just means no decisions are made at all. They had help from organizations that give advice to co-ops, and now they have been running it successfully for nine years. If you're unfamiliar with this process, they point out many designers already use horizontal decision-making in working together with clients or participatory design. But, as they comment, if it is only applied on a project basis and not to the organization itself, you will never break the hierarchical structure.

Where do they get money?

All of the income from the cooperative comes from design work, but it has not been an easy ride. They set out to work for environmental and social organizations, but these rarely have money to spend, and at the start of their collective they almost had no

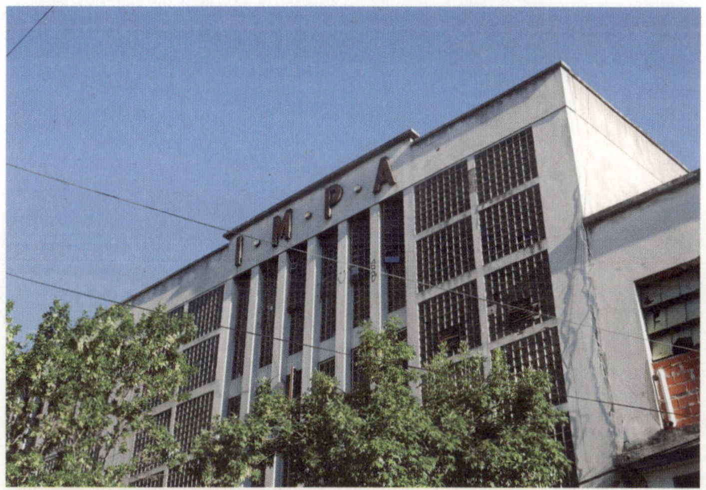

↑   IMPA factory building where Cooperativa de Diseño is housed, Buenos Aires, 2018.
→   Photography and communication for the Atamisqui community, 2019.

income for one year. But their practice does not need to make a profit, as long as salaries can sustain basic needs and labour rights such as vacation time, health care and parental leave. Working for social organizations is difficult and that sometimes means putting in extra work, but they don't strictly distinguish between for-profit and non-profit clients. As they say 'It is not charity or something that we do in our spare time. Work for social movements has to be paid as every other job.'[22]

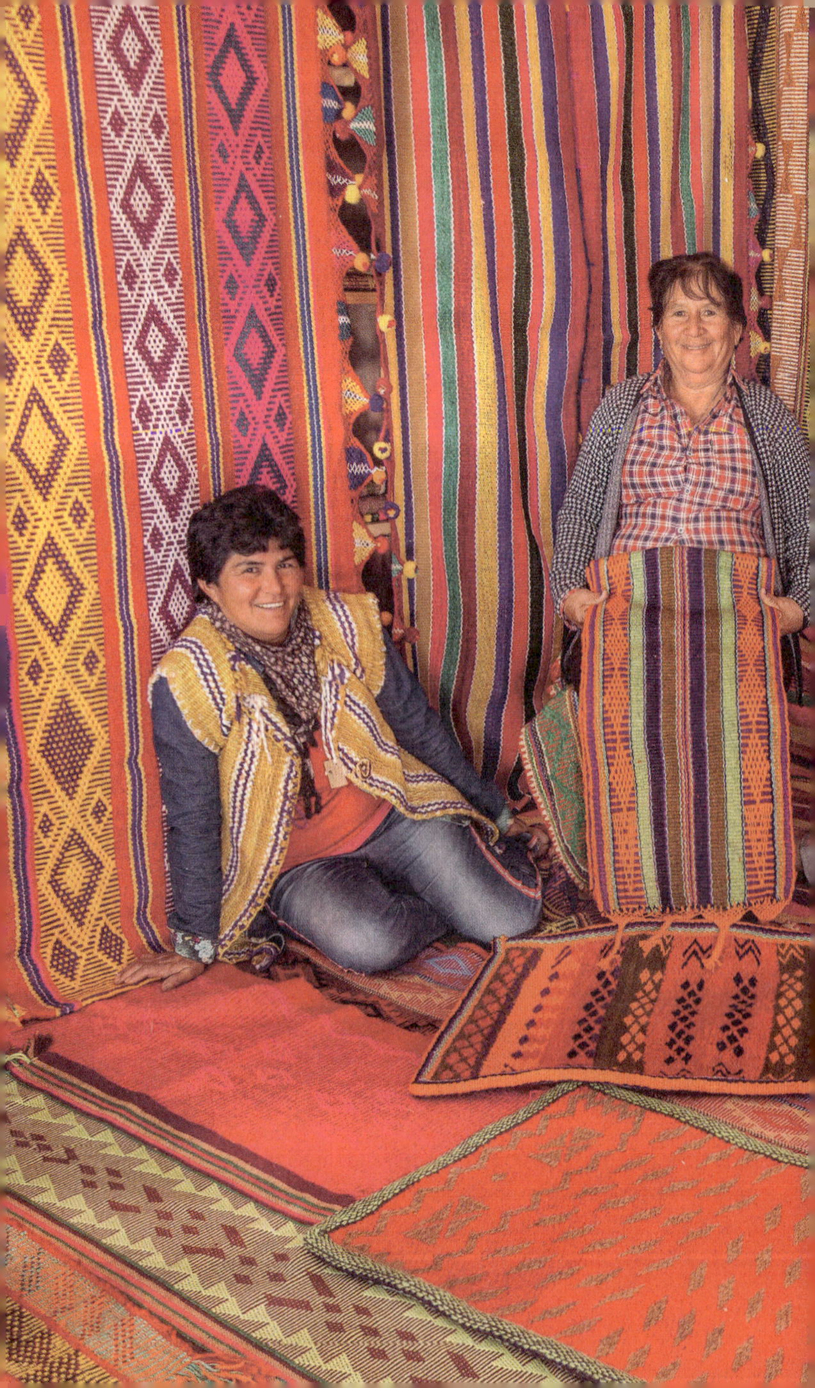

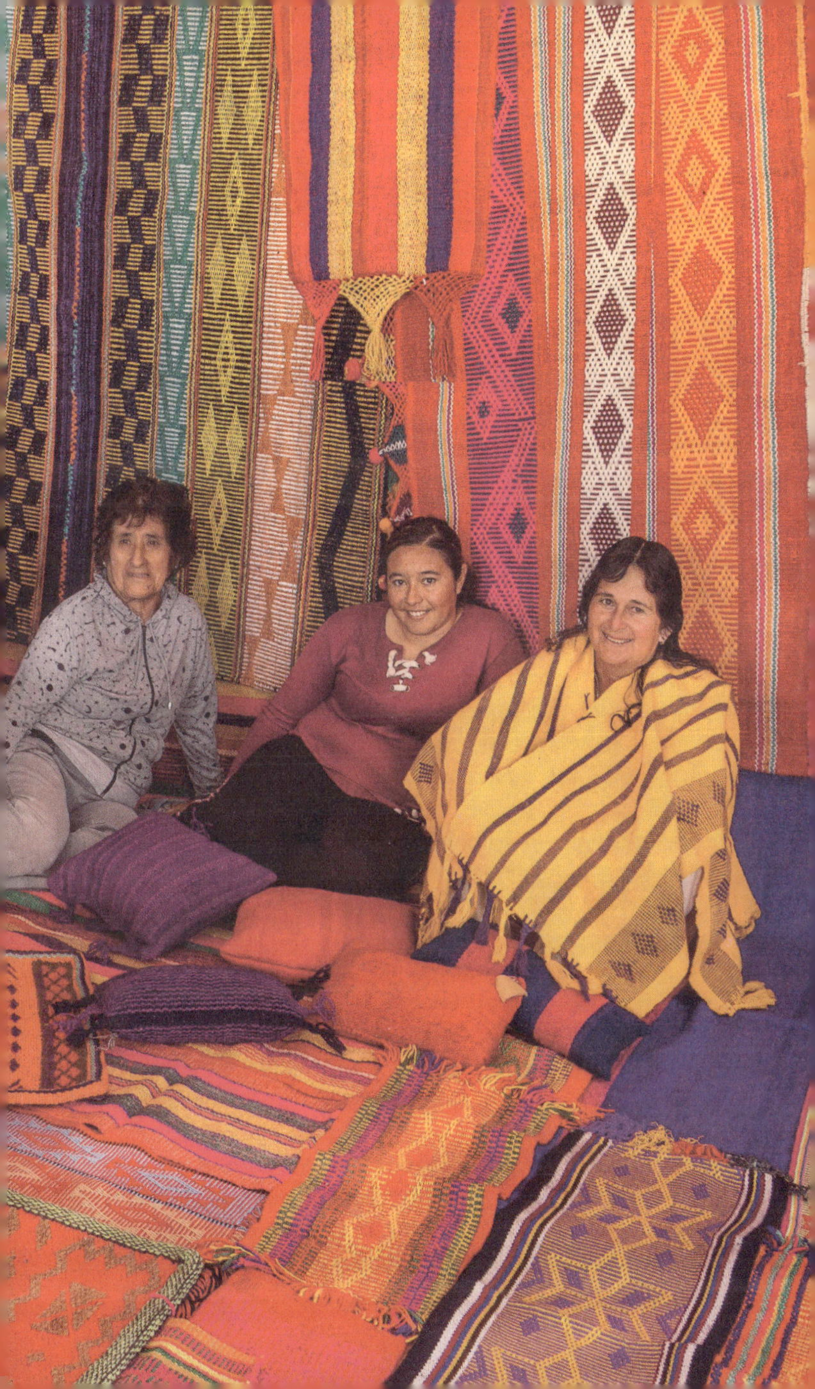

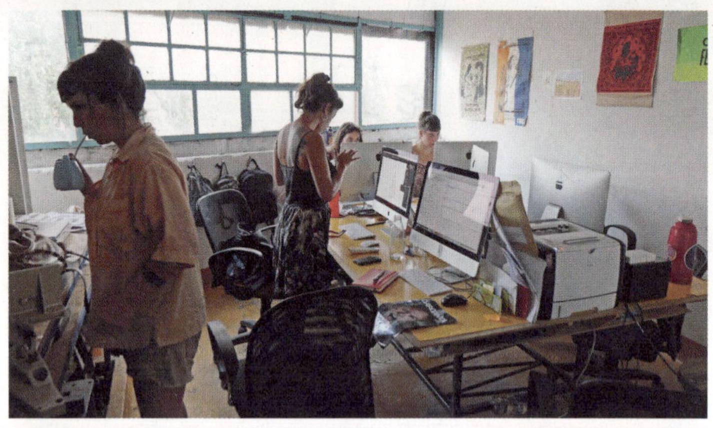

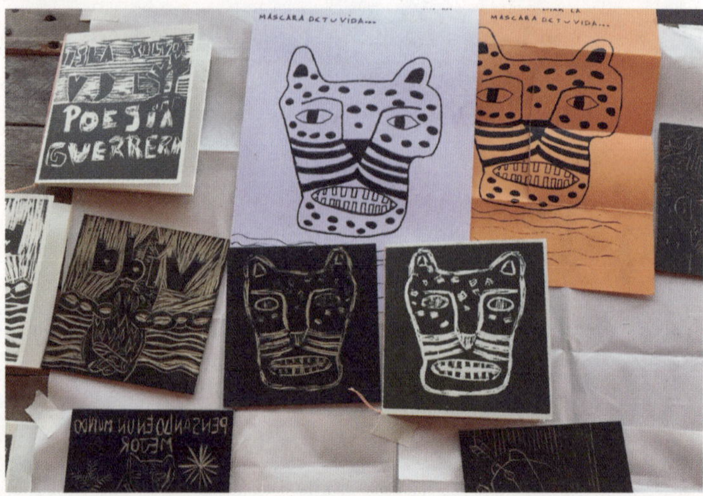

To build an ethical design collective and to live from it at the same time is really hard.

EMILIA, DESIGNER

How do they divide the collective income?

Experience in running the co-op has produced some interesting insight about sharing income. Within the collective, design work is not valued higher in wages than tasks such as administration or going to a bank. It is all necessary to run the cooperative. That doesn't mean everyone earns the same income. Not everyone has the same needs, and part of equality is acknowledging that a mother needs more than someone without children, and that a person who owns a house needs less income than someone who rents. For the co-op every individual's needs have to be considered. Dividing income is finding a balance between the needs of the co-op and those of its members. As they say, it's a messy process, but it also creates honesty and mutual understanding.

How is a design collective only run by women different?
A design studio run exclusively by women is not an everyday occurrence in the male-dominated design world, especially not a cooperative studio run only by women. This is no coincidence. A lot of their design work is dedicated to the women's movement. For example, they designed T-shirts with feminist slogans that were used by protesters in the huge grassroots movement's *Ni Una Menos* (not one [woman] less) marches, which started in Argentina in 2015 in response to violence against women. Latin America is known for its *machismo*, and has the highest rate in femicide in the world. That horrendous statistic has led to large women's movements and massive protests in Latin America on women's day. The collective is always involved in gender issues and women's rights. One of their projects is a website 'How to have an abortion', with key information about safety. They conducted research into how children's toys construct gender identity, and they made a documentary series for adolescents about gender called *Pibxs*.[23]

What else can designers learn from their practice?
Cooperativa de Diseño might seem from the outside like a collective that only does strict political work for non-profits, but that would be too simplistic. They also produce commercial work like packaging for worker-owned factories. Perhaps in some countries packaging design is regarded as one of the most commercial and least interesting graphic design work, commissions from which the more anti-commercial designers would steer clear. Not the

↑   Studio space, 2018.
←   Community workshop 'winds of freedom'.

Cooperativa. They see the importance of helping the worker-owned factory that can benefit from better design. In that sense the collective is looking for how their design can have the greatest impact and serves popular interest. In that spirit they want to share their experiences working as a cooperative in a network with other cooperatives, whether they are designers or metal workers, to show that you can create a vibrant local economy that does not merely serve the profits of corporations, but keeps value within the community. They see it as part of their work to discuss with designers how they too can strengthen social economies, rather than just look for cool clients. But they admit it will not be easy 'to build an ethical design collective and to live from it at the same time is really hard'.[24]

cooperativadedisenio.com

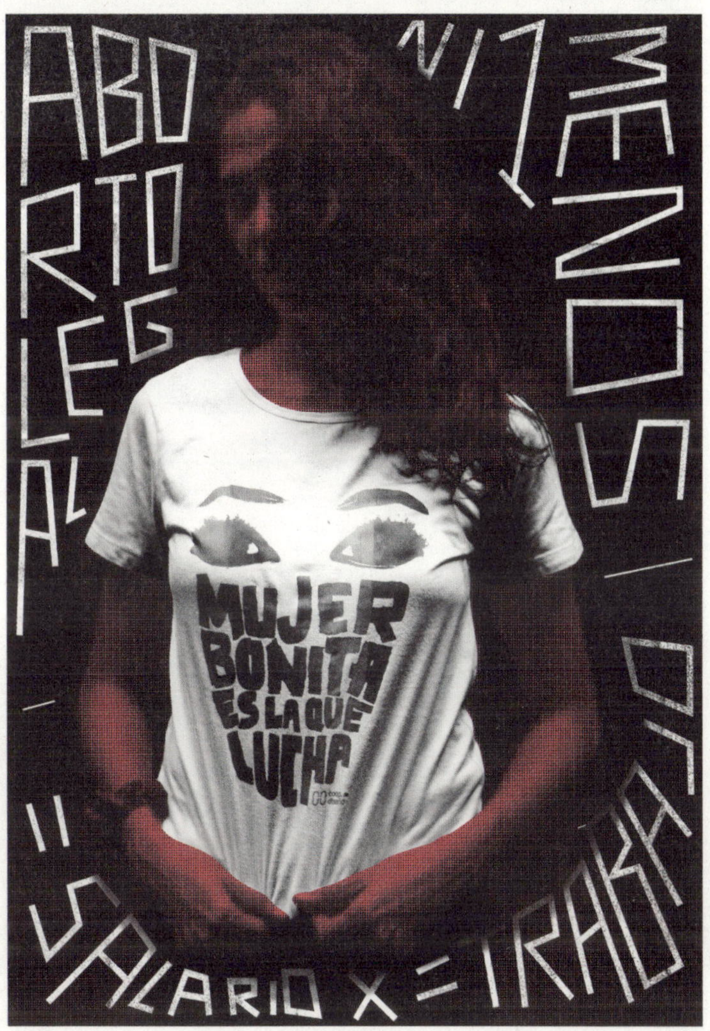

↑   'A pretty woman is one who fights' (T-shirt text), 2019.
←   'Who chooses your gender identity?', campaign for Pibxs, 2020.

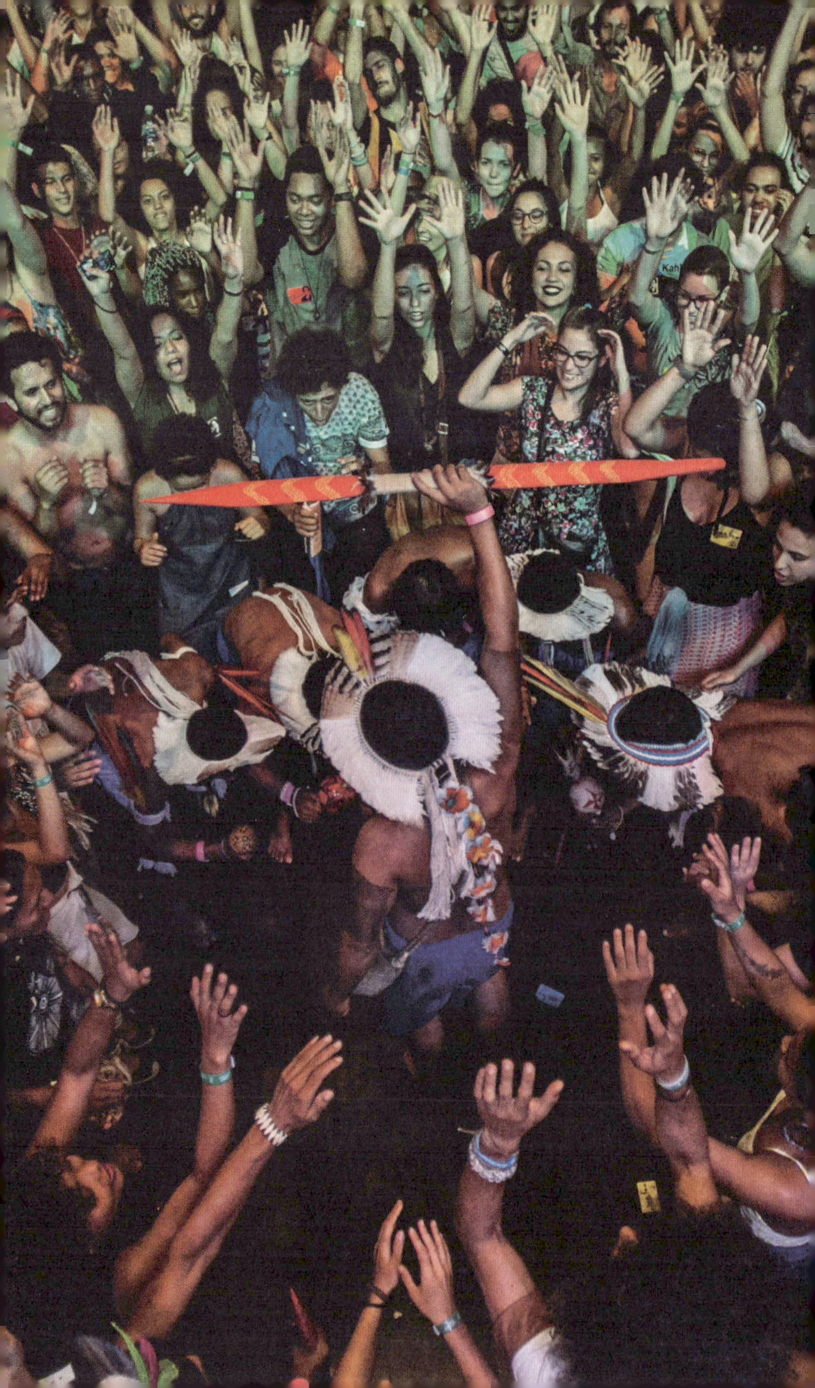

MÍDIA NINJA

Mídia NINJA (an acronym for Independent Narratives, Journalism and Action) from Brazil are a citizen journalism and media activist collective with over 200 members. They consider themselves media activists and journalists in the digital age, using social media to give a voice to those that are not heard. When protests broke out in 2013 due to a rise in bus fares, the police cracked down hard and violently, but Brazil's main media outlets flat out ignored the protests. NINJA journalists were the first to report about the protests, and they bypassed the mainstream media by live-streaming their footage across the world for free. Since then, they have ceaselessly reported on indigenous struggles, protests, corruption, the climate crisis, and the deforestation of the Amazon, all shared as media commons, free to use for everyone.

Mídia NINJA questions the neutrality that journalists claim in Brazil's corporate journalism with its 'false myth of impartiality'.[25] The media in Brazil are dominated by a handful of media conglomerates, owned by the country's wealthiest families, which serve the interests of the ruling class. Mídia NINJA's attempts to democratize media in Brazil has been successful. Using their extensive social-media network of more than eight million followers, they actively mobilize others to get involved in politics and activism to protect natural resources and repressed communities. As they say, 'The Internet changed journalism and we are part of this transformation. We live in a peer-to-peer culture that allows people to share information without traditional mediators.'[26]

How are they organized?
Mídia NINJA is the media and journalism arm of Fora do Eixo (off-axis), a cultural network that started in 2000 with a few students that organized music festivals outside of the axis Rio de Janeiro–

← Photo by Mídia NINJA.

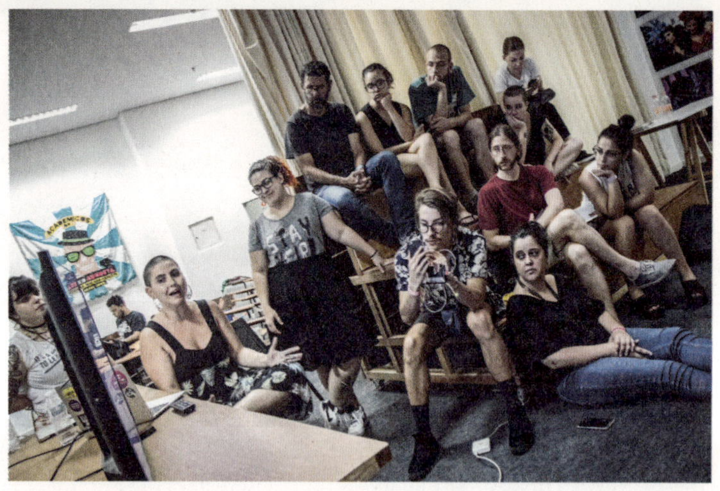

São Paulo (hence the name) on a shoe-string budget. Within twenty years the collective grew into a movement with two thousand members, twenty-five collective houses, and activities in fifteen countries. Fora do Eixo was founded on ideas to challenge capitalist relations and on a firm belief in free access to information. They have their own currency, the FdE card, their own university, a collective bank, and members live in collective houses. Fora do Eixo uses a diagonal hierarchy structure. where most of its activities are horizontally organized through assemblies, but dedicated management and coordination functions do exist to better organize the enormous number of activities. Fora do Eixo is not without its own problems, as running such a huge social organization is a feat in itself, but it remains founded on solidarity principles in search for alternatives to capitalism, and no members are able to profit from or capitalize on the work of the collective.

How do they live and work?

During a trip to Brazil, I visited two houses of Mídia NINJA where they live and work, sometimes with 20–30 people in one house. Their collective houses are a pleasant cacophony of writers, photographers, designers, and filmmakers working tirelessly to

↑   Design activist meeting, Mídia NINJA, 2018.
→   Chat groups within Mídia NINJA, 2020.

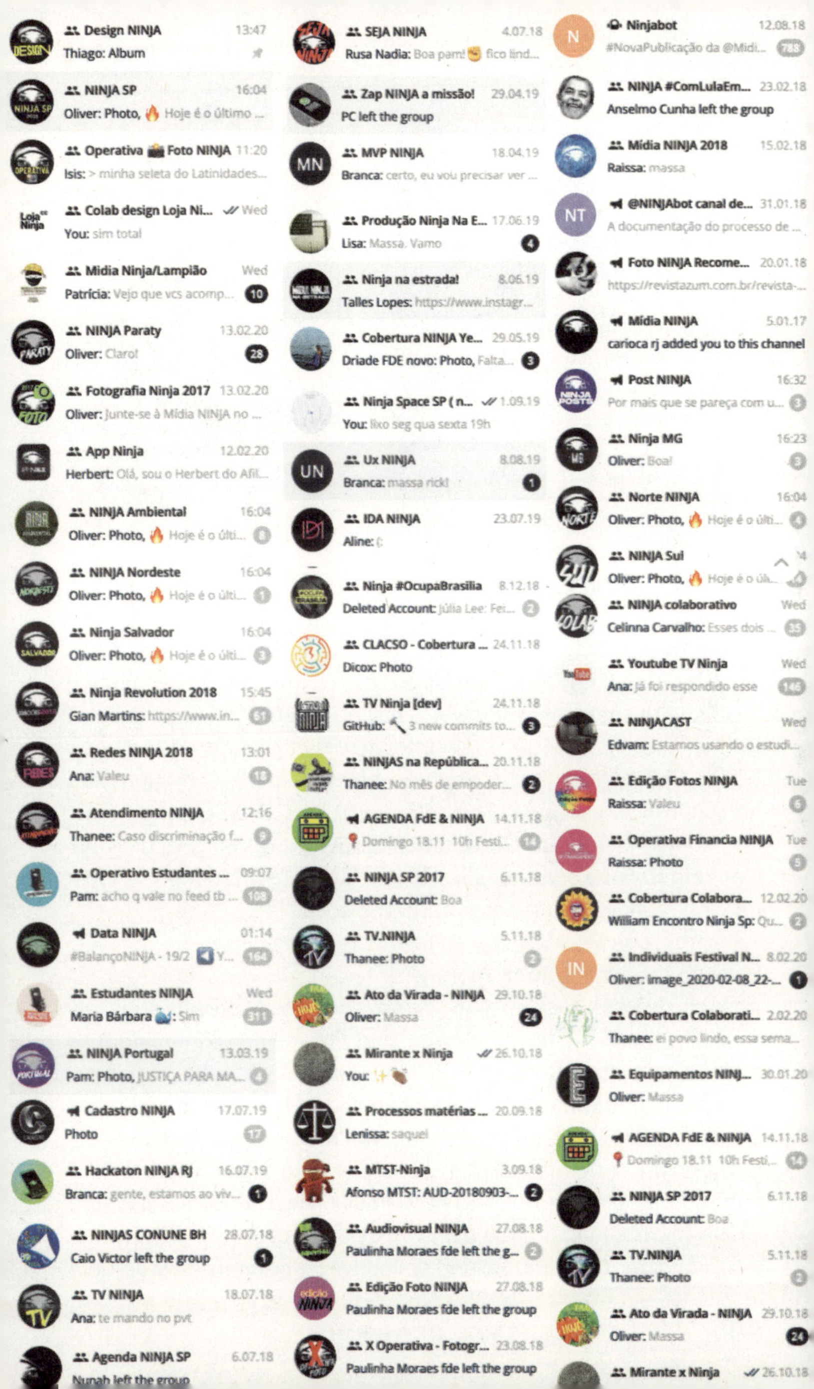

Design NINJA — 13:47
Thiago: Album

NINJA SP — 16:04
Oliver: Photo, 🔥 Hoje é o último …

Operativa 📷 Foto NINJA — 11:20
Isis: > minha seleta do Latinidades…

Colab design Loja Ni… — ✔✔ Wed
You: sim total

Mídia Ninja/Lampião — Wed
Patrícia: Vejo que vcs acomp… — 10

NINJA Paraty — 13.02.20
Oliver: Claro! — 28

Fotografia Ninja 2017 — 13.02.20
Oliver: Junte-se à Mídia NINJA no …

App Ninja — 12.02.20
Herbert: Olá, sou o Herbert do Afil…

NINJA Ambiental — 16:04
Oliver: Photo, 🔥 Hoje é o últi… — 1

NINJA Nordeste — 16:04
Oliver: Photo, 🔥 Hoje é o últi… — 1

Ninja Salvador — 16:04
Oliver: Photo, 🔥 Hoje é o últi… — 3

Ninja Revolution 2018 — 15:45
Gian Martins: https://www.in… — 51

Redes NINJA 2018 — 13:01
Ana: Valeu — 13

Atendimento NINJA — 12:16
Thanee: Caso discriminação f… — 7

Operativo Estudantes … — 09:07
Pam: acho q vale no feed tb … — 100

Data NINJA — 01:14
#BalançoNINJA - 19/2 Y… — 164

Estudantes NINJA — Wed
Maria Bárbara 💧: Sim — 311

NINJA Portugal — 13.03.19
Pam: Photo, JUSTIÇA PARA MA… — 4

Cadastro NINJA — 17.07.19
Photo — 17

Hackaton NINJA RJ — 16.07.19
Branca: gente, estamos ao viv… — 1

NINJAS CONUNE BH — 28.07.18
Caio Victor left the group — 1

TV NINJA — 18.07.18
Ana: te mando no pvt

Agenda NINJA SP — 6.07.18
Nunah left the group

SEJA NINJA — 4.07.18
Rusa Nadia: Boa pam! 😍 fico lind…

Zap NINJA a missão! — 29.04.19
PC left the group

MVP NINJA — 18.04.19
Branca: certo, eu vou precisar ver …

Produção Ninja Na E… — 17.06.19
Lisa: Massa. Vamo — 4

Ninja na estrada! — 8.06.19
Talles Lopes: https://www.instagr…

Cobertura NINJA Ye… — 29.05.19
Driade FDE novo: Photo, Falta… — 3

Ninja Space SP (n… — ✔✔ 1.09.19
You: lixo seg qua sexta 19h

Ux NINJA — 8.08.19
Branca: massa rick! — 1

IDA NINJA — 23.07.19
Aline: (:

Ninja #OcupaBrasília — 8.12.18
Deleted Account: Júlia Lee: Fe… — 2

CLACSO - Cobertura … — 24.11.18
Dicox: Photo

TV Ninja [dev] — 24.11.18
GitHub: 🔧 3 new commits to… — 3

NINJAS na República… — 20.11.18
Thanee: No mês de empoder… — 2

AGENDA FdE & NINJA — 14.11.18
📍 Domingo 18.11 10h Festi… — 14

NINJA SP 2017 — 6.11.18
Deleted Account: Boa

TV.NINJA — 5.11.18
Thanee: Photo — 2

Ato da Virada - NINJA — 29.10.18
Oliver: Massa — 24

Mirante x Ninja — ✔✔ 26.10.18
You: ✨ 👏

Processos matérias … — 20.09.18
Lenissa: saquei

MTST-Ninja — 3.09.18
Afonso MTST: AUD-20180903-… — 2

Audiovisual NINJA — 27.08.18
Paulinha Moraes fde left the g… — 2

Edição Foto NINJA — 27.08.18
Paulinha Moraes fde left the group

X Operativa - Fotogr… — 23.08.18
Paulinha Moraes fde left the group

Ninjabot — 12.08.18
#NovaPublicação da @Midi… — 745

NINJA #ComLulaEm… — 23.02.18
Anselmo Cunha left the group

Mídia NINJA 2018 — 15.02.18
Raissa: massa

@NINJAbot canal de… — 31.01.18
A documentação do processo de …

Foto NINJA Recome… — 20.01.18
https://revistazum.com.br/revista-

Mídia NINJA — 5.01.17
carioca rj added you to this channel

Post NINJA — 16:32
Por mais que se pareça com u… — 3

Ninja MG — 16:23
Oliver: Boa! — 3

Norte NINJA — 16:04
Oliver: Photo, 🔥 Hoje é o últi… — 4

NINJA Sul — 4
Oliver: Photo, 🔥 Hoje é o úl…

NINJA colaborativo — Wed
Celinna Carvalho: Esses dois … — 35

Youtube TV Ninja — Wed
Ana: Já foi respondido esse — 145

NINJACAST — Wed
Edvam: Estamos usando o estudi…

Edição Fotos NINJA — Tue
Raissa: Valeu — 6

Operativa Financia NINJA — Tue
Raissa: Photo — 5

Cobertura Colabora… — 12.02.20
William Encontro Ninja Sp: Qu… — 2

Individuais Festival N… — 8.02.20
Oliver: image_2020-02-08_22-… — 1

Cobertura Colaborati… — 2.02.20
Thanee: ei povo lindo, essa sema…

Equipamentos NINJ… — 30.01.20
Oliver: Massa

AGENDA FdE & NINJA — 14.11.18
📍 Domingo 18.11 10h Festi… — 14

NINJA SP 2017 — 6.11.18
Deleted Account: Boa

TV.NINJA — 5.11.18
Thanee: Photo — 2

Ato da Virada - NINJA — 29.10.18
Oliver: Massa — 24

Mirante x Ninja — ✔✔ 26.10.18

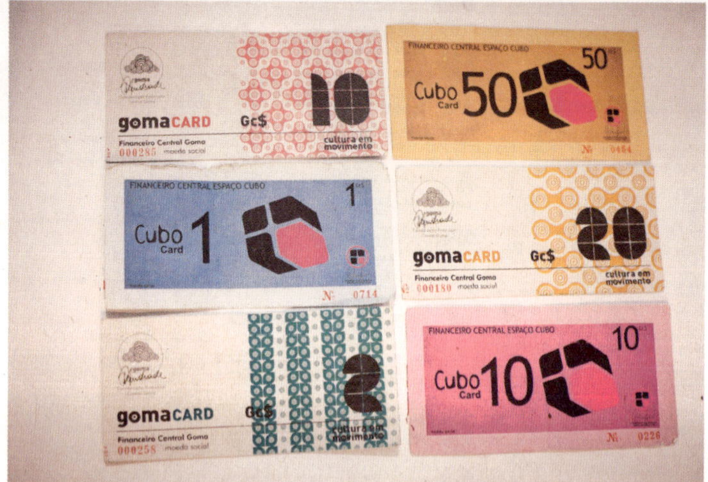

The Fora do Eixo currency, the Cubo Card or $FdE.

direct content to their hundreds of social media accounts. Within the collective the roles switch. One person may be designing one moment, and cleaning or cooking the next. By European standards they live in austere conditions, sleeping on mattresses in common rooms with make-shift showers, having little or no possessions. Rafael Vilela points out in an interview that compared to Brazil, where 13.7 million live in extreme poverty, these conditions are considered privileged.[27] The activists of NINJA work long hours, and there seems little distinction between working and living. Cooking is done communally. Houses also often function as locations for concerts, and are vibrant with social life.

How do they make their money?

As Mídia NINJA does not earn money with their activities, they rely on microdonations from followers and the selling of merchandise and tickets to music events. NINJA also receives grants from international institutions that support human rights activism and press freedom, although they don't accept donations or grants that interfere with the content. NINJA members receive no salaries, but their basic needs are covered, and each house has a collective account where members can draw money from for expenses. Many members consider the freedom and collective community environment

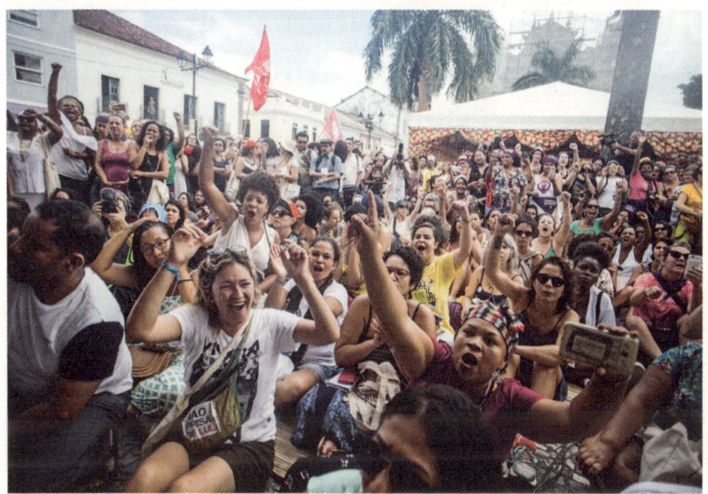

Mídia NINJA at the World Social Forum, Salvador, Bahia, Brazil, 2018.

to work on activist projects as a dream come true, even if it's only for a few years. Rafael Vilela notes how they see the community itself as a the most important source of value, which serves its members by continuously creating activist and socially meaningful activities while building strong social bonds.

They have their own currency. How does that work?

Alternative economies are not new to Latin America. During the dictatorships of the 1970s, people set up solidarity economies and barter networks to survive.[28] When Fora do Eixo had difficulty making ends meet in organizing a festival, they started to issue their own currency: the Cubo Card or $FdECard. The idea was that bands could spend their $FdE to have an album recorded, or a music video made, so money would stay within the community. Difficulties of managing such a currency occurred when they had given out too many credits, and they had to learn how to keep the currency's value stable. They partnered with local restaurants, taxi services, and clothing stores that started to accept the currency. It was a concept to generate resources for independent cultural production. Today, paper bills have been replaced with digital cards, but Fora do Eixo have been using their own currency for more than seventeen years now.

The Internet changed journalism and we are part of this transformation. We live in a peer-to-peer culture that allows people to share information without traditional mediators.

MÍDIA NINJA

What about their design work?

Mídia NINJA has many graphic designers within the collective to cover the overwhelming number of films, websites, graphics, and amount of social media content they produce. But roles aren't fixed and members can receive training in graphic design to give it their best shot. Dedicated designers might live in different houses or regions, and collaborate using the many Telegram channels that are the pulsing heart of Mídia NINJA. Hundreds of channels keep members connected across different projects, regions, cities, interests, or disciplines. One of the projects NINJA designers are involved in is the campaign #designativista (design activism), an Instagram hashtag to call upon graphic designers from Brazil to publish work against the Bolsonaro regime. Another one is the 342amazonia app that was developed together with Greenpeace. 342amazonia allows users to join collective activist action against deforestation to protect the Amazon.

Linking activists and others together is what the NINJAs are very good at. Currently they are busy connecting graphic designers to activist and social groups across Brazil with an app that functions like a dating app, so that the great distances between designers living in the cities and rural social movements are bridged digitally. The app is part of a new activist strategy coming out of the pandemic called *Floresta Ativista* (activist forest), an ecosystem with forty apps that is based on social technologies developed from twenty years of collective work, making activism more accessible. NINJA calls it a powerful tool for building solutions to the common challenges of a post-pandemic generation. Fora do Eixo has been challenging existing labour conditions and capitalism in Brazil by creating new solidarity economies and social structures for activism.

They have proven that new forms of community can exist, and that it is possible to organize alternative structures that challenge the economic status quo in Brazil.

midianinja.org

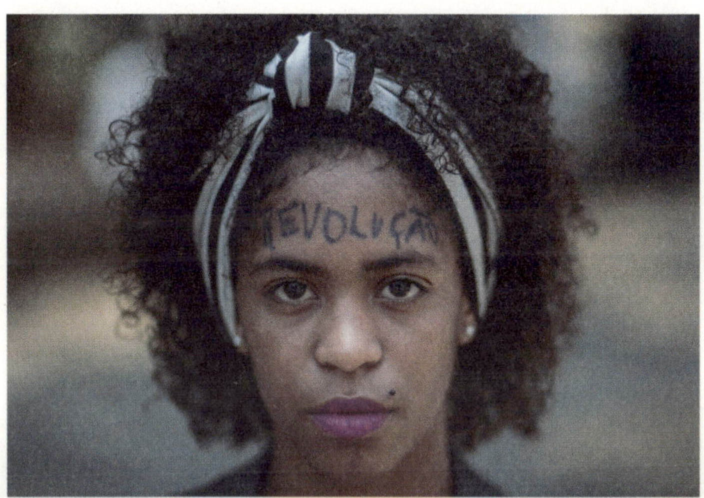

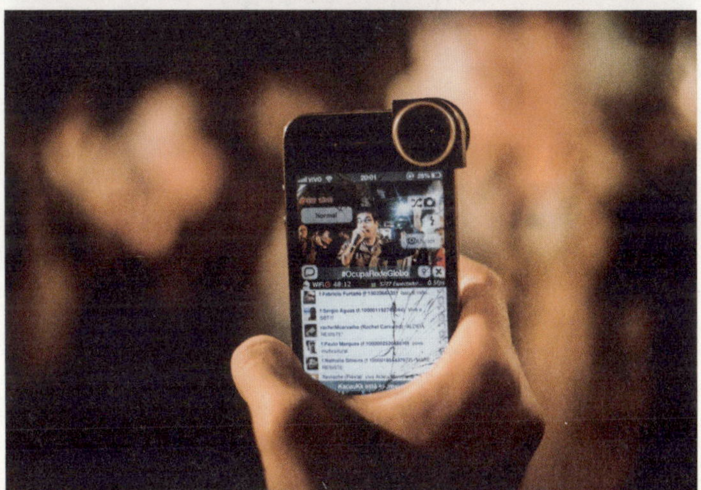

Photos by Midia NINJA, 2013.

OPEN SOURCE PUBLISHING

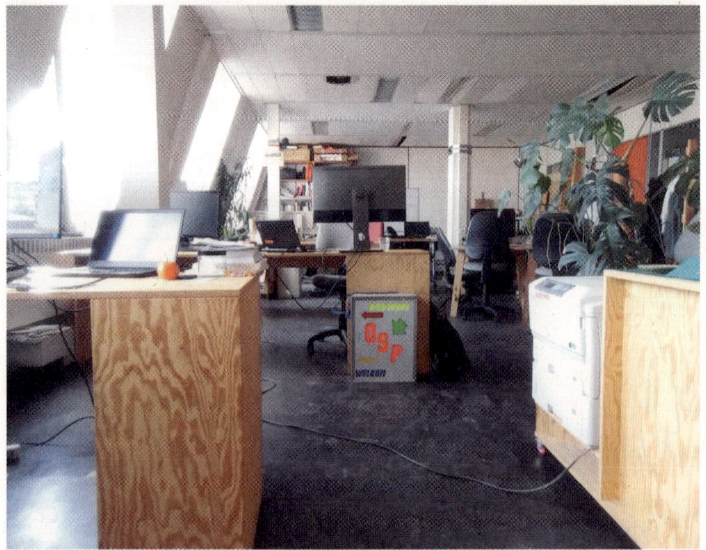

OSP office, Brussels.

Five graphic designers in Brussels started the following experiment in 2006: is it possible to make graphic design using only Free/Libre Open Source Software? They started by adjusting the tools of graphic design, and eventually also started to make their own.[29] It turned out to be a successful experiment, and fifteen years later Open Source Publishing (OSP) is still going strong. Meanwhile the original members have made way for a new crew, and OSP now consists of three core members and four acting in a more satellite role. Besides their office their main platform is the website, which offers a wealth of typefaces, publications, workshops, knowledge, and texts, all of which are free to use, adapt, and redistribute. The openness and generosity are a refreshing change from the conservative ideas that most graphic designers have about copyright. The experiment to design with Free/Libre Open Source Software (FLOSS) goes beyond discussions about technology or copyright: OSP 'thinks of design as a space for dialogue and tension between cultures'.[30]

How are they organized and what do they do on a daily basis?
OSP is a bilingual Belgian non-profit organization. Maybe one day OSP will set up a cooperative for its commissioned works and keep the non-profit association for its educational and self-initiated activities, as they say in an interview. Since cooperatives in Belgium are also meant to make profit, they are not all fully comfortable with this notion. Working for OSP is not a fulltime job and all members have other commitments, such as teaching or other design practices. At their studio, OSP do typeface design, software development, workshops, and publications. These different methods are not separate but part of an ecological approach towards design and cultural production.

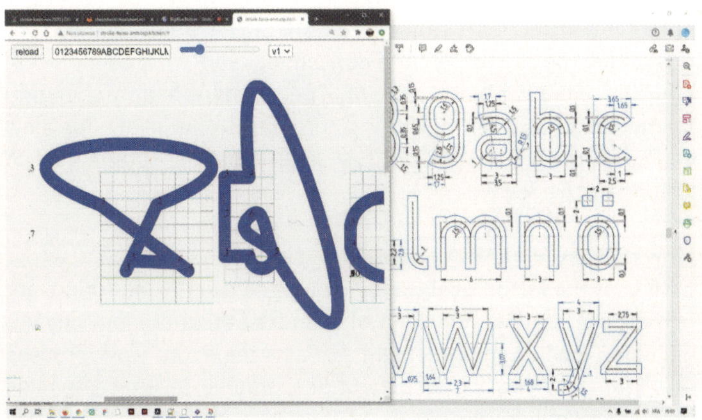

Stroke fonts workshop, 2020.

How are they funded?
OSP is not able to sustain income for all its members at the moment, and they all have incomes from other practices. Commissioned work is the main source of income, although for some self-initiated projects and research they are financed through subsidies. Payment of the members is based on how work is divided

within projects. Clients are asked to pay 50 percent of the budget within a month after the start of a project. 25 percent of the budget is kept within OSP, and the rest is divided among the members working on the project. This 25 percent is meant to pay fixed costs such as rent and administration, and to finance self-initiated projects.

What about their type design practice?
At OSP, type design is 'more than the work of solitary masters passing on their secret trade to devoted pupils', an image that is carefully preserved in the closed world of type design, obscuring the fact that typography today is lightweight and widespread.[31] It certainly contrasts with the invitation of Free Software to anyone to run, copy, distribute, study, change, and improve. Type design is inherently generative, especially since digital files have everything to gain from being copied and re-mixed, says OSP. They prefer to work with their constraints and affordances, rather than rely on a contradictory business model that invests more in copyright enforcement than in creative development itself. Unfortunately, type design can be extremely time-consuming work, that cannot exist ethically without reimbursement. Their hope is that a changing relationship between user and producer can allow for new economic models that do not restrict use, but encourage it while valuing the work itself.

How do they work with clients?
OSP uses the word 'collaborator' instead of 'client', since they work in dialogue as a team instead of from a position of hierarchy. An online collaboration agreement explains the entire work process in full transparency.[32] Unlike traditional graphic design companies they don't do three proposals from which a client can choose. By collaborating on an equal basis, they work towards a common goal. An OSP design team always consists of two or more members, so that no one works alone. An external team member keeps an eye on planning and budgets. As member Gijs de Heij writes, 'Collaboration is inherently inefficient. Openness and compatibility take work and effort, perhaps it's not a bad thing this is reflected in the

→   Poster for Balsamine, 2020.

137 FAÇONS DE MOURIR

VIRGINIE STRUB – KIRSH CIE

du 29.09
au 9.10
Création
théâtre

du 7 au 17.11
Création
théâtre
d'ombres et de
marionnettes

AU PIED DES MONTAGNES

UNE TRIBU COLLECTIF

XX TIME

FRANÇOISE BERLANGER

du 30.09
au 07.12
Concert
performé

du 10
au 15.11
Création
Théâtre
Musique

LES SŒURS H

IN MY BIG FIREWORKS I PLAY TO YOU THE FINAL BOUQUET

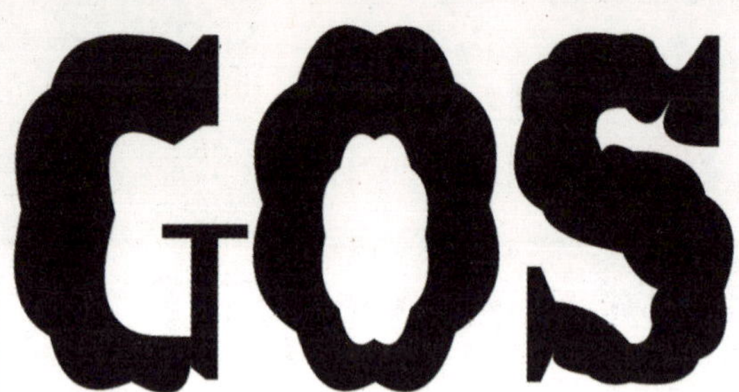

Advance Width Metrics For Umi-Mincho_Baka -2-
File Edit Element View Metrics Window Help
latn(dflt)   GOS   New Lookup Subtable...
Name: G   O   S
Width: 2048   2048   2048
LBearing: 68.1   -0.13   128.8
RBearing: 48   -1.87   97.28
Kern:

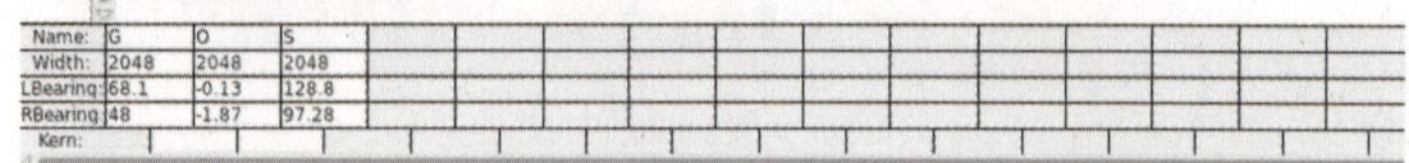

tools we use.'[33] Their motto for projects is 'release early, release often', a saying from software development. During each stage of the project folders and files are put online, documenting the work, so the public can witness the design process. They say a good documentation is essential because it determines what power the collaborators, and all future users, have.

What software do they use?

OSP believes their work is a way of testing the possibilities and limitations of open-source software in a professional design environment, without expecting the same experience as we are used to from proprietary software. They see Free and Open-Source Licenses as a 'hack' of the traditional copyright system. Open-source alternatives can be found for all popular design software. Gimp or Krita are alternatives to Adobe Photoshop, Inkscape is an alternative to Adobe Illustrator, and Scribus can replace Adobe Indesign. OpenShot can be used for video editing, and FontForge for type design. To exchange large numbers of files or huge ones, OSP use Nextcloud, a libre cloud software. For collective text they recommend etherpad. Gijs de Heij notes that an important advantage of open-source software is that the user has continuous access to the files. If proprietary software is discontinued, or updates are too expensive, or license fees become too high, the designer or collaborator might not be able to access the files anymore.

What is their user and copyright policy?

The licenses OSP uses on its production are all copyleft. This licensing model was first used in 1976, and later described in the GNU Manifesto by Richard Stallman in 1985. It means that anyone is free to reuse, modify, and redistribute their materials, even for commercial purposes. It doesn't mean you give up authorship, but that you invite others to be influenced by others and to acknowledge this. OSP urges everyone to use intellectual property to open up this material under the same copyleft licenses, and to convince your partners to do so as well. The goal of these licenses is that the entire documentation of a project, both its process and its final result, becomes available for the community to build upon.

← Type sketches from the OSP website.

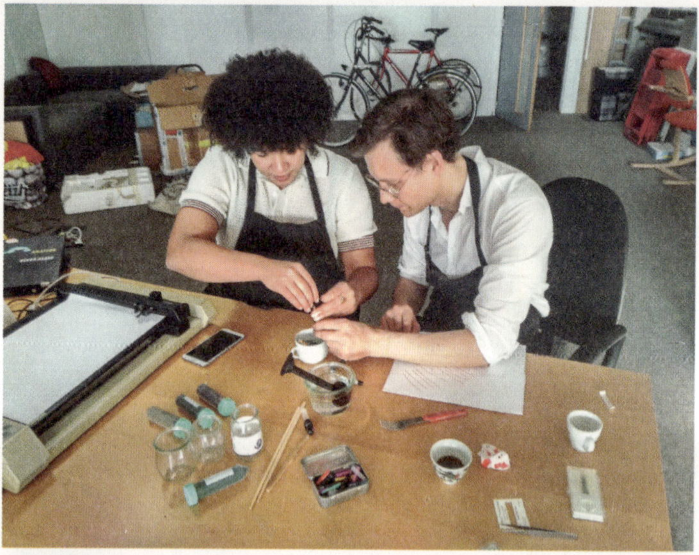

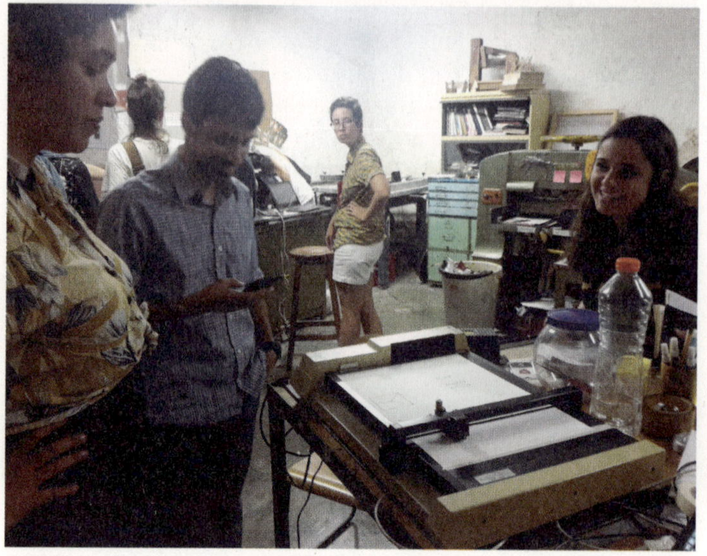

What's their advice to designers who are looking to change their practice?
OSP's experience of designing with Free Software has shown that 'owning' our tools is not the same as 'mastering' them. The designers at OSP proceed from a position that few graphic designers can completely ignore: the work in all its dimensions (cultural, social, and economic) is highly connected to politics and ideology. OSP calls for a generous artistic practice that recognizes that culture is above all based on the circulation of ideas, and on the fact that any work is derivative by nature, in the sense that it is informed by preceding works. Code is poetry, code is culture.

osp.kitchen

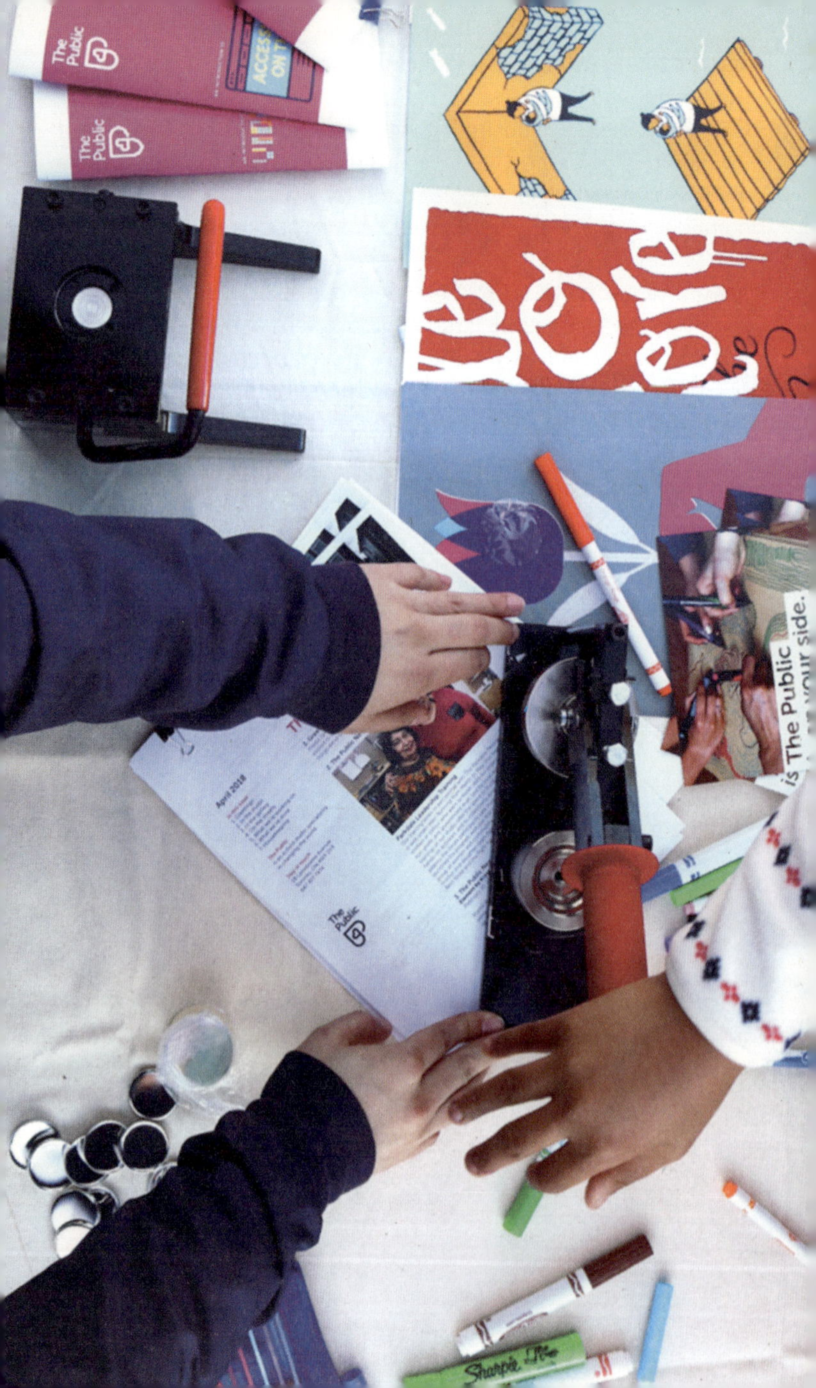

The Public
The Public
ACCESS
ON T
love
is The Public
your side.
April 2018
The Public
Sharpie

THE PUBLIC

In the middle of Parkdale, a tight-knit neighbourhood in the centre of Toronto, Canada, stands a red storefront building that houses The Public: a community-centred, social justice design studio run by Sheila Sampath, LJ Robinson, Natalia Saavedra, Jenny Chan and Anabel Khoo. The designers all identify as people of colour and/or queer or trans. Their background is important because those lived experiences continue to inform their work. The Public calls itself 'an activist design studio specialized in changing the world', 'working for grassroots community organizations, larger non-profits, unions, and community-led businesses that share our values'.[34]

Upon starting in 2008, the designers at The Public had the intention of bringing better design to activist communities. In retrospect they see this starting point as 'contributing to inequitable power structures'.[35] Their experiences made them realize that a distinction between designers and non-designers fails to appreciate the existing creativity that resides within justice-seeking communities. An insight that led them to radically shift from designing to facilitating design by means of co-creation. Now they see themselves as organizers, facilitators, and cultural workers that can empower others to develop their creativity.

What do they do on a day-to-day basis?
The Public is a full-service design agency that produces and co-produces everything from flyers and banners to short videos and web platforms. Their work consists of 'traditional' design work following a client-supplier model, co-design work rooted in principles of community self-determination, and self-initiated work. The latter includes a community gallery, programming open-source resources, and a residency programme. All projects serve a public

← Workshop at a street festival.

social cause or support activist organizations, or socially embedded work. Their real passion is co-design work, which requires them to become fluent in activities like facilitation and community-care that designers aren't always taught as core competencies. Their space, and access to that space, is a part of their community practice; for example, if someone from the neighbourhood enters the studio and asks for water or they need a place to rest or dispose of a needle, they consider that also part of their work, notes creative director Sheila Sampath.[36]

Where do they get money?
The Public operates as a social enterprise, which is a revenue-generating organization whose objective is to have a social impact. The Public's five members pay themselves a living wage. All excess income goes into community programming. Their income is sufficient but they've also had some lucky breaks. The storefront is rented from Sheila's brother-in-law at a reduced rate. Emotional labour and community work is not usually part of the billable hours of designers, but they find that there is a spirit of mutual care between them and their clients; folks want to pay fairly for this work and respect them as workers. Sheila Sampath says they have even had clients who have told them they are undervaluing their work and offered to pay more for their services.[37]

What role do they play in the community?
The Public's studio has been in Parkdale since 2016. The community has been under threat of gentrification, and residents have united in several grassroots organizations, with over thirty community-based initiatives and hundreds of community members. A local currency programme was set up and also a community-based food distribution and a community land trust model.[38]

The Public understands how design studios and galleries are often complicit in gentrification. The neighbourhood is not just a temporary studio location, but part of a long-term commitment to strengthen social bonds through cultural production. A lot of the work that The Public does are workshops and trainings based on mutual aid principles. That means they see their work as reciprocal, exchanging creativity and knowledge within the community.

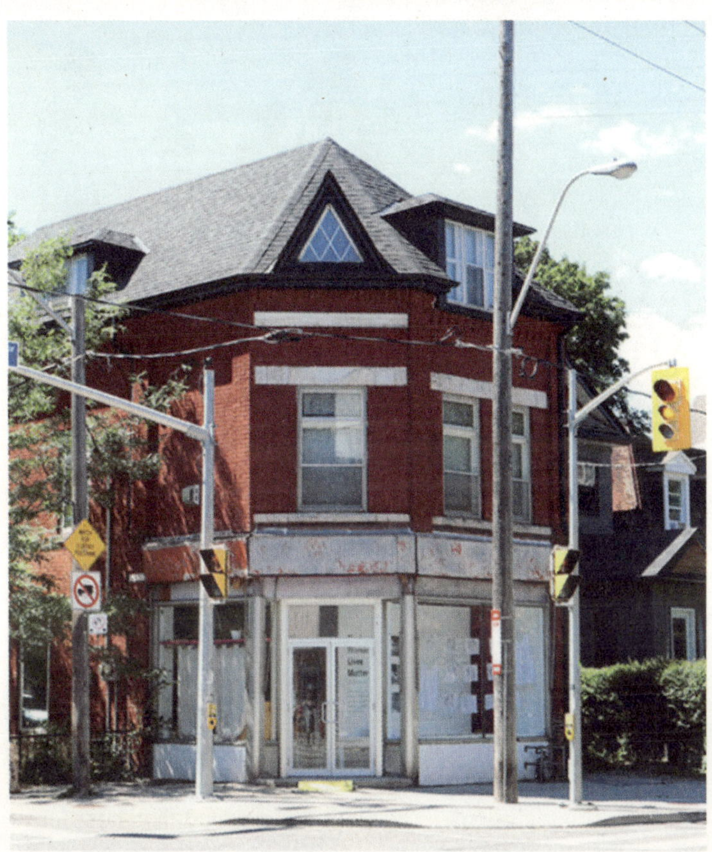

The storefront building in Parkdale, Toronto, where The Public is housed.

What helps is that their storefront functions as a community gallery, located right in front of a bus stop.

'Lately there's been a lot of design studios that do pro-bono or liberal work, but there's no care. They're not invested in the communities they're designing for, and we are', says studio manager Anabel Khoo. 'We don't want to be gatekeepers. For me, my perfect world would be one where everyone could do what we do.' Designer Natalia Saavedra adds, 'I want us to keep supporting Parkdale and be part of the community as a radical and beautiful space that can be used by more folks.'[39]

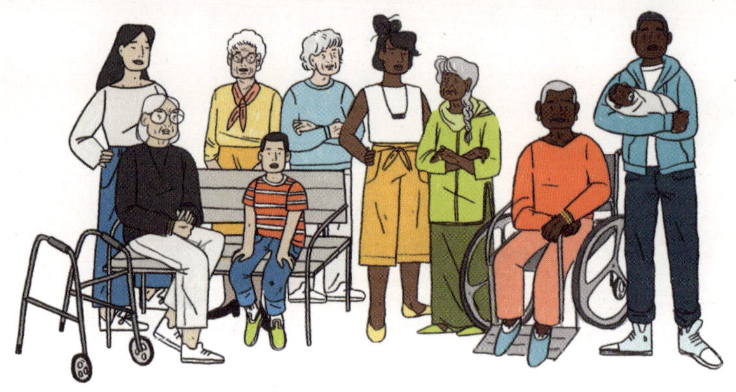

How do care and love become qualities of design work?
The Public runs a studio based on care, not on competition, which is actually a deeply intuitive process, writes Sheila Sampath:

> We know that when we make something, it should be beautiful, but the process and meaning matter more. It's so much more than what you can see. It's what you feel, and what you do, who you do that with, and how you hold them through that process.[40]

They refer to their work as 'a labour of love' and that 'heart' is at the core of The Public, which shows in their logo as well. For some, terms like love and care may seem incompatible with running a design business, but The Public practices this on a daily basis: by making sure their designs aren't harmful, by collaborating and co-creating, and sharing design skills with people who haven't historically been given permission to identify as designers so they can feel confident designing themselves, by embracing a culture of care in a studio is also about fostering a space where celebration and pleasure is as much of a priority as meeting a deadline.[41] Anabel says how she has always been drawn to the 'joyful energy' of The Public. After working for more than a decade, their wish is to keep their relationships in the neighbourhood growing, and to share the creativity and care with more people. Sheila writes,

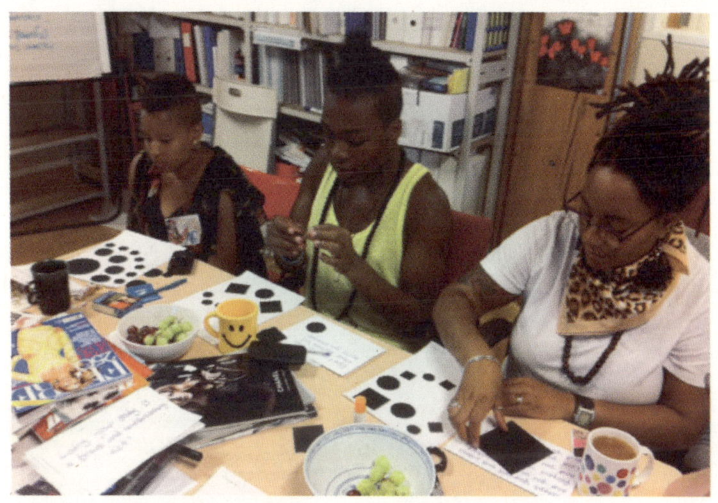

Lately there's been a lot of design studios that do pro-bono or liberal work, but there's no care. They're not invested in the communities they're designing for, and we are.

ANABEL KHOO, THE PUBLIC

If we're trying to negate the harm and violence of this world, we have to do it with care. And actually the 'how' isn't that complex, people *do* know how, it's actually very innate to care for each other. We unlearn care through capitalism, we learn that a deadline is more important than our mental health, that getting ahead of someone is more important than making sure that when you move forward they're standing next to you. Care is re-learning to interact intuitively with the world around us.[42]

What advice can they give designers about engaging in activism? When designers think of activism, they often imagine a poster for a political cause, or they seek out a situation which they assume 'needs their help'. The Public has more than a decade of experience in socially embedded work, and tells other designers that before they engage in radical world-building or designing better

I love using art as a pathway to healing, because art is something that you have to take care of yourself in order to participate in, and it's also an act of care.

KAYA JOAN, THE PUBLIC INTERN

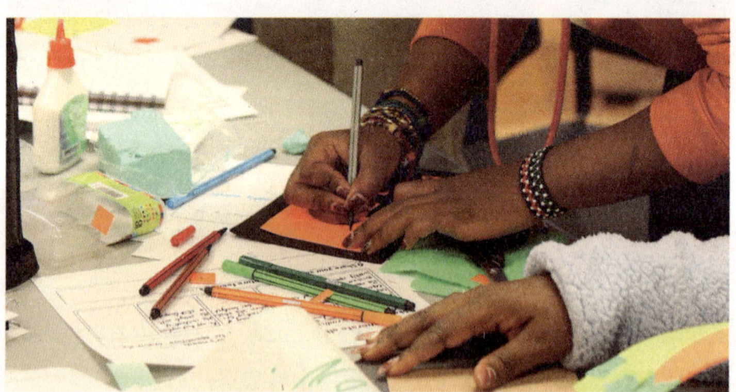

systems, they have to acknowledge and honour the ways many communities are already doing that. Eliminating the distinction between designers and non-designers is one way in which The Public practice this insight. If designers understand their role as facilitators of design rather than as individual creatives, this allows them to expand their activities to education and emotional labour, all of which is highly creative work. Sheila emphasizes that this work is striving towards obsolescence; working towards a future where this work isn't necessary.

> I want us to not have to do that work one day because we will have achieved those things collectively and broadly. So my dream is to not have to do this work, to not have wage labour. That's the long-term dream.[43]

thepublicstudio.ca

↑ Beyond Human-Centred Design workshop for Engineers Without Borders, 2019.
→ Poster to end immigration detention, 2014. Made with Tings Chak.

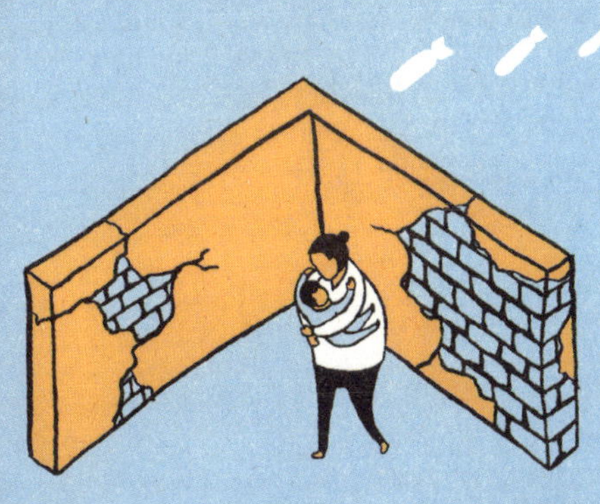

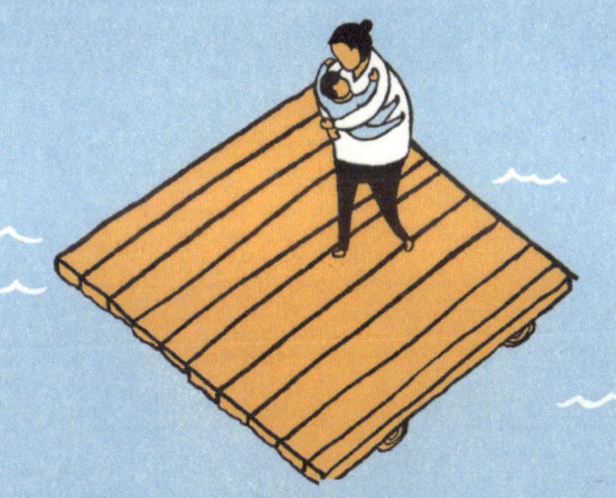

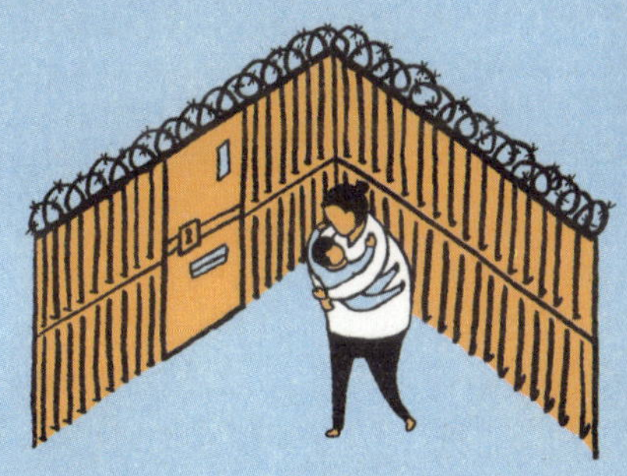

Migration with dignity:
end immigration detention.

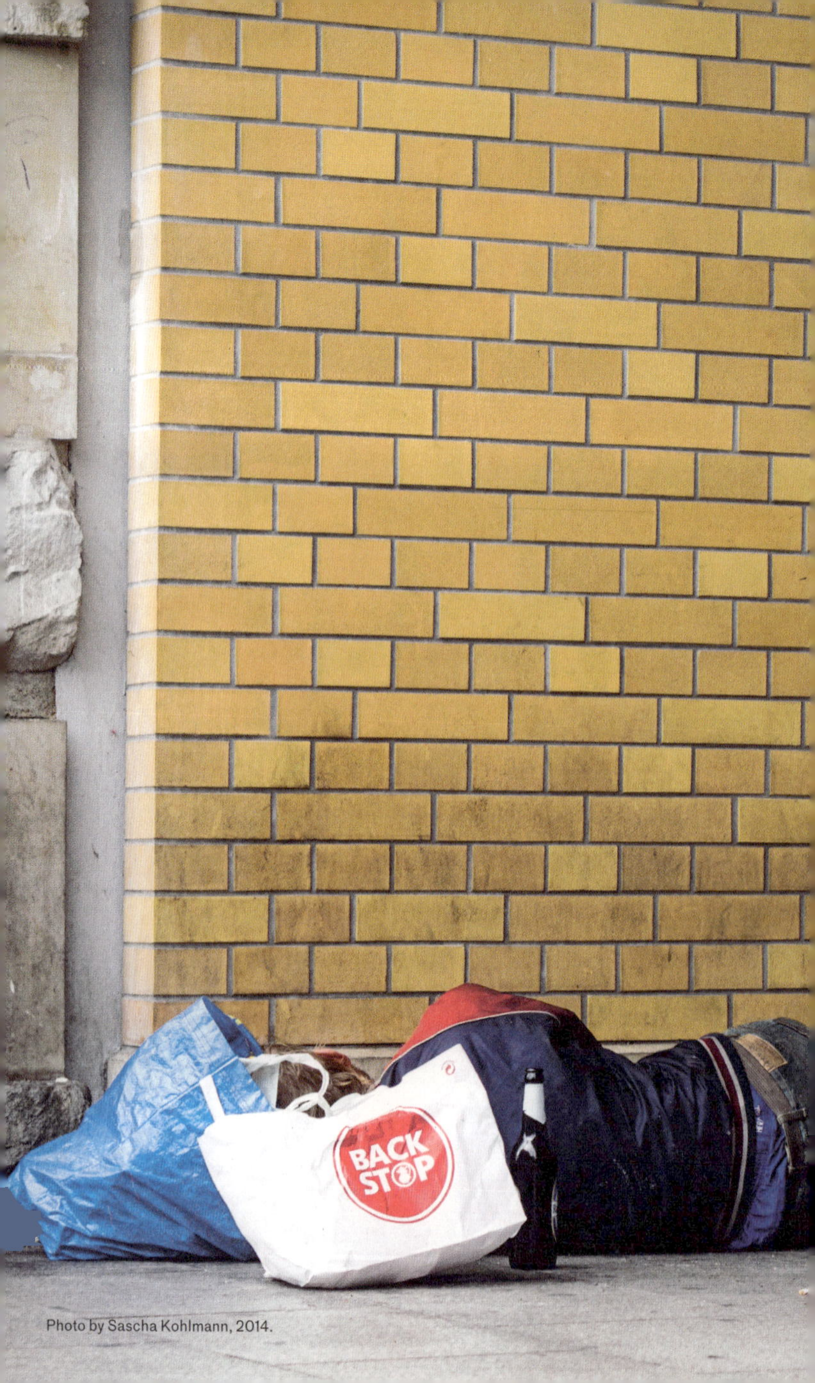

Photo by Sascha Kohlmann, 2014.

PART 4

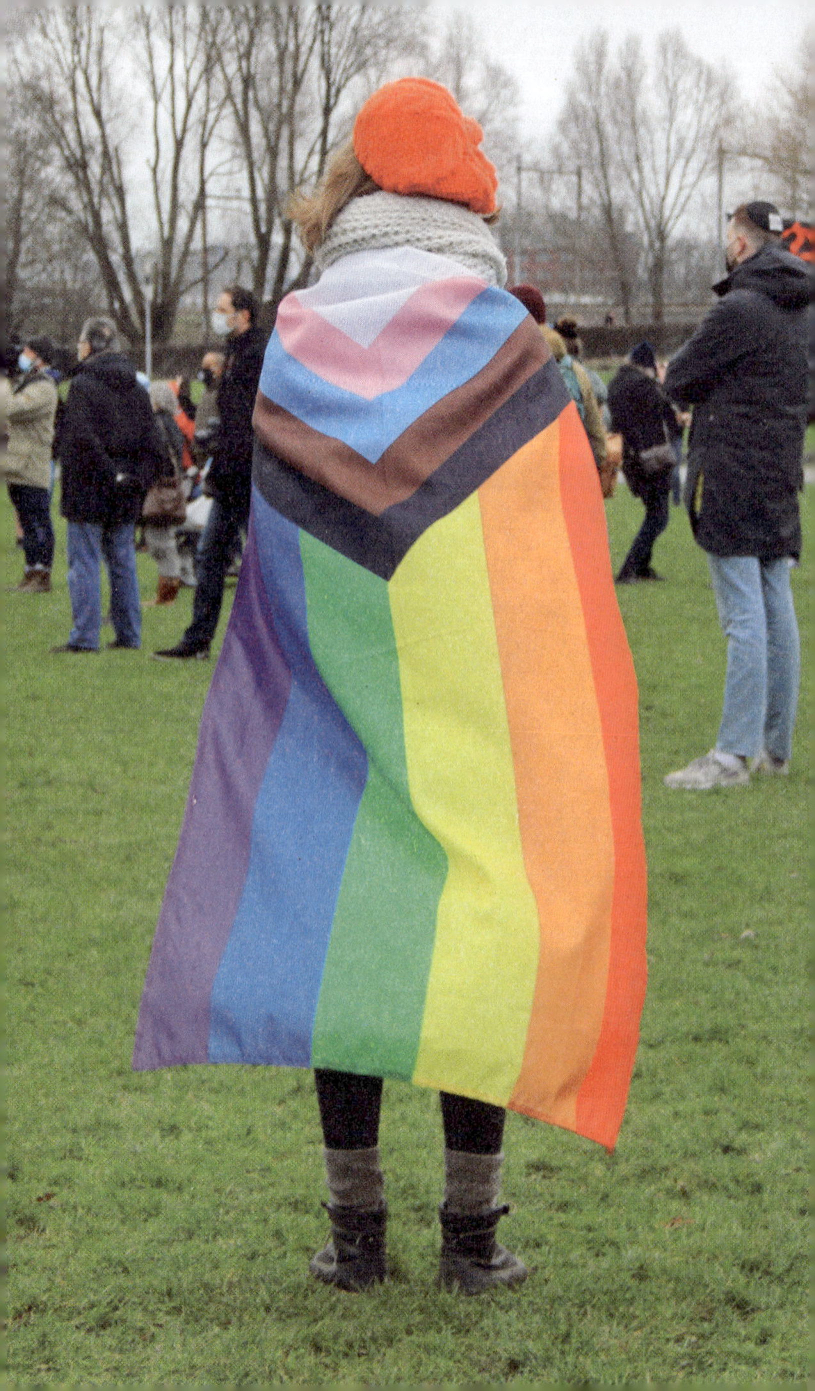

OUTRO

This book has taken up quite a bit of the reader's time to explore how design is related to capitalism. This was necessary because the relationship is too often reduced to simple divisions such as advertising vs. graphic design, or for-profit vs. non-profit clients. Such a simplified understanding of capitalism's role in design inevitably leads to easy fixes, as we have read in the chapters 'The Designer as Futurist' and 'The Designer as Philanthropist'. On the other hand, the realization that capitalism can appropriate all forms of creativity for profit, can easily demotivate and lead to designers doing nothing at all. Using the various roles of the designer, *CAPS LOCK* has attempted to portray a more nuanced, but far from complete image of the relationship between capitalism and graphic design. This preliminary analysis helps us to imagine effective strategies that can be used to resist, counter, and escape capitalism.

The chapters 'The Designer as Scribe' and the 'Designer as Engineer' demonstrated how the design of money, stock market information, bureaucratic documents, and financial records are indispensable for the functioning of international markets. Western scientific ideas about mapmaking, standards, and infographics have come to dominate other forms of knowledge. The fact that these are considered 'neutral', emphasizes how colonialism influenced knowledge systems and how this has helped spread capitalism all over the world. Numerical notation, efficient production, and global standards are necessary to combat global issues such as the climate crisis and inequality. Designers can however place more emphasis on the social relations that they facilitate, rather than understanding every design process exclusively as an industrial process that solves a communication problem for a client. For example, to consider the possibility that templates or industrial

← Anti-fascist demonstration in Amsterdam, 2020. Photo by Laura Colom Urrea.

pre-sets aren't the only options, and that not all visual communication has to result in a new designed object.

'The Designer as Brander' and the 'Designer as Salesperson' retrace how graphic design and advertising are not separate disciplines but have always been intertwined. Graphic design provides capitalism with the ideas, images, and aesthetics to keep increasing demand, especially if that demand is not based on actual needs. Branding and advertising have always existed in some form, and eliminating them does not solve the underlying issue: that the role of the salesperson and brander has overtaken other roles, and everything from education to energy, healthcare and even air is being branded and sold. Graphic design can help to resist the urge to view every social encounter as a sales opportunity.

The chapters on the designer as worker, as entrepreneur, amateur, and as educator provide insights into how the working life of a designer, from an amateur, to a student, to a professional, is shaped by capitalism. Even in its rough outline it becomes clear that the design work is characterized by fierce competition and overwork and that it fetishizes individual achievements. Unhealthy conditions that lead to mental health issues, toxic work environments, and weak social bonds. Too often this aspect is left out of design debates, as if exploitative working conditions within design are the norm. You cannot achieve a more ethical graphic design by having unpaid interns make anti-capitalist posters. In other words: practice what you preach. Here we must stop and think about how to build mutual solidarity among designers, and work together instead of being in constant competition. Different core values can shift away from the capitalist winner-takes-all mentality, and embrace the potential value of a design discipline where everyone can share in the value that designers collectively create.

The closing chapters explored some of the strategies that designers have come up with in response to capitalism. The designer as a hacker is a useful role to critically engage with our means of production. Do we slavishly use tools that multinationals provide, based on patents, copyrights, and renting proprietary software? Or do we create our own tools, or choose to use those made collectively in the digital commons, like the many open-source tools available. A critical use of technology could empower users, allowing them to expand, customize, and learn from digital production rather than being confined or manipulated by them.

Similarly, designing for good, or speculative design, has inspired more designers to actively find ways to contribute to a public cause. A combination of artistic expression and good intentions have swayed museums and conferences to celebrate these as the most valuable emerging forms of design. Speculative design and social design have attracted corporations who appropriate these ideas to create positive press and boost stock value. It becomes clear that forms of futurism or philanthropy in design need to be embedded in communities and linked to real-life situations, in order for the designer to assume full responsibility for the ideas that are put forward. Otherwise, designers and their clients will be part of the enclosure process, and simply profit from crises, instead of supporting structural change.

In the last chapter we found that even claims to design activism serve capitalism, or end up being appropriated indirectly. The fact that activist design is still separated from work that pays the bills, and is seen as outside the designer's personal relationships with colleagues, family, and the community, is central to understanding the problem.

Six design collectives were introduced that show it is possible to practice design more ethically, and still pay the bills. Their experiences show that real-life circumstances require not only a moral compass, but also a personal and practical approach. Common Knowledge (UK) and Cooperativa de Diseño (AR) have embraced the cooperative form, working without bosses and with equal compensation. Open Source Publishing (BE) design typefaces, print work, and websites using only open-source software and publishes everything without copyrights. Collectives such as Mídia NINJA (BR) bring together hundreds of creatives in design and media production, living in communal spaces, following social ideals and using their own currency. Others build strong relationships in their communities, for instance Brave New Alps (IT) and The Public (CA), where they collaborate through workshops and collective projects. The stories of these six design practices are both inspiring and hopeful, and although there are more of these examples, the truth is that they still exist on the outer fringes of design. The challenge is how these tactics can be scaled up to a strategy so they make up a sizable portion of the graphic design discipline, without becoming appropriated for capitalist purposes.

ALT/ESCAPE

We find ourselves dominated by an economic and political system that is to 'too big to fail'. A system that has created a class of ultra-rich billionaires, while the number of people living in extreme poverty is increasing. Because of its enormous impact on people and the planet, capitalism is a system that ultimately threatens life itself. As designers we find ourselves creating endless promotional images for products we don't need, working all-nighters for low wages, while dreaming of becoming star designers. But we are not famous, and we are not only individuals. There are millions of designers all over the world. For centuries our creativity has greased the chain of promotion and consumption, contributing to the wealth of stockholders, a polluted environment, and feelings of depression and anxiety. While freshly discarded flyers and letterheads decorate landfills, we cheerfully present another unnecessary corporate identity for another business, knowing very well it will be rebranded, or merge and disappear within a few years.

There is no way around it, if we want to create a more equal and sustainable world, we have to get rid of capitalism. It is not enough to be a good citizen and vote every few years, and passively wait for some post-capitalist utopia to happen. Anti-capitalist alternatives such as state socialism and communism have been tried, and so far, have turned out to be just as repressive and exploitative as capitalism. A political and societal change will require both mass political organizing, activism, and creating alternative practices to show it can be done differently. On the left side of the political spectrum, some believe that the only solution for an ethical future is to fully embrace technology and economic growth. The idea being that automating all jobs and giving everyone a universal basic income would leave humanity with time to create, to philosophize, to be lazy, and socialize. That would be an amazing future indeed, but if such a system would somehow materialize today, it would almost certainly be limited to the Global North, automatically turning the rest of the world in production regions to pay for what

 CAPS LOCK – Part 4

would be essentially a 'luxury communism'[1] for the few.

Human societies are inherently complex systems with an unimaginable diversity in languages, cultures, and ideas. The modernistic logic of conforming everyone on the planet to one political or economic system is in itself an oppressive concept. That doesn't mean everything should be local or small-scale, because that would testify to a deep lack of understanding of the complexities of today's society. We live in a highly complex economic reality, and global systems of exchange of information and resources are necessary for many different reasons. The climate crisis does require economic degrowth, but this should be seen in local contexts. Europeans are amongst the world's biggest polluters with 20.5 tons CO_2 per capita,[2] while the average Ethiopian emits 0.1 tons of CO_2 per capita.[3] Instead of a one-size-fits-all approach, some regions need accelerated economic growth, while others need degrowth.

CAPS LOCK started with Marx's analysis of capitalism. One of his central ideas is that the economy is not made out of numbers or money, but a collection of social relations between people. That means designers can start experimenting with forging more ethical and sustainable relations, and thereby make new economies in their immediate community. I know that isn't immediately possible for everyone. Many designers are unemployed, unable to survive, or cannot escape working for wages. But there are always small steps one can take. Educate yourself on labour rights, refuse unpaid internships, demand fair wages, boycott all-male panels and conferences that lack diversity, refrain from doing unpaid work, try to organize with colleagues, and speak up against exploitation and malpractices. In the long term, a more comprehensive approach is needed to build new forms of design economies.

COMMON SENSE

Commoning is a strategy that already exists in many parts of society. As previous chapters explained, the commons are from before the very beginning of capitalism, when collective lands called commons were meant for collective or communal uses. These lands were necessary for peasants to survive, where they could grow food and tend cattle, but they were also the places where social life happened. These commons were owned collectively, and were cared for by the peasant community, balancing human needs and ecological sustainability. When you think about it, the commons are a very logical way of organizing society, and these shared spaces were essential to economic and social life before capitalism. Many indigenous cultures have similar ideas of commons known under other names.

Over time the idea of the commons has grown to include not just land, but also water, forests, rivers, and immaterial resources such as knowledge, education, health care, art, science, and digital networks. What unites them is that (at some point) they were freely accessible to everyone and owned collectively rather than privately. Having resources such as water, knowledge, or land accessible to everyone is a very anti-capitalist idea. Under capitalism everything is owned privately. Contrary to capitalism's obsession with the individual, the commons are based on collective use and collective living As Antonio Negri notes 'One cannot live alone, in loneliness, once cannot produce alone, and one cannot love alone.'[4]

A commons is not just about sharing resources, it is a process, a verb: commoning. The idea behind commoning is that shared spaces and resources require continuous care and tending for, and even need to be defended. Just like a river is a collective resource from which many can benefit (drinking water, transport, fishing, washing, irrigation), it also needs to be collectively cared for, in order not to become polluted, or drained by irrigation, or overfished. The reason why so many anti-capitalist initiatives refer to the commons, is that it provides a practical way to create non-capitalist societies on a small scale. Silvia Federici writes that '...a commons-based economy [enables] us to resist dependence on wage labour and subordination to capitalist relations'.[5] In some way, commoning is the continuous act of creating and caring for non-commercial societies.

How do you practice commoning in design? Creating commons doesn't mean creating free typefaces, or publishing graphic design works online for free. If a corporation uses your open-source typeface for a campaign, you are not creating commons, you are just giving capitalism your stuff for free. Just like an urban garden needs to be defended and cared for—otherwise it will be bought by urban developers, or its soil will be depleted when overused—design commons needs to be cared for and defended. Researcher J.M. Pedersen explains this process through 'reciprocity in perpetuity'.[6] Just as the river is a balance between a healthy ecology and providing food and water for the community, giving out free typefaces without any restrictions on use or adaptation doesn't create a healthy design ecology. If designers use free typefaces, they could also add to the commons by sharing their work as well, or help to expand character sets to include more languages. Commons are not about giving everything for free without limit, but extending user rights under certain conditions, which as Fournier writes: 'must not endanger the sustainability of the resource system'.[7]

Bianca Elzenbaumer of Brave New Alps writes in her PhD thesis how commoning could provide a shift from competition to care in the graphic design practice.[8] She points out that a commons-based approach to design also implies there is no strict divide between unpaid work and paid work, but that all work should be valued equally. We see this with the examples from the collectives in the last chapter, which involve the communities in their work (Brave New Alps, The Public, Cooperativa de Diseño), or collectively create new social economies (Mídia NINJA).

There are many examples of commoning in- and outside of design. Social centres, urban gardens, digital commons like the P2P Foundation,[9] and the international farmers organization Via Campesina.[10] This strategy means that designers will have to start creating shared spaces and resources that can create value for people so they don't have to rely on working for a boss for a wage. Only by claiming the value of design work for designers, we can start to create common-based economies that allow more and more designers to survive outside of or without capitalism.

The commons offers an interesting framework to practice ethical forms of graphic design, but it doesn't provide easy answers. Like other roles discussed in this book, commons are continuously created, but are also continuously at risk of being enclosed. The World Bank and Wikinomics have already used the concept of commons for capitalist purposes.[11] Neoliberal politics has issued budgets cuts on health care and welfare, using narratives such as the Big Society in the UK, and the *participatiesamenleving* (participation society) in the Netherlands. While giving tax breaks to corporations, governments demand of citizens to take care of each other by volunteering and providing community aid. We need to be watchful that a push towards a commons-based economy doesn't lead to neoliberal politics of enclosing more collective resources.

That is why commons should be understood 'not as a noun but as a verb, it is an activity without end, without limit' as Max Haiven writes.[12] Just like the common lands that were enclosed, and its users violently expelled from them, the commons that are created today have to be cared for and defended. This requires designers to become organized, using tactics such as mutual aid and horizontal organization, which tie in with earlier concepts in *CAPS LOCK*. If done well, the commons allows for a more wholesome view on society, where value is created collectively, outside of capitalism, and used to care for all members of the community. Its continued need for care and social organization requires stronger social relations among designers and their communities.

The brave collectives convince us that alternatives are not only possible, but there are many ways in which ethical design can exist. They can be completely digital like Common Knowledge, community-based like The Public, or large-scale like Mídia NINJA. We find examples in Europe, North America, and Latin America. If you're inspired to try it yourself, understand that it will not be easy. It will be a slow process, and it will likely not make you rich or famous. If you are willing to take the chance to create an initiative for a more ethical design practice, you can help and inspire others. Perhaps they will try their own versions, and with them you can build a commons with other designers who share knowledge, resources and help each other. When there are many more designers doing that around the world, we are on our way to building a society based on sustainability, social justice, and equality for all.

Ruben Pater

Notes

Intro

1 oxfam.org/en/press-releases/worlds-billion-aires-have-more-wealth-46-billion-people, accessed 10 February 2021.

2 *World Social Report 2020: Inequality in a Rapidly Changing World* (S.I.: United Nations Department of Economic and Social Affairs, 2020).

3 technologyreview.com/2020/12/17/1013213/hunger-starvation-food-policy-history, accessed 10 February 2021.

4 Guy Julier, *Economies of Design* (London: SAGE publishing, 2017), p. 2.

5 Ruben Pater, *The Politics of Design: A (Not So) Global Manual for Visual Communication* (Amsterdam: BIS Publishers, 2016).

PART 1

The Designer as Scribe

1 Johanna Drucker and Emily McVarish, *Graphic Design History: A Critical Guide* (Hoboken: Pearson, 2009), p. 7.

2 Seth Siegelaub and Armand Mattelart, *Communication and Class Struggle: I. Capitalism, Imperialism: An Anthology in 2 Volumes* (New York: International General, 1979), pp. 12–14.

3 Drucker and McVarish, *Graphic Design History*, pp. 53–55.

4 Johanna Drucker, *Graphesis* (Cambridge, MA, and London: Harvard University Press, 2014), p. 84.

5 Liz Alderman, 'Our Cash-Free Future Is Getting Closer', *The New York Times*, 6 July 2020.

6 Lisa Gitelman, *Paper Knowledge: Toward a Media History of Documents* (Durham: Duke University Press, 2014), pp. 1–2.

7 Ibid., p. 4.

8 Jenny Noyes, 'Almost 20 Million Bank Account Records Lost by Commonwealth Bank', *The Sydney Morning Herald*, 2 May 2018.

9 David Graeber, *Debt: The First 5000 Years* (New York: Melville House, 2011), p. 217.

10 One of the first newspapers is considered to be the correspondence by one of the wealthiest families in Europe, the German Fugger family, called the *Fuggerzeitung* (Fugger newspaper), 1568–1605.

11 Martin Luther King Jr., 'The Three Evils of Society' speech at the National Conference on New Politics, Chicago, 31 August 1967.

12 Drucker and McVarish, *Graphic Design History*, p. 106.

13 Interview with Kris Sowersby from Klim Foundry via e-mail, July 2019.

14 gapminder.org/dollar-street, accessed 10 February 2021.

15 Adam Smith, *The Wealth of Nations* (Buffalo: Prometheus Books, 1991), pp. 11–12.

16 Graeber, *Debt*, p. 589.

17 Jon Astbury, 'In for a Penny: The Design Evolution of Money', *The Architectural Review*, 9 April 2014.

18 Graeber, *Debt*, p. 227.

19 Drucker and McVarish, *Graphic Design History*, p. 34.

20 De Heij, 'Designing Banknote Identity', p. 23.

21 Alan Rappeport, 'Harriet Tubman $20 Bill Is Delayed Until Trump Leaves Office, Mnuchin Says', *The New York Times*, 22 May 2019.

22 'Specification of the £1 Coin: A Technical Consultation', *HM Treasury*, 12 September 2014.

23 Ibid.

24 Yuval Noah Harari, *Sapiens: A Brief History of Humankind* (London: Vintage UK, 2015), p. 162.

25 De Heij, 'Designing Banknote Identity', p. 40.

26 Graeber, *Debt*, p. 809.

27 De Heij, 'Designing Banknote Identity', p. 24.

28 Graeber, *Debt*, p. 889.

29 David Pallister, 'How the US Sent $12bn in Cash to Iraq: And Watched It Vanish', *The Guardian*, 8 February 2007.

30 Graeber, *Debt*, p. 956.

31 From an e-mail exchange with Jan van Toorn in July 2019.

32 David Harvey, *A Companion to Marx's Capital* (London: Verso Books, 2010), p. 110.

33 Patrick Mat, '50 years Later: How the Credit Card Has Changed America', *Mercury News*, 14 August 2016. mercurynews.com/2008/09/12/50-years-later-how-the-credit-card-has-changed-america/, accessed 6 August 2019.

34 Jennifer Wheary and Tamara Draut, *Who Pays? The Winners and Losers of Credit Card Deregulation* (New York: Demos, 2007), p. 1.

35 Ibid.

36 Max Haiven, *Cultures of Financialization: Fictitious Capital in Popular Culture and Everyday Life* (London and New York: Macmillan Palgrave, 2014), p. 49.

37 De Heij, 'Designing Banknote Identity', p. 168.

38 Drucker and McVarish, *Graphic Design History*, p. 64.

39 Haiven, *Cultures of Financialization*, p. 102.

40 Rachel O'Dwyer, *Stop Making Money: Valuation and Non-Monetary Utopias*, presentation at Transmediale 2018, Berlin.

41 Cathy O'Neil, *Weapons of Math Destruction: How Big Data Increases Inequality and Threatens Democracy* (New York: Crown Books, 2016), p. 124.

42 Louis Matsakis, 'How the West Got China's Social Credit System Wrong', *WIRED.com*, 29 July 2019. wired.com/story/china-social-credit-score-system/, accessed 7 August 2019.
43 See chapter 'The Designer as Hacker'.
44 James Bridle, *New Dark Age: Technology and the End of the Future* (London and New York: Verso Books, 2018, p. 63.
45 De Heij, 'Designing Banknote Identity', p. 58.
46 christiannold.com/archives/1, accessed 10 February 2021.
47 en.wikipedia.org/wiki/Time-based_currency, accessed 10 February 2021.
48 timebank.cc/, accessed 10 February 2021.

The Designer as Engineer

1 James C. Scott, *Two Cheers for Anarchism: Six Easy Pieces on Autonomy, Dignity and Meaningful Work and Play* (Princeton: Princeton University Press, 2012), p. 35.
2 Witold Kula, *Measures and Men* (Princeton: Princeton University Press, 1986), p. 29.
3 James C. Scott, *Seeing Like a State: How Certain Schemes to Improve the Human Condition* (New Haven: Yale University Press, 1998), p. 28.
4 Ibid., pp. 24, 29–30.
5 Ibid., p. 31.
6 Robin Kinross, *A4 and Before: Towards a Long History of Paper Sizes* (Wassenaar: NIAS, 2009).
7 Alexis C. Madrigal, 'Episode 1: Welcome to Global Capitalism', *Medium*, 7 April 2017, medium.com/containers/episode-1-welcome-to-global-capitalism-f9f56c92f414, accessed 21 August 2019.
8 Michael Hardt and Antonio Negri, *Assembly* (New York: Oxford University Press, 2017), p. 177.
9 Gavin Weightman, 'The History of the Bar Code', *Smithsonian Magazine*, 23 September 2015, smithsonianmag.com/innovation/history-bar-code-180956704, accessed 19 November 2019.
10 Christian Parenti, *The Soft Cage: Surveillance in American from Slavery to the War on Terror* (New York: Basic Books, 2003), p. 99.
11 Benedict Anderson, *Imagined Communities: Reflections on the Origin and Spread of Nationalism* (London: Verso Books, 1983), p. 42.
12 See the collaborative translation project of the encyclopaedia of Diderot and d'Alembert at quod.lib.umich.edu/d/did/, accessed 12 January 2021.
13 Scott, *Two Cheers for Anarchism*, p. 34.
14 Scott, *Seeing Like a State*, 1998, p. 65.
15 Michael Wines, 'The Long History of the U.S. Government Asking Americans Whether They Are Citizens', *The New York Times*, 12 July 2019, nytimes.com/2019/07/12/us/the-long-history-of-the-us-government-asking-americans-whether-they-are-citizens.html, accessed 16 August 2019.
16 See chapter 'The Designer as Scribe'.
17 Parenti, *The Soft Cage*, pp. 19–25.
18 Alison Millington, '23 countries where money can buy you a second passport or "elite residency"', *Business Insider*, 27 December 2018, businessinsider.nl/countries-where-you-can-buy-citizenship-residency-or-passport-2018-9?international=true&r=US, accessed 16 August 2019.
19 Text from femkeherregraven.net/liquid.
20 *I, Daniel Blake*, 2016. Directed by Ken Loach, Sixteen Films.
21 David Graeber, *The Utopia of Rules* (New York: Melville House, 2015), p. 51.
22 Michel Foucault, *Mental Illness and Psychology* (New York: Harper and Row, 1976); *Discipline and Punish: The Birth of the Prison* (New York: Pantheon Books, 1977).
23 This is no figure of speech. In the Netherlands the head of state is a King.
24 Quoted from: Graeber, *The Utopia of Rules*, p. 150.
25 Only eight countries in the world have full equal rights for women. statista.com/chart/17290/countries-with-most-equal-rights-for-women/, accessed 9 January 2021.
26 Drucker, Graphesis, pp. 21–22.
27 Drucker and McVarish, *Graphic Design History*, p. 106.
28 Edward Tufte, *The Visual Display of Quantitative Information* (Cheshire: Graphics Press, 2001), p. 32.
29 William Playfair, *The Commercial and Political Atlas*, 1768, p. 17.
30 Drucker, *Graphesis*, 2014, p. 94.
31 rethinkingeconomics.org, accessed 6 March 2021.
32 Rob Evans, 'Half of England is Owned by Less Than 1% of the Population', *The Guardian*, 17 April 2019.
33 Graeber, *Debt*, p. 24.
34 Max Haiven, 'The Commons Against Neoliberalism, the Commons of Neoliberalism, the Commons Beyond Neoliberalism', in *The Handbook of Neoliberalism*, ed. Simon Springer, Kean Birch, and Julie MacLeavy (New York: Routledge, 2016), p. 259.
35 Ibid.
36 David Turnbull, *Maps Are Territories: Science is an Atlas: A Portfolio of Exhibits* (Chicago: University of Chicago Press, 1993), p. 26.
37 Scott, *Seeing Like a State*, p. 47.
38 Ibid., p. 46.
39 Laura Gottesdiener, 'The Great Eviction: The Landscape of Wall Street's Creative Destruction', *The Nation*, 1 August 2013.
40 Walter D. Mignolo, *The Darker Side of Western Modernity: Global Futures, Decolonial Options* (Durham: Duke University Press, 2011), p. 3.
41 Anderson, *Imagined Communities*, 1983, p. 174.
42 Wood, *The Origins of Capitalism*, pp. 110–111
43 Mignolo, *The Darker Side of Western Modernity*, p. 155.
44 Walter D. Mignolo, *The Darker Side of the Renaissance: Literacy, Territoriality & Colonization*

(Ann Arbor: University of Michigan Press, 1995), p. 270.

45 Mignolo, *The Darker Side of Western Modernity*, pp. 183–184.

46 Tom Keefer, 'A Short Introduction to the Two Row Wampum', *Briar Patch Magazine*, 10 March 2014, briarpatchmagazine.com/articles/view/a-short-introduction-to-the-two-row-wampum, accessed 30 August 2019.

47 Scott, *Two Cheers for Anarchism*, p. 53.

48 P. Utrilla et al., 'A Palaeolithic Map from 13,660 calBP: Engraved Stone Blocks from the Late Magdalenian in Abauntz Cave (Navarra, Spain)', *Journal of Human Evolution* 57, no. 2 (2009).

The Designer as Brander

1   Pater, *The Politics of Design*, p. 135.

2   Harari, *Sapiens*, pp. 26–27.

3   Graeber, *Debt*, pp. 188–189.

4   Boris Badenov, 'As many enemies as there are slaves: Spartacus and the politics of servile rebellion in the late republic', *Libcom.org*, 8 June 2010, libcom.org/history/many-enemies-there-are-slaves%E2%80%99-spartacus-politics-servile-rebellion-late-republic, accessed 17 January 2021.

5   Simone Browne, *Dark Matters: On the Surveillance of Blackness* (Durham: Duke University Press, 2015), p. 99.

6   Instructions for branding set out by *de Middelburgsche Commercie Compagnie*, or the Trade Company of Middelburg, a Dutch charter company that later displaced the WIC in slave trading. Quoted from Browne, *Dark Matters*, p. 99.

7   Ibid., p. 100.

8   Ben Haring, 'Identity Marks in Ancient Egypt: Scribal and Non-Scribal Modes of Visual Communication', in *Non-scribal Communication Media in the Bronze Age Aegean and Surrounding Areas: The semantics of a-literate and proto-literate media (seals, potmarks, mason's marks, seal-impressed pottery, ideograms and logograms, and related systems)*, eds. A.M. Jasink, J. Weingarten and S. Ferrara (Florence: Firenze University Press, 2017), p. 241.

9   Philip B. Meggs and Alston W. Purvis, *Meggs' History of Graphic Design* (Hoboken: Wiley, 2011), p. 412.

10 Ellen Lupton and J. Abbott Miller, *Design, Writing, Research: Writing on Graphic Design* (London: Phaidon Press, 1999), p. 177.

11 Naomi Klein, *No Logo: Taking Aim at the Brand Bullies* (New York: Vintage Canada, 2009), pp. 7.

12 ama.org/topics/branding.

13 Klein, *No Logo*, p. 345.

14 Ibid., p. 345.

15 Charles Zuber, 'The Logo That Lasted', *Design Online*, 2017, designonline.org.au/the-logo-that-lasted/, accessed 18 January 2021.

16 Ned Dymoke, '5 of the Richest Companies in History', *The Big Think*, 17 October 2018, bigthink.com/culture-religion/5-of-the-richest-companies-in-history?rebelltitem=2#rebelltitem2.

17 Klein, *No Logo*, p. 221.

18 Meggs and Purvis, *Meggs' History of Graphic Design*, p. 425.

19 Drucker and McVarish, *Graphic Design History*, p. 269.

20 Aaron Kenedi, 'Marks Men: An Interview with Ivan Chermayeff, Tom Geismar, and Sagi Haviv of Chermayeff & Geisma', *Printmag*, 14 September 2011, printmag.com/post/marks-men-an-interview-with-ivan-chermayeff-tom-geismar-and-sagi-haviv-of-chermayeff-geismar-2, accessed 18 January 2021.

21 Milan Babic, Eelke Heemskerk and Jan Fichtner, 'Who is More Powerful – States or Corporations?', *The Conversation*, 10 July 2018, theconversation.com/who-is-more-powerful-states-or-corporations-99616, accessed 18 January 2021.

22 Gary Shteyngart, *Super Sad True Love Story: A Novel* (New York: Random House, 2010).

23 European Economic and Social Committee, *Fake Products Cost 800,000 Jobs Annually*, 18 July 2017, eesc.europa.eu/en/news-media/news/fake-products-cost-800000-jobs-annually, accessed 23 December 2019.

24 Nicolas Maigret and Maria Roszkowska, *The Pirate Book* (self-published, 2015), p. 121.

25 ec.europa.eu/growth/content/too-good-be-true-real-price-fake-products_en, accessed 8 March 2021.

26 Maigret and Roszkowska, *The Pirate Book*, p. 217.

27 Quoted from Maigret and Roszkowska, *The Pirate Book*, p. 161.

28 Klein, *No Logo*, p. 36.

29 Ibid., p. 29.

30 Marina Vishmidt, Vinca Kruk and Daniel van der Velden, eds., *Uncorporate Identity: Metahaven* (Zurich: Lars Muller, 2010), p. 490.

31 UNCTAD, *World Investment Report 2019: Special Economic Zones* (New York: United Nations Publications, 2019), xii.

32 Klein, *No Logo*, p. 201.

33 Trevor Paglen and A.C. Thompson, *Torture Taxi: On the Trail of the CIA's Rendition Flights* (London: Icon Books, 2006).

34 Richard L. Florida, *The Rise of the Creative Class: And How It's Transforming Work, Leisure, Community and Everyday Life* (New York: Basic Books, 2002).

35 Chip Kidd, 'An Interview with Milton Glaser', *Believer Magazine*, 1 September 2003, believermag.com/an-interview-with-milton-glaser/, accessed 14 October 2019.

36 William K. Tabb, *The Long Default: New York City and the Urban Fiscal Crisis* (New York: Monthly Review Press, 1982), pp. 11–12.

37 Ibid., p. 39.

38 David Harvey, *A Brief History of Neoliberalism* (Oxford: Oxford University Press, 2005), p. 45.

39 Tabb, *The Long Default*, p. 30.

40 Harvey, *A Brief History of Neoliberalism*, p. 2.

41 Kidd, 'An Interview with Milton Glaser'.

42 Information from the Amsterdam marketing website iamsterdam.com/en/business/investment-opportunities, accessed 13 October 2019.

43 2016 figures. nos.nl/artikel/2171069-airbnb-ruim-verdubbeld-in-amsterdam-1-7-miljoen-overnachtingen; amsterdamsdagblad.nl/gemeente/aantal-ontruimingen-corporatie-woningen-historisch-laag-in-amsterdam.

44 yuriveerman.nl/Van-wie-is-de-stad, accessed 13 October 2019.

45 Wouter van Loon and Thijs Niemantsverdriet, 'Airbnb-verhuur Amsterdam stijgt verder door', *NRC Handelsblad*, 8 May 2019.

46 underconsideration.com/brandnew/.

47 Louise Story, 'Anywhere the Eye Can See, It's Likely to See an Ad', *The New York Times*, 15 January 2007.

The Designer as Salesperson

1 James Rorty, *Our Masters Voice: Advertising* (New York: The John Day Company, 1934), p. 134.

2 'The Entire History of Advertising', *Softcube Blog*, 4 August 2020, softcube.com/the-entire-history-of-advertising/, accessed 19 January 2021.

3 See the enclosure of the commons in chapter 'The Designer as Engineer'.

4 Anne McClintock, *Imperial Leather: Race, Gender, and Sexuality in the Colonial Context* (New York: Routledge, 1995), p. 210.

5 Ibid., p. 208.

6 Ibid., p. 210.

7 Ibid., p. 211.

8 Ibid., p. 223.

9 Ibid., p. 209.

10 Edward Bernays, *Propaganda* (New York: Horace Liveright, 1928), p. 52.

11 Vance Packard, *The Hidden Persuaders* (New York: David McKay, 1957), p. 114.

12 Thomas C. Frank, *The Conquest of Cool: Business Culture, Counterculture, and the Rise of Hip Consumerism* (Chicago: University of Chicago Press, 1997), p. 46.

13 Ibid., p. 106.

14 Klein, *No Logo*, pp. 29–33.

15 Ibid., p. 32.

16 Ibid., p. 24.

17 Nick Bell, 'Brand Madness: The Steamroller of Branding', *Eye Magazine* 14, no. 53 (2004).

18 David Harvey, *The Condition of Postmodernity: An Inquiry into the Origins of Cultural Exchange* (Hoboken: Wiley-Blackwell, 1991), pp. 16, 17, 343.

19 Ibid., p. 22.

20 Story, 'Anywhere the Eye Can See'.

21 Harvey, *A Companion to Marx's Capital*, pp. 39–41.

22 Karl Marx, *Capital, Vol. 1 & 2* (Hertfordshire: Wordsworth, 2013), pp. 46–55.

23 Harvey, *A Companion to Marx's Capital*, p. 46.

24 Berger, *Ways of Seeing* (London: Penguin Books, 1972), p. 139.

25 Deyan Sudjic, *The Language of Things* (London: Penguin Books, 2008), p. 63.

26 Berger, *Ways of Seeing*, p. 132.

27 *World's billionaires have more wealth than 4.6 billion people*, Oxfam International, 20 January 2020, oxfam.org/en/press-releases/worlds-billionaires-have-more-wealth-46-billion-people, accessed 20 January 2021.

28 *First Things First Manifesto*, 1964, designishistory.com/1960/first-things-first/, accessed 20 January 2021.

29 Ibid.

30 Bill Morton, 'An Overview of International NGOs in Development Cooperation', *United Nations Development Programme*, 2011.

31 Joanna Boehnert, *Design, Ecology, Politics: Towards the Ecocene* (London and Oxford: Bloomsbury, 2018), p. 46.

32 Oli Mould, *Against Creativity* (London: Verso Books, 2018).

33 Boehnert, *Design, Ecology, Politics*, pp. 5–6.

34 *First Things First Manifesto*.

35 Daniel van der Velden, 'Research and Destroy', *Metropolis M* no. 2, April/May 2006.

36 See chapters 'The Designer as Worker' and 'The Designer as Entrepreneur'.

37 David Ogilvy, *On Advertising* (New York: Vintage Books, 1985), p. 25.

38 Nick Srnicek, *Platform Capitalism* (Cambridge, UK: Polity Press, 2017), p. 70.

39 Charles Arthur, 'Marissa Mayer's appointment: What does it mean for Yahoo?', *The Guardian*, 16 July 2012, theguardian.com/technology/2012/jul/16/marissa-mayer-appointment-mean-yahoo, accessed 19 January 2021.

40 Shoshana Zuboff, *The Age of Surveillance Capitalism* (New York: Hachette, 2019), p. 271.

41 Ibid., pp. 292–301.

42 Maurits Martijn and Jesse Frederik, 'Dit is de nieuwe internetbubbel: Online advertenties', *De Correspondent*, 19 January 2019.

43 Martijn and Frederik, 'De (on)zin van online advertenties.'

44 See chapter 'The Designer as a Hacker' for more strategies.

45 Paul Mason, *Postcapitalism* (London: Allen Lane, 2015), p. 128.

46 Frances Thomson and Sahil Dutta, *Financialisation: A Primer*, The Transnational Institute, 13 September 2018, tni.org/en/publication/financialisation-a-primer, accessed 19 January 2021.

47 Patrick Greenfield, 'Apple apologises for slowing down older iPhones with ageing batteries', *The Guardian*, 29 December 2017.

48 Marjanne van Helvert, ed., *The Responsible Object: A History of Design Ideology for the Future* (Amsterdam: Valiz Publishers, 2016), p. 110.

49 Naomi Klein, *The Shock Doctrine* (New York: Metropolitan Books, 2007).

50 Which affected 500,000 and killed more than 2,000 people.

51 See bcw-global.com and en.wikipedia.org/wiki/Burson_Cohn_%26_Wolfe.

52 Armin, 'News: News Corp New Corporate Logo', *Brand New*, 29 May 2013. underconsideration.com/brandnew/archives/news_news_corp_new_corporate_logo.php, accessed 19 January 2021.

53 Peeling Back the Truth on Bananas, Food Empowerment Project, 28 April 2020, foodispower.org/our-food-choices/bananas/, accessed 19 January 2019.

54 Daniel Kurtz-Phelan, 'Big Fruit', *The New York Times*, 2 March 2008.

55 Declassified diplomatic cable from 29 December 1929, web.archive.org/web/20120609172903/http://www.icdc.com/~paulwolf/colombia/caffery29dec1928.htm, accessed 19 January 2021.

56 Gabriel Fonnegra, Bananeras testimonio vivo de una epopeya (Bogotá: Tercer Mundo, 1980).

57 Vishmidt, Kruk and Van der Velden, *Uncorporate Identity*.

58 Stefanie Goodman, 'Labor Abuse and Exploitation: The Dark Side of Ecuador's Banana Industry', *Borgen Magazine*, 12 November 2020, borgenmagazine.com/labor-abuse-and-exploitation-the-dark-side-of-ecuadors-banana-industry/, accessed 20 January 2021.

59 A YouGov poll between July and October 2020, today.yougov.com/topics/food/explore/brand/Chiquita, accessed 20 January 2021.

60 Ogilvy, op. cit., p. 216.

61 David Evan Harris, 'São Paulo: A City Without Ads', *Adbusters*, 3 August 2007, adbusters.org/article/sao-paulo-a-city-without-ads/, accessed 19 January 2021.

62 Araw Mahdawi, 'Can Cities Kick Ads? Inside the Global Movement to Ban Urban Billboards', *The Guardian*, 12 August 2015.

63 Paul Skeldon, 'Young Affiliates: Nearly a Fifth of British Children Aspire to be Social Media Influencers', *Telemedia Magazine*, 31 January 2019, telemediaonline.co.uk/young-affiliates-nearly-a-fifth-of-british-children-aspire-to-be-social-media-influencers/, accessed 19 January 2021.

64 Berger, *Ways of Seeing*, p. 139.

65 Boehnert, *Design, Ecology, Politics*, p. 6.

66 Victor J. Papanek, *Design for the Real World: Human Ecology and Social Change* (New York: Pantheon Books, 1972).

PART 2

The Designer as Worker

1 news.gallup.com/poll/1720/work-workplace.aspx, accessed 20 January 2021.

2 AIGA Design Census 2019, designcensus.org/, accessed 20 January 2021.

3 Vivek Chibber, *Understanding Capitalism: The ABCs of Capitalism* (New York: Jacobin Foundation, 2018).

4 James E. Thorold Rogers, *Six Centuries of Work and Wages: The History of English Labour* (London: Allen and Unwin, 1949), pp. 542–543.

5 Andrea Komlosy, *Work: The Last 1,000 Years* (London: Verso Books, 2018), p. 106.

6 Silvia Federici, *Caliban and the Witch: Women, the Body and Primitive Accumulations* (New York: Autonomedia, 2004), p. 25.

7 See chapter 'The Designer as Engineer'.

8 Harry Magdoff, 'The Meaning of Work: A Marxist Perspective', *The Monthly Review*, 1 October 2006, monthlyreview.org/2006/10/01/the-meaning-of-work-a-marxist-perspective/, accessed 28 July 2020.

9 Komlosy, *Work*, p. 28.

10 Thanks to Silvio Lorusso for suggesting this bible quote.

11 Max Weber, *The Protestant Ethic and the Spirit of Capitalism* (New York: Routledge, 2001), p. 44.

12 Kathi Weeks, *The Problems with Work* (Durham: Duke University Press, 2011), p. 11.

13 Edwin Chadwick, *The Sanitary Condition of the Labouring Population, Poor Law Commissioners*, Home Office, 1842.

14 Scott, *Two Cheers for Anarchism*, p. 68.

15 Weeks, *The Problems with Work*, p. 63.

16 Kate Hodal, 'One in 200 People is a Slave: Why?', *The Guardian*, 25 February 2019.

17 Emily Guendelsberger, *On The Clock: What Low-Wage Work Did to Me and How It Drives America Insane* (Boston: Little, Brown, and Company, 2019), p. 87.

18 Guy Julier, *Economies of Design* (London: SAGE Publication, 2017), p. 22.

19 These examples are from my own fourteen years work of experience at design studios in the Netherlands and in the US.

20 Adrian Shaughnessy, *How to Be a Graphic Designer, without Losing Your Soul* (Princeton: Princeton Architectural Press, 2005), p. 33.

21 Ibid., p. 35.

22 Van der Velden, 'Research and Destroy'.

23 Shaughnessy, *How to Be a Graphic Designer, without Losing Your Soul*, p. 122.

24 Julia Anixter, 'Equal Pay in Design: How Do We Make It a Reality?', *AIGA.org*, 12 April 2016, aiga.org/equal-pay-day-for-women-in-design, accessed 20 January 2021.

25 Brave New Alps, *Designers' Inquiry*, 2013, brave-new-alps.com/designers-inquiry/.

26 Meg Miller, 'What Does It Mean to Unionize When You're Your Own Boss?', *AIGA Eye on Design*, 22 October 2019, eyeondesign.aiga.org/what-does-it-mean-to-unionize-when-youre-your-own-boss/, accessed 20 January 2021.

27 Shaughnessy, *How to Be a Graphic Designer, without Losing Your Soul*, p. 76.

28 'Nike workers don't earn 20 cents an hour or work 80 hours a week', *Africa Check*, 14 August 2019, africacheck.org/fact-checks/fbchecks/nike-workers-dont-earn-20-cents-hour-or-work-80-hours-week, accessed 20 January 2021.

29 Marx, *Capital, Vol. I*, pp. 120–160.
30 Gary Becker, 'The Economic Way of Looking at Life' (9 December 1992), in *Nobel Lecture: Economics 1991–1995*, ed. Tosten Persson (Singapore: World Scientific Publishing, 1997), pp. 38–58.
31 'Rising inequality affecting more than two-thirds of the globe, but it's not inevitable: New UN report', *UN News*, 21 January 2020, news.un.org/en/story/2020/01/1055681, accessed 21 January 2021.
32 '5 shocking facts about extreme global inequality and how to even it up', *Oxfam*, 21 October 2019, oxfam.org/en/5-shocking-facts-about-extreme-global-inequality-and-how-even-it, accessed 21 January 2021.
33 Dominic Rushe, 'US bosses now earn 312 times the average worker's wage, figures show', *The Guardian*, 16 August 2018.
34 Precarious Workers Brigade, *Training for Exploitation? Politicising Employability and Reclaiming Education* (London: Journal of Aesthetics & Protest Press, 2017), p. 12.
35 Aggie Toppins, 'Designers, Please Pay Your Interns', *AIGA Eye on design*, 4 January 2018, eyeondesign.aiga.org/designers-please-pay-your-interns/, accessed 20 January 2021.
36 Seb Chan, 'Museum Resolution: Do Away with Salary Cloaking', *The Walker Reader*, 12 March 2021. walkerart.org/magazine/soundboard-museum-resolutions-seb-chan, accessed 20 January 2021.
37 Evening Class, 'Open Letter: Against Undisclosed Salaries', *The Pluralist*, 23 April 2020, thepluralist.info/Open-Letter-Against-Undisclosed-Salaries, accessed 20 January 2021.
38 'Anthony Burrill tells us about his numerous Etsy WORK HARD rip-offs', *It's Nice That*, 26 November 2015, itsnicethat.com/articles/anthony-burril-plagiarism-work-hard-be-nice-to-people, accessed 20 January 2021.
39 From the website of designer Ben Barry: v1.benbarry.com/, accessed 20 January 2021.
40 Evening Class survey.
41 *BNO Branchemonitor: De Nederlandse ontwerpsector in beeld en getal*, January 2020, p. 11.
42 *AIGA Design Census 2019*, designcensus.org/, accessed 20 January 2021.
43 Sarah Pflug, 'Overwork isn't heroic: Tips from creatives on how to be a success without overdoing it', *Creative Boom*, 3 September 2018, creativeboom.com/tips/how-to-be-successful-without-working-too-hard/, accessed 20 January 2021.
44 Shaughnessy, *How to Be a Graphic Designer, without Losing Your Soul*, p. 74.
45 Zoë Schlanger, 'Daylight Saving Time as Americans know it was instituted by corporate lobbies, not farmers', *Quartz*, 4 November 2017, qz.com/1120488/daylight-saving-time-as-americans-know-it-was-instituted-by-corporate-lobbies-not-farmers/, accessed 13 August 2019.
46 ourworldindata.org/working-hours, accessed 25 January 2021.
47 James Suzman, 'Why "Bushman Banter" was Crucial to Hunter-Gatherers' Evolutionary Success', *The Guardian*, 29 October 2017.
48 *AIGA Design Census 2019*, designcensus.org/, accessed 20 January 2021.
49 Harvey, *A Companion to Marx's Capital*, pp. 274–275.
50 Van der Velden, 'Research and Destroy'.
51 Richard Sennett, *The Corrosion of Character: The Personal Consequences of Work in the Capitalism* (New York: W.W. Norton & Co., 1998), p. 44.
52 Shaughnessy, *How to Be a Graphic Designer, without Losing Your Soul*, p. 37.
53 Precarious Workers Brigade, *Training for Exploitation?*, p. 9.
54 Silvio Lorusso, *Entreprecariat: Everyone is an Entrepreneur: Nobody is Safe* (Eindhoven: Onomatopee, 2019).
55 Mark Fisher, *Capitalist Realism: Is There No Alternative?* (New York: Verso Books, 2009), p. 19.
56 Brave New Alps, *Designers' Inquiry*, p. 24.
57 Fisher, *Capitalist Realism*, p. 36.
58 Lynn Berger, 'In onze prestatiemaatschappij is iedereen een marathonloper (maar waar rennen we heen?)', *De Correspondent*, 4 August 2020, decorrespondent.nl/11458/in-onze-prestatiemaatschappij-is-iedereen-een-marathonloper-maar-waar-rennen-we-heen/381769102-565bca5a, accessed 20 January 2021.
59 Guy Debord, *Oeuvres*, ed. Jean-Louis Rançon (Paris: Gallimard, 2006), marxists.org/reference/archive/debord/1963/never-work.htm, accessed 21 January 2021.
60 Weeks, *The Problems with Work*, p. 79.
61 Ibid., p. 98.
62 Komlosy, *Work*, p. 68.
63 Precarious Workers Brigade, *Training for Exploitation?*, p. 16.
64 These solutions are inspired by the document 'Some Solutions' by Evening Class, UK, 2018.
65 Miller, 'What Does It Mean to Unionize When You're Your Own Boss?'
66 Johana Bhuiyan, 'The Google Walkout: What Protesters Demanded and What They Got', *LA Times*, 6 November 2019.
67 Jack Shenker, 'Strike 2.0: How Gig Economy Workers are Using Tech to Fight Back', *The Guardian*, 31 August 2019.
68 vloerwerk.org, accessed 11 February 2021.
69 uvwunion.org.uk/design-culture-workers, accessed 21 January 2021.
70 Perrin Drumm, 'Can We Design a More Perfect Design Union?', *AIGA Eye on design*, 19 June 2018, eyeondesign.aiga.org/can-we-design-a-more-perfect-design-union/, accessed 21 January 2021; 'This is What Starting a Design "Union" Looks Like', *AIGA Eye on design*, 19 June 2018, eyeondesign.aiga.org/this-is-what-starting-a-design-union-looks-like/, accessed 5 July 2018.
71 uvwunion.org.uk/design-culture-workers, accessed 21 January 2021.
72 More about co-ops here backspace.com/

notes/2005/09/collectives-for-designers.
php, accessed 21 January 2021.

73 'Understanding the Seven Cooperative
Principles', *NCREA*, 1 December 2016,
electric.coop/seven-cooperative-princi-
ples%E2%80%8B, accessed 21 January
2021.

74 Danielle Aubert, 'The Politics of the Joy of
Printing in Detroit*', *Infinite mile Detroit*,
no. 29, June 2016, infinitemiledetroit.com/
THE_POLITICS_OF_THE_JOY_OF_
PRINTING_IN_DETROIT.html,
accessed 21 January 2021.

75 See chapter 'The Designer as Activist'.

76 Nick Srnicek and Alex Williams, *Inventing the
Future: Postcapitalism and a World Without
Work* (London: Verso Books, 2015), p. 93.

77 See chapter 'The Designer as Activist'.

78 Ibid.

The Designer as Entrepreneur

1 Steven Heller and Lita Talarico, *The Design
Entrepreneur: Turning Graphic Design Into
Goods That Sell* (Beverly: Rockport
Publishers, 2008).

2 Perrin Drumm, 'Equity Investing is Expensive,
Risky, and Slow: So Why Are All These
Designers Trying to Become Venture Capitalists?', *AIGA Eye on design*, 28 August 2017,
eyeondesign.aiga.org/equity-investing-is-
expensive-risky-and-slow-so-why-are-all-
these-designers-trying-to-become-venture-
capitalists/, accessed 22 January 2021.

3 Michael T. Deane, 'Top 6 Reasons New Businesses Fail', *Investopedia*, 28 February 2020,
investopedia.com/financial-edge/1010/
top-6-reasons-new-businesses-fail.aspx,
accessed 22 January 2021.

4 See chapter 'The Designer as Futurist'.

5 Mould, *Against Creativity*, p. 28.

6 Read more about the early internet in the
chapter 'The Designer as Hacker'.

7 Newton Lee, *Facebook Nation: Total
Information Awareness* (New York: Springer,
2012), p. 201.

8 *AIGA Design Census 2019*.

9 'We Surveyed Gender Representation at
Design Conferences Again—and Not Much
Has Changed', *Eye on design*, 16 January
2020, eyeondesign.aiga.org/we-surveyed-
gender-equity-at-design-conferences-again-
and-not-much-has-changed/, accessed 20
January 2021.

10 Lucienne Roberts et al., eds., *Graphic
Designers Surveyed* (London:
GraphicDesign&, 2015).

11 Haiven, *Cultures of Financialization*, p. 50.

12 More on mental health see chapter 'Designer
as Worker'.

13 itsnicethat.com/news/graphic-designers-
surveyed-results-150116.

14 *Graphic Design forum*, graphicdesignforum.
com/t/micro-managing-boss-or-just-a-
regular-creative-director/13149/7, accessed

15 Haiven, *Cultures of Financialization*,
pp. 129–130.

16 'Educated, Overworked, Underpaid: Graphic
Designers Surveyed', *It's Nice That*, 15
January 2016, itsnicethat.com/news/
graphic-designers-surveyed-results-150116,
accessed 22 January 2021.

17 Sarah Boris, 'The Design Industry Needs to
Take a Stand Against Free Pitching', *EYE
on design*, 15 May 2019, eyeondesign.aiga.
org/the-design-industry-needs-to-take-a-
stand-against-free-pitching/, accessed 22
January 2021.

18 'Anti-Competitive Agreements', *European
Commission*, 16 April 2012, ec.europa.eu/
competition/consumers/agreements_
en.html, accessed 22 January 2021.

19 Heller and Talarico, *The Design Entrepreneur*,
p. 40.

20 Richard Sennett, 'The Workshop', in *The
Craftsman* (London: Penguin Books, 2008),
p. 113.

21 Drucker and McVarish, *Graphic Design
History*, p. 74.

22 Fredric Jameson quoted in: Harvey,
The Condition of Postmodernity, p. 63.

23 Gerry Beegan and Paul Atkinson, 'Professionalism, Amateurism and the Boundaries of
Design', *Journal of Design History* 21,
no. 4 (2008).

24 'What is a labour union?', *Evening class*, 27
June 2018.

25 Two trillion is two million-million,
$2,000,000,000,000.

26 Aggie Toppins, 'Can We Teach Graphic
Design History Without the Cult of Hero
Worship?', *AIGA Eye on design*, 29 May 2020,
eyeondesign.aiga.org/can-we-teach-graph-
ic-design-history-without-the-cult-of-hero-
worship/, accessed 22 January 2021.

27 Shaughnessy, *How to be a graphic designer,
without losing your soul*, p. 64.

28 See chapter 'The Designer as Worker'.

29 Lily Smith, 'T-Mobile is suing a company for
using magenta: Can it really "own" a color?',
Fast Company, 29 November 2019, fastcom-
pany.com/90436680/t-mobile-is-suing-a-
company-for-using-magenta-can-it-really-
own-a-color, accessed 25 January 2021.

30 Haiven, 'The Commons Against
Neoliberalism', p. 264.

31 Erik Olin Wright, 'Destination Beyond
Capitalism', in *How to Be an Anticapitalist
in the Twenty-First Century* (London: Verso
Books, 2019), p. 173.

32 creativecommons.org, accessed 25 January
2021.

33 en.wikipedia.org/wiki/Copyleft, accessed 22
January 2021.

34 Sarah Grey, 'Four Myths About the 'Freelancer Class', *Jacobin Magazine*, 5 July 2015,
jacobinmag.com/2015/05/freelance-in-
dependent-contractor-union-precariat,
accessed 22 January 2021.

35 *Occupational Outlook Handbook*, US Bureau

for labor statistics, 1 September 2020, bls.
gov/ooh/arts-and-design/graphic-design-
ers.htm#tab-3, accessed 22 January 2021.

36 Depending on country or state this may vary.

37 'Amsterdammer verlamd na ernstig fietsongeluk: "Ik mis de oude Lars heel erg"', *NH
Nieuws*, 23 March 2017.

38 Silvio Lorusso, 'Fake It till You Make It: Genesis of the Entrepreneurial Precariat', *Entreprecariat, Institute of Network Cultures*, 22 May
2018, networkcultures.org/entreprecariat/
fake-it-till-you-make-it-genesis-of-the-
entrepreneurial-precariat/, accessed 22
January 2021.

39 'Van werkenden loopt zzp'er meeste risico op
armoede', *CBS*, 5 March 2019, cbs.nl/nl-nl/
nieuws/2019/10/van-werkenden-loopt-zzp-
er-meeste-risico-op-armoede, accessed 22
January 2021.

40 Sam Levin, 'Uber drivers often make below
minimum wage, report find', *The Guardian*, 1
March 2018.

41 Lorusso, *Entreprecariat*.

42 Bianca Elzenbaumer, *Designing Economic
Cultures*, thesis (London: Goldsmiths,
University of London, 2013), p. 77.

43 Sasha Costanza-Chock, *Design Justice:
Community-Led Practices to Build the Worlds
We Need* (Cambridge, MA: MIT Press, 2020),
p. 162.

44 Richard Sennett, 'Drift', in *The Corrosion of
Character: The Personal Consequences of
Work in the New Capitalism* (New York: W.W.
Norton & Co., 1998), p. 37.

45 Shaughnessy, *How to be a graphic designer,
without losing your soul*, p. 25.

46 See osp.kitchen and commonknowledge.
coop, accessed 22 January 2021.

47 velvetyne.fr, accessed 22 January 2021.

48 uvwunion.org.uk/en/sectors/designers-
cultural-workers, accessed 22 January 2021.

49 Elzenbaumer, *Designing Economic Cultures*,
p. 124.

The Designer as Amateur

1 Papanek, *Design for the Real World*, p. 3.
2 Costanza-Chock, *Design Justice*, p. 13.
3 Papanek, *Design for the Real World*, p. 3.
4 Costanza-Chock, *Design Justice*, p. 14.
5 Ibid., p. 99.
6 Beegan and Atkinson, 'Professionalism,
Amateurism and the Boundaries of Design',
p. 305.
7 See chapter 'The Designer as Educator'.
8 Sennett, 'The Workshop', pp. 120–125.
9 Drucker and McVarish, *Graphic Design
History*, p. 161.
10 Beegan and Atkinson, 'Professionalism,
Amateurism and the Boundaries of Design',
p. 305.
11 *AIGA Design Census 2019*, designcensus.org,
accessed 20 January 2021.
12 Michael Rock, 'On Unprofessionalism', *2 x 4*,
1994, 2x4.org/ideas/1994/on-unprofession-

alism/, accessed 27 January 2021.
13 Costanza-Chock, *Design Justice*, p. 73.
14 Pierre Bourdieu, *Distinction: A Social Critique
of the Judgement of Taste* (New York:
Routledge, 1986).
15 Tibor Kalman, interview by Charlie Rose, 24
December 1998, charlierose.com/videos/
17661, accessed 27 January 2021.
16 Rick Poynor, *No More Rules* (New Haven: Yale
University Press, 2003), p. 89.
17 Mr. Keedy, 'Style Is Not a Four Letter Word',
in *Looking Closer 5: Critical Writings on
Graphic Design,* ed. Michael Bierut, Steven
Heller and William Drenttel (New York:
Allworth Press, 2006), pp. 102.
18 Lindsay Ballant, 'Bernie, Hillary, and the
Authenticity Gap: A Case Study in Campaign
Branding', *Medium*, 1 March 2016, quoted
in: Michael Bierut, 'I'm With Her', Design
Observer, 28 March, 2017, designobserver.
com/feature/im-with-her/39523, accessed
27 February 2021.
19 Mark Bovens, Paul Dekker and Will Tiemeijer,
eds., *Gescheiden werelden: Een verkenning
van sociaal-culturele tegenstellingen in
Nederland* (The Hague: SCP/WRR, 2014).
20 Gitelman, *Paper Knowledge*, p. 52.
21 Paul Atkinson, 'Do It Yourself: Democracy
and Design', *Journal of Design History* 19,
no. 1 (2006).
22 Teal Triggs, 'Scissors and Glue: Punk
Fanzines and the Creation of a DIY Aesthetic',
Journal of Design History 19, no. 1 (2008), p. 72.
23 Atkinson, 'Do It Yourself', p. 1.
24 Beegan and Atkinson, 'Professionalism,
Amateurism and the Boundaries of Design',
p. 307.
25 Ellen Lupton, *D.I.Y.: Design it Yourself*
(Princeton: Princeton Architectural Press,
2006), p. 19.
26 See chapter 'The Designer as Entrepreneur'.
27 See chapter 'The Designer as Scribe'.
28 Gitelman, *Paper Knowledge*, p. 47.
29 OECD statistics, 2020, stats.oecd.org/,
accessed 22 January 2021.
30 Robert Neuwirth, *Stealth of Nations: The
Global Rise of the Informal Economy* (New
York: Pantheon Books, 2011), pp. 17–18.
31 Andrea Bandoni, 'The Digital Age Reaches
the Fringes A Public Fab Lab in Brazil and
Its (Possible) Implications for Design', in *The
Responsible Object: A History of Design
Ideology for the Future*, ed. Marjanne van
Helvert (Amsterdam: Valiz, 2016), p. 224.
32 Neuwirth, *Stealth of Nations*, p. 178.
33 Pater, *The Politics of Design*, pp. 58–60.
34 Joshua Zane Weiss, 'Belief in the Potential
Object: Technological Disobedience in Cuba',
Walker Reader, 7 March 2018, walkerart.org/
magazine/ernesto-oroza-technological-diso-
bedience-cuba, accessed 22 January 2021.
35 Costanza-Chock, *Design Justice*, p. 142.
36 hardworkinggoodlooking.com/about,
accessed 22 January 2021.
37 w3.org/standards, accessed 27 January 2021.
38 See chapter 'The Designer as Engineer'.

39   For example, the Dutch graphic design trade organization BNO provides legal aid for freelancers and has salary guidelines for designers. bno.nl/page/english, accessed 27 January 2021.

40   Rock, *On Unprofessionalism*.

41   designjustice.org, accessed 21 January 2021.

42   Costanza-Chock, *Design Justice*, p. 9.

The Designer as Educator

1   Peter Gray, 'Play Theory of Hunter-Gatherer Egalitarianism', in *Ancestral Landscapes in Human Evolution: Culture, Childrearing and Social Wellbeing*, ed. Darcia Narvaez et al. (Oxford: Oxford University Press, 2014), pp. 192–215.

2   See chapter 'The Designer as Scribe'.

3   F.D. Harvey, 'Literacy in the Athenian Democracy', *Revue des Études Grecques* 79, nos. 376-378 (July-December 1966), pp. 585–636.

4   ourworldindata.org/literacy, accessed 28 January 2021.

5   Sennett, 'The Workshop', pp. 122–125.

6   Drucker and McVarish, *Graphic Design History,* pp. 104–105.

7   See chapter 'The Designer as Entrepreneur'.

8   Sennett, 'The Workshop', pp. 137–153.

9   'Academy of Art', *Encyclopaedia Britannica*, britannica.com/art/academy-of-art#ref41269, accessed 22 January 2021.

10   Harvey, *A Companion to Marx's Capital*, p. 152.

11   Gilles Deleuze, 'Postscript on the Societies of Control', *L'Autre journal no. 1*, May 1990.

12   Ben Maldonado, 'Eugenics on the Farm: Ellwood Cubberley', *The Stanford Daily*, 4 February 2020. stanforddaily.com/2020/02/04/eugenics-on-the-farm-ellwood-cubberley/, accessed 28 January 2021.

13   Ivan Illich, *Deschooling Society* (New York: Harrow Books, 1973), p. 22.

14   Ibid., p. 7.

15   Elzenbaumer, *Designing Economic Cultures*, p. 99.

16   Precarious Workers Brigade, *Training for Exploitation?*

17   Meggs, *Meggs' History of Graphic Design*, p. 181.

18   From the statutes of the Century Guild, 1882.

19   'Central School of Arts and Crafts', Mapping the Practice and Profession of Sculpture in Britain & Ireland, 1861–1951, sculpture.gla.ac.uk/view/organization.php?id=msib2_1212166601, accessed 22 January 2021.

20   Elizabeth Carolyn Miller, 'William Morris, Arts and Crafts, and the Idea of Eco-Socialist Design', in *The Responsible Object: A History of Design Ideology for the Future*, ed. Marjanne van Helvert (Amsterdam: Valiz, 2016), pp. 29–30, 35.

21   Jenny Farrell, '100 Years of Bauhaus: Building for a Society of Equals', *People's Worlds*, 25 March 2019, peoplesworld.org/article/100-years-of-bauhaus-building-for-a-society-of-equals, accessed 22 January 2021.

22   Walter Gropius, *Bauhaus manifesto*, 1919, bauhausmanifesto.com.

23   Tatiana Efrussi, 'After the Ball: Hannes Meyer Presenting the Bauhaus in Moscow', *Bauhaus Imaginista Edition* 3: Moving Away, 2018, bauhaus-imaginista.org/articles/2083/after-the-ball, accessed 28 January 2021.

24   aiga.org/history-timeline, accessed 28 January 2021.

25   See chapter 'The Designer as Philanthropist'.

26   Decolonizing Design, 'Decolonising Design Education: Ontologies, Strategies, Urgencies', in *Extra-Curricular*, ed. Jacob Lindgren (Eindhoven: Onomatopee, 2018), p. 77.

27   Mould, 'A History of Creativity', in *Against Creativity*, p. 21.

28   Arthur Frederick Wingate, 'Working for Morris & Co.', *JWMS* 11, no. 2 (Spring 1995), pp. 31–32.

29   Guy Standing, *The Precariat: The New Dangerous Class* (London etc.: Bloomsbury, 2011), p. 68.

30   Carlos Aguilar, 'Calarts Students Launch Protest as Annual Tuition Rises to Over $50K', *Cartoon Brew*, 15 March 2015, cartoonbrew.com/schools/calarts-students-launch-protest-as-annual-tuition-rises-to-over-50k-171415.html, accessed 22 January 2021.

31   calarts.edu, accessed 28 January 2021.

32   Paulo Freire, *Pedagogy of the Oppressed* (New York: Bloomsbury Academic, 2000).

33   thewomansbuilding.org, accessed 13 February 2021.

34   antiuniversity.org, accessed 22 January 2021.

35   Naomi Klein, 'Naomi Klein: How Big Tech Plans to Profit from the Pandemic', *The Guardian*, 13 May 2020.

36   Jacob Lindgren, ed., *Extra-Curricular* (Eindhoven: Onomatopee, 2018).

37   futureofdesigneducation.org, accessed 22 January 2021.

38   Cameron Tonkinwise. Twitter post, 13 July 2020, twitter.com/camerontw/status/1282483355620003840, accessed 22 January 2021.

39   Liz Stinson, 'The Trick to Recession-proofing Your Design Practice? Try Something New', *EYE on design*, 3 October 2019, eyeondesign.aiga.org/the-trick-to-recession-proofing-your-design-practice-try-something-new, accessed 22 January 2021.

40   Illich, *Deschooling Society*, p. 18.

PART 3

The Designer as Hacker

1   Drucker and McVarish, *Graphic Design History*, p. 336.

2   A glossary for computer programmers from 1975 called The Jargon File, in: Ben Yagdo, 'A Short History of "Hack"', *The New Yorker*, 6 March 2014.

3   Pekka Himanen, *The Hacker Ethic: A Radical*

Approach to the Philosophy of Business (New York: Random House, 2001), viii.

4   Silvia Federici, 'Feminism and the Politics of the Commons', in *Uses of a Whirlwind: Movement, Movements, and Contemporary Radical Currents in the United States*, ed. Craig Hughes, Stevie Peace and Kevin Van Meter for the Team Colors Collective (Edinburgh, Oakland and Baltimore: AK Press, 2010), pp. 283–294.

5   Dmytri Kleiner, *The Telekommunist Manifesto* (Network Notebooks 03), ed. Geert Loving and Sabine Niederer (Amsterdam: Institute of Network Cultures, 2010), p. 15.

6   'The new investors in underwater sea cables', *Internet Health report*, April 2019, internethealthreport.org/2019/the-new-investors-in-underwater-sea-cables, accessed 22 January 2021.

7   Bridle, *New Dark Age*, p. 246.

8   Aditya Mukerjee, 'I Can Text You A Pile of Poo, But I Can't Write My Name', *Model View Culture* 18 (17 March 2015), modelviewculture.com/pieces/i-can-text-you-a-pile-of-poo-but-i-cant-write-my-name, accessed 22 January 2021.

9   Keith A. Spencer, 'The Neoliberal Politics of Emoji', *Salon*, 23 July 2017, salon.com/2017/07/23/the-neoliberal-politics-of-emoji/, accessed 22 January 2021.

10   Marshall McLuhan, *The Medium is the Massage: An Inventory of Effects* (London: Penguin Books, 1967), p. 8.

11   Ibid., p. 16.

12   Manuel Castells, *The Information Age: Economy, Society and Culture, Volume 1: The Rise of the Network Society, 2nd ed.* (Oxford: Wiley Blackwell, 2010).

13   klomp.tv/#/053204149098/, accessed 22 January 2021.

14   Zuboff, *The Age of Surveillance Capitalism*, p. 84.

15   Bridle, *New Dark Age*, p. 236.

16   Jamie Doward and Alice Gibbs, 'Did Cambridge Analytica influence the Brexit vote and the US election?', *The Guardian*, 4 March 2017.

17   Forum on Information & Democracy, informationdemocracy.org/principles/, accessed 22 January 2021.

18   '250 Recommendations on How to Stop "Infodemics"', *Forum on Information & Democracy*, 12 November 2020, informationdemocracy.org/2020/11/12/250-recommendations-on-how-to-stop-infodemics/, accessed 22 January 2021.

19   Disnovation, profilingtheprofilers.com, accessed 22 January 2021.

20   Matthew Ström, 'The Paradox at the Heart of A/B Testing', *matthewstrom.com*, 9 January 2020, matthewstrom.com/writing/ab-testing-paradox, accessed 22 January 2021.

21   Tristan Harris, '*How Technology is Hijacking Your Mind—from a Magician and Google Design Ethicist*', *Medium*, 18 May 2016, medium.com/thrive-global/how-technology-hijacks-peoples-minds-from-a-magician-and-google-s-design-ethicist-56d62ef5edf3#.qsgtv1l6b, accessed 22 January 2021.

22   Franco Bifo Berardi, 'Time, Acceleration, and Violence', *e-flux journal* 27 (September 2011), e-flux.com/journal/27/67999/time-acceleration-and-violence, accessed 22 January 2021.

23   Bridle, *New Dark Age*, pp. 147–148.

24   Jesus Diaz, 'This Machine Can Tell You if Your Photos Suck or Rule', *Gizmodo*, 22 November 2021, gizmodo.com/this-machine-can-tell-you-if-your-photos-suck-or-rule-5862074, accessed 13 February 2021.

25   Neural Filters, *Adobe.com*, helpx.adobe.com/photoshop/using/neural-filters.html, accessed 22 January 2021.

26   Hannah Sparks and Suzy Weiss, 'Every Bikini Photo You See Is Probably Fake', *The New York Post*, 16 July 2018.

27   Bradely Johnson, 'World's Largest Advertisers: Spending is Growing (and Surging in China)', *AdAge*, 5 December 2017, adage.com/article/cmo-strategy/world-s-largest-advertisers-2017/311484, accessed 22 January 2021.

28   Bridle, *New Dark Age*, p. 126.

29   Denis Metev, '39+ Smartphone Statistics You Should Know in 2020', *Review42*, 21 November 2021, review42.com/smartphone-statistics, accessed 22 January 2021.

30   Hito Steyerl, *The Wretched of the Screen* (Berlin: Sternberg Press, 2012), p. 36.

31   Anja Groten, 'Hacking & Designing: Paradoxes of Collaborative Practice', in *The Critical Makers Reader: (Un)learning Technology*, ed. Loes Bogers and Letizia Chiappini (Amsterdam: Institute of Network Cultures, 2019), p. 239.

32   Bridle, *New Dark Age*, p. 3.

33   Brian Barrett, 'An Artist Used 99 Phones to Fake a Google Maps Traffic Jam', *WIRED*, 3 February 2020, wired.com/story/99-phones-fake-google-maps-traffic-jam/, accessed 22 January 2021.

34   Aymeric Mansoux and Roel Roscam Abbing, *Seven Theses on the Fediverse and The Becoming of Floss* (Amsterdam: Institute of Network Cultures, 2020), p. 137.

35   '"Every non-free program is an injustice": Richard Stallman on the Free Software Movement', *e-flux*, 1 October 2018, conversations.e-flux.com/t/every-non-free-program-is-an-injustice-richard-stallman-on-the-free-software-movement/8474, accessed 22 January 2021.

36   osp.kitchen/foundry, accessed 22 January 2021.

37   See chapter 'The Designer as Entrepreneur'.

38   Haiven, 'The Commons Against Neoliberalism, the Commons of Neoliberalism, the Commons Beyond Neoliberalism', p. 264.

39   Steven Levy, *Hackers: Heroes of the Computer Revolution* (Newton: O'Reilly, 2010).

40   'Ethical Design Manifesto', 2017, ind.ie/ethical-design, accessed 22 January 2021.

41   Groten, 'Hacking & Designing', p. 240.

42 Hijacking the Outdoor Digital Billboard, by Defcon 16 hacking panel, youtube.com/watch?v=tpZ_NDx35u8, accessed 22 January 2021.

43 Groten, 'Hacking & Designing', p. 238.

The Designer as Futurist

1 Peter Bil'ak in: Jon Sueda, 'On Speculation', *All Possible Futures*, 2014, allpossiblefutures.net/on-speculation-3-2, accessed 28 January 2021.

2 Melissa Bauman, 'How Accurate Were Predictions for the Future?', *RAND Review*, 14 July 2020, rand.org/blog/rand-review/2020/07/how-accurate-were-predictions-for-the-future.html, accessed 22 January 2021.

3 Uncertain Commons, *Speculate This!* (Durham and London: Duke University Press, 2013).

4 Anthony Dunne and Fiona Raby, *Speculative Everything* (Cambridge, MA: MIT Press, 2013), pp. 3–5.

5 David M. Higgins and Hugh C. O'Connell, 'Introduction: Speculative Finance/Speculative Fiction', *The New Centennial Review* 19, no. 1 (Spring 2019), pp. 1–10.

6 Thomson and Dutta, *Financialisation*.

7 Marcia Klotz, 'Of Time Loops and Derivatives: Christopher Nolan's Interstellar and the Logic of the Futures Market', *CR: The New Centennial Review* 19, no. 1 (2019), pp. 277–297.

8 'Buffett warns on investment 'time bomb', *BBC News*, 4 March 2003, news.bbc.co.uk/2/hi/business/2817995.stm, accessed 22 January 2021.

9 Zuboff, *The Age of Surveillance Capitalism*, p. 14.

10 Ibid., pp. 8, 100, 128.

11 Anthony Dunne, *Hertzian Tales: Electronic Products, Aesthetic Experience, and Critical Design* (Cambridge, MA: MIT Press, 2005), p. 84.

12 Dunne and Raby, *Speculative Everything*, p. 9.

13 Julian Bleecker, *Design Fiction: A Short Essay on Design, Science, Fact and Fiction*, 2009, blog.nearfuturelaboratory.com/2009/03/17/design-fiction-a-short-essay-on-design-science-fact-and-fiction/.

14 allpossiblefutures.net/, accessed 13 February 2021.

15 Fredric Jameson, 'Future City', *New Left Review 21* (2003), pp. 76.

16 Fisher, *Capitalist Realism*, p. 18.

17 Ibid., p. 21.

18 Facebook earns 97% of its revenue from ads. Google earns 88% from ads. Jeff Desjardins, 'The Tech Takeover of Advertising in One Chart, *Visualcapitalist*, 22 September 2017, visualcapitalist.com/the-tech-takeover-of-advertising-in-one-chart/, accessed 22 January 2021.

19 Michael Mogensen, 'NIUN: Saudi Futures', *Journal of Futures Studies*, 11 October 2018, jfsdigital.org/2018/10/11/niun-saudi-futures, accessed 22 January 2021.

20 thefuturelaboratory.com, accessed 22 January 2021.

21 youtube.com/watch?v=w-tFdreZB94&ab_channel=MicrosoftinBusiness, accessed 22 January 2021.

22 uber.com/nl/en/elevate, accessed 22 January 2021.

23 Shell's own speculative design is called 'Shell Scenarios', shell.com/energy-and-innovation/the-energy-future/scenarios/what-are-scenarios.html, accessed 22 January 2021.

24 Françoise Vergès, 'Capitalocene, Waste, Race, and Gender', *e-flux journal* 100 (May 2019), e-flux.com/journal/100/269165/capitalocene-waste-race-and-gender/, accessed 10 March 2021.

25 Pedro Oliveira and Luiza Prado, 'Cheat Sheet for a Non- (or Less-) Colonialist Speculative Design', *Medium*, 10 September 2014, medium.com/a-parede/cheat-sheet-for-a-non-or-less-colonialist-speculative-design-9a6b4ae3c465, accessed 22 January 2021.

26 moma.org/interactives/exhibitions/2013/designandviolence/about, accessed 22 January 2021.

27 Wouter van Noort, 'De tirannie van ons kortetermijndenken', *NRC Handelsblad*, 28 January 2021.

28 en.wikipedia.org/wiki/Seven_generation_sustainability, accessed 30 January 2021.

The Designer as Philanthropist

1 Papanek, *Design for the Real World*, p. 151.

2 Darin Buzon, 'Design Thinking is a Rebrand for White Supremacy: How the Current State of Design is Simply a Digitally Status Quo', *Medium*, 2 March 2020, dabuzon.medium.com/design-thinking-is-a-rebrand-for-white-supremacy-b3d31aa55831, accessed 22 January 2021.

3 Facebook company's motto until 2014.

4 What Design Can Do Refugee Challenge, 2014, whatdesigncando.com/stories/challenge-what-design-can-do-for-refugees, accessed 22 January 2021.

5 Rob Reich, *Just Giving: Why Philanthropy Is Failing Democracy and How It Can Do Better* (Princeton: Princeton University Press, 2018), p. 24.

6 Krystin Gollihue, 'The History of Global Charitable Giving: Why We Need to Remember', *Philanthropy Journal*, 18 July 2016, pj.news.chass.ncsu.edu/2016/07/18/the-history-of-global-charitable-giving-why-we-need-to-remember, accessed 22 January 2021.

7 Carl Rhodes and Peter Bloom, 'The Trouble with Charitable Billionaires', *The Guardian*, 24 May 2018.

8 Reich, *Just Giving*, p. 9.

9 Donovan Alexander, 'Mark Zuckerberg's $5 Billion Project to End Disease Within a Generation', *Interesting Engineering*, 6

January 2019, interestingengineering.com/
mark-zuckerbergs-5-billion-project-to-end-
disease-within-a-generation, accessed 22
January 2021.

10   'Facebook, Google and Microsoft "avoiding
     $3bn in tax in poorer nations"', *BBC News*, 26
     October 2020 bbc.com/news/business-
     54691572, accessed 22 January 2021.

11   Tal Axelrod, 'Dell CEO rejects Ocasio-
     Cortez's tax plan at Davos', *The Hill*, 23
     January 2019, thehill.com/policy/finance/
     domestic-taxes/426695-dell-ceo-rejects-
     ocasio-cortezs-tax-plan-at-davos, accessed 1
     February 2021.

12   Dean Spade, *Mutual Aid: Building Solidarity
     During This Crisis (and the Next)* (New York
     and London: Verso Books, 2020), p. 21.

13   Fisher, *Capitalist Realism*, p. 21.

14   Papanek, *Design for the Real World*, p. 107.

15   Ibid., p. 69.

16   Van Helvert, *The Responsible Object*, p. 158.

17   Dung-Sheng Chen et al., 'Social Design: An
     Introduction', *International Journal of Design*
     10, no. 1 (2015), pp. 1–5.

18   Danah Abdulla, 'A Manifesto of Change or
     Design Imperialism? A Look at the Purpose
     of the Social Design Practice', in *A Matter of
     Design: Making Society through Science and
     Technology*, ed. Claudio Coletta et al. (Milan:
     STS Italia Publishing, 2014), p. 247.

19   archive.designigniteschange.org, accessed
     22 January 2021.

20   Abdulla, 'A Manifesto of Change or Design
     Imperialism?', p. 252.

21   Ibid., pp. 252, 246.

22   Natasha Jen, 'Why Design Thinking is
     Bullshit', *It's Nice That*, 23 February 2018.
     itsnicethat.com/articles/natasha-jen-
     pentagram-graphicdesign-230218,
     accessed 22 January 2021.

23   designthinking.ideo.com/, accessed 22
     January 2021.

24   Evgeny Morozov, *To Save Everything, Click
     Here: The Folly of Technological Solutionism*
     (New York: PublicAffairs, 2013), pp. 5–6.

25   Natasha Iskander, 'Design Thinking Is
     Fundamentally Conservative and Preserves
     the Status Quo', *Harvard Business Review*, 5
     September 2018.

26   Buzon, *Design Thinking is a Rebrand for White
     Supremacy*.

27   This and following quotes from Maggie
     Gram, 'On Design Thinking', *N+1 magazine*
     35 (Fall 2019), nplusonemag.com/issue-35/
     reviews/on-design-thinking/, accessed 22
     January 2021.

28   What Design Can Do Refugee Challenge
     website, 2015, whatdesigncando.com/
     stories/challenge-what-design-can-do-for-
     refugees/, accessed 22 January 2021.

29   Ibid.

30   Ruben Pater, 'Treating the refugee crisis as
     a design problem is problematic', *Dezeen*, 21
     April 2016, dezeen.com/2016/04/21/ruben-
     pater-opinion-what-design-can-do-refugee-
     crisis-problematic-design/, accessed 22

January 2021.

31   Ibid.

32   The annual budget of FRONTEX, the EU's
     border agency was 142 million euros in 2015.
     frontex.europa.eu/faq/key-facts/, accessed
     22 January 2021.

33   At the time of writing, nominations have
     been removed from the What Design Can
     Do website. This article still lists some of
     the nomination material: fastcompany.
     com/3061335/25-smart-designs-that-
     could-help-ease-the-refugee-crisis#!/
     vizhome/GreenCitiesScore/Sheet1,
     accessed 22 January 2021.

34   makersunite.eu, accessed 22 January 2021.

35   'Mediterranean "world's deadliest border"
     for migrants, says UN', *Deutsche Welle*, 25
     November 2017, dw.com/en/mediterranean-
     worlds-deadliest-border-for-migrants-says-
     un/a-41525468, accessed 22 January 2021.

36   Ivan Illich, 'To Hell with Good Intentions',
     lecture at CIASP Canada, 1968, dial-infos.
     org/alterinfos/spip.php?article5168,
     accessed 22 January 2021.

37   Teju Cole, 'The White-Savior Industrial
     Complex', *The Atlantic*, 21 March 2012,
     theatlantic.com/international/archive/2012/
     03/the-white-savior-industrial-complex/
     254843/, accessed 22 January 2021.

38   Teju Cole, Twitter post, 8 March 2012, twitter.
     com/tejucole/status/177809396070498304,
     accessed 22 January 2021.

39   Cole, 'The White-Savior Industrial Complex'.

40   Costanza-Chock, *Design Justice*, pp. 20–22.

41   Ibid., p. 23.

42   Peter Kropotkin, *Mutual Aid: A Factor of
     Evolution*, 1902, theanarchistlibrary.org/
     library/petr-kropotkin-mutual-aid-a-factor-
     of-evolution, accessed 22 January 2021.

43   Dean Spade, 'Solidarity Not Charity: Mutual
     Aid for Mobilization and Survival', *Social Text*
     142, vol. 38, no. 1 (March 2020), 131–151.

44   Wikipedia.org/mutual_aid, accessed 22
     January 2021.

45   en.wikipedia.org/wiki/Free_Breakfast_for_
     Children, accessed 22 January 2021.

46   mutualaiddisasterrelief.org/, accessed 22
     January 2021.

The Designer as Activist

1   Ann Thorpe, 'Defining Design as Activism',
    2011, designactivism.net/wp-content/
    uploads/2011/05/Thorpe-definingdesign
    activism.pdf, accessed 1 February 2021.

2   Uday Dandavate, 'Design Activism', *Medium*,
    16 September 2019, medium.com/sonicrim-
    stories-from-the-edge/design-activism-
    496db463e5ee, accessed 1 February 2021.

3   Ibid.

4   sonicrim.com, accessed 1 February 2021.

5   Carl DiSalvo, *Adversarial Design* (Cambridge,
    MA, and London: MIT Press), 2012.

6   Eric Ressler, 'Causewashing is the New
    Greenwashing', *Cosmic*, 17 May 2018,

7   designbycosmic.com/insights/articles/
cause-washing-is-the-new-greenwashing,
accessed 15 February 2021.

7   thinkbeforeyoupink.org, accessed 1
February 2021.

8   Russel Weigandt, 'The Problem with Brand
Support of Black Lives Matter', *Medium*, 19
June 2020, medium.com/swlh/the-
problem-with-brand-support-of-black-lives-
matter-7444f5a85122, accessed 15
February 2021.

9   Papanek, *Design for the Real World*, p. 88.

10   See chapter 'The Designer as Hacker'.

11   brave-new-alps.com/about, accessed 14
February 2021.

12   Interview with Brave New Alps by the author,
conducted in March 2020.

13   See chapter 'The Designer as Hacker'.

14   'Understanding the Seven Cooperative
Principles', *NCREA*, 1 December 2016,
electric.coop/seven-cooperative-
principles%E2%80%8B, accessed 21
January 2021.

15   Interview with Gemma Copeland by the
author, conducted in December 2020.

16   Ibid.

17   Ibid.

18   Ola Kohut, 'Digital tools for self-organized
change: Interview with Gemma Copeland',
Autark, 17 October 2019, blog.autark.xyz/
interview-with-gemma-copeland, accessed 1
February 2021.

19   Interview with Gemma Copeland by the
author, conducted in December 2020.

20   Ibid.

21   Ibid.

22   Interview with Emilia Pezzati from Cooperativa de Diseño by the author, January 2021.

23   youtube.com/pibxs, accessed 15 February
2021.

24   Interview with Emilia Pezzati from Cooperativa de Diseño by the author, January 2021.

25   midianinja.org.

26   Ibid.

27   Diego Garcia, 'Extreme Poverty Affects 13.7
Million Brazilians, Says IBGE', *Folha de St.
Paolo*, 13 November 2020,
www1.folha.uol.com.br/internacional/en/
business/2020/11/extreme-poverty-affects-
137-million-brazilians-says-ibge.shtml,
accessed 19 March 2021.

28   Andrew C. Whitworth-Smith, 'Solidarity
Economies, Networks and the Positioning
of Power in Alternative Cultural Production
and Activism in Brazil: The Case of Fora
do Eixo' (diss. University of California, San
Diego, 2014).

29   Interview with Gijs de Heij, February 2021.

30   Collaboration ecotones, ecotones.caveat.
be/osp.html, accessed 15 February 2021.

31   osp.kitchen/foundry, accessed 15 February
2021.

32   Collaboration ecotones, ecotones.caveat.
be/osp.html, accessed 15 February 2021.

33   Interview with Gijs de Heij, February 2021.

34   Interview with Sheila Sampath, February
2021 and thepublic.ca/studio, accessed 15
February 2021.

35   Sheila Sampath, 'We Can Build in Different
Ways', *Studio Magazine* Fall/Winter 2020,
studiomagazine.ca/articles/2020/11/
we-can-build-in-different-ways,
accessed 14 February 2021.

36   Interview with Sheila Sampath, February
2021.

37   Ibid.

38   parkdalepeopleseconomy.ca, accessed 15
February 2021.

39   thepublicstudio.ca/news/a-labour-of-love-
the-public-team, accessed 15 February 2021.

40   Ibid.

41   Ibid.

42   Ibid.

43   thepublicstudio.ca/news/a-labour-of-love-
the-public-team, accessed 15 February 2021.

PART 4

Outro

1   Brian Merchant, 'Fully Automated Luxury
Communism', *The Guardian*, 18 March 2015.

2   statista.com/statistics/986392/co2-
emissions-per-cap-by-country-eu, accessed
11 February 2021.

3   worldometers.info/co2-emissions/ethiopia-
co2-emissions, accessed 11 February 2021.

4   Nico Dockx and Pascal Gielen, *Commonism:
A New Aesthetics of the Real* (Amsterdam:
Valiz, 2018), p. 110.

5   Federici, 'Feminism and the Politics of the
Commons'.

6   J.M. Pedersen, 'Properties of Property: A
Jurisprudential Analysis', *The Commoner*
(Special Issue on Commoning), 14 (Winter
2010), pp. 138–210.

7   Valérie Fournier, 'Commoning: On the Social
Organisation of the Commons',
M@n@gement 16, no. 4 (2013), pp. 433–453.

8   Elzenbaumer, *Designing Economic Cultures*.

9   p2pfoundation.net/, accessed 17 March
2021, p. 2.

10   viacampesina.org/en, accessed 17 March 2021.

11   Federici, 'Feminism and the Politics of the
Commons'.

12   Haiven, 'The Commons Against
Neoliberalism', pp. 271–283.

Bibliography

A–C

Abdulla, Danah. 'A Manifesto of Change or Design Imperialism? A Look at the Purpose of the Social Design Practice.' In *A Matter of Design: Making Society through Science and Technology*. Edited by Claudio Coletta et al., pp. 245–260. Milan: STS Italia Publishing, 2014.

Alderman, Liz. 'Our Cash-Free Future Is Getting Closer.' *The New York Times*, 6 July 2020.

'Amsterdammer verlamd na ernstig fietsongeluk: "Ik mis de oude Lars heel erg".' NH Nieuws, 23 March 2017.

Anderson, Benedict. *Imagined Communities: Reflections on the Origin and Spread of Nationalism*. London: Verso Books, 1983.

Arthur, Charles. 'Marissa Mayer's Appointment: What Does It Mean for Yahoo?' *The Guardian*, 16 July 2012.

Astbury, Jon. 'In for a Penny: The Design Evolution of Money.' *The Architectural Review*, 9 April 2014.

Atkinson, Paul. 'Do It Yourself: Democracy and Design.' *Journal of Design History* 19, no. 1 (2006).

Bandoni, Andrea. 'The Digital Age Reaches the Fringes: A Public Fab Lab in Brazil and Its (Possible) Implications for Design.' In *The Responsible Object: A History of Design Ideology for the Future*. Edited by Marjanne van Helvert, pp. 209–226. Amsterdam: Valiz, 2016.

Becker, Gary. 'The Economic Way of Looking at Life' (9 December 1992). In *Nobel Lecture: Economics* 1991–1995. Edited by Tosten Persson, pp. 38–58. Singapore: World Scientific Publishing, 1997.

Beegan, Gerry, and Paul Atkinson, 'Professionalism, Amateurism and the Boundaries of Design.' *Journal of Design History* 21, no. 4 (2008).

Bernays, Edward. *Propaganda*. New York: Horace Loveright, 1928.

Bhuiyan, Johana. 'The Google Walkout: What Protesters Demanded and What They Got.' *LA Times,* 6 November 2019.

Boehnert, Joanna. *Design, Ecology, Politics: Towards the Ecocene*. London and Oxford: Bloomsbury, 2018.

Bourdieu, Pierre. *Distinction: A Social Critique of the Judgement of Taste*. New York: Routledge, 1986.

Bovens, Mark, Paul Dekker and Will Tiemeijer, eds. *Gescheiden werelden: Een verkenning van sociaal-culturele tegenstellingen in Nederland*. The Hague: SCP/WRR, 2014.

Bridle, James. *New Dark Age: Technology and the End of the Future*. London and New York: Verso Books, 2018.

Browne, Simone. *Dark Matters: On the Surveillance of Blackness*. Durham: Duke University Press, 2015.

Castells, Manuel. *The Information Age: Economy, Society and Culture, Volume 1: The Rise of the Network Society*. 2nd ed. Oxford: Wiley Blackwell, 2010.

Chadwick, Edwin. *The Sanitary Condition of the Labouring Population*, Poor Law Commissioners, Home Office, 1842.

Chen, Dung-Sheng, et al. 'Social Design: An Introduction.' *International Journal of Design* 10, no. 1 (2015), pp. 1–5.

Chibber, Vivek. *Understanding Capitalism: The ABCs of Capitalism*. New York: Jacobin Foundation, 2018.

Costanza-Chock, Sasha. *Design Justice: Community-Led Practices to Build the Worlds We Need*. Cambridge, MA: MIT Press, 2020.

D–F

Decolonizing Design. 'Decolonising Design Education: Ontologies, Strategies, Urgencies.' In *Extra-Curricular*. Edited by Jacob Lindgren. Eindhoven: Onomatopee, 2018.

Deleuze, Gilles. 'Postscript on the Societies of Control.' *L'Autre journal* no. 1, May 1990.

DiSalvo, Carl. *Adversarial Design*. Cambridge, MA, and London: MIT Press, 2012.

Dockx, Nico, and Pascal Gielen, *Commonism: A New Aesthetics of the Real*. Amsterdam: Valiz, 2018.

Doward, Jamie, and Alice Gibbs. 'Did Cambridge Analytica Influence the Brexit Vote and the US Election?' *The Guardian*, 4 March 2017.

Drucker, Johanna. *Graphesis*. Cambridge, MA, and London: Harvard University Press, 2014.

Drucker, Johanna, and Emily McVarish. *Graphic Design History: A Critical Guide*. Hoboken: Pearson, 2009.

Dunne, Anthony. *Hertzian Tales: Electronic Products, Aesthetic Experience, and Critical Design*. Cambridge, MA: MIT Press, 2005.

Dunne, Anthony, and Fiona Raby. *Speculative Everything*. Cambridge, MA: MIT Press, 2013.

Elzenbaumer, Bianca. *Designing Economic Cultures*. Thesis. London: Goldsmiths, University of London, 2013.

Evans, Rob. 'Half of England is Owned by Less Than 1% of the Population.' *The Guardian*, 17 April 2019.

Federici, Silvia. 'Feminism and the Politics of the Commons.' In *Uses of a Whirlwind: Movement, Movements, and Contemporary Radical Currents in the United States*. Edited by Craig Hughes, Stevie Peace and Kevin Van Meter for the Team Colors Collective, pp. 283–294. Edinburgh, Oakland and Baltimore: AK Press, 2010.

Federici, Silvia. *Caliban and the Witch: Women, the Body and Primitive Accumulations*. New

York: Autonomedia, 2004.

Fisher, Mark. *Capitalist Realism: Is There No Alternative?* New York: Verso Books, 2009.

Florida, Richard L. *The Rise of the Creative Class: And How It's Transforming Work, Leisure, Community and Everyday Life*. New York: Basic Books, 2002.

Fonnegra, Gabriel. *Bananeras testimonio vivo de una epopeya*. Bogotá: Tercer Mundo, 1980.

Foucault, Michel. *Mental Illness and Psychology*. New York: Harper and Row, 1976.

—. *Discipline and Punish: The Birth of the Prison*. New York: Pantheon Books, 1977.

Fournier, Valérie. 'Commoning: On the Social Organisation of the Commons.' *M@n@gement* 16, no. 4 (2013), pp. 433–453.

Frank, Thomas C. *The Conquest of Cool: Business Culture, Counterculture, and the Rise of Hip Consumerism*. Chicago: University of Chicago Press, 1997.

Freire, Paulo. *Pedagogy of the Oppressed*. New York: Bloomsbury Academic, 2000.

G–J

Gitelman, Lisa. *Paper Knowledge: Toward a Media History of Documents*. Durham: Duke University Press, 2014.

Gottesdiener, Laura. 'The Great Eviction: The Landscape of Wall Street's Creative Destruction.' *The Nation*, 1 August 2013.

Graeber, David. *Debt: The First 5000 Years*. New York: Melville House, 2011.

—. *The Utopia of Rules*. New York: Melville House, 2015.

Gray, Peter. 'Play Theory of Hunter-Gatherer Egalitarianism.' In *Ancestral Landscapes in Human Evolution: Culture, Childrearing and Social Wellbeing*. Edited by Darcia Narvaez, et al., pp. 192–215. Oxford: Oxford University Press, 2014.

Greenfield, Patrick. 'Apple Apologises for Slowing Down Older iPhones with Ageing Batteries.' *The Guardian*, 29 December 2017.

Groten, Anja. 'Hacking & Designing: Paradoxes of Collaborative Practice.' In *The Critical Makers Reader: (Un)learning Technology*. Edited by Loes Bogers and Letizia Chiappini, pp. 237–244. Amsterdam: Institute of Network Cultures, 2019.

Guendelsberger, Emily. *On The Clock: What Low-Wage Work Did to Me and How It Drives America Insane*. Boston: Little, Brown, and Company, 2019.

Haiven, Max. 'The Commons Against Neo-liberalism, the Commons of Neoliberalism, the Commons Beyond Neoliberalism.' In *The Hand Book of Neoliberalism*. Edited by Simon Springer, Kean Birch, and Julie MacLeavy, pp. 271–283. New York: Routledge, 2016.

—. *Cultures of Financialization: Fictitious Capital in Popular Culture and Everyday Life*. London and New York: Macmillan Palgrave, 2014.

Harari, Yuval Noah. *Sapiens: A Brief History of Humankind*. London: Vintage UK, 2015.

Hardt, Michael, and Antonio Negri, *Assembly*. New York: Oxford University Press, 2017.

Haring, Ben. 'Identity Marks in Ancient Egypt: Scribal and Non-Scribal Modes of Visual Communication.' In *Non-scribal Communication Media in the Bronze Age Aegean and Surrounding Areas: The semantics of a-literate and proto-literate media. seals, potmarks, mason's marks, seal-impressed pottery, ideograms and logograms, and related systems)*. Edited by A.M. Jasink, J. Weingarten and S. Ferrara. Florence: Firenze University Press, 2017.

Harvey, David. *The Condition of Postmodernity: An Inquiry into the Origins of Cultural Exchange*. Hoboken: Wiley-Blackwell, 1991.

—. *A Brief History of Neoliberalism*. Oxford: Oxford University Press, 2005.

—. *A Companion to Marx's Capital*. London: Verso Books, 2010.

Harvey, F.D. 'Literacy in the Athenian Democracy.' *Revue des Études Grecques* 79, nos. 376–378 (July-December 1966), pp. 585–636.

Heller, Steven, and Lita Talarico. *The Design Entrepreneur: Turning Graphic Design Into Goods That Sell*. Beverly: Rockport Publishers, 2008.

Helvert, Marjanne van, ed. *The Responsible Object: A History of Design Ideology for the Future*. Amsterdam: Valiz Publishers, 2016.

Higgins, David M., and Hugh C. O'Connell, 'Introduction: Speculative Finance/Speculative Fiction.' *The New Centennial Review* 19, no. 1 (Spring 2019), pp. 1–10.

Himanen, Pekka. *The Hacker Ethic: A Radical Approach to the Philosophy of Business*. New York: Random House, 2001.

Hodal, Kate. 'One in 200 People is a Slave: Why?', *The Guardian*, 25 February 2019.

Illich, Ivan. *Deschooling Society*. New York: Harrow Books, 1973.

Iskander, Natasha. 'Design Thinking Is Fundamentally Conservative and Preserves the Status Quo.' *Harvard Business Review*, 5 September 2018.

Jameson, Fredric. 'Future City.' *New Left Review* 21 (2003), pp. 65–79.

Julier, Guy. *Economies of Design*. London: SAGE Publication, 2017.

K–M

Keedy, Mr. 'Style Is Not a Four Letter Word.' In *Looking Closer 5: Critical Writings on Graphic Design*. Edited by Michael Bierut, Steven Heller and William Drenttel, pp. 94–103. New York: Allworth Press, 2006.

Kinross, Robin. *A4 and Before: Towards a Long History of Paper Sizes*. Wassenaar: NIAS, 2009.

Klein, Naomi. *The Shock Doctrine*. New York: Metropolitan Books, 2007.

—. *No Logo: Taking Aim at the Brand Bullies*. New York: Vintage Canada, 2009.

—. 'Naomi Klein: How Big Tech Plans to Profit from the Pandemic.' *The Guardian*, 13 May 2020.

Kleiner, Dmytri. *The Telekommunist Manifesto*

(Network Notebooks 03). Edited by Geert Loving and Sabine Niederer. Amsterdam: Institute of Network Cultures, 2010.

Klotz, Marcia. 'Of Time Loops and Derivatives: Christopher Nolan's Interstellar and the Logic of the Futures Market.' *CR: The New Centennial Review* 19, no. 1 (2019), pp. 277–297.

Komlosy, Andrea. *Work: The Last 1,000 Years.* London: Verso Books, 2018.

Kula, Witold. *Measures and Men.* Princeton: Princeton University Press, 1986.

Kurtz-Phelan, Daniel. 'Big Fruit.' *The New York Times*, 2 March 2008.

Lee, Newton. *Facebook Nation: Total Information Awareness.* New York: Springer, 2012.

Levin, Sam. 'Uber drivers often make below minimum wage, report finds.' *The Guardian*, 1 March 2018.

Levy, Steven, *Hackers: Heroes of the Computer Revolution.* Newton: O'Reilly, 2010.

Lindgren, Jacob. ed. *Extra-Curricular.* Eindhoven: Onomatopee, 2018.

Loon, Wouter van, and Thijs Niemantsverdriet. Airbnb-verhuur Amsterdam stijgt verder door.' *NRC Handelsblad*, 8 May 2019.

Lorusso, Silvio. *Entreprecariat: Everyone is an Entrepreneur: Nobody is Safe.* Eindhoven: Onomatopee, 2019.

Lupton, Ellen. *D.I.Y.: Design it Yourself.* Princeton: Princeton Architectural Press, 2006.

—, and J. Abbott Miller. *Design, Writing, Research: Writing on Graphic Design.* London: Phaidon Press, 1999.

Mahdawi, Araw. 'Can Cities Kick Ads? Inside the Global Movement to Ban Urban Billboards.' *The Guardian*, 12 August 2015.

Maigret, Nicolas, and Maria Roszkowska. *The Pirate Book.* Self-published, 2015.

Mansoux, Aymeric, and Roel Roscam Abbing. *Seven Theses on the Fediverse and The Becoming of Floss.* Amsterdam: Institute of Network Cultures, 2020.

Martijn, Maurits, and Jesse Frederik. 'Dit is de nieuwe internetbubbel: Online advertenties', *De Correspondent*, 19 January 2019.

Marx, Karl. *Capital, Vol. 1 & 2.* Hertfordshire: Wordsworth, 2013.

Mason, Paul. *Postcapitalism.* London: Allen Lane, 2015.

Mat, Patrick. '50 years Later: How the Credit Card Has Changed America.' *Mercury News*, 14 August 2016.

McClintock, Anne. *Imperial Leather: Race, Gender, and Sexuality in the Colonial Context.* New York: Routledge, 1995.

McLuhan, Marshall. *The Medium is the Massage: An Inventory of Effects.* London: Penguin Books, 1967.

Meggs, Philip B., and Alston W. Purvis, *Meggs' History of Graphic Design.* Hoboken: Wiley, 2011.

Merchant, Brian. 'Fully Automated Luxury Communism.' *The Guardian*, 18 March 2015.

Mignolo, Walter D. *The Darker Side of the Renaissance: Literacy, Territoriality & Colonization.* Ann Arbor: University of Michigan Press, 1995.

Mignolo, Walter D. *The Darker Side of Western Modernity: Global Futures, Decolonial Options.* Durham: Duke University Press, 2011.

Miller, Elizabeth Carolyn. 'William Morris, Arts and Crafts, and the Idea of Eco-Socialist Design.' In *The Responsible Object: A History of Design Ideology for the Future.* Edited by Marjanne van Helvert, pp. 29–48. Amsterdam: Valiz, 2016.

Morozov, Evgeny. *To Save Everything, Click Here: The Folly of Technological Solutionism.* New York: PublicAffairs, 2013.

Morton, Bill. 'An Overview of International NGOs in Development Cooperation.' *United Nations Development Programme*, 2011.

Mould, Oli. *Against Creativity.* London: Verso Books, 2018.

N–R

Neuwirth, Robert. *Stealth of Nations: The Global Rise of the Informal Economy.* New York: Pantheon Books, 2011.

Noort, Wouter van. 'De tirannie van ons korte-termijndenken.' *NRC Handelsblad*, 28 January 2021.

Noyes, Jenny. 'Almost 20 Million Bank Account Records Lost by Commonwealth Bank.' *The Sydney Morning Herald*, 2 May 2018.

O'Neil, Cathy. *Weapons of Math Destruction: How Big Data Increases Inequality and Threatens Democracy.* New York: Crown Books, 2016.

Ogilvy, David. *On Advertising.* New York: Vintage Books, 1985.

Packard, Vance. *The Hidden Persuaders.* New York: David McKay, 1957.

Paglen, Trevor, and A.C. Thompson. *Torture Taxi: On the Trail of the CIA's Rendition Flights.* London: Icon Books, 2006.

Pallister, David. 'How the US Sent $12bn in Cash to Iraq: And Watched It Vanish.' *The Guardian*, 8 February 2007.

Papanek, Victor J. *Design for the Real World: Human Ecology and Social Change.* New York: Pantheon Books, 1972.

Parenti, Christian. *The Soft Cage: Surveillance in American from Slavery to the War on Terror.* New York: Basic Books, 2003.

Pater, Ruben. *The Politics of Design: A (Not So) Global Manual for Visual Communication.* Amsterdam: BIS Publishers, 2016.

Pedersen, J.M. 'Properties of Property: A Jurisprudential Analysis.' *The Commoner. Special Issue on Commoning*, 14 (Winter 2010), pp. 138–210.

Playfair, William. *The Commercial and Political Atlas*, 1768.

Poynor, Rick. *No More Rules.* New Haven: Yale University Press, 2003.

Precarious Workers Brigade, *Training for Exploitation? Politicising Employability and Reclaiming Education.* London: Journal of Aesthetics & Protest Press, 2017.

Rappeport, Alan. 'Harriet Tubman $20 Bill Is Delayed Until Trump Leaves Office, Mnuchin Says.' *The New York Times*, 22 May 2019.

Reich, Rob. *Just Giving: Why Philanthropy Is Failing Democracy and How It Can Do Better.* Princeton: Princeton University Press, 2018.

Rhodes, Carl, and Peter Bloom. 'The Trouble with Charitable Billionaires.' *The Guardian*, 24 May 2018.

Roberts, Lucienne, et al., eds. *Graphic Designers Surveyed.* London: GraphicDesign&, 2015.

Rogers, James E. Thorold. *Six Centuries of Work and Wages: The History of English Labour.* London: Allen and Unwin, 1949.

Rorty, James. *Our Masters Voice: Advertising.* New York: The John Day Company, 1934.

Rushe, Dominic. 'US Bosses Now Earn 312 Times the Average Worker's Wage, Figures Show.' *The Guardian*, 16 August 2018.

S–Z

Scott, James C. *Seeing Like a State: How Certain Schemes to Improve the Human Condition.* New Haven: Yale University Press, 1998.

—. *Two Cheers for Anarchism: Six Easy Pieces on Autonomy, Dignity and Meaningful Work and Play.* Princeton: Princeton University Press, 2012.

Sennett, Richard. *The Corrosion of Character: The Personal Consequences of Work in the Capitalism.* New York: W.W. Norton & Co., 1998.

—. 'The Workshop.' In *The Craftsman.* London: Penguin Books, 2008.

Shaughnessy, Adrian. *How to Be a Graphic Designer, without Losing Your Soul.* Princeton: Princeton Architectural Press, 2005.

Shenker, Jack. 'Strike 2.0: How Gig Economy Workers are Using Tech to Fight Back.' *The Guardian*, 31 August 2019.

Shteyngart, Gary. *Super Sad True Love Story: A Novel.* New York: Random House, 2010.

Siegelaub, Seth, and Armand Mattelart. *Communication and Class Struggle: I. Capitalism, Imperialism: An Anthology in 2 Volumes.* New York: International General, 1979.

Smith, Adam. *The Wealth of Nations.* Buffalo: Prometheus Books, 1991.

Spade, Dean. *Mutual Aid: Building Solidarity During This Crisis (and the Next).* New York and London: Verso Books, 2020.

—. 'Solidarity Not Charity: Mutual Aid for Mobilization and Survival.' *Social Text* 142, vol. 38, no. 1 (March 2020), 131–151.

Sparks, Hannah, and Suzy Weiss. 'Every Bikini Photo You See Is Probably Fake.' *The New York Post*, 16 July 2018.

'Specification of the £1 Coin: A Technical Consultation', *HM Treasury*, 12 September 2014.

Srnicek, Nick, and Alex Williams. *Inventing the Future: Postcapitalism and a World Without Work.* London: Verso Books, 2015.

Srnicek, Nick. *Platform Capitalism.* Cambridge, UK: Polity Press, 2017.

Standing, Guy. *The Precariat: The New Dangerous Class.* London etc.: Bloomsbury, 2011.

Steyerl, Hito. *The Wretched of the Screen.* Berlijn: Sternberg Press, 2012.

Story, Louise. 'Anywhere the Eye Can See, It's Likely to See an Ad.' *The New York Times*, 15 January 2007.

Sudjic, Deyan. *The Language of Things.* London: Penguin Books, 2008.

Suzman, James. 'Why "Bushman Banter" was Crucial to Hunter-Gatherers' Evolutionary Success.' *The Guardian*, 29 October 2017.

Tabb, William K. *The Long Default: New York City and the Urban Fiscal Crisis.* New York: Monthly Review Press, 1982.

Triggs, Teal. 'Scissors and Glue: Punk Fanzines and the Creation of a DIY Aesthetic.' *Journal of Design History* 19, no. 1 (2008), pp. 69–83.

Tufte, Edward. *The Visual Display of Quantitative Information.* Cheshire: Graphics Press, 2001.

Turnbull, David. *Maps Are Territories: Science is an Atlas: A Portfolio of Exhibits.* Chicago: University of Chicago Press, 1993.

Uncertain Commons, *Speculate This!* Durham and London: Duke University Press, 2013.

UNCTAD. *World Investment Report 2019: Special Economic Zones.* New York: United Nations Publications, 2019.

Utrilla, P., et al. 'A Palaeolithic Map from 13,660 calBP: Engraved Stone Blocks from the Late Magdalenian in Abauntz Cave (Navarra, Spain).' *Journal of Human Evolution* 57, no. 2 (2009), pp. 99–111.

Velden, Daniel van der. 'Research and Destroy.' *Metropolis M* no. 2, April/May 2006.

Vishmidt, Marina, Vinca Kruk and Daniel van der Velden, eds. *Uncorporate Identity: Metahaven.* Zurich: Lars Muller, 2010.

Weber, Max. *The Protestant Ethic and the Spirit of Capitalism.* New York: Routledge, 2001.

Weeks, Kathi. *The Problems with Work.* Durham: Duke University Press, 2011.

Wheary, Jennifer, and Tamara Draut, *Who Pays? The Winners and Losers of Credit Card Deregulation.* New York: Demos, 2007.

Whitworth-Smith, Andrew C. *Solidarity Economies, Networks and the Positioning of Power in Alternative Cultural Production and Activism in Brazil: The Case of Fora do Eixo.* Diss. University of California, San Diego, 2014.

Wines, Michael. 'The Long History of the U.S. Government Asking Americans Whether They Are Citizens.' *The New York Times*, 12 July 2019.

Wingate, Arthur Frederick. 'Working for Morris & Co.' *JWMS 11*, no. 2 (Spring 1995), pp. 31–32.

World Social Report 2020: Inequality in a Rapidly Changing World. S.l.: United Nations Department of Economic and Social Affairs, 2020.

Wright, Erik Olin. 'Destination Beyond Capitalism.' In *How to Be an Anticapitalist in the Twenty-First Century.* London: Verso Books, 2019.

Yagdo, Ben. 'A Short History of "Hack".' *The New Yorker*, 6 March 2014.

Zuboff, Shoshana. *The Age of Surveillance Capitalism.* New York: Hachette, 2019.

ONLINE SOURCES

A–C

'5 shocking facts about extreme global inequality and how to even it up.' *Oxfam*, 21 October 2019. oxfam.org/en/5-shocking-facts-about-extreme-global-inequality-and-how-even-it, accessed 21 January 2021.

'250 Recommendations on How to Stop "Infodemics".' *Forum on Information & Democracy*, 12 November 2020. information democracy.org/2020/11/12/250-recommen-dations-on-how-to-stop-infodemics/, accessed 22 January 2021.

'Aantal ontruimingen corporatiewoningen historisch laag in Amsterdam.' 13 February 2018. amsterdamsdagblad.nl/gemeente/aantal-ontruimingen-corporatiewoningen-historisch-laag-in-amsterdam.

Aguilar, Carlos. 'Calarts Students Launch Protest as Annual Tuition Rises to Over $50K.' *Cartoon Brew,* 15 March 2015, cartoonbrew.com/schools/calarts-students-launch-protest-as-annual-tuition-rises-to-over-50k-171415.html, accessed 22 January 2021.

AIGA Design Census 2019, *designcensus.org*, accessed 20 January 2021.

aiga.org/history-timeline, accessed 28 January 2021.

Alexander, Donovan. 'Mark Zuckerberg's $5 Billion Project to End Disease Within a Generation.' *Interesting Engineering*, 6 January 2019. interestingengineering.com/mark-zuckerbergs-5-billion-project-to-end-disease-within-a-generation, accessed 22 January 2021.

allpossiblefutures.net, accessed 13 February 2021.

ama.org/topics/branding.

Anixter, Julia. 'Equal Pay in Design: How Do We Make It a Reality?' *AIGA.org*, 12 April 2016. aiga.org/equal-pay-day-for-women-in-design, accessed 20 January 2021.

'Anthony Burrill tells us about his numerous Etsy WORK HARD rip-offs.' *It's Nice That*, 26 November 2015. itsnicethat.com/articles/anthony-burril-plagiarism-work-hard-be-nice-to-people, accessed 20 January 2021.

'Anti-Competitive Agreements.' *European Commission*, 16 April 2012. ec.europa.eu/competition/consumers/agreements_en.html, accessed 22 January 2021.

antiuniversity.org, accessed 22 January 2021.

archive.designigniteschange.org, accessed 22 January 2021.

Armin, 'News: News Corp New Corporate Logo.' *Brand New*, 29 May 2013. underconsideration.com/brandnew/archives/news_news_corp_new_corporate_logo.php, accessed 19 January 2021.

Aubert, Danielle. 'The Politics of the Joy of Printing in Detroit*.' *Infinite mile Detroit*, no. 29, June 2016. infinitemiledetroit.com/THE_POLITICS_OF_THE_JOY_OF_PRINTING_IN_DETROIT.html, accessed 21 January 2021.

Axelrod, Tal. 'Dell CEO rejects Ocasio-Cortez's tax plan at Davos.' The Hill, 23 January 2019. thehill.com/policy/finance/domestic-taxes/426695-dell-ceo-rejects-ocasio-cortezs-tax-plan-at-davos, accessed 1 February 2021.

Babic, Milan, Eelke Heemskerk and Jan Fichtner. 'Who is More Powerful – States or Corporations?' *The Conversation*, 10 July 2018. theconversation.com/who-is-more-powerful-states-or-corporations-99616, accessed 18 January 2021.

backspace.com/notes/2005/09/collectives-for-designers.php, accessed 21 January 2021.

Badenov, Boris. 'As many enemies as there are slaves: Spartacus and the politics of servile rebellion in the late republic.' *Libcom.org*, 8 June 2010. libcom.org/history/many-enemies-there-are-slaves%E2%80%99-spartacus-politics-servile-rebellion-late-republic, accessed 17 January 2021.

Barrett, Brian. 'An Artist Used 99 Phones to Fake a Google Maps Traffic Jam.' *WIRED*, 3 February 2020. wired.com/story/99-phones-fake-google-maps-traffic-jam/, accessed 22 January 2021.

Bauman, Melissa. 'How Accurate Were Predictions for the Future?' *RAND Review*, 14 July 2020. rand.org/blog/rand-review/2020/07/how-accurate-were-predictions-for-the-future.html, accessed 22 January 2021.

bcw-global.com.

Bell, Nick. 'Brand Madness: The Steamroller of Branding.' *Eye Magazine* 14, no. 53 (2004). eyemagazine.com/feature/article/the-steam roller-of-branding-text-in-full

Berardi, Franco 'Bifo'. 'Time, Acceleration, and Violence.' *e-flux journal* 27 (September 2011). e-flux.com/journal/27/67999/time-accelera-tion-and-violence, accessed 22 January 2021.

Berger, Lynn. 'In onze prestatiemaatschappij is iedereen een marathonloper (maar waar rennen we heen?).' *De Correspondent*, 4 August 2020. decorrespondent.nl/11458/in-onze-prestatiemaatschappij-is-ieder een-een-marathonloper-maar-waar-rennen-we-heen/381769102-565bca5a, accessed 20 January 2021.

Bierut, Michael. 'I'm With Her.' *Design Observer*, 28 March 2017. designobserver.com/feature/im-with-her/39523, accessed 27 February 2021.

Bleecker, Julian. *Design Fiction: A Short Essay on Design, Science, Fact and Fiction*, 2009. blog.nearfuturelaboratory.com/2009/03/17/design-fiction-a-short-essay-on-design-science-fact-and-fiction/.

bno.nl/page/english, accessed 27 January 2021.

Boris, Sarah. 'The Design Industry Needs to Take a Stand Against Free Pitching.' *EYE on design*, 15 May 2019. eyeondesign.aiga.org/the-design-industry-needs-to-take-a-stand-against-free-pitching/, accessed 22 January 2021.

Brave New Alps. *Designers' Inquiry*, 2013. brave-new-alps.com/designers-inquiry/.

brave-new-alps.com/about, accessed 14 February 2021.

'Buffett warns on investment "time bomb".' *BBC News,* 4 March 2003. news.bbc.co.uk/2/hi/

business/2817995.stm, accessed 22 January 2021.

Buzon, Darin. 'Design Thinking is a Rebrand for White Supremacy: How the Current State of Design is Simply a Digitally Status Quo.' *Medium*, 2 March 2020. dabuzon.medium.com/design-thinking-is-a-rebrand-for-white-supremacy-b3d31aa55831, accessed 22 January 2021.

calarts.edu, accessed 28 January 2021.

'Central School of Arts and Crafts.' Mapping the Practice and Profession of Sculpture in Britain & Ireland, 1861–1951. sculpture.gla.ac.uk/view/organization.php?id=msib2_1212166601, accessed 22 January 2021.

Chan, Seb. 'Museum Resolution: Do Away with Salary Cloaking.' *The Walker Reader*, 12 March 2021. walkerart.org/magazine/sound board-museum-resolutions-seb-chan, accessed 20 January 2021.

christiannold.com/archives/1, accessed 10 February 2021.

Cole, Teju. 'The White-Savior Industrial Complex.' *The Atlantic*, 21 March 2012. theatlantic.com/international/archive/2012/03/the-white-savior-industrial-complex/254843/, accessed 22 January 2021.

Cole, Teju. Twitter post, 8 March 2012, twitter.com/tejucole/status/177809396070498304, accessed 22 January 2021.

commonknowledge.coop, accessed 22 January 2021.

creativecommons.org, accessed 25 January 2021.

D–F

Dandavate, Uday. 'Design Activism.' *Medium*, 16 September 2019. medium.com/sonicrim-stories-from-the-edge/design-activism-496db463e5ee, accessed 1 February 2021.

Deane, Michael T. 'Top 6 Reasons New Businesses Fail.' *Investopedia*, 28 February 2020. investopedia.com/financial-edge/1010/top-6-reasons-new-businesses-fail.aspx, accessed 22 January 2021.

designjustice.org, accessed 21 January 2021.

designthinking.ideo.com/, accessed 22 January 2021.

Desjardins, Jeff. 'The Tech Takeover of Advertising in One Chart, *Visualcapitalist*, 22 September 2017. visualcapitalist.com/the-tech-takeover-of-advertising-in-one-chart/, accessed 22 January 2021.

Diaz, Jesus. 'This Machine Can Tell You if Your Photos Suck or Rule.' *Gizmodo*, 22 November 2021. gizmodo.com/this-machine-can-tell-you-if-your-photos-suck-or-rule-5862074, accessed 13 February 2021.

Disnovation, profilingtheprofilers.com, accessed 22 January 2021.

Drumm, Perrin. 'Can We Design a More Perfect Design Union?' *AIGA Eye on design*, 19 June 2018. eyeondesign.aiga.org/can-we-design-a-more-perfect-design-union, accessed 21 January 2021.

Drumm, Perrin. 'Equity Investing is Expensive, Risky, and Slow: So Why Are All These Designers Trying to Become Venture Capitalists?' *AIGA Eye on design*, 28 August 2017. eyeondesign.aiga.org/equity-investing-is-expensive-risky-and-slow-so-why-are-all-these-designers-trying-to-become-venture-capitalists, accessed 22 January 2021.

Dymoke, Ned. '5 of the Richest Companies in History.' *The Big Think*, 17 October 2018, bigthink.com/culture-religion/5-of-the-richest-companies-in-history?rebellt item=2#rebelltitem2.

ec.europa.eu/growth/content/too-good-be-true-real-price-fake-products_en, accessed 8 March 2021.

ecotones.caveat.be/osp.html, accessed 15 February 2021.

'Educated, Overworked, Underpaid: Graphic Designers Surveyed.' *It's Nice That*, 15 January 2016. itsnicethat.com/news/graphic-designers-surveyed-results-150116, accessed 22 January 2021.

Efrussi, Tatiana. 'After the Ball: Hannes Meyer Presenting the Bauhaus in Moscow.' *Bauhaus Imaginista* Edition 3: Moving Away, 2018. bauhaus-imaginista.org/articles/2083/after-the-ball, accessed 28 January 2021.

en.wikipedia.org/wiki/Burson_Cohn_%26_Wolfe.

en.wikipedia.org/wiki/Copyleft, accessed 22 January 2021.

en.wikipedia.org/wiki/Free_Breakfast_for_ Children, accessed 22 January 2021.

en.wikipedia.org/wiki/Seven_generation_ sustainability, accessed 30 January 2021.

en.wikipedia.org/wiki/Time-based_currency, accessed 10 February 2021.

'Ethical Design Manifesto.' 2017, ind.ie/ethical-design, accessed 22 January 2021.

European Economic and Social Committee. *Fake Products Cost 800,000 Jobs Annually*, 18 July 2017. eesc.europa.eu/en/news-media/news/fake-products-cost-800000-jobs-annually, accessed 23 December 2019.

Evening Class, 'Open Letter: Against Undisclosed Salaries.' *The Pluralist*, 23 April 2020. thepluralist.info/Open-Letter-Against-Undis closed-Salaries, accessed 20 January 2021.

'"Every non-free program is an injustice": Richard Stallman on the Free Software Movement.' *e-flux*, 1 October 2018. conversations.e-flux.com/t/every-non-free-program-is-an-injus-tice-richard-stallman-on-the-free-software-movement/8474, accessed 22 January 2021.

'Facebook, Google and Microsoft "avoiding $3bn in tax in poorer nations".' *BBC News,* 26 October 2020. bbc.com/news/business-54691572, accessed 22 January 2021.

Farrell, Jenny. '100 Years of Bauhaus: Building for a Society of Equals.' *People's Worlds*, 25 March 2019. peoplesworld.org/article/100-years-of-bauhaus-building-for-a-society-of-equals/, accessed 22 January 2021

fastcompany.com/3061335/25-smart-designs-that-could-help-ease-the-refugee-crisis#!/vizhome/GreenCitiesScore/Sheet1, accessed 22 January 2021.

femkeherregraven.net/liquid/.

First Things First Manifesto, 1964, designishistory.com/1960/first-things-first/, accessed 20 January 2021.

Forum on Information & Democracy, information democracy.org/principles/, accessed 22 January 2021.

frontex.europa.eu/faq/key-facts/, accessed 22 January 2021.

futureofdesigneducation.org, accessed 22 January 2021.

G–J

gapminder.org/dollar-street, accessed 10 February 2021.

Garcia, Diego. 'Extreme Poverty Affects 13.7 Million Brazilians, Says IBGE.' *Folha de St. Paolo*, 13 November 2020. www1.folha.uol. com.br/internacional/en/business/2020/11/ extreme-poverty-affects-137-million-brazil ians-says-ibge.shtml, accessed 19 March 2021.

Gollihue, Krystin. 'The History of Global Charitable Giving: Why We Need to Remember.' *Philanthropy Journal*, 18 July 2016. pj.news. chass.ncsu.edu/2016/07/18/the-history-of-global-charitable-giving-why-we-need-to-re member, accessed 22 January 2021.

Goodman, Stefanie. 'Labor Abuse and Exploitation: The Dark Side of Ecuador's Banana Industry.' *Borgen Magazine*, 12 November 2020. borgenmagazine.com/labor-abuse-and-exploitation-the-dark-side-of-ecuadors-banana-industry/, accessed 20 January 2021.

Gram, Maggie. 'On Design Thinking.' *N+1 magazine* 35 (Fall 2019). nplusonemag.com/ issue-35/reviews/on-design-thinking/, accessed 22 January 2021.

Graphic Design forum. graphicdesignforum.com/ /micro-managing-boss-or-just-a-regular-creative-director/13149/7, accessed 21 January 2021.

graphicdesignforum.com/t/q-for-in-house-graphic-designers-only-mostly-print/6957/17, accessed 22 January 2021.

Grey, Sarah. 'Four Myths About the 'Freelancer Class.' *Jacobin Magazine*, 5 July 2015, jacobin mag.com/2015/05/freelance-independent-contractor-union-precariat, accessed 22 January 2021.

Gropius, Walter. *Bauhaus manifesto*, 1919. bauhausmanifesto.com.

hardworkinggoodlooking.com/about, accessed 22 January 2021.

Harris, David Evan. 'São Paulo: A City Without Ads.' *Adbusters*, 3 August 2007. adbusters.org/ article/sao-paulo-a-city-without-ads, accessed 19 January 2021.

Harris, Tristan. 'How Technology is Hijacking Your Mind—from a Magician and Google Design Ethicist', *Medium*, 18 May 2016. medium.com/ thrive-global/how-technology-hijacks-peoples-minds-from-a-magician-and-google-s-design-ethicist-56d62ef5edf3#.qsgtv1l6b, accessed 22 January 2021.

Hijacking the Outdoor Digital Billboard. youtube. com/watch?v=tpZ_NDx35u8, accessed 22 January 2021.

iamsterdam.com/en/business/investment-opportunities, accessed 13 October 2019.

Illich, Ivan. 'To Hell with Good Intentions.' Lecture at CIASP Canada, 1968. dial-infos.org/alterin fos/spip.php?article5168, accessed 22 January 2021.

itsnicethat.com/news/graphic-designers-surveyed-results-150116.

Jen, Natasha. 'Why Design Thinking is Bullshit.' *It's Nice That*, 23 February 2018. itsnicethat. com/articles/natasha-jen-pentagram-graph icdesign-230218, accessed 22 January 2021.

Johnson, Bradely. 'World's Largest Advertisers: Spending is Growing (and Surging in China).' *AdAge*, 5 December 2017. adage.com/ article/cmo-strategy/world-s-largest-advertisers-2017/311484, accessed 22 January 2021.

K–M

Kalman, Tibor. Interview by Charlie Rose, 24 December 1998. charlierose.com/ videos/17661, accessed 27 January 2021.

Keefer, Tom. 'A Short Introduction to the Two Row Wampum.' *Briar Patch Magazine*, 10 March 2014. briarpatchmagazine.com/articles/view/ a-short-introduction-to-the-two-row-wampum, accessed 30 August 2019.

Kenedi, Aaron. 'Marks Men: An Interview with Ivan Chermayeff, Tom Geismar, and Sagi Haviv of Chermayeff & Geisma.' *Printmag*, 14 September 2011. printmag.com/post/marks-men-an-interview-with-ivan-chermayeff-tom-geis mar-and-sagi-haviv-of-chermayeff-geismar-2, accessed 18 January 2021.

Kidd, Chip. 'An Interview with Milton Glaser.' *Believer Magazine*, 1 September 2003. believ ermag.com/an-interview-with-milton-glaser/, accessed 14 October 2019.

klomp.tv/#/053204149098/, accessed 22 January 2021.

Kohut, Ola. 'Digital tools for self-organized change: Interview with Gemma Copeland.' *Autark*, 17 October 2019. blog.autark.xyz/ interview-with-gemma-copeland, accessed 1 February 2021.

Kraniotis, Leen. 'Airbnb ruim verdubbeld in Amsterdam: 1,7 miljoen overnachtingen.' 2 May 2017. nos.nl/artikel/2171069-airbnb-ruim-verdubbeld-in-amsterdam-1-7-miljoen-overnachtingen.

Kropotkin, Peter. *Mutual Aid: A Factor of Evolution*, 1902. theanarchistlibrary.org/library/petr-kropotkin-mutual-aid-a-factor-of-evolution, accessed 22 January 2021.

Lorusso, Silvio. 'Fake It till You Make It: Genesis of the Entrepreneurial Precariat.' *Entreprecariat, Institute of Network Cultures*, 22 May 2018. networkcultures.org/entreprecariat/fake-it-till-you-make-it-genesis-of-the-entrepreneurial-precariat, accessed 22 January 2021.

Madrigal, Alexis C. 'Episode 1: Welcome to Global

Capitalism.' *Medium*, 7 April 2017. medium. com/containers/episode-1-welcome-to-global-capitalism-f9f56c92f414, accessed 21 August 2019.

Magdoff, Harry. 'The Meaning of Work: A Marxist Perspective.' *The Monthly Review*, 1 October 2006. monthlyreview.org/2006/10/01/the-meaning-of-work-a-marxist-perspective/, accessed 28 July 2020.

makersunite.eu, accessed 22 January 2021.

Maldonado, Ben. 'Eugenics on the Farm: Ellwood Cubberley.' *The Stanford Daily*, 4 February 2020. stanforddaily.com/2020/02/04/eugenics-on-the-farm-ellwood-cubberley/, accessed 28 January 2021.

marxists.org/reference/archive/debord/1963/never-work.htm, accessed 21 January 2021.

Mat, Patrick. '50 years Later: How the Credit Card Has Changed America.' *Mercury News*, 14 August 2016. www.mercurynews.com/2008/09/12/50-years-later-how-the-credit-card-has-changed-america/, accessed 6 August 2019.

Matsakis, Louis. 'How the West Got China's Social Credit System Wrong.' *WIRED.com*, 29 July 2019. wired.com/story/china-social-credit-score-system/, accessed 7 August 2019.

'Mediterranean "world's deadliest border" for migrants, says UN.' *Deutsche Welle*, 25 November 2017. dw.com/en/mediterranean-worlds-deadliest-border-for-migrants-says-un/a-41525468, accessed 22 January 2021.

Metev, Denis. '39+ Smartphone Statistics You Should Know in 2020.' *Review42*, 21 November 2021. review42.com/smartphone-statistics, accessed 22 January 2021.

midianinja.org.

Miller, Meg. 'What Does It Mean to Unionize When You're Your Own Boss?' *AIGA Eye on Design*, 22 October 2019. eyeondesign.aiga.org/what-does-it-mean-to-unionize-when-youre-your-own-boss/, accessed 20 January 2021.

Millington, Alison. '23 countries where money can buy you a second passport or "elite residency".' *Business Insider*, 27 December 2018. business-insider.nl/countries-where-you-can-buy-citizenship-residency-or-passport-2018-9?international=true&r=US, accessed 16 August 2019.

Mogensen, Michael. 'NIUN: Saudi Futures.' *Journal of Futures Studies*, 11 October 2018. jfsdigital.org/2018/10/11/niun-saudi-futures, accessed 22 January 2021.

moma.org/interactives/exhibitions/2013/design-andviolence/about, accessed 22 January 2021.

mutualaiddisasterrelief.org/, accessed 22 January 2021.

Mukerjee, Aditya. 'I Can Text You A Pile of Poo, But I Can't Write My Name.' *Model View Culture* 18 (17 March 2015). modelviewculture.com/pieces/i-can-text-you-a-pile-of-poo-but-i-cant-write-my-name, accessed 22 January 2021.

Neural Filters. Adobe.com, helpx.adobe.com/photoshop/using/neural-filters.html, accessed 22 January 2021.

'Nike workers don't earn 20 cents an hour or work 80 hours a week.' *Africa Check*, 14 August 2019. africacheck.org/fact-checks/fbchecks/nike-workers-dont-earn-20-cents-hour-or-work-80-hours-week, accessed 20 January 2021.

Occupational Outlook Handbook, *US Bureau for labor statistics*, 1 September 2020. bls.gov/ooh/arts-and-design/graphic-designers.htm#tab-3, accessed 22 January 2021.

Oliveira, Pedro, and Luiza Prado. 'Cheat Sheet for a Non- (or Less-) Colonialist Speculative Design.' *Medium*, 10 September 2014. medium.com/a-parede/cheat-sheet-for-a-non-or-less-colonialist-speculative-design-9a6b4ae3c465, accessed 22 January 2021.

osp.kitchen, accessed 22 January 2021.

ourworldindata.org/literacy, accessed 28 January 2021.

ourworldindata.org/working-hours, accessed 25 January 2021.

oxfam.org/en/press-releases/worlds-billionaires-have-more-wealth-46-billion-people, accessed 10 February 2021.

p2pfoundation.net/, accessed 17 March 2021.

parkdalepeopleseconomy.ca, accessed 15 February 2021.

Pater, Ruben. 'Treating the refugee crisis as a design problem is problematic.' *Dezeen*, 21 April 2016. dezeen.com/2016/04/21/ruben-pater-opinion-what-design-can-do-refugee-crisis-problematic-design/, accessed 22 January 2021.

'Peeling Back the Truth on Bananas', *Food Empowerment Project*, 28 April 2020, foodispower.org/our-food-choices/bananas/, accessed 19 January 2019.

Pflug, Sarah. 'Overwork isn't heroic: Tips from creatives on how to be a success without overdoing it.' *Creative Boom*, 3 September 2018. creativeboom.com/tips/how-to-be-successful-without-working-too-hard/, accessed 20 January 2021.

quod.lib.umich.edu/d/did/, accessed 12 January 2021.

Ressler, Eric. 'Causewashing is the New Greenwashing.' *Cosmic*, 17 May 2018. designbycosmic.com/insights/articles/causewashing-is-the-new-greenwashing, accessed 15 February 2021.

rethinkingeconomics.org, accessed 6 March 2021.

'Rising inequality affecting more than two-thirds of the globe, but it's not inevitable: New UN report.' *UN News*, 21 January 2020. news.un.org/en/story/2020/01/1055681, accessed 21 January 2021.

Rock, Michael. 'On Unprofessionalism.' *2 x 4*, 1994. 2x4.org/ideas/1994/on-unprofessionalism/, accessed 27 January 2021.

Sampath, Sheila. 'We Can Build in Different Ways.' *Studio Magazine* Fall/Winter 2020. studiomagazine.ca/articles/2020/11/we-can-build-in-different-ways, accessed 14 February 2021.

Schlanger, Zoë. 'Daylight Saving Time as Americans Know It Was Instituted by Corporate Lobbies, Not Farmers.' *Quartz*, 4 November 2017. qz.com/1120488/daylight-saving-time-as-americans-know-it-was-instituted-by-corporate-lobbies-not-farmers/, accessed 13 August 2019.

'Shell Scenarios.' shell.com/energy-and-innovation/the-energy-future/scenarios/what-are-scenarios.html, accessed 22 January 2021.

Skeldon, Paul. 'Young Affiliates: Nearly a Fifth of British Children Aspire to be Social Media Influencers.' *Telemedia Magazine*, 31 January 2019, telemediaonline.co.uk/young-affiliates-nearly-a-fifth-of-british-children-aspire-to-be-social-media-influencers/, accessed 19 January 2021.

Smith, Lily. 'T-Mobile is suing a company for using magenta: Can it really "own" a color?' *Fast Company*, 29 November 2019. fastcompany.com/90436680/t-mobile-is-suing-a-company-for-using-magenta-can-it-really-own-a-color, accessed 25 January 2021.

sonicrim.com, accessed 1 February 2021.

Spencer, Keith A. 'The Neoliberal Politics of Emoji.' *Salon*, 23 July 2017. salon.com/2017/07/23/the-neoliberal-politics-of-emoji/, accessed 22 January 2021.

statista.com/statistics/986392/co2-emissions-per-cap-by-country-eu, accessed 11 February 2021.

stats.oecd.org, accessed 22 January 2021.

Stinson, Liz. 'The Trick to Recession-proofing Your Design Practice? Try Something New.' *EYE on design*, 3 October 2019, eyeondesign.aiga.org/the-trick-to-recession-proofing-your-design-practice-try-something-new, accessed 22 January 2021.

Ström, Matthew. 'The Paradox at the Heart of A/B Testing.' *matthewstrom.com*, 9 January 2020. matthewstrom.com/writing/ab-testing-paradox, accessed 22 January 2021.

Sueda, Jon. 'On Speculation.' *All Possible Futures*, 2014. allpossiblefutures.net/on-speculation-3-2, accessed 28 January 2021.

technologyreview.com/2020/12/17/1013213/hunger-starvation-food-policy-history, accessed 10 February 2021.

'The Entire History of Advertising.' *Softcube Blog*, 4 August 2020. softcube.com/the-entire-history-of-advertising, accessed 19 January 2021.

'The new investors in underwater sea cables.' *Internet Health report*, April 2019. internethealthreport.org/2019/the-new-investors-in-underwater-sea-cables, accessed 22 January 2021.

thefuturelaboratory.com, accessed 22 January 2021.

thepublic.ca/studio, accessed 15 February 2021.

thepublicstudio.ca/news/a-labour-of-love-kaya-joan, accessed 15 February 2021.

thepublicstudio.ca/news/a-labour-of-love-the-public-team, accessed 15 February 2021.

thewomansbuilding.org, accessed 13 February 2021.

thinkbeforeyoupink.org, accessed 1 February 2021.

'This is What Starting a Design "Union" Looks Like.' *AIGA Eye on design*, 19 June 2018. eyeondesign.aiga.org/this-is-what-starting-a-design-union-looks-like, accessed 5 July 2018.

Thomson, Frances, and Sahil Dutta, 'Financialisation: A Primer', *The Transnational Institute*, 13 September 2018, tni.org/en/publication/financialisation-a-primer, accessed 19 January 2021.

Thorpe, Ann. 'Defining Design as Activism.' 2011. designactivism.net/wp-content/uploads/2011/05/Thorpe-definingdesignactivism.pdf, accessed 1 February 2021.

timebank.cc., accessed 10 February 2021.

today.yougov.com/topics/food/explore/brand/Chiquita, accessed 20 January 2021.

Tonkinwise, Cameron. Twitter post, 13 July 2020. twitter.com/camerontw/status/1282483355620003840, accessed 22 January 2021.

Toppins, Aggie. 'Can We Teach Graphic Design History Without the Cult of Hero Worship?' *Eye on design*, 29 May 2020. eyeondesign.aiga.org/can-we-teach-graphic-design-history-without-the-cult-of-hero-worship/, accessed 22 January 2021.

Toppins, Aggie. 'Designers, Please Pay Your Interns.' *Eye on design*, 4 January 2018. eyeondesign.aiga.org/designers-please-pay-your-interns/, accessed 20 January 2021.

uber.com/nl/en/elevate, accessed 22 January 2021.

underconsideration.com/brandnew/.

'Understanding the Seven Cooperative Principles.' *NCREA*, 1 December 2016. electric.coop/seven-cooperative-principles%E2%80%8B, accessed 21 January 2021.

uvwunion.org.uk/design-culture-workers, accessed 21 January 2021.

uvwunion.org.uk/en/sectors/designers-cultural-workers, accessed 22 January 2021.

v1.benbarry.com/, accessed 20 January 2021.

'Van werkenden loopt zzp'er meeste risico op armoede.' *CBS*, 5 March 2019. cbs.nl/nl-nl/nieuws/2019/10/van-werkenden-loopt-zzp-er-meeste-risico-op-armoede, accessed 22 January 2021.

Veerman, Yuri. 'Van wie is de stad: Political Campaign 2018.' yuriveerman.nl/Van-wie-is-de-stad, accessed 13 October 2019.

velvetyne.fr, accessed 22 January 2021.

Vergès, Françoise. 'Capitalocene, Waste, Race, and Gender.' *e-flux journal* 100 (May 2019). e-flux.com/journal/100/269165/capitalocene-waste-race-and-gender/, accessed 10 March 2021.

viacampesina.org/en, accessed 17 March 2021.

vloerwerk.org, accessed 11 February 2021.

w3.org/standards, accessed 27 January 2021.

'We Surveyed Gender Representation at Design Conferences Again—and Not Much Has Changed.' *AIGA Eye on design*, 16 January 2020. eyeondesign.aiga.org/we-surveyed-gender-equity-at-design-conferences-again-and-not-much-has-changed/, accessed 20 January 2021.

web.archive.org/web/20120609172903/icdc.com/~paulwolf/colombia/caffery29dec1928.htm, accessed 19 January 2021.

Weigandt, Russell. 'The Problem with Brand Support of Black Lives Matter.' *Medium*, 19 June 2020. medium.com/swlh/the-problem-with-brand-support-of-black-lives-matter-7444f5a85122, accessed 15 February 2021.

Weightman, Gavin. 'The History of the Bar Code.' *Smithsonian Magazine*, 23 September 2015, smithsonianmag.com/innovation/history-bar-code-180956704, accessed 19 November 2019.

Weiss, Joshua Zane. 'Belief in the Potential Object: Technological Disobedience in Cuba.' *Walker Reader*, 7 March 2018. walkerart.org/magazine/ernesto-oroza-technological-disobedience-cuba, accessed 22 January 2021.

whatdesigncando.com/stories/challenge-what-design-can-do-for-refugees, accessed 22 January 2021.

Wikipedia.org/mutual_aid, accessed 22 January 2021.

women.statista.com/chart/17290/countries-with-most-equal-rights-for-women/, accessed 9 January 2021.

Wines, Michael. 'The Long History of the U.S. Government Asking Americans Whether They Are Citizens.' *The New York Times*, 12 July 2019, nytimes.com/2019/07/12/us/the-long-history-of-the-us-government-asking-americans-whether-they-are-citizens.html, accessed 16 August 2019.

'Work and Workplace.' news.gallup.com/poll/1720/work-work-place.aspx, accessed 20 January 2021.

World's billionaires have more wealth than 4.6 billion people, *Oxfam International*, 20 January 2020, oxfam.org/en/press-releases/worlds-billionaires-have-more-wealth-46-billion-people, accessed 20 January 2021.

worldometers.info/co2-emissions/ethiopia-co2-emissions, accessed 11 February 2021.

youtube.com/pibxs, accessed 15 February 2021.

youtube.com/watch?v=w-tFdreZB94&ab_channel=MicrosoftinBusiness, accessed 22 January 2021.

Zuber, Charles. 'The Logo That Lasted.' *Design Online*, 2017. designonline.org.au/the-logo-that-lasted/, accessed 18 January 2021.

Image Credits and Sources

54 commons.wikimedia.org/wiki/File:Hyper
    inflation_in_Germany_in_1923.jpg.
55 reddit.com/r/travel/comments/c7h3z8/
    money_market_in_hargeisa_somaliland.
56 newnumismatics.weebly.com/visa.html.
58 Illustration by Ruben Pater.
59 Illustration by Ruben Pater. Source ccsi.
    co.uk/artwork/artwork-full-colour.php.
60 99percentinvisible.org/episode/the-fresno-
    drop.
61 © American Express and © VISA.
62 Darren Cullen.
65 © Intuit. mint.intuit.com.
66 © Apple Computer. apple.com/apple-pay.
67 © Venmo; © Tikkie.
69 © Caroline Woolard. carolinewoolard.com/
    project/exchange-café.
72 © Lawrence Weiner. e-flux.com/announce
    ments/37598/e-flux-presents-time-currency
    -current-times.
72 © Ithaca Hours by Paul Glover. Source:
    Cornell University.
72 © This Ain't Rock and Roll. brixtonpound.
    org/product/b10-featuring-david-bowie.
73 © Christian Nold. christiannold.com/
    archives/1.
73 © Joseph Beuys. metamart.at.
73 © Zachary Gough. maxhaiven.com/
    political-economy-art-school.

The Designer as Engineer

74 Photo by Theodor Jung. Nitrate negative,
    LC-USF33- 004027-M1 [P&P]. Farm
    Security Administration — Office of War
    Information Photograph Collection. loc.gov/
    resource/fsa.8a13939.
76 Usage des Nouvelles Mesures. Système
    métrique et monétaire. 17.2 x 10.7 cm. Musée
    Carnavalet, Histoire de Paris. Autre titre:
    Calendriers. Divers.
78 nms.ac.uk/explore-our-collections/stories/
    world-cultures/gold-weights-from-ghana.
81 Photo from the Leipzig Spring Fair 1932,
    probably taken by staff at the Deutsche
    Institut für Normung, DIN. Via *Westfalen Post*.
83 Lt Dennis Dauphin, Lt Gary Dean Springer,
    and Sgt Joe Cook. themightyninth.org/
    War%20Stories/CONEX/CONEX.htm.
83 Drawing US Military. webdoc.sub.gwdg.de/
    ebook/p/2005/CMH_2/www.army.mil/cmh-
    pg/books/vietnam/logistic/chapter8.htm.
84 Patent by Joe Woodland, 1949. patents.
    google.com/patent/US2612994
85 Illustration by Ruben Pater.
87 Typometers © Rotring, 1983 and © Faber
    Castells, 1984.
88 en.wikipedia.org/wiki/File:US_Census_1860_
    Dundee_Roll.jpg
89 commons.wikimedia.org/wiki/File:
    Signalementskaart_Veenhuizen_Ommer
    schans_gevangene_3488.jpg
90 © US Census Bureau. flickr.com/photos/
    uscensusbureau/6878357486.
91 Detail from US Census Bureau form, 2018.

Image © US Census Bureau.
92 © Virginia Historical Society. Via Tucker
    McLachlan. librarycatalog.virginiahistory.
    org/final/portal.aspx?lang=en-US
93 © Virginia Historical Society. Via Tucker
    McLachlan. librarycatalog.virginiahistory.
    org/final/portal.aspx?lang=en-US
94 Femke Herregraven.
95 © Rijksoverheid Ministerie BZK, 2014.
    rijksoverheid.nl/binaries/rijksoverheid/
    documenten/brochures/2015/12/04/ken
    merken-nederlandse-paspoorten-en-
    nederlandse-identiteitskaart/kenmerken
    fld-2014-ned.pdf.
96 maz-online.de/Brandenburg/Stasi-Schnip
    sel-Beauftragte-fordern-Rekonstruktion
97 brenmarco.com.
99 appleinsider.com/articles/12/12/06/redacted-
    version-of-apple-htc-settlement-reveals-
    licensed-patents-little-else.
100 © US Census Bureau. flickr.com/photos/
    uscensusbureau/7024456499.
100 © Stadsarchief Amsterdam. archief.
    amsterdam/uitleg/indexen/56-gezins
    kaarten-1893-1939.
102 commons.wikimedia.org/wiki/File:1786_
    Playfair_-_20_Chart_of_the_National_Debt_of_
    England_(from_3e_edition,_1801).jpg
104 © Yale Babylonian Collection en.wikipedia.
    org/wiki/YBC_7289.
104 en.wikipedia.org/wiki/Cartesian_
    coordinate_system.
105 Frank Bunker Gilbreth, 1868–1924; Lillian
    Moller Gilbreth, 1878–1972, joint author;
    American society of mechanical engineers.
    archive.org/details/processcharts00gilb/
    page/12/mode/2up.
106 commons.wikimedia.org/wiki/File:
    Nightingale-mortality.jpg.
106 William Edward Burghardt Du Bois. Paris,
    1900–1900. Ink and watercolour, 710 × 560
    mm. Library of Congress.
108 Signs from different sources compiled by
    Ruben Pater.
111 William R. Shepherd, *Historical Atlas*, 1923.
    en.wikipedia.org/wiki/Open-field_system#/
    media/File:Plan_mediaeval_manor.jpg.
112 managementhelp.org/blogs/strategic-
    planning/2011/05/20/strategic-intuition/
    napoleon-plotting-strategy-with-map.
113 © La Région Auvergne-Rhône-Alpes.
    patrimoine.auvergnerhonealpes.fr/img/
    67a64624-1df7-44a3-a6fc-8b0cb3b1866c.
114 © Stadsarchief Amsterdam. geheugen
    vanoost.amsterdam/page/28334/uittreksel-
    uit-het-kadaster-van-de-diamantslijperij.
116 Henry Holiday, Ocean-Chart. From: Lewis
    Carroll, *The Hunting of the Snark*, 1876.
    snrk.de/the-ocean-chart.
118 Abraham Ortelius. Print coloured by hand,
    1571–1584. Koninklijke Bibliotheek PPN
    369376781. commons.wikimedia.org/wiki/
    File:Atlas_Ortelius_KB_PPN369376781-
    002av-002br.jpg
119 Photo by Ryan Vizzions. ryanvizzions.com.
120 Antonio de Herrera. Koninklijke Bibliotheek,

engraving on paper, 21 x 16 cm. commons.
wikimedia.org/wikiFile:AMH-8118-KB_Map_
of_Southeast_Asia.jpg.
122 © Iconoclasistas. Iconoclasistas.net
124 © Native Land. Nativeland.ca
125 United States Department of the Interior, 1
broadside: 1 illustration; 62 x 49 cm. Library
of Congress loc.gov/item/2015657622.
128 Photo by Francis Stewart, War Relocation
Authority photographer, (NARA record:
8464475) National Archives at College Park.
commons.wikimedia.org/wiki/File:Tule_
Lake_Relocation_Center,_Newell,_California._
Filing_clerk,_Hana_Uyeno._-_NARA_-
_536682.jpg

The Designer as Brander

130 Photo by Arthur Rothstein. 1 negative nitrate;
35 mm. Library of Congress. loc.getarchive.
net/media/branding-a-calf-quarter-circle-u-
roundup-montana-3.
132 © Hank Willis Thomas, *Scarred Chest*, 2003
Lambda photograph. Courtesy of the artist
and Jack Shainman Gallery, New York.
134 John H. Felch and William Riches. commons.
wikimedia.org/wiki/File:Branding_slaves.jpg.
135 © Collection Museum voor Wereldculturen.
c.18 cm. TM-H-2978, before 1877. hdl.
handle.net/20.500.11840/201347.
136 © English Heritage. british-history.co.uk.
137 © Wenceslas Hollar Digital Collection,
1607–1677, 28 x 17 cm,. commons.wikimedia.
org/wiki. File:Wenceslas_Hollar_-_Arms_of_
knights_of_the_Garter_4.jpg
138 Illustration Josef Hoevenaar. Via
Boekwinkeltjes.nl.
141 reddit.com.
141 robinchu.com.
142 Compiled from various sources by Ruben
Pater.
144 reddit.com
146 Logotypes © Respective companies.
148 Source unknown.
150 Photo by Rob DiCaterino. commons.wikimedia.
org/wiki/File:Line_at_Apple_Store_in_NYC.jpg.
151 pics.me.me/so-many-options-walmart-
dress-code-freedom-of-choice-walmart-
36380922.png
152 Logotypes © Philips.
154 Pinterest.
157 © Globo. globoplay.globo.com/v/9348268.
160 Photo by Slleong. Bokeo Province Laos.
commons.wikimedia.org/wiki/File:Golden_
Triangle_Special_Economic_Zone_7.jpg.
161 Photo by Paul Spijkers. en.wikipedia.org/
wiki/Southern_Air_Transport#/media/File:
Southern_Air_Transport_Boeing_747-200_
Spijkers.jpg
162 Logotypes © respective companies.
Collected and compiled by Ruben Pater.
163 legionmagazine.com/en/2020/07/rise-
in-military-contracting-hides-human-
monetary-costs.
164 Logotypes © Milton Glaser, © Koeweiden

Postma, © Cros & Machine, © KesselsKramer.
167 *NY Daily News*.
169 Images collected and compiled by Ruben
Pater.
171 Photo by Kevin McGill. commons.wikimedia.
org/wiki/File:I_amsterdam_(9259130734).jpg
172 Poster and photo by Yuri Veerman.
175 Ruben Pater.
176 Clay Butler. sidewalkbubblegum.com/
aha-graffiti.
178 Krakershandleiding, early 1969. A4-sized
(oblong) booklet. 14 stapled offset-printed
pages (7 double-sided sheets, black and
white), and a screenprinted cover (featuring
drawings by Tjebbe van Tijen and Rob
Stolk). Published by Federatie Onafhanke-
lijke Vakgroepen and Buro De Kraker.
2or3things.tumblr.compost/159570069131/
krakershandleiding-squatters-manual.

The Designer as Salesperson

180 commons.wikimedia.org/wiki/File:Great_
Depression_Salesman.png
182 viewing.nyc/vintage-photograph-of-broad
way-advertising-in-times-square-circa-1909/
Library of Congress.
184 Photo by Carole Raddato. 2014.commons.
wikimedia.org/wiki/File:Wine_selling_
advertisement_and_prices,_%22Ad_Cu
cumas%22_shop,_ancient_roman_painting_
in_Herculaneum,_Italy_(45563843984).jpg
185 John Orlando Parry, *A London Street Scene*,
1835, watercolour, Alfred Dunhill Collection.
commons.wikimedia.org/wiki/File:
Parrywatercolour.jpg
186 John Everett Millais and Pears' Soap.
commons.wikimedia.org/wiki/File:
Bubbles_by_Sir_John_E_Millais.png
187 Pears' Soap. en.wikipedia.org/wiki/Pears_
(soap)#/media/File:Pears-1884.jpg
189 © Coca-Cola. jaideepdoshi.wordpress.com/
2013/09/25/coke-priming.
192 Photo by Lyzadanger. The New Fred Meyer
on Interstate on Lombard (7404 N Interstate
Ave, Portland, OR 97217). commons.wikimedia.
org/wiki/File: Fredmeyer_edit_1.jpg.
195 © Primal, © Bling, © Fillico.
197 Photo by Chris Bentley. flickr.com/photos/
cementley/18772787060.
197 Photo by Matt Murphy. flickr.com/photos/
86332492@N00/2618224557.
198 Photo by Rosaria Forcisi. rosariaforcisi.com.
201 See Red Women's Workshop. Disc Jockey,
The state & sexist advertising causes illness,
don't let these men invade your homes, 1973.
Screenprint 78.5 x 53.5 cm.
202 flickr.com/photos/42353480@
N02/5558126028.
204 Published by Ken Garland, 1964.
206 Jonathan Barnbrook.
209 Adbusters.
210 patents.google.com.
213 patents.google.com.
214 patents.google.com.

216 Newspapers compiled by Ruben Pater.
218 flickr.com/photos/42353480@
     N02/3917267245.
219 © Miller Lite.
221 Logotypes © Newscorp.
222 © Chiquita International.
225 Library of Congress. 1 colour map; 60 x 60
     cm. wdl.org/en/item/62/view/1/1.
226 © Chiquita International.
229 Via carlosbgil.wordpress.com/category/
     book-reviews.
230 © Chiquita International.
234 Photo by Margaret Bourke-White. commons.
     wikimedia.org/wiki/File:American_way_of_
     life.jpg

PART 2

The Designer as Worker

236 Men working at a printing press, proofing
     copy, inking, and setting type. Wood
     engraving after a woodcut by Stradanus,
     c.1580. Wellcome Collection gallery
     commons.wikimedia.org/wiki/File:Men_
     working_at_a_printing_press%2C_proofing_
     copy%2C_inking%2C_and_Wellcome_
     V0023786.jpg
238 Prole.info.
240 © Collection International Institute of Social
     History. commons.wikimedia.org/wiki/
     File:Kinderarbeid_in_drukkerij_(ca.1900).jpg
243 Jean-François Millet, *Les glaneuses*, 1857,
     oil on canvas, 83.5 x 110 cm. Collection
     Musée d'Orsay RFG 592. commons.wikimedia.
     org/wiki/File:Jean-Fran%C3%A7ois_Millet_
     -_Gleaners_-_Google_Art_Project_2.jpg
245 Photo by Waldon Fawcett. Library of Congress,
     LOT 10589. commons.wikimedia.org/wiki/
     File:Employees_at_printing_presses_in
     _the_Bureau_of_Engraving_and_Printing_
     LCCN91796393.jpg
246 Photo by Russell Lee, 1946. Department of
     the Interior. Solid Fuels Administration
     For War. NARA record: 2489414. commons.
     wikimedia.org/wiki/File:Mrs._Furman_
     Currington,_wife_of_miner,_hangs_up_laundry_
     in_kitchen_of_her_6_room_house_which_
     rents_for_$15.00_per..._-_NARA_-_541256.jpg
247 commons.wikimedia.org/wiki/File:Ford_
     assembly_line_-_1913.jpg.
248 flickr.com/photos/42353480@
     N02/5757760150.
249 Source: Economic Policy Institute (EPI).
251 © Motorola.
252 Photo by Sukrafte. commons.wikimedia.org/
     wiki/File:Bilio's_Design_Studio.jpg.
253 Photo by 霍天賜. pexels.com/photo/
     lampshade-between-computer-and-white-
     book-shelves-3775620.
254 Alex Medina.
256 Chris Gergley, Maquila Solidarity Network,
     Adbusters, 2005.
258 Source unknown.
259 Source Economic Policy Institute (EPI), 2018.

259 Source Economic Policy Institute (EPI), 2016.
261 payinterns.nyc
262 Evening Class, evening-class.org.
264 Anthony Burrill. anthonyburrill.com
265 Ben Barry. v1.benbarry.com
266 Ruben Pater.
269 Photo by Dorothea Lange. Federal Security
     Administration. Social Security Board. NARA
     record: 10582293. commons.wikimedia.org/
     wiki/File:Jobless_Men_Lined_up_for_the_
     First_Time_in_California_to_File_Claims_
     for_Unemployment_Compensation_-_NARA_-
     _7716670_(page_1).jpg
271 Ruben Pater.
272 See Red Women's Workshop. Capitalism
     also depends on domestic labour (1975)
     Screenprint 53.5 x 69 cm.
274 Ekomedia.
277 Source unknown.
278 Industrial Workers of the World, iww.org.
280 Socialist Appeal. flickr.com/photos/
     135433887@N02/50261977013.
282 Kheel Center for Labor-Management
     Documentation and Archives, Cornell
     University Library. flickr.com/photos/
     kheelcenter/5279691680.
283 infinitemiledetroit.com/THE_POLITICS_OF_
     THE_JOY_OF_PRINTING_IN_DETROIT.html.
286 Photo by Lewis Wickes Hine, National Child
     Labor Committee collection, Library of
     Congress, Prints and Photographs Division. 1
     photographic print. 1 negative: glass; 5 x 7 in.
     loc.gov/pictures/item/2018674998.
287 Photo by GMB Akash. © GMB Akash/panos
     pictures.

The Designer as Entrepreneur

290 Photo by kaysgeog. flickr.com/photos/
     23351536@N07/50034520026.
292 © *The New York Times*. nytimes.com/
     interactive/2018/04/24/upshot/women-
     and-men-named-john.html.
294 Logos © respective institutions.
297 Mu Mu Store.
298 Book covers collected and compiled by
     Ruben Pater.
301 © Victoria and Albert Museum. Albumen print
     photograph c.1884. collections.vam.ac.uk/
     item/O1266772/hammersmith-socialist-
     league-photograph/
303 © Robohead. robohead.net.
304 © DreamWorks. infous.biz/dreamworks-
     home-entertainment-vhs.html.
305 flickr.com/photos/biwook/145765624.
306 The Pirate Bay.
307 en.wikipedia.org/wiki/Copyleft.
308 medium.com/@jesscreatives/why-you-
     should-stop-using-fiverr-3889e9c8a6bb.
310 vice.com/en/article/evyy8k/fiverr-ad-white-
     man-black-woman.
313 kisbridgingloans.co.uk.
314 Photo by Steve Jurvetson. commons.
     wikimedia.org/wiki/File:Elon_Musk_at_
     the_2016_Tesla_Annual_Shareholders%27_

Meeting_(26780147923).jpg

315 Photo by Adam Jones. commons.wikimedia. org/wiki/File:Cooperative_Miner_in_Cerro_ Rico_Mountain_-_Potosi_-_Bolivia_04_ (3781815149).jpg

The Designer as Amateur

316 © Stedelijk Museum Alkmaar. alkmaar. nieuws.nl/nieuws/1352/verzet-tijdens-woii-een-mannenzaak.

318 Photo by Hardworking Goodlooking.

321 Photo by Sgt. David J. Hercher. zh.wikipedia. org/zh-my/File:USMC-060916-M-4680H-002.jpg.

322 © Trustees of the Guild of Handicraft Trust hippingcampdenschool.org.uk/content/ special-exhibits/c-r-ashbee/c-r-ashbee-1863-1942.

323 grupaok.tumblr.com/post/35207198471/ vkhutemas-students-1927.

324 Ernesto Oroza. ernestooroza.com.

327 Ernesto Oroza. ernestooroza.com.

328 Mark Perry. garage.vice.com/en_us/article/ 7xy7qb/1970s-punk-unseen-photos.

333 © Collectie NIOD. beeldbankwo2.nl/nl/ beelden/detail/4fe11f10-025a-11e7-904b-d89d6717b464/media/7e4b4b3d-b3f9-88d5-d45e-944ddf957c57.

335 Photo by Hardworking Goodlooking.

337 Ernesto Oroza. ernestooroza.com.

338 Photos by Hardworking Goodlooking.

339 Photo by Hardworking Goodlooking.

The Designer as Educator

340 Blandine Molin.

342 Iconoclasistas. iconoclasistas.net.

345 Laurentius de Voltolina, *Liber ethicorum des Henricus de Alemannia*, 14th century. Kupfer stichkabinett Berlin, painting on parchment, 18 x 22 cm. commons.wikimedia.org/wiki/ File:Laurentius_de_Voltolina_001.jpg.

347 Photo by Frances Benjamin Johnston, 1864–1952. Cyanotype. Library of Congress Prints and Photographs Division Washington, D.C. 20540 USA loc.gov/item/2001699123.

348 State Government Photographer, c.1935, Glass Negatives, The History Trust of South Australian, South Australian Government. commons.wikimedia.org/wiki/File:Students_ working_in_Printers_Trade_School_Workshop (GN13197).jpg

350 getty.edu/research/exhibitions_events/ exhibitions/bauhaus/new_artist/history/ principles_curriculum.

351 The Black Mountain College Research Project Papers, Visual Materials, North Carolina State Archives, Raleigh, NC. commons.wikimedia.org/wiki/File:BMCRP_ VM_Bx92_SnelsonK_Fuller_4ee--Sum1949-unk-EugGodfrey-MJSlick-unk_ (6506085371).jpg.

353 Photo by Alvin Arthur.

355 Photo by Fernanda Haiabe. cartoonbrew.com/ schools/calarts-students-launch-protest-as-annual-tuition-rises-to-over-50k-171415.html.

357 Blandine Molin.

359 © School of the Damned.

361 Photo by Jim Brady.

364 Photo by Arvid Jense; Photo by Alvin Arthur.

365 Photo by Jim Brady; © School of the Damned.

PART 3

The Designer as Hacker

366 Photo by Mídia NINJA.

368 NASA, 1964. Melba Roy heads the group of NASA mathematicians, known as 'computers,' who track the Echo satellites. en.wikipedia. org/wiki/Melba_Roy_Mouton#/media/ File:Melba_Roy_-_Female_Computer_-_GPN-2000-001647.jpg.

370 Photo by Simon Waldherr, 2019. commons. wikimedia.org/wiki/File:CERN_Computer_ Center_03.jpg

371 © Blackberry. blackberry.com/us/en/ company/newsroom/media-gallery.

373 © MIT Museum. wired.com/2014/11/ the-tech-model-railroad-club/

373 commons.wikimedia.org/wiki/File:Steve_ Jobs_y_Wozniak_en_1976_en_los_inicios_de_ Apple.jpg

374 Ruben Pater.

376 Ruben Pater.

378 A.B.C. Telegraphic Code 5th Edition, via Atlantic-cable. commons.wikimedia.org/ wiki/File:1901_Eastern_Telegraph_cables.png.

379 submarinecablemap.com.

381 Dennis de Bel and Roel Roscam Abbing.

382 Rogier Klomp. Klomp.tv.

383 Rogier Klomp. Klomp.tv.

384 Disnovation.org.

386 Ruben Pater.

387 Ruben Pater.

388 seenthis.net.

389 Disnovation.org.

391 Simon Weckert. simonweckert.com.

392 © Chaos Communication Congress. nzzas. nzz.ch/gesellschaft/partisanen-des-internets-ld.1349130?reduced=true.

395 Disnovation.org.

The Designer as Futurist

396 Gabriel von Max. Internet Archive Book Images. commons.wikimedia.org/wiki/ File:Gabriel_von_Max_-_Consulting_the_ Fortune-teller.jpg.

398 Next Nature. nextnature.net.

401 © Joseph Voros 2000. ; © the Computer History Museum, 2017. youtube.com/ watch?v=vHdhwCw4isg.

402 © bitcoinprice.com/binance-futures.

403 © PredictIt.

404 © Dassault System. futurism.com/

luxembourg-establishes-e220-million-
fund-for-space-mining.

407 © AKQA. akqa.com.

409 © respective film production companies.
Collected by Ruben Pater.

410 © NIUN. jfsdigital.org/2018/10/11/niun-
saudi-futures.

410 © Microsoft. youtube.com/watch?v=w-
tFdreZB94

410 © Shell. shell.com/energy-and-innovation/
the-energy-future/scenarios/what-are-
scenarios.html

412 Source: De Correspondent/Global Carbon
Tracker and LocalFocus.

413 Photo by Bill Anders, December 24, 1968, at
mission time 075:49:07, while in orbit
around the Moon, showing the Earth rising
for the third time above the lunar horizon.
NASA. commons.wikimedia.org/wiki/
File:NASA-Apollo8-Dec24-Earthrise.jpg.

414 Solen Feyissa. flickr.com/photos/solen-
feyissa/50040111491.

416 Rick Guidice. License: Public Domain
Source: NASA Ames Research Center.
pxhere.com/en/photo/108910.

The Designer as Philanthropist

418 © Library of Congress Prints and Photographs Division. loc.gov/item/2018654467.

420 © madelaineberlis.com/2015/11/25/219.

423 Broder, S. & United States. Office of War
Information. 1 poster: col; 71 x 56 cm. digital.
library.unt.edu/ark:/67531/metadc590.

424 William Ellis, A *Journal of a Tour Around
Hawaii: The Largest of the Sandwich Islands*,
1822–1823, Philadelpha: Crocker & Brewster.
commons.wikimedia.org/wiki/File:A_
Missionary_Preaching_to_Natives,_on_the_
lava_at_Kokukano,_Hawaii,_sketch_by_
William_Ellis.jpg.

425 Ryan Walker. flickr.com/photos/
internetarchivebookimages/14578124037.

426 © (RED), red.org.

428 Boring Dystopia.

430 citl.illinois.edu/paradigms/design-thinking.

430 commons.wikimedia.org/wiki/File:Design_
Thinking_process_in_the_Chapters_
Dialogue_project.png (middle), weloop.org/
en/our-services/ecodesign.

432 © What Design Can Do.
whatdesigncando.com.

433 © What Design Can Do.
whatdesigncando.com.

435 Photo by Michael Dietrich. flickr.com/
photos/wsobotka/34804876542

435 © TNI. tni.org/en/publication/
expanding-the-fortress.

439 Photo by Ducho Dennis, The Black Panthers.
itsabouttimearchive.com.

440 Nicole Marie Burton.

442 i.redd.it/361x9ogtp6101.jpg.

The Designer as Activist

444 Photo by Mídia NINJA.

446 Photo by Paula Kindsvater. commons.
wikimedia.org/wiki/File:Ni_una_menos_
parana_pkindsvater_16.jpg

449 Twitter surveys, image via Facebook.

451 Photo by Javier Collao. commons.wikimedia.
org/wiki/File:Intervenci%C3%B3n_art%
C3%ADstica_en_Plaza_Dignidad._
Santiago,_Chile.jpg

451 Photo by Ken Ohyama. commons.wikimedia.
org/wiki/File:2014_Hong_Kong_protests_
DSC0211_(16098934251).jpg

452 Photo by Augustin-Hippolyte Collard, 1871.
Musée Carnavalet, Histoire de Paris, 21,7 x
31,1 cm, PH15424.CC0 Paris Musées /
Musée Carnavalet.

454 Photo by Jahfrann. instagram.com/
JAHFRANN. *EN LLEGADA (on arrival)*, 2020.

456–463 Brave New Alps.

464–471 Common Knowledge.

472–481 Cooperativa de Diseño.

482–489 Mídia NINJA.

490–497 Open Source Publishing.

498–505 The Public.

PART 4

506 Photo by Sasha Kohlmann. flickr.com/
photos/skohlmann/14840319621.

508 Photo by Laura Colom Urrea.

Index

CAPS LOCK – Part 4

CAPS LOCK — Part 4